SEATTLE
BEST PLACES

SEATTLE
BEST PLACES

The most discriminating guide to
Seattle's restaurants, shops, hotels, nightlife, sights,
outings, and annual events

David Brewster
Stephanie Irving

Sasquatch Books

Library of Congress Cataloging-in-Publication Data

Brewster, David, 1939-
Seattle best places : the most discriminating guide to Seattle's
restaurants, shops, hotels, nightlife, sights, outings, and annual
events/David Brewster, Stephanie Irving—5th ed.
p. cm.
Includes indexes.
ISBN 0-912365-42-0 (pbk.) : $11.95
1. Seattle (Wash.)—Description—Guide-books. 2.Seattle Region (Wash.)—
Description and travel—Guide Books. I. Irving,
Stephanie, 1962-. II. Title
F899.S43B74 1991
917.97'7720443—dc20   90-24948
                                                                  CIP

Cover illustration by Don Baker
Illustrations by Jerry Nelson
Design by Jane Jeszeck
Maps by Karen Schober
Typeset by The Typeworks, Vancouver, BC

The Best Places guidebooks have been published continuously since 1975. Books
in the Best Places series read as personal guidebooks, but our evaluations are
based on numberous reports from locals and traveling inspectors. Final judg-
ments are made by the editors. Our inspectors never identify themselves (except
over the phone) and never take free meals or other favors. Readers are advised
that places listed in previous editions may have closed or changed management,
or are no longer recommended by this series. The editors welcome information
conveyed by useres of this book, as long as they have no financial connection with
the establishment concerned. A report form is provided at the end of the book.
Northwest Best Places, Seattle Best Places, Portland Best Places and other
Sasquatch Books are available at bulk discounts for corporate gifts, conventions,
and fund-raising sales for clubs and organizations. See order form in back of book.

Sasquatch Books
1931 Second Avenue
Seattle, WA 98101
(206)441-5555

TABLE OF CONTENTS

HOW TO USE THIS BOOK

Star rating system. We rate restaurants and lodgings on a scale of zero-to-four stars (with half stars in between), based on uniqueness, enjoyability, loyality of local clientele, excellence of cooking, performance measured against the place's goals, cleanliness, and professionalism of service. **All places in the book are recommended, even those with no stars.**

(no stars)	Worth knowing about, if nearby
★	A good place
★★	Excellent, some wonderful qualities
★★★	Distinguished, many outstanding features
★★★★	The very best in the region (four establishments so honored in this edition)
½	Half-stars fall between these designations
unrated	New at presstime

Price Range. *Expensive*—a dinner for two, appropriate fro this restaurant, and including wine or a drink (but not tip), would run more than $75; a double-occupancy hotel room would be more than $90. *Inexpensive*—the dinner for two would be less than $30; the double room, less than $50. *Moderate*—between Expensive and Inexpensive.

Map Indicators. The letter-and-number code listed just after the phone number is keyed to coordinates on the fold-out map included in this book. Single letters (F7) refer to the Downtown Seattle map; double letters (FF7) refer to the Greater Seattle map on the flip side.

Credit Cards. American Express (AE), Diner's Club (DC), MasterCard (MC), VISA (V).

Address. Addresses are in Seattle unless otherwise specified. If an establishment has two Seattle-area locations, we list both addresses; if there are more than two we list the original, downtown, or biggest branch with "and branches" written after the address.

Phone Numbers. All area codes are 206, except where indicated. Telephone numbers listed with a 1- preceding them are long-distance numbers, but still within the 206 range.

Indexes. There is a full index by page number in the back. You'll also find handy categorical indexes fronting the "Bars" and "Nightclubs" sections of the Nightlife chapter, and the Restaurants chapter. Bars are indexed by neighborhood and important features; nightclubs by neighborhood and type of music; restaurants by neighborhood, cuisine/important features, and star rating.

KIDS and **FREE** symbols throughout the book signal attractions and events that are, respectively, especially good for children or free of charge.

INTRODUCTION

Seattle, as you have no doubt heard *ad nauseam*, is one swell place to live in, and not too shabby to visit. It's become such a "hot" city that it is beginning to emit rays of doubt, a natural reaction to a steady, decade-long emanation of hype. Accordingly, this guidebook, purporting to put a large chunk of the best things about this city within its covers, has a little explaining to do.

Well, it is a fine place to live in, though getting endangered. Housing prices are now right up there with the other most expensive cities. That development, which happened in the past three years or so, kicked away one of the keys to the city's livability for a broad spectrum of classes. The city has a vibrant, participatory politics, but it has not been able to get its act together for solving growing congestion (particularly bad in the booming suburbs), or for reinvesting in education. Its economy is humming along, thanks to Boeing and the Microsoft and medical/biotechnological sectors, but this new economy is so busy making money or jetting around the world that it hasn't yet created a class of people sufficiently interested in the arts and the public quality of life in their own city. The natural environment is wondrous, but a cheapskate attitude about taxes means that we are underinvesting in its protection.

For a visitor, Seattle remains a middling sort of place. The town has never exactly wanted to be a tourist town along the lines of San Francisco. One of the liveliest issues in the city these days, for instance, concerns all the tourists flooding into the Pike Place Market in the fair weather. They drive away the regular business, merchants say, and a regular customer is not only steady but he or she buys more than a gawker from Iowa. To its credit, Seattle has never wanted to create Fisherman's Wharf kinds of "tourist ghettos," which is one reason why visitors to Seattle love the place: they feel like they belong here and are welcome. They actually are welcome, mostly, as long as they don't get too numerous. In the summer of 1990, the city staged its poor man's version of the Olympics, the Goodwill Games, and it taught the town an important civic lesson. Business dried up. The regulars were so worried about the batallions of tourists (inflated figures, it turned out) that they stayed away from their favorite restaurants in droves. This city likes its visitors, like everything else, in moderation.

Accordingly, tourism in Seattle is more elusive than in most large cities. The attractions don't have big signs, like a Disneyland. They are more likely to be modest-seeming things like the zoo, tucked away in a north end park where everyone seems to be jogging or playing soccer. But take a second glance: elephants are roaming through their own 5-acre Asian forest, in a display that is humane, rare, and far more happy than other large zoos.

By now you have probably suspected that all these windy observations are mostly a clever way of saying that you need this book, whether you're a visitor, a newcomer, or a settled resident. Quite true. But this is also a way of explaining why we put this book together as we do.

For starters, it is not a book for tourists. It is aimed at the people who live here, who provide repeat business (the most demanding) for places, and who like out-of-the way places of high character and individualism. Paradoxically, that makes it just right for *Seattle* tourists. The best places in this city of veiled attractions, where you have to peer through the misty atmosphere, are those the local denizens favor: places of good value, unfranchised, touched with local history, growing out of the soil of this region where growing things is the dominant religion. Beyond that, we tend to favor places with lively individualists in command, with Asian accents that reflect the longstanding internationalism and tolerance of the town, and those graced by natural beauty.

Our method for gathering this harvest, which we reap every two or three years, is to send a team of about two dozen knowledgeable reviewers out into the fields, looking for new discoveries and checking up on old favorites or aspirants. Then we ask others who are savvy about certain categories to make sure our visits square with their inside assessments. We try to express these views candidly, using a star-rating system for restaurants and hotels, so that the book reads like a personal guidebook. But it is more properly thought of as a consensus of numerous visits. The ideal would be the seasoned judgement of a person who has dined at a certain restaurant 20 times or so over the past few years, learning its foibles, its true strengths, its unique characteristics.

Doing a book like this every few years, we naturally draw some conclusions about changes during that time. Here are a few. The "outer city" portions of Seattle, particularly on the Eastside, are now producing metropolitan attractions of their own, as witness a four-star restaurant in the Cascade foothills hamlet of Fall City. Restaurants are slipping a bit, returning to more conservative formats, as the yuppie spending binge of the '80s fades away. Rising prices downtown are forcing out some variety, as individualistic places cannot afford midtown rents and are moving to the near periphery, such as First Avenue. The city's remarkable arts renaissance is still with us, though there is a little too much complacent coasting. Local ale is great, and a city with great ales can't be all bad. City streets are not safe enough, and that is costing establishments in nighttime business. The city is coffee-crazy for some reason we don't understand, but enough for us to start a new section, Dessert, Coffee, and Tea, in the Nightlife chapter. The whole region, thanks to that cursed "hotness," has become too expensive. (Best cure: eat at Asian restaurants, of which there are hundreds more each year.) Retailers are catching up with Nordstrom. And the neighborhood commercial districts are starting to fill up with distinctive places.

All our inspectors remain anonymous during visits and do not accept free meals or services, but now that their words are all in we can thank some of them: Lisa Anderson, Heather Barbieri, Brenda Bell, Carol Brown, Carlene Canton, Alf Collins, Connie Cooper, Robert Cumbow, Anne Depue, John Doerper, Susan English, Stuart Grover, Kitty Harmon, Linda Johns, Erika Lim, Theresa Morrow, Kristen Nelson, Rose Pike, Cathy Ragland, Eric Scigliano, Jane Steinberg, Debra Sykes, Carmi Weingrod, Larry West, Kathy Witowsky, and Adam Woog.

Four others who deserve special mention are: Barry Foy and Don Roberts who worked as a team copyediting and proofreading this book to near perfection; Kathryn Robinson, the former *Best Places* editor, offering her sage advice and submitting impeccable reviews; and Emily Hall, an invaluable editorial assistant, who wins the award for learning more about Seattle in a year than any other person in this city.

And thanks to you as well, in advance, for sending us a report form, tips on new places, and corrections or complaints. These reports help keep the town, and us, on our toes.

David Brewster
Stephanie Irving

RESTAURANTS

8

▼
RESTAURANTS CONTENTS

INDEX: STAR RATING
9

INDEX: LOCATION
11

INDEX: FOOD AND OTHER FEATURES
14

TOP 300 RESTAURANTS
21

INDEX: STAR RATING

★ ★ ★ ★
The Herbfarm
Labuznik
Rover's

★ ★ ★ ½
Cafe Sport
Cafe Sport/Bellevue
Dahlia Lounge
Gerard's Relais de Lyon

★ ★ ★
Adriatica
Cafe Juanita
Cafe Lago
Fullers (Seattle Sheraton
   Hotel)
Georgian Room (Four
   Seasons Olympic)
The Hunt Club (Sorrento
   Hotel)
Il Bistro
Le Gourmand
Ray's Boathouse
Saleh al Lago
Union Bay Cafe

★ ★ ½
Al Boccalino
Ayutthaya
Botticelli Cafe
Bravo
Cafe Alexis (Alexis Hotel)
Canlis
Chez Shea
Il Terrazzo Carmine
Izumi
Kaspar's by the Bay
Mezza Luna Ristorante
Nikko
Place Pigalle
Pleasant Beach Grill and
   Oyster House
Ristorante Allegria
Ristorante Stresa
Romio's Pizza
Sea Garden
Septieme
Settebello
Szmania's
Thai Restaurant
Wild Ginger

★ ★
Anthony's HomePort
Aoki
Arrowhead Cafe

Asuka
Bahn Thai
Beeliner Diner
Cactus
Cafe Hue
Campagne
Chanterelle Specialty
   Foods
Chau's Chinese Restaurant
The Chile Pepper
Chinook's
Crêpe de Paris
Cutters Bayhouse
DaVinci's Flying Pizza
Domani
El Puerco Lloron
Eques (Hyatt Regency
   Hotel)
Filiberto's
The 5-Spot and Counter-
   balance Room
Giorgina's Pizza
Giulio Ristorante Italiano
Grand Central Baking
   Company
Hien Vuong
I Love Sushi
Islabelle Caribbean Food
Italia
Java Restaurant
Karam's
Kikuya
Kokeb
La Rive Gauche
Landau's
Le Tastevin
Lofurno's
Machiavelli's
Madison Park Cafe
Maltby Cafe
Mandarin Garden
Maple Leaf Sports Grill
Marrakesh
Mikado
Pacifica
Palm Court (Westin Hotel)
Palomino
Panda's
Pasta & Co.
Pasta Bella
Pegasus Pizza and Pasta
Phoenecia Restaurant
The Pink Door
Phnom Penh Noodle Soup
   House
A Pot of Phnom Penh
   Restaurant & Karoake
R & L Home of Good
   Barbeque

Rain City Grill
raison d'être
Ristorante Buongusto
Ristorante Stresa
The Roost
Salvatore Ristorante
   Italiano
The Santa Fe Cafe
Satsuma
Shucker's (Four Seasons
   Olympic Hotel)
Siam on Broadway
Taj Mahal India Restaurant
Takara
Tandoor Restaurant
Teger's
Thai Terrace
Toscana
Toyoda Sushi
Trader Vic's
Triples
Trolleyman Pub
Truffles
Two Bells Tavern
Wang's Garden
Yarrow Bay Restaurant and
   Beach Cafe

★ ½
A. Jays Delicatessen and
   Restaurant
A. Jays Eatery
Andrés Gourmet Cuisine
Après Vous Cafe
Ave! Al Ristorante Italiano
B & O Espresso
Bagel Oasis
Big Time Pizza
Brooklyn Cafe and
   Oyster Bar
brusseau's
Buddy's Homesick Cafe
Burk's Cafe
Bush Garden
Byzantion
Cafe Sabika
Cafe Sophie
Cajun Corner Cafe (Alexis
   Hotel)
Caveman Kitchens
Ciao Italia
Cucina! Cucina!
du jour
Duck Cafe
Duwamps Cafe and Seattle
   Brewing Company
El Toreador
Ezell's Fried Chicken

F.X. McRory's Steak, Chop, and Oyster House
Fountain Court Off Main
Four Swallows
Gravity Bar
Green Village
Hi-Spot Cafe
Hisago
House of Hong
Il Paesano
Jake O'Shaughnessey's
Julia's 14 Carrot Cafe
Julia's in Wallingford
Kamalco
Kells
Kohan
Koraku
La Cocinita de Tlaquepaque
La Flambée
La Fleur
Linyen
Little Italy West
Maximilien-in-the-Market
McCormick and Schmick's
McCormick's Fish House and Bar
Mediterranean Kitchen
Metropolitan Grill
Musashi's Sushi & Grill
New Jake O'Shaughnessey's
Olympia Pizza and Spaghetti
The Oven
Panko's
Paparazzi Ristorante
Phad Thai
Piecora's
Piecora's New York Pizzeria
Pogacha
Provinces Asian Restaurant and Bar
Queen City Grill
Restaurant Shilla
Ristorante Pony
Salute
Salute in Città (WestCoast Vance Hotel)
Sea Thai
Seattle Bagel Bakery
Seoul Olympic Restaurant
Still Life in Freemont Coffeehouse
Stravinsky
Streamliner Diner
Surrogate Hostess
Szechwan Garden
Tatsumi
TestaRossa
Thai Chef
Thai Heaven

Thai Palace
Tlaquepaque
Togetsu
Tosoni's Cafe
Tump Nak Thai
Union Square Grill
Viet My
Vonnie's, A Garden Cafe
Western Coffee Shop

★

Abruzzi
Alki Bakery & Cafe
Angelina's Trattoria (see Trattoria Mitchelli)
Arita
Armadillo Barbecue
Arnie's Northshore
Bai Tong
Bangkok Cafe
Bella Luna
Best Wok
Blacksheep Cafe and Catering
Cafe Los Gatos
Cafe Open
Caffè Minnie's
Casa-U-Betcha
Catfish Corner
Chandler's Crabhouse and Fresh Fish Market
Chautrelles
Coho Cafe
Continental Restaurant and Pastry Shop
Copacabana
Cousins of Kirkland
Cyclops
Duke's Bar & Grill
Emmett Watson's Oyster Bar
Empress of China
Fremont Classic
Gordo's
Greenlake Jake's
Guido's Pizzeria
Han Il
Harbor City Barbecue House
Hot Lips Pizza
Hunan Garden
India Taj
Ivar's Acres of Clams and Fish Bar
Ivar's Captain's Table
Kaleenka Russian Cafe
Kamon on Lake Union
Kamon of Kobe
Kirkland Roaster & Ale House
Lake Union Cafe

Lake Washington Grillhouse and Taproom
Lakeside Cafe
Lao Chearern
Le Bonaparte
Leschi Lakecafe
A Little Bit of Saigon
Little Saigon
Louie's Cuisine of China
Macheesmo Mouse
The Maddox Grill
Mae's Phinney Ridge Cafe
Maneki
Matzoh Momma
Pacific Northwest Brewing Company
Peerless Pies
Peter's on the Park
Pho 88
Pho Hoa
Pizzeria Pagliacci
Pizzuto's Italian Cafe
Pollo Rico
Prego (Stouffer Madison Hotel)
Rama on Post
Rattlers Grill
The Restaurant
The Ritz Cafe
Rosellini McHugh's Nine-10 Restaurant
Singapore
Spot Bagels
Stella's Trattoria (see Trattoria Mitchelli)
Stone Way Cafe
Subito
Sunlight Cafe
Sunset Cafe
Sushi-Ten
Swingside Cafe
Tanooki Cafe
Thai Thai Restaurant
Thompson's Point of View
Three Girls Bakery
Tokyo Japanese Restaurant
Tommy Thai
Trattoria Mitchelli
Umberto's
Viet Nam Vietnamese Cuisine
Wanza

NO STARS

Bakeman's Restaurant
Duke's Chowder House and Outrageous Canoe Club
El Palacio
Globe Cafe
Gourmet City Restaurant

INDEX: LOCATION

RESTAURANTS

McCormick's Fish House
and Bar
Metropolitan Grill
Palm Court (Westin Hotel)
Palomino
Pasta & Co.
Peerless Pies
Prego (Stouffer Madison
Hotel)
raison d'être
Rama on Post
Romio's Pizza
Rosellini and McHugh's
Nine-10 Restaurant
Salute in Città (WestCoast
Vance Hotel)
Seattle Bagel Bakery
Shucker's (Four Seasons
Olympic Hotel)
Thirteen Coins
Tlaquepaque
Trader Vic's
Union Square Grill
Western Coffee Shop
Wild Ginger

EASTLAKE
Julia's 14 Carrot Cafe
Lake Union Cafe
Rattlers Grill

EDMONDS
Anthony's Homeport
Arnie's Northshore
brusseau's
Chanterelle Specialty
Foods
Ciao Italia
Provinces Asian Restaurant
and Bar

ELLIOTT AVENUE
Ivar's Captain's Table

FALL CITY
The Herbfarm

FIRST HILL
A. Jays Delicatessen and
Restaurant
The Hunt Club (Sorrento
Hotel)

FISHERMAN'S TERMINAL
Chinook's

FREMONT
Fremont Classic
Ponti Seafood Grill

Still Life in Fremont
Coffeehouse
Swingside Cafe
Trolleyman Pub

GREEN LAKE
Cafe Los Gatos
Duke's Chowder House
and Outrageous
Canoe Club
Greenlake Jake's
Guido's Pizzeria
Panko's
Saleh al Lago
Spud Fish and Chips

GREENWOOD/PHINNEY RIDGE
Arita
Buddy's Homesick Cafe
El Toreador
Lakeside Cafe
Mae's Phinney Ridge Cafe
Phad Thai
The Santa Fe Cafe

INTERNATIONAL DISTRICT
Bush Garden
Chau's Chinese Restaurant
Green Village
Green Village 2
Han Il
Harbor City Barbecue
House
Hien Vuong
House of Dumplings
House of Hong
Koraku
Linyen
A Little Bit of Saigon
Little Saigon
Maneki
Mikado
Nikko
Phnom Penh Noodle Soup
House
Pho 88
Sea Garden
Szechwan Garden
Viet Nam Vietnamese
Cuisine

ISSAQUAH
Kohan
La Costa
Mandarin Garden
The Roost

KENMORE
Lake Washington Grill-
house and Taproom

KENT
Caveman Kitchens

KIRKLAND
Anthony's Homeport
Cafe Juanita
Cousins of Kirkland
DaVinci's Flying Pizza
Giulio Ristorante Italiano
Izumi
Kirkland Roaster &
Ale House
Ristorante Stresa
Spud Fish and Chips
Tommy Thai
Yarrow Bay Restaurant and
Beach Cafe

LAKE CITY WAY
New Peking
Taj Mahal India Restaurant
Toyoda Sushi

LESCHI/MADRONA
Hi-Spot Cafe
Leschi Lakecafe

MADISON PARK/
MADISON VALLEY
Cactus
The Duck Cafe
Madison Park Cafe
Mezza Luna Ristorante
Peter's on the Park
Rover's

MAGNOLIA/INTERBAY
Cafe Open
Lofurno's
Romio's Pizza
Szmania's

MALTBY
Maltby Cafe

MERCER ISLAND
Haruko's
Subito

MONTLAKE
Cafe Lago
Teger's

MOUNT BAKER/
SEWARD PARK
Pizzuto's Italian Cafe

RESTAURANTS

WATERFRONT (ALASKAN WAY)
Ivar's Acres of Clams and Fish Bar
Seattle Bagel Bakery

WEST SEATTLE/ALKI
Alki Bakery & Cafe
Angelina's Trattoria (see Trattoria Mitchelli)

B&O Espresso
Coho Cafe
Luna Park Cafe
Pegasus Pizza and Pasta
The Restaurant
Salty's on Alki
Spud Fish and Chips

WESTLAKE
Adriatica
Arrowhead Cafe

Triples

WHITE CENTER
Thai Thai Restaurant

WOODINVILLE
Armadillo Barbecue
Newman's Bear Creek Cafe
Pacifica
Tokyo Japanese Restaurant #2

INDEX: FOOD AND OTHER FEATURES

AFTERNOON TEA
The Georgian Room (Four Seasons Olympic Hotel)
The Hunt Club (Sorrento Hotel)

ALL NIGHT
Caffè Minnie's
Stella's Trattoria (see Trattoria Mitchelli)
Thirteen Coins

BAGELS
Bagel Oasis
Matzoh Momma
Seattle Bagel Bakery
Spot Bagels

BAKERY
Alki Bakery & Cafe
B&O Espresso
Chanterelle Specialty Foods
Continental Restaurant and Pastry Shop
Grand Central Baking Company
Peerless Pies
Septieme
Surrogate Hostess
Three Girls Bakery

BARBECUE
Armadillo Barbecue
Caveman Kitchens
Han Il
Harbor City Barbecue House
R&L Home of Good Barbeque

BREAKFAST
A. Jays Delicatessen and Restaurant
A. Jays Eatery
Alki Bakery & Cafe
B&O Espresso
Cafe Open
Caffé Minnie's
Continental Restaurant and Pastry Shop
DaVinci's Flying Pizza
The Duck Cafe
Emmett Watson's Oyster Bar
Gravity Bar
Greenlake Jake's
Hi-Spot Cafe
House of Dumplings
Julia's 14 Carrot Cafe
Julia's in Wallingford
Julia's Park Place
Lakeside Cafe
Luna Park Cafe
Madison Park Cafe
Mae's Phinney Ridge Cafe
Maltby Cafe
Matzoh Momma
Maximilien-in-the-Market
Paparazzi Ristorante
Peerless Pies
The Restaurant
Seattle Bagel Bakery
Septieme
Stone Way Cafe
Streamliner Diner
Sunlight Cafe
Sunset Cafe
Surrogate Hostess
Swingside Cafe
Trattoria Mitchelli
Truffles
Vonnie's, A Garden Cafe
Western Coffee Shop

BREAKFAST, ALL DAY
A. Jays Delicatessen and Restaurant
A. Jays Eatery
Caffé Minnie's
Mae's Phinney Ridge Cafe
Stone Way Cafe
Western Coffee Shop

BREWPUBS
Duwamps Cafe and Seattle Brewing Company
Pacific Northwest Brewing Company
Trolleyman Pub

BRUNCH
Anthony's Homeport
Après Vous Cafe
Arnie's Northshore
Arrowhead Cafe
Beeliner Diner
Bella Luna
Brooklyn Cafe and Oyster Bar Lounge
brusseau's
Cactus
Chandler's Crabhouse and Fresh Fish Market
Chinook's
Cutters Bayhouse
Cyclops
Duwamps Cafe and Seattle Brewing Company
The 5-Spot and Counter-balance Room
Grand Central Baking Company
The Hunt Club (Sorrento Hotel)
Lake Union Cafe

INDEX: FOOD AND OTHER FEATURES

RESTAURANTS

The Two Bells Tavern

ESPRESSO
B&O Espresso
Bagel Oasis
Botticelli Cafe
Cafe Open
Grand Central Baking
    Company
Islabelle Caribbean Food
Italia
Mae's Phinney Ridge Cafe
Pasta Bella
Peerless Pies
Septieme
Still Life in Fremont
    Coffeehouse
Sunlight Cafe
Surrogate Hostess
Vonnie's, A Garden Cafe
Western Coffee Shop

ETHIOPIAN/EAST AFRICAN
Kokeb
Wanza

FIREPLACE
Cafe Sophie
Eques (Hyatt Regency
    Hotel)
Gerard's Relais de Lyon
The Hunt Club (Sorrento
    Hotel)
Pleasant Beach Grill and
    Oyster House
Teger's

FISH 'N' CHIPS
Benji's
Chinook's
Emmett Watson's
    Oyster Bar
Gordo's
Ivar's Acres of Clams and
    Fish Bar
Ivar's Captain's Table
Leschi Lakecafe
Spud Fish and Chips

FRENCH
Campagne
Crêpe de Paris
Fountain Court Off Main
Gerard's Relais de Lyon
La Flambée
La Fleur
La Rive Gauche
Le Bonaparte
Le Gourmand
Le Tastevin

Maximilien-in-the-Market
Rover's
Septieme

GAME
Newman's Bear Creek Cafe

GAMES
Duwamps Cafe and
    Seattle Brewing
    Company (darts)
The Two Bells Tavern
    (backgammon)

GERMAN/AUSTRIAN
Szmania's
Tosoni's Cafe

GOURMET TAKEOUT/DELI
brusseau's
Chanterelle Specialty
    Foods
du jour
Truffles

GREEK
Byzantion
Continental Restaurant and
    Pastry Shop
Lakeside Cafe

GRILL
Jake O'Shaughnessey's
Kirkland Roaster & Ale
    House
The Maddox Grill
Maple Leaf Sports Grill
McCormick and Schmick's
McCormick's Fish House
    and Bar
Metropolitan Grill
The New Jake
    O'Shaughnessey's
Queen City Grill
Rain City Grill
The Roost

HANGING OUT
B&O Espresso
Continental Restaurant and
    Pastry Shop
Cyclops
The Globe Cafe
Gravity Bar
Septieme
Still Life in Fremont
    Coffeehouse
Surrogate Hostess
Trolleyman Pub

HOME COOKING
Beeliner Diner
Buddy's Homesick Cafe
Cafe Open
Cousins of Kirkland
The 5-Spot and Counter-
    balance Room
Streamliner Diner
Western Coffee Shop

INDIAN (INDIA)
India Taj
Taj Mahal India Restaurant
Tandoor Restaurant

INDONESIAN
Java Restaurant

INVENTIVE ETHNIC
Chanterelle Specialty
    Foods
Coho Cafe
Cutters Bayhouse
Cyclops
Dahlia Lounge
Duwamps Cafe and Seattle
    Brewing Company
Eques (Hyatt Regency
    Hotel)
The Georgian Room (Four
    Seasons Olympic Hotel)
Gravity Bar
Julia's 14 Carrot Cafe
Julia's in Wallingford
Pacific Northwest Brewing
    Company
raison d'être
Ristorante Pony
Sunset Cafe
Surrogate Hostess
Teger's

IRISH
Kells

ITALIAN
Al Boccalino
Angelina's Trattoria (see
    Trattoria Mitchelli)
Ave! Al Ristorante Italiano
Bella Luna
Botticelli Cafe
Bravo
Cafe Juanita
Cafe Lago
Ciao Italia
Cucina! Cucina!
Domani
Filiberto's
Fremont Classic

INDEX: FOOD AND OTHER FEATURES

RESTAURANTS

Dahlia Lounge
Fountain Court Off Main
Fullers (Seattle Sheraton
  Hotel)
The Georgian Room (Four
  Seasons Olympic Hotel)
The Herbfarm
The Hunt Club (Sorrento
  Hotel)
Le Gourmand
Pacifica
Place Pigalle
Rover's
Union Bay Cafe

OUTDOOR DINING

Anthony's Homeport
Après Vous Cafe
Asuka
Big Time Pizza
Cactus
Campagne
Caveman Kitchens
Chandler's Crabhouse and
  Fresh Fish Market
Chinook's
Copacabana
Cucina! Cucina!
The Duck Cafe
Duke's Chowder House
  and Outrageous
  Canoe Club
Duwamps Cafe and Seattle
  Brewing Company
El Puerco Lloron
Emmett Watson's Oyster
  Bar
Fremont Classic
Gordo's
Greenlake Jake's
The Hunt Club (Sorrento ·
  Hotel)
Il Terrazzo Carmine
Italia
Ivar's Acres of Clams and
  Fish Bar
Ivar's Captain's Table
Kells
Leschi Lakecafe
Madison Park Cafe
The New Jake
  O'Shaughnessey's
Pacific Northwest Brewing
  Company
PaneVino
Panko's
Peerless Pies
Peter's on the Park
The Pink Door
Place Pigalle
Pleasant Beach Grill and
  Oyster House

Ponti Seafood Grill
Ray's Boathouse
Ristorante Buongusto
Ristorante Stresa
The Ritz Cafe
Salty's at Redondo
Salty's on Alki
Septieme
Shucker's (Four Seasons
  Olympic Hotel)
Spot Bagels
Spud Fish and Chips
Streamliner Diner
Surrogate Hostess
Thai Palace
Vonnie's, A Garden Cafe
Yarrow Bay Restaurant and
  Beach Cafe

OYSTER BARS

Brooklyn Cafe and
  Oyster Bar
F.X. McRory's Steak, Chop,
  and Oyster House
McCormick and Schmick's
McCormick's Fish House
  and Bar
Pleasant Beach Grill and
  Oyster House
Shucker's (Four Seasons
  Olympic Hotel)
Triples

PAN-ASIAN

Provinces Asian Restaurant
  and Bar
Wild Ginger

PIZZA

Abruzzi
Ave! Al Ristorante Italiano
Bella Luna
Big Time Pizza
Bravo
Cafe Lago
Cucina! Cucina!
Filiberto's
Fremont Classic
Giorgina's Pizza
Guido's Pizzeria
Hot Lips Pizza
Italia
Little Italy West
Mezza Luna Ristorante
Olympia Pizza and
  Spaghetti
Palomino
Pegasus Pizza and Pasta
Piecora's
Piecora's New York
  Pizzeria

Pizzeria Pagliacci
Pizzuto's Italian Cafe
Pogacha
Romio's Pizza
Salute
Salute in Città (WestCoast
  Vance)
TestaRossa

POLYNESIAN

Trader Vic's

PRIVATE ROOMS

Anthony's Homeport
Cafe Juanita
Domani
Duwamps Cafe and Seattle
  Brewing Company
F.X. McRory's Steak, Chop,
  and Oyster House
Fountain Court Off Main
Gourmet City Restaurant
Kirkland Roaster
  & Ale House
Landau's
Le Bonaparte
Linyen
Mandarin Garden
McCormick and Schmick's
Metropolitan Grill
The New Jake
  O'Shaughnessey's
Palm Court (Westin Hotel)
PaneVino
Peter's on the Park
Phoenecia Restaurant
The Ritz Cafe
Salty's at Redondo
Salty's on Alki
Satsuma
Subito
Triples
Umberto's

ROMANTIC

Cafe Alexis (Alexis Hotel)
Cafe Juanita
Cafe Sophie
Chez Shea
Copacabana
Il Bistro
Pasta Bella
Place Pigalle
Septieme
Toscana
Trolleyman Pub

RUSSIAN

Kaleenka Russian Cafe

F.X. McRory's Steak, Chop,
and Oyster House
Metropolitan Grill

SUSHI
(see also Japanese)
Arita
Asuka
I Love Sushi
Kamon of Kobe
Kamon on Lake Union
Kikuya
Musashi's Sushi & Grill
Nikko
Sushi-Ten
Takara
Tatsumi
Toyoda Sushi

TAKEOUT ONLY (OR MOSTLY)
The Blue Mesa
Caveman Kitchens
Chanterelle Specialty
Foods
du jour
Gordo's
Grand Central Baking
Company
La Cocinita de Tlaquepaque
Pasta & Co.
Pizzeria Pagliacci
Salute Deli
Tatsumi Express
Toscana Deli
Toshi's Teriyaki
Truffles

TAVERN
Trolleyman Pub
The Two Bells Tavern

TERIYAKI
(see also Japanese)
Arita
Musashi's Sushi & Grill
Panko's
Tanooki Cafe

THAI
Ayutthaya
Bahn Thai
Bai Tong
Bangkok Cafe
Lao Charearn
Phad Thai
Rama on Post
Sea Thai
Siam on Broadway
Thai Chef
Thai Heaven

Thai Palace
Thai Restaurant
Thai Terrace
Thai Thai Restaurant
Tommy Thai
Tump Nak Thai

VEGETARIAN
*(see also Middle Eastern
and all Asian categories)*
Cafe Los Gatos
Cyclops
The Globe Cafe
Gravity Bar
Hien Vuong
Julia's 14 Carrot Cafe
Julia's in Wallingford
Julia's Park Place
Kamalco
Kokeb
Little Italy West
Macheesmo Mouse
Mediterranean Kitchen
The Oven
Peerless Pies
Singapore
Still Life in Fremont
Coffeehouse
Streamliner Diner
Sunlight Cafe
Surrogate Hostess
Tandoor Restaurant
Tanooki Cafe
Thai Thai Restaurant
Wanza

VIETNAMESE
André's Gourmet Cuisine
Cafe Hue
Hien Vuong
A Little Bit of Saigon
Little Saigon
Pho 88
Pho Hoa
Viet My
Viet Nam Vietnamese
Cuisine

VIEW
Alki Bakery & Cafe
Anthony's Homeport
Arnie's Northshore
Asuka
Cafe Sophie
Campagne
Canlis
Chandler's Crabhouse and
Fresh Fish Market
Chez Shea
Chinook's
Copacabana

Cucina! Cucina!
Cutters Bayhouse
du jour
Duke's Chowder House
and Outrageous
Canoe Club
Kamon of Kobe
Kamon on Lake Union
Kaspar's by the Bay
Kirkland Roaster &
Ale House
Lake Union Cafe
Leschi Lakecafe
Maximilien-in-the-Market
Pegasus Pizza and Pasta
The Pink Door
Place Pigalle
Prego (Stouffer Madison
Hotel)
Ray's Boathouse
Ristorante Stresa
Salty's at Redondo
Salty's on Alki
Spud Fish and Chips
Triples
Yarrow Bay Restaurant and
Beach Cafe

WHEELCHAIR, NON-ACCESSIBLE
Adriatica
Après Vous Cafe
Arrowhead Cafe
Chez Shea
Java Restaurant
Little Italy West
Pink Door
Place Pigalle
Prego
Ristorante Buogusto
Romio's
Rover's
Salty's on Alki
Seoul Olympic Restaurant
Shucker's
Szechwan
Toscana
Viet My
Yarrow Bay Restaurant and
Beach Cafe

TOP 300 RESTAURANTS

A. Jays Eatery

*2619 1st Ave, 441-1511
(map: C8)
Inexpensive; beer and
wine; MC, V; local
checks only
Breakfast, lunch every
day*

A. Jays Delicatessen and Restaurant

*1320 Madison St,
328-3993 (map: HH7)
Inexpensive; no alcohol;
MC, V; local checks only
Breakfast, lunch, dinner
every day*

When owner Alan J. Rugoff moved down the street to these more modern quarters, folks worried that his breakfasts just wouldn't be the same; the location is large and modern, but the friendly atmosphere hasn't changed at all (it just holds more people), and neither has the food. For breakfast, the blue corn pancakes are especially good, as are the apple pancakes and latkes. Omelets are generous and filling. For lunch, the menu lists burgers, sandwiches, and good soups—perfect for the demographic mix of babies and business suits the place attracts. Right now A. Jays serves only breakfasts and lunches, but at press time a second A. Jays on Capitol Hill just opened. Here Rugoff has installed a full deli-style dinner menu (in addition to food to go), including New York classics from stuffed cabbage to smoked whitefish.

Abruzzi

*604 Pike St, 624-8122
(map: K5)
Inexpensive; beer and
wine; no credit cards;
local checks only
Lunch, dinner Mon-Sat*

In business since 1956, Abruzzi comes closer in atmosphere to a North End Boston pizza joint than any other Seattle pizzeria, right down to the brusque service. "All I know," says one customer, "is I like the way the crust is light and crispy-thin and snaps slightly when you bite into it, but is still puffy-chewy around the edges." Indeed, the crust is very thin, very Neapolitan, and dressed sparingly with very fresh ingredients. Extra oil if you request it. Order a whole pie or just a slice.

Adriatica

*1107 Dexter Ave N,
285-5000 (map: B2)
Expensive; full bar; DC,
MC, V; checks OK
Dinner every day*

This is Mediterranean food brought to the city, polished to perfection but with an earthy lustiness all but forgotten in many contemporary restaurants of comparable style. The crowd is urban and sophisticated, the site a glossy refurbished house perched on a hillside (up a long flight of stairs, not wheelchair accessible) overlooking the broad expanse of Lake Union. All is overseen in cordial style by owner/host Jim Malevitsis, who leaves the kitchen in the estimable hands of chef Nancy Flume. Her skill there is evidenced by a remarkable record of consistency.

Most diners start with fried calamari and garlic dip, probably the best-known appetizers in the city, but as successful are the taramosalata spread on bread or the delicate, paper-thin carpaccio. The horiatiki (Greek salad) is a refreshing standout among the six salads. The menu runs to savory grilled meats, expertly done pastas, and some of the finest fish in the city, cooked to perfection and presented under inspired sauces (like an extraordinary swordfish with olive butter, diced tomatoes, and pine nuts). A baklava-like dessert—dates and walnuts and brandy baked in phyllo with cognac and almond whipped cream—is rich and delicious. Tiny problems—a disappearing busboy, no tables for two near the window—tend to diminish in light of the big picture. An extensive cellar includes more than 20 champagnes and 300 wines.

Al Boccalino

1 Yesler Way, 622-7688
(map: O8)
Moderate; beer and wine;
AE, MC, V; checks OK
Lunch Mon-Fri, dinner
Mon-Sat

No, it's not the name of that Italian boy down the street who used to date your daughter. Al Boccalino is an extremely promising southern Italian restaurant, at the tag end of Yesler Way in Pioneer Square. Co-owner Luigi DeNunzio (you'll remember him from Il Terrazzo) has gathered recipes from his native Apulia, the heel of the Italian boot, and with chef Tim Roth produces renditions of these to make your palate sing and your cholesterol level soar into the stratosphere. Petti di polli trifolati (egg-dipped and tenderly sautéed chicken breast topped with paper-thin slices of prosciutto and Gruyère, then sauced with cognac and truffles) is magnificent, served, as are all entrées, with a cheesy dish of polenta and fresh vegetables. An entrée as simple as sautéed prawns is invested with the fullest flavors of olive oil and garlic. The somewhat pricey menu ranges beautifully from salmon to lamb. In short, this is a winner its first month. Even the decor agrees: chic mottled mustard and raw brick walls, with gleaming dark-wood accents, and a skewed shape to the rooms, which creates the desired atmosphere of intimacy and intrigue.

Alki Bakery & Cafe

2726 Alki Ave SW,
935-0616 (map: HH9)
Inexpensive; full bar;
MC, V; local checks only
Breakfast, lunch, dinner
every day

West Seattle's beachside cafe is where many Alkians come summer or winter to watch the action on the strip against a background of ferries and barges plying the waters of the Sound. It's a long and narrow cafe, with a bakery take-out counter in front (the beach is right across the street). Great for an early morning nosh. The dinner menu's limited, but the seafood's often fresh, and there are regulars who swear by the wilted spinach salad with its hot sweet-and-sour dressing and the fresh fruit flan for dessert. Parking's tough.

André's Gourmet Cuisine

14125 NE 20th St,

André Nguyen, a young Vietnamese-born chef who earned his stripes at Fullers, Daniel's Broiler, and the

RESTAURANTS

*Bellevue, 747-6551,
(map: GG2)
Moderate; beer and wine;
MC, V; no checks
Lunch Mon-Fri, dinner
Mon-Sat*

Lakeside, has brought inexpensive, innovative Eurasian cuisine to Bellevue. From a menu about equally divided between Vietnamese and European selections, you choose carefully prepared food that's served with a color-conscious nouvelle flair. Some puzzling lapses, though. We had scallops served in a scallop-shaped ceramic bowl and bathed in a buttery, beautifully balanced mushroom and cream sauce with fresh dill; they were meltingly excellent. Oddly, they came with a side of Chef Boy-ar-dee-style spaghetti. Lamb au garlic featured four tender pink slices of lamb seasoned with a whisper of rosemary and topped with broiled garlic cloves, but sitting in a bland, eggy sauce. Some of the Vietnamese combinations explode with vibrant, complex spicings; others are merely routine. We'll come back, though, because what André does well, he does wonderfully.

Anthony's Homeport

*135 Lake Ave NW (and
branches), Kirkland,
822-0225 (map: EE3)
Moderate; full bar; AE,
DC, MC, V; checks OK
Dinner every day,
brunch Sun*

In a city where most seafood restaurants come in multiples and are based more on marketing concepts than culinary ideas, Anthony's Homeport stands out. Although the original on Kirkland's waterfront has cloned itself onto other nearby shores (Everett, Des Moines, Edmonds, Shilshole Bay), they're still banking hard on the quality of their seafood, which is excellent: robust cioppino filled with fleshy mussels and Manila clams; sautéed scallops with garlic, parsley, and a splash of lemon juice; a fine rendition of fish 'n' chips; a simple, exact piece of grilled salmon. Sunday brunch is ordered off a menu—what a refreshing surprise at a waterside restaurant—and lunches are served in all branches but Kirkland. (Kirkland has a fine private room that seats 40.) The views, of course, over whatever body of water happens to be outside your particular branch's window, are peerless.

Aoki

*621 Broadway E,
324-3633 (map: GG6)
Inexpensive; beer and
wine; MC, V, AE;
checks OK
Dinner Tues-Sun*

It was really only a matter of time before sushi came to Broadway, and in Aoki it has found itself a stylish home. There's a hip Broadway crowd, picking a little of this and a little of that off a menu that provides Anglo and Asian yuppies with a new kind of fast food: robata (grilled) items, very fresh sushi and sashimi, and gyoza. This style of eating—grazing—is the best way to approach Aoki (although it will empty your wallet as surely and slyly as Spanish tapas), since full dinners are less impressive. The teriyaki, for instance, is almost always overdone. But the nasu, or baby eggplant, is grilled until the skin is charred and the flesh tender, and then skinned and cut into the shape of a fish—delicious. Reports are likewise delirious on the grilled mackerel and garlic rice.

Après Vous Cafe

1530 Queen Anne Ave N, 284-9827, (map: GG7)
Moderate; beer and wine; AE, DC, MC, V; checks OK
Lunch, dinner Mon-Sat, brunch Sat-Sun

★½

Situated on Queen Anne Hill, on the second floor of a historic brick building (just down the hall from an aerobics studio), this little café serves bounteous portions of simple, honest food. Brunches are a delight, ranging from inventive scrambles to sinful baked goods from the White Orchid Bakery, which also provides an array of rich desserts. In fact, a lot of folks like the Après Vous best as a late dessert and coffee drop-in spot. The attempt at spartan elegance makes for a cold feeling, so we try to sit out on the fair-weather terrace.

Arita

8202 Greenwood Ave N, 784-2625 (map: DD8)
Inexpensive; beer and wine; MC, V; no checks
Lunch Mon-Fri, dinner Mon-Sat

★

Followers of Japanese restaurants in Seattle, give an ear: this Greenwood restaurant is where Daiki and Hatsuko Matsueda (original owners of Hakata up in Lake City) have gone. They've created an environment that gratifies the senses: lilting Japanese flute music flutters in the background, a sweet soy-ginger-onion aroma fills the air, decor is serene and handsome. The teriyakis are quite acceptable and much less cloying than we've had elsewhere, though the rest of the menu's a bit more health-conscious: a cleansing miso soup, udon noodles in dashi stock, a perfectly crafted plate of yakisoba. There's no sushi bar but the sashimi is very fresh nonetheless. Terrific prices, as Japanese food goes—you won't pay much over $30 for two.

Armadillo Barbecue

13109 NE 175th St, Woodinville, 481-1417 (map: AA1)
Inexpensive; beer and wine; AE, MC, V; checks OK
Lunch, dinner every day

★

A West Texas barbecue joint plopped down in West Woodinville might not measure up to the standards of an oil-state expatriate, but never mind. People come here for camaraderie, an icy beer (from the 70-plus selection), and a refill of the smoky sauce with its rich hot tang. The pork is lean and tender and the chicken's extra moist, *and* they both come with a side of molassesy beans and cakey corn bread. The salads are merely passable. Brothers Bob and Bruce Gill have done up "222 Pork Avenue" with a freewheeling, slightly perverse sense of humor. Specials of the day (Cement Soup, for example) are scrawled on the front windows (rumor has it they no longer serve Lizard Gizzards), there's always an old codger or two at the window table picking his teeth, and the menu includes some inspired descriptions (Beef short rib: "Hearty hunks of heifer slow-cooked to kill the taste").

Arnie's Northshore

*1900 N Northlake Way
(and branches), 547-3242
(map: FF7)
Moderate; full bar; AE,
DC, MC, V; local
checks only
Lunch Mon-Fri, dinner
daily, brunch Sun*

The idea is to stay with the simple seafood preparations, like halibut grilled in mustard sauce or mesquite-grilled prawns, which use flash-frozen fish—a process that seems to preserve flavor better than fresh. Avoid the more complicated pastas and sauced dishes, which often fail miserably, and you'll find yourself enjoying good value and a world-class view. The Edmonds (771-5688) branch sits on Puget Sound, south of the Kingston ferry dock; the original is in Mukilteo (355-2181).

Arrowhead Cafe

*1515 Westlake Ave N,
283-8768 (map: A1)
Moderate; full bar; MC,
V; checks OK
Breakfast, lunch every
day, dinner Mon-Sat,
brunch Sat-Sun*

Owner Greg Beckley gave a rakish new look to the interior of the narrow, arrowhead-shaped building that once housed Liz's Tavern: butter-colored walls, Deco sconces, stylish black-and-white checkerboard floor tiles. The air is rich with swing and bluesy jazz, and the waitstaff dashes around taking good and friendly care of guests. The name and the ingredients (Navajo fry bread, hominy, melons) say Southwest, but the food, when it's heaped in front of you, is imaginative and unprescribed. Beckley (Ray's Boathouse, McCormick's Fish House) and chef Curtis Fontana (Campagne, Bravo) have made the menu purposefully short until the place gets off the ground (open only a few months at press time). The Anasazi mud pie is nachos by way of New Mexico, and the grilled papaya, melon, and onion that sided a dinner of grilled fresh scallops with a hint of blue cheese were a refreshing twist. Fruit is used here in all sorts of unusual ways, from a breakfast side of a mild apple sausage to a watermelon salad drizzled with raspberry purée and walnut oil, sprinkled with black pepper, and tossed with sweet red onions (an admirable creation that's been getting raves).

Asuka

*1000 2nd Ave, 682-8050
(map: M7)
Expensive; full bar; AE,
MC, V; checks OK
Lunch Mon-Fri, dinner
Mon-Sat*

Last year, Jun Miwa, the new owner of this beautifully modern Japanese restaurant moved the restaurant and its excellent staff to a new downtown location. There's no longer a tempura bar; however, you'll find superior sushi, private tatami rooms, and a skyline view of the city. Classic Japanese dishes are augmented by more unusual lobster arrangements. Provided you have ordered a day in advance you can be served omakase, a multicourse "chef's choice" dinner. The food is very subtle and quite good, though the prices are particularly high here. The decor is especially beautiful, with the private, rice paper-paneled dining rooms prefabricated in Japan. It makes an elegant place for consummating business deals, in the Japanese manner.

Service is better mid-week. In summers, you can sit outside in the pretty courtyard.

Ave! Al Ristorante Italiano
4743 University Way NE,
527-9830 (map: FF6)
Inexpensive; beer and
wine; MC, V; no checks
Lunch Mon-Fri, dinner
every day

★½

Bruno Zabaglio (former owner of Bella Neapolis) and Bruno Pace brought good pasta to the Fast-Food Ave. The restaurant is open and airy, simple and bistrolike, with oil lamps on the tables and travel posters on the walls. Evenings are crowded and cacophonous, with families and college students accounting for a sizable percentage of the patrons. The menu is broad, with most items—pastas, pizzas, and enormous calzones— nicely under $10. One breathless reviewer schooled in Italy deems the lemon, wine, and caper sauce a thing of poetry; another likes the pesto and marinara. Bruno's single-serving pizzas are light and authentically Neapolitan: billowing crusts, bright sauce, fresh toppings, scant cheese. You can split one for an appetizer. The wine list is uneven, but you can count on the house red. And great cappuccino.

Ayutthaya
727 E Pike St, 324-8833
(map: K1)
Inexpensive; beer and
wine; AE, MC, V;
no checks
Lunch, dinner Mon-Sat

★★½

One of the best Thai restaurants in town also has the nicest atmosphere, at least in terms of contemporary aesthetics, and attracts a mixed clientele: couples in their finery, young families, and savvy businesspeople. Soft pastel colors and clean, smooth lines create a calming antidote to the fiery food, which is prepared carefully and authentically by the Fuangaromya family (members of which also own Thai Restaurant in Lower Queen Anne). One of the few Thai restaurants where it's good to make reservations; there's little waiting room. The showy seafood is excellent, perhaps a sizzling platter of shrimp spiked with basil, chile, and garlic that's a show in itself. With the exception of the fried noodles (too sweet), everything is good: Naked Bathing Rama, a Thai meat-and-potato dish called massaman beef in a toned-down curry sauce, exceptionally delicate grilled chicken in coconut milk. Local businesspeople are catching on to the best lunch deal in town, so arrive early. Service is patient and sweet.

B & O Espresso
204 Belmont Ave E,
322-5028 (map: GG6)
Inexpensive; no alcohol;
no credit cards; no checks
Breakfast, lunch, dinner
every day

Legendary for espresso, extraordinary desserts, and serious conversation, this vigorous Capitol Hill coffeehouse buzzes from morning to midnight. Even with the expansion into the old B & O deli space, the interior maintains a lingering countercultural feel. It's a peaceful place for breakfast, for a cup of steamed latte con orange and a tart, or a plate of fried new potatoes

2352 California Ave SW,
935-1540 (map: II9)
No alcohol; no credit
cards; checks OK
Breakfast, lunch, dinner
every day

with peppers and onions. Lately, they've been serving lunches—thoughtful, out-of-the-ordinary creations like Chinese hot noodles, artichoke salad, and Egyptian lentil soup—and you can eat contentedly off that menu until 8pm. Desserts and coffee are where the B & O really shines; these are some of the best homemade desserts in town (not cheap, though—dessert and coffee can easily run $10 for two). As for the coffee, this is one of the few places in town that make their regular coffee by diluting espresso. The service, though quick, is on the taciturn side (another trick from New York). The newer West Seattle B & O is a smaller, brighter, homogenized version of the original—a more limited dessert selection (they're made on Capitol Hill) and a far less interesting crowd. A third coffee-and-biscotti outlet recently opened in the former Veneto's space in the Broadway Market.

Bagel Oasis
2112 NE 65th St,
526-0525 (map: EE6)
Inexpensive; no alcohol;
no credit cards; local
checks only
Breakfast, lunch every
day

Not long ago, there wasn't a respectable bagel to be found in the city. Now, finicky bagel lovers are trying to rate which of the dozen are the best. For a few months, Bagel Oasis was the noshingest place in town. When the young crew has its timing right, the right-out-of-the-oven bagels have a defiant, chewy-crunchy crust and a voluptuous, spongy center. The timing's not always accurate, and the bagels, upon occasion, have been too dry. Most often, however, they're big, yeasty, and, when laced with garlic or onion, assertively flavored. Co-owner Peter Ryan learned his craft in the bagelries of the Big Apple, though he has no qualms about offering such unkosher concoctions as ham and swiss with mayo and sprouts on a whole-wheat bagel. The meats are mostly Boar's Head, the lox Port Chatham, the omelets cooked to perfection.

Bahn Thai
409 Roy St, 283-0444
(map: A5)
Inexpensive; beer and
wine; AE, MC, V;
no checks
Lunch Mon-Fri, dinner
every day

Unquestionably one of Seattle's oldest and best-loved Thai establishments. *Bahn* means house, and the restaurant appointed with teak and blue linen occupies the main floor of what was once an old Queen Anne home. Owners Benchai and Prathan Eal (fondly known as Benny and Pete) greet with honest smiles and know many of the regulars on a first-name basis. The phad Thai is some of the most flavorful in the city, and believe us, we've tried them all. Beyond the staples, sample the larb gai (shredded chicken on raw cabbage served at room temperature). The juicy white meat reflects a piquant marinade of mint, fresh basil, lime, and flecks of dried red chiles. Spicier fare is the beef panang, with a generous portion of curried beef laced with garlic and basil. Service is fast but courteous enough to let you linger over a Thai beer.

Bai Tong
15859 Pacific Hwy S,
Sea-Tac, 431-0893
(map: O06)
Inexpensive; beer and
wine; MC, V; no checks
Lunch, dinner Mon-Sat

Get beyond the drive-in setting—inside, the staff, who speak little English, cater to a mostly Thai crowd, some of them Thai International Airways employees on their way in or out of town. They sit cross-legged on the bamboo matted floor in the back room (reserved for groups of 6 to 12) eating noodle soups and reading Thai newspapers, which the restaurant provides. If you're not Thai you might not get such treatment, but you should get the unusual gai hor bai toey, a chicken breast marinated in curry, soy, garlic, and coconut milk, folded in imported toey leaves, and deep-fried until sweetly crisp on the outside and moist inside. The peanut sauce with satay or steamed spinach is a bit too sweet and sticky; better is the chicken with a brothy red curry sauce that's especially good when soaked up with the steamy jasmine rice. No fooling around with one, two, or three stars here; when it arrives at your table it comes at a solid four stars. On recent visits the service has been unbearably slow.

Bakeman's Restaurant
122 Cherry St, 622-3375
(map: N8)
Inexpensive; full bar; no
credit cards; no checks
Breakfast, lunch, dinner
Mon-Fri

Here's a local treasure, an institution among Seattle's office workers, who form fast-moving lines every day for working-class sandwiches. Big, honest chunks of dark or light roast turkey on homemade white bread are a favorite, but there's also a great meat loaf sandwich, homemade soup, and chili. Eat in or take out— maybe over to Waterfall Park. They're open until 7pm, but the real draw is those sandwiches. Very cheap.

Bangkok Cafe
345 15th Ave E,
324-9443 (map: HH6)
Inexpensive; no alcohol;
AE, MC, V; no checks
Lunch Mon-Fri, dinner
every day

When the Bangkok Cafe is good, it is very, very good. For flat-out flavor (not necessarily spicing) the Bangkok gets our attention—especially the curries. Chef Gloy Tsui's impressive repertoire includes a half-dozen of her mother's curries: seafood dressed in a subtle coconut-milk green curry, roasted duck cooked in a sublime red curry. The crisp orange duck came perked up with broccoli, tomatoes, and onion. Even dishes that have become old standbys are distinctive here; one reviewer claims the phad Thai is superior in taste and texture to others. The long-awaited liquor license is still just that, but the to-go menu is extensive.

Beeliner Diner

2114 N 45th St, 547-6313
(map: FF7)
Inexpensive; beer and
wine; no credit cards;
checks OK
Mon-Fri, dinner
every day

The 5-Spot and Counterbalance Room

1502 Queen Anne Ave N,
285-SPOT (map: GG7)
Full bar; no credit cards;
local checks only
Brunch every day, lunch
Mon-Fri, dinner
every day

Bella Luna

14053 Greenwood Ave N,
367-5862 (map: CC8)
Moderate; full bar; AE,
MC, V; checks OK
Lunch, dinner every day,
brunch Sat-Sun

Best Wok

19 148th Ave NE,
Bellevue, 747-7031
(map: HH2)
Full bar; AE, MC, V;
local checks only
Lunch, dinner Tues-Sun

KIDS Peter Levy's Beeliner was the city's first of what is now classified as almost a trend—genuine fake diners dishing out genuine real (and improved) American food. This is where meat loaf and macaroni and cheese have gone, along with flaky crusted chicken potpie, charcoal-grilled pork chops, Parker House rolls, roast chicken with mashed potatoes, and the Blue Plate Special. Grab a booth or a counter stool (best for overhearing the hash slingers bark orders in Dinerese), order a libation off a list marked "cheap white wine," sink into a creamy slice of coconut cake to finish. It isn't perfect (watch for tepid soup, dry chops, and intentionally obnoxious service), but it's got personality to burn.

The new 5-Spot, at the top of Queen Anne's Counterbalance, is a suitably noisy place to bring the tots, Granny, or the canasta girls for a quick supper of just about anything you want (anything, that is, that's Made in the USA). Or just drop by for a nip in the Counterbalance Room.

The latest of the Mitchelli empire, way up in North Seattle (which seems like Alaska to some) is Dany Mitchell's biggest diversion from his three other trattorias. He succeeded in turning a North End Round Table Pizza restaurant into a stylish Italian restaurant warmed by a fireplace. It's the first of the four to offer remarkably good pizzas—the Italian kind, where you can actually taste the different ingredients. The rest of the menu has a new look, too, in part owing to Collins Jones, who revamped (finally) many of the old standbys and added a few now signature, items (like the Marco Polo, with fresh spinach linguine melded with a concoction of green olives, walnuts, garlic, and roasted red peppers) that you won't find elsewhere. It closes a bit earlier than the wee hours of the other Mitchelli outposts—10pm on weekdays, 11pm on weekends.

There are a half dozen glitzier Chinese restaurants in the neighborhood, but Best Wok still packs them in. Expect to wait in line, even on weeknights. The staff is used to crowds and handles them smoothly, in keeping with the restaurant's general master plan of efficiency. The place is spotless and tidily arranged, with a Bellevue gloss to it—businesslike, few surprises. The 70-plus-item menu won't surprise you either, and like most Chinese restaurants in the area, they have a timid approach to Sichuan and Hunan standards; hot-and-sour soup and hot and spicy bean cake have nary a hint of hot pepper and are mild enough to feed a baby. Though tamely seasoned, the food is attractively prepared, with crunchy fresh vegetables and a satisfactory amount of meat and shrimp.

Big Time Pizza

7281 W Lake Sammamish Pkwy NE, Redmond, 885-6425 (map: FF1)
Inexpensive; beer and wine; no credit cards; checks OK
Lunch, dinner every day

Big Time Pizza may be named like a chain, it may look like a chain (in a 7-Eleven strip mall at the end of Highway 520), it may at times even *act* like a chain—but it isn't. And the pizza doesn't taste like it's been faxed to your table. Here, the pies are all about flavor and nuance, enlightenment and restraint—like our favorite, the Pesto Plus, a harmonious blend of pesto, mushrooms, artichoke hearts, and sun-dried tomatoes. Or the Double Tomato, in which both Romas and sun-drieds (along with artichoke hearts, rosemary, mushrooms, and fresh basil) are baked into a layer of melted fontina. Crusts are aromatic and chewy, toppings are applied with an even hand and an epicurean's light touch. Owner Bill Tamiesie also makes focaccia bread, breadsticks, calzones, and terrific (try the Greek) salads. At press time he was gearing up for a move to a bigger space a few doors down, with enough room that you'll even be able to sit down and eat. There's also a playground next door, where there will be a few tables in the summer.

Blacksheep Cafe and Catering

18132 Bothell Way NE, Bothell, 485-1972 (map: BB4)
Inexpensive; beer and wine; MC, V; checks OK
Breakfast, lunch every day, dinner Tues-Sat

KIDS It's not easy to find, but this deli-style hangout at Bothell Landing just across from the Burke-Gilman Trail is a very people-conscious place: large wooden shareable tables, limited use of saturated fats, no preservatives, and an airy nonsmoking environment. The food is always healthy, and sometimes that means hearty, too (one night's special was a Moroccan stew). Thick white tuna sandwiches, turkey sliced fresh from a roasted bird, excellent low-cal curried chicken salad, and homemade lemon Dijon salad dressings. Desserts are whole-wheat sweet. Bikes and trikes welcome.

Botticelli Cafe

101 Stewart St, 441-9235 (map: I7)
Inexpensive; no alcohol; no credit cards; checks OK

This very polished, very Italian four-table aperitif bar is a place to linger over one of Seattle's finest espressos or irresistible panini (toasted Italian sandwiches). If you so much as peek in the door you might be coaxed in by Angelo Belgrano and expected to stay awhile. Unfortunately, Angelo's not here as often as he used to

Breakfast, lunch
Mon-Sat

★★½

be, since the opening of PaneVino in Pioneer Square (see listing). His stand-ins speak the requisite language but lack Angelo's charm. Still, the excellent sandwiches are enough of a draw—Sicilian focaccia bread toasted warm with fresh mozzarella, artichoke hearts, Roma tomatoes, and sweet red peppers and drizzled with thyme, oregano, and extra-virgin olive oil. Expect exceptional quality and freshness. Espresso, Italian mineral waters, and fresh fruit ices are for sipping.

Bravo
10733 Northup Way,
Bellevue, 827-8585
(map: GG3)
Moderate; full bar; AE,
MC, V; checks OK
Lunch Mon-Fri, dinner
every day

★★½

The brightest star from the (pizzeria) Pagliacci people is Bravo, home of—among other things—the best lunch in Bellevue. The pizza comes from a wood-fired oven, which makes for a very crisp crust, and the toppings would be at home in Santa Monica. The pasta is cooked firm, with good fresh sauces. A few fresh seafood and veal selections round out the menu. The restaurant sprawls like a Roman-bath grotto into many rooms, and the help sometimes seems to have gotten lost in the maze, but you will eat well at good prices in this happy marriage of West Coast cuisine and Italian cooking. A piano bar is in full swing Thursday through Sunday nights. There's an excellent, well-priced selection of Italian wines.

Brooklyn Cafe and Oyster
Bar Lounge
1212 2nd Ave, 224-7000
(map: K7)
Moderate; full bar; AE,
MC, V; checks OK
Lunch, dinner Mon-Sat

★½

The name Brooklyn Cafe seems to promise a New York theme, but it actually comes from the renovated Brooklyn building attached to the Washington Mutual Tower in which the cafe is located, not from the New York borough. It's a handsome restaurant; the booths are immense, the counter chairs are large enough to fly, and the service level is high. The menu seems formulaic (steaks, chicken, fresh seafood), although it has gotten better, especially since they ditched the silly little plate/big plate setup and added free valet parking. We've sampled a wonderfully grilled halibut. The fresh oyster bar—brimming with numerous different mollusks—is one of the best in town. Desserts are from Au Gavroche. On Seahawk Sundays, they're open for brunch.

brusseau's
117 5th Ave S, Edmonds,
774-4166
Inexpensive; beer and
wine; MC, V; local
checks only

Jerilyn Brusseau is Edmonds's own culinary ambassador to the world and has become a star on the TV talk show circuit. Maybe because these activities require so much of her time, or possibly because she spoiled us with her high standards, the salads can seem perfunctory, and recently the vegetable soup was pale

*Breakfast, lunch, early
dinner every day,
brunch Sun*

and flavorless. On the other hand, the French toast
(more like a gigantic slice of bread pudding) was the
same wonderful creation as in years past. When the
kitchen's on, you can still get a thick and hearty vegetable soup and well-stocked clam chowder. Even with
the occasional blunders, people enjoy this pleasant
neighborhood cafe. Overall, the food is good and the
baked goods better.

Buddy's Homesick Cafe
*8420 Greenwood Ave N,
784-6430 (map: DD8)
Inexpensive; full bar;
MC, V; checks OK
Lunch, dinner every day*

Kathy Casey, the young chef who a few years back put
Fullers in the Seattle Sheraton on the world's culinary
map, has brought her expertise to another kind of venture. It's called Buddy's Homesick Cafe, in homage to
the home cooking we're all homesick for. The Casey-
designed menu certainly reminds us of something Mom
might have dreamed up in the '50s: pot roast with cran-
berries, turkey with all the trimmings, meat loaf,
chicken-fried steak—this is what we now call Comfort
Food, a name that brings to mind soft, gloppy foods like
mashed potatoes and milk shakes (both of which, incidentally, are done very well at Buddy's). The setting
is rather unsettling—turquoise Naugahyde boothes and
Jetsonesque decor—but the casual, retro atmosphere
makes Buddy's ideal for kids, who will love the PB&J
with banana sandwich and the Crackerjack sundae. The
bar's for the grown-ups.

Burk's Cafe
*5411 Ballard Ave NW,
782-0091 (map: EE8)
Moderate; beer and wine;
MC, V; checks OK
Lunch, dinner Tues-Sat*

The building, constructed in 1891 to house Ballard's
first tavern, has been beautifully restored to house the
estimable Creole and Cajun cooking of Terry "Burk"
Burkhardt's. There's both file and okra gumbo,
homemade sausage, local crayfish in season, oyster po-
boys, and specials that sometimes include fresh catfish
(no bargain). Every table has its own crock of pickled
okra. All the dinners come, classically, with red beans
and rice. The rice is basmati from Texas, an exceptional long-grained variety that, combined with wild rice
and onion, is quite flavorful. Finish with a slice of the
best pecan pie in town (the chocolate peanut butter's
not bad either). The cafe can be too crowded for comfort during peak hours (and service can take forever
even when it's not full). Parking is no fun during lunch.

Bush Garden
*614 Maynard Ave S,
682-6830 (map: R7)
Moderate; full bar; AE,*

Bush Garden is one of the most popular Japanese restaurants in town, favored for its extensive menu, long
hours, numerous tatami rooms, and free parking. Most
of all, people return because it's the best value for their

MC, V; no checks
Lunch Mon-Fri, dinner
every day

money. Don't get us wrong, it's *not* cheap, just reasonable prices for good quality meals. Inside, it's ornate to the point of excess, with a babbling stream, paper lanterns and umbrellas, and lots of rattan. As for the food, you might experience excellent sashimi, tasty black cod kasuzuke, wonderful clam soup, and light tempura. While their efforts shine in the food department, they dull a bit elsewhere: substandard sake, ugly plastic teapots, and disposable chopsticks. Service is usually friendly. The late-night snacks in the cocktail lounge, the salmon chazukai (tea poured over salmon and rice) for example, are very good.

Byzantion
601 Broadway E,
325-7580
(map: GG6)
Inexpensive; beer and
wine; AE, MC, V;
no checks
Breakfast, lunch, dinner
every day

It's probably the best Greek food in Seattle, but that has never meant much in Seattle. What you can expect at Byzantion is hearty country food in generous portions, in a glowing, thoroughly intimate environment (the Russian mural on the wall is a leftover bit of atmosphere from this space's former tenant, the Russian Samovar). Order the spanakopita, flaming saganaki, or lamb—always dependable. Vegetables, too, are often outstanding. There are major flaws: we've been served raw chicken kebabs, mushy moussaka, and dry dolmades, by a waitress who slaughtered the pronunciation of virtually every item on the menu. Breakfasts are quite good, especially the feta omelets and Greek-style hash browns. Parking's atrocious.

Cactus
4220 E Madison Ave,
324-4140 (map: GG5)
Moderate; beer and wine;
MC, V; local checks only
Lunch, dinner Mon-Sat,
brunch Sat-Sun

It's rare that a restaurant has a line out its door during its opening week. Not only did Cactus's patrons wait the first week, they're still waiting. So it is at Cactus, where chef Marco Casabeaux—Italian born, Argentinian raised, and Spanish-trained—consolidates his talents in this colorful new Madison Park bistro. The terra-cotta floors and center table piled with peppers, Serrano ham, and garlic create a Mexican utopia. The menu travels further afield. The antojitas, called tapas here as in Spain, include Moorish-style dishes such as roasted eggplant with cumin and cilantro pesto. Quinoa salad is a South American version of tabouli (annoyingly gritty on one visit). The Navajo frybread, posole, and enchiladas are pure New Mexico. The Yucatan-style grilled fish comes directly from the Mexican Gulf Coast. The pork steak adobo, a hefty pork loin marinated in achiote seed, peppers, orange juice, garlic, and herbs and then grilled, is authentic in all but one respect—there's not enough of it. Skip the worshipful tableside preparation of guacamole ($5.25 to watch your waiter mash an avocado). Instead, poke into the excellent and unusual cactus salad (a jumble of greens and Southern vegetables such as jicama, squash, and grilled nopales—prickly pear cactus sans thorns). A festive atmosphere with sidewalk tables in summer.

Cafe Alexis (The Alexis Hotel)

1007 1st Ave, 624-3646
(map: M8)
Expensive; full bar; AE,
DC, MC, V; checks OK
Lunch Mon-Sat, dinner
every day

★★½

For the past five or so years Cafe Alexis has managed the unlikely: culinary consistency in the face of chef inconsistency. The latest in the kitchen parade is Charles Ramseyer, a Four Seasons Hotels recruit whose fall menu as we went to press was superb: grilled New York steak with cabernet onion marmalade, lamb sausage with fennel in warm huckleberry coulis, peppered ahi with saffron risotto cakes. On one visit a bowl of warm potato-pear bisque was flavorful and beautifully textured; an appetizer of sun-dried tomato pesto with mozzarella and prawns on crostini fingers gave the impression of earthy pizza bread, even as it awakened long-sleeping taste buds with its sophisticated flavors. Then we tasted Ramseyer's specials, one a tender flank of salmon in mustard cream sauce, the other, a slightly overcooked venison with a side of spaetzle. On the whole, delicious food, exactingly executed.

Unfortunately, such blue-ribbon dinners seem increasingly out of place at the Alexis. No longer does service in this cozy brocade drawing room of a restaurant bear the patina of exquisite professionalism; servers have been youthful and awkward on recent visits. And any reservation system that loses not one but *two* reservations is past due for some serious tinkering. If you can overlook these problems, you'll have a meal to remember, all the way through to the fruity homemade ice cream for dessert. Until they solve them, however, we're compelled to withhold the third star Ramseyer's food definitely merits.

Cafe Hue

312 2nd Ave S, 625-9833
(map: P8)
Inexpensive; beer and
wine; MC, V; checks OK
Lunch, dinner every day

Cafe Hue's (pronounced *way*) combination of Vietnamese and French cuisine is not as surprising as it may sound. Chef Kieutay Nguyen blends traditional Viet dishes with French touches and an ambience more conducive to lingering than that of most Vietnamese noodle houses. There are meals to satisfy both sides. The salade Niçoise is served comme il faut to please the strictest Francophile. The menu, however, tends more toward the Asian. There is a hearty hu tieu xao (rice noodles with shrimp and turkey). An example of

Nguyen's touch is the oc nhoi, or French escargot. The snail is ground with turkey and ginger and packed back into the shell, with a strand of lemongrass tied to the meat for easy extraction. At a dollar per, it's as much of a bargain as you could ask for. Nguyen studied the art of French pastry in Saigon, and her desserts deserve an extra few minutes. Have a superpotent Vietnamese coffee or a glass of wine from their good list, and relax in Hue's comfy chairs.

Cafe Juanita
*9702 NE 120th Pl,
Kirkland, 823-1505
(map: DD3)
Moderate; limited bar;
MC, V; checks OK
Dinner every day*

Owner Peter Dow has threaded happily among tables of pasta eaters in this charming white house restaurant for over 10 years now. He's often seen presenting a bottle of his own 1988 Cavatappi sauvignon blanc or his Nebbiolo (he makes them both on the premises) and fresh baked bread flaked with green olives and rosemary, or perhaps describing with gusto the home-bottled vinegar that makes the cafe's salads so wonderful. Pasta is Dow's forte. A recent primo piatto—cheese ravioli redolent with garlic—was delightful. Dow's chalkboard menu is built around three rarely changing main dishes (chicken in a near-luminous pistachio cream sauce, lamb chops grilled in garlic, rosemary, and olive oil, and sturdy lasagne). The predominantly rich standards are accompanied by a half-dozen rotating specials: the spiedini misti (two skewers of lamb and Italian sausage, chicken marinated in herbs and olive oil and chicken livers), perfectly roasted, and a succulent veal chop sauced with a stirring blend of veal stock, brandy, and sage. Each came with tender spears of asparagus.

The wine list carries one of the best selections of inexpensive Italian wines we've seen locally. For dessert, be sure to include Dow's crème de monforte, a wonderful, dense variation of crème caramel he perfected after an Italian sojourn. Or book the private room for a party of up to 25—it's particularly cozy, with its fireplace and sofa. Reservations need not be made a month ahead anymore, but it's a good idea to plan a week or so in advance (weekdays are more accessible).

Cafe Lago
*2305 24th Ave E,
329-8005 (map: GG6)
Moderate; beer and wine;
no credit cards;
checks OK*

The earnest Cafe Lago is a relatively new kid in town, yet what we've seen so far, we've not only liked, but admired. Carla Leonardi and Jordi Viladas hail from Tuscany and Calabria (by way of Connecticut), respectively, and here have combined the flavors of both cuisines. This exuberant and friendly little restaurant in

Dinner Tues-Sun

atmosphere comes closer than almost any place in town to the essence of a genuine Italian trattoria, from the rough red wine served in water glasses to the basket of Ciro Pasciuto's chewy, rustic bread that arrives on the paper-covered table as soon as you sit down. The simple menu, which changes twice a week or so, includes real Italian antipasti (braseola and coppa instead of salami, fontina *and* fresh mozzarella instead of provolone, and roasted red peppers so sweet they dissolve on the tongue). One-person-pizzas bake in the wood-fired oven in the back and emerge with a crisp (not shatteringly so) crust and an outstanding herbed tomato sauce and fresh mozzarella. Combinations here are reminiscent of very old Renaissance-style recipes, redolent of a clean, not candied, sweetness or a simple spiciness (the fresh ravioli filled with butternut squash and crumbled Amaretto cookies topped with a little melted butter, for instance, or the four cheese lasagna with a hint of nutmeg). Lombardi plans to add secondi piatti in the near future, including wood-oven roasted chicken and spiral sausage. We found glitches (overcooked pasta on one dish, and one night they seemed to run out of things faster than we could order them), but borne with such good cheer in these early weeks (and *such* a homemade tiramisu), that these shortcomings are more than forgivable. We're guessing these problems will quickly become a distant memory.

Cafe Los Gatos
6411 Latona Ave NE,
527-9765 (map: EE7)
Inexpensive; no alcohol;
AE, MC, V; local
checks only
Dinner Tues-Sat

In the cuisines of Central and South America, plain staples like beans, chicken, and squash ascend provocatively under the influence of delicate infusions of anise and clove, cilantro and lime, cayenne and cardamom, chiles and chocolate. Yolanda Gradi and Peter Brickman honor these traditions in their Latona neighborhood "cafe of the cats," a tiny (12 seats), vivid splash of backstreet Havana.

They prepare five dishes nightly, mostly slow-cooking stews and one-dish pots au feu, each from a different Hispanic culture. Every night there's a fish, meat, veggie, and a chicken selection—the menu rotates every month—plus one special. One Mexican main dish, estofado de cerdo, is a pork stew studded with almonds, bananas, grapes, and peaches—sweet echoes of Costa Rica and North Africa, accompanied by copious helpings of allspice-fragrant black beans and rice. A fillet of Chilean sea bass in chile sauce was fresh and terrific. The gallopin' gatos in the kitchen eschew animal fat and grease in meat as well as vegetarian entrées. The result is meals that are always healthy, always exotic, but that may falter in the realm of particulars (the occasional overcooked fish or unbalanced seasoning). Still, Cafe Los Gatos's spirit and substance (and excellent desserts) are right where they should be. Alas, no cerveza.

Cafe Open
2005 W Dravus St,
284-4552 (map: GG8)
Inexpensive; no alcohol;
no credit cards; local
checks only
Breakfast, lunch
every day

Set—not *sit*—a spell in Cafe Open and pretty soon you'll feel like you've just dropped into a neighbor's kitschy kitchen for a cup of coffee. It's a good, friendly place, known for simple breakfasts that begin the day for half of Interbay. One Queen Anne dweller likes the veggie omelet, a filling three-egg pouch stuffed with onions, peppers, mushrooms, tomatoes, and Cheddar cheese. Cafe Open will make omelets out of any combination of ingredients, including Cascioppo Brothers sausage; other morning meals include waffles, French toast, oatmeal, biscuits and gravy, and cinnamon rolls (wheat or white). Wash it all down with espresso. Hours can be somewhat irregular, but on the day this is being written, it's open breakfast and lunch. Generally speaking, we prefer breakfast; other items can waver in quality, like the veggie lasagne—the downside of "home cooking." The upside is that if you really love something—and from time to time you will—they might give you the recipe.

Cafe Sabika
315 E Pine St, 622-3272
(map: K1)
Moderate; beer and wine;
MC, V; checks OK
Dinner Tues-Sat

John and Gloria Rios run this homey place almost like their home dining room: she does the legwork from table to table, he's visible tossing sautés around, stirring sauces, banging pans in the open kitchen. They've found a perfectly quirky showcase for their own patented brand of charm. Once in a while they pop a bottle of champagne, break into song, and have their own kitchen party between orders. (Sometimes they simply decide to close for a week or so—call ahead.) But for all the informality of the place (like their Chateau Rios on Lopez Island), the meals are elegant (reminiscent of Chateau Rios on Roy Street) and classic: butter-tender beef Wellington with his masterful béarnaise, snapper sparked with cilantro and garlic, and excellent smoked duck linguine. He smokes his own game hens—a succulent whole hen that's lightly and thus evocatively smoked, then baked to skin-crispiness and covered with an apricot brandy sauce that's the perfect complement. There are minor inconsistencies here: the smoked duck salad with raspberry vinaigrette we found short on the main ingredient. Regardless, this welcoming bistro-style Basque cafe is the kind of place you'd like to eat at every night. You can even sit on a little staging platform in the window and gaze out at the rain—and become a part of the Rioses' magical world.

Cafe Sophie

*1921 1st Ave, 441-6139
(map: H8)
Moderate; beer and wine;
MC, V; checks OK
Lunch Tues-Sat, dinner
Tues-Sun, brunch Sun*

Nothing is subtle at this unabashedly garish restaurant, from the opulent interior—draped booths, fringed lamps, a back room with deep red walls, a fireplace, a view of the Sound—to the elaborate list of desserts, usually some combination of white chocolate and framboise. Least memorable about Shane Dennis's place is the food. That said, we'd still return. Two things make this place work: the exquisite desserts, which are made daily on the premises (some aren't even available until 8pm, so it caters to a later-than-usual downtown crowd, and the fact that Cafe Sophie doesn't take itself too seriously. A sense of humor is imperative to turn a former funeral home into a refined restaurant, and model the ladies' washroom after one in a bordello.

Cafe Sport

*2020 Western Ave,
443-6000 (map: H9)
Moderate; full bar; AE,
DC, MC, V; checks OK
Breakfast, lunch, dinner
every day*

Cafe Sport/Bellevue

*Winter Garden in
Bellevue Place, Bellevue,
453-1111 (map: HH3)
Moderate; full bar; AE,
DC, MC, V; checks OK
Lunch Mon-Fri, dinner
Mon-Sat*

Even before Chef Diana Isaiou was moved to the new Cafe Sport Bellevue and was succeeded by her assistant Camille Convy, we began to notice a loss of the subtleties that once distinguished this as a four-star restaurant. We've heard complaints about inattentive service, overcooked steaks, sauces that don't quite come together—things that might plague other restaurants but shouldn't be a problem at the Sport. Still, complaints come mingled with an equal number of accolades, as Cafe Sport remains the standard-bearer for a consistently fresh blend of New American and Pacific Rim cuisines and stands as one of Seattle's most distinctive restaurants.

In spirit, downtown Cafe Sport is two restaurants. First there is the "cafe," where you can eat a casual lunch (better have reservations) or eat at a booth in the bar, noisily populated by the maddeningly fit patrons of the adjacent Seattle Club. Perhaps a third of the patrons order the black bean soup, a cilantro-and-lime-laced version, coarsely pureed, to be sopped up with chewy bread. Hot chicken breast sandwich—slabs of perfectly grilled poultry served with basil mayonnaise and a mound of shoestring potatoes, fabulously messy to eat—and the famous Dungeness crab cakes (still the best in town) are similarly popular. Lately, though, the kitchen seems a little bored by these favorites, and they might emerge without their usual luster. Breakfast dishes of omelets and meats and waffles can be among the best in town (though one recent report of a cold omelet and absentee service leaves us skeptical as to the priorities these days).

In the evening, you can enjoy the "restaurant" experience: lights are dimmed, and it all becomes a bit more formal, though far from stuffy (some would wish maybe a little *more* formal). For starters, try the antipasto plate loaded with marinated vegetables, a whole roasted head of garlic, and goat cheese. Entrées show the restaurant's respect for fresh ingredients, Asian flavors, and especially good seafood. Each entrée is paired with a recommended wine—a very helpful feature. Among our favorite desserts are a dark chocolate terrine with white chocolate sauce and the city's best silky-thick crème caramel.

Happily, the new Sport on the Eastside in Kemper Freeman's Bellevue Place (we like to call it Son of Sport) seems to promise the accommodating, unobtrusive service and brilliant innovation that once marked the downtown original. At press time, Cafe Sport/Bellevue had been open only three weeks. Chef Isaiou has opened the new place, not with the pan-Asian touches that illuminate the downtown menu but with a Mediterranean–Middle Eastern inclination. It reads a little more self-consciously prettified than downtown does, but we may just need to get used to it.

Caffè Minnie's
101 Denny Way,
448-6263 (map: C9)
Moderate; beer and wine;
AE, DC, MC, V; local
checks only
Breakfast, lunch, dinner
every day

This isn't cuisine, this is just food—good food—served anytime. Lunch at Minnie's found us delving into big salads (with good croutons), hefty portions of lasagne, pollo alla Parmigiana sandwiches (chicken breasts on crunchy, buttery garlic bread smothered with marinara and mozzarella and broiled). One reviewer nearly swooned over the accompanying grilled red potatoes dusted with Parmesan and spices. At dinner we were served a so-so Italian burger (marinara, Gorgonzola, and mushrooms—minus, mysteriously, the mushrooms), and service was, well, unpredictable, but given the breadth and depth of this 24-hour menu, we'll forgive. Breakfast (granola to eggs Benedict to Dutch-baby pancakes) and dinner (humanely raised veal, pasta) are served round the clock.

Cajun Corner Cafe
(The Alexis Hotel)
90 Madison St, 682-5019
(map: M8)
Inexpensive; full bar; AE,
DC, MC, V; local
checks only
Lunch, dinner Mon-Sat

It's Cajun food, in a just plain regular room with no out-landish pretensions, despite its proximity to the cushy Alexis. You'll find traditional New Orleans muffuletta sandwiches, spicy, smoky andouille sausage, gumbo, po-boy sandwiches, red beans and rice, and blackened just about everything—occasionally overcooked, rarely underseasoned, but don't let that scare you off. It's a good–cheer spot, a place to stuff yourself silly, nosh on the tidbits, or sink into a wicked wedge of sweet potato–pecan pie; you won't pay much for this home cooking, which you can eat until 2am.

Campagne
86 Pine St, 728-2800
(map: J8)
Expensive; full bar; AE,
DC, MC, V; no checks
Lunch Mon-Sat, dinner
every day

At press time, owner Peter Lewis had brought in chef Tamara Murphy (formerly of Dominique's Place) to re-place Susan Vanderbeek as the head of the kitchen, and since she had been behind the line only two weeks, it was difficult to tell what changes she will bring to the kitchen. Peter's province is the front—a light, quietly elegant space in the Inn at the Market courtyard, with wood floors, Oriental rugs, and a view of the bay—and the highly individualistic wine list (from which you can actually order a good white burgundy by the glass). Provençal food is still the focus; however, our sam-plings have been wildly uneven. We've had a few stun-ning meals here: a starter of sole-and-salmon sausage, a main course of melting and meaty duck breast marinated with juniper berries, and at lunch "tuna sand-wiches" of Eastern sea scallops layered with fresh tuna. But the latest version of the menu has not been as stellar: a steamed bass garnished with shellfish and served in a saffron-tomato sauce was virtually devoid of any herbal aroma; a bland cassoulet arrived, un-garnished, with underdone beans. (No excuse for such slipups when you're charging these prices.)

Canlis
2576 Aurora Ave N,
283-3313 (map: GG7)
Expensive; full bar; AE,
DC, MC, V; checks OK
Dinner Mon-Sat

For a town filled with restaurants, Seattle has remark-ably few that qualify as institutions. At the top of this short list is Canlis, around for nearly 40 years. It's lasted this long because it delivers exactly what it promises: good food, fine service, and a great view. There's a timeless quality about the place, from the twinkling lights around Lake Union below to the crowd at the piano bar to the kimono-clad waitresses, many of whom are in their third decade here. You won't find the latest in trendy dining at Canlis, but there is no better place for the annual thick steak accompanied by a noble cabernet. There's no shortage of seafood, either, including lobster bisque, Canlis's signature sautéed prawns, salmon, or scallops, all superbly prepared. This perfection has its price: the menu is à la carte, and the tariff is among the highest in town. The high prices carry over to the wine list, which is so extensive it has a table of contents.

Casa-U-Betcha
2212 1st Ave, 441-1026
(map: G8)
Moderate; full bar; AE,
MC, V; no checks
Lunch Mon-Fri, dinner
every day

Every so often a restaurant's decor is as tangible an element as its cuisine. So it is at Seattle's first "taco club," which was actually conceived in Portland five years ago. Diners sit in lizard-skin vinyl booths, in front of backlit fiberglass, or within sight of an unavoidable 15-foot inverted pyramid. The menu is daunting, but order with courage. This is a meal that defies description—perhaps Mexican/South American/Northwest? Some dishes try to cover it all in one bite, such as the Mexican Sushi (avocado, jicama, smoked salmon, sweet rice, wasabi, and black bean paste rolled in a tortilla). Skip it. This colorful eating odyssey should begin with the blue corn and red chile polenta, served with a surprisingly creamy, mustardy crab sauce. Instead of the Mexican staples, opt for the combinations that may or may not take you south of the border, such as feijoada completa, a Brazilian stew of various meats in (lots of) black beans, or one of the grilled meats. We also like the Northwest Caesar salad, which usually has an ample amount of smoked salmon substituting for the less popular anchovian version. The bar is cozier for dining than the overwhelming main room—which tends to get as loud as the decor in prime dinner hours—and has an admirable selection of tequilas and spiked Jell-O drinks.

Catfish Corner
2726 E Cherry St,
323-4330 (map: HH6)
Inexpensive; no alcohol;
no credit cards;
checks OK
Lunch, dinner every day

KIDS Here's a small neighborhood cafe with comfortable booths, a jolly regular clientele, and restorative soul food: sweet Louisiana catfish, deep-fried just right and perfect with a few hush puppies and maybe some pie. The potato salad is very good. Great for take-out, too.

Cave Man Kitchens
807 West Valley Hwy,
Kent, 854-1210
Inexpensive; no alcohol;

The late Dick Donley was a tinkerer with both machines and food. He spent years experimenting with methods of smoking ribs, chicken, turkey, sausage, ham, and salmon over alder and (when available) applewood. What he finally achieved was outstanding—

MC, V; checks OK
Lunch, dinner every day

especially the moist smoked turkey. Donley's six children carry on after him, and nothing has changed. There is no inside seating, but in warm weather you can eat outside on picnic tables and go across the street to the neighborhood store for beer. Most people take out, loading up on the smoked goods and accompaniments such as beans, potato salad, coleslaw, and a terrific bread pudding with butterscotch whiskey sauce.

Chandler's Crabhouse and Fresh Fish Market
901 Fairview Ave N,
223-2722 (map: D1)
Moderate; full bar; AE,
DC, MC, V; local
checks only
Lunch, dinner every day,
brunch Sun

It's shiny, all right, the kind of place where the patrons are as pretty as the view of Lake Union, which is as pretty as the waiters serving you, who are as pretty as the salmon on your plate. You wade through an obstacle course on the way to your table (fresh fish market here, loud pickup bar there) but once seated in the dramatic glass-walled vault you'll be in for decently treated seafood and an absolutely winning view of the spinnakers on the lake. The menu is crab-heavy—fresh cracked Dungeness, crab cakes, and the rarely seen soft-shelled blues (in season)—with other shellfish, Maine lobster, and a fresh fish list every day. A recent order of king salmon arrived moist and perfectly cooked in a creamy (bland) sauce, with grilled onions and zucchini on the side and a superfluous pile of overcooked pasta, while across the table sat an overcooked hunk of sturgeon in a splendid garlic sauce. The bread, an onion rye from Brenner Brothers, is excellent, though we recently had to wait much too long for it (our waiter, too, for that matter). Sunday brunch is a fine time to visit, for order-off-the-menu omelets, crab cakes, and such. At the other end of the day you can order off the crab bar menu until 1am.

Chanterelle Specialty Foods
316 Main St, Edmonds,
774-0650
Inexpensive; beer and
wine; MC, V; local
checks only
Breakfast, lunch Tues-
Sun, dinner Tues-Sat

Stunning, inventive creations come out of Jochen Bettag's Edmonds kitchen, the most exciting of which is his seafood sausage. The place is stocked with gourmet foodstuffs, salads, et al., which can be packaged to go. You order and pay up front, but because of the freshness and vibrance of the food, that doesn't detract from the experience. Pesto-cheese eggs for breakfast are light and flavorful; spanakopita is dripping with spinach, pine nuts, and feta cheese. Every night Bettag offers a half-dozen entrées, a couple of soups, and several salads. Prices are great.

Chau's Chinese Restaurant
310 4th Ave S, 621-0006

Chau's gets a big zero for atmosphere and even less for cleanliness, and yet some insist that Jimmy Yick serves

(map: Q7)
Inexpensive; beer and
wine; MC, V; no checks
Lunch Mon-Fri, dinner
every day

★★

up the best Cantonese seafood this side of the Far East, taking advantage of this region's abundant selection of undersea edibles. Customers in the know head straight for the steamed oysters with garlic sauce (huge fresh oysters piled high with chopped garlic and cooked just right, no longer raw but still redolent of the open ocean) or heady and flavorful wok-baked Dungeness crab with ginger and green onions remain enthusiastic. Reports are dismal on the rest of the fare, so skip the dime-a-dozen items like sweet-and-sour pork and fried rice (these get little or none of the chef's attention). Try Chau's with a large group: a 10-course seafood banquet can cost as little as $15 per person (in a room that accommodates up to 80 people). Food is served until 11:30pm.

Chautrelles

321 E Pine St, 624-1648
(map: K1)
Moderate; beer and wine;
AE, MC, V; checks OK
Lunch Tues-Fri, dinner
Tues-Sat

★

Laurie and Gregg Monette's sparsely decorated neighborhood restaurant on Capitol Hill showed lots of promise when it opened two years ago. Little problems were encountered this year: old bread, withering centerpiece roses, a sweet but unpolished waitress, dishes that lacked subtlety. The lingcod was sauced with a strong list of ingredients—sun-drieds, capers, black olives, shallots, and lemon—but the olive oil was the dominant flavor; the caramel-apple pie had the appeal of a candy apple run through a Cuisinart. The chef has a tendency to undercook the seafood to the point of rawness. Strong points are the salads especially the one that featured sautéed mushrooms, crispy bacon, and goat cheese in a robust rosemary garlic vinaigrette, or another with seared scallops and candied garlic with a raspberry shallot dressing. Chautrelles has plenty of well-heeled fans, who visit often enough to know what to order.

Chez Shea

Pike Place Market,
467-9990 (map: J8)
Expensive; beer and wine;
AE, MC, V; checks OK
Dinner Tues-Sun

★★½

In many ways, Chez Shea is the quintessential Market restaurant: the freshest ingredients, a real love for the bounty of the region, and a cozy elegant setting with half-moon windows overlooking the Market rooftops to the Sound and the Olympics. Candles and subdued lighting provide just enough illumination to keep conversations low and the experience romantic. It's hard to believe a bustling kitchen headed by chef Craig Packard is just behind the bamboo screen. The four-course meals are prix-fixe ($32); you pick from one of the four entrées. The three other courses come as executive chef Shea designs—three times a season. Recent meals have not been up to the same high standards of imagination we remember from previous visits. The courses that surrounded the entrée seemed perfunctory: a light tomato and red pepper terrine pepped up with a vinaigrette, followed by a stark naked white risotto garnished with only a sprig of parsley, and a salad built of only red lettuce and two precious slices of tomato. For entrées, the pan-roasted beef tenderloin in wine, basil, and garlic sauce was butter-knife tender, topped with Gorgonzola and walnuts and perfectly rare (as requested); however, the yellowfin ahi (though competently cooked) was oversauced with mediocre béarnaise. The wine list, while not long, has an excellent mix of top West Coast and European vintages, carefully chosen by manager Lotta Hashizume.

The Chile Pepper
*5000 University Way NE,
526-5004 (map: FF6)
Inexpensive; beer and
wine; no credit cards;
checks OK
Lunch, dinner Mon-Sat*

Hidden behind the inauspicious exterior and the fast-foodish-sounding name is Seattle's best and most distinctive Mexican restaurant. The Chile Pepper serves authentic regional cuisine of mountainous Guanajuato, home state of proprietor Rodolfo and his chef and mother, Catalina Gonzales. The chicken mole poblano is neither the Oaxacan chocolate nor the bland peanut sauce found elsewhere, but rather a rich, redolent infusion of tomatillo, sesame, almonds, cinnamon, cloves, laurel, and diverse other spices. The puerco en adobo is an equally complex balance of fiery, sweet, and tangy flavors, topped by that signature cinnamon. Their chile relleno is usually the best in town—piquant, deep-red dried chiles anchos lightly battered and cleanly fried, with sweet, sour, and spicy accents in the usual cheese filling—but a recent sample was not up to the usual standard. Service seems to be sliding, too.

Chinook's
*1735 W Thurman St,
283-4665 (map: FF8)
Moderate; full bar; AE,
MC, V; checks OK
Lunch, dinner every day,
brunch Sat-Sun*

It's big, busy, and formulaic, but this time the Anthony's Homeport folks seem to be using the right bait at the Port of Seattle's $13 million renovation of Fishermen's Terminal. The industrial-strength design with very high ceilings, steel countertops, visible beams, and ventilation ducts, matched with an appealing collection of action-packed fishing photos, fits well with the bustle around the working marina. The 125-item menu ranges from broiled and fried seafood to Japanese stir-fries and big, juicy burgers. We suggest you nab a few things off the regular menu (tempura onion rings and a half-dozen oysters) and the rest from the daily special sheet (Copper River salmon char-grilled with sun-dried tomato basil butter or petrale sole baked with soy sauce and topped with toasted almonds). We have found a few of the charbroiled selections slightly overcooked. For dessert, try a big piece of blackberry cobbler. The problems are with the staff, often young and forgetful.

Ciao Italia
512 5th Ave S, Edmonds, 771-7950
Moderate; beer and wine; MC, V; no checks
Dinner Tues-Sun

★½

KIDS Gino and Tama Borriello have taken over the old Bel Piemonte site and infused it with a new openness and ambience. It is now a pleasure to be here (families too). Diners coo over the calamari, quickly poached and served with a pesto marinade. The pizza margherita was sensational—a light crust and a well-herbed sauce. However, the minestrone was weak and disappointing and the dinner salads heavy with oil and vinegar. More memorable were the creamy, verdant pollo pesto, a tender veal spiked with artichokes and mushrooms, the penne with ricotta, mozzarella, and Parmesan, and eggplant in marinara sauce. A comfortable spot where children are always *benvenuti.*

Coho Cafe
4533 California Ave SW, 935-5930 (map: JJ9)
Inexpensive; beer and wine; MC, V; checks OK
Lunch Tues-Fri, dinner Tues-Sat

★

One of the first of West Seattle's new wave of restaurants since the new bridge went in. Coho's white stucco exterior strikes a contemporary note with hip accents such as an attractive salmon logo, little window displays, and a curious red neon CHEF sign in the window. The food is neither flashy nor expensive; nevertheless, it is often creative, honest, and essentially healthy. And over the past two years owner/chef Richard Davis (formerly of La Fleur and The Ritz Cafe) has cultivated a growing list of regulars who return for such dishes as the slightly sweet duck breast with oyster mushrooms, cassis, and a white zinfandel sauce or the chicken pasta made with fusilli, dark chicken meat, walnuts, onions, mushrooms, and a smoky, cumin-flavored cream sauce. The menu changes seasonally and is adaptable to special diets. A couple of times a year, Davis hosts special edition dinners demonstrating the various uses of the wild mushrooms he gathers from Western Washington forests.

Continental Restaurant and Pastry Shop
4549 University Way NE, 632-4700 (map: FF6)
Inexpensive; beer and wine; MC, V; no checks

KIDS Simple, friendly, and airy, this U District classic has the atmosphere of a Greek storefront cafe. Breakfast (served all day) with eggs, wonderful Greek fries, and a souvlaki skewer is a great bargain. Later in the day try the lentil soup or dolmades, with galatoboureko for dessert, if it's Friday. You can buy authentic in-

Breakfast, lunch, dinner every day

Copacabana
Pike Place Market,
622-6359 (map: J8)
Inexpensive; beer and
wine; AE, DC, MC, V;
no checks
Lunch, dinner Mon-Sat
(summer);
Lunch Mon-Sat, dinner
Fri-Sat (winter)

Cousins of Kirkland
140 Central Way,
Kirkland, 822-1076
(map: FF3)
Inexpensive; beer and
wine; MC, V;
local checks only
Breakfast every day,
lunch Mon-Fri

Crêpe de Paris
Rainier Square,
623-4111 (map: L6)
Moderate; full bar; AE,
DC, MC, V; no checks
Lunch, dinner Mon-Sat

gredients from the adjoining deli and make your own pastries, too. Great people-watching.

Seattle's only Bolivian restaurant doesn't quite recall the authenticity of Ramon Paleaz's original Pike Place Market dive—the one with the counter that tilted so much that servers had to jam forks beneath the plates to keep them upright—but the splendid sun deck (great for viewing Elliott Bay and Pike Place) comes close. The family recipes are still used: the spicy shrimp soup; salteñas, juicy meat-and-raisin-stuffed pastries; huminta, a piquant corn pie topped with cheeses; poached halibut with sautéed onion and tomato in a mild saffron sauce. Like the Spanish, Bolivians seem to cook everything to death, and everything here is a tad pricier than you'd expect.

The three owners, Dr. Albert Reichert, Lo Reichert, and Mitchell Cameil, are first cousins from, not Kirkland, but Massachusetts and Paris. More than cousins (sisters, brothers, and uncles, too) contribute to this family-run lunch place awash with natural light, whose Art Deco decor and high ceilings give it an airy appeal. You can get the expected deli fare here, but you should at least sample Franny's blintzes (cottage and cream cheeses folded into homemade crepes). Cousins' breakfasts are great. They showcases a good seafood omelet, though it's only served on weekends. It's become increasingly popular with families, especially since the whole restaurant is designated no smoking.

Annie Agostini's 13-year old Rainier Square crêperie is more of a bistro than a fancy French restaurant these days. The place bustles at lunch but is all but deserted in the evenings, except when the cabaret is on (most Thursdays to Saturdays), and then reservations are advised. Crêpes are still a generous part of the menu though you have to look on the back page to find them. Fillings range from ratatouille Provencal, chicken and mushrooms, and spinach and cheese to boeuf bourguignon, all wrapped in light, almost crisp, Breton crêpes. The mainstays on the front page, however, emphasize lighter classic French cooking (emphasizing seafood) as well as large salads, sandwiches, and simple pasta dishes. Desserts lean toward the classics or fruit-and-ice-cream filled sweet crêpes. Crêpe de Paris is perfect for a relaxed lunch in the heart of the shopping district, and for dinner theater fare, you won't find any better. Each cabaret show runs for a month or two.

Cucina! Cucina!

901 Fairview Ave N (and branches), 447-2782 (map: D1)
Moderate; full bar; AE, MC, V; checks OK
Lunch, dinner every day

Cucina! Cucina! is overwhelming! overwhelming! There's the place: a slick Italianate chamber sectioned into parts—the open kitchen, the upper bar, the lower bar, the dining area, the broad deck—with Lake Union shimmering outside the window. There are the patrons, looking like they're going right from here to the Academy Awards (and making, incidentally, just one hell of a racket). And the menu, which with its multitudinous antipasti, zuppe, insalate, pizze, paste, and griglie makes you tired just looking at it. Everybody's confused, the waitstaff perhaps most of all. Some of the nibbles have been quite good: the crackly focaccia bread, whose aroma perfumes the whole place, is garlicky and delicious. The five-cheese (mozzarella, provolone, Gorgonzola, fontina, and pecorino Romano) pizza, made in the wood-burning oven, is a creamy, smoky delight. But spices overwhelmed both the roast trout and the tomato sauce over angel hair pasta. Cucina! Cucina! has cloned itself in Tukwila (17770 Southcenter Parkway, 575-0520) and in Bellevue (800 Bellevue Way, 637-1177). The Eastside's version in Bellevue Place is equally loud and fun, distinctly less glitzy, but it lacks the dramatic compartmentalization of the Lake Union establishment. No reservations; open until 1am.

Cutters Bayhouse

2001 Western Ave, 448-4884 (map: J8)
Moderate; full bar; AE, DC, MC, V; checks OK
Lunch, dinner every day, brunch Sun

This stylish restaurant overlooking Elliott Bay on the north edge of the Pike Place Market is jammed morning, noon, afternoon, and night. The hodgepodge menu echoes the interior design, which includes a bar, brasserie, deli, cafe, and restaurant. You can order just about anything—Chinese, Hawaiian, Cajun, Italian, salads, pastas, seafood, and more; what's surprising is that most everything is good. We've enjoyed the fresh lingcod with hazelnut sauce served with focaccia (the thick Italian bread that makes the whole restaurant smell like garlic, even at Sunday breakfast) and the bar nibbles that are served until 1am nightly. The bar also has a good selection of wines by the glass. The view is wonderful both outside and in, where the upwardly mobile types congregate after aerobics at the Seattle Club across the street.

Cyclops

2416 Western Ave,
441-1677 (map: F9)
Inexpensive; no alcohol;
no credit cards; no checks
Lunch, dinner Tues-Sun,
brunch Sat-Sun

Geof Spencer swore off restaurants after a stint as a chef at the raison d'être years ago. Gina Kaukola checked coats at the Re-Bar. Together, they saved the former Cafe Mars by putting an eyeball in the Mars logo and calling it Cyclops. That's the spirit of Cyclops: adventurous, free-form, challenging restaurant conventions, and open late. Where else in Seattle can you find a packed house at 2:30 on Sunday morning? Where the only criteria for guest chef are "a pretty good idea and lots of friends"? And the food, well, who knows on those nights, but most of the time you might call it working-class vegetarian: lemony tabouli, creamy hummus scooped with pita, veggie sandwiches, and spinach salad with feta. At night you'll find a couple of specials—maybe a turkey potpie, or artichokes stuffed with rice and served with steamed vegetables. And the homemade desserts are baked right there. In fact, Geof might just waft a hot apple pie by your nose for a sure-sell sniff. Fresh fruit and espresso shakes are some other favorites. At press time they were just beginning to serve breakfast.

Dahlia Lounge

1904 4th Ave, 682-4142
(map: H6)
Moderate; full bar; AE,
DC, MC, V; checks OK
Lunch Mon-Fri, dinner
Mon-Sat

Over the past year, the Dahlia has blossomed into one of Seattle's finest restaurants. Tom Douglas (who brough national acclaim to Cafe Sport a few years ago) opened his own downtown restaurant in the former 1904 location. The two story vermillion space with floral upholstered booths and artful papier-maché fish lamps is far better suited to cold rainy nights than to the late-sun evenings of summer. Recent meals suggest that he has produced yet another restaurant that brilliantly captures the pioneer spirit of Northwest cuisine. Douglas cooks the kind of food he likes to eat; if it has to be defined, it's somewhere between the comfort food of the '50s and Northwest cuisine of the '90s. Who else would dare feature roast pork with sweet potato hashbrowns, delicate Dungeness crab cakes with Wild West Salsa, or charred rare tuna puttanesca with egg noodles on the same menu? Douglas not only gets away with it, he does a superb job a delighting foodies with tastes they never expected to like; the hoisin barbecued salmon with fried rice was simultaneously light and spicy; the roast duck with green peppercorn sauce came with a soothing butternut squash risotto; and a special one night was a properly cooked steak with a rich anchochile-based barbecue sauce and moist jalapeño cornbread. Lunches run a similarly unexpected multi-ethnic course, from tomato and sweet red pepper soup with sorrel cream to a pita sandwich filled with grilled chicken, hummus and tzatziki to simple gnocchi with a pesto and plum tomato sauce. The desserts are light on chocolate (except the moist chocolate polenta cake with white chocolate sauce) and heavy on invention—the pear tart (layers of delicate puff pastry with almond paste, pears, and whipped cream surrounded by caramel sauce) was ethereal. Douglas's relaxed, casual, and professional tone (he likes to chat with the diners) has rubbed off on his outstanding staff.

DaVinci's Flying Pizza
89 Kirkland Ave,
Kirkland, 889-9000
(map: DD3)
Inexpensive; full bar; AE,
MC, V; local checks only
Breakfast Sat-Sun,
lunch, dinner every day

Kirkland doesn't *need* any more zany pizza joints on its waterfront, but Michael Brown's (of Browny's fame) is actually a good one—in spite of the acid-trip decor (beheaded mannequins, flying pizzas) and the barbecue smoked-chicken pizzas. Much better are the classic pies on a bready crust, a clean marriage of flavors. Better still are the pastas including unquestionably the area's finest slab of lasagna (layers of cheese, saffron marinara, and a duxelles paste of mushrooms and herbs). Salads are satisfying and desserts heavenly. The retractable garage door in the front room opens the whole place onto the sidewalk in summer. There's a breakfast of frittatas, pancakes, and French toast on weekends and dancing in the lively bar Wednesdays, Fridays, and Saturdays.

Domani
604 Bellevue Way NE,
Bellevue, 454-4405
(map: HH3)
Moderate; full bar; AE,
MC, V; no checks
Lunch Mon-Fri, dinner
every day

An Eastsider's choice for lunch that has been improving steadily over the past couple of years, most recently due to chef Geoff Foubert, who took over in January 1990. It's a smart setting with skylights, raw wood, and a lot of greenery. Foubart keeps Domani's menu adventurous: the calamari San Remo (sautéed calamari steaks served with white wine, garlic, and chopped tomato) is one of our favorite dishes. The tortellini with sausage, mozzarella, and prosciutto is dependable, and the Caesar outstanding. An address right across from Bellevue Square makes Domani a great place for a meeting: two private rooms hold 20 and 60.

du jour
1919 1st Ave, 441-3354
(map: I8)
Moderate; beer and wine;
MC, V; checks OK

High-toned, high pretensions, high prices. This sparkling, upscale European deli on First Avenue lures you in with its lineup of fancy, overpriced salads prettily displayed in the front window. You proceed through the cafeteria line while cheerful servers grace your plate

*Breakfast, lunch, dinner
Mon-Sat*

★½

with precious portions of salads and ethnic-tinged luncheon items and sell those exquisite accompaniments (dense Milano rolls, truffles) as if they were going to receive a commission on them. And the espresso is mediocre at best. But we keep coming back—for the city's best soda bread at breakfast, and a cup of tea and a butter cookie nibbled at those tables in the back, where the view of the bay is irresistible.

The Duck Cafe
*4021 E Madison St,
329-7037 (map: GG5)
Moderate; no alcohol;
MC, V; checks OK
Breakfast Mon-Fri,
lunch every day, brunch
Sat-Sun*

★½

This 11-table cafe a few blocks from the beach at Madison Park has quietly become one of the top weekend brunches in Seattle. There's a wide-ranging selection of omelets, each named after a different quacker (Bufflehead, Ruddy Duck), as well as hotcakes, coffee cake, and a terrific bowl of oatmeal. The servings aren't as big as we remember, but as long as they give us more of those crunchy, oniony cottage fries they're forgiven. Lunchtime brings such fare as delicious curried chicken salad in hefty portions. Sidewalk tables in summer.

Duke's Bar & Grill
*236 1st Ave W,
283-4400 (map: GG7)
Moderate; full bar; AE
DC, MC, V; local
checks only
Lunch Mon-Fri, dinner
every day*

*10116 NE 8th St,
455-5775 (map: HH4)
Moderate; full bar; AE
DC, MC, V; local
checks only
Lunch Mon-Sat, dinner
every day*

★

The original Duke's on Queen Anne is one of the city's prime schmoozing and networking spots, with good drinks and coffee and serviceable-to-better lunch and dinner fare that runs to Caesar salads (some say the city's most garlicky), London broil, fresh seafood, pastas, and hearty sandwiches. The Bellevue outpost, its parking lot jammed with BMWs and Mercedeses, serves the same see-and-be-seen function. We hear reports of generous sandwiches (heaped with relishes and melted cheese) on good sourdough, toothsome buckwheat linguine off the specials sheet one night, perfectly sauced (though overcooked) seafood, and terrific desserts. A lot of this can be nibbled in the bar—the best part of Duke's—into the wee hours.

Duke's Chowder House and Outrageous Canoe Club
*901 Fairview Ave N
382-9963 (map: D1)
Inexpensive; full bar; AE
MC, V; local checks only
Lunch, dinner every day*

*7850 N Green Lake Dr,
522-4908 (map: EE7)*

The formatting of Duke's Chowder Houses marks Duke's as one of the city's most versatile restaurant chains, from the formal Yacht Club to the beachy Canoe Club where a kayak suspends from a ceiling beam, boats pass by the large windows, and pretty young women show off their shoulders. There's a lot of energy at the Canoe Club, where the staff seems to have as much fun as the customers. The food runs from decent variations of burgers (with great Creole-spiced

Full bar; AE, MC, V;
checks OK
Lunch, dinner every day,
breakfast Sat-Sun

fries) to sandwiches (try the Caribbean Club made with grilled lingcod and banana mango chutney) to selections from a fresh specials sheet every day. In truth, you're here because, well, everyone else is. A large dining room cut in two by a walkway leading to an outdoor deck features a long bar, complete with a TV tuned to sports. On Lake Union, none of the windows have shades, providing a nice but sometimes glaring view. Ask to borrow a pair of sunglasses.

Duwamps Cafe and Seattle Brewing Company

301 Queen Anne Ave N,
281-8200 (map: A8)
Moderate; full bar; MC,
V; checks OK
Lunch Mon-Fri, dinner
Mon-Sat, brunch Sat-Sun

★½

Phil and Susan Rogers, late of the Napa Valley Brewing Company and Calistoga Inn, have brought a little California to the city which for a few brave months in 1852 was known as Duwamps. The space they chose in the office district of Lower Queen Anne is a renowned restaurant graveyard, but they've San Franciscified the place with dark wood and faux-mustard walls, and the crowds are starting to gather. Sadly, the kitchen's ambitions have so far exceeded its capacities. The menu is sophisticated and appealing, with appetizers that sound particularly fetching (house-cured salmon gravlax with aquavit capers and dill; rare filet mignon, sliced thin, with fresh grated horseradish; spicy crab cakes with tomato ginger chutney) and a list of inventive sandwiches, pizzas, calzones, pastas, and seafood. Many items feature some alluring twist—apples and calvados with medallions of turkey, trout, and hazelnuts in the escarole salad—but bland, awkward execution can deflate high hopes. One lunch special, farafalle pasta with lamb sauce, was eatable but nominally unexciting. Fish stew, a russet liquid with a hint of tomato flavor, came very lightly seasoned, with the shrimp boiled tough. Other dishes—specifically a sauceless and liberally garlicked mozzarella pizza and a simple split roast chicken—have been splendid. The bread, cut off of Ciro Pasciuto's dark-crusted La Panzanella loaf, is some of the best in Duwamps. This is a microbrewery, and early brewings are promising. All four variations (plus two guest beers) are on tap in the darts-and-TV bar upstairs. A banquet room behind the brewery holds up to 35.

El Palacio

5212 Rainier Ave S,
725-9139 (map: JJ5)
Inexpensive; no alcohol;
MC, V; no checks
Lunch, dinner every day

El Palacio offers some of Seattle's more genuine Mexican food: homemade flour and corn tortillas, thick and chewy; delicious salsa made fresh daily (tomatoes, onion, lime juice, garlic, and cilantro); good enchiladas (in red sauce only); and authentic special dishes like puerco con carne. Norteño music—much preferable to the tunes on the jukebox—wails from the tiny kitchen, which is in view of the diners. Owners Estela and José Molina are from Chihuahua and Bolivia, respectively, via California, and they're especially proud of their seafood specialties. Chicken enchiladas and carne asada (marinated, grilled strips of beef tucked inside tortillas) are also excellent. But El Palacio's fajitas resemble what Tex-Mex restaurants usually call carne guisada—meat and peppers cooked in a tomato sauce. Save your pesos for the fried ice cream (only $1.50). Kids of any age love it.

El Puerco Lloron
1501 Western Ave,
624-0541 (map: J9)
Inexpensive; beer and
wine; AE, MC, V;
no checks
Lunch, dinner every day

KIDS For authenticity of decor and cooking (at cheaper than authentic prices), few Mexican places in Seattle beat "The Crying Pig," on the Pike Market Hillclimb. The metal card tables and folding chairs, complete with scars and Cerveza Superior logos, were imported from a cafe in Tijuana. The vivid hues of ordinary Mexico—pink, aqua, yellow—were splashed on the ceiling and walls, and the ersatz fare found in American Mexican restaurants is shunned. Everything here is handmade with fresh ingredients. The masa for the tortillas—from American corn, and therefore yellower—is ground daily. The menu is short, but the prices are astonishingly low. Two popular items are tacos de carne asada (soft-shelled tacos the way the Mexicans make them, filled with freshly grilled strips of steak) and taquitos, a plate of three small corn tortillas stuffed with your choice of meat. It's all delicious, especially the fresh chiles rellenos. Dinner ends at 7pm on Sundays, 9pm the rest of the week.

El Toreador
9747 4th Ave NW,
784-4132 (map: DD8)
Inexpensive; full bar;
MC, V; no checks
Lunch Mon-Fri, dinner
every day

KIDS El Toreador is a popular family place with a big indoor fountain, a strolling guitarist, and fresh, warm tortillas dispensed at the door to soothe the agonies of waiting. Although its stock in trade is the usual menu of Cal-Mex standards, this Holman Road fixture does it all much better, and certainly in larger quantity, than most. And some items—the green tomatillo sauce in the enchiladas verdes and chalupas; the stuffed corn-meal patties (sopes); the camarones mojo de ajo (garlic shrimp); the unusually good, limey guacamole—are downright buenissimo. Don't expect the same delights from the Redmond El Toreador; there's no relation.

RESTAURANTS

Emmett Watson's Oyster Bar

*Pike Place Market,
448-7721 (map: H8)
Inexpensive; beer and
wine; no credit cards;
checks OK
Breakfast Wed-Sat, lunch
Mon-Sat*

Occupying a cheery back-alley cranny in the Soames-Dunn Building, the namesake restaurant of Seattle's curmudgeonly journalist embodies some of the spirit of this town. You might like the tiny flowered courtyard when warm noontime sunlight washes down onto the tables, but you can take refuge inside at one of the (uncomfortable) booths when it's wet outside. Oysters on the half shell (Quilcenes, Minterbrooks, Shoalwater Bays) are sensational with one of the 50 brews available. Some prefer the salmon soup (a clean, clam-based broth with big chunks of the pink fish), the clam chowder, the spicy shrimp soup, or the true cod fish 'n' chips. Breakfasts are hearty, featuring omelets and an oyster-laden Hangtown Fry. Service couldn't be slower. Open until 5:30pm.

Empress of China

*707 148th Ave NE,
Bellevue, 747-8700
(map: HH3)
Moderate; full bar; AE,
DC, MC; no checks
Lunch, dinner every day*

It's difficult to tell from its appearance whether this is a fancy Chinese restaurant or one of coffeshop caliber. Get beyond the candy dispensers to the beige Naugahyde dining room in this large restaurant, overlook the fact that they'll hand you fork and knife without asking if you want chopsticks, and you'll have a very good Chinese meal in Bellevue: a tender, not overly salted kung pao beef; shrimp rolled in rice noodles, deep-fried, and served with a sweet rich lemon sauce; and a superb and unusual blend of steamed eggplant with ground pork in a not-too-hot garlic sauce. Service is impeccable—but when it's very busy, they may forget to remove the requested chopsticks from the paper sleeve for you.

Eques (Hyatt Regency Hotel)

*NE 8th and Bellevue
Way, Bellevue, 451-3012
(map: HH3)
Moderate; full bar; AE,
DC, MC, V; no checks
Breakfast Mon-Sat,
dinner every day,
brunch Sun*

Formal but nonetheless warm and pleasing in pastel tones and natural wood, Eques dispels the presumption that hotel dining is bound to disappoint. The menu is divided: the right side lists the daily specials, which let Chef Peter Kelly exhibit his culinary creativity; the left side presents tried and true Eques classics, which have earned that status by virtue of diners' repeated requests and raves. We can only hope that the duck and spinach salad with mustard dressing moves over to the left side and becomes available every night. Another favorite is veal medallions with artichoke hearts in red wine and Gorgonzola, a meltingly tender combination. Their rendition of chowder—infused with puréed salmon—is an excellent choice, as is the spinach fettucine served with blackened tuna with lemon thyme cream. Prices in this glitzy Bellevue Place spot are quite reasonable and the service properly subdued. Children's portions are available at half price, although the atmosphere—with a roaring fire in the fireplace and a classical guitarist in the background—is only for the best behaved.

Ezell's Fried Chicken
501 23rd Ave, 324-4141
(map: HH6)

4216 University Way NE,
548-1455 (map: FF6)
Inexpensive; no alcohol;
no credit cards; no checks
Lunch, dinner every day

KIDS A Central District take-out chicken spot that puts the Colonel to shame, Ezell's features good old fried chicken, regular or Creole-spicy, without the grease or inch-thick breading that ruins most others' offerings. Homemade yeast rolls, potato salad, and divine sweet potato pie round out the whole experience. There's another on the Ave, which serves the same in a larger space, but is not quite as good.

F.X. McRory's Steak, Chop, and Oyster House
419 Occidental Ave S,
623-4800 (map: P9)
Moderate; full bar; AE,
DC, MC, V; checks OK
Lunch Mon-Fri, dinner
every day

You can't get to or from the Kingdome without tripping up on McRory's, so it's crammed before and after events there. (A back room, incidentally, makes a handy place for a pregame gathering for up to 55 guests.) It's part of the Tim Firnstahl and Mick McHugh formula, which goes something like this: Wait for your table in the bar, known for its bourbon and sports figures (but our favorite place for a prime rib sandwich or Cobb salad at lunch); then proceed to the oyster bar, awkwardly situated in the entrance, for some fresh bivalves on the half shell; then on to your table in the dining room, where the specialty is beef and lamb finished in bourbon casks. Chops, roasts, mixed grills, stews, and large salads are the other choices—largely good, slightly overpriced. The crowd takes its toll on the service—the waitstaff has been known to get argumentative if told they brought the wrong dish. You can usually eat in the bar all the way into the night.

Filiberto's
14401 Des Moines Way S,
Burien, 248-1944
(map: OO7)
Moderate; full bar; AE,
DC, MC, V; checks OK
Lunch Tues-Sat, dinner
Tues-Sun

Filiberto's is the most authentic and, on a good day, among the best of the local (and we mean local) Italian restaurants. The look is cheery and trattoria-perfect, with even the dishwashing section in back finished in imported tile. Service can be erratic, but the food seems to have gotten more consistent, with good attention to the basics. The long menu emphasizes Roman and other midregion preparations of pasta, veal, poultry, and rabbit, right down to the real stracciatella alla Romana egg-drop soup (not too salty, as it often is in Rome). Three special treats: the huge, very well-priced selection of Italian wines in a take-your-pick glass case (here's where you'll find that unforgettable label with the forgotten name), Filiberto's pizza oven—the realest in Seattle—and a bocce court out back (if you're lucky you'll get asked to play).

Fountain Court off Main
22 103rd Ave NE, Bellevue, 451-0426 (map: HH3) Expensive; full bar; AE, MC, V; checks OK Lunch Mon-Fri, dinner Mon-Sat

Concept exceeds performance at this quietly inviting haven in old Bellevue. They have the theatrics of elegances mastered, portions are ample and sauces rich, and a lot of care is taken with presentation. But the cuisine—a mixture of French country and Northwest styles—is wildly uneven; some dishes are done to exacting standards while others are profoundly disappointing. The sauce on the vegetable fettuccine was too glutinous but the sole paupiettes stuffed with shrimp were nearly perfect. Presentation is precise and lovely. The service is less so, sometimes hovering, other times neglectful—cordial but unschooled. When both the service and the food connect, though, the Fountain Court experience can be a fine one. It's an engaging place, an elegant old Bellevue home with a courtyard. Private parties of up to 40 are nicely handled in the loft.

Four Swallows
4569 Lynwood Center Rd, Bainbridge Is, 842-3397 Inexpensive; beer and wine; MC, V; local checks only Dinner Tues-Sun

Islanders can't get enough of Geraldine Ferraro's cheery English-style pub on the south end of Bainbridge Island, in a Tudor building that houses the island's only movie theater. With its high booths, comfortable couch, and fresh flowers, the Four Swallows is appreciated by locals for its friendliness and, lately, good food. The menu's small (so is the kitchen), but it's always exactly right: a platter of perfectly ripe pears, slices of kiwi fruit, goat cheese rolled in pine nuts, crackers, and a large head of roasted garlic, or a plate-sized pizza margherita (tomato sauce, fresh basil, and three cheeses). One recent special (there are usually two) was a savory heap of fall-off-the-bone pork with black beans, sour cream, salsa, and tortillas. The tiny kitchen is not in a hurry, but when the food does get to your table it arrives in good hands. The Four Swallows is not on the way to anywhere except, for some, home. The chocolate pâté is worth the detour.

Fremont Classic
4307 Fremont Ave N, 548-9411 (map: FF7) Inexpensive; beer and

Not yet a classic, but in the minds of many Fremonters it's pretty darn close. Two years ago, Paul Kohlenberg opened this tiny, two-room trattoria in a former neighborhood residence. The Kansas City pizza zaps you

wine; MC, V; checks OK
Lunch Mon-Fri, dinner
every day

with barbecue sauce and bite-size chunks of chicken.
No nibbling here: the Classic is a place where real
people with real appetites come to eat. The pastas are
decent and three times the size most people can handle
in one sitting. Even the desserts—a mocha cheesecake
or blackberry cobbler (in season)—land with a thud,
twice as big as they need to be. If the tables are full, order at the counter and gorge yourself out on the patio.

Fullers
(Seattle Sheraton Hotel)
1400 6th Ave, 447-5544
(map: K5)
Expensive; full bar; AE,
MC, V; checks OK
Lunch Mon-Fri, dinner
Mon-Sat

Fullers has been at the top of many lists for many
years, as one after another of its phenomenal chefs has
skyrocketed to fame. These days it's Caprial Pence,
who's moving into her fourth year as the city's star
chef. Her hallmarks are beautiful presentation (a rose-
colored crepe, red from sweet peppers, folded blos-
somlike around a light Dungeness crab mousse, tied
with a scallion in a square knot, and accented with a
deep green basil coulis), Asian accents (gravlax of
salmon and ahi tuna in a sauce of mustard, cardamom,
and lime, with a dab of wasabe), and an obvious understanding of subtlety. Maybe a bit *too* subtle lately: our
kasu cod, perfectly cooked and strikingly presented
atop a deep purple cabbage salad cooked in red wine,
sake, and ginger, lacked its usual garlicky punch. The
roasted sweetbreads atop a few common greens lacked
dimension except for wild mushrooms. At other times,
Pence is more aggressive with her sauces, especially
when there's fruit involved. Try the rack of lamb in an
outrageous marionberry sauce or the slices of roasted
duck laid like stepping-stones across a pool of deep-red
cranberry onion compote. Sometimes the entrées—
which are as visually pleasing as the Mark Tobey painting above your table or the Pilchuck glass on display—
don't always measure up in complexity. The service,
which can be fawning to the point of intrusiveness,
seems to be more responsive to the diners' wishes
when there's something (or someone) to celebrate.
Still, we commend any chef (or at least the marketing
department) who's gutsy enough to offer a table in the
kitchen (two seatings, at 6pm and 9pm) and invite
guests to dine behind the line.

Georgian Room
(Four Seasons
Olympic Hotel)
411 University St,
621-7889 (map: L6)

The Georgian Room at the Four Seasons Olympic
Hotel is a grand, elegant space with high ceilings, huge
chandeliers, and all the accoutrements of formal dining,
right down to the silver-domed covers on the plates of
food and the fresh napkins placed in your lap. Live

Expensive; full bar; AE, DC, MC, V; checks OK Breakfast every day, lunch Mon-Fri, dinner Mon-Sat

piano music tinkles unobtrusively from the center of the room. The waitstaff, though they lack the polish one would expect from a fine hotel, are young and eager to please.

Chef Kerry Sear, originally from England by way of Chartwell's of the Four Seasons in Canada, is the Georgian Room's new hotshot executive chef. He's turning what was once not much more than a formidable hotel dining experience into an evening elegant, innovative, and very unexpected. Sear doesn't take anything for granted, so there are lots of surprises: tempura basil sprigs garnish a salad of bitter greens, a pear consommé is the broth for a wild-mushroom ravioli soup, lamb rib eye with foie gras and whipped potatoes is unconventionally stacked in the middle of your plate. This 3-D approach is a major departure from the pretty little food compositions so in vogue a couple of years ago. The best way to sample Sear's talents is to order the four-course chef's menu ($35). For $20 more, the dinner is complemented by carefully selected wines by the glass (1981 Sauternes, 1985 Bordeaux), making a wonderful value. Recently, we started with corn pasta cakes with scallops in avocado butter, garnished with crispy corn pasta bits for extra height (Sear's fetish). From the main menu came lobster and imaginative blackened tomato lasagne with smoked tomatillo butter. The sweetbreads consommé was clear and perfect, garnished with a tiny ear of baby corn and a sprig of fresh rosemary—elegant without being precious. Red bell pepper and smoked salmon bisque was a fine example of why this restaurant is so good: the texture was silky smooth, the color a brilliant orange red, and the flavor a seamless combination of the sharp bit of pepper and the velvet smokiness of the fish. Venison was served on a bed of wild mushroom risotto—just a bit too al dente, but the meat was on the pink side and surprisingly moist. Portions are ample but not overwhelming. Dessert (included in the chef's menu) might be tart tatin in fluffy-crisp puff pastry and a butter caramel sauce, or a layered sorbet cake with mango sauce. Hot soufflés are available, but they need to be ordered early in your meal. If chef Kerry Sear continues to challenge conventional food ideas (the current chef's menu is wonderfully promising), Seattle diners may soon flock to the Georgian Room to rub elbows with the older travelers and important-looking business types already there.

Gerard's Relais de Lyon
17121 Bothell Way NE,
Bothell, 485-7600
(map: AA4)
Expensive; full bar; DC,
MC, V; checks OK
Dinner every day

★★★½

Tucked away beneath the tall pines off Bothell Way, Gerard Parrat's Lyonnaise restaurant has not only survived but has (modestly) grown in its almost 15 years. The only thing you need to do to forget where you are is walk through the door, for to eat here is to return the senses to France, in a country inn appointed with crisp linen, Wedgwood china, leaded glass, fresh flowers, and a fireplace. Still, even dedicated local diners are unaware that in the Relais de Lyon we have a restaurant as good as any in the country. A large helping of voluptuous lobster bisque leaves the faintest possible taste lingering on the tongue; a galantine of duck with a centerpiece of caramelized shallot wrapped in lamb and accented with pistachios and pickled hazelnuts was breathtaking. Presentation is important, but Parrat never overreaches: a simple circular mesa of succulent, subtly spicy ratatouille was topped with thin, quarter-size rounds of rare lamb loin in a reduction of pan juices. But for all its sophistication of assembly and presentation, Parrat's cuisine remains firmly within his Lyonnaise heritage with lighter, more finicky tastes: rabbit fricassee with chanterelles, cabbage-stuffed partridge in puff pastry; potato and corn blinis topped with his own smoked salmon and caviar. To appreciate the full extent of Parrat's talents, try the six-course menu découverte or a 10-course menu dégustation—a good deal at $55 (though the wine list is rather pricey). The only quibbles are that the tables are too close together and the restaurant can get quite noisy. Plan on spending at least three hours over dinner—this is a meal worth savoring, and there's no reason for the staff to rush you.

Giulio Ristorante Italiano
12513 NE 144th St,
Kirkland, 821-1051
(map: CC3)
Moderate; beer and wine;
AE, DC, MC, V; local
checks only
Dinner Mon-Sat

★★

Proprietor Giulio Pellegrini is no relation to Seattle's famed gustatory philosopher, Angelo Pellegrini, though he says it was the latter's autobiography that drew him to Seattle, more specifically, Kirkland. A native of Patrica, Italy (south of Rome), who drifted wistfully from a painting to a cooking career, Giulio still brings an artistic enthusiasm and spontaneity to his work, strolling the floor, chatting up patrons, and soliciting critiques from his cultishly fervent fans. The mainstream menu is just the starting point for Giulio's offerings, and a good thing—the one entrée we tried from it was an insipid veal Marsala. More energy goes into specials. We enjoyed the generous, spicy sweetbreads on polenta; other frequent choices are pepper steak in balsamic vinegar, veal with scampi and chanterelles in season, homey soups such as pastina with chicken and pasta e fagioli, and rack of lamb on weekends. Located in a remote Kirkland shopping center, the restaurant is done up a little kitschy, extremely Italian. The net effect, matching Pellegrini's own friendly informality, is hearty and soulful rather than refined or subtly balanced.

The Globe Cafe
1531 14th Ave, 324-8815
(map: HH6)
Inexpensive; no alcohol;
no credit cards;
checks OK
Lunch, dinner Tues-Sun

You've got to love a place that supplies marbles and an Etch-a-Sketch along with daily newspapers. That's the way of the Globe, a vegetarian coffeehouse where you're expected—no, encouraged—to linger (and sometimes not by your own volition). The walls are covered with local artwork, and the house ethics are impressive: it recycles, avoids waste, and uses no animal products except milk (and believe us, avoid the soy lattes). The rest is glorified vegetarian homefare with only an occasional flash of inspiration. Desserts in the past have run to the whole-wheat genre; however, with the new owners (who have installed a new oven) the variety of bread and baked goods is improving.

Gordo's
6226 Seaview Ave NW,
784-7333 (map: EE9)
Inexpensive; no alcohol;
no credit cards; no checks
Lunch, dinner every day

Gordo's at Shilshole is a sunny-day spot, the type of place that, corn dogs and all, conjures up memories of childhood summers at the beach. They've got a couple of roadside picnic tables set up outside (there's no inside seating), but we recommend grabbing the greasy (that's the point here) goods and heading up to Golden Gardens. Lots of customers swear by Gordo's burgers, but we go for the no-nonsense fish 'n' hot fries. You'll want to save room for one of the scrumptious milk shakes, made to order with undeniably tender loving care and lots of fresh fruit.

Gourmet City Restaurant
12319 Roosevelt Way
NE, 365-8288
(map: CC6)
Inexpensive; full bar; AE,
MC, V; local checks only
Lunch Mon-Sat, dinner
every day

Gourmet City recently took over the old China North spot. It looks a bit different: Johnny Ing and Chen Shiou Sheng (both seven-year veterans—waiter and chef, respectively—of Andy and Jemmy's Wok in nearby Northgate) cleaned up the place and added some wall aquariums (they kept the adjustable banquet room, which seats 20 to 40 diners). Early reports indicate that Andy and Jemmy taught them well. Everything's nicely seasoned, from the expected (hot-and-sour soup, Mongolian beef) to the unexpected (braised sea cucumber). Lunch specials ($3.95) aren't bad (soup, egg roll, fried rice, and a choice of a shrimp, pork, chicken, or beef dish), but the waitstaff brightens up when you order à la carte instead.

**Grand Central
Baking Company**
*214 1st Ave S, 622-3644
(map: P8)
Inexpensive; beer and
wine; MC, V; checks OK
Lunch Mon-Sat
(restaurant), lunch every
day (deli)*

This bakery has put Grand back in its name. Following a brief hiatus in 1989, the *new* Grand Central Baking Company opened its doors with renewed vigor. Previously, locals knew the place for its honey-sweetened cinnamon rolls; today, thanks to baker Thomas Solis (and now Leslie Mackie) and raves from *Bon Appétit* and *The New York Times*, fans from all over stop by daily to rip into a variety of rustic breads. One is the Como Loaf, a moist, crusty loaf of Italian-style bread that is definitely the rising star (better than the chicken salad it sandwiched on a recent visit). Whole-grain and walnut loaves practically have fan clubs. Slide your tray past the cafeteria's counters and make your decision: a Vashon Summer Salad of wild greens and herbs from the island and topped with artichoke hearts, olives, cucumbers, and a heap of baby shrimp; a slice of focaccia steaming with tomatoes, onions, and black olives; or creamy Italian cheese soup. The sweet baked goods—memorable molasses cookies, for one—are grand finales. Service is often indifferent.

Gravity Bar
*113 Virginia St, 448-8826
(map: I7)
Inexpensive; no alcohol,
no credit cards; local
checks only
Breakfast, lunch, dinner
every day*

*415 Broadway E,
325-7186 (map: GG6)
Breakfast, lunch, dinner
every day*

Unless glowing neon and wheatgrass juice are already part of your daily routine, you'll probably feel like you're walking into a private Plutonian party as you enter this electric-hip juice bar. But don't let it stop you: this is good, vegetarian, body-mind-soul food—a Pesto Rica salad of brown rice tossed with pesto and sundried tomatoes and salad veggies; open-faced pine-nut, pesto, and chèvre sandwiches; a bowl of brown rice, tofu, and steamed vegetables in a lemon-tahini dressing; miso soup with buckwheat noodles. Things like that. Wash it all down with a shot of the slime-colored wheatgrass potion and a chaser of carrot-pineapple juice. Service is ridiculously slow in both locations: **Broadway stays open until 11 on weekends (but watch out for the after-movie rush); Virginia Street closes at 2am.**

Green Village
*721 S King St, 624-3634
(map: R6)
Inexpensive; beer and
wine; MC, V; no checks
Lunch, dinner Wed-Mon*

Green Village 2
*514 6th Ave, 621-1719
(map: Q7)*

Sizzling rice soup is just what it says—sizzling—at this lively little favorite in the heart of Chinatown. The waitress brings a big bowl of broth swimming with shrimp and veggies and ceremoniously dumps in a plate of crisp-fried rice. Mix frying oil and water and—*sizzle*—so hot it's still warm by the time you're nearly done. The menu is a mix of Sichuan and curry dishes, and the choice of over 100 items can make for an interesting first few minutes. It's best and cheapest to come

Inexpensive; no alcohol;
no credit cards; no checks
Lunch, dinner Mon-Sat

with a crowd. The prawns and noodles are delightful, the hot-and-sour soup one of the better versions we've tasted locally, and the Sichuan shredded pork spicy but not ear-smoking hot. The interior features one of those wonderful upper balconies that used to be in all Seattle Chinatown restaurants, this one lined with wicker chairs and hung with Christmas lights. Try the fast-food version on Sixth Avenue.

Greenlake Jake's
7918 E Green Lake Dr N,
523-4747 (map: EE7)
Inexpensive; beer only; no
credit cards; checks OK
Breakfast, lunch, dinner
every day

KIDS Blueberry-muffin lovers swear by this short-order eatery, which also serves the usual eggs and hash browns for breakfast and homemade corned beef hash, plus tasty burgers that have achieved cult status with the active set at Green Lake. Portions are big enough for athletes, prices are very cheap, and lines are out the door on Saturday mornings. You can eat outside.

Guido's Pizzeria
7902 E Green Lake Dr N,
522-5553 (map: EE7)
Inexpensive; no alcohol;
no credit cards;
checks OK
Breakfast, lunch, dinner
every day

2108 NE 65th St,
525-3042 (map: EE6)
Inexpensive; beer and
wine; no credit cards;
checks OK

Guido's is a friendly, no alcohol, mostly take-out pizza joint right in the heart of Green Lake's teeming north-west corner, purveying tasty thin-crust (or thicker Sicilian-style) slices or whole pies with a nice tomato sauce and a light hand with the toppings. Calzones, espresso, sun tea, homemade desserts, and a salad you really want to eat are the sidelights. Now Guido's is also a friendly, beer or wine only, mostly eat-in pizza bistro in the former Schumacher's space in Ravenna.

Han II
409 Maynard Ave S,
587-0464 (map: Q6)
Inexpensive; full bar;
MC, V; checks OK
Lunch, dinner every day

In the renovated Bush Asia Center, Han II is a gather-ing spot for the city's Koreans, and on a given night one may find the inner dining room occupied by a boisterous wedding banquet, while in the atriumlike narrow room that overlooks Hing Hay Park, young couples feed each other barbecued short ribs lifted sizzling from a hot grill in the middle of the table. The menu is extensive, and the appetizers (incendiary kim chee, soothing bean sprouts, crisp jellied seaweed) are superb, but other dishes on a recent visit were wildly inconsistent. Oc-topus in a spicy sauce was good, the mollusk perfectly cooked and the sauce fiery, but barbecued beef—cooked in the kitchen, not at the table—was un-conscionably undercooked and shoe-leather tough;

likewise the spicy crab soup, which featured a rich, flavorful broth marred by overcooked crab of questionable freshness. Portions are large, and although the menu offers a smattering of Chinese and Japanese dishes, stay with the Korean. The lunch specials are relatively cheap and quite filling. With your basic order of pork, chicken, or beef you get Korean pickles and two tempura prawns.

**Harbor City
Barbecue House**
*707 S King St, 621-2228
(map: R6)
Inexpensive; no alcohol;
no credit cards;
checks OK
Lunch, dinner every day*

Often overlooked, Harbor City had the first *real* Chinese barbecue oven in town—a large, drumlike contraption large enough to roast a whole pig as it hangs vertically and turns slowly. The results are some of the most tender, moist morsels we've found in Seattle. Stop the chef from pouring barbecue sauce all over it; it can be a very leaky affair if you take it to go. Besides, meat that good doesn't need to be soaked in sauce.

The Herbfarm
*32804 Issaquah–Fall
City Rd, Fall City,
784-2222
Expensive; wine only;
MC, V; checks OK
Lunch Fri-Sun, dinner
Fri-Sat*

The Herbfarm is far more than a destination restaurant, even though it's a 30-minute drive east of Seattle and the waiting list these days is often months long. The Herbfarm is more like Mecca, a trusty haven of gourmandism rendered nearly mythic by inaccessability and reputation. The farm itself is a rustic, beautifully maintained collection of gardens, out of which chef/owner Ron Zimmerman and his chefs, Jerry Traunfeld and Bill Kraut, compose prix-fixe ($35) six-course herbal luncheons and occasional nine-course ($75 and up) herbal dinners. A complex reservations system requires that you make your August lunch plans in April, or else wait until the last minute (1pm on Friday) to try for one of the six seats left open each week.

Complications (and prices) notwithstanding, these herbal adventures are worth it. Each meal begins with a guided tour of the grounds. The guests—just 26 at a time—are seated in a dining room, decorated to echo the efflorescence of the gardens. A summer menu might include stuffed zucchini blossoms with tomatoes and thyme-flower sauce, Copper River salmon with lemon verbena and tuberous begonia sauce, a sorbet of lavender and violets, and a 35-ingredient salad with roasted hazelnut vinaigrette, rose geranium ice cream with a sauce for fruit-scented sage. Each course is prepared and served with such care and love that the whole experience can be quite inspirational—and educational. In fact, with all the lore and technique these chefs share, it can seem like more of a seminar than a luncheon. You will take several new discoveries home with you, and find yourself reaching again for snips of herbs you haven't used in years.

Hi-Spot Cafe

*1410 34th Ave, 325-7905
(map: HH6)
Inexpensive; beer and
wine; MC, V; checks OK
Breakfast, lunch
Wed-Mon*

One of the earlier exemplars of the laid-back neighborhood coffeehouse genre in this town is back and going strong. The long lines are still there, but the miserable service and disappointing food went out with the former owners. Amanda Wood and Michael Kingsley have turned this charming Madrona house back into the comfortable, welcoming eatery it always deserved to be. The favorite meal here is breakfast (you'll wait in line on weekends), which is made with a concern for purity and health; though they don't go overboard on health food. The cinnamon rolls are as popular as the omelets and pancakes. Lunches feature sandwiches such as grilled turkey, tomato and avocado, BLTs and burgers, and homemade soup (always vegetarian). Burgers are big and tasty, served with the works. No more dinners, alas, but at breakfast everybody's talking, laughing, lingering—even the waiting (there's often an entertaining magician) has gotten more pleasant.

Hien Vuong

*502 S King St, 624-2611
(map: Q7)
Inexpensive; no alcohol;
no credit cards; no checks
Lunch, dinner Wed-Mon*

★★

Simple food has never been so exquisite. The place is nothing much, just a cubbyhole across from Uwajimaya. It's the food that draws, for its freshness and vibrancy of flavors. The beef noodles come in a light but miraculously resonant broth. Papaya with beef jerky combines grated, still-green papaya with delicate shreds of spiced, dried beef in a tangy dressing. The shrimp rolls are some of the best in town: very fresh shrimp with romaine, mint, and cilantro wrapped in rice paper, with scallion ends peeking out like little green tails. It comes with a rich, brown peanut sauce for dipping. All the hot dishes come to your table straight off the stove. Crisp, clean, and delightful. Two can eat dinner for under $10.

Hisago

*543 NE Northgate Way,
363-1556 (map: DD6)
Inexpensive; wine only;
AE, MC, V; no checks
Lunch Tues-Fri, dinner
Tues-Sun*

From the outside, Hisago looks anything but promising: another storefront in another strip mall near Northgate. But inside, the restaurant is clean, attractive, and spare, with a sushi bar near the entrance, tatami rooms on the far side, and a gorgeous red embroidered kimono hanging on the wall. The sushi is skillfully prepared and very fresh; you can order it off a

Kohan

*1590 NE Gilman Blvd,
Issaquah, 392-4301
Inexpensive; no alcohol;
MC, V; no checks
Lunch Mon-Fri, dinner
Mon-Sat*

sushi card or in several dinner options. The tempura tends to be overbattered and undercooked, but the rest of the entrées and appetizers are good, including stir-fried mahi-mahi with vegetables or the gyoza (Japanese potstickers). The five combination dinners offer diners a chance to sample a variety of dishes. Servings are generous, prices are relatively low for Japanese food, and the food is consistently good. There's a carbon copy, Kohan, in Issaquah.

Hot Lips Pizza

*930 3rd Ave (and
branches), 467-6760
(map: M7)
Inexpensive; beer and
wine; no credit cards;
checks OK
Lunch Mon-Sat, dinner
Mon-Fri*

Most pizza made locally is Neapolitan-style, with a thin crust and familiar toppings. Thick-crusted Sicilian and deep-dish Chicago pizza also have their niches. The Hot Lips product is completely different. It's got a soft but hearty hand-thrown crust, and fabulous toppings sure to horrify purists: feta cheese, kalamata olives, garden-grown herbs preserved in olive oil, fresh basil, fontina from Sweden, and blue cheese from Oregon. These end up in combinations heretofore not even dreamed of, like the Tex-Mex (chorizo, jack cheese, pasilla chile sauce, and fresh salsa) or the Northwest (Oregon sharp Cheddar, red delicious apples, and crushed filberts). Grab a quick slice to go, order a giant 19-incher for the office (they deliver within about a four-block radius), or enjoy the lively atmosphere in the upstairs dining room. Hot Lips is an Oregon chain that just added links in Redmond (7297 W Lake Sammamish Parkway NE, 885-6425), the U District (4222 University Way NE, 548-9354), and Capitol Hill (2407 10th Avenue E). Closes at 9pm weekdays, 6pm Saturdays.

House of Dumplings

*510 S King St, 340-0774
(map: Q7)
Inexpensive; no alcohol;
no credit cards;
checks OK
Breakfast, lunch, dinner
Wed-Mon*

Until House of Dumplings opened, you had to leave the country to find a traditional Chinese breakfast. Local Chinese were resigned to making periodic pilgrimages to Vancouver, BC, whenever they got a craving for hot soy milk, youtiao (fried dough sticks), and shaobing (sesame buns), the centuries-old staples of the morning meal. Early on, this small eatery in the International District had a throng of regulars who couldn't seem to stop coming until they had tried the other 46 items on the menu as well. Just about every down-home favorite is listed: potstickers, steamed buns with various fillings, scallion cakes, turnip cakes, and a number of Taiwanese specialties. We only wish House of Dumplings had a better system for taking orders (you line up at the counter) and serving the food. A harried server took so long finding one eater's table that the fried items had cooled to tepid by the time they arrived. The lines are not out the door anymore, if only because the novelty has worn off (there are other Chinese breakfast places now); however, generally the food is good, especially if it gets to your table hot, and the prices are astonishingly low. Weekdays are the days to go—weekend mornings bring chaos.

House of Hong

409 8th Ave S, 622-7997
(map: R6)
Inexpensive; full bar; AE,
DC, MC, V; no checks
Lunch, dinner, every day

KIDS Faye Hong, whose family previously made the Atlas Cafe a local favorite, operates a more elegant model of what most folks still mean by "Chinese restaurant"—uncorrupted Cantonese cuisine, not especially exciting but usually reliably and speedily prepared. The setting is a match: handsome dusty pink in a courtyardlike indoor layout, yet still a place you feel comfortable taking the kids. Which is just what the regulars do on weekends, for one of the district's better dim sums (come before the 11am opening). At 75 items, Hong's is also one of the most diverse. Even simple classics like ginger beef dumplings and ha gow are refined in flavor and texture and are wheeled in piping hot. We found the dough in the baked humbos cloyingly sweet, somewhat balanced by an overly salty filling, and the steamed dumplings are more dependable than the fried (which we find too greasy). Dinners are likewise steady and dependable, with seafood carrying the banner: prawns in lobster sauce are ambrosial, steamed black cod in ginger oil a special delight. Others praise the earthy quality of the home-cooked fare (salted fish and fried rice), the order-ahead banquets (in a private room), and the parking lot—no small plus in this crowded district. Food until midnight on weekends.

Hunan Garden

11814 NE 8th St,
Bellevue, 451-3595
(map: HH3)
Inexpensive; full bar; AE,
DC, MC, V; no checks
Lunch Mon-Fri, dinner
every day

Hunan food is the latest Chinese regional cuisine to go mainstream, and Hunan Garden has led the pack. Keeping in mind that real Hunan cooking—blazing hot and liberal with oil—would leave the average Western palate in a shambles, we recommend Hunan Garden for its pleasant ambience and a selection of modified Hunan dishes that range from indifferent to very good. Scallops in tangy sauce and homestyle bean curd are solid choices, and Sichuan selections like kung pao chicken (made with a generous amount of cashews) are quite tasty. Insist on three stars if you like your food spicy. Incidentally, you and your server may have a real communication gap, and the chipped glasses and serving plates have seen better days.

**The Hunt Club
(Sorrento Hotel)**
900 Madison St,
622-6400 (map: M4)
Expensive; full bar; AE,
DC, MC, V; checks OK
Breakfast, lunch, dinner
every day,
brunch weekends

Dark with burnished mahogany paneling and deep red bricks, this is one of the most pleasant restaurants in the city, especially in the winter. When the days are longer (June through September) we prefer to eat outdoors in the courtyard. Barbara Figueroa, the chef who came from LA's Spago a couple of years ago, seems to have settled into a comfortable routine, offering the kinds of dishes (roast Oregon rabbit in fruit-and-port sauce; an excellent rack of Ellensburg lamb done with rosemary and mustard) that make the traveling executive feel well fed, as well as the kind of outrageous combinations that make nouvelle cuisine the object of so many ambivalent feelings (a wonderful smoked duck and oyster mushroom timbale with a gentle sweet Marsala demiglaze sauce that made the duck taste more like dessert; distinctive rolls of smoked halibut around peppered crab mousse tied with a bow of nori and sided with a dipping dashi sauce).

Figueroa's menu, which of course changes seasonally, makes excellent use of fresh, usually Northwest, ingredients, though a recent lobster splurge dressed with a well-balanced tomato tarragon concassé showed her competence with foods from other waters. The lobster bisque, on the other hand, left a slightly bitter aftertaste. Some dishes play with more of an Asian theme: deep-fried shrimp wontons with an ocean salad of seaweeds tossed with black sesame seeds and a black mushroom chile dipping sauce. This kitchen has a tendency toward overcomplication: entrées occasionally come with so many little surprises you find yourself wondering what it all is and why it's sharing the same plate. But as you work your way around the plate from a tender bite of lamb to a brussels sprout to eggplant stuffed with lamb sausage and Oregon blue cheese to black beans it can also be a pleasant journey, with no need to surmise why. Overall, it would be difficult to imagine getting an unsatisfying meal at the Hunt Club.

After dinner, savvy patrons retire to the lobby bar for dessert and coffee (a fine place to go even if you haven't dined at the restaurant, complete with fireplace and cozy sofas). Afternoon tea with pastries and finger sandwiches is served here every day. Desserts, while usually fine, sometimes falter by working too hard at being different.

I Love Sushi
11818 NE 8th St,

Tadashi Sato is head chef at the slickest sushi house with the dumbest name in Bellevue. He produces im-

*Bellevue, 454-5706
(map: HH3)
Moderate; full bar; AE,
DC, MC, V; local
checks only
Lunch Mon-Sat, dinner
every day*

peccable morsels of the freshest sushi: hot, crisp pieces of salmon skin and shreds of flesh, rolled up with bright green radish sprouts (the Alaska Roll); furumaki made of pink fish cake, mushrooms, cucumbers, and seaweed; tuna sashimi that arrives in the shape of a rose. You can feel equally safe straying from the sushi menu toward such delights as Tiger Eye (squid stuffed with smoked salmon, then sliced and fried) or Sato-san's deep-fried soft-shelled crab. Everything is à la carte, so beware the final tab. Most everything is seafood. Do ask if what you want is fresh, since waiters are quite forthcoming (if sometimes difficult to understand). Excellent food.

Il Bistro

*93-A Pike St, 682-3049
(map: J8)
Expensive; full bar; AE,
DC, MC, V; no checks
Dinner every day*

This Pike Place Market walk-down makes fine use of its low ceilings and warrenlike space. Rounded arches, white plaster, low amber lights, much rich, dark oak, and a few Oriental rugs on the walls combine for a mood that's part Moorish, part Continental, and irresistibly cozy. Small wonder the bar is a cherished refuge on damp winter nights; soft recorded jazz and fine brandy and malt whiskey selections abet lingering.

Against such ambience, the food plays neither a starring nor a subordinate role. The menu's range has grown somewhat beyond the Italian classics, in keeping with local tastes. Seafoods—shellfish in particular—have come to play a larger and more distinguished role, and exotic mushrooms appear even in mainstream entrées like the veal Marsala. Il Bistro's celebrated standbys, a tangy cioppino and meltingly marinated rack of lamb, are still here, and its pastas are varied if somewhat tame. The penne con melanzane is one of the more distinctive: eggplant and generous dollops of mozzarella hugging the robust pasta tubes, held together by the usual savory Bistro red sauce, with an unexpectedly smoky undercurrent.

A few minor extras fall short. Il Bistro's light-brown sourdough bread is too gummy, and undeserving of the sauces it sops. And a ghastly Mondavi cabernet offered by the glass has no place in a restaurant as good as this (though better alternatives are also poured). However, desserts are good, and one as simple as marionberry blackcurrant sorbet can be lovely, charting an exhilarating course from tart to very sweet.

Il Paesano

5628 University Way NE,

Il Paesano is an endearing little box of a trattoria featuring the inexpensive, everyday food of Italy. The menu

526-0949 (map: FF6)
Moderate; beer and wine;
MC, V; local checks only
Dinner Mon-Sat

comprises a list of pastas (wonderfully rich lasagne, rigatoni alla carbonara, spaghettini alla puttanesca), a few meat entrées, and excellent pizzas on crackerlike crusts (one serves well as an appetizer for a couple). On a recent meal we found the salads uneventful, the gnocchi with marinara sauce delicious, the spaghetti overcooked, the zabaglione for dessert stunning, and the bill ($35 for two, all told) the biggest delight of all. Mostly we found—and always find—the atmosphere infectiously festive.

Il Terrazzo Carmine
411 1st Ave S, 467-7797
(map: O9)
Expensive; full bar; AE,
DC, MC, V; local
checks only
Lunch Mon-Fri, dinner
Mon-Sat

Carmine's Grill
83 S King St, 622-6743
(map: P9)
Expensive; full bar; AE,
DC, MC, V; local
checks only
Lunch Mon-Fri, dinner
Mon-Sat

Floor-to-ceiling floral drapes dominate the comfortable room, an opera is often playing, and in the summer you can eat out on the outdoor patio, where a fountain is supposed to drown out the noise of the viaduct (unfortunately, it doesn't—if it's rush hour and you want to talk, go inside). There are more gold chains around necks here than in any other Seattle restaurant, but the elegance is subdued and the clientele somewhat older and upscale, all enjoying the great presentation, consistently flavored dishes, excellent wine, and sometimes odd service. Be sure to take notice of the antipasti on the way in; they're all laid out for perusal, and the taste matches the presentation. We've had stunning veal picatta (lightly sauced and zipped with capers), superb pillows of ravioli filled with venison, and rich tender medallions of venison sautéed with wild mushrooms and Marsala. The half chicken roasted with oregano sauce is *meriviglioso*. Service, however, can be a bit confused (and tends to favor regulars and celebrities). It's nice that the waiters have authentic accents, but there are times when we'd like to understand them (or vice versa)—at one visit we ended up with a few desserts we didn't order, though we'll probably order the profiteroles again. If you choose carefully and take advantage of the extensive Italian wine list, the food is certainly worth the considerable expense (a dinner for four may average $160), and the ambience is, as ever, *molto invitante*.

Owner Carmine Smeraldo recently opened Carmine's Grill on King Street. It's not primarily an Italian restaurant, and offerings include grilled anything, from half chickens to duck to fish. It's slightly less expensive than its big brother up the street, but don't get your hopes up—it's still not cheap.

All places in this book are recommended; even "no stars" are worth knowing about.

India Taj

625 1st Ave, 233-0160
(map: N8)
Inexpensive; beer and
wine, soon; AE, MC, V;
checks OK
Lunch Mon-Sat, dinner
every day

A four-foot-by-four-foot white marble rendition of the Taj Mahal dominates this Pioneer Square restaurant, where the menu is basic Indian and the bread is sublime. Sink your teeth into the kulcha (a puffy, oniony bread), the nan (a hot slab baked in a tandoor oven), or the pudina paratha (a thin bread with a fiery spread of mango, hot pepper, peas, and potatoes). Tandoori chicken was unusually moist; rice Pulao was inconsistent, but when it was good, it was done to perfection. The buffet table tends to be unimpressive and on the greasy side. Stick to the à la carte menu for fresher, more dependable options.

Islabelle Caribbean Food

1501 N 45th St, 632-8011
(map: FF7)
Inexpensive; no alcohol;
no credit cards;
checks OK
Lunch, dinner Tues-Sun

This shot of sunshine that once shimmered on the industrial north shore of Lake Union has moved up to a busier location on 45th Street. Now it has tables (albeit only a few, and tiny), so you can eat in and savor all the sensual tropical appeal of the place: sun-splashed colors on industrial-metal walls, the exotic aromas of tamarinds and cumin, plantains and garlic. Caribbean food is rare in Seattle, which makes Islabelle a beautiful island indeed. From Lorenzo Lorenzo's repertoire of spicy Caribbean classics come tender, marinated halibut, broiled and served with cumin-fragrant black beans and two domes of rice; a marinated pork sandwich; the mighty yet subtle Caribbean Burger, topped with homemade salsa, sautéed onion, bright slices of tomato, and fresh, leafy watercress. The food is so good you might even savor the humbler side dishes—foo-foo balls (mashed plantains and seasoned garlic) and little salads of tomato and olive dressed with vinegar and oil—as essential, inevitable complements to the spicy chicken. There has been talk on and off for months of returning breakfast items to the menu; at press time we began to hear these rumors again—we hope they're true. What we remember was very good.

Italia

1010 Western Ave,
623-1917 (map: L8)
Moderate; beer and wine;
AE, DC, MC, V; local
checks only
Lunch, dinner Mon-Sat

Ever since Scott Craig (formerly of Chez Shea) took over the helm of this upscale cafeteria, the usual lunchtime bustle has been slowly moving into the night. Here, in this cavernous space that's simultaneously part art gallery, part gourmet food store, and part concert hall (Cafe Concerts on many Tuesdays at 5:30pm), there's a dichotomy to the food. At lunch, Italia has an excellent pizza with a crackerlike crust that lets the tomato sauce and cheese (sometimes with smoked chicken, pancetta, leek, or chèvre) take over. Other lunch faves are the usual and often indifferent gourmet foods—pasta salads, sandwiches, and pasta or torta specials. But nighttime, when it's rarely jammed (but increasingly popular), is when Italia's food shines. Craig's new dinner menu includes specialties like the roast garlic with chevre and crostini antipasto, a salad with wild greens spruced up with fennel, risotto with fresh asparagus, sage, and tomato. One recent visit presented us with an outstanding chicken breast sautéed with cucumber (now THAT'S interesting), tomatoes, and basil, with a side of gnocchi. Herbs are important here. So is the sometimes obscure art—second Thursday of each month there's an art lecture that's fast becoming a Seattle tradition. The wine list is good, including a good selection by the glass. On warm evenings, sit at a sidewalk table and watch the horse carriages pass by.

Ivar's Acres of Clams and Fish Bar

Pier 54, 624-6852
(map: L9)
Moderate; full bar; AE,
MC, V; checks OK
Lunch, dinner every day

Ivar's Captain's Table

333 Elliott Ave W,
284-7040 (map: A9)
Moderate; full bar; AE,
MC, V; checks OK
Lunch Mon-Fri, dinner
every day, brunch Sun

★

Ivar Haglund was a legend in this town—entre-preneurial dynamo, master of the corny pun ("Keep Clam"), prolific fish fryer. He has passed away (God rest his sole), but his legacy lives on in the form of three waterside restaurants, two take-out fish bars, and fast-food outposts all over the city (not recom-mended here). Best and most complete is the Captain's Table, with several seafood dishes—Quilcene oy-ster–stuffed snapper, halibut au gratin—served in a room with sensational Elliott Bay views. Best loved, however, is Northlake's Indian Salmon House (401 NE Northlake Way, 632-0797), a replica of an Indian long-house where salmon and black cod are properly broiled over a smoky alder fire and served with corn bread. It's not very consistent, but Seattleites often take guests here anyway. Acres of Clams is the most centrally lo-cated for tourists, the slickest, and therefore the laziest—you might encounter overcooked salmon or flawed service. Kids will be delighted with the menu-masks at each restaurant. The Salmon House and Acres of Clams both have take-out adjuncts with out-door seating; wonderful for cod 'n' chips or (excellent) clam nectar, enjoyed in quintessentially Seattle set-tings. Good happy-hour deals.

Izumi

12539 116th Ave NE,
Kirkland, 821-1959
(map: DD3)

Chef Hiroyuki Matsushima's Izumi gets consistent raves from Japanese eaters in the area, many of whom consider it the best moderately priced Japanese eatery in greater Seattle. Located at Totem Lake West Shop-

Moderate; beer and wine; AE, MC, V; local checks only
Lunch Tues-Fri, dinner Tues-Sun

ping Center, Izumi rubs shoulders with hamburger joints and ersatz Mexican chain restaurants. Katsui Yanagibashi of Tokyo chose the spot back in 1985 because there were no other Japanese restaurants for miles. He continues to live in Tokyo (where he owns another restaurant) but drops by Kirkland a few times a year to assure that his standards are being maintained. Chef Matsushima himself wields the sushi knife, with conspicuous flair and exacting standards. His waitstaff is friendly and efficient, making Izumi the kind of place where families feel right at home. Lunches are tasty and reasonably priced—try the Izumi makunouchi, served in a lidded lacquer box with six sections. The sections are fastidiously packed with sushi topped with shrimp, fish, vegetables, and tempura prawns.

Jake O'Shaughnessey's
100 Mercer St, 285-1897 (map: A6)
Moderate; full bar; AE, DC, MC, V; checks OK
Dinners every day

Jake's, now under the sole ownership of Tim Firnstahl, is waiting to be redeveloped out of existence, but that could take months or years. Until then, the cavernous bar remains listed in *Guinness Book of World Records* for its 774 different bourbons, and the dining room retains its noisy, saloonlike atmosphere (nothing, however, compared with the boisterous bar). It also continues to feature aged beef and baked russets, though it's turning increasingly in the direction of fish. Either direction, the food is bland and the lack of flavor is pointed up by strong sauces and spicing that merely emphasizes that there isn't anything underneath. The fish is often overcooked, and the quality-control people cruising the floor may leave you feeling supervised. But even with the overwritten menu, Jake's goes a long way to convince you that a formula restaurant can have a soul. In this case it's in the bar, where you'll undoubtedly be sent for at least 15 minutes regardless of empty tables in the dining area.

Java Restaurant
8929 Roosevelt Way NE, 522-5282 (map: DD6)
Moderate; beer and wine; AE, MC, V; local checks only
Dinner every day

An exotic dining experience, highly romantic, in a spotless, comfortable house full of unique and personal artifacts, with service (by a family of Chinese Indonesians) that's deeply polite and pleasing. The food is a fair sampling of Indonesian fare; the specialty is satay—skewers of marinated grilled meat or prawns to be dipped in peanut sauce. The lamb satay is extraordinarily rich and tender. The rijsttafel (rice table) is a colorful, delicious sampling of side dishes ranging from pickled cucumber to curries to broiled chicken with a choice of sauces, the flavors of which are both pungent and light. The peanut sauce is mild (unlike the Thai version), the sweet-and-sour sauce has both delicacy and punch. Vegetarian gado gado, topped with the delectable peanut sauce, and Javanese sweet-sour broiled chicken are also worth ordering. The interestingly textured casaba chips, offered as an appetizer, are novel but bland and not compelling enough to be the only choice. Skip them, likewise the gummy desserts.

Julia's 14 Carrot Cafe
*2305 Eastlake Ave E,
324-1442 (map: GG7)
Inexpensive; beer and
wine; MC, V; checks OK
Breakfast every day,
lunch Mon-Sat, dinner
Tues-Sat*

Julia's in Wallingford
*4401 Wallingford Ave N,
633-1175 (map: FF7)
Inexpensive; beer and
wine; MC, V; checks OK
Breakfast every day,
lunch, dinner*

★½

KIDS There are two things you can count on in Seattle: rain and a Sunday morning line at Julia's. It's warm, steamy, noisy, and plain, serving homemade "health food" renditions of dishes pulled from a couple of dozen cuisines—Sichuan beef, Greek salad, several pastas—in bountiful portions. Dinner is more consistent, but breakfast is the fabled meal, with big build-your-own omelets, thin and tangy sourdough pancakes, grilled potatoes with scallions and cheese, hefty cinnamon rolls, and Scotch oatmeal, plus exotic inventions like Tahitian toast (grilled, egg-dipped sourdough bread with sesame butter, served with fresh fruit and yogurt). At the Wallingford Julia's there are suggestions of a California nouvelle cuisine influence in the dishes, along with a slightly more upscale ambience. Both are clearly overrated—imagination and execution of specials have dropped off since Wallingford opened, prices keep creeping up, and you practically have to camp out on the doorstep for a breakfast two-top. But Julia's is as essential to Seattle as water. Plenty of vegetarian choices; no smoking. Success has prompted the opening of a third branch in Ballard, Julia's Park Place (5410 Ballard Avenue NW, 783-2033).

Kaleenka Russian Cafe
*1933 1st Ave, 728-1278
(map: I8)
Moderate; beer and wine;
MC, V; checks OK
Lunch, dinner Mon-Sat*

Capable Russian hands prepare hearty food in this cozy restaurant hung with Russian tapestries and hats. Most of the food—the flavorful eight-vegetable borscht, for instance—has a Ukrainian accent, but James and Lydia Venichenko Barrett have added some regional specials from Georgia, Uzbekistan, and Armenia. Lunch is served cafeteria-style and is heavy on the carbohydrates. Load up on the vareniky (dumplings stuffed with farmer cheese and potato) or the pilmeny (stuffed with meat and swimming in rich homemade beef broth and dolloped with sour cream). Dinner is a more formal affair, with a larger menu that dips into those other regions. Try the chicken Kiev, or the galubtzi, a luscious roll of beef, pork, and rice wrapped in cabbage leaves and baked in a slightly sweet, rich, sour-cream tomato sauce. Mahnte—lamb-filled dumplings—were slightly less successful but came with two wonderful Uzbek breads: obi-non, a flatbread sprinkled with sesame seeds and served hot with butter, and samsa, round pastries stuffed with lamb and served with a dill sour cream dipping sauce. Wash it all down with a selection of Eastern European and Soviet beers and wines.

Kamalco
414 E Pine St, 323-7565
(map: K1)
Inexpensive; beer and
wine; AE, MC, V;
no checks
Lunch Tues-Fri, dinner
every day

★½

Kamalco is short on atmosphere but long on good Middle Eastern food for the discerning, impoverished patron: zahrah (lightly breaded fried cauliflower dipped in lemony tahini sauce), Lebanese whipped cheese, tasty baba ghanouj, garlicky spit-roasted chicken over pilaf. Like his brother, who runs the Mediterranean Kitchen across town on Lower Queen Anne, Hakmat Aboul-Hosn uses garlic with abandon. Have a private party here (there are two small rooms to choose from). Portions are enormous.

Kamon on Lake Union
1177 Fairview Ave N,
622-4665 (map: D1)
Moderate; full bar; AE,
DC, MC, V; checks OK
Lunch Mon-Fri, dinner
every day

Kamon of Kobe
2444 NE
Bellevue–Redmond Rd,
Bellevue, 644-1970
(map: GG2)
Moderate; full bar; AE,
MC, V;
checks OK
Lunch Mon-Fri, dinner
every day

Like the others at the south end of Lake Union, this is a gorgeous restaurant. At night the obsidian shine of the lake contrasts with the wispy shades of pink and celadon inside. Beautiful brass and bamboo, friendly lighting, and a gleaming sushi bar are part of the inviting interior. But Kamon is not just another pretty face. It's three: a neon sushi bar, a tatami room where you can get an international menu with a smattering of ersatz French, Italian, and Chinese dishes, and a teppanyaki room with Japanese grills at each table. While the faultless, very fresh offerings at the sushi bar and the quick and skillful chefs leave us confident that this Japanese-based firm, Shalon International (Benihana, Morgan's Lakeplace) knows what it's doing, there are some disturbing tendencies elsewhere. The menu is being adjusted to suit a broader clientele; for instance, a halibut dish stuffed with steamed oysters has been changed to fish and fried oysters. We suggest ordering strictly Japanese, perhaps even sticking to the long list of sushi preparations; try the sushi platter during happy hour for under $3. Kamon of Kobe in Bellevue, with its vinyl banquettes, is looking a bit tired of late. The food is good, but it lacks the vigor that gives the Lake Union branch its appeal.

---

*Look for **KIDS**—it means your child will especially enjoy this place or attraction.*

Karam's

340 15th Ave E,
324-2370 (map: GG6)
Inexpensive; beer and
wine; AE, MC, V;
checks OK
Dinner Mon-Sat

The cuisine of the Middle East enjoys a lot of representation in this town, and Karam's does very well by it. The restaurant is a small, airy place at the Group Health end of 15th Avenue East, and owners Anis and Julie Karam are very much in evidence—he in his spotless whites, tin of sumac poised over a plate of baba ghanouj, she laboriously forming falafel patties. They have wisely kept their repertoire down to four entrées each night: a marinated lamb shish kabab, juicy and grilled to a turn; spicy falafel balls drizzled with garlicky tahini; seasoned fish of the day (the halibut is excellent); and marinated half chicken. It all comes with lentil soup or a minty salad, and curried rice with pine nuts. They've collected quite a corps of regulars, who go nuts when Anis augments the menu with something special, say, homemade goat's milk cream cheese with garlic, mint, and oregano. Very dependable.

Kaspar's by the Bay

2701 1st Ave, 441-4805
(map: E8)
Moderate; full bar; AE,
MC, V; checks OK
Lunch Mon-Fri,
dinner Mon-Sat

★★½

Something's right when a restaurant can survive a year without a phone listing (missed the deadline by a week). It's certainly not the ambience, with Muzak wafting through an office-tower dining room dominated by spiky greenery, country pine antiques, and bleached plank walls. At night, the sterile decor (so out of place in Belltown), faded by candlelight and coupled with the twinkling vista of the bay or—turn to the north—the skyline, transforms into a far more inviting atmosphere. Fortunately, view is not the only draw to Kaspar Donier's fifth-floor Continental restaurant. Donier, who came down from Vancouver's Le Pavillon in the Four Seasons, has proven again and again that good food can overcome flaws in ambience (and gaffs in service). A meal might start with translucent chanterelle, morel, and oyster mushroom ravioli with a sumptuous shallot chardonnay sauce. The menu is the kind of suspiciously multicultural thing you rarely see anymore in this age of specialization: veal scallopini with mushroom risotto, a moist chicken with feta wrapped in grape leaves, and a deftly balanced sauce on linguine tossed with pea pods and strips of beef tenderloin. Eclectic though it all seems, Donier's kitchen manages to execute dishes from this menu with distinction and flavorful exactitude. Desserts are perfectly in tune with the rest of the meal: a refreshingly tart lemon mousse with a raspberry sauce, for example. For

Looking for a particular place? Check the index at the back of this book for individual restaurants, nightclubs, lodgings, shops, attractions, and more.

lunch, try one of the outrageous pizzas (barbecue sauce, artichokes, chicken, and mozzarella on a dill crust on one visit; lamb, spinach, feta, artichokes, and mozzarella on a paprika crust the next).

Kells
Post Alley, Pike Place Market, 728-1916 (map: H8) Moderate; full bar; MC, V; no checks Lunch, dinner Mon-Sat

This Irish pub–style restaurant in Post Alley fits perfectly into the rich ethnic mix of Pike Place Market. The food is straightforward but often surprisingly good: meat pies, leg of lamb, a warming bowl of coddle, broiled fish, and roasted chicken—hearty, hot, and accompanied by particularly good soda bread. They get a little fancier with their specials. We had some wonderful sole stuffed with a crab mousse and garnished with pretty vegetables. The staff is a friendly bunch of Irishmen. Drop by for a pint of ale in the cozy bar; there's live Irish music Wednesday through Saturday nights.

Kikuya
8105 161st Ave NE, Redmond, 881-8771 (map: EE2) Moderate; beer and wine; MC, V; no checks Lunch Tues-Fri, dinner Tues-Sat

Stuck in the back of an undistinguished shopping center in Redmond is this small, family-run, informal Japanese restaurant where the food is wonderful. No kimonos or tatami rooms here—the draw is the excellent sushi bar. As for the rest, it's the kind of place where you order good, honest, simple things—spicy yakisoba (which you can see the chef cooking), gyoza, donburi, and a tempura you can always count on. The fresh, full-flavored meats and fish aren't overseasoned; they're allowed to command the entrée. Everything comes with pickled cucumbers, miso soup, a simple salad, and green tea. Kikuya, a favorite with local Japanese, doesn't take reservations. There's frequently a line at the door, and once seated you may find the service disarmingly rushed.

Kirkland Roaster & Ale House
111 Central Way, Kirkland, 827-4400 (map: EE4) Moderate; full bar; AE, DC, MC, V; checks OK Lunch, dinner every day

This was the fifth formula restaurant from the McHugh/Firnstahl dynasty before their final parting. It's just Firnstahl's now, and as formulas go, nobody does it better. Located smack in downtown Kirkland, the restaurant is nested between a winery (Covey Run) and a brewery (Hale's Ales). Inside, the bar boasts blazing mirrors, brass spigots, and a dozen or more fine, distinctive beers and ales on tap. The dining rooms offer two views: one of Moss Bay, the other of chickens, beef, lambs, and hams roasting slowly in the 9-foot-high vertical spit roaster. With that as a visual first course, we can't imagine ever needing to order an appetizer. The meats are the house specialty and are consistently your best choice. Some of the other dishes are less successful, although the clam chowder is especially good, thick and hearty and chewy with clams. Service is generally good; the staff seems a little too eager and formulaic itself. A private room holds 40.

Kokeb
926 12th Ave, 322-0485
(map: HH6)
Inexpensive; full bar; AE,
DC, MC, V; no checks
Dinner every day

KIDS There are now at least two other Ethiopian places in town—proving that Seattle has truly arrived as a culinary crossroads—but the first remains the best. It's plain and inexpensive, with a steady clientele of Seattle University students and faculty. The food is distinctive and exotic, and because it's eaten with the fingers, it appeals to children. Be forewarned, though: nearly all of the entrées are spicy. The base of a meal, literally, is injera, a flat, spongy bread. A round of this on a platter holds an entire party's entrée choices, soaks up their sauces, and is eaten to climax the meal. Each entrée comes with a choice of two vegetables and a bland homemade cottage cheese called eyeb, a welcome counterpart to the spicy main dishes. Service can be blasé, but this food is worth the wait.

Koraku
419 6th Ave S, 624-1389
(map: Q7)
Inexpensive; no alcohol;
no credit cards; no checks
Lunch Mon-Fri

Two war brides started Koraku years ago, and early every morning they go across to Uwajimaya to buy the freshest ingredients for simple country-style meals. Off a five-item menu and a list of daily specials, they cook for Japanese tastes: pungent fried mackerel; yakisoba, a grand dish of wheat noodles with vegetables and pork served hot and glistening with oil; tuna teriyaki; and salmon cooked shioyaki-style (rubbed with salt before cooking). Open only for lunch (closes at 5:30pm), the homey storefront is especially dear to the hearts of Japanese businessmen and is often standing room only. Pleasant, plain, and fun.

La Costa
240 NW Gilman Blvd,
Issaquah, 392-8980
Inexpensive; full bar; AE,
DC, MC, V; local
checks only
Lunch, dinner every day

KIDS What appears to be no more that an American roadside diner is in fact nothing less than an authentic Mexican eatery that's oft haunted by the editor of *La Voz* and others searching for the real thing. Mexican standards are meticulously prepared with fresh ingredients. Even the variations on the Latin offerings are dutifully executed, allowing every flavor to come through. The service is speedy, efficient, and friendly. The place is justly popular (especially with families) but doesn't take reservations, so expect a wait at peak hours. Finally, we can rave about a Mexican restaurant in—well, *near*—Seattle.

La Flambée

16150 NE 85th,
Redmond, 869-5559
(map: HH3)
Moderate; beer and wine;
MC, V;
checks OK
Lunch Mon-Fri, dinner
every day

Oddly, Laura Bady named her restaurant after a notable French restaurant in Paris. From the outside it's not exactly reminiscent of Paris (in fact, it's more of a modest storefront in Redmond), and the menu is only half French, due in part to Ali Chalal (Le Petit Cafe) who helped Bady design the menu for her first restaurant. He's since left the Eastside for more urban ventures; however, the new chef, Rod Smith, competently prepares the original menu, from farm-raised coho salmon with a sweet fruit sauce to Chalal's signature spicy couscous and chicken. The wine list is small but high quality, something that seems true of every aspect of La Flambée, from the use of tumblers instead of goblets to the courteous and attentive (but not effusive) service. Quiet and charming, this restaurant may have been too out of the way for Chalal, but it certainly isn't for the rest of us.

La Fleur

5414 Sand Point Way
NE, 527-3400
(map: FF6)
Moderate; full bar; MC,
V; checks OK
Dinner every day

Mindy Hankins came on board a few years ago, and ever since, this Sand Point favorite has been showing signs of solid improvement. As always, the space looks great, a quiet room with exposed brick, flower prints, dark antiques, and intimate booths. With Hankins in the kitchen, the food now reflects proprietor Steven Goddard's commitment to seasonal cuisine. Unfortunately, the delivery occasionally falls short of the promise. Pan-fried soft-shelled crabs with chile aioli ended up being too much texture and not enough flavor; breading and frying obliterated the subtlety of the crab. A better appetizer was polenta with herbed goat cheese and roasted peppers. A particularly satisfying entrée was six thick lamb rib chops, cooked exactly as requested and served robed in an excellent garlic-chive-cream sauce rich and flavorful enough to complement the lamb. Fresh swordfish came with a sauce of ginger, leek, and sesame butter—a good example of Hankins's simple but innovative touch. Side dishes are good, the wine list is intelligent, and desserts are a letdown. Regulars look upon La Fleur as a sort of private club, but Goddard welcomes everyone.

La Rive Gauche

2214 2nd Ave, 441-8121
(map: G7)
Moderate; full bar; AE,

An effervescent collage of lively jazz piano, echoing lights and voices, and the inimitable charm of a casual Left Bank bistro. Jean-Paul and Nina Kissel have created an atmosphere comfortable enough for dropping in for a bowl of French onion soup or a full four-course meal. The short menu stars simple neighbor-

DC, MC, V; checks OK
Dinner Mon-Sat

★★

hood food of France: an excellent bouillabaisse, gigot d'agneau, a complex cassoulet, and Paris's ubiquitous steak and frites. The linger-awhile mood prevails with Kissel at the helm, neighborhood regulars at the bar, and more recently the handsome Pierre Savoie behind the piano on Fridays and Kendra Shank on Saturdays (that is, when she's not in Paris). The prix-fixe dinner ($24) may include a pâté plate with a mild terrine or a rich chicken liver mousse, a wild green salad studded with goat cheese and walnuts, succulent halibut poached in a rich tarragon butter sauce sided with sautéed garlic potatoes, and a much-raved-about hard-crusted French bread. In the past, the kitchen's been uneven, but recently reports have only been favorable. The Kissels have long understood atmosphere. They also know chocolate; confirm that by ending the evening with a layered slice of bittersweet chocolate hazelnut torte.

Labuznik

1924 1st Ave, 441-8899
(map: I8)
Expensive; full bar; AE,
DC, MC, V; no checks
Dinner Tues-Sat

★★★★

Artistic temperment has always been part of the charm of Labuznik and its perfectionist owner Peter Cipra. Customers who've known Labuznik since its inception 14 years ago claim that service is as exact and professional as ever (if tinged with hauteur—except on the occasion when Cipra's wife, Susan, takes you in hand with her usual graciousness).

While other chefs have followed fads and experimented with showy Mediterranean, Japanese, and nouvelle influences, Cipra has stuck steadfastly by the stolid traditions of his native Czechoslovakia. His restaurant is the apotheosis of meat and potatoes, with sublime dumplings and unexciting sauerkraut on the side. You have to admire the confidence of a chef who dares ignore color in presentation; his uniformly monochromatic meals are elegant and comforting.

Concentrating as he does on a narrow, near-changeless menu, it's no surprise that Cipra has found the very best meats, and simple preparations that clear the stage to parade their virtues. Nevertheless, nightly specials seem to awaken his inspiration more than do the menu standbys. For example, a richly sauced seasonal special of pork medallions with fresh chanterelles (served in season) was intoxicating, while staple Tournedos Black and White and veal Orloff were excellent but unexciting. Minor flaws: the twin hindquarters of the hallowed Bohemian roast duck came inconsistently roasted, one noticeably browner and crisper than the other, and the usually delicious fish soup was conspicuously oversalted. Labuznik's wine list, while not the bargain it was once renowned as, is still a wise and succinct selection from moderate to very high price levels.

Lake Union Cafe

3119 Eastlake Ave E,
323-8855 (map: GG7)
Moderate; full bar; AE,
DC, MC, V; no checks
Dinner every day,
brunch Sun

Reborn, yet again, as a jazz supper club and Seattle's first restaurant to dare to offer a free ride to or from home (within a 10-mile radius); a lot of hoopla for a restaurant that has undergone at least five incarnations over the past decade. Behind it all is a menu of the steak-seafood-pasta genre. The pastas are the obvious favorites; try the mushroom ravioli gratinée in a garlicky tomato sauce. Specials (which change weekly) may include pork tenderloin with pecans, breast of chicken, grilled fillet of Northwest salmon, or mesquite-grilled swordfish. The Sunday champagne brunch (remember the legendary feast from the Great American Food and Beverage Company?) is still an extravaganza of seafood, ham, turkey, sausages, bacon, fruit, desserts, and made-to-order omelets and crepes. You'll want to get a window table in the glassed-in porch that faces Lake Union.

Lake Washington Grillhouse and Taproom

6161 NE 175th St,
Kenmore, 486-3313
(map: BB5)
Moderate; full bar; AE,
DC, MC, V; checks OK
Lunch Mon-Sat, dinner
every day, brunch Sun

Roadhouses boomed at the turn of the century as rest stops to ease long trips between towns. Firnstahl's newest establishment, self-dubbed the last roadhouse, is a little more than just a stopping place and a little less than an enterprising restaurant. The ambience is colored with collections of old beer taps, local business cards, and menus from defunct Seattle-area restaurants, more entertainment than the speedy service requires. Firnstahl brings spit-roasted ham, chicken, or lamb (you've seen them before at Kirkland Roaster & Alehouse) and an impressive array of draft microbrews to the north end of Lake Washington near the Kenmore marina. Everything comes with French fries and an occasional scoop of coleslaw. There's nothing exactly wrong with the middlebrow menu, which has the look of an upscale Denny's, but there's little attention to detail: most of the meats are overdone, and worse, so is the salmon. The service is customer-conscious, ready to do anything to make you (and your family) comfortable and happy. The Taproom's a lively after-work watering hole.

Lakeside Cafe

7419 Greenwood Ave N,
783-6945 (map: EE8)
Inexpensive; beer and
wine; MC, V; checks OK
Lunch, dinner Mon-Sat,
breakfast Sat

KIDS One of the brightest spots in Seattle's neighborhood ethnic dining scene is one of its best Greek restaurants. The place exudes the humble comforts of a Greek taverna, right down to the lusty verve of your animated hostess, Katarina Avgoustious, who encourages guests to stay for one more glass of retsina. The deep-fried calamari appetizer is meal-sized, with tender, perfectly fried squid and a side of pungent skordalia for dipping. That and a horiatiki salad—a heaping mound of tomatoes, cucumbers, kalamata olives, peppers, romaine, and feta cheese—can make a complete dinner for two, along with the good pita. The moussaka is especially good, each layer distinct yet the whole a pillow of richly blended flavors. The baklava is disappointing, so try Mr. Avgoustious's cheesecake. The music is appropriately manic.

Landau's

500 108th Ave NE,
Bellevue, 646-6644
(map: GG3)
Moderate; full bar; AE,
DC, MC, V; checks OK
Lunch Mon-Fri, dinner
Mon-Sat

A year ago, Landau's was a budget-busting showpiece of a restaurant: all polished granite, enormous flower arrangements, plush carpeting, and satiny upholstery, located in the Koll Center in downtown Bellevue. And to some extent it is still a place for moneyed retirees to hang out. However, recently Mary Jane Landau has worked hard at reducing the pretension (the crack waiters are no longer of the bow-and-scrape school) and has rewritten the menu to include more pastas and a detailed daily fresh sheet (so the pricing is less exclusive). A noble attempt to become less intimidating, though the details of a fine restaurant are still evident: for instance, complimentary bite-sized hors d'oeuvres begin the meal and artfully arranged petit fours end it. The menu has broad appeal, with classic Continental dishes (lamb chops, scallops of veal, roast duck breast) and a few more trendy items tweaked for the 1980s palate (smoked salmon linguine, black bean soup, tequila chicken). We've come to expect a delicacy of flavor here—no bang-up spicings—and true finesse. In truth, the biggest changes are really in the bar, where a few nostalgic photographs have been hung on the walls and an express menu (at deli prices) serves up a businessperson's choice of soup, salads, pastas, or a fresh roasted turkey sandwich with all the trimmings. For later in the day, the bar has 16 different vodkas, complimentary hors d'oeuvres, and a small list of bar eats, from tempura chèvre to beer-battered halibut. Private parties here (for 8 to 50 people) are grand.

RESTAURANTS

Lao Charearn

121 Prefontaine Pl S,
223-9456 (map: O8)
Inexpensive; beer only;
no credit cards;
checks OK
Lunch, dinner Mon-Sat

This unprepossessing little restaurant on Prefontaine Place is already too crowded (especially at lunch), but word continues to spread about its delightful Lao and Thai food. Order the Lao spring rolls, filled with a peppery mixture of ground pork, cabbage, carrots, and cellophane noodles, tightly wrapped and deep-fried to a deep, nutty brown. The hot-and-sour shrimp soup, a tingling lime and lemongrass broth, arrives in a hot pot belching fire through its chimney. One eater's favorite is the chicken, fresh spinach, and peanut sauce with rice—but we prefer the gai yarng, chicken marinated in coconut milk and spices and then grilled to a char. The preparation takes a while, but it's the best dish on the menu. There's also a selection of beef and chicken curries and a tasty Lao phud cashew chicken loaded with peppers, onions, and a lot of cashews. A small private room for 15 to 20 people can be reserved—great for lunch meetings.

Le Bonaparte

S 216th St and Marine
View Dr, Des Moines,
878-4412 (map: QQ7)
Expensive; full bar; AE,
DC, MC, V; no checks
Lunch Mon-Fri, dinner
every day, brunch Sun

By mining the territory between traditional French and nouvelle cuisines, this restaurant-in-a-house has been known to draw diners from the entire region to the shoreline of Des Moines. But as things begin to slip, fewer are inspired to make an evening of it. Owner-chef Jacques Mason normally has up to four game birds (squab, duck, quail, pheasant) prepared in different sauces. Not all of them are successful. A recent lamb dish was overpowered by Pernod. There are, however, some surprising touches, the veal dishes are often exemplary, and the chocolate Marie Antoinette gâteau made without flour continues to wow even reluctant chocoholics. The service has been known to attempt to cover up incompetence with snobbery. Le Bonaparte is especially lovely in summer, when you can eat on the veranda in the shade of venerable old fruit trees. On Sundays, a five-course brunch features everything from omelets and fruit to seafood and escargot. Chef Mason puts together imaginative customized menus for private groups of up to 70.

Le Gourmand

425 NW Market St,
784-3463 (map: FF8)
Expensive; beer and wine;
AE, MC, V; checks OK
Dinners Wed-Sat

Inside an unlikely Ballard storefront on an unlikely street for a French restaurant lives the spirit of Parisian dining. Owners Robin Sanders (she's back after a short stint at her own restaurant) and Bruce Naftaly have created a calm, intimate dining space, simply appointed with fresh linens and candles, and filmy curtains to obscure the traffic on busy NW

Market Street. The fancy French names (paupiette de porc, boeuf à la ficelle) are mere disguises for what we've come to label as Northwest cuisine: seasonal mushrooms, blossoms, and bottom fish that arrive daily from Naftaly's carefully chosen list of local suppliers, all generously embellished with Naftaly's forte, sauce. Each meal comes with a choice of appetizer (Whidbey Island steamed mussels in tomato, garlic, basil broth, or zucchini and mint soup). Entrées may include an unbelievably tender venison with a dark elderberry and pinot noir stock, simultaneously tart and sweet, and roast rack of lamb coated with mustard-seed crumbs or beef tenderloin stewed in its own stock infused with shallot butter and homemade mustard—both accompanied by a platter of wintery greens (Russian kale, red and green chard, New Zealand spinach, and amaranth). Finish with a wild-greens salad feathered with calendulas, nasturtiums, and rose petals. A divine crème brulée served in a wide saucer and garnished with chopped hazelnuts and brandied raspberries nearly gilds the lily. Not every meal brings forth the invention these two are capable of, but with Sanders's return, she and Naftaly can spend more time in the kitchen being inventive and less time, well, at work.

Le Tastevin

19 W Harrison St,
283-0991 (map: A8)
Expensive; full bar; AE,
DC, MC, V; checks OK
Lunch Tues-Fri, dinner
Mon-Sat

A French fixture in Seattle for over 14 years, Le Tastevin has boasted ardent regulars since 1976—and the airy, trellised space hidden on Lower Queen Anne is large enough to hold many of them at once. Owners Jacques Boiroux, who wields a heavy hand in the kitchen beside chef Rick Hanson, and Emile Ninaud, who works the dining room, have maintained an admirable record of quality, emphasizing slightly lightened versions of traditional French fare. The problem, we suspect, stems from the fact that the menu isn't as showy as it used to be. Gone is the Tastevin salad, but the stellar prawns villemarie (in a creamy, Pernod-spiked sauce), thankfully, are still a fixture. We still enjoy the wonderfully textured pheasant pâté, ever-so-satisfying bouillabaisse, and meltingly tender sweetbreads. Though we've also had less memorable dishes, like the salmon kulibiac (with mushrooms and dill baked in a pastry shell) and the coquilles St. Jacques—too uninspired to justify these kinds of prices. We recommend that you dine in the bar, where the weight of the high dinner prices has been lessened with a lighter, lower-priced appetizer menu for the urban crowd. The extraordinary wine cellar, presided over by Ninaud, boasts everything from moderate Northwest selections to rare French vintages. There are interesting iced, flavored vodkas to start, and at the end of the meal, check out the exquisite cognacs and dessert wines (such as a 50-year-old raisin sherry), many of which are very reasonably priced. The desserts are very good.

Leschi Lakecafe

102 Lakeside Ave S,
328-2233 (map: HH6)
Inexpensive; full bar; AE,
DC, MC, V; checks OK
Lunch, dinner every day

This place simply tries too hard. You are besieged with information about the historic site, the sources of seafood, exactly how the tea is brewed, and on and on. Despite the overload, the staff is less than helpful when you ask a question they are not programmed for, and service can be shaky even with all the drilling. The result is a place that ends up making you nervous and a little embarrassed for all the effort to produce passable food. The seafood is good, if they get the orders right, and the beer selection in the bar is very extensive. Best to come for fish 'n' chips, sit outside (it's very pretty), and stay away when the crowds arrive, by boat and BMW.

Linyen

424 7th Ave S, 622-8181
(map: R6)
Inexpensive; full bar; AE,
DC, MC, V; no checks
Dinner every day

Elaine Young is an anomaly in the International District: a Caucasian woman running a Chinese restaurant. She's built it into one of the favorites in the neighborhood, however, and certainly has done more in the way of snazzy decor than most. The cuisine is Cantonese, light and tasty, and quality is consistently high (though we hear complaints about the egg rolls). Avoid the limited printed menu (except for the lemon chicken, which has fans all over town) and head straight for the specials off the board by the door: crab in black bean sauce, spicy clams, potstickers, and chicken wrapped in parchment paper. Ask for what is fresh and haggle for the best. You'll get it. Young is an affable host and attracts quite a late-night "who's who" in the restaurant (until 1:30am) and bar (with its own dart team). There are three private rooms in the restaurant and a larger banquet room across the street.

A Little Bit of Saigon

1036 S Jackson St,
325-3663, (map: R4)
Inexpensive; beer and
wine; MC, V; checks OK
Breakfast, lunch, dinner
every day

Hidden around the back of Asian Plaza, A Little Bit of Saigon is probably the biggest Vietnamese place in town. It nicely fulfills the first rule of ethnic restaurants: it's a favorite of native eaters, but friendly and accommodating to outsiders. And it hones squarely to the rule that, while Thai food gets trendier and pricier,

Pho 88
1038 S Jackson St,
325-0180, (map: R4)
Inexpensive; no alcohol;
no credit cards;
checks OK
Breakfast, lunch, dinner
every day

Vietnamese restaurants remain the cheapest places to eat well. A little Bit of Saigon's menu is weighted somewhat toward the meat dishes and pho (beef and noodle soups) of North Vietnam, but you can also make a whole meal out of the excellent appetizers (skewers of marinated pork with lemongrass, lemon juice, and garlic; and excellent spring rolls). Sublime pho is the focus of their sister take-out shop next door, Pho 88; they're open until 7pm, perfect for a quick, light dinner.

Little Italy West
Corner of Winslow Way
and Madison Ave,
Bainbridge Island,
842-0517
Inexpensive; beer and
wine; no credit cards;
local checks only
Dinner every day

Of the three Italian eateries on Bainbridge, this trattoria is the islanders' favorite. Even in its new space on Winslow Way (same blue corrugated building on the corner, different street), the steamy little plate is often jam-packed. And the food is hot and plentiful. An order of cioppino (the soup's a meal in itself) comes with a side of garlic bread and a small place of pasta (recently, rotini in marinara). Pizzas are consistent, thin-crusted, crisp, and light, with 20 toppings (pesto, Canadian bacon, and sun-dried tomatoes or cappocolla, garlic, and anchovies). The calzones are fat, bursting with cheese. The pastas are big, heaping plates of chicken pesto or clams in wine sauce. Other entrées include a silky adaptation of the classic chicken piccata, finished with cream to smooth the lemony kick. This is all to be savored with a delightful nebbiolo, or to be ordered to go and enjoyed on the ferry ride back to the mainland.

Little Saigon
606 S Weller St,
382-9888 (map: R7)
Inexpensive; beer and
wine; MC, V; no checks
Lunch, dinner Tues-Sun

It's an upscale restaurant that's priced like a dive—most dishes cost under $4. Start with the cold shrimp rolls: whole shrimp, a few stray bits of pork, rice noodles, and practically a whole garden of greens, all tightly rolled inside a snowy rice pancake, ready for dipping into a hoisin-flavored sauce. (By contrast, the meat rolls are dry and uninteresting.) Then on to the cook-it-yourself items: thinly sliced beef that has been marinated in sesame oil and chiles, to be cooked at your table on a little domed hibachi, then piled with fresh noodles and greens into rice pancakes; or the seafood hot pot, for which you dip raw shrimp, oysters, scallops, sliced geoduck, and octopus into a wok full of a fire-spiced boiling broth. The rest of the menu ranges widely (fried macaroni?) and can be inconsistent.

Lofurno's
2060 15th Ave W,

It's nothing from the outside, but through Lofurno's narrow doors is an irresistible neighborhood Italian res-

283-7980 (map: GG8)
Moderate; full bar; AE,
MC, V; checks OK
Dinner every day

Lofurno's to Go
3410 W McGraw St,
Seattle, WA,
285-TOGO (map: GG9)
Moderate; no alcohol;
AE, MC, V; checks OK
Dinner Wed-Sat

taurant, pulled from a better time and place—say, Chicago, 1948. Phil Lofurno is a restaurateur's restaurateur, and he's installed all the necessities: jazz piano in the lounge, a bluesy combo smoldering on Sunday and Monday nights, high-backed booths, veteran bartenders, career waiters. The pasta is just what it oughta be, heavy on the garlic (to the delight of most of the diners) and red sauce (a welcome antidote to the light Northern Italian fare all over town). The creamy carbonara is terrific, the house salad loaded with Gorgonzola. There's a long list of veal preparations, including one rolled in raisins and pine nuts with a mushroom-and-Marsala cream sauce. If you're just plain hungry and want to skip the atmo and go directly to the pasta, try the take-out outlet, open 5pm until 9:30pm Wednesday through Saturday—its menu is almost identical to the restaurant's.

Louie's Cuisine of China
5100 15th Ave NW,
782-8855 (map: EE8)
Inexpensive; full bar; AE,
MC, V; checks OK
Lunch Mon-Fri, dinner
every day

Louie's has a labyrinthian layout with more twists and turns than a Chinese dragon (including two private rooms for parties). And it's usually jammed with loyal patrons. There's a large bar, attractive and comfortable furnishings, and a menu that safely stays within the long tradition of Chinese-American cuisine, from spare ribs to garlic chicken. Superb service.

Luna Park Cafe
2918 SW Avalon Way,
935-7250 (map: JJ9)
Inexpensive; beer and
wine; MC, V; checks OK
Breakfast, lunch, dinner
every day

Luna Park came along just in time to save its baloney-and-cheese West Seattle neighborhood from fading into culinary oblivion. Nearly two years ago, John Bennett (who owns the jukebox store next door) opened this swell joint and filled it with '50s decorative flotsam: a soda fountain, Naugahyde booths, and—what else?—jukeboxes at every booth. You can order light (a Corona and spinach salad) or not (a patty melt and a mocha milk shake) and use the jukebox to select a fitting accompaniment. For a while the place received raves. But the good tide began to ebb: service slowed to a crawl and the food lost its sheen. Recent visits happily suggest a renaissance, though: big slabs of French toast, a pancake sandwich (with an egg and link sausage), and a number of decent omelets.

Macheesmo Mouse
4129 University Way NE,
633-4658 (map: FF6)
Inexpensive; beer only; no

The concept is dynamite: a futuristic fast-food outlet with a health-conscious menu. So good for you, in fact, that Group Health's *View* magazine recently chose the Mouse as home of Seattle's healthiest lunch.

credit cards;
local checks only
Lunch, dinner every day

211 Broadway E,
325-0072 (map: GG6)

Macheesmo Mouse is a West Coast chain (with its origin in the Rose City) purveying low-fat, low-salt, fresh food preparations—and nothing fried. Judging by the number of branches that have opened around the Northwest, the Mouse is doing the right thing, in the right place. The menu runs the burrito/taco/beans/tortilla line, but they've recently added a salad and side dish option to the dinners, a few enchiladas, and a kid's plate. Everything comes with black beans and either some nutty brown rice or mixed vegetables, all served in a dizzying space that mixes retro-'50s constructivist with postmodern, er, Portland. But for your buck (and your calorie) you can't get more bang anywhere else in the neighborhood. No smoking. A Bellevue branch is scheduled to open in March 1991 at 31 Bellevue Way.

Machiavelli
1215 Pine St, 621-7941
(map: HH7)
Moderate; full bar; MC,
V; checks OK
Dinner Mon-Sat

In keeping with the trend that's been sweeping the country of late—an Italian restaurant in every neighborhood—Ristorante Machiavelli has made Pine Street and 12th Avenue its home. It's terrific. We favor the atmosphere in the bar nook downstairs to the slightly sterile restaurant room itself, but atmosphere becomes a minor point when owner Tom McElroy brings out tortellini with a robust meat sauce; garlic chicken with a crackling rosemary-redolent skin; a stunning mushroom pizza on a thin crust (the perfect appetizer for two). The canolli, billed as Northwest's best, isn't; better is the tiramisu. You and your family will roll out.

The Maddox Grill
638 NW Richmond Beach
Rd, 542-4766
Moderate; full bar; AE,
MC, V; local checks only
Lunch Mon-Fri, dinner
every day,
brunch Sat-Sun

Browny's in Richmond Beach, named for original owner Michael "Browny" Brown, was succeeded in mid-1989 by The Maddox Grill, named for new owner Rick Maddox. The restaurant still stands alone in the parking lot of a North Seattle mini-shopping center. Inside, wooden latticework creates an airy, almost gazebolike environment. Fresh fish, respectfully prepared, and friendly, attentive service continue to be the restaurant's strong suits, although recent visits show signs of inconsistency. We found the marlin steaks cooked exactly right, grilled just long enough to leave them moist but not underdone, and gently seasoned by mesquite charcoal. A pineapple chutney, properly restrained to avoid overpowering the delicate marlin, added interest. Less successful were the calamari (rubbery from overcooking) and the tiger shrimp (upstaged by an aggressive though tasty black bean sauce). The New England–style clam chowder, a longtime favorite at Browny's, was a shade watery. The wine list, moderate in price and depth, naturally favors whites. Fresh fish appears in the weekend brunch menu as well: crab and artichoke omelets and grilled salmon are featured.

Madison Park Cafe
1807 42nd Avenue E,
324-2626 (map: GG6)
Inexpensive; beer and
wine; MC, V; checks OK
Breakfast Tues-Sun,
lunch Tues-Sat

It's best in summer, when you can sit out in the sun-dappled brick courtyard and enjoy a lovingly crafted breakfast: a well-pulled café au lait, delectable spinach-and-tomato baked eggs, and the best hot, buttery, flaky scones in town. At lunch, fresh salads, fancy cream soups, and imaginative pastas and quiches (hard to find anymore!) draw a loyal, well-heeled crowd from the surrounding neighborhoods. The waitpeople always seem to remember who you are and are quite patient with children. They're not open for dinner, as this mother-mother operation spends most evenings catering private parties.

Mae's Phinney Ridge Cafe
6412 Phinney Ave N,
782-1222 (map: EE8)
Inexpensive; full bar;
MC, V; local checks only
Breakfast, lunch, dinner
every day

When the greasy, boozy old Phinney Ridge Cafe finally gave up the ghost, Mae moved in and resurrected the place. Mae is actually three women whose collective résumé includes stints at Julia's and the Surrogate Hostess, and whose specialty, therefore, was destined to be breakfast (served well into the afternoon). Sure enough, there are platefuls of homemade biscuits and sausage gravy, buttermilk pancakes and nine-grain toast, oatmeal with a shot of espresso. Try the warm, oversized, sticky, yeasty cinnamon rolls instead of the lifeless hash browns. Lunch features thick burgers, homemade fries, and real milk shakes. The towering fudge-crowned sundaes are built in the inimitable Moo Room, done up with a jukebox, a soda fountain, and sundry bovine paraphernalia.

Maltby Cafe
8809 212th St SE (Maltby
Rd), Maltby, 483-3123
Inexpensive; beer and
wine; MC, V;
local checks only
Breakfast, lunch
every day

Four women have taught the old Maltby schoolhouse cafeteria a new lesson: how to cook. It's now a tough-to-find country cafe, contemporary in design but not overly trendy. Unhurried breakfasts feature delicious, fluffy, rich omelets (the sauces and spices in the Italian omelet were not too tangy or spicy), good new potatoes, and old-fashioned oatmeal with nuts, raisins, and cream. The giant cinnamon rolls are so legendary that the cafe often runs out (go early). If you do miss breakfast, lunch is even better. You can take a seat at one of the nine counter stools for a thick Reuben sandwich (they cook their own corned beef), grilled tuna on a huge slab of bread, big toothsome hamburgers, or a bowl of homemade soup, and local beer for lunch. Leave your cigarettes at home. Long lines are the norm now, so you may want to call ahead if you're going to take it to go.

Mandarin Garden
*40 E Sunset Way,
Issaquah, 392-9476
Inexpensive; beer and
wine; MC, V; local
checks only
Lunch Tues-Sat, dinner
Tues-Sun*

This Issaquah restaurant has the distinction of producing spiciness where promised—a rarity among Chinese restaurants in the area, and all the more admirable since chef and owner Andy Wang is a native of Shanghai. The minimal decor and the down-at-heels ambience mask Wang's understanding of Sichuan, Hunan, and Mandarin cooking and warm, efficient service. Praiseworthy dishes include melt-in-your-mouth kung pao chicken, mixed seafood Sichuan, and variations on bean curd. Two private rooms (one holding up to 50 guests) are available for banquets. Peking duck should be ordered a day in advance.

Maneki
*304 6th Ave S, 622-2631
(map: Q6)
Inexpensive; full bar; AE,
MC, V; no checks
Dinner Tues-Sun*

In a city where restaurants are always changing, it's delightful to go to one that is timeless. Maneki reminds us of a comfortable Japanese inn, with eight or 10 tables on one side, tatami rooms on the other (accommodating private parties of up to 30), and a tiny sushi bar in back (as far as we remember this was Seattle's first sushi bar). Though nothing will knock you over, the menu is extensive and offers several interesting à la carte options: butter-sautéed geoduck, kasuzuke black cod, teriyaki salmon. Tempura is usually pretty good, crispy and cooked through; the sunomono salads with seafood and cucumber slices in vinegar are refreshing and delicious; sushi, entertainingly cut by sushi chef Kozo, is quite fresh. The real treat is to see families who have been coming here for two generations.

Maple Leaf Grill
*8909 Roosevelt Way NE,
523-8449 (map: DD6)
Inexpensive; beer and
wine; MC, V; checks OK
Dinner, Mon-Sat*

Every neighborhood craves a place like this: part sports tavern, part grill, it's a successful neighborhood eatery where Northeast Seattleites mingle over burgers and beer or chicken and white wine. What you'll find is an Art Deco space with lots of old wood, nine local brews on tap, a couple of TVs with the game on and the volume turned down, Ry Cooder on the stereo, and a blackboard full of wonderful specials (grilled black bass, spicy seafood stew, grilled chicken with papaya chutney, and several pasta dishes) that change frequently. Chef Harrison Ripley, of the late

Green Lake Grill, has a fondness for chile peppers, but not everything is spicy. Even the burgers are special, served with Yakima Gouda cheese (and, on request, on Como bread from the Grand Central Bakery), accompanied by a stack of fresh French fries. The wild-greens dinner salad with blue cheese ($3.25) is a great value, with very fresh, hearty greens and ample Oregon blue crumbled on top. The meals leave little room for desserts—no loss, have a glass of dessert wine or port from the well-chosen wine list instead. The helpful folks behind the bar are friendly, just like the congenial Maple Leaf neighborhood itself.

Marrakesh
605 15th Ave E,
328-4577 (map: GG6)
Moderate; full bar; AE,
MC, V; no checks
Dinner Tues-Sun

The traditional code of desert hospitality in Morocco demands that a host treat all guests with graciousness and concern. That code is well preserved at this bit of Fez on 15th, where host Ben Alaoui (formerly of the other Moroccan restaurant in town, Mamounia) assures that your meal will begin with the customary finger-washing ceremony and end with the sprinkling of rosewater over your hands. In between you will experience a cuisine—without benefit of utensils—that seems a paradigm of the generosity of desert hospitality and a reflection of the lushness and fertility of the Maghreb itself. At the Marrakesh, $14.50 buys a substantial five-course meal—a whitewashed version here if you're familiar with the model, but offering some wonderful moments, and achieved with fewer fatty sauces. Everyone begins with harira Marrakshia, the ubiquitous lentil soup of North Africa and the Middle East, here made with a tomato base. The meal continues through a Moroccan eggplant salad (served too cold on our visit) and a dry and rather uninteresting bastela royale (poultry pie), at which point you choose your entrée. The couscous and honey-prune chicken are lackadaisical versions, so we suggest the braised hare: tender, lean Vashon Island rabbit in a rich, warm paprika sauce. Or visit with a large group and order the mechoui—Morocco's famous roast lamb. Hosting a group may, in fact, be Marrakesh's best function—the private room is fine for a party, and the relaxed festivity of the place is great for get-togethers in need of an ice breaker. Don't plan on whispering sweet nothings, however; the din can really escalate in here, especially when the bedizened belly dancer starts to sway. Last year, Ben Alaoui opened a similar version of this restaurant in northwest Portland.

Matzoh Momma

509 15th Ave E,
324-6262 (map: GG6)
Inexpensive; beer and
wine; MC, V; checks OK
Breakfast, lunch, dinner
every day

KIDS This may be the best of a sparse selection of Jewish deli-restaurants in the Seattle area. The menu offers standard kosher fare (matzoh balls, great latkes with sour cream and applesauce, cheese blintzes), along with deli salads (three-bean, fresh coleslaw, chicken) and Jewish deli items (kosher wines, pickles, herring, etc.). The take-out and catering operations continue to thrive. Some prices are high, but the chicken soup is a tasty bargain, and the sandwiches are delectable. At night amateur and professional musicians entertain, making Matzoh Momma a gathering place for North Capitol Hill residents.

Maximilien-in-the-Market

Pike Place Market,
682-7270 (map: J8)
Moderate; full bar; AE,
DC, MC, V; no checks
Breakfast, lunch, dinner
Mon-Sat, brunch Sunday

Francois and Julia Kissel's French market cafe in the Main Arcade is such a splendid *place*—full of noble antiques and blessed with a view of Elliott Bay—but the fare has been increasingly inconsistent and we've heard several reports of moody service. In addition to croissants, espresso, and so on, breakfasts include a soufflé and homemade sage sausage. At lunch, there are two salads (Niçoise, and one with napa cabbage, shrimp, and salmon), maybe an omelet, steamed mussels with wine and cream, dilled meatballs with nutmeg sauce, and excellent fish 'n' chips. Dinners include grilled sweetbreads in mustard caper sauce, a halibut and red snapper soup, and chicken with apples and veal sausage. Finish with bread pudding, topped with Francois's incomparable caramel sauce—desserts are a consistent strong point at Maximilien's. The upstairs bar area is available for rent by parties of up to 30.

McCormick and Schmick's

1103 1st Ave, 623-5500
(map: L8)
Moderate; full bar; AE,
DC, MC, V; checks OK
Lunch Mon-Fri, dinner
every day

A kind of Tadich's North, this seafood restaurant is an encyclopedia of San Francisco clichés: dark wood paneling, booths, glittering bar, and waiters with black bow ties. You'd think they'd been grilling lamb chops and salmon steaks since the turn of the century. Don't smirk—they do it well, if not with perfect consistency. Just remember to keep it simple: order seafood, and stay away from the pasta. Start with roasted garlic and some fresh oysters; then get the fresh fish of the day, usually done in a tasty, uncomplicated sauce. The straightforward work at the grill also includes meat, game, and poultry. At lunch it's too busy for its own good—service adopts a hurry-up attitude, and they make you sit in the hall until your whole party assembles—but dinners are more relaxed, with the bar suppers a nice feature for solo diners. A private room holds up to 15 guests.

McCormick's Fish House and Bar
722 4th Ave, 682-3900
(map: N6)
Moderate; full bar; AE,
DC, MC, V; checks OK
Lunch Mon-Fri, dinner
every day

This may be the best of the downtown fish houses (not that that's saying much), and it certainly is the most popular. Lunch is noisy and frenetic, the bar jams up with City Hall–types after 5pm, and even dinners feel crowded, particularly during the tourist season. Somehow, the waiters remain cheerful amid the bustle. The formula here is simple: the heavy-on-seafood menu, printed daily, offers several types of fish prepared in largely simple ways (grilled with a flavored butter, sautéed with another butter, baked more elaborately). Preparation can be uneven—we've had both tough tuna and near-perfect halibut—but you can usually rely on decent cooking (especially when you order your fish broiled) and generous portions. Oysters are fine, salads pedestrian, the wine list carefully chosen and overpriced, the beautifully fresh sourdough bread always a treat.

Mediterranean Kitchen
4 W Roy St, 285-6713
(map: GG7)
Inexpensive; beer and
wine; AE, DC, MC, V;
no checks
Lunch Tues-Fri, dinner
every day

The Oven
213 Broadway E, Seattle
98102, 328-2951 (GG6)
Inexpensive; no alcohol;
no credit cards; no checks
Lunch, dinner every day

This is the most garlicky kitchen in town. But there are other distinctions, notably the presence of owner-chef Kamal Aboul-Hosn, a Lebanese who serves fare from the entire Mediterranean basin. His zahrah (cauliflower florets with a light tahini dressing) are the best in town; we also appreciate the North African couscous (with carrots, potatoes, onions, and a spoon-tender lamb shank braised in a tomato-based sauce) and a Lebanese farmer's dish of broiled chicken wings and rice in—naturally—garlic sauce. Enormous quantities (even with the appetizers) at very low prices have earned this place institution status (the couscous lasted us through two more lunches). It's the place to go with an appetite; you'll actually be turned away at the door if all you want is soup or appetizers. The Kitchen's fast-food branch, The Oven on Broadway, is a cavernous eatery and like the original in more ways than one: the beef or chicken shawarma is generously marinated in lemon and garlic, and none cost over $5.

Metropolitan Grill
818 2nd Ave, 624-3287
(map: N7)
Expensive; full bar; AE,
DC, MC, V; checks OK
Lunch Mon-Fri, dinner
every day

This handsome haunt in the heart of the financial district does a booming business among stockbrokers and Asian tourists. The soul of the restaurant is its steaks, and you'd do well to stick to them, since they really do live up to the hoopla. Pastas and appetizers are less well executed, but a growing list of large, appealing salads (and terrific clam chowder) presents a good alternative to beef for the lunch crowd. There's a lot of table-hopping going on here, which puts the poker-faced waiters in even nastier spirits. Financiers like to use the Met's private room (holds about 32 people) as a dependable venue for private dinners.

Mezza Luna Ristorante
3130 E Madison St,
325-8068 (map: GG6)
Moderate; beer and wine;
AE, MC, V; local
checks only
Dinner every day

A restaurant of remarkably democratic appeal, Mezza Luna is filled on any given evening with families and aristocrats, Madison Park denizens and destination diners alike. The stark decor defies any notion of a family-style restaurant, yet a casual atmosphere reigns; likely as not you'll find owner Michael Failla—as well as most of his guests—in jeans. The open kitchen in the corner produces straightforward, classic dishes from Scott Carsberg (formerly of Settebello) using quality ingredients and care in preparation and presentation. Pizza toppings range from the simple, beautiful margherita to noble assemblages of smoked venison sausage and peppers in a spicy tomato sauce, grilled eggplant with smoked mozzarella, and goat cheese with pesto and prosciutto (cooked in a wood-burning oven). Pastas tend to vary in quality and punch (from bland to prohibitively garlicky). On weekends the kitchen turns out a much-requested grilled veal shank served with sautéed chanterelles, pancetta, and a side of grilled polenta—a mix of Northwest bounty and an Italian touch. Prices tend to mount dangerously here, so watch the extras (like the San Pellegrino water at your table, which is *not* gratis), but for an unpretentious meal in a neighborhood restaurant, you won't miss the lire.

Mikado
514 S Jackson St,
622-5206 (map: Q7)
Moderate; full bar; AE,
MC, V; local checks only
Dinner Mon-Sat

You can still eat well (or mostly well) at Mikado, but either its food is merely good, no longer surpassing. It is still a very cozy place for one so large, broken up into a warren of distinct, intimate dining settings and styles. You sit at Formica tables and order from any of the menu genres; it is usually a mistake to dine here; far better to sit at the sushi or robata bar, where the Japanese diners congregate. If you must settle for the main dining room, grab a stuffed-vinyl corner booth. If you're in a large party, reserve a straw-matted, low-seated tatami room; the food perks up in this traditional setting, and a big steaming pot of toban-yaki—meat, fish, shrimp, and vegetables cooked at your table—is a marvelously sociable antidote to winter blahs. If you're solo or in a pair, consider the robata-yaki (grill) or the sushi bar, and compose a meal of the fresh hors d'oeuvres that are Mikado's strongest suit; prepara tions and service at either of these make for a splendid mealtime show. At our last visit, the sashimi was fine though not exceptional, the eel was too soft and old, and the saba too tough. Vegetables have arrived cold. Still, the service was quick, maybe a bit *too* quick with the check, and the veteran waitresses delight in decoding Japanese cuisine for novices.

Musashi's Sushi & Grill
1400 N 45th St, 633-0212
(map: FF7)
Inexpensive; beer and
wine; no credit cards;
local checks only
Lunch Tues-Fri, dinner
Tues-Sat

It's a small, stylish Wallingford restaurant that's easy to find: it'll be the one with the line stretching out onto the sidewalk. Mitsuko Woo made some smart choices right from the start: she limited the menu to a few well-chosen items, plus sushi—very fresh smoked salmon and yellowtail, octopus, great California rolls—that don't cost half a week's wages for a few ethereal bites. Consequently, Musashi's enjoys a devoted following. Some come for the good curries, others for the chicken teriyaki (some say it's the best teriyaki sauce in town), and others for the artful bento boxes: Japanese "brown bag" specials that include skewers of roasted vegetables and chicken, rice, sweet omelet slices, kami kamaboko (fish cake), and a generous sampler of sashimi, all beautifully presented in black lacquer boxes, for $7 (also available to go).

The New Jake O'Shaughnessey's
401 Bellevue Square,
Bellevue, 455-5559
(map: HH3)
Moderate; full bar; AE,
DC, MC, V; checks OK
Lunch, dinner every day

When Seattle restaurateurs Mick McHugh and Tim Firnstahl tossed a coin off the Space Needle to decide how to divvy up their restaurant empire, McHugh got the New Jake's at Bellevue Square, and we bet he's still smiling about it. The partners had opened the New Jake's in 1985 to meet the demands of a growing Eastside clientele. It's a move that paid off; these days, lunch and dinner business are both brisk. While the trademark, reputation-building beef and lamb remain popular menu items, the emphasis is shifting toward seafood and lighter fare. Fresh salmon is available daily and the lunchtime fish 'n' chips is a steady favorite. Whatever else you order at dinner, start off with the steamed fresh shellfish appetizer, a pot full of fresh clams and mussels simmered in light cream, vermouth, and butter just for dipping—it's worth asking for more sourdough bread. Other Jake's classics include the roast leg of lamb sandwich with mustard sauce and the original Boston butt pork chop. For dessert, attempt the Snicker's pie, a concoction of praline ice cream, roasted peanuts, and caramel sauce, topped with whipped cream and served on a cookie crumb crust.

The bar, with late-night appetizers, is hopping on Friday and Saturday nights. There's outdoor dining in summer and a private dining room that seats up to 60 guests. Reservations are recommended.

New Peking

7845 Lake City Way NE,
523-1010 (map: EE6)
Inexpensive; beer and
wine; MC, V; no checks
Lunch Mon-Sat, dinner
every day

Peking House

17505 15th Ave NE,
365-6500 (map: BB6)
Inexpensive; full bar;
MC, V; local checks only
Dinner every day

It used to be that for authentic Chinese food you had to go to the International District, but the trend toward Sichuan, Mandarin, and Hunan cuisines has altered that rule. The New Peking has been in the North End for a decade, serving mostly excellent, authentic northern Chinese dishes. Owner Chih-kin Ding runs the Peking House (decorated in the McChinese-red style) and his wife, Helen, oversees the original New Peking. Both restaurants have identical menus featuring six pages of meat, seafood, vegetable, and noodle dishes emphasizing spiciness. Eggplant and pork with garlic hot sauce is served as spicy-hot as you want, if they know you mean it. Crispy duck is glorious proof of why the Chinese consider this fowl the ultimate feast; marinated three days in a special blend of spices, the duck is moist, tender, and incredibly flavorful. Pay attention to what you order—not all is outstanding. We've heard recent reports of bland potstickers and a Mongolian beef that, while spicy, lacked invention. In addition, the all-you-can-eat crowd cheapens the overall effect of the evening. With such enormous portions, who cares?

Newman's Bear Creek Cafe

13120 NE 177th Pl,
Woodinville, 485-9372
(map: BB1)
Expensive; beer and wine;
AE, MC, V; local
checks only
Dinner Tues-Sat

A game restaurant is a brave endeavor, particularly in rural Woodinville. Dennis Newman (trained at the Culinary Institute of America) specializes in meats from venison and quail to antelope, bison, and elk, sautéed or grilled in their own juices and bathed in their own reduced sauces. Newman is committed to quality suppliers, so the ingredients will be good, if erratic in preparation. Be prepared for strong flavors and steep prices. We had an excellent buffalo fillet in mushroom gravy but received it well done after requesting it medium rare. There were other quibbles, too: the side of pasta was merely filler, the salad was far too sparing, and the accompanying rolls, though fresh and herbed, were sweet enough for dessert. Newman has added a selection of more reasonably priced Italian fare; however, you'll do better if you stick to the game in this pretty restaurant overlooking a garden.

Send us your feedback and tips on the report form at the back of this book.

Nikko

*1306 S King St, 322-4905
(map: II6)
Moderate; full bar; AE,
DC, MC, V; no checks
Dinner Mon-Sat*

Most sushi aficionados agree that owner–sushi chef Shiro Kashiba, a master showman who claims position as Seattle's first sushi chef, is Seattle's best. From 6pm on, Shiro packs the house with diners queued up at the sushi bar to watch the expert craft bite-size Japanese delicacies—squid gut, fish liver, fish skin—with remarkable alacrity. Trouble is, neophytes to Japanese cuisine (or those who don't favor ordering in the traditional Japanese way, by asking the chef to prepare whatever's freshest) receive the same first-rate fish with second-rate presentation and third-rate service. Likewise, one must move with care into the conventional menu: single orders of sukiyaki arrive precooked from the kitchen; the menu is too light on vegetables and tofu; and tempura varies from light and lacy to gummy within. If you can't wait for a seat at Nikko's bar, you have a choice of the dining tables or tatami rooms (one of which can hold a private party of 40). Either place, ask for the Japanese menu for more esoteric (and more carefully prepared) items, including snack-size portions of wonderful things like steamed clams with sake and cold spinach with soy and sesame. Strangers to this not-so-secret restaurant may be surprised by the somewhat seedy entryway, which looks a bit worn, a bit tired. Perhaps Shiro is, too.

Olympia Pizza and Spaghetti

*1500 Queen Anne Ave N
(and two others),
285-5550 (map: GG7)
Inexpensive; beer and
wine; no credit cards;
checks OK
Lunch, dinner every day*

KIDS Nimble-fingered guys in striped shirts construct these pies, piling spicy pepperoni, fresh mushrooms, outstanding fennel-flavored Italian sausage, shrimp, and other flavorful stuff on freshly made dough, then topping it all with a thick glaze of creamy mozzarella. Your pizza will take a nine-minute ride through the oven on a conveyor belt, then be whacked into slices by cooks wielding scimitars. Olympia also offers a first-rate green salad, decent pastas, and sub sandwiches, but you go there for the pizza. You'll probably have to wait in line. A good place for kids.

Pacific Northwest Brewing Company

*322 Occidental Ave S,
621-7002 (map: O8)
Moderate; full bar; AE,
MC, V; no checks
Lunch, dinner Tues-Sun,
every day in summer*

English-born Richard Wrigley lives in New York but came out here for a short bit to open his third brewpub (the first two were in New York and Boston), to tap into Seattle's cultish infatuation with homebrew. His bitter English-style beers (the Golden Ale has less of a bite than the Blond) don't have the kind of following yet that Wrigley would like, but the restaurant has caught on with the Pioneer Square lunch crowd and is rapidly becoming a popular pregame place. Big, shiny brass beer tanks brighten up the otherwise cold and noisy room, and diners can watch the brewmasters work, then heft a few. Diners choose from bratwurst steamed in ale, hot sausage and shellfish gumbo (with lots of fire), and daily specials that usually include a number of pastas. Try the fish cakes, made with salmon and cod moistened with a green peppercorn mayonnaise, or the grilled chicken, blue cheese, bacon, and pesto mayo club on walnut rye bread. Service is efficient and friendly, and when Wrigley *is* in town he'll be greeting you at the door.

Pacifica
14450 Woodin-
ville–Redmond Rd,
Woodinville 487-1530
(map: CC2)
Moderate; full bar; AE,
MC, V; local checks only
Lunch Tues-Sat, dinner
Tues-Sun, brunch Sun

What Pacifica does well, it does very well—the staff is educated in cooking and wines (good thing, as this has become a popular stopping point during tours of the nearby wineries). A recent chowder was excellent (though heavy-handed on the pepper); the Caesar, as the waiter had warned, was not what we expected. In contrast, seafood entrées were faultless: the Atlantic sea scallops with chanterelles and the fresh halibut with a mild lime sauce were sublime. It seems that people come here not only to consume good food and good wine but also to talk about it. Order a full bottle of wine: this restaurant seems to favor those who at least appear to be aficionados. Superb cheesecake.

Palm Court (Westin Hotel)
1900 5th Ave, 728-1000
(map: H5)
Expensive; full bar; AE,
DC, MC, V; checks OK
Lunch Mon-Fri, dinner
Mon-Sat

The setting, in the Westin Hotel, is superb: four glass pavilions diminishing in size to one that holds a single table seating up to 12. All the glass and some imaginative lighting give the place two personalities: at night, intimacy with a certain sheen; at lunch, gardenlike, with many potted palms and banks of pink-leaved caladiums. Attention to detail—bottled water, silver crumb scoops, and so on. The cuisine is prettily Continental and mostly successful—a Muscovy duck breast with orange cranberry sauce, medallions of beef tenderloin with a Madeira sauce and a heap of colorful peppers, rack of lamb with minted coriander au jus. On recent visits we've sampled overcooked beef and meager salad portions (salads, by the way, are outstanding). Desserts, too, are good (the chocolate Concord cake is very smooth), and the wine list is excellent. Upstairs a lovely private room seats 13 to 35 and has its own marble bar.

Looking for a particular place? Check the index at the back of this book for individual restaurants, nightclubs, lodgings, shops, attractions, and more.

Palomino

*1420 5th Ave (Pacific
First Centre), 623-1300
(map: J5)
Expensive; full bar; AE,
DC, MC, V; local
checks only
Lunch Mon-Sat, dinner
every day*

In the heart of metropolitan Seattle, Palomino jumped out of the starting gate at a full gallop. One year later, Rich Komen (Cutters Bayhouse, Triples) has managed to keep his newest restaurant a nose ahead of encroaching competition with a concept that seems, even on the third floor of the Pacific First Centre, to work. Dozens of chefs, garbed in whites and toques, bustle with reckless proficiency in open kitchens. An open-fired, 900-degree wood oven roasts most of the fish, an alder-fired oven takes care of the wafer-thin pizzas with a light hand on the toppings, and a Milanese girarrosto roasts chicken, duck, pork loin, and sausage. The vast dark-wood space accented by spiky-fronded palms and Pilchuck glass sconces makes diners feel like there's a lot going on here. The sheer volume of bodies (beautiful bodies) makes up the main attraction. Then there's the food, which hovers somewhere between Mediterranean and pure Italian. Favorites include anything from the ovens or roasting spit, such as the flash-roasted Alaskan king salmon with shallot, peppercorn, and brandy sauce or the fall-apart garlic chicken with bursts of rosemary and fresh lemon. There's a good beer list featuring many of the local microbrews (and Red Hook's cask-conditioned ale) and a wine list that is well priced. The tiramisu will not only pick you up, it will send you flying over the finish line.

Panda's

*7347 35th Ave NE,
526-5115 (map: EE6)
Inexpensive; beer and
wine; AE, MC, V; local
checks only
Lunch Mon-Sat, dinner
every day*

Panda's is the best Chinese restaurant in the North End. After many meals we have not had a bad or even ordinary dish yet. Occupying a small storefront in a new strip mall, Panda's has a contemporary look, with an open kitchen and high-backed stools at the counter. As three cooks work the wok line, a hostess covers delivery orders on the phone, someone else bags them up, and two drivers run in and out in a constant flurry of motion. Free delivery in northeast Seattle is unbelievably fast and probably quadruples the output from the small kitchen. Smoked tea duck is smoky and moist, served with hoisin sauce and soft steamed buns. Lover's Eggplant is thick slices of eggplant battered and fried to golden perfection, a sort of Chinese tempura. The Mushu pork is nicely done here: the vegetables are crisp and distinct, the pork strips are tender, and the accompanying pancakes are homemade. Chicken salad with fresh cucumbers and noodles features a tangy vinegar sauce. Beef and asparagus in black bean garlic sauce shows how skilled the cooks are—neither the asparagus nor the beef is cooked a moment too long. All noodles, dumplings, buns, and sauces are made on the premises. The waitstaff is friendly and helpful and can be trusted to make good suggestions, especially for the adventurous.

PaneVino

303 Occidental Ave S,
343-0233 (map: N8)
Moderate; full bar; MC,
V; checks OK
Lunch Tues-Fri, dinner
Tues-Sun

unrated

Sitting out on the cobbled patio, the sun filtering through the shade trees, with *tre gatti* parading around with strong Italian accents (one of them, Thor Taggart, hails from Seattle)—it doesn't get much better than this. Inside this airy restaurant, there are hardwood floors, a 20-foot ceiling, and turn-of-the-century brick walls. Angelo Belgrano (Botticelli Cafe) wants his new Italian restaurant in the former Cafe Felipe spot in Pioneer Square to be the kind of place where people go to hang out day or night—until 2, 3, 4am. On Fridays and Saturdays food's served until 11:30, but the bar's open as late as there are people (the alcohol stops at 2am). Indeed, this is the kind of place we'd like to go often— and would, if we could afford these kinds of prices. Early bites (open for three weeks at press time) of the risotto al radicchio were as rich and comfortable as you'd ever want. The crema di pomodoro con crostini—a creamy tomato soup with slices of crusty rustica bread—was delightful, though the prizewinner among the primi piatti was the pennette alle chanterelle (a small plate of penne with veal, fresh tomato, Parmesan, garlic, and chanterelles). The appetizers are not terribly inspired. Request advice about the wine, and Thor, the resident wine expert, will make suggestions based on your order (there are 21 wines by the glass). Hopefully, when the bar opens with less expensive eats like Botticelli-style panini (grilled sandwiches) and roasted fowl, PaneVino will become the kind of place where everyone wants to be.

Panko's

4850 Green Lake Way N,
632-6301 (map: FF7)
Inexpensive; no alcohol;
no credit cards;
checks OK
Breakfast, lunch Tues-
Sun, dinner Tues-Sat

★½

The neighborhood folk fill up regularly at this former gas station near Green Lake. It's wholesome with a Japanese twist—we're inclined to think of it as the '90s version of Toshi's. Whatever, this little spot opened with promises of $1 lattes and delicious scones. The lattes are indeed a buck, but it's the fair-priced dinners (spicy ginger prawns with brown rice and vegies, a good-sized hunk of teriyaki salmon) for which people return. You can place your order at the counter or from one of the tables. On warm days, try the small Japanese garden out back.

Paparazzi Ristorante

2202 N 45th St, 547-7772
(map: FF7)
Moderate; beer and wine;
AE, MC, V; checks OK
Dinner every day, brunch
Sat-Sun

The Italian name belies and English pub–like interior and a genteel atmosphere where a laudable list of local microbrews is eagerly recited. The menu, with 20 entrées (rather unwieldy for an 18-table venture) focuses on pasta, fish, chicken, and veal. Skip the appetizers, they're too much of nothing special and they spoil your dinner. The entrées are generous enough themselves and come with a well-thought-out salad or soup. The penne marinara was undeniably the largest pasta dish we've *ever* encountered. The pasta was heaped with acres of steaming clams, mussels, squid, salmon, and scallops in a pungent tomato sauce. The grilled swordfish pleases as well. Paparazzi continues to be a well-kept Wallingford secret (even with its proximity to the Guild 45th theaters), full of promise and surprises—like the spanking new wine and espresso bar that makes waiting that much nicer (and stopping in for dessert after a movie that much easier). At press time, the new grill in the kitchen had allowed new chef Leslie Dillon to round out the menu with lighter items like grilled fresh swordfish with nectarine salsa or free-range veal with fresh chanterelles. Breakfast (weekends only) is a good alternative to the busy morning spots nearby.

Pasta & Co.

1001 4th Ave (and
branches), 624-3008
(map: M6)
Inexpensive; beer and
wine; MC, V; local
checks only
Breakfast, lunch, early
dinner Mon-Fri

The leading fresh-pasta emporium in Seattle features pasta made to absorb sauces a shade thinner than usual, and fine deli foodstuffs (sun-dried tomatoes, European and domestic olive oils, the makings of antipasto plates), to be purchased and enjoyed according to the advice of reliable proprietor Marcella Rosene. Though both the Bellevue Square (279 Bellevue Square, 453-8760) and original University Village (2640 NE University Village Mall, 523-8594) branches do a healthy business in ready-to-eat take-out items, the only one that really counts as a restaurant is the central downtown deli, with its sit-down stools and stylish glass walls. Every lunch hour, throngs of discriminating execs enjoy repasts from Marcella's vast repertoire: Chinese vermicelli salad, a corn-and-pepper medley glistening with wonderful oil, hazelnut tortellini in a velvet cream sauce, a simple toss of spirelli pasta and fresh basil, black bean soup. Order it up in a deli line, then pray for a seat (late lunchers may be out of luck). You pay for the quality—a lunchtime three-salad sampler is $6.50—but when you compare it with expense-account places with half the commitment to freshness, you'll decide it's a bargain. For breakfast, order an omelet and pick up a fruit muffin, moist and not sweet. Service tends toward the exasperated.

Pasta Bella

5909 15th Ave NW,
789-4933 (map: EE8)
Inexpensive; beer and
wine; AE, DC, MC, V;
local checks only
Dinner every day

In a haphazardly festive room—almost rococo with dark green walls, renditions of Roman columns, and gilt mirrors—you come quite close to finding all the elements of the *perfetto* Italian meal. That is, if Italian waiters would be found dressed in Hawaiian shirts and purple hightops. This popular restaurant uses fresh ingredients such as woodsy Northwest mushrooms and vine-ripened Roma tomatoes and does a nice job on a dozen or so fresh, robust pasta dishes (including a knockout pollo al limone), a relaxed, slightly flirtatious atmosphere that lets you settle back and order just one more glass of wine, and astonishingly low prices. We like the antipasto plate (includes caponata, an Italian ratatouille) and the fragrant, rich chicken Marsala. Finish with a memorable latte and a wedge of something freshly baked from the kitchen.

Peerless Pies

Pike Place Market,
443-1801 (map: H8)
Inexpensive; no alcohol;
MC, V; checks OK
Breakfast, lunch, dinner
every day

Pies are honest food. As much as people fool with it, real American pie is Mom food, and very hard to duplicate. That's where Peerless Pies comes in, grabbing the corner on what ex-Starbuckeroos Gordon Bowker and Zev Siegl hope is the last untapped comfort food for a long while. Crusts are flaky, flavorful, and rich and stuffed with fillings both savory (clam, chicken, Yankee beef) and sweet (excellent apple-walnut-raisin and other fruit varieties, chocolate-pecan, and lemon meringue). Buy one whole or by the slice, with a scoop of slaw and a bite-sized dessert, if you're eating in. The Pike Place Market original has three peers: Broadway (434 Broadway E, 323-0476), Columbia Center (701 Fourth Avenue, #114, 386-5855), and University Village (4508 University Village Plaza NE, 523-7992).

Pegasus Pizza and Pasta

2758 Alki Ave SW,
932-4849 (map: II9)
Inexpensive; beer and
wine; MC, V; checks OK
Dinner every day

KIDS Alki dwellers will be the first to tell you that the best reason to venture to West Seattle is still the Greek pizza at Pegasus. It's feta and mozzarella, olives, onions, fresh spinach, ground beef, and sunflower seeds, all mounded on a buttery, gritty-textured (like good homemade anadama bread) crust, and served on a cake plate. Toppings, including the dense, potent tomato sauce, are applied with epicurean restraint. The setting is very Seattle: a lot of windows, great views of Puget Sound, matching furniture, friendly waiters. They've nearly doubled the seating area, but that's done little to curb the line at the take-out window.

Peter's on the Park
4000 E Madison St,
323-7686 (map: GG6)
Moderate; full bar; MC,
V; checks OK
Lunch Tues-Fri, dinner
Tues-Sat

The next generation of Peter Canlis's restaurant clan has produced this trendy little spot in trendy little Madison Park. The menu is a supperish version of Canlis's, strong on pastas and steaks but with burgers thrown in to help with the family crowd. Our meal was nothing special: although the steak was well aged, the oysters Rockefeller were bland. The service is cheery. It's the kind of crowd that loves to table hop and compare recent tennis scores. A private room holds 30.

Phad Thai
8530 Greenwood Ave N,
784-1830 (map: DD8)
Inexpensive; beer and
wine; MC, V; no checks
Lunch Mon-Fri, dinner
every day

There's years of experience behind Seattle's newest Thai restaurant. Husband-wife team Dolly Armstrong (formerly of Angel's Thai on Broadway) and Wichai Saksrisanguan (from Thai Tahnee—one of Seattle's first Thai establishments—and Bahn Thai) put their expertise to work in this unassuming eatery with a huge menu: exceptionally well balanced chicken in peanut sauce cooled with Thai white rice, perfectly cooked scallops with onions, carrots, green pepper, powerful Thai basil, wine, and sultry spices, and a generous portion of vegetable curry. Thai curries are less heavy than other curries and usually produce a special lift—this was transcendent. Dolly takes kids in stride. On a recent visit, she sent plain, crunchy steamed broccoli to the table to curb the children's appetite. For dessert, dare to try a steaming bowl of sticky, sweet black-rice pudding in coconut milk. A treat.

Philadelphia Fevre Steak & Hoagie Shop
2332 E Madison St,
323-1000 (map: GG6)
Inexpensive; beer only;
AE, MC, V; no checks
Lunch, dinner Mon-Fri

Seattleites don't quite get it, the appeal of white bread, red meat, manufactured cheese, packaged dessert, and terse service. Put it all together, though, and you've got a guaranteed nostalgia trip for every displaced Easterner. It's called Philadelphia Fevre, a comfy roost run by Philly transplant Renee LeFevre. Tasters agree she makes the meanest Philadelphia steak sandwich in town: a pile of thinly sliced ribeye steak, grilled with onions and served on an Italian roll. OK, so what if it's a bit softer than *over there*. Add some white American cheese and hot cherry peppers, and you've got a pepper cheese steak. The list of additions goes on (provolone and pizza sauce, mushrooms and cheese), and we've rarely been disappointed. LeFevre's hoagies (Genoa salami, prosciutto, cappocolla, provolone) are almost triple the size of the cheese steaks and are all dressed with lettuce, tomato, and raw onions doused with your choice of oil or mayonnaise. Cheese fries are a whimsical accompaniment—crinkly fried potatoes drowning in something that acts and tastes a whole lot like Cheez Whiz. You'll be embarrassed at how much you love them, and you can make them part of your early dinner; the grill shuts down just before 7pm. Finish with—sigh—a TastyKake.

Pho Hoa
4406 Rainier Ave S,
723-1508 (map: JJ6)
Inexpensive; no alcohol;
no credit cards; no checks
Breakfast, lunch, dinner
every day

We're not usually in the business of saluting chain restaurants, but this one has two mitigating qualifications and one compelling one: it's a very small chain, based in the Vietnamese-American heartland of Orange County; it's such a heartening reuse of an old Kentucky Fried Chicken shack; and it serves the best bowl of pho in Seattle. Pho (pronounced like the French *feu*) is the ubiquitous breakfast, lunch, and anytime quick meal of Vietnam, a soup of rice noodles, scallions, and beef in a clear broth that, like a good bagel, is one of the irreducible perfect food forms. Pho Hoa, like a good Saigon soup stand, serves only pho, in 15 different forms (depending on beef cut added, from rare steak to tendon to beef balls). But it's the broth that figuratively as well as literally carries the pho, and Pho Hoa's is bracingly rich and fragrant, with a mysterious infusion of spices. Bowl sizes vary from ample to enormous, all ridiculously cheap. On the side is the full complement of garnishes—lime, fresh herbs, chiles, bean sprouts—to finish your soup to taste. Though alcohol's lacking here, as in most Vietnamese restaurants, fresh-squeezed orange juice, soy milk, and super-concentrated Vietnamese coffee more than fill its place.

Phoenecia Restaurant
100 Mercer St, 285-6739
(map: A6)
Moderate; beer and wine;
MC, V; checks OK
Dinner Tues-Sat

Owner/chef Hussein Khazaal has built his reputation on excellent service, highest-quality Mediterranean delicacies, and a warmth and generosity practically unknown in other Seattle restaurants. He greets his diners warmly, fusses over them, and makes sure they're being taken care of. The restaurant, in the Hansen Baking complex (yes, it's still around), is an elegant spot done up in cerulean and purple and divided into separate rooms to accommodate private parties. The menu has been cut back in recent years, but the essentials are still there: smoky baba ghanouj, creamy hummus, delicate lamb kebabs, and tender and spicy Egyptian chicken (it's not on the menu, but ask for it anyway). Khazaal serves some of the best Mediterranean cuisine in town. Too bad he has to limit his printed menu to what will work for the hurry-up pre-curtain crowd. The best plan for fully appreciating Phoenecia is to bring a crowd of friends in and order one of Khazaal's famous *meezas* (feasts), for $18 to $25 per person. For the next couple of hours you will be served an embarrassment of incredible food, probably enough for twice the size of your group. Khazaal will pull out all the stops: seafood, poultry, lamb, vegetables, couscous, flaky desserts—incredible variety and dishes you aren't likely to find anywhere else. When (and if) the Hansen Baking complex is remodeled into condominiums, Khazaal will move Phoenecia to a new location, but he's been assured by the landlords that, as of press time, that's at least a year away. Also at press time, Hussein was on the verge of opening Cafe Phoenecia in Pike Place Market (a space for which he waited 12 years), which will offer an inexpensive version of his Queen Anne establishment's fare—even box lunches.

Piecora's
1401 E Madison St,
322-9411 (map: GG6)
Inexpensive; beer only;
no credit cards; checks
OK
Lunch, dinner every day

Over a decade ago, two brothers from New York brought the real East Coast pie to this shore. Unfortunately, the brotherly Piecora partnership didn't last very long, hence another similarly named venture in Ravenna (see review). That said, Piecora's (the original) is a marvelous place to be. It's a warm room, full of good neighborhood vibes, with the boyish pizza tossers installed by the window. There are 20-odd toppings, but it's the garlicky sauce and the crisp crust that get raves. Pizza's served (and delivered, within reasonable distance) until midnight on weekends.

Piecora's New York Pizzeria
2614 NE 55th St,
526-5698 (map: FF6)
Inexpensive; beer and
wine; no credit cards;
checks OK
Dinner every day

KIDS The other Piecora's is owned by Richie Piecora and his partner, Dennis O'Brien, who purvey hearty, hand-tossed pies with a dozen or so fresh toppings—Cascioppo Brothers spicy Italian sausage, Portuguese anchovies, fragrant chopped garlic, roasted red peppers. The sauce is garlicky and mozzarella cheese is mounded on generously. The pizza comes in one size—a whopping 18 inches—or you can get half or a slice to go. They do a substantial take-out business, but ever since the back area was opened with tables and dressed up a bit with a few Italian flags, more people have been choosing to eat in. The menu also includes salads, wonderful heroes, and bulging calzones.

The Pink Door

1919 Post Alley,
443-3241 (map: I8)
Moderate; full bar; MC,
V; no checks
Lunch, dinner Tues-Sat

We like this Post Alley spot despite its flaws. The idea is exemplary: an inexpensive trattoria with cheap wine, reasonably good pasta, and a sort of built-in cachet (you enter through the pink door on Post Alley; there's no sign). At lunch, the large room grows noisy around a burbling fountain, and the service becomes forgetful. To be safe, stick with the pasta selections—especially anything with the puttanesca sauce, or the spinach fettucini with salmon and cream. In warm weather, Jackie Roberts opens a splendid outdoor cafe on the roof with a pleasant view of the Sound. At night when the pace slows down, the tables are lit by candlelight, the service becomes more attentive, and you can dine—prix fixe—on four courses (no choices). Later, you can order appetizers in the bar and watch the entertainment (sometimes cabaret). The quality of cooking is still uneven, but certain dishes—a full-bodied cioppiono, wonderful bubbling lasagne, a Gorgonzola soup we'll never forget—can shine. The place overflows with Italian kitsch, but it's cheerful.

Pizzeria Pagliacci

4529 University Way NE
(and branches), 632-1058
(map: FF6)
Inexpensive; beer and
wine; AE, MC, V; local
checks only
Lunch, dinner every day

Pizzerias have fiefdoms. If you live anywhere near the Ave, Broadway, or Lower Queen Anne, you pay tribute to Pagliacci's thin and tangy cheese pizzas—or you ought to. It's all tasty, all hand thrown, and available by the slice or by the pie. The crust is thick and rectangular or thin and round—the result of careful research by the owners—and very good. A true test of this exceptional crust is the original, which is unadorned except for a light, fresh tomato sauce and mozzarella. (A general rule of thumb: Get what's right out of the oven, as the crust doesn't survive the wait very well.) The Calabrian-style calzones, turnovers stuffed with vegetables, meats, and cheeses, are wonderful; salads are generally disappointing. There are take-out windows and inside tables at all three Pagliaccis (no table service, alas). Service can crawl.

Pizzuto's Italian Cafe

5032 Wilson Ave S,
722-6395 (map: JJ5)
Inexpensive; beer and
wine; MC, V; checks OK
Lunch Mon-Fri, dinner
Mon-Sat

KIDS It's the Seward Park version of the neighborhood Italian restaurant that every Seattle neighborhood now seems to have—here done in cheerful, bustling fashion. A diverse crowd munches on standard pasta (though one reviewer loved the spaghetti all'Amatriciana, made with bacon, onions, and hot peppers), flavorful homemade minestrone, and veal and chicken dishes (not the restaurant's strong suits). We come for the pizza, handmade from the dough up, with a lovely

Neapolitan-style thin crust and fresh toppings. Service is quick (as it needs to be with this many regulars); the whole place is a smoking section.

Place Pigalle
Pike Place Market,
624-1756 (map: J8)
Expensive; full bar; MC,
V; no checks
Lunch, dinner Mon-Sat

This spiffy bistro boasts breathtaking views over Elliott Bay, windows that open to the breeze (in summer, a few tables are perched outside on the walkway), and a thoughtful, inventive menu. Seafood is as fresh as it should be with Pike Place Fish just an alley away. It shows up in the form of daily specials (salmon in brandy–bing cherry sauce) and seasonal dishes (spot prawns grilled with shiitake mushrooms, radicchio, and scallions and served with a salad of arugula). A parade of talented chefs has passed through the Place's tiny kitchen en route to fame and glory; now it's Will Mac-Namara's turn, and he's retained perennial favorites such as the rich French onion soup and the lightly gingered calamari in a mustard cream. Most of the rest of the dishes, which change with the seasons, toss tradition right out the window: pan-roasted duck breast with demiglaze and fresh plum and jalapeño chutney, rabbit filled with crimini mushrooms and panettas and served with a roasted bell pepper–calamata olive relish. Dishes have been always artful, always entertaining, always fresh, and usually disarmingly successful (the bing cherry sauce on the salmon was a bit overpowering; the steak with Walla Walla sweet onions, arugula, and a charred leek tarragon mustard vinaigrette was rich in taste but meager in portion). Service ranges from attentive to aloof. You can eat outdoors in the skyway in summer or perch at the tiny bar with a local ale and lounge the afternoon away.

Pleasant Beach Grill and Oyster House
4738 Lynwood Center
NE, Bainbridge,
842-4347
Moderate; full bar; MC,
V; local checks only
Dinner every day,
brunch Sun

Bainbridge Island's only white-linen restaurant remains quietly tucked away in a large Tudor house on the south end of the island. Islanders have always favored the pine-paneled bar warmed by a fireplace and with two couches as the place to sink into a drink and dessert (a luscious slice of rich shortcake crowned with crimson berries, or an excellent chocolate mousse). In the past the food's been uneven, but recent meals have proved delightful, from the Eastern scallops and prawns brochette with lime, soy, and ginger butter sauce to an excellent 10-ounce slab of New York pepper steak with green peppercorn, mustard, and brandy sauce. Of course there are oysters on the half shell; however, the namesake oysters are baked with garlic butter, Parmesan, and brandy. Stick with simple grills and seafoods, enjoy the ample portions and skilled service. The dining room's pleasant, but in the summer, ask for the terrace. In winter, reserve a table in the comfortable bar.

Pogacha
119 106th Ave NE,
Bellevue, 455-5670
(map: HH3)
Inexpensive; beer and
wine; AE, MC, V;
no checks
Lunch Mon-Fri, dinner
Tues-Sat

★½

Pogacha, a sauceless Croatian relative of Italian pizza, is the specialty of the house in this odd, sterile Bellevue strip-mall space. The light, crisp—but chewy on the inside—disks are baked in the brick oven centerpiece and topped with any of a half-dozen combinations, which include mushrooms, pesto, salami, red onions, basil, tomatoes, and various cheeses. It's really good pizza. There are also some generously sauced pastas, hearty peasant soups, and good salads, and buttery pastries by the score. A terrific wine-by-the-glass program is an unexpected delight.

Pollo Rico
420 Broadway E,
325-8712 (map: GG6)
Inexpensive; no alcohol;
AE, MC, V; no checks
Lunch, dinner Mon-Sat

This all-cheap, all-chicken spot in the heart of Broadway, started by Colombian restaurateur Alfred Kure, was recently purchased by Mary Garcia. Still, not one of the 14 dishes, each hails from a different Latin country, costs more than $6.25. There's So'O-yosopy (chicken and rice soup) from Paraguay, Argentinean chicken in orange sauce, Colombian chicken tamales wrapped in banana leaves, Bolivian empanadas, and pollo guisado (chicken sautéed with garlic and vegetables) from Ecuador. We favor the pollo a la criolla, full of chunks of onion and firm flavors that taste like they've been gently mingling for days; and the arroz con pollo, a fluffy confetti of chicken, steamed rice, capers, green onions, red peppers, and (if you ask for them) little chunks of searing Peruvian peppers. Kure spoons this lush dish out of a pan he's been adding to all evening. He also does the cooking, so your order might take a while, or arrive at the table well after your companions'. Stay clear of the harshly lit back room, and the pollo and salsa de coco (which tastes like chicken with coconut frosting) and your experience will be tasty and exotic—long past due on this well-traveled stretch of street.

Ponti Seafood Grill
3014 Third N,
284-3000 (map: FF8)
Moderate; full bar; AE,
DC, MC, V; checks OK

On the ship canal, in the shadow of the Fremont bridge, Jim and Connie Malevitsis (Adriatica) opened their second restaurant with Richard and Sharon Malia (remember the former Malia's Northwest) in the final weeks of 1990. It's a large space split into more comfortably-

*Lunch Mon-Fri, dinner
every day, brunch Sun*

unrated

sized rooms with a view from nearly every seat. As for the food, chef Alvin Binuya (formerly of Cafe Sport) helped to create a menu featuring seafood tweaked with influences of Italian, Middle Eastern, Asian, and French. Early samplings revealed excellent salads (a warm spinach and smoked prawn with a light vinaigrette and a mixed green salad spiked with Oregon blue cheese, carmelized walnuts, and pomegranate seeds), tender scallops seared with a tomato-basil vinegar alongside a snappy Asian cabbage slaw. Portions are probably a little smaller than we'd like and the chipper service a bit disorganized, but nothing that a little time can't fix. Desserts are outstanding especially the chocolate bread (croissant) pudding with a creme anglaise.

A Pot of Phnom Penh Restaurant & Karoake
*3758 Rainier Ave S,
725-2768, (map: JJ6)
Inexpensive; beer and
wine; AE, MC, V;
no checks
Lunch, dinner Tues-Sun*

Phnom Penh Noodle Soup House
*414 Maynard Ave S,
682-5690, (map: R6)
Inexpensive; no alcohol;
no credit cards; no checks*

The original Noodle Soup House is a two-story hole-in-the-wall facing onto colorful Hing Hay Park and serving one of the most intelligently streamlined menus in town: seven varieties of Cambodian rice-noodle soup, each very distinct from the rest and quite delicious. It has become a haven for both local Cambodians and a loyal outside following, and bred a much more ambitious sister establishment. The new Pot of Phnom Penh is a sprawling place done up in oddly harmonious scheme of pale pink and green. It offers the same wonderful soups, plus a full menu of Sino-Khmer dishes, beer and wine (a rarity at Indochinese eateries), and when there's enough of a crowd, the universal karaoke. The differences between its stir fries, chop sueys, and hot-and-sour soup and the Chinese originals are real but subtle; too subtle, perhaps, since this Pot eschews prahok, the essential, extremely pungent Cambodian fermented fish paste. The center piece is a "special sate spicy firepot," with a savory broth in place of the usual boiling water, in which diners steep their various meats, seafoods, and vegetables. We fared well on a chef's special soup with a bit of everything tasty, and sauteed pork and greens in a thick, comforting, garlic-laden gravy. The fruit shake is a jackfruit lover's delight.

Prego
(Stouffer Madison Hotel)
*515 Madison St, 28th
floor, 583-0300
(map: M6)*

Beyond the quiet hush that characterizes so many hotel restaurants, Prego, high up in the Stouffer Madison Hotel, opens to a view of Seattle's seaport with good—make that great—food and unassuming atmosphere, and no bothersome crowds. It's an ideal spot for an im-

Moderate; full bar; AE, DC, MC, V; checks OK Lunch Mon-Fri, dinner every day

portant business lunch or a cautious date. The kitchen leans toward seafood—we suggest the pan-fried bass in a sweet hazelnut sauce or tricolored saffron linguine with mussels and clams.

Provinces Asian Restaurant and Bar
201 5th Ave S, Edmonds, 744-0288 (map: AA7) Inexpensive; full bar; AE, DC, MC, V; local checks only Lunch Mon-Sat, dinner every day

Five years ago, Asian fare was either Chinese, Japanese, Cambodian, or Vietnamese. The thought of a pan-Asian restaurant was an aberration most foodies would have snubbed their nose at. Today, such culinary journeys work well. Pan-Asian food in a clean-lined restaurant has caught on, first in Seattle (Wild Ginger) and now in Edmonds. Cambodian-Chinese Ken Lee opened his restaurant early in 1990, and it's one of the few Asian places with a license to serve booze. Favorites include Hong Kong–style pan-fried noodles topped with vegetables, beef, chicken and prawns served on a medium-pizza-sized platter, and the Triple Mushrooms (black, straw, and oyster). Portions vary, however: the prawns in black bean sauce with pea pods was meager. Desserts make no attempt to stay within the continent, originating instead at Seattle's own Pacific Desserts—and that's fine with us.

Queen City Grill
2201 1st Ave, 443-0975 (map: G8) Moderate; full bar; AE, MC, V; checks OK Lunch Mon-Fri, dinner every day

You sink into a glossy, high-backed booth and disappear from the world to schmooze with friends. In a très chic little drop-in space with mottled ochre walls, tall booths, and Art Deco wall sconces, Peter Lamb (owner of Il Bistro) and Steven Good have peeled off the veneer of formality to allow a more casual style of eating out. We encountered aloof and unprofessional service detracts on an otherwise be an enjoyable evening. Chef Paul Michael has a way with the grill, from the swordfish to the New York steak, and he occasionally brings his Texas know-how and barbecue sauce to an andouille sausage lunch. All is simply prepared, and the dishes don't rely on sauces for interest. They'd do well to be a bit more generous with the portions, however. At lunch, reservations are recommended. Good wine, good service at lunch, and lotsa garlic.

R & L Home of Good Barbeque
1816 E Yesler Way, 322-0271 (map: HH6)

Mary Collins Davis runs the oldest and, we say, the best barbecue joint in the city. Lean and tasty alder-smoked ribs, chicken, links, and sliced beef are served in sandwiches, or as a full dinner with potato salad or

Inexpensive; beer and wine; no credit cards; no checks Lunch, dinner Tues-Sat

 ★★

tremendous baked beans. The thinnish sauce, mild or hot, is excellent. No atmo, very consistent, great peach cobbler.

Rain City Grill
2359 10th Ave E, 325-5003 (map: GG6) Moderate; full bar; MC, V; no checks Lunch Mon-Fri, dinner every day

★★

It's all very Seattle: multicolored umbrellas, four walls of stormy gray, and wooden fish swimming above each booth. But as with the notorious weather talk, it's easy to tire of the overstated theme. Grilled items, particularly the fish, are generally good. The pastas are usually outstanding, though lately the pasta itself tasted store-bought—for these prices it should be very fresh. However, the salads (warm spinach doused in orange-sesame dressing tinged with wasabe or a sweet poppy seed-teriyaki chicken combination) and the desserts (chocolate torte with a white chocolate sauce) were terrific, and for them we've returned countless times.

raison d'être
113 Virginia St, 728-1113 (map: I7) Expensive; full bar; AE, MC, V; checks OK Breakfast, lunch, dinner every day

★★

Stacey Coleman and Shelley Kimball spend so much of their time in their restaurant that they get bored. That explains the decor change every year or so, usually just paint and new artwork. However, this year has seen probably the most significant changes, and not just in color (it's shocking chartreuse these days) but in philosophy. They're pulling away from espresso (too many espresso carts have appeared in this neighorhood) and graduating toward late-night drink festivities (the Floribunda Martini comes poured over ice cubes containing frozen flowers and is presented with a spray of rose water). The small restaurant now divides the city's socioeconomic classes with a waist-level wall separating suit-clad lawyers in a marble-topped dining area from punk-fashionable twentysomethings at the tall social tables with changeable landscapes beneath the glass. In essence, however, the raison is still the raison, serving beautifully *designed* food at fine-art prices, presented by servers who know a pretty plate but don't really have an understanding of what's behind it—they leave that to the kitchen. (The spacy service can be part of the allure.) One summer's menu offered a definite Asian twist: a colorful spread of steamed garden vegetables with a ginger miso dipping sauce; a Chinese BBQ pork loin open-faced sandwich on toasted homemade bread with garlic butter, dashed with sides of apple chutney, hot mustard, and purple mustard; and a chilled bowl of lemony blueberry soup painted with crème fraiche and a pansy. Breakfasts are superb—corned beef hash with sweet plum catsup and a poached egg, dark blue buckwheat waffles, eggs Benedict with perfectly whipped hollandaise, and fresh fruits artfully displayed (you pay fancy prices for these elegant preparations). This is a wonderful spot to begin a day or to linger when day is done (the kitchen's open until 11:30pm and you can get nibbles even later). And, yes, they still pull one of the finest espressos in town.

Rama on Post
83 Spring St, 340-9047
(map: M8)
Inexpensive; full bar; AE,
MC, V; local checks only
Lunch, dinner Mon-Sat

In a city loaded with Thai eateries, this pretty two-year-old restaurant has landed one of the better locations, between Pike Place Market and the ferry terminal. Portions may not be quite as generous as at some other Thai places, but everything is fresh and beautifully presented. Spiciness, and the prices, are toned down for the lunch crowd, so if you like it hot, ask. You won't go wrong with any of the lightly cooked seafood dishes variously prepared with ginger, basil, mint, lime, onions, and/or diced chiles. The seafood salad is outstanding ($7.95 at lunch); it's a toss of snapper, clams, prawns, and squid. Or try the pan-fried oysters dashed with lime. At press time there was mention of putting in a satay bar, not unlike the one at Wild Ginger up the street. For our money, however, Rama is already a better deal.

Rattlers Grill
1823 Eastlake Ave E,
325-7350 (map: GG7)
Moderate; full bar; AE,
DC, MC, V; local
checks only
Lunch Mon-Fri, dinner
every day

With its drop-dead desert deco interior (Georgia O'Keeffe paintings, large cactus, and pastel colors), a Lake Union location (formerly Casa Lupita), and one of the most ambitious Southwestern menus in town, Rattlers has given a shake to the growing number of New Mexican–style restaurants. They don't miss a trick here: piles of fresh flour tortillas cooked on a griddle in the dining area, excellent salsas (tomatillo is especially good), and flawlessly prepared side dishes (such as the black beans, which accompany three-quarters of the dishes, and ceviche). We could do without the guacamole that's mashed at the table (an unfortunate new trend). Watch out, it's very easy to fill up on the moist, sweet corn cakes (more like muffins) and the butter-smeared hot tortillas. As for dinner, meats are the star attraction here: beef, pork, chicken, and duck grilled over applewood and mesquite and served with one of three sauces: verde (made with Anaheim chiles), rojo (all red chiles, no tomato), or mole (red chiles and bittersweet Mexican chocolate). Unfortunately, this is where Rattlers falls short. The carnitas in the fajitas were a bit dry, and the red chile sauce, though made from scratch, was too tentative for our tastes. Ambitions are high here; however, execution and service need to be a little more picante.

Ray's Boathouse
6049 Seaview Ave NW,
789-3770 (map: EE9)
Moderate; full bar; AE,
DC, MC, V; checks OK
Lunch Mon-Fri, dinner
every day, lunch Sat-Sun
(cafe only)

You'd have thought Seattle had lost its best friend, the way folks carried on after a dock fire overcooked this institution in 1987. But the self-confident Ray's has bounced back, and it feels unchanged—same attention to very fresh seafood, same casual cafe/bar up a flight, same three-week wait for a Saturday night two-top, same peerless (and unabashedly romantic) vista of the Sound, the Olympics, the sunset. In composing your meal, concentrate on the simple fresh items that Ray's has proven it can do: grilled rockfish splashed with white wine, capers, and lemon juice; smoked black cod, meltingly broiled; scallop sauté (and little danger of overcooking here). Ray's appetizers prove tempting and substantially sized; tender deep-fried calamari in an airy tempura batter was accompanied by a delicate aioli, and steamed Manila clams were bathed in a fragrant broth of white wine and dill. The superb wine list (beautifully organized by country and varietal, with a page devoted to splits) and the extremely professional service help nudge the whole experience into the realm your final tab warrants. Fish doesn't come any fresher or better.

If the reservation wait for the dining room proves weeks long, try the upstairs cafe. Walk-ins are often successful, and the prices are more moderate.

The Restaurant
2716 Alki Ave SW,
935-6550 (map: II9)
Inexpensive; full bar; AE,
MC, V; checks OK
Breakfast, lunch, dinner
every day

Although they do a brisk burger-and-salad lunch trade and some fine seafood specials at dinner, it's the all-day breakfast that has made The Restaurant on the beach at Alki a West Seattle tradition. It'll be just packed—with a line, most likely—and kind of clattery and cramped like a diner (no good for restless children or intimate interludes), but everyone agrees that the omelets and other scrambles and excellent fried potatoes (all under $6) are worth it. Besides, in summer you could swear that was California out the window. Very friendly service.

Restaurant Shilla
2300 8th Ave, 623-9996
(map: F5)

Shilla's owners have done their best to convert an oversized motel coffee shop into a convincing Japanese/Korean restaurant, complete with tatami rooms.

Moderate; full bar; AE, DC, MC, V; no checks Lunch Mon-Fri, dinner every day

Lunches are easy on the purse ($5 to $7), but standards are better at dinner. Avoid the sushi and order the Korean national dish, bul ko ki, and you can cook it yourself—sliced beef, chicken, ribs, squid, or even seldom-ordered organ meats—at a table fit with a hibachi barbecue. Seven kinds of kim chee are made on the premises. At dinner it's all a little pricier than you'd find in the International District, but some consider it some of the better Korean food in the city.

Ristorante Allegria
11100 NE 8th St, Bellevue, 453-1981 (map: HH2) Expensive; full bar; AE, MC; checks OK Lunch Mon-Fri, dinner Mon-Sat

Allegria means happiness, and there's plenty of it in this classic Italian restaurant. It's not of the jam-packed, red-checked-tablecloth variety; Allegria is elegantly stark, with white table linens, stucco walls, and tables spaced comfortably apart. The knowledgeable and well-trained waitstaff and the location (just off 405 on NE Eighth Street in Bellevue) predict an uptown experience, and that's what is delivered. Best of all, the food lives up to any and all unspoken promises made by the surroundings. Owners Bruce Zabaglio (who owns Ave!) and Brian Douay (who used to cook at Ave!) operate Allegria under more formal (and expensive) pretenses. Their previous experience has taught them well. The seafood is excellent—start with the sauté di pesce misto (clams, mussels, calamari, prawns, and scallops in olive oil, garlic, and white wine sauce) or the gamberi al limone (prawns in lemon sauce with red pepper and garlic). The pasta is cooked to perfection (including the special round ravioli stuffed with smoked salmon in a light tomato, basil, and cream sauce), and the sauces are so good that even the most proper of Allegria's diners can be caught discreetly dipping bits of bread to get the last drop. They do an excellent job with Italian standards such as veal parmigiania and chicken Marsala. Don't waste time looking for street parking on NE Eighth—use the underground lot and have the ticket validated.

Ristorante Buongusto
2232 Queen Anne Ave N, 284-9040 (map: GG7) Moderate; full bar; MC, V; checks OK Lunch Tues-Fri, dinner Tues-Sun

Finally, Queen Anne has a restaurant that's worth climbing the Counterbalance for. Two brothers, Salvio and Roberto Varchetta, under the watchful direction of mamma Melina, have transformed the former (and awkward) Petit Prince space into an inviting restaurant that's quickly become more of a special-occasion restaurant than a drop-in trattoria. First off, you can't drop in (unless it's very late), as reservations have become a must on any night. On three recent visits at least two festive groups were celebrating a birthday. Patrons come for appetizers like garlicky pan-fried calamari, refreshingly simple slices of fresh tomato and mozzarella and cleansing basil, or antipasti plates of grilled or pan-fried marinated vegetables prepared by mamma herself. Dinners are steaming hot: veal scallopine topped with wild mushrooms in a savory sauce sided with a heap of thin-sliced zucchini, or a simple penne in a green onion and zucchini sauce easily sopped up with Ciro Pasciutto's chewy bread. There are only a few desserts to pick from each night, none outstanding except the very moist carrot cake. In the summer, the outdoor terrace gets plenty of noise from busy Queen Anne Avenue behind the tall fence.

Ristorante Pony
621½ Queen Anne Ave N, 283-8658 (map: GG7) Moderate; full bar; MC V; no checks Lunch, dinner Tues-Sun, brunch Sat-Sun

★½

Serving robust, inventive pastas and Mediterranean dishes, the Pony draws neighborhood regulars and theater-goers from Lower Queen Anne. We used to like to drop into this tiny (cramped), romantic place for after-theater dessert, but we don't anymore, now that owner Lois Pierris discourages dessert-only by implementing a $4 minimum after 5:30pm. Things tend toward the overrich and, sometimes, underseasoned, but daily specials are good choices: perhaps spanakopita, mussels and pasta with saffron, or lasagna primavera. Excellent homemade desserts are the other strong point, served until midnight on weekends. American-style breakfasts on weekends.

The Ritz Cafe
429 15th Ave E, 328-0440 (map: GG6) Moderate; full bar; AE MC, V; no checks Lunch M-F, dinner every day, brunch Sun

One of the most agreeable things about The Ritz Cafe, besides its wide-ranging menu, is the high-backed booths upstairs on the second level. Even when the cafe is packed with Saturday-night revelers, these upholstered hideaways give a sense of cozy seclusion; you can schmooze with your dinner companions almost unaware, but for a pleasant ambient hum, that you are in a public place. In addition, the restaurant competently juggles 20 reasonably priced entrées, from superbly sauced barbecued ribs to perfectly cooked shark on a superfluous bed of fettucine. A big bowl of steamer clams and mussels that preceded the meal was a little unusual in that its liquor was laced with red burgundy instead of the usual dry white wine. It's hard to go really wrong here, unless the kitchen or the waitstaff— a most unusual and generally hardworking crew—has an off night. As we went to press, new owners had stepped in. Their new young chef, Laura Dewell, is in the process of revamping the menu in a more Euro-Mediterranean direction. In good weather, you can dine outdoors on the patio. All in all, the Ritz still provides a sophisticated social scene, in the (mostly gay) piano bar up front. The crowd seems a microcosmic mix of the hill's polyglot population.

Romio's Pizza
2001 W Dravus St (and branches), 284-5420 (map: GG8)
Inexpensive; beer and wine; MC, V; local checks only
Lunch, dinner every day

Gasp! This fine Interbay institution is as busy a neighborhood eatery as we've ever seen; the last thing it needs is press. Even more, it delivers—literally and figuratively—a magnificent product. The pies, with a thick, crisp (yet chewy inside) crust, feature ingredients that are almost abnormally flavorful. In the Zorba, each part—onion, tomato, feta, Greek olives, gyro meat, and homemade tzatziki—contributes nobly to the whole. Romio's signature pizza, with garlic, artichoke hearts, sun-dried tomatoes, and pesto, achieves an integration of flavors and textures that seems somehow inevitable. Order it on a garlic crust (which they tend to run out of early) and you've got yourself a bona fide GASP! Other branches are downtown (917 Howell, 622-6878) and at Pioneer Square (616 First Avenue, 621-8500).

The Roost
120 Gilman Blvd NW, Issaquah, 392-5550
Moderate; full bar; AE, DC, MC, V; checks OK
Lunch, dinner every day, brunch Sun

After a bumpy opening last year, The Roost is taking off. The initial problems—uneven service, building inefficiencies, and a lawsuit that forced a name change from Cooper's Roost—have been taken care of. McHugh's first solo venture since splitting with longtime partner Tim Firnstahl has the nestlike appeal of a studied hunting and fishing lodge, right down to a river-rock fireplace and a well-stocked bar with a prodigious beer list. The menu balances salads, big roasted meats, and fresh local (is there anything else?) seafood. It's convivial enough for kids.

Rosellini and McHugh's Nine-10 Restaurant
910 2nd Ave, 292-0910 (map: M7)
Moderate; full bar; AE, MC, V; local checks only
Lunch Mon-Fri, dinner Mon-Sat

Victor Rosellini reigned for 50 years as the dean of Seattle restaurateurs (Rosellini's Six-10, Rosellini's Four-10). Mick McHugh, the jolly and prolific restaurateur of F.X. McRory's fame, began as Rosellini's protégé. Their collaboration in this large grill in the heart of downtown recalls both enterprises—McRory's in the well-populated bar, Rosellini's in the men's-club-like dining room. Both hosts are well in back-slapping, hand-shaking evidence.
The Nine-10's institution status has little to do with its food, however. Salads, frittatas, burgers, pastas,

filet mignon, and hearty fish—it's manly food, dished up in manly portions and without excessive attention to execution. Thus, the carbonara is impressive in size but its sauce is an unintegrated failure; the halibut in herb hollandaise is a fat, healthy, and undercooked fillet. The appetizer sheet is pure 1959 (large prawn cocktails, to wit). But as far as we can tell, nobody minds—the place is packed with business dealers at lunch, and the politicians who used to frequent the Four-10 for party scoop now get it in the Nine-10 bar after work. Stay with the tried-and-true Four-10 classics (crab and shrimp salad, the sourdough burger, canneloni, and a marvelous cup of minestrone) and avoid anything approximating invention. Waiters are of the Rosellini bow-and-scrape school.

Rover's
2808 E Madison St,
325-7442 (map: GG6)
Expensive; beer and wine;
AE, DC, MC, V;
checks OK
Dinner Mon-Sat

★★★★

In a frame house in Madison Valley, Rover's is more than just a fine neighborhood restaurant. Over the past three years Chef Thierry Rautureau has created a restaurant that reaches beyond—far beyond—the boundaries of any neighborhood. It's a place for which most people would not only drive across town, but drive *into* town. The semiformal setting offers quiet intimacy, but the simultaneously unobtrusive and attentive service puts you at ease. Dinners—marvelously sauced, classically French-inspired treatments of Northwest fare—are served with a generous hand. Rautureau's forte is seafood, and he's adept at finding the best quality ingredients, local or not. Recently we tried an outstanding Columbia River sturgeon with Maine lobster, served on a bed of ocean salad (a product of Japan imported by Mutual Fish consisting of seaweed, agar, Japanese mushrooms, sesame, rice vinegar, and white sesame seed). Ample portions of the two seafoods, perfectly prepared, were complemented by a rich, fresh black truffle sauce. Steamed halibut was served with caviar, braised leeks, and lobster sauce. Other choices might include boned squab with wild mushrooms and huckleberry sauce or Washington rabbit with plum tomato relish and sherry shallot sauce. Ellensburg lamb loin was generous, as we've come to expect, with a sauce redolent of the savory lamb, chanterelles, goat cheese, and rosemary. The stunning and plentiful entrées were diminished only by the tininess of the accompanying saucer of vegetables: one peapod artfully splayed, two slivers of summer squash, a baby bok choy leaf, a tablespoon of rice—very Zen, little else. The seasonal appetizers, like the entrées, are imaginative. Late-summer offerings have included grilled eggplant and tomato terrine with a tomato and balsamic vinegar marinade. Nothing is treated perfunctorily: Rautureau can even make a cliché dessert inspiring. His crème brulée was the silkiest custard imaginable, gently flavored with ginger and a hint of lavender. Wines are carefully chosen from the Northwest and France, with many half-bottles available. Or try a five-course feast from the menu de gustation, Rautureau's masterpiece, for a fixed price ($39.50, $35.50 for the vegetarian version). A gem.

Saleh al Lago

6804 E Green Lake Way N, 522-7943/524-4044 (map: EE7)
Expensive; full bar; AE, DC, MC, V; local checks only
Lunch Mon-Fri, dinner Mon-Sat

Saleh Joudeh, a Syrian who studied medicine in the central Italian city of Perugia, puts out some of the best Italian food in Seattle, of a style slightly heavier and spicier than Northern Italian, in a very stark—almost businesslike—space. On the recently revised menu, some dishes have been re-portioned as appetizers, allowing more opportunity to sample Joudeh's creations. The ravioli al burro nero, now an appetizer, is a preparation of pasta stuffed with ricotta and spinach that takes on a deeper hue with the addition of a rich brown garlic sauce. And although the menu changes periodically, several favorites always have a berth: the calamari antipasto (a garlicky sauté of squid) and simple yet exquisite risotto verde (arborio rice with spinach, cream, and Parmesan). The assaggini plate is a wonderful array of tidbits that, though Italian in spirit, takes full advantage of Northwest ingredients, such as chanterelles, perfectly marinated. Seafood is usually prepared simply and with care—a recent halibut special was accompanied but not overwhelmed by tomatoes and seasonal mushrooms—though the emphasis here is decidedly meat-oriented. Try the veal medallions; we like the quattro formaggi, with its dense, delicate cream sauce of fontina, Bel Paese, Romano, and Gorgonzola. The space is a split-level design dividing the tile-floored cafe (with big windows on busy Green Lake Way) and the raised, carpeted dining room. The cafe is ideal for a drink, snack, or late-night dessert and espresso; it opens in summer onto a sunny patio.

Salty's on Alki

1936 Harbor Ave SW, 937-1600 (map: II8)
Moderate; full bar; AE,

There are a couple of good reasons to visit Gerry Kingen's twin waterside restaurants, but food and quiet ambience are not among them. It's generally noisy (and crowded), and the food lacks finesse (a leaden tempura

DC, MC, V; checks OK
Lunch Mon-Fri, dinner
every day, brunch Sun

Salty's at Redondo

28201 Redondo Beach Dr
S, Redondo, 946-0636
Moderate; full bar; AE,
DC, MC, V; checks OK
Lunch Mon-Sat, dinner
every day, brunch Sun

Salute

3410 NE 55th St (and
branches), 527-8600
(map: EE6)
Moderate; beer and wine;
MC, V; no checks
Dinner Tues-Sat

Salute in Città
(WestCoast Vance Hotel)

606 Stewart St, 728-1611
(map: I5)
Moderate; full bar; AE,
MC, V; no checks
Continental breakfast,
lunch, dinner every day

★½

batter obscured perfectly good prawns) and suffers under the place's ambitions to serve an overpriced dish from every ethnic category, and an all-you-can-eat brunch every Sunday. You go instead for the view—a rare, postcard perspective of the whole grand sweep of Seattle's skyline—or for a party in the sensational private room (also with a view), which seats up to 300. Chef Marc Rosenfield does a good job with the catering operation, making Salty's one of the nicest places in town to have a party.

Raffaele Calise has got himself a mini chain, what with spinoffs of his Salute all over town: a takeout-only deli in Wedgwood called Salute Deli (7500 35th Avenue NE, 522-8580), a fancier version next door to the original called La Dolce Vita (3426 NE 55th Street, 523-3313), and his newest Salute in Città, on the eastern fringe of downtown. His original, the exuberant, charming Salute (credited with setting off the Italian food craze in this town), is still the most popular—where breathless crowds keep returning for the reasonably priced meals, playboy waiters, and fine pizza (on those nights when the kitchen slows down to bake the dough enough). Rabid popularity has almost spoiled it, with long waits and a "dish it up, move 'em out" attitude—but lately pastas have been coming out nicely al dente, sauces fresh and fine-tuned. Many items are still not inspired, but we'll vouch (any day) for the antipasto misto, a terrific spaghetti marinara, and a plate of cold squid simply dressed.

The neighborhood quickly grew fond of the "sweet life" next door. It has less native charm than Salute and a more ambitious menu. Our service was on autopilot, and the food was a fine saltimbocca, overcooked Piemonte grill (marinated lamb, chicken, and veal grilled and served with mustard brandy cream and fried polenta), a far too bland polenta, and an overdressed Caesar. All in all, La Dolce Vita is priced too high for its mediocre offerings—particularly when Italian food is a lire a dozen in this town.

Salute in Città is clearly meant to be a downtown version of the original, and they've made a noble stab at re-creating the kitschy, candlelit ambience of the original. On early visits we found the service appallingly slow, the food mostly perfunctory.

Inspectors for the Best Places series accept no free meals or accommodations; the
book has no sponsors or advertisers.

Salvatore Ristorante Italiano

*6100 Roosevelt Way NE,
527-9301 (map: EE6)
Moderate; beer and wine;
MC, V; checks OK
Lunch Mon-Fri, dinner
Mon-Sat*

You'll be struck by the Italian heartiness of this north-east neighborhood place. A whole wall is painted with a bright mural of a village street scene, peopled with art-fully pasted-in photos of crew and friends. Much of the warmth, however, stems from Salvatore himself, who brings his amore for the Southern Italian food of Basil-icata—one of the country's lesser-known regions—to his North End landing. The penne puttanesca was a fine example of the region's fondness for red pepper, while the linguine alle cozze with an unusual meld of herbs and rich sweet mussels was spiced with restraint. All in all, you will not be disappointed, especially if you're here on an evening when the dessert menu perks up with a tiramisu.

The Santa Fe Cafe

*2255 NE 65th St,
524-7736 (map: EE6)
Moderate; full bar; AE,
MC, V; checks OK
Lunch Tues-Fri, dinner
every day, brunch Sun*

*5910 Phinney Ave N,
783-9755 (map: EE7)
Moderate; full bar; MC,
V; checks OK
Lunch Tues-Fri, dinner
every day, brunch Sun*

Southwestern food is still hot stuff in Seattle—figur-atively, if not literally—as evidenced by the prolifera-tion of new restaurants that elevate hearty New Mexi-can fare into high-style cuisine. The Santa Fe Cafe is the doyenne of this crowd and the least pretentious. After nine years, the original restaurant in Ravenna now has two other siblings: the slightly more spacious branch on Phinney Ridge and the new take-out spot, Blue Mesa (2205 Queen Anne Avenue N, 282-6644), on Queen Anne. Besides that, nothing else has changed, not the ubiquitous artichoke ramekin, not the popular carne adovada. The menu is a paean to New Mexican red and green chiles, which the owners (formerly from Albuquerque) have shipped here by the truckload, a ton a month in the high season. Con-sequently the seasonings are fresh-tasting but mild enough (except for the green chile sauce and the chile-spice adovada). Try one of the unusual custards: a savory molten garlic custard with red chile sauce for starters, a sweet banana flan with raspberry purée to finish. Excellent draft ales from regional micro-breweries and, of course, margaritas. No smoking at either spot.

Satsuma

*14301 Ambaum Blvd
SW, Burien, 242-1747
(map: NN7)
Inexpensive; beer and
wine; AE, MC, V;
no checks*

Plain as a box on the outside, this tranquil Burien hideaway has captured the interest of the local Japa-nese, who come to enjoy the cooking of Tak Suetsugu, formerly of the Mikado. The tempura is light as air, the sushi merely creditable. For a twist, try the Washing-ton roll, with smoked salmon, tamagoyaki (similar to an omelet), cucumber, and strips of Washington apple. The black cod kasuzuke, marinated in sake lees and

Lunch Tues, Wed, Fri,
dinner Tues-Sun

Sea Garden
509 7th Ave S, 623-2100
(map: R6)
Inexpensive; full bar; AE,
MC, V; no checks
Lunch, dinner every day

Sea Thai
2313 N 45th St, 547-1961
(map: FF7)
Inexpensive; beer and
wine; AE, MC, V;
no checks
Lunch Tues-Fri, dinner
Tues-Sun

Seattle Bagel Bakery
1302 Western Ave,
624-2187 (map: L8)

broiled, is a velvety ambrosia. Tatami rooms are available, including one that holds 20—great for a private function. Service is gracious.

The Sea Garden has emerged as one of Seattle's finest Chinese eateries. Over the past few years it's draped linen over its Formica-topped tables, and prettied it up a bit with a coat of pastel; but, elegance or not, we've always been enamored with their ability to keep such consistently excellent seafood so reasonably priced. It's subtle, elegant Cantonese fare, the tamely spiced food we all enjoyed before we developed our culinary crush on fiery Sichuan or Hunan food. The seafood is scrupulously fresh, from the steamed crab in black bean sauce (taken from the holding tank minutes before arriving at your table) to the thinly sliced geoduck with a soy-based dipping sauce (which could have used a little more zing), and an excellent braised black cod. Such standards as wonton soup and chow mein are infused with new subtleties; all are served with fresh vegetables and, if requested, no MSG. The place is usually filled with Asians (but that's been changing lately) and, after midnight, the all-night mah-jongg crowd from the District. The upstairs room can be used for private parties of up to 50.

As the price of Thai food begins to sneak out of the good deal department, Sea Thai remains one of the city's best values. This unobtrusive spot in Wallingford is clean and attractive in its interior sparsity. The service is always cheerful and gracious, the food consistently delicous. The Hot Sea-Thai Soup (not to be confused with Hotsy-Totsy) comes in a Sterno-heated iron pot; inside there's a piquant broth crowded with mussels, shrimp, mushrooms, and a secret Thai ingredient that defies translation. Another appetizer, mee krob, is pleasantly less sweet than elsewhere. Main dishes are generous in their portions. The yum woon saen is a salad of "silver noodle" (thin, slippery bean threads) spiced with lime juice and bulging with lots of greens, prawns, pork, chicken, onions, and peanuts. Try the Thai iced tea, simultaneously strong and sweet. A good selection of nonmeat dishes.

Seattleites rarely match Manhattanites in their lust for the doughy rings, but this spot in the little non-neighborhood between Pioneer Square and Pike Place

Inexpensive; beer and wine; no credit cards; local checks only
Breakfast, lunch every day

★½

Market comes close to inspiring the same passion. The only way it differs from what you might find in New York is that it's clean, airy, nonsmoking, and full of sunlight. Sometimes warm, always fresh, these little wonders of raisin, pumpernickel, cheese and garlic, or poppy seed can be eaten alone or split open and heaped with cream cheese and lox without smothering the taste of the bagel.

Seoul Olympic Restaurant
1200 112th Avenue NE, Bellevue, 455-9305
(map: HH3)
Inexpensive; full bar; AE, MC, V; checks OK
Lunch, dinner every day

★½

Some of the best Korean food in the Seattle area is in a nondescript office complex in Bellevue. There's a whole page of untranslated Korean-only entrées, and if you ask what they are, the waitress will just shake her head and say "too hot" or "not cooked" or "too strange." Well, you don't need to *read* Korean to order the Korean barbecued beef (grilled beef that's been marinated in soy sauce, sugar, and wine). Traditionally, you grill your own, which you can do here in the small barbecue room in back. Adventuresome eaters who do end up randomly ordering off the Korean-only page may find themselves faced with a hearty soup of beef, tripe, and tubular animal innards.

Septieme
2331 2nd Ave, 448-1506
(map: G8)
Inexpensive; beer and wine; no credit cards; checks OK
Breakfast, lunch, dinner every day

★★½

In the Paris of the *septième arrondissement*, a vigorous intellectual culture exists in tiny cafes, where the propriétaires let the literati linger, and conversation is fueled with coffee and rich pastries. Septième is Kurt Timmermeister's tribute to the student life he remembers there. He features the same lush pastries, the same easy atmosphere, the same compact quarters. Last March he improved on the space and moved just down the street into the old McGraw Kittinger Case Insurance building, where a small brick courtyard furthers the European appeal. Septième pays attention to what's important: rich and delicious lattes served in china teacups (or bowls for the real addicts), on white linen-covered tables. You choose from a spread of beautiful pastries at the counter, and they're delivered to you on pretty, gold-rimmed white china plates with heavy silver forks. Fans rhapsodize about them, and they're all baked in-house. Timmermeister has added specialty sandwiches (a recent high-rise creation featured eggplant, roasted red peppers, tapenade, and truly fresh mozzarella layered between slices of chewy Italian bread) and an excellent Caesar salad ($5). Septieme opens early and closes late (at midnight every night but Sunday).

Settebello

1525 E Olive Way,
323-7772 (map: I1)
Expensive; full bar; AE,
MC, V; checks OK
Lunch Mon-Fri, dinner
Mon-Sat

Ristorante Stresa

2220 Carillon Point,
Kirkland, 889-9036
(map: EE3)
Moderate; full bar; AE,
DC, MC, V; checks OK
Lunch (pizzeria) every
day, dinner Mon-Sat

Shuckers (Four Seasons Olympic Hotel)

411 University St,
621-1984 (map: L6)
Moderate; full bar; AE,
DC, MC, V; local checks
Lunch Mon-Sat, dinner
every day

Siam on Broadway

616 Broadway E,
324-0892 (map: GG6)
Inexpensive; beer and

Owner Luciano Bardinelli has endeavored to put his "beautiful seven" on a more conventional keel. He's succeeded reasonably well—but with the number of Northern Italian spots that have opened in the interim—including another of his own, Ristorante Stresa in Kirkland—that's hardly cause for excitement. Menu and presentation have made a decided turn (or return) toward the mainstream. Salads remain lively, fresh, and presented with trademark elegance, but the pasta and veal dishes we've tried have been uninspired. The frutta di mare, with clams and mussels well served by a tangy light tomato sauce, stands out. Settebello's finest pleasures are relatively simple ones: authentic Italian bread and classic Italian soups, such as pappa di pomodoro and pasta e fagioli, that are more often seen in grandmas' kitchens than on restaurant menus. They soften both the chill of winter and the chilling effect of the prices. Settebello's service, which was notorious for veering schizzily between effusive and frigid, seems to be settling into a more comfortable mode, though you may languish waiting for it to arrive.

Stresa, named after Bardinell's hometown in Italy, features a menu that echoes Settebello's; however, the preparations are disappointingly unattended to. The veal scallopini decorated with peeled lemon slices, with flower-shaped whipped potatoes, suffered slightly from an unappealing mix of greens. The seafood risotto was decent; the pizza only so so. The decor is unoffensive though the centerpiece of the scheme is the stunning view of Yarrow Bay and its marina. The small patio is especially nice when the weather complies.

For seafood downtown, you can't do better than Shuckers in the Four Seasons Olympic. It's also the most attractive and surely the most convenient for downtown lunches. The specials change daily to reflect the fresh fish available, but notable constant items include Irish soda bread muffins (and other good breads) and a slightly sweet geoduck stew. They get decent oysters on the half-shell (particularly the Belons), but the fish preparations are inconsistent and expensive. Weather permitting, you can sit outside in a tiny space.

Among Seattle's burgeoning collection of Thai restaurants, Chai Asavadejkajorn and John Sariwatanarong's tiny Siam on Broadway stands out as clean, friendly, and smoothly run. The menu doesn't stray far from the

wine; AE, MC, V;
checks OK
Lunch Mon-Fri, dinner
every day

Bangkok standards, but the food is distinctive and the bustling atmosphere like no other Thai eatery in Seattle. The open kitchen makes a fun diversion—it's probably the only place in town where you can enjoy Thai cooking from a front-row seat (and undoubtedly will if you don't make reservations at least 24 hours in advance for a table in back). Regulars agree that this restaurant takes its hot chiles seriously, especially in the soups. However, a three-star chicken curry was no hotter than the two-star soup during a recent visit. Try the yum wuun sen, a salad of bean threads with pork, squid, and onion. The bean threads are steamed to just the right crispness and piquant with fresh lime and cilantro. Or choose the whole pan-fried pompano (butterfish) topped with a glistening sauté of onions, mushrooms, green and red chiles, and a wow of garlic.

Singapore
17549 15th Ave NE,
365-3474 (map: BB6)
Inexpensive; beer and
wine; MC, V; local
checks only
Lunch Mon-Fri, dinner
Mon-Sat

Huang Lin-Chan, an emigrée from the tropical island nation of Singapore, brings you the best flavors from all of the ethnic groups that make up that equatorial entrepot. Wear washable clothes and be prepared to dine with your fingers as you savor multiethnic cuisine blending several varieties of Chinese cooking—Cantonese, Sichuan, Mandarin, and Fujian—with sambals (sweet and sour) of the Malay peninsula, curry (of southern India), and the peanut sauces of Indonesia. You could order familiar Chinese fare, but you shouldn't miss your chance to sample satay with peanut pineapple sauce, fish in coconut milk curry, or gado gado—an Indonesian vegetable medley with peanut sauce. Essential to any meal here are Singapore rice noodles, light and fluffy, with minced meats and vegetables and a hint of curry powder. The main event, though, will be the arrival of a plate of heaping chile-sauce crab, the house special: a whole cracked Alaskan crab buried in spicy sauce made with crushed Chinese black beans. Gobble it up with alternating mouthfuls of steamed rice. At meal's end you will get warm lemon tea to wash well-licked fingers.

Spot Bagels
1815 N 45th St,
633-SPOT (map: FF7)
Inexpensive; no alcohol;
no credit cards;

Two wacky dalmations, Alex and Zane, are the spots behind the name of Jay Glass's outrageous bagelry in Wallingford Center. It started with an espresso shop in Minneapolis, sort of, except Jay Glass didn't want to move to Minneapolis. And since the last thing Seattle—for that matter, Wallingford—needs is another coffee shop (thank you, Jay), he decided to fill the city's next

checks OK
Bagels, lunch every day

craving. Sure enough, these kosher babies (they're even boiled in purified water) are as addictive as caffeine itself: the Joy of Garlic has whole cloves of garlic both in and on these chewy treats, the Orange Joy is made with oranges and their juice, and the Firehouse Jalapeño will ring the alarm. Stack them with turkey, smoked ham, pastrami, or lox and you've got a meal. There's seating outside in the courtyard when the weather's nice, or grab a dozen to go (you can find them fresh daily at PCC and Larry's, too). This spot closes at 6pm weekdays, 5pm weekends.

Spud Fish and Chips
2666 Alki Ave SW,
938-0606 (map: II9)
Inexpensive; no alcohol;
no credit cards; no checks
Lunch, dinner every day

KIDS After 50 years, Spud is still a swell, family fish-frying enterprise. It's spawned locations in summertime's highest-density neighborhoods—Green Lake's northeast shore (6860 Green Lake Way N, 524-0565, map: EE7) and Juanita Drive in Kirkland (9700 NE Juanita Drive, Kirkland, 823-0607, map: DD4)—but only the original Alki Beach outpost gets our vote for consistency and quality control. Fresh, large pieces of lingcod are coated with a crispy cornmeal blend, lightly deep-fried in clean vegetable oil, and served atop a pile of those namesake spuds, peeled, cut, and fried fresh every day. Some people go for the prawns and chips or clams and chips or oysters and chips, but we can't seem to get past the fish. Eat inside, outside, or across the street by the water.

Still Life in Fremont Coffeehouse
709 N 35th St, 547-9850
(map: FF7)
Inexpensive; beer and
wine; no credit cards;
checks OK
Breakfast, lunch, dinner
every day

A big, light space with floor-to-ceiling windows, mismatched wooden dining room tables and chairs, a big '40s radio, and Dick Powell and June Allyson's old coffee table. Add to these good art, good weekend entertainment, and good vibes—remember those? The star of the little menu is the Special Sub ($4.50), bursting with good ham, provolone, wine-cured salami, tomatoes, onions—oh, you know, the works. The soups are stunning, some of the best in town, and creative, too: thick purée of carrot, spicy chicken peanut, potato leek. Top it off with a good beer, so-so espresso, and a sweet, and leave reflecting on your good fortune that there is, in fact, still life in Fremont.

Stone Way Cafe
3620 Stone Way N,
547-9958 (map: FF7)
Inexpensive; no alcohol;
no credit cards;

On Saturdays or Sundays, it seems almost everyone from Wallingford to Phinney Ridge makes a morning pilgrimage to this steamy little cafe on Stone Way. Breakfast favorites include corned beef hash, biscuits and gravy, and a wide variety of omelets. At lunch the

checks OK
Breakfast every day,
lunch Mon-Fri

burgers are handmade and grilled to order and the soups are wonderful (chicken or beef noodle, vegetable—nothing too exotic or threatening). Owner Charlene Iverson will tell you what to order for your kids, and then later can recite you your check from memory. Best of all is the blackberry pie—hot and sweet, not cloying, topped with vanilla ice cream.

Streamliner Diner

397 Winslow Way,
Bainbridge, 842-8595
Inexpensive; beer and
wine; no credit cards;
local checks only
Breakfast every day,
lunch Mon-Sat (light
lunch Sun)

You don't need a better excuse than breakfast to hop the ferry to Bainbridge Island. The Streamliner Diner (an easy walk from the Winslow ferry) has been an Island institution for eight years now, having built its reputation on extraordinarily satisfying breakfasts and inventive entrées—mom food with a creative twist. The lines are quite long now on weekends, and locals gripe about creeping prices and smaller portions, but don't let that deter you. With its kitchen-table decor and sweet saxophone swing coming through the sound system, this no-smoking restaurant still oozes small-town personality. Breakfasts include inventive omelets, incomparable buttermilk waffles with real maple syrup, nutritious homemade granola, and Potatoes Deluxe— the famed spiced potatoes stir-fried with vegetables and topped with Cheddar cheese. Lunches are natural homemade soups, salads, quiches, and sandwiches. A delightful spot on any morn.

Subito

2448 76th Ave SE,
Mercer Island, 232-9009
(map: I14)
Moderate; beer and wine;
MC, V; checks OK
Lunch Mon-Fri, dinner
Mon-Sat

With the dearth of good restaurants on Mercer Island, it's not hard to become the island's best. After 2½ years of settling in, Eric Napoleone has succeeded in avoiding Mercerfication—the tendency to cater to otherwise bland tastes as so many other island restaurants do. The tangy antipasti are excellent, and the marinara, Bolognese, and cream sauces do well with the pasta, chicken, and veal dishes. Chef Napoleone has found the establishment's niche and narrowed his menu to traditional Italian (OK, so there are a few burgers for the kids, on request). The insalata di mare catches five types of seafood in a lemon-jalapeño vinaigrette in a net of lettuce, red bell peppers, and fresh vegetables. The Fettucine Mario (herbed artichokes and chicken in cream sauce) is satisfying. The cool, contemporary dining space beams with enthusiastic servers, big, colorful paintings, and a moderately priced wine list (including numerous microbrewed beers). A semiprivate room in back works nicely for parties of 15.

Sunlight Cafe

*6403 Roosevelt Way NE,
522-9060 (map: EE7)
Inexpensive; beer and
wine; no credit cards;
checks OK
Breakfast, lunch, dinner
every day*

More for Birkenstocks than for BMWs, the Sunlight Cafe is a pleasant slice of the 1960s that continues to thrive because what it does, it does well. For breakfast and weekend brunch there are bountiful fruit salads, crunchy whole-wheat sesame waffles, blueberry pancakes, and quiches. Lunch features flavorful soups and hearty, dense homemade breads. Dinners include lasagne, enchiladas, and, best of all, stir-fried vegetables with a yogurt cheese sauce. All selections are meatless, and there is no smoking, but the evil bean is served in abundance—including espresso at bargain prices.

Sunset Cafe

*1306 Union Ave NE,
Renton, 235-1458
(map: MM3)
Inexpensive; beer and
wine; no credit cards;
checks OK
Breakfast, lunch Mon-
Sat, dinner Mon-Fri*

The most endearing restaurant in Renton is in a little oblong box in the Sunset Shopping Center in Renton Highlands. It's a modest place dressed in a conundrum of country craft grapevine wreaths and corn husk streams, which gained recognition after being chosen as having Seattle's best dessert at the 1989 Bite. Indeed, the desserts are good, but this chromey cafe with black and white tiles has since become a melting pot of good—very good—food. There are almost two dozen entrées on the regular menu (including a hand-tossed New York–style pizza); however, the most interesting inventions are the specials. For example, Sunset Pork, medallions of pork with apple brandy sauce and a julienne of vegetables, or plain-sounding roast chicken that's delightful stuffed with an apple almond filling and topped with a riesling and golden raisin sauce. All meals come with soup or salad and mouthwatering homemade bread sticks. Wednesday and Thursday nights are Cajun-style.

Surrogate Hostess

*746 19th Ave E,
324-1944 (map: GG6)
Inexpensive; beer and
wine; no credit cards;
local checks only
Breakfast, lunch, dinner
every day*

*1907 E Aloha St,
328-0908 (map: GG6)
Inexpensive; no alcohol;
MC, V; local checks only
Breakfast, lunch
every day*

KIDS It's nearly impossible not to have a conversation at the Surrogate Hostess, where patrons enjoy the inventive homemade food, meet friends, read the newspaper, and watch their kids at long, communal tables. It also has a reputation as something of a repository of yuppie angst. Talk of uneven food and sullen service has drifted our way during the last couple of years, but regulars report that conditions are once again on the upswing. There are usually several good (sometimes overdressed) salad choices—along with a pasta or potato dish, an excellent quiche, a pâté, and two soups a day. Breakfast at the Surrogate is a big Seattle tradition—unique egg dishes (scrambled with sherry and cream cheese, for instance), beautiful coffee cakes made with seasonal fruits, great hot cereal, sensational, light cinnamon rolls. The bakery is, in fact, the Surrogate's primary strength. Exceptional, imaginative desserts change daily, though you can always count on the best commercial chocolate chip cookie in town (a bargain at 60 cents). The Surrogate can also hostess your next party for you. You can get your goods to go at the retail store around the corner; they're open until 3pm every day and stock good frozen dinner entrées.

Sushi-Ten
2217 140th Ave NE,
Overlake, 643-6637
(map: CC6)
Moderate; beer and wine;
MC, V; no checks
Lunch Mon-Fri, dinner
every day

Every now and then this sushi bar breaks tradition and opens up to an all-you-can-eat crowd. Call ahead to make sure you've got the right night and warn sushi-chef Masashi Seki that you're on your way. At the sushi bar, you name your favorites (tuna, yellowtail, the ubiquitous California roll) and they'll come until you stop. It's probably the only sushi bar around that actually gets rambunctious at times. The rest of the restaurant (where you can order plump gyoza, light-batter tempura, and sparingly doused teriyaki chicken, or salmon) is more conducive to leisurely conversation.

Swingside Cafe
4262 Fremont Ave,
633-4057 (map: FF7)
Inexpensive; beer and
wine; no credit cards;
checks OK
Breakfast, lunch, dinner
Wed-Sat, brunch Sun

This is an unassuming nook in unassuming Fremont that's been through a couple of misfit incarnations recently. But the current owners, who display a fascination with baseball (on the wall) and an interest in jazz (in the air), have created the kind of place it should have been long ago. The kind of place Fremonters want to frequent. Come as one and sit at the wall counter with a newspaper, or as two (but definitely no parties larger than four) for a scrumptious breakfast of huevos rancheros, buckwheat pancakes, or one of their signature frittatas and a side of apple sausage. It's less crowded at lunch and dinner (the TV can be somewhat intrusive in this small casual space), but early samplings of the three different meals suggest the tiny Swingside is big with ambition. The limited-income lunch menu features Red Long's barbecue sauce over chicken ($4.95) and pita bread stuffed with marinated lamb, tzatzuki, hummus, tomatoes, and lettuce ($5.95); dinner converts to an authentic-tasting jambalaya, a hazelnut pesto linguine, and a couple of specials, most recently linguine with calamari in a tomato-based sauce and a large helping of lamb stew. It's not outstanding, but it's all competently prepared and, best of all, fairly priced.

Szechwan Garden

88 Yesler Way, 343-9988
(map: N8)
Moderate; beer and wine;
AE, MC, V; no checks
Lunch Mon-Fri, dinner
Mon-Sun

The Lu family, proprietors of the Green Village in the International District, also operates this brightened basement spot in Pioneer Square, which specializes in the spicy cuisine of China's Sichuan province. We find the dinners consistently pleasing and the lunches often quite busy. For an appetizer, try the superb hot cucumber salad or an excellent version of hot-and-sour soup. The hot shredded pork was delicious and the seafood dishes are another highlight, especially the wonderfully tender Sichuan scallops. One regular suggests that you leave the ordering to your waiter, who will bring you the best the kitchen has to offer that night. Diners who really want their spicy dishes hot need only say so.

Szmania's

3321 W McGraw St,
284-7305 (map: G8)
Moderate; full bar; DC,
MC, V; checks OK
Lunch Mon-Fri, dinner
Mon-Sat, brunch Sat

Szmania's (pronounced *smahn-ya's*) at press time has just joined the culinary tradition established in Seattle by chefs such as Bruce Naftaly of Le Gourmand and Mark Manley of Union Bay Cafe, who bravely ply their trade in residential hinterlands far from urban centers. Ludger (late of the Four Seasons Olympic) and Julie Szmania wisely chose Magnolia, a high-rent neighborhood with virtually no restaurants to serve it. This restaurant's sleek contemporary style (very much wheelchair accessible) feels altogether out of sync with the dry cleaners and pizza parlors of folksy Magnolia Village, but this is not criticism.

Ludger Szmania cooks wonderfully and with suggestions of his native Germany, from an appetizer of toothsome chanterelle risotto to entrées such as cinnamon smoked chicken bread with herb sauce and smoked pork loin with homemade sauerkraut. One special, salmon in mushroom sauce, was rich and meltingly textured. Szmania also has respect for pasta, which he might combine with pesto cream and serve with blackened scallops or toss with lightly grilled prawns with a fragrant smoked tomato sauce. It all seems underpriced, with entrées hovering at about $13. there are problems—an overdressed Caesar, an almost comically forgetful waiter—but with a pro like Szmania at the helm, these defects will surely be addressed.

Taj Mahal India Restaurant

12343 Lake City Way
NE, 367-4694
(map: CC6)
Inexpensive; beer and
wine; DC, MC, V;

A simple place where the flavor of India comes not through the decor but the food. From the peanuts and coconut in the delicious appetizer dahl aloo chaati (a spicy potato dumpling in cool yogurt sauce) to the bowl of anise seeds served to departing patrons, this 11-table (but possibly expanding in the near future) Lake

no checks
Lunch Mon-Fri, dinner
every day

City restaurant demonstrates the Indian love of nuts and seeds as food and flavoring. With each dinner you get a flavorful lentil broth (somewhat salty); pappadum, a fragile lentil cracker; ketchumber (a fancy name for a very ordinary salad); an aromatic, colorful mound of rice pilau cooked to the tooth; a choice of chapati (a whole-wheat flat bread) or puri (a globelike deep-fried whole-wheat puff). All that precedes your order: butter chicken cooked in a tandoor and bathed in a buttery, pungent sauce, or the tandoori pomfret (fresh white fish flown in from the Indian Ocean). In a town with shockingly few Indian restaurants, this place is inexpensive and delightful. If only Chef Bernard would believe patrons who request their food *hot.*

Takara
1501 Western Ave (Pike
Place Hillclimb),
682-8609 (map: J8)
Moderate; beer and wine;
AE, MC, V; no checks
Lunch Mon-Fri, dinner
Mon-Sat

Kuma-san is a funny man who is very dexterous with a sashimi knife. As he jokes and laughs with the customers, his hands are busy cutting, seemingly without effort, perfect slices of fish and shellfish. Thin strips of daikon radish appear magically. He lays down the knife and forms roses and phoenixes from nori slivers, thinly sliced fish, rice, salmon roe. There is a long list of à la carte items, such as deep-fried tofu with daikon sauce, a black cod tidbit marinated in sake paste for three days, and wonderful soups. Delicious, traditional, and reasonably priced, dishes of tempura, teriyaki, and a small steak round out the menu, though Kuma-san is more known for his exotic preparations: fermented monkfish liver, deep-fried sole skeleton, and sea cucumber sashimi. He is also one of the few cooks in Seattle certified to handle fugu—a fish that is literally deadly in the hands of the untrained (the meat must remain untouched by bits of the toxic organs)—though it's not available here, as no one will import it.

Tandoor Restaurant
5024 University Way NE,
523-7477 (map: FF6)
Inexpensive; beer and
wine; AE, MC, V;
no checks
Lunch, dinner every day

Seattle lacked a good, reasonably priced Indian restaurant until the Mroke family, owners of Da Tandoor in Vancouver, BC, opened Tandoor in the University District. Since then, a couple of others have joined the ranks, including a downtown version of the Mrokes's own, Moti Mahal. One of India's most distinctive contributions is tandoori-style cooking. Meat or fish is marinated overnight in yogurt spiced with chili powder, turmeric, ginger, and garlic. The next day the chicken is sprinkled with saffron and chili powder before being roasted in a charcoal-fired clay oven. The result is moist, smoky, and wonderful. A good introduction to this cuisine is the murgh tikka masala, a boneless chicken that's ever so tender. The tandoor fish was a bit too salty for our tastes, but we sopped up the papri chaat appetizer—diced potatoes, chick peas, and yogurt with a wonderful tamarind sauce—with crispy pappadums. Elsewise, try the eggplant bhattha (roasted eggplant mashed and seasoned). The service is personable and helpful, and the waitstaff will (if plied) explain the intricacies of the cuisine.

Tanooki Cafe
6311 Roosevelt Way NE,
526-2935 (map: EE7)
Inexpensive; beer and
wine; MC, V; local
checks only
Lunch Mon-Sat, dinner
every day

The Tanooki Cafe, like its neighbor the Sunlight, comes from the brown rice and stir-fry school of nutritious cooking—but here with a Japanese bent. At this no-smoking, low-priced restaurant there are no sushi chefs or knife-wielding grill masters; rather, just fresh, quickly cooked, earthy food. There are yaki bowls of chicken, beef, salmon, shrimp, or tofu on rice, and yakisoba with herbed noodles and a garlicky, tomato-based soy sauce. They sometimes overcook the meat or undercook the vegetables, but the clean, simple decor—sort of Japanese-goes-Scandinavian— and clean, simple food have more loyal fans than almost any place in town.

Tatsumi
4214 University Way NE,
548-9319 (map: FF6)
Moderate; full bar; MC,
V; no checks
Lunch Mon-Sat, dinner
every day (except 4th
Sunday of the month)

Tatsumi Express
4214 University Way NE,
548-1507 (map: FF6)
Inexpensive; no alcohol;
no credit cards; no checks
Lunch, dinner Mon-Sat

Just when we had given up hope of ever finding a good meal in the fast-food wasteland of the Ave, Tatsumi opened—a slick, classy, clean-lined winner. There's a sushi bar in one corner and a "bamboo forest" (complete with running water) in another, but the presentation of the food impresses us most. Tempura is light, crisp, and perfectly done, and served on paper folded like a bird. It holds many surprises: fan-sliced eggplant, slivers of jicama, shiso leaf, decoratively cut carrot. The sashimi is first-rate and might include creamy smooth squid, opalescent red snapper, and firm, fresh octopus. The menu continues to include more variety than we've seen in some time, with large sections devoted to seafood, meat, donburi, noodles, and combination dinners. If there's a weak point, it's the sauces. Moist breast slices in the chicken teriyaki were drenched in a puddle of runny juice, not in the traditional thick, redolent sauce, and black cod kasuzuke held little of the winey tang from the sake lees. The place has a rare polish, from smiling servers to shiny lacquerware dishes. Try out your Spanish on the sushi chef.

For those wanting a quicker, cheaper bite of Tatsumi's teriyaki, udon, sushi, or stir-fries, next door's Tatsumi Express is a fast-food version of the original.

Teger's
2302 24th Ave E,
324-3373 (map: GG6)
Moderate; beer and wine;
MC, V; checks OK
Dinner Wed-Sat, lunch or
breakfast by request

★★

A red neon sign, flashing Christmas lights, and proximity to the modest Montlake storefront library do little to draw attention to this quintessential neighborhood place. Every dinner starts with a glass of sherry and ends with a Hershey's kiss. With Cordon Bleu–trained owner Janice Matthews (who also owns the new Lake Union Bed & Breakfast) back in the kitchen and working up new menus—she had briefly relinquished control—the food is consistently pleasing and elegantly executed. Thursday is neighborhood night: $7.95 gets you an entrée, soup or salad, and a glass of wine. If you want a vegetarian meal, be sure to call ahead (ditto if you'd like to sit on the small terrace out back, or if you'd like her to cater a special occasion). One night, Matthews's vegetarian invention was a flavor-jammed caponata. As would be expected in a small, one-person kitchen, all meals come with the same appetizer of the night (maybe a heavenly sweet creamy tomato basil soup) and side dishes (on one night, a homey potatoes-and-cheese concoction, peas with basil, and a slice of ripe melon). The excellent desserts are large enough for two: Kahlua cheesecake with black raspberry chambord, Bananas Foster, or a *Gourmet*-award–winning bread pudding. It's best to make reservations, as Matthews stocks the kitchen according to how many she's expecting; also, come winter, the regulars return to their fireside tables.

TestaRossa
210 Broadway E,
328-0878 (map: GG6)
Inexpensive; beer and
wine; AE, DC, MC, V;
checks OK
Lunch Mon-Sat, dinner
every day

★½

The main draw at this sparkling, bright Broadway eatery is stuffed pizza—the closest analogy we can draw being four and 20 blackbirds baked in a pie. These rich pies ooze all manner of fabulous treats: San Remo sun-dried tomatoes, roasted eggplant and red peppers, fennel sausage, pine nuts, Montrachet cheese, pesto, artichoke hearts. All this bounty is laced together with milky top-quality domestic mozzarella and reggianito cheese from Argentina, and then bathed in a rich tomato sauce. The crust, its taste alive with yeast, delivers flavor as well as texture. The basic stuffed pizza easily serves three, especially if those three have nibbled through the wait on focaccia or pumate spread, a pleasing mix of sun-dried tomatoes, ricotta, cream cheese, and garlic. The smokeless atmosphere buzzes cheerfully. TestaRossa is open until midnight on Friday and Saturday, and until 11pm the rest of the week.

Thai Heaven
352 Roy St, 285-1596
(map: A5)
Inexpensive; full bar; AE,
MC, V; local checks only
Lunch, dinner every day

Once home to a French restaurant, the big house on the northeast corner of Roy Street and Nob Hill is now Thai heaven—figuratively speaking. And it's giving the venerable Bahn Thai down the way a run for its baht. The food here is fresh and the service cheerful and suspiciously fast (in fact, if the food weren't so good you'd suspect it was preprepared). Owner Eddie Meko is the Monty Hall of Thai cooking—bustling around, greeting regulars with a foghorn voice and a friendly clap on the shoulder. He has an uncanny knack of remembering orders without notes. A noteworthy appetizer is fish cake, curry, and green beans with a tangy-hot cucumber vinegar pepper sauce. The seafood entrées, such as garlic prawns or prig king prawns with a curry basil sauce, go far beyond their modest-sounding names. There's a healthy (though unimaginative) selection of vegetarian dishes. The Thai iced tea is delicately flavored and happily less sweet than elsewhere. Try it sweetened with a shot of rum.

Thai Palace
2224 8th Ave, 343-7846
(map: F5)
Inexpensive; full bar; AE,
DC, MC, V; no checks
Lunch Mon-Fri, dinner
every day

Thai Chef
1645 140th Ave NE,
Bellevue, 562-7955
(map: GG2)
Inexpensive; beer and
wine; AE, MC, V;
no checks
Lunch Mon-Fri, dinner
every day

One step beyond the carport of the Quality Inn at Eighth and Blanchard are the aroma and music of Thailand. Of all the Thai restaurants inundating Seattle, this is probably the most misjudged. Get yourself through the featureless hotel lobby, however, and you'll be in for some delicious surprises. We like the potak, owner Sakada Itti's innovation of a traditional fish soup; the seafood—shrimp, clams, fish, squid—and vegetables are almost background to a thin, very delicafe sauce for spooning over rice. The big pluses at Thai Palace include its full liquor license (unlike most Thai restaurants, which are not fully licensed); order a margarita—the lime and salt mix as well with this cuisine as they do with Mexican. There's also a big bright courtyard for summer dining, a banquet room in the back that seats 50, and lightning-quick service. The Bellevue outpost, run by Itti's wife, Rachanee Phaladiganon, is very popular with the electronics crowd. Be sure to make reservations at the Eastside one; now that they serve beer and wine, people tend to linger longer than usual.

All places in this book are recommended; even "no stars" are worth knowing about.

Thai Restaurant
101 John St, 285-9000
(map: B8)
Inexpensive; full bar; AE,
MC, V; no checks
Lunch Tues-Fri, dinner
Tues-Sun

Now that you don't have to stand a half hour in the rain, now that you can sit in the waiting area adorned with fresh flowers, there's barely a wait—rarely long enough to count the fish in the tank. The staff's incredibly efficient; they swirl by in their cool, bright shirts (reportedly bought on the streets of Bangkok), trailing the essences of coconut, peanut, and orange. Start with the mee krob, a nest of crunchy noodles fried with a tangy citrus flavor and topped with red pepper, a sweet plum sauce, bean sprouts, shreds of red cabbage, and tofu. The spring rolls are wrapped in a tender rice pancake, filled with lettuce and surimi; they're good dipped in plum sauce and dabbed in chopped peanuts. Judging by the number of servings of phad Thai that come streaming out of the kitchen, it must be the most popular dish. The squid sautéed with garlic and pepper sauce is outstanding, its tender squid contrasting nicely with the crunchy bits of garlic. And we like the Thai Special Salad: barely blanched fragments of green beans tossed with chicken slivers in a sassy, peanut-flavored sauce. Hotness is quite undependable here: someone in the kitchen likes playing with fire.

Thai Terrace
21919 66th Ave W,
Mountlake Terrace,
774-4556
Inexpensive; beer and
wine; AE, MC, V;
no checks
Lunch Mon-Fri, dinner
Mon-Sat

Mountlake Terrace Mall is an unlikely place to find good food, much less good Thai food. Thai Terrace is an exception. Everything is unquestionably fresh. The vegetables glisten with their original colors and are never limp. All dishes are prepared to order, even the soups. The subtle vegetarian spring rolls and the crisp Pinkies (shrimps wrapped in wonton skin and fried) are nice antidotes to the fiery ricochet from the tender squid in chile sauce or the excellent phad Thai when spiced with anything more than one star. The silver noodles are a gold mine. In Thai tradition, end the meal with homemade coconut ice cream and sticky black rice in coconut milk—an especially light version.

Thai Thai Restaurant
11205 16th Ave SW,
246-2246 (map: NN8)
Inexpensive; beer and
wine; V; local checks only
Lunch Mon-Fri, dinner
Mon-Sat

Hidden in the far wastes of White Center is a clean, friendly Thai restaurant whose food draws many discriminating Thai natives. It would surely set the town raving if it were better located, like its downtown competitors. Proprietor Sam Sudthaya doesn't stint with the peppers or spices, and he crafts salads and other presentations from a 100-item menu with a little more of the famous Thai elegance than your usual Thai noodle house. His stuffed-chicken Angel Wings are the best in town, crisp, tasty, and fried with minimum grease. And his soups and curries are rich and fragrant enough to justify the detour.

Thirteen Coins
18000 Pacific Hwy S,
243-9500 (map: OO6)

125 Boren Ave N,
682-2513 (map: F2)
Moderate; full bar; AE,
DC, MC, V; checks OK
Breakfast, lunch, dinner
every day (all day)

Around-the-clock dining and short-order food have made these twin diners popular for many years (helped by the fact that they occupy neighborhoods—by *The Seattle Times* building and the airport, respectively—without much else to choose from). Grill cooks work in the open, turning out (mediocre) sandwiches, salads, and a long list of pasta, fish, and meat dishes. Portions are large, the bread is good, and service is quite willing to meet you halfway.

Thompson's Point of View
2308 E Union St,
329-2512 (map: HH6)
Inexpensive; full bar;
MC, V; checks OK
Lunch, dinner every day

Carl Thompson's soul-food restaurant produces favorites with Creole undertones in a space that's smoky, accessible, and conducive to a nice, lingering evening. The entrée of choice, lightly breaded catfish, is moist with a crisp skin and accompanied by excellent long-simmered red beans and rice. Side dishes can be the best part of the meal—delicious potato salad, black-eyed peas, sweetened yams, and Southern-style greens that are slightly sweet and cooked to death the way they'd be in a north Georgia roadside diner. Or try the mouth-watering, challenging Thompson burger, a massive soul-food sandwich with sliced hot links, crisp bacon, a grilled beef patty, cheese, and condiments on an egg bun. Sometimes things come dry and overcooked, sometimes service is annoyingly slow. A section of the restaurant can be walled off for private parties.

Three Girls Bakery
Pike Place Market,
622-1045 (map: J8)
Inexpensive; no alcohol;
no credit cards;
local checks only
Breakfast, lunch
Mon-Sat

A Sanitary Market institution, the Three Girls Bakery serves up very hearty soups (a bargain meal at $2 a cup) and terrific thick sandwiches, particularly the honey-cured ham. A seat at the crowded lunch counter is the preferred place to do your eating (and a little chewing-of-the-fat with your wisecracking server); otherwise it's stand in line at the take-out window. Pick up a loaf of Seattle sourdough or a chocolate macaroon while you're there.

Tlaquepaque
1122 Post Alley
467-8226 (map: M8)
Moderate; full bar; AE,
DC, MC, V; checks OK
Lunch, dinner every day

Don't come here if you're looking for quiet conversation: Tlaquepaque is about as quiet as a Mexican plaza on Cinco de Mayo. Mariachi music, crowds of chatty patrons, and the occasional whoops and hollers, which ensue when some poor soul orders a Tequila Popper, blend into a general festive cacophony. In spite of all

La Cocinita de Tlaquepaque
1123 Post Alley,
467-6608 (map: M8)
Inexpensive; no alcohol;
AE, DC, MC, V;
checks OK
Lunch, dinner every day

 ★½

Togetsu
217 Yesler Way,
623-3977 (map: O7)
Moderate; full bar; AE,
DC, MC, V; no checks
Lunch Tues-Fri, dinner
Tues-Sun

 ★½

Tokyo Japanese Restaurant
Across from Factoria
Cinema inside
Loehman's, Bellevue,
641-5691 (map: II2)
Moderate; beer and wine;
MC, V; no checks
Lunch Mon-Fri, dinner
every day

Tokyo Japanese Restaurant #2
17321 140th Ave NE,
Woodinville, 820-7676
Moderate; beer and wine;
MC, V; no checks
Lunch Tues-Fri, dinner
Tues-Sun

 ★

the fuss, however, the food is pretty authentic, running to the fancier meats and seafoods of Mexico's Gulf Coast. A hearty pollo laredo topped with melted cheese and served with fresh vegetables, fabulous mesquite-broiled fajitas, and cabrito (milk-fed baby goat) defy the usual Cal-Mex lineup of burritos and such (which aren't on the menu but are available on request). On Saturdays and Sundays, the dinner menu is served all day. The colorful, rough-walled space in the Cornerstone sector of Post Alley is the perfect home for all this noisiness (you can rent the upstairs level for a festive gathering of 75), and it's packed during happy hour. A little deli across the alley sells tortillas and salsas, and tasty breakfast and lunch tidbits to go.

Togetsu may well be one of the better Japanese eateries in town; some sources say you can get the meal of your life here. However, there are probably only a few in town who know it—those who take the time to befriend the chef and give him a free hand to plan a feast (and cheerfully expect to pay an arm and a leg). For the rest of us, the food is not so exacting. The bento boxes at lunch, though elaborately assembled, seem a bit prefab. In general, dinners are carefully prepared and beautifully presented. But we wonder what we could be getting if we told them *who* we are. It isn't elegant, but it's pleasant and bright inside, with fresh flowers on the tables and lattice dividers between the booths. We know chef Yoshio Yari can perform; we just wish he would all the time.

Jin Sato, who managed the Mikado in its heyday, now owns two very reliable (sometimes outstanding) Japanese restaurants. They're both on the eastside and both both jammed with families virtually every night. Couples should opt to eat at the tiny sushi bar where selections are fresh and service very professional. There's an excellent selection of sakis from virtually every prefecture of Japan.

Tommy Thai
*8516 122 Ave NE,
Kirkland, 889-2447
(map: EE3)
Inexpensive; beer and
wine; MC, V; local
checks only
Lunch Tues-Fri, dinner
Tues-Sun*

Tommy Changkrchang has a winning manner. He likes to come out into the dining room to chat with the customers and look at the fish in the aquarium. Over the past year, he's turned his stark Kirkland restaurant into one of the best bets for Thai food east of the Lake. We like the deep-fried shrimp cakes, especially when livened with an unusual cucumber–hot pepper–sweet plum sauce. The calamari thickened with a rich garlicky sauce was also excellent. In fact, the only letdown was the ubiquitous phad thai. Tommy's considering making the entire restaurant nonsmoking, but for no-smokers are sequestered by the far wall.

Toscana
*1312½ NE 43rd St,
547-7679 (map: FF6)
Moderate; beer and wine;
MC, V; checks OK
Dinner Wed-Mon*

Toscana Deli
*1312 NE 43rd St,
547-7679
(map: FF6)
Inexpensive; beer and
wine; MC, V; checks OK
Lunch, dinner Mon-Sat*

Toscana is a New York restaurant in Seattle. As you enter from the alley, a cloud of warm, moist, garlicky, cheesy air hits you in the face. Then Angelo rushes over, takes your coat, seats you, and brings out the wine—a disarming and completely charming entrance. The food reminds us a little of home cooking—sometimes flawed (medallions of veal too slippery in the piccata, agnolotti kind of dry inside, broccoli cooked to the chartreuse stage), sometimes exquisite (beautiful gnocchi, garlicky sautéed squid to order again and again, delicious toasted herb bread)—but less the point of the evening than the atmospheric whole, masterfully created by Angelo himself. Be sure to end with his zabaglione. Watch out—prices that seem reasonable add up quickly here.

Toscana's success among Italian food aficionados prompted Angelo to open the Toscana Deli, where it's all available at half the price, and with a salad to boot. There's also a good selection of sandwiches, pastas, bread, and even an Italian hamburger.

Tosoni's Cafe
*14320 NE 20th N,
Bellevue, 644-1668
(map: GG2)
Moderate; beer and wine;
MC, V; local checks only
Dinner Tues-Sat*

It's an unabashedly weird combination—Austrian and Italian food, with some dishes from the South Seas—but it's prepared and served with such surefooted confidence in a place that's so irresistibly full of the personality of its owner that each meal is somehow a success, if not a model of studied perfection. Calamari marinara is wonderfully tender strips of squid in a bland tomato sauce, enlivened with kalamata olives. (We found the acidity of a forthright Alto Adige Pinot Grigio—from a terrific list that includes at least 25 wines under $20—to be a tasty, reasonable complement for this.) The changing menu (dinners only, now) might include Wiener schnitzel, mango chicken, a nicely done veal

136

▼

RESTAURANTS

saltimbocca, a simple salmon and prawn combination, tournedos Genovese, halibut Tuscany, and a Caesar salad that packs a two-fisted anchovy and garlic punch. Desserts are good, especially a slice of the sumptuous custard–fresh fruit cake. Service is professional, but kind of chummy with regulars—and everybody's a regular. No smoking.

Toyoda Sushi
12543 Lake City Way NE, 367-7972
(map: DD6)
Moderate; beer and wine; MC, V; checks OK
Dinner Wed-Mon

Stacks of wooden sake cups with people's names burned onto them is evidence that there are a lot of regulars at this North End Japanese restaurant—and, may we add, with reason. The owner, Natsuyoshi Toyoda (formerly of Aoki), is extremely conscious of freshness, and the fish is exquisitely so, even on Sunday. The kasuzuke black cod (marinated in sake lees), the saba shioyaki (mackerel grilled with salt), and the kakifry (deep-fried oysters) are all absolutely superb. There are some things on this menu not found elsewhere—for instance, yamakake (raw tuna with grated mountain potato) and hamachi no kamayaki (yellowtail with sweet potato). Five dollars gets you six big, browned gingery dumplings. Service is lightening fast, even when the place is busy, which is often.

Trader Vic's
1900 5th Ave, 728-8520
(map: H5)
Expensive; full bar; AE, DC, MC, V; no checks
Lunch Mon-Fri, dinner every day

Seattleites have grown rather tired of this timeless institution, with its relentless Polynesian theme and dated menu. But it is still a good spot, with friendly service, and a manager, Harry Wong, who knows everybody and everything. And the meats coming out of the Chinese ovens, particularly the succulent barbecued smoked pork, are quite tasty. Salads and fresh oysters are recommended at lunch. Order one of the monster drinks, laced with seven different rums, and the place will float in an agreeable Polynesian haze.

Trattoria Mitchelli
84 Yesler Way, 623-3885
(and branches)
(map: N8)
Moderate; full bar; AE, DC, MC, V; checks OK
Breakfast, lunch, dinner every day

Dany Mitchell has earnestly built himself a restaurant empire: Angelina's Trattoria, Bella Luna (see listing), Stella's Trattoria. He alone has provided Seattle with places where you can host a lively impromptu party in the bar or restaurant at almost any time of night. In general, the notoriously bad service is as much a fixture as the pasta alle vongole—which, by the way, isn't bad, but it's not nearly as good as the ravioli in butter and garlic (our current favorite dish) or anything made with veal (usually fresh and tender) or breakfasts of Italian frittatas and cheesy omelets. The rest of the food is mediocre, but mediocrity never had such an appealing bohemian backdrop as at the original trattoria in Pioneer Square. Stella's (4500 Ninth Avenue NE, 633-1100, map: FF6) in the University District Metro Cinema multiplex is open all night—a private room serves 50. West Seattle's Angelina's (2311 California Avenue SW, 932-7311, map: JJ9), geared more toward yuppie families, closes the earliest of them all, 11pm on weekends. The dense, chewy scoop of caramèllo ($1.35) topped with whipped cream is an after-dinner staple at all of them.

Triples

1200 Westlake Ave N,
284-2535 (map: GG7)
Moderate; full bar; AE,
MC, V; checks OK
Lunch Mon-Sat, dinner
every day

Triples is one of Rich Komen's formula ventures, a restaurant with such a splendid view of Lake Union and a bar so full of yuppie singles that skeptics may doubt there's a serious kitchen behind the hype. There is, though, and every night it turns out half-a-dozen innovative entrées. The seafood is always right on target—we tried a meltingly tender grilled shark with West African peanut sauce and an even better Idaho trout basted with basil sauce. The grilled salmon and halibut are also commendable. Sushi, sashimi, and fresh oysters are available in the bar but are uneven in quality. Service can be embarrassingly slow and amateurish, especially around noon, when the restaurant is packed with business-lunchers. This is a marvelous place, incidentally, for a business meeting or a party in one of three private rooms—one has a knockout view of Lake Union and holds up to 250.

Trolleyman Pub

3400 Phinney Ave N,
548-8000 (map: FF7)
Inexpensive; beer only;
MC, V; local checks only
Lunch, dinner Mon-Sat
(open Sun, but no food)

If taproom manager Pamela Hinkley hadn't been so persistent, Seattle's first brewpub would have been just that: a microbrewery pouring utterly fresh Red Hook beers at the end of a brewer's tour. Hinkley's insistence resulted in the addition of food prepared by an ex–Dahlia Lounge cook—and for beer drinkers who love to linger over an ESB or a Ballard Bitter, these light meals are the perfect accompaniment. The food, like the beer, is seasonal; a different soup graces the menu each day. Try the wonderful, assertively spicy black bean chili served with pools of cool sour cream or the hearty sausage lasagne. You can sit at the long, curved wooden bar, nestle in front of the fireplace on an overstuffed couch, or join your friends at one of the long community tables.

Look for **FREE**—*it means this attraction or event is free of charge.*

Truffles

3701 NE 45th St,
522-3016 (map: FF7)
Inexpensive; beer and
wine; AE, MC, V;
checks OK
Breakfast, lunch, dinner
Mon-Sat, brunch Sun

Truffles is part of a kitchen and gourmet food store that is also one of Seattle's more imaginative catering businesses. Located near University Village, the cafe offers a bright, pretty atmosphere and wide-ranging fare that includes soups and tasty salads (such as a superb Sapnish black bean with tuna, cilantro, and sweet red pappers, or potato salad with aioli dressing). There are deli items, too: sandwiches mad with Truffles' own breads (roast beef on orange walnut whole-grain bread), and entrées such as a moist chutney roasted chicken. You can put together a gourmet to-go meal in a snap. Owner Bobbi Smythe is a dedicated perfectionist with excellent taste.

Tump Nak Thai

419 Denny Way,
441-5024 (map: D7)
Inexpensive; full bar;
MC, V; no checks
Lunch Mon-Fri, dinner
every day

In a sea of uniform (and almost uniformly good) Thai restaurants in this town, Tump Nak Thai manages to stand out. It features an elegant khan toke room, a variation on the traditional dining style of the northern capital of Chiang Mai, which provides something of the same ceremonial comfort as Japanese tatami. Diners sit without shoes on the carpeted floor, backs against wedge-shaped cushions of bright tribal fabrics, legs stretched into deep pits beneath the tables. Interestingly, we would prefer to have the food Chiang Mait–style fiery hot and to sit Buddha-style at a low table, as the Thais do. The whole effect is tempered by the typically Thai pink and lavender furnishings, which strike a pleasantly incongruous note against the brass and dark wood of what was once a rollicking Western bar. The khan toke room serves largely the same Bangkok-style menu as the conventional outer dining rooms, at slightly higher prices, along with a few Northern specialties. Pla lard prik, crisp-fried pompano with a stinging chile-paste topping, is a prime seafood choice; curries are also done very well here. The standout, ho mok pla, is a salmon fillet steamed in a banana leaf and bathed in delicate, lemongrass-scented coconut custard. Meat lovers choose the neau yuang, a steak marinated in strong, fresh coriander and garlic and charcoal broiled to a tender medium-rare, or the panang ped, duck in a rich curry sauce flavored with lime leaf and dotted with sweet red bell pepper. Proprietors Chaiyong and Tirapol Juhtara and Nisa and Tom Kungkaya promise to add more Chiang Mai specials as Seattle grows accustomed to them.

The Two Bells Tavern

*2313 4th Ave, 441-3050
(map: F7)
Inexpensive; beer and
wine; no credit cards;
no checks
Lunch, dinner every day*

Everybody likes this new-wave, slightly seedy, urban tav-cum-eatery for its engaging blend of artsy atmosphere and cheap, delicious food. There's always a daily homemade soup or sandwich, a good Caesar, a couple of cold plates, a hot beer sausage sandwich (two split wieners facedown in sweet-hot mustard with Swiss cheese melting over the top), and, of course, the famed burger, a thick hunk of beef and plenty of onions on crusty French bread, with good chunky potato salad. Weekend breakfasts offer very untavernly things like orange nutmeg French toast and salsa omelets. There are 25 kinds of beer. We wonder what would happen to the arts scene in town if there weren't a Two Bells to so cheaply nourish the artists.

Umberto's

*100 S King St, 621-0575
(map: P9)
Moderate; full bar; AE,
MC, V; local checks only
Lunch Mon-Fri, dinner
every day*

Umberto's is at its best for lunch on a gloomy winter day when nothing sounds better than hot pasta and the lively company of a Pioneer Square crowd. The charming room—brick walls, tile floors, light wood, handsome banners—will warm you up faster than a puttanesca sauce. The antipasti are a departure from the salami/olive version you get in some pseudo-Italian places. Umberto's eggplant wrapped around provolone is especially good, mussels and calamari both fresh and tender, orzo pasta interesting. The tender veal sautéed with peas, apples, port, walnuts, and Gorgonzola worked well. Things fall apart with the pastas. Such dishes as cannelloni with spinach and crab in cream sauce are passable, but they miss the mark with a too-heavy sauce and rather bland flavor. Do bulk up on the good chewy bread, and do order dessert. Umberto's (like most Pioneer Square establishments) bustles before Seahawks games. Instead of waiting, try the "to-go box" ($6.95), packed with an Italian soda, fresh fruit, and a choice of grilled Italian sandwiches or salads—even a napkin and utensils. Private rooms hold up to 75.

Union Bay Cafe

*3505 NE 45th St,
527-8364 (map: FF6)
Moderate; beer and wine;
AE, MC, V; checks OK
Dinner Tues-Sun*

Part local hangout, part serious restaurant, this comforable Laurelhurst storefront offers seasonal fare in a low-key setting. Chef/owner Mark Manley is likely to leave his open kitchen to wander among the linen-topped tables, discussing his carefully chosen dishes. The menu, which changes daily, is small and emphasizes fresh seafood. Appetizers might include tender squid with lime and roasted garlic aioli or chanterelles sautéed with leeks, garlic, and port. Fresh tomato basil soup showed only the barest hint of basil. Recent seasonal entrées have included white sturgeon grilled with sun-dried tomato, garlic, olives, and mustard greens. The fish was still moist, but its subtle flavor wanted a richer sauce and more of it. Lamb chops with eggplant and sun-dried tomato were two small, perfectly cooked chops, this time nicely enhanced by the understated sauce. Other offerings are the popular pepper steak, imaginative preparations of duck, and grilled salmon. Seasonal produce shows up again in desserts (nectarine and huckleberry crisp and fresh fig tart with blackberry sauce, for instance), but the smooth and creamy chocolate mousse is a standout. The small wine list offers some interesting choices by the glass.

Union Square Grill
*621 Union St (Two Union Square Bldg),
224-4321 (map: K6)
Moderate; full bar; AE,
DC, MC, V; checks OK
Lunch Mon-Fri, dinner
every day*

★½

Consolidated Restaurants' (Elliott's Oyster House, Hiram's at the Locks, Metropolitan Grill) new downtown brasserie is a looker—white tablecloths, burnished wood, Deco appointments, mirrored everything—and in its first month of business, it's clear a lot of financial fat cats approve of the plush booths. The food, however, misses more than it hits. Out of noble aspirations—French brasserie fare—emerge limp pommes frites, bland and ungarnished roast chicken, swampy cream-sauced fish. Its finest hour is probably the bouillabaisse, whose russet broth conceals nuggets of monkfish, halibut, squid, prawns, clams, mussels, and scallops—but which still, on our visits, has been seasoned with an artless hand and fraught with chewy fish. Add to this that everything's overpriced by $3 to $5 and the service is chatty and salesmanlike, and you've got a restaurant that's a nice place to be, but you wouldn't want to eat there. Parking's validated, but finding the restaurant from the garage is an adventure in itself.

Viet My
*129 Prefontaine Pl S,
382-9923 (map: O7)
Inexpensive; no alcohol;
no credit cards; local
checks only
Lunch, dinner Mon-Fri*

★½

When Chau Tran arrived in Seattle, she began cooking out of her home for appreciative friends. When her living room was no longer large enough, she opened this little storefront on Prefontaine, where she serves authentic, delicious Vietnamese dishes: chicken curry with rice, rice-paper rolls with shrimp and pork, and an incredible seafood soup. Tran imports many of her ingredients from her homeland, and aficionados can taste the difference. Consult the list of specials taped to the wall and plan on a wait—Chau is a one-woman show, so lunch may take a while. Very inexpensive.

Viet Nam Vietnamese Cuisine
*660 S King St, 467-6426
(map: Q6)
Inexpensive; no alcohol;
no credit cards; no checks
Lunch, dinner, every day*

This is the Tai Tung of Vietnamese eateries, open almost any time you could possibly crave a good bowl of pho or plate of go'i cuioen. That makes it a merry multinational crossroads in late evening, when the big family tables give way to dating couples. Beyond such convenience, Viet Nam offers an unusually large selection (77 dishes), covering all the Vietnamese regions and genres. The spicy Hue version of beun bao Huiee glows with the red pepper of the classic soup. The tempting dessert menu sets you up for disappointment, however: on a recent visit, there was only one—beanh flance (flanlike custard)—available in the whole cooler.

Vonnie's, A Garden Cafe
*120 Blanchard St,
441-1045 (map: G8)
Inexpensive; beer and
wine; AE; checks OK
Lunch, dinner Mon-Fri,
brunch Sun*

An engaging and sophisticated courtyard restaurant half a level below Blanchard Street is Belltown's best-kept secret for inexpensive little lunches and dinners in a casual urban setting. Sunlight slants through the graceful wrought iron on the windows, and herbs grow in the windowsills. The food is satisfying and earthbound. Pastas are surprisingly well executed, as, for the most part, are soups, sandwiches, salads, and brunch foods (a butter-textured cheesecake's outstanding). Skip the weird stuffed French toast but don't skip brunch. In summer, eat outside in the courtyard with a burbling fountain.

Wang's Garden
*1644 140th Ave NE,
Bellevue, 641-6011
(map: HH2)
Moderate; full bar; AE,
DC, MC, V; local
checks only
Lunch Mon-Sat, dinner
every day*

Chef and owner C.C. Wang has been devoting full time to managing and cooking for Wang's Garden since he sold his other Wang's last year. The food—lemon chicken, sizzling rice seafood soup, sesame beef, beef orange—seems to be benefiting from his complete attention. Peking duck, requiring a 24-hour-in-advance order elsewhere, can be prepared with only a 30-minute warning here. The imperial dinner (for a preestablished per-person price) is course after course of seasonal and house specialties. Statues of Buddha and tranquil fountains greet you at the door. A banquet room seats 50.

Wanza
*6409 Roosevelt Way NE,
525-3950 (map: EE6)
Inexpensive; beer and
wine; MC, V; checks OK
Lunch Mon-Sat, dinner
every day*

A pleasant little Ethiopian restaurant with pink tablecloths that lend a touch of elegance. As usual, the dishes are mounded upon injera, the spongy, flat national bread, which is especially good here. Staple dishes are peppery (though not quite peppery enough) lamb, beef, or chicken wats, served with the standard seasoned vegetable accompaniments. Wanza also offers a few more unusual treats: bederjan (delicious baked eggplant) and shifinfin (the chef's choice, a beef stew served with injera). That's followed by a coconut and Amaretto tortoni for dessert.

Western Coffee Shop

911½ Western Ave,
682-5001 (map: M8)
Inexpensive; no alcohol;
no credit cards;
local checks
Breakfast, lunch
every day

It's just a slice of a coffee shop down on Western Avenue, where you dig into hearty platefuls of breakfast and other good chow to the lonesome twangs of real cowboy music. Fluffy, generously filled omelets; homemade corned beef hash redolent of cloves and topped with poached eggs and Parmesan; sandwiches made of moist, nutty egg salad or meat loaf as flavorful as a good terrine; thick, hand-packed espresso milk shakes—all done up on one four-burner electric stove, a griddle, and a toaster. Servers are slow (but boy, are they well dressed!), and the place is small—four booths and 10 stools. Unisex bathrooms. A hangout for artists and architects.

Wild Ginger

1400 Western Ave,
623-4450 (map: J8)
Moderate; full bar; AE,
DC, MC, V; checks OK
Lunch Mon-Sat, dinner
every day

A glimpse at this self-proclaimed Asian menu—Chinese broccoli, Japanese eggplant, squid Singapore, Mongolian steak—made us wonder whether they weren't reaching in too many directions, especially in a city infused with myriad Cambodian, Thai, Chinese, and Vietnamese restaurants. But taste the food, and hesitations vanish. Rick Yoder, who spent two years in the South Pacific and Southeast Asia, came up with something entirely unique: the first, at this moment the only, satay bar in the country. Capitalizing on that and the restaurant's family-style approach, the Ginger manages to maintain a level of quality that is consistently good and occasionally excellent. If there are only two of you, sit at the Honduran mahogany satay bar. Of the satays, the grilled marinated prawns with soy black vinegar sauce was our favorite, as the peanut sauce on the chicken skewers (purposefully mild) was too bland. The vegetables and seafood are favorites: a plate of asparagus with black bean sauce was good enough to stand on its own as an entrée, the special whole steamed sand dabs (tongue sole) were delicate yet flavorful, and the scallops excellent. Even so, we'd return for the panang beef curry—hot with ginger and red chile—or the fragrant crisp duck with a hint of anise. Owner Yoder balances every facet of the restaurant

Looking for a particular place? Check the index at the back of this book for individual restaurants, hotels, B&Bs, shops, bars, parks, museums, galleries, neighborhoods, messenger services, nightclubs, and more.

performance with an eye for detail. The thrill of the startlingly different satay bar has worn off a bit since the opening just over a year ago, but many are fond of this eclectically Southeast Asian restaurant that happens to be run by a couple of Westerners.

Yarrow Bay Restaurant and Beach Cafe
1270 Carillon Point, Kirkland, 889-0303 or 889-9052 (map: EE3) Moderate; full bar; AE, DC, MC, V; local checks only Lunch Mon-Fri (restaurant only), dinner every day

Three out of the four owners of Ray's Boathouse (Russ Wohlers, Earl Lasher, and Jack Sikma) opened this Kirkland beachside restaurant about a year ago. It is really two restaurants with one winning Seattle-top view across Lake Washington, and one kitchen from which wild-caught seafood and organically grown produce emerge as stunningly healthful meals. In ways, it's reminiscent of the praiseworthy Shilshole formula. Upstairs, in the formal dining room with teak booths and Edward R. Curtis photographs, the entrées are a bit more celebratory and run from $15 to $27. They do most things well here, but we'd suggest staying with the simpler, single-itemed entrées, such as the moist, mesquite-grilled Alaskan king salmon. The mixed seafood grill (each fish with its own sauce) reflected too much of a shotgun philosophy; the plate had a cluttered appeal and each fish (unevenly cooked) was sauced differently (and sometimes inappropriately).

Downstairs, in the Beach Cafe, you come as you are, sit on the west-facing deck over Lake Washington or at any of the teak-trimmed tables (we like the angled booths at sunset), and choose from equally sophisticated dishes at less sophisticated prices: ravioli stuffed with three cheeses, hazelnuts, and roasted garlic hidden in a mustard and salmon cream sauce; Whidbey Island mussels dijonnaise (an appetizer upstairs, meal-sized on the water level); or fried calamari with an aioli dipping sauce. On a recent visit, the half portion of spinach salad doused with a tangy Dijon-shallot vinaigrette and tossed with fresh mushrooms, bacon, egg, and Parmesan and a plate of mesquite-grilled chicken glazed with herb butter were more than enough for two hungry eaters. The wine list (same on both levels) is well conceived, with a few good-valued zinfandels, semillons, and gewurztraminers.

Wondering about our standards? We rate establishments on value, performance measured against the place's goals, uniqueness, enjoyability, loyalty of clientele, cleanliness, excellence and ambition of the cooking, and professionalism of the service. For an explanation of the star system, see the how to use this book.

NIGHTLIFE

NIGHTLIFE CONTENTS

BAR, PUB, AND TAVERN INDEX: TYPE

(See also Entertainment in this chapter)

BARGAIN/FREE HAPPY HOUR HORS D'OEUVRES
Le Tastevin
Sam's Bar & Grill
(Bellevue Hilton Hotel)

DRINKS WITH A VIEW
Adriatica
Anthony's Homeport
Arnie's Northshore
Athenian Inn
Benjamin's
Cafe Sport
Canlis
Chandler's Crabhouse
Coleman Bar and Grill
Cutters Bayhouse
Ernie's Bar and Grill (The Edgewater)
Hiram's at the Locks
Morgan's Lakeplace Bistro
The Pink Door
Ray's Boathouse
The Red Robin Burger and Spirits Emporium

Salty's on Alki
Salty's on Redondo
Space Needle
Triples

GAY BARS
The Ritz Cafe
Thumpers

HAPPY HOURS
Arnie's Northshore
Big Time Brewery and Alehouse
Coleman Bar and Grill
College Inn Pub
Comet Tavern
Duke's
Fitzgerald's on 5th (Westin Hotel)
Il Terrazzo Carmine
Mecca Saloon
Murphy's Pub
Tlaquepaque

PIANO BARS
Canlis
Ernie's Bar and Grill (The Edgewater)
The Fireside Room (Sorrento Hotel)
Fitzgerald's on 5th (Westin Hotel)
Garden Court (Four Seasons Olympic Hotel)
Sam's Bar & Grill (Bellevue Hilton Hotel)

SPORTS BARS
Sneaker's

WINE BARS
Adriatica
Cafe Sport
Le Tastevin
McCormick & Schmick's
University Bar & Grill

BAR, PUB, AND TAVERN INDEX: LOCATION

BAINBRIDGE ISLAND
Four Swallows
Pleasant Beach Grill and Oyster House

BALLARD/SHILSHOLE
Anthony's Homeport
Hattie's Hat
Hiram's at the Locks
Louie's Cuisine of China
Ray's Boathouse
The Sloop

BELLEVUE
Duke's Bar and Grill
Benjamin's
Morgan's Lakeplace Bistro
New Jake's
O'Shaughnessey's
The Pumphouse

Sam's Bar and Grill
(Bellevue Hilton Hotel)

BELLTOWN/DENNY REGRADE
Two Bells Tavern
The Virginia Inn

CAPITOL HILL
Comet Tavern
Deluxe Bar and Grill
Ernie Steele's
The Red Robin Burger and Spirits Emporium
The Ritz Cafe
Roanoke Park Place Tavern
Thumpers

DES MOINES
Anthony's Homeport

DOWNTOWN
The Bookstore...A Bar (The Alexis Hotel)
Cafe Sport
Cloud Room (Camlin Hotel)
Coleman Bar and Grill
The Dog House
Duke's Bar and Grill
The Fireside Room (Sorrento Hotel)
Fitzgerald's on 5th (Westin Hotel)
Garden Court (Four Seasons Olympic Hotel)
McCormick & Schmick's

McCormick's Fish House
and Bar
Noggin's Brewpub
Palomino
Shuckers (Four Seasons
Olympic Hotel)
Vito's

EASTLAKE
Eastlake Zoo

EDMONDS
Anthony's Homeport

FIRST HILL
The Fireside Room
(Sorrento Hotel)

FREMONT
The Fabulous Buckaroo
Red Door Alehouse
318 Tavern
The Trolleyman

INTERNATIONAL DISTRICT
Kau Kau Restaurant
Linyen

FEDERAL WAY
Salty's on Redondo

GREEN LAKE
Latona by Green Lake

KIRKLAND
Anthony's Homeport
Kirkland Roaster & Ale
House
Smokie Jo's

LAKE UNION
Adriatica
Anthony's Homeport
Arnie's Northshore
Benjamin's
Canlis
Chandler's Crabhouse
Franco's Hidden Harbor
Triples

LESCHI
Leschi Lakecafe

MADISON PARK/VALLEY
The Red Onion Tavern

MERCER ISLAND
Roanoke Inn

NORTH END
Cooper's Northwest Ale
House

PIKE PLACE MARKET
Athenian Inn
Cafe Sport
Cutters Bayhouse
Il Bistro
Kells
The Pink Door
Place Pigalle
Tlaquepaque

PIONEER SQUARE
F.X. McRory's Steak,
Chop, and Oyster
House
Il Terrazzo Carmine
J & M Cafe
Metropolitan Grill

Pacific Northwest Brewing
Company
Sneakers

QUEEN ANNE/SEATTLE CENTER
Duke's Bar and Grill
Harry's Burger
Establishment and Good
Time Bar
Jake O'Shaughnessey's
Le Tastevin
Mecca Saloon
Queen Anne Bar and Grill
Space Needle
Targy's Tavern

UNIVERSITY DISTRICT
University Bar and Grill
The Red Robin Burger and
Spirits Emporium

RAVENNA
The Duchess Tavern

UNIVERSITY DISTRICT
Big Time Brewery and
Alehouse
The Blue Moon Tavern
College Inn Pub
The Unicorn

WATERFRONT
Cutters Bayhouse
Ernie's Bar and Grill (The
Edgewater)

WALLINGFORD
Murphy's Pub
Pacific Inn

WEST SEATTLE
Salty's on Alki

BARS, PUBS, AND TAVERNS

Adriatica
1107 Dexter Ave N,
285-5000 (map: C3)
Full bar

Everyone's favorite bar, atop everyone's favorite restaurant. All the ingredients are in place: a view of Lake
Union and the Cascades, excellent drinks and wines,
the best squid and skordalia appetizer in town, and a
romantic mood you could cut with a knife.

All places in this book are recommended; even "no stars" are worth knowing about.

Anthony's Homeport
6135 Seaview Ave NW
(and branches), 783-0780
(map: EE9)
Full bar

A lot of glass, a lot of bar action, seafood hors d'oeuvres, and a view that won't quit. Next door to Ray's Boathouse and not nearly as crowded or pretentious. Edmonds, Kirkland, Des Moines, and, most recently, Everett also have Anthony's outposts.

Arnie's Northshore
1900 N Northlake Way,
547-3242 (map: FF7)

300 Admiral Way,
Edmonds, 771-5688
Full bar

A spiffy sailor's hangout on Lake Union with a great two-for-one appetizers deal during happy hour, although the taped soft rock can be a pain. If you get there early, you'll have a good view from the bar.

Athenian Inn
1517 Pike Pl, 624-7166
(map: J8)
Full bar

A Market authentic, the modest Athenian's smoky bar is open early, commands a superb view of Elliott Bay, and attracts a wide selection of geezers. The beer list (with 16 brews on tap) will break your arm.

Benjamin's
809 Fairview Pl,
621-8262 (map: D1)

10655 NE 4th St,
Bellevue, 454-8255
(map: HH3)
Full bar

Is the view better from the inside looking out, or from the outside looking in? Sparkly patrons decorate the scene at these glitzy outposts. The newer, at Lake Union's southern extremity, receives high marks for its good wine list. No happy-hour specials.

Big Time Brewery and Alehouse
4133 University Way NE,
545-4509 (map: FF6)
Beer and wine

Three or four traditional American ales, all brewed on the premises, are on draft in Reid Martin's old-style tavern, which sports a collection of vintage brewery signs. You can even look in on the brewing process from inside the pub. To soak up the beer there is a brief menu that includes homemade chili and sandwiches.

The Blue Moon Tavern
712 NE 45th St,
545-8190 (map: FF7)
Beer and wine

In 1990, this lair of legends and gutter dreams—swarming with beat ghosts, living poets, and scruffier survivors of the U District's glory days—was under threat of demolition. A year-long battle secured a 40-year lease with the developers, who now will build the condos *on top* of this landmark tavern. Here, Camels are smoked and Grant's ales drunk without making a fuss over them. Sunday is Grateful Dead night, Monday is opera night, Friday afternoons is jazz, and even the graffiti is famous.

Seattle Best Places *lists the finest establishments throughout Seattle and the Eastside, north to Edmonds, south to Federal Way, and west to Bainbridge Island.*

The Bookstore...A Bar (The Alexis Hotel)
1007 1st Ave, 624-4844
(map: L8)
Full bar

A refined European-style bookstore is now a refined European-style bar. You can come for great snacks off the Cafe Alexis menu, dessert and coffee, or a microbrew, but in its heart it's a Tanqueray kind of place. Intimate, cozy—great for rainy days.

Cafe Sport
2020 Western Ave,
443-6000 (map: H8)
Full bar

For sensational Beautiful People mingling, tidbit munching, martini drinking, and people watching, station yourself at one of the booths in this most stylish Art Deco restaurant-bar and let the evening unfold. The wine list is carefully chosen; the food (which you can order in here) is inspired.

Canlis
2576 Aurora Ave N,
283-3313 (map: FF7)
Full bar

The only bar in Seattle that requires men to wear sport coats. If you feel like hearing some good jazz piano and rubbing shoulders with the wealthy, this view spot above Lake Union is for you.

Chandler's Crabhouse
901 Fairview Pl,
223-2722 (map: GG7)
Full bar

Showy, viewy, classic 1930s fish house. Good black-pepper prawns and one of the few places to regularly serve Alaskan king crab. Good beer selection, too.

Cloud Room (Camlin Hotel)
1619 9th Ave, 682-0100
(map: I4)
Full bar

As warm and pleasant as Rob and Laura Petrie's living room on the "Dick Van Dyke Show," the Cloud Room piano bar features glitz straight out of New Jersey. The drinks are well mixed, and you can count on the piano man to know "our song." Even on days when you're not in the clouds, most of the views are obscured by surrounding buildings.

Coleman Bar and Grill
808 Post Alley, 447-0129
(map: M8)
Full bar

Quaint, classic New Orleans–style atmosphere with a thirtysomething charm. A comedy improv theater presenting short skits and "happenings" makes an otherwise dull Tuesday come to life. Wednesday through Saturday the club tones down to a slow pace, featuring light jazz. Weekly happy-hour specials.

College Inn Pub
4006 University Way NE,
634-2307
(map: FF6)
Beer and wine

The dark, cozy basement of the College Inn is the closest thing hereabouts to a campus rathskeller, since such is strictly verboten at the university a block away. Students who've reached the age of majority drink microbrewed ales by the pitcher, attack mounds of nachos, play pool to loud records, and convene for more serious symposia in the private room in back.

Send us your feedback and tips on the report form at the back of this book.

BARS, PUBS, AND TAVERNS

Comet Tavern
922 E Pike St, 323-9853
(map: HH6)
Beer and wine

This amiably scruffy Capitol Hill institution just doesn't give a dang what you think of it, which, of course, is the source of its charm. We can't guess which of its denizens (arts types, traveling politicians, students from Seattle U) are responsible for the inspired graffiti on the walls, but we know that Jiffy Pop tastes better here than anywhere else. No video games.

Cooper's Northwest Ale House
8065 Lake City Way NE,
522-2923 (map: DD7)
Beer and wine

The decor is a bit shiny, and the TV intrudes, but Cooper's has four dart boards and an outstanding draft selection: 22 taps, 21 of them Northwest microbrews. The Ballard Bitter–battered fish 'n' chips are terrific.

Cutters Bayhouse
2001 Western Ave,
448-4884 (map: H8)
Full bar

It's a formula bar/restaurant appealing to the young, the rich, and the restless. The place is always hopping, so service can get inattentive (and you might have to stand during the after-work crunch). Cutters invented grazing, but it's a white-wine-and-vegetable-plate kind of place.

Deluxe Bar and Grill
625 Broadway E,
324-9697 (map: GG7)
Full bar

The time-honored Deluxe is where the more mainstream Broadway boulevardiers go for stuffed baked potatoes and electric iced teas. Often annoyingly crowded, although the retractable wall in front allows you to sit on the sidewalk and watch the steady stream of passersby.

The Dog House
2230 7th Ave,
624-2741 (map: F5)
Full bar

A late-night (all-night) Seattle institution that's ended many a novelty evening for otherwise regular folks. The patrons at this organ bar do carry on, so come prepared to let your hair down.

The Duchess Tavern
2827 NE 55th St,
527-8606 (map: EE6)
Beer and wine

This is the kind of neighborhood tavern that former university students remember fondly decades after graduation. It's a bit more open and airy than in the past, and there are 21 beers on tap (about half are micros). The darts, the pool table, and the 1960s rock make it the perfect stop for a pitcher after the game. The pizza is remarkably tasty.

Duke's Bar and Grill
236 1st Ave W,
283-4400 (map: HH7)

The singles march on through, especially on Friday and Saturday nights. Superior bartenders, a big wine list, and tasty snacks are part of the draw—although it's the

---

10116 NE 8th St,
Bellevue, 455-5775
(map: HH3)
Full bar

only place we've ever been offered "apps." There's Duke memorabilia all over the walls.

Eastlake Zoo
2301 Eastlake Ave,
329-3277 (map: GG7)
Beer and wine

Young pool hustlers and older barflies have haunted the Zoo for 16 years. The place livens up with retro rock 'n' roll and R&B bands on Sundays and cools down with classic 1970s rock hits on weekdays. Plenty to do besides drink beer—play pool, shuffleboard, darts, or pinball (no video games). Free pool until 2:30pm.

Ernie Steele's
300 Broadway E,
324-0229 (map: GG7)
Full bar

Never mind the 50-year-old smoke; this is a Broadway institution, full of folks who look like they belong in one. Ernie Steele's is the last refuge of the asocial drinker. And don't eat here, for goodness sake.

Ernie's Bar and Grill
(The Edgewater)
2411 Alaskan Way,
728-7000 (map: F9)
Full bar

After last year's remodel, there's no more counter circling the baby grand; instead, the place has a more woodsy feel (duck wallpaper and all), and all the tables now have that view—that spectacular view. There's music in the piano bar up front on Tuesdays through Saturdays, and customers request, and sometimes sing, their favorites. Great view, lousy food.

F.X. McRory's Steak, Chop,
and Oyster House
419 Occidental Ave S,
623-4800 (map: P9)
Full bar

McR's has plenty of Old World charm, as well as more Gilded Age bravura and more bourbon than you can imagine. It's a favorite among the town's professional athletes. Fresh oysters and a solid beer collection, too. Go with a Seattle Prep grad who talks sports—loudly.

The Fabulous Buckaroo
4201 Fremont Ave N,
634-3161 (map: FF8)
Beer and wine

Beautiful Upper Fremont has its own laid-back, jolly roadhouse, as good a burger- as a beer-stop. The motorcycle helmet rack by the door is usually full.

The Fireside Room
(Sorrento Hotel)
900 E Madison St,
622-6400 (map: HH7)
Full bar

This clubby little bar evokes a leisurely world of hearthside chats in overstuffed chairs, an unrushed perusal of the daily newspaper, a hand of whist. Most pleasant for an after-theater drink, especially Wednesday through Saturday (when the piano man is tickling the ivories), although service can be dreamy. Appetizers are available until midnight.

If you are traveling in the Pacific Northwest, consult Northwest Best Places, the only reliable guide to superior restaurants, lodgings, and attractions in Washington, Oregon, and British Columbia.

BARS, PUBS, AND TAVERNS

Fitzgerald's on 5th (Westin Hotel)
1900 5th Ave, 728-1000 (map: H6)
Full bar

A long, narrow alcove off the Westin lobby, sleek and dark. Happy-hour hors d'oeuvres are just $2.50. There's a dance floor with a DJ.

Franco's Hidden Harbor
1500 Westlake Ave N, 282-0501 (map: GG7)
Full bar

The tinsely Lake Union spots may fade in and out of fashion, but Franco's—jammed, jolly, and full of regulars—will always hold that certain appeal for Mr. Big Businessman. The double martini is a bargain.

Garden Court (Four Seasons Olympic Hotel)
411 University St, 621-1700 (map: L6)
Full bar

Spacious and grand, the formal Garden Court is the pièce de résistance of the Olympic Hotel. You come here to celebrate with expensive champagne, to dance on a parquet floor to the strains of a society combo (piano bar during the week), to hobnob with the pearls-and-basic-black set. Have lunch, high tea, a drink and hors d'oeuvres, or coffee and torte among the palms.

Harry's Burger Establishment and Good Time Bar
610 1st Ave N (Hansen Baking Co.), 282-2002 (map: A7)
Full bar

More garish than the parrot caged in the corner, Harry's serves the cheapest well drink in Seattle—$1.49—with the disclaimer (printed on the wall) that you get what you pay for. A lot of people turn 21 here.

Hattie's Hat
5231 Ballard Ave NW, 784-0175 (map: EE8)
Full bar

Deep in the heart of Scandinavian Ballard is Hattie's Hat, home of Aunt Harriet's Room and its massive back bar brought 'round the Horn at the turn of the century. We suspect the thirsty Scandinavian fishermen aren't here for the antiques, though.

Hiram's at the Locks
5300 34th Ave NW, 784-1733 (map: FF9)
Full bar

A nice place to sit and sip and watch the nautical world pass through the Hiram M. Chittenden Locks. There's a grassy patio outside for toasting Seattle's occasional fair weather.

Il Bistro
93-A Pike St, 682-3049 (map: J8)
Full bar

Tucked into the alleyway under the clock at Pike Place Market, this glowing, sophisticated bar gives you a glimpse of Seattle people actually being out in the evening. Right after work it can be crowded and noisy, so we like to come late at night for a half-bottle of champagne or a poetically crafted martini. The crowd, too, is mixed: politicos, romancers, and restaurateurs.

Il Terrazzo Carmine
411 1st Ave S,
467-7797 (map: O9)
Full bar

The romantic bar in the Merrill Place building's commendable country Italian restaurant, Il Terrazzo Carmine, is a superb place to wind up a day in Pioneer Square or an evening at the Empty Space Theater.

J & M Cafe
201 1st Ave S,
624-1670 (map: O8)
Full bar

Pioneer Square's most popular saloon, with a long bar and crowded counter, and decent hofbrau sandwiches and burgers. The place to meet someone on Friday or Saturday night—if the line doesn't drive you away.

Jake O'Shaughnessey's
100 Mercer St (Hansen
Baking Co.), 285-1897
(map: A7)
Full bar

It's loud and rambunctious, and it caters to a young crowd. But then, Jake's *is* Irish. Built to look like an old bar with heart, it felt like one almost from the day it opened. The array of single-malt Scotches and the fine Irish coffee are known far and wide, as is the bartender tenor, Robert Julien.

Kau Kau Restaurant
626 S King St, 682-9988
(map: R7)
Full bar

The downstairs Jackson Street outpost of the famous International District barbecue joint is the bar of choice for district business owners. The hors d'oeuvres (including roast duck) are excellent, the drinks are fine, and the waitresses are jolly.

Kells
1916 Post Alley,
728-1916 (map: J8)
Full bar

Rousing sing-alongs to live Celtic music boom throughout the licensed pub side of this Irish restaurant Wednesday through Saturday. Good coddle and soda bread.

Kirkland Roaster & Ale House
1111 Central Way,
Kirkland, 827-4400
(map: EE3)
Full bar

This is the Kirkland version of the Firnstahl bars that have proven so rabidly successful elsewhere. They continue to do here what they do best—pour boutique beer and fancy bourbon down the throats of yupscale folks who like to get loud. But here there's a really delightful extra gimmick: a winery on one side (Covey Run), and a brewery (Hale's) on the other.

Latona by Green Lake
6423 Latona Ave NE,
525-2238 (map: EE7)
Beer and wine

It used to be a darkened haunt for hard drinking; now it's a light, bright, new and improved microbrew-and-cheesebread-lovers kind of place. And, to make things extra cozy in this tiny Greenlake nook, good local jazz and folk musicians (Thursday through Sunday) make the best of a tight situation.

If you've found a place around town that you think is a Best Place, send in the report form at the back of the book. If you're unhappy with one of the places, please let us know why. We depend on reader input.

BARS, PUBS, AND TAVERNS

Le Tastevin
19 W Harrison St,
283-0991 (map: GG8)
Full bar

Choose from a famous selection of connoisseur ports, sherries, and wines served by the glass, or excellent cocktails, in the bar adjoining this French restaurant. They have the best happy-hour hors d'oeuvres in the city, served Monday through Thursday, a spread that includes roast beef, cheeses, and beautiful salads.

Leschi Lakecafe
102 Lakeside S,
328-2233 (map: HH6)
Full bar

Ah, the sporting life. The Lakecafe serves the jogging-sailing-cycling constituents of the charming Leschi neighborhood with McHugh's usual vast selection of beers and booze. It's best in summer, when the umbrella'd tables in the courtyard are the hottest tables in town (and folks can munch on fish 'n' chips from the take-out window at Koby's, the Lakecafe's adjunct business), but the action is no less lively inside the rest of the year.

Linyen
424 7th Ave S,
622-8181 (map: R6)
Full bar

The haunt of local Democratic Party pols and young International District hangers-out, the bar in the back of Elaine Young's Chinese institution is ever buzzing late into the night.

Louie's Cuisine of China
5100 15th Ave NW,
782-8855 (map: FF8)
Full bar

A favorite of bartenders around town, Louie's in Ballard is just the opposite of the usual dreary, fake-Chinese bar. Light and sleek, with polished wood tables, cushioned bamboo chairs, and ceiling fans, Louie's has a friendly atmosphere, efficient barkeeps, and free hors d'oeuvres during happy hour.

McCormick & Schmick's
1103 1st Ave, 623-5500
(map: L8)
Full bar

Bankers like it because it looks like a bank. Dark-stained mahogany and cut glass provide just the right atmosphere for stockbrokers and lawyers after Irish coffees and stiff well pours. Good downtown location.

McCormick's Fish House and Bar
722 4th Ave, 682-3900
(map: N6)
Full bar

Polished wood and brass, stand-up counters and fresh oysters make this the closest thing to a class San Francisco bar. McCormick's crawls with attorneys and bureaucrats after work.

Mecca Saloon
526 Queen Anne Ave N,
285-9728 (map: GG7)
Full bar

A no-nonsense backroom bar with reasonably priced well drinks, old regulars, and friendly service. To the folks at the Mecca, those flashy buildings down the street—the Coliseum and the Space Needle—are still news.

Metropolitan Grill
818 2nd Ave,
624-3287 (map: M7)
Full bar

Kind of smoky, and the drinks are weak, but where else in Seattle does a Dow Jones stock exchange board hang in the bar? Listen up—you might overhear a good commodities tip from the next table.

Morgan's Lakeplace Bistro
2 Lake Place Dr,
Bellevue, 455-2244
(map: HH3)
Full bar

Bellevue, surprisingly, has a dearth of good bars, and Morgan's has become a lot of people's choice. It's best in summer, when the doors (overlooking condo-ringed Lake Bellevue) open up and you can join the Vuarnet set out on the terrace. Good bar menu.

Murphy's Pub
1928 N 45th St, 634-2110
(map: FF7)
Beer and wine

There's nothing self-conscious about this jolly Irish pub. Somewhat collegiate, often packed, always good-humored, it's filled with smoke and an unintimidating crowd of Wallingfordians (and beyond). Murphy's is devoted to two recreations: folk music, from the real Irish stuff to Neil Young impersonations, and a zillion beers and ales from a million countries.

New Jake O'Shaughnessey's
401 Bellevue Square,
Bellevue, 455-5559
(map: HH3)
Full bar

A little shiny, a little young, but this Firnstahl establishment in Bellevue Square is hoppin', especially on weekends. A good list of late-night appetizers.

Noggin's Brewpub
400 Pine St, Westlake
Center, 682-BREW
(map: J6)
Beer and wine

This is an outpost of a brewpub we know well in Victoria, BC (Spinnaker's). Wide selection of home-brewed British- and German-style lagers, burgers, and seafood snacks that have established a fine reputation up north. This uptown, Art Deco space in downtown's Westlake mall gets jumpin' Tuesdays through Sundays with local rock and rockabilly bands setting the groove.

Pacific Inn
3501 Stone Way N,
547-2967 (map: FF7)
Beer and wine

Should you come for the brew (six kinds on tap, 36 bottles and cans) or for the tasty cayenne-flavored fish 'n' chips? Most everyone enjoys both at this Wallingford workingman's mainstay.

Pacific Northwest Brewing Company
322 Occidental Ave S,
621-7002 (map: O8)
Beer and wine

See Restaurants chapter.

Map locators refer to the fold-out map included in this book. Single letters refer to the Downtown Seattle map; double letters refer to the Greater Seattle map.

▼

BARS, PUBS, AND TAVERNS

Palomino
Pacific First Centre,
623-1300 (map: J5)
Full bar

See Restaurants chapter.

The Pink Door
1919 Post Alley,
443-3241 (map: J8)
Full bar

We know it's kitschy, but imbibing blue martinis on the prettiest rooftop terrace in town to the strains of Tony Yazzolino's accordion music happens to be one of our weaknesses. Even with the rooftop expansion it's still tough to get a seat after work. A variety of musical acts come by in the evenings, including multipersonalitied cabaret singer Julie Cascioppo, who does Liza Minnelli better than the crooning superstar herself.

Place Pigalle
Pike Place Market,
624-1756 (map: J8)
Full bar

Tucked into the corner of this secret gem is a slightly bohemian bar, with a well-selected list of beers, ales, wines, and eaux-de-vie. A comfortable spot to drink alone or *à deux*.

Pleasant Beach Grill and Oyster House
4738 Lynwood Center NE, Bainbridge Island,
842-4347

Bainbridge Island's fancy-white-tablecloth restaurant has a simply splendid bar—cozy, woody, and full of friendly regulars. Visit in winter on the couch in front of the fire, when the rain is drizzling down the window-panes, for a warming brandy.

The Pumphouse
11802 NE 8th St,
Bellevue, 455-4110
(map: HH3)
Full bar

This dim, unassuming joint on the refreshingly wrong side of Bellevue's tracks offers a long menu of eats to enjoy with the local drafts. It's kind of a ribald crowd, but always harmless and friendly.

Queen Anne Bar and Grill
612 1st Ave N (Hansen Baking Co.), 284-8381
(map: GG7)
Full bar

The tiny bar of this bustling walk-up restaurant has an arty feel and a certain theaterish charm: impromptu cast parties from The Rep or Intiman across the street often happen here, and the barkeep knows the dirt on all the actors in town.

Ray's Boathouse
609 Seaview Ave NW,
789-3770 (map: EE9)
Full bar

One visit to the jammed upstairs view-deck cafe will assure you that Ray's doesn't lack fans. On a weekend you'll probably have to wait to get in, but it's easier than trying to get into the main dining room, which often requires reservations in advance. Service can be harried, the cafe food is fresh but not particularly inventive, and the crowd is just having way too much fun. The view's the thing, right off a postcard, and that redeems the whole into something much better than the sum of its parts. Outstanding wine list, too.

Red Door Alehouse
3401 Fremont Ave N,
547-7521 (map: FF7)
Beer and wine

The atmosphere is somewhat bland, though the large outdoor beergarden in the back, the wide beer selection (22 on tap, including Northwest microbrews), and the good, small menu (with steamed mussels and burgers) help pack this neighborhood pub.

The Red Onion Tavern
4210 E Madison St,
323-1611 (map: GG6)
Beer and wine

Perfect in winter, when you can drink a beer around the huge stone fireplace, this Madison Park institution is also known for its pool tables and its pizza. Mellow local crowd.

The Red Robin Burger and Spirits Emporium
3272 Fuhrman Ave E
(and branches), 323-0917
(map: FF7)
Full bar

Seattle's collegiate Algonquin Club is now one outpost of the formula Red Robin burger-and-cocktail chain, but the place itself, overlooking Portage Bay, is a marvelous spot for watching the boats drift by. If you like circus burgers, exotic cocktails, and enormous desserts, you'll also be happy at any of the seven clones around town.

The Ritz Cafe
429 15th Ave E,
328-0440 (map: GG6)
Full bar

This well-appointed, even-tempered gay bar and restaurant is under new ownership, but it's the same nice crowd around the piano bar and the same pedestrian parade outside the front window.

Roanoke Inn
1825 72nd Ave SE,
Mercer Island, 232-0800
(map: II4)
Beer and wine

This venerable old country tavern is a swell place to relax with a cool beer after a bike ride around Mercer Island. It feels like a summer home, and very genteel: in the john, there are blackboards in the stalls.

Roanoke Park Place Tavern
2409 10th Ave E,
324-5882 (map: GG6)
Beer and wine

A gathering ground where the junior gentry of north Capitol Hill can feel like just folks. Good burgers and beers, but loud music often drowns out conversation. Beware the influx of students on Thursday nights.

Salty's on Alki
1936 Harbor Ave SW,
937-1600 (map: II9)

Salty's on Redondo
28201 Beach Dr, Federal
Way, 946-0636
Full bar

The spacious West Seattle bar spills over onto the bay-level patio (warmed, thankfully, by high-rise heat lamps), where you can order from a lengthy menu of seafood appetizers and gaze at the twinkling lights of Seattle.

Books in the Best Places series read as personal guidebooks, but our evaluations are based on numerous reports from local experts. Final judgements are made by the editors. Our inspectors never identify themselves (except over the phone) and never accept free meals or other favors. Be an inspector. Send us a report.

▼

BARS, PUBS, AND TAVERNS

**Sam's Bar and Grill
(Bellevue Hilton Hotel)**
*100 112th Ave NE,
Bellevue, 455-3330
(map: HH3)
Full bar*

A cocktail lounge and sports bar in downtown Bellevue, Sam's caters to 40ish Bellevue businessmen and hotel guests who come to game. Half-price hors d'oeuvres are offered from 4pm to 6pm.

**Shuckers (Four Seasons
Olympic Hotel)**
*411 University St,
621-1700 (map: L6)
Full bar*

Here you'll find The Establishment and celebrity hotel guests enjoying Northwest oysters and shrimp or talking to the bartender's bartender, David Williams, who likes fixing drinks so much he wrote a book about it. There's a light afternoon menu of seafood and good local beers.

The Sloop
*2830 NW Market St,
782-3330 (map: EE8)
Beer and wine*

The big sloop painted on the east side of the building tells you that you're at one of maritime Ballard's favorite taverns. They don't pour the hometown ale anymore—maybe because Ballard Bitter left them for Fremont. Hale's refreshes the pool and dart players these days.

Smokie Jo's
*106 Kirkland Ave,
Kirkland, 827-8300
(map: EE3)
Beer and wine*

The one place in Kirkland where a laid-back crowd of regulars forgets the dress code and enjoys a great selection of draft beer.

Sneakers
*567 Occidental Ave S,
625-1340 (map: P9)
Full bar*

This long, narrow sports bar is squeezed in between some warehouses down by the Kingdome. The food isn't very good, but it's priced so you can sit and nibble while you drink and stare at the bank of TV screens jammed between sports memorabilia and ticker tape.

Space Needle
*Seattle Center, 443-2100
(map: C6)
Full bar*

If enjoying a truly sensational view means sipping the most expensive drink you'll ever have in your life, then spring the $3.75 for the hop to the top (only restaurant patrons ride free) . . . and then drink slowly. The restaurant food is just not worth it.

Targy's Tavern
*600 W Crockett St,
285-9700 (map: GG7)
Beer and wine*

The kind of place where the best thing on the menu is the Rolaids, Targy's is the unofficial Upper Queen Anne Community Center, full of character and characters and a rinky-dink charm not everyone will appreciate. Sixteen kinds of beer and the best electric darts in town.

All places in this book are recommended; even "no stars" are worth knowing about.

318 Tavern
318 Nickerson St,
285-9763 (map: FF7)
Beer and wine

An unpretentious tunnel of a place right by the funky Fremont Bridge, the 318 is justly famous for its heaping baskets of deliciously gut-wrenching burgers and fries. The beer, the pool tables, and the CD jukebox? Merely pleasing diversions.

Thumpers
1500 E Madison St,
328-3800 (map: HH7)
Full bar

The cozy ambience of the fireplace and oak paneling attracts a loyal gay crowd. Sample the well-chosen selection of appetizers (calamari, pâté, tempura vegetables) and enjoy a wonderful view of downtown Seattle.

Tlaquepaque
1122 Post Alley,
467-8226 (map: M8)
Full bar

It's standing-room-only in this colorful Tex-Mex bar, where a deadly specialty called a "popper"—a blend of tequila, Kahlua, and ginger ale that is slapped on the bar until it foams up, then chugged—incites the fashionable drunks into an unholy frenzy. Roving photographers and an eclectic lineup of happy-hour entertainment add to the chaos.

Triples
1200 Westlake Ave N,
284-2535 (map: GG7)
Full bar

Rich Koman's lakeside enterprise is the creamiest singles scene for the city's sophisticates. All the ingredients are here: dressy patrons, Lake Union backdrop, decent bar food (sushi, sashimi, oysters), and a wealth of drinking selections. Just *try* to find a seat after work.

The Trolleyman
3400 Phinney Ave N,
548-8000 (map: FF7)
Beer only

Fremont's Red Hook Brewery opened this taproom just for serving its own celebrated product; it's in the same building (a restored turn-of-the-century trolley barn) as the microbrewery. The space, right on the Lake Washington Ship Canal, is light and airy, with a big fireplace and piano. There's also a light snack menu. Don't plan to carouse too late—hours are limited to midday through early evening. No smoking, either.

Two Bells Tavern
2313 4th Ave,
441-3050 (map: F7)
Beer and wine

Even the most self-conscious hipster lets it all hang out at Two Bells. Good selection of local microbrews and imported gems, plus sporadic but always creative bookings of solo guitar acts, unusual art exhibits, and poetry readings. Great burgers grilled until 9pm.

The Unicorn
4550 University Way NE,
634-1115
(map: FF6)
Beer and wine

The Unicorn's publican, Angus Robson, wants you to know that the focus of his U District haunt is the food, which is why he offers table seating only and charges a $4 food minimum (roast beef and Yorkshire pudding, meat pies, Cornish pasties, and the like). Mellow Celtic and American folk music, excellent beers.

University Bar and Grill
4553 University Way NE, 632-3275 (map: FF6)
Full bar

It's a little chilly in the decor department, and the New Age Muzak in the background can wear on the nerves, but it's one of the only grown-up bars in this student-crowded neighborhood. Grab a table by the window and catch the scene on the Ave. Hard liquor, 22 wines by the glass, and a nice list of ports and sherries.

The Virginia Inn
1937 1st Ave, 728-1937 (map: I8)
Beer and wine

What do you get when you mix arty Belltown dwellers, chic-seeking suburbanites, and babbling pensioners in a historic, brick-tile-and-avant-garde-art tavern? You get the VI, a very enlightened, very appealing, vaguely French-feeling tav with a fine list of libations (including pear cider) and character to burn.

Vito's
927 9th Ave, 682-2695 (map: M4)
Full bar

If you like a well-constructed cocktail (like a gigantic martini) and enjoy watching a professional bartender in action, this old-timey joint is the place to go. All dark wood and maroon leather, it attracts police detectives, lawyers, the sports crowd, and judges on the road to intemperance.

ENTERTAINMENT INDEX: MUSIC/TYPE

AFRICAN POP
Kokeb
Re-bar
University Bistro

ALTERNATIVE
Backstage
Central Tavern and Cafe
The New Melody Tavern
Off Ramp
OK Hotel
Re-bar
Rendezvous
University Sports Bar and Grill
Vogue

CAJUN
The New Melody Tavern
New Orleans Restaurant

COMEDY
Bailey's Eatery and Bar
Comedy Underground
Giggles

COUNTRY
Backstage
The Beanery
Old Ballard Firehouse
The Timberline

DISC JOCKEYS
Borderline
Celebrity Bar and Grill
HD Hotspurs
The Infinity Lounge
    (Doubletree Plaza
    Hotel)
Kokeb
Neighbours
Oz
Re-bar
Romper Room

Spinnaker's
The Timberline

FOLK/ACOUSTIC
Murphy's Pub
The New Melody Tavern
OK Hotel
Poor Richard's Saloon
Square on Yesler

GAY
Neighbours
Off Ramp
The Timberline
Wildrose

JAZZ
The Attic
Dimitriou's Jazz Alley
La Rive Gauche
Lake Union Cafe
Lofurno's
The New Melody Tavern

New Orleans Creole
  Restaurant
Old Timer's Cafe
Patti Summers First and
  Pike
Wildrose

OPEN MIKE/VARIETY
Murphy's Pub
University Bistro

REGGAE
The Attic
University Bistro
Vogue

RHYTHM/BLUES
The Attic
Backstage
Chicago's
Doc Maynard's
The Far Side
Jules Maes Ice House

The Kirkland Stage
Larry's Greenfront
Old Ballard Firehouse
Old Timer's Cafe
Owl Cafe
Parker's
Pike Place Bar and Grill
Poor Richard's Saloon
Scarlet Tree
The Square on Yesler
University Bistro
University Sports Bar and
  Grill

ROCK
The Attic
Backstage
Central Tavern and Cafe
Doc Maynard's
The Far Side
Hollywood Underground
The Kirkland Stage
Old Ballard Firehouse

Parker's
Waldo's

SALSA/LATIN
Hollywood Underground

TOP 40
Celebrity Bar and Grill
Charlie's Bar and Grill
Deeter's (The Greenwood
  Hotel)
Meeker's Restaurant
  and Lounge
Oz
Pier 70 Restaurant and
  Chowder House
Sharky's
Top of the Hilton
  (Hilton Hotel)

VIDEO ROCK
The Attic
Latitude 47
Spinnaker's

ENTERTAINMENT INDEX: LOCATION

BALLARD/SHILSHOLE
Backstage
The New Melody Tavern
Old Ballard Firehouse
Owl Cafe
Sharky's
Spinnaker's

BELLEVUE
Bailey's Eatery and Bar
Charlie's Bar and Grill
Deeter's (The Greenwood
  Hotel)

BELLTOWN/DENNY REGRADE
La Rive Gauche
Oz
Rendezvous
Vogue

CAPITOL HILL
Kokeb
Neighbours

Tugs Belmont
Wildrose

DOWNTOWN
Dimitriou's Jazz Alley
Off Ramp
Top of the Hilton
  (Hilton Hotel)

FREMONT
Poor Richard's Saloon

INTERBAY
Lofurno's

KENT
The Beanery
HD Hotspurs
Meeker's Restaurant
  and Lounge

KIRKLAND
The Kirkland Stage
Waldo's

LAKE UNION
Jillian's Billiard Club and
  Cafe
Lake Union Cafe
Latitude 47

MADISON PARK
The Attic

MONTLAKE
Sandy Bradley's Potluck
  (MOHAI)

NORTH END
The Far Side
Parker's

PIKE PLACE MARKET
Patti Summers First
  and Pike
Pike Place Bar and Grill

PIONEER SQUARE
Borderline
Celebrity Bar and Grill
Central Tavern and Cafe
Comedy Underground
Doc Maynard's
Hollywood Underground
Larry's Greenfront
New Orleans Restaurant
Old Timer's Cafe
The Square on Yesler

QUEEN ANNE/SEATTLE CENTER
Chicago's
Oz

Romper Room

ROOSEVELT
Scarlet Tree

SOUTH END
Jules Maes Ice House

TUKWILA
The Infinity Lounge
   (Doubletree Plaza
   Hotel)

UNIVERSITY DISTRICT
Giggles

University Bistro
University Sports Bar
and Grill

WALLINGFORD
Honey Bear Bakery
Murphy's Pub

WATERFRONT
OK Hotel
Pier 70 Restaurant and
   Chowder House

ENTERTAINMENT

The Attic
4226 E Madison St,
323-3131 (map: GG6)

A neighborhood (Madison Park) hangout with live music every weekend (always danceable, usually rock 'n' roll or reggae).

Backstage
2208 NW Market St,
781-2805 (map: FF8)

Blues, rock, progressive folk, reggae, jazz, and the lot—by nationals and internationals as well as the best Northwest artists—make this one of the hottest and most eclectic clubs in town. Mellow 25-to-40 audience. Good sound but some sightline problems in this downstairs club.

Bailey's Eatery and Bar
821 NE Bellevue Way,
Bellevue, 455-4494
(map: HH3)

Very maroon and very mellow nightclub with soft, romantic jazz during the week. But if you drop in on a Friday or Saturday night you'll be faced with a noisy, jammed club being taunted by a stand-up comedy act.

The Beanery
19611 E Valley Hwy,
Kent, 872-8575
(map: RR3)

Plenty of beer drinkin' and good country music five days a week in this lively cocktail lounge. On the sixth (Monday) The Beanery goes ballroom.

Borderline
608 1st Ave, 624-3316
(map: N8)

Pioneer Square's progressive dance club. The prowling collegiate crowd likes to get pretty rowdy.

Celebrity Bar and Grill
315 2nd Ave S,
467-1111 (map: P8)

Red neon and mirrors have zapped the old Jazz Alley digs into a hipper-than-hip dinner/dance club for upscales and upstarts. Impressive ethnic mix, distressing architectural mix: disco mirrors, Roman pillars, New Orleans railings. No dress code, but remember to look sharp (doormen do pick and choose).

Central Tavern and Cafe
207 1st Ave S, 622-0209
(map: O8)

A large (by Seattle club standards, anyway), funky, and comfortable Pioneer Square establishment that bills itself as Seattle's only second-class tavern. Features local rock plus leading national alternative bands (some bad postpunk noise bands). Grant's, Ballard Bitter, Guinness, and a dozen other brews on tap. It's dark and hot, with a very young clientele all expressing their nonconformity in black-on-black clothing.

Charlie's Bar and Grill
11021 NE 8th St,
Bellevue, 455-4535
(map: HH3)

A popular after-work spot for Bellevue's businessmen and -women, who gather around the complimentary hors d'oeuvres. And just as the last business suit staggers out the door, a younger, twentysomething crowd takes its place on Charlie's two roomy dance floors, ready to shake its collective groove thang to generic Top 40 fare.

Chicago's
315 1st Ave N, 282-7791
(map: A7)

Classy, brassy, with plenty of room for dancing and mingling. Chicago's lives up to its name by featuring live R&B (always top-notch local players) every Friday and Saturday, with no cover, ever. Happy hours, too.

Comedy Underground
222 S Main St, 628-0303
(map: P8)

You can't get into this palace of yuks without waiting in line. National and local acts, all high quality. Be prepared for audience involvement. Downstairs from the athlete's hangout Swannies.

Deeter's (The Greenwood Hotel)
625 116th Ave NE,
Bellevue, 455-9444
(map: HH2)

A loungy, Top 40 place, with live bands Monday through Saturday until 1:30am and a chicly attired pack of suburbanites and tourists on the prowl. Dance to disco before the band starts. The hors d'oeuvres buffet packs the place during happy hour.

Dimitriou's Jazz Alley
2033 6th Ave,
441-9729 (map: H5)

Swank, intimate, and not a bad seat in the house, this spacious jazz club is one of the nicest on the West Coast—an absolute treasure. Owner John Dimitriou, a veteran jazz producer, presents leading national acts six nights a week. A larger stage, a back alley entrance, and a new, much improved sound system

---

Map locators refer to the fold-out map included in this book. Single letters refer to the Downtown Seattle map; double letters refer to the Greater Seattle map.

means a small music charge at the door. The best seats are up in the extended mezzanine, but wherever you sit you can always count on top quality acts like Katie Webster, Ahmad Jamal, and Tito Puente.

Doc Maynard's
610 1st Ave, 682-4649
(map: N8)

A regular bar, with weekend rock 'n' roll and R&B bands and a regular crowd of what look like either fraternity guys or Eastside investment advisers ready to slam and shimmy. Being in Pioneer Square, it's usually packed and lively.

The Far Side
10815 Roosevelt Way
NE, 362-1480
(map: CC6)

A north Roosevelt tavern-club with original rock 'n' roll bookings Monday through Saturday.

Giggles
5220 Roosevelt Way NE,
526-5653 (map: FF6)

A tad more collegiate than its Pioneer Square cousin, the Comedy Underground, Giggles is a large, plain, brick room with some dozen specialty beers on tap and cheap eats. The club features up-and-coming comedy acts—usually not as funny as a good Lawrence Welk rerun, but it depends on the night.

HD Hotspurs
315 S Washington St,
Kent, 854-5653
(map: QQ4)

This popular south suburban dance room with DJs features Top 40 music Monday through Sunday, plus excellent barbecued ribs until 2am Friday and Saturday.

Hollywood Underground
323 2nd Ave S,
628-8964 (map: P8)

Stumble in after you've been to the Celebrity (it's right down the street) and put the yang back in your yin with serious bootie-shakin' funk, rap, and hip-hop selections. Rustic and unpretentious; the Tinseltown theme is limited to antique film projectors and posters of movie stars. Wednesday is salsa night, with live music and dance workshops.

Honey Bear Bakery
2106 N 55th St, 545-7296
(map: FF7)

See Dessert and Coffee and Tea in this chapter.

The Infinity Lounge
(Doubletree Plaza Hotel)
16500 Southcenter Pkwy,
Tukwila, 575-8220
(map: OO5)

A popular place for disco; nightly DJs playing Top 40 all night long.

The facts in this edition were correct at presstime, but places close, chefs depart, hours change. It's best to call ahead.

Jules Maes Ice House
5919 Airport Way S,
763-0570 (map: JJ7)

During the week, Jules Maes is a very working-class joint with all the attributes of any self-respecting two-bit diner: a long bar with four or five human installations, a collection of weird old jetsam on the walls, a jukebox, and electric darts. To survive weekends of empty bar stools, the club has opened its doors to an earsplitting array of local alternative rock and R&B—while regulars long for country.

Jillian's Billiard Club and Cafe
731 Westlake Ave N,
223-0300 (map: D1)

It isn't whether you can play or not, but rather how good you look while cueing up. Here's a pool hall concept that began in Boston two years ago and, to the disappointment of true-to-smoke-and-beer pool sharks, has spread into three other cities (Miami, Seattle, and Cleveland). Beer, wine, champagne, and a light menu are served, though mineral water and espresso are the drinks du jour. Private lessons are de rigueur.

The Kirkland Stage
218 Central Way,
Kirkland, 822-8511
(map: DD3)

This rugged establishment is a beer-drinker's delight, with happy-hour schooners at $1.10 a pop and $4 pitchers. Bands playing rock 'n' roll oldies, R&B, and blues on Fridays and Saturdays keep the beer flowing well into the night.

Kokeb
926 12th Ave, 322-0485
(map: HH6)

At 10pm on Friday or Saturday nights, this Ethiopian restaurant closes its kitchen and shuffles the tables around to reveal a brightly lit dance floor. A whole new batch of patrons packs the floor (especially Saturdays), moving to the latest in African pop music from Algeria to Zimbabwe.

La Rive Gauche
2214 2nd Ave, 441-8121
(map: G7)

Friendly, appealing, and casual atmosphere for late-night weekend rovers looking for a nightcap. Cabaret jazz singer Kendra Shank offers an all-French set of Edith Piaf–styled gems. One of the rare downtown spots to serve its entire dinner menu until midnight.

Lake Union Cafe
3119 Eastlake Ave E,
323-8855 (map: HH7)

The newest club to start a regular jazz lineup, with some second-echelon performers, some national successes, and some regionalites on the rise. Admission (proportionate to the importance of the act) can run as high as $15—but that's for the entire night, as they don't turn the house.

Larry's Greenfront
209 1st Ave S,

Another Pioneer Square joint: any flotsam might drift in, wrapped in a three-piece suit or a one-piece sleep-

624-7665 (map: O8)

ing bag. Larry's specializes in local blues bands in the evening, Bloody Mary breakfasts at the top of the morning (Sundays).

Latitude 47
1232 Westlake Ave N,
284-1047 (map: GG7)

Three large video screens play rock videos interspersed with sports and news in the lounge.

Lofurno's
2060 15th Ave W,
283-7980 (map: GG8)

The piano bar downstairs at this popular Italian restaurant books some of the better players in town; Sunday and Monday nights the jazz jam occasionally led by veteran Buddy Catlett waxes hot. Upstairs in the swing ballroom one Thursday a month, you can dance yourself right back to the 1930s; the rest of the time it is available for private parties, by reservation only.

Meeker's Restaurant and Lounge
1401 W Meeker St, Kent,
854-0500

This huge Top 40 room brings in the best of the local rock cover bands and a few originals. This is the place to make the singles scene.

Murphy's Pub
2110 N 45th St, 634-2110
(map: FF7)

See Bars, Pubs and Taverns in this chapter.

Neighbours
1509 Broadway,
324-5358 (map: HH6)

Originally a strictly gay dance club; the Neighbours crowd is now about half and half. Music is Top 40 and disco, and the dance floor stays packed, even since they started lightly frisking folks on the way in (a result of recent bomb threats). There is a buffet Friday and Saturday nights.

The New Melody Tavern
5213 Ballard Ave NW,
782-3480 (map: EE8)

This great barn of a place used to house oompah bands, but since banjo man Dave LeMargee bought it, the New Melody has opened its floor to bluegrass, avant-garde jazz, Cajun, folk music, square dances, the gamut. Hale's Ale is on tap, and an earthy, high-spirited clientele of all ages gathers at this lively watering hole.

New Orleans Restaurant
114 1st Ave S,
622-2563 (map: N8)

This Creole/Cajun restaurant with French Quarter decor in Pioneer Square is a good place to catch ragtime, Dixieland, zydeco, jazz, and R&B acts. Tuesday nights are devoted to Cajun music and weekends generally bring in internationally known jazz acts.

OK Hotel
212 Alaskan Way S,

Well hidden in the bowels of the Alaskan Way viaduct, this incidental cafe-cum-gallery-cum-performance-

621-7903 (map: N8)

space is where the stylishly laid-back meet for breakfast and late morning coffee, to return later to the speakeasy-looking space way in the back for eclectic jazz and neofolk performances. Food is served til 2am.

Off Ramp
109 Eastlake Ave E,
628-0232 (map: G1)

Three rooms house three different endearingly tacky walks of life: a cafe, a small bar, and a late-night club, showcase-style. The club regularly books original and alternative music Monday through Thursday and women's disco on Friday and Saturday; on Sundays, anything goes, from leather conventions to drag shows.

Old Ballard Firehouse
5429 Russell Ave,
784-3516 (map: EE8)

Granted, no one has ever gazed into Ballard's watery eyes and pleaded, "Never change." But the Firehouse, with its menu of music including Cajun, blues, rock, country, reggae, and jazz, is doing its part to transform the sleepy community into a place you'd want to check out. Big dance floor, pizzas, impressive big-name bookings (Charlie Musselwhite, Sleepy LaBeef), and interesting locals.

Old Timer's Cafe
620 1st Ave, 623-9800
(map: N8)

Local blues and jazz seven nights a week. Full bar and typical Pioneer Square wood and brass decor.

Owl Cafe
5140 Ballard Ave NW,
784-3640 (map: FF8)

Aging hippies and socially aware youths frequent this cozy Ballard nightspot. The entertainment features blues of all shades, from down-home delta to R & B.

Oz
131 Taylor Ave,
448-0888 (map: D6)

Specially designed for club hounds-in-waiting, this club for people 18 and not much older features lip-sync contests, blaring Top 40 hits, and occasional live "as seen on MTV" bands. Dress code: No sweats, spandex, or torn jeans.

Parker's
17001 Aurora Ave N,
542-9491 (map: BB7)

Everyone from Tommy Dorsey to Ray Charles has played Parker's. During the 1950s, it hosted early Seattle rockers the Kingsmen and the Wailers; in the 1970s it was the major rock emporium The Aquarium; in the 1980s, it was a Top 40 dinner-and-dance place (the food's not half bad). And in the 1990s Parker's is a great place to be if you don't want to be in the present, as it regularly features blasts from the past like the Platters, the Mamas and the Papas, Head East, and the Tubes. The club has a dance floor the size of Duvall, a parking lot the size of Rhode Island, a superb sound system, and not a bad seat in the house.

Patti Summers First and Pike
Pike Place Market,
621-8555 (map: J8)

A favorite hangout for young jazz musicians, who flutter their wings with professionals such as Floyd Standifer at the Sunday night jam session. Wednesday through Saturday, owner Patti Summers, an earthy jazz and blues singer (she used to play the lounge circuit with husband Gary Steele), performs in her apron between stints behind the bar and in the kitchen. Corner Market Building.

Pier 70 Restaurant and Chowder House
2815 Alaskan Way,
624-8090 (map: D9)

Singles is the game at this "thanks for the dance" Top 40 emporium looking out on the bay.

Pike Place Bar and Grill
90 Pike St, 624-1365
(map: J8)

A Pike Place Market hideout that's often forgotten, but shouldn't be. This corner bar is never without a handful of regulars listening to the piano player and exchanging stories about the way things used to be. Listen closely.

Poor Richard's Saloon
3405 Fremont Ave N,
547-1065 (map: FF8)

A tavern with folk/acoustic/blues and an occasional dash of Dixieland. The culinary specialty is chili.

Re-bar
1114 Howell St,
233-9873 (map: I2)

Initially designed as an out-of-the-way spot for anti-nightclub scenemakers. Problem is, the arty, low-budget club was branded too cool, too fast. So, to thin out uncontrollable weekend mobs, the club's owners have been known to wade through the crowd and hand out maps directing curiosity seekers to other clubs around town. Those without maps stick around to dance (or, shall we say, pose) to the latest in world beat, European disco, funk, hip-hop, reggae, and experimental music spun by the town's best DJs. Tuesdays are live music nights.

Rendezvous
2320 2nd Ave,
441-5823 (map: G7)

You get the best of both worlds here. Just as you enter, to the right, is a smoky bar lined with some of the friendliest drunks you'll ever want to meet. Continue on through the 1940s dining room into a tiny former film-screening room—affectionately called the Jewel-box Theater—where some of the city's most alternative alternative bands play to ultrahip fans. For old times' sake there are weekly movie screenings, sometimes of early jazz films.

Romper Room
106 First Ave N,

Seattle's newest dance club and bar, the Romper Room, opened on the lowest end of Queen Anne near

284-5003 (map: A7)

First and Denny. Keith Robbins, who operated the popular Watertown club in Belltown until its demise has given it that same sort of low-tech feel that once characterized the Watertown.

Sandy Bradley's Potluck (Museum of History and Industry)
2700 24th Ave E,
324-1126 (map: GG6)

Last year, Sandy Bradley and the Canote twins moved their nationally syndicated musical potluck (broadcast and produced locally by KUOW) from Murphy's Pub to a larger, family-oriented auditorium at MOHAI. These hour-long acoustic/folk shows—pepped up with a lot of comedic banter—begin at 11am (be there by 10:30). Sandy's guests, usually culled from who's in town for the weekend, keep the program fresh each week; she may be coupled with chanting monks from Tibet, the principal flutist of the Boston Symphony, Ranch Romance, or the Total Experience Gospel Choir. The admission fee of $5 for adults and $3 for kids includes nibbles from a table full of baked goods.

Scarlet Tree
6521 Roosevelt Way NE,
523-7153 (map: EE6)

It may not be glamorous, but this shakin' little bar north of the U District is hot, funky, and ready to romp to rhythm and blues. Frequented by students, Ravenna residents, and blues fans.

Sharky's
7001 Seaview Ave NW,
784-4070 (map: EE9)

This hopping, high-volume club in The Beach House (formerly the Windjammer) is still owned by Ballard's Mitchell Brothers (they also own neighboring Shilshole eateries Charlie's and Spinnaker's), but it's been spiffed up a bit and renamed. The middle-class Top 40 rock-by-the-water seems to work well here. Live bands Tuesday through Sunday; mellow on Monday.

Spinnaker's
6413 Seaview Ave NW,
789-8777 (map: EE9)

Of all the Shilshole nightspots, this high-tech, neon establishment has the best view. Video disco jams the joint on weekends. Weeknight drink specials keep the club busy, especially on Mondays, when they feature lip-sync contests, and Wednesdays, when ladies fill up on 75 cent glasses of champagne and the men show what they're made of in the Levi's 501 jeans contest. Don't come here with a date.

The Square on Yesler
111 Yesler Way,
447-1514 (map: N8)

Housed in Party Central, this restaurant/bar still maintains its intimate, unassuming atmosphere with good R&B. But the crowds move in on Thursdays, "acoustic night," when local rock, blues, and alternative music stars play unplugged and personal.

ENTERTAINMENT

The Timberline
2015 Boren Ave,
622-6220 (map: G3)

Shake a leg to the best western swing music in town at this lively, gay and lesbian disco. Line-dancing and two-step lessons happen throughout the week; there's square dancing on Fridays.

Top of the Hilton
(Hilton Hotel)
1301 6th Ave,
624-0500 (map: K5)

Top 40, skyscraper views, and singles.

Tugs Belmont
Pine St and Belmont Ave,
323-1145 (map: HH6)

The new Tugs is in the old Squid Row spot, but it hardly looks familiar. No more tables, as it's mostly dancing (you can even dance on the small stage), with DJs playing underground industrial disco, sometimes even retro-disco—you know, those tunes you thought you'd never hear again—to a slightly gay, slightly collegiate crowd.

University Bistro
4135 University Way NE,
547-8010 (map: FF6)

Local rock, blues, reggae, and African pop acts. The room has the look of the straight and narrow, right out of a '70s acid haze. One of the only nightclubs with a broad, good menu. Clientele runs the gamut, depending on the entertainment.

University Sports Bar
and Grill
5260 University Way NE,
526-1489 (map: FF7)

This was once the only escape for noncollegiate types along the University "Ave." Now that the club has begun booking raucous rock and R&B on the weekends, the university crowd has regained control and a good bit of the sidewalk and parking lot out front as well. Another great place to turn 21.

Vogue
2018 1st Ave, 443-0673
(map: H8)

Ultrachic, with an unwritten dress code to keep it that way, the Vogue features new-wave art, video, up-to-the-minute dance music, and alternative thrash 'n' bash live bands. Patrons display black from their boots to the roots of their hair. If you like to dance, better bring along a crash helmet and knee pads.

Waldo's
12657 NE 85th St,
Kirkland, 827-9292
(map: EE2)

Hey, old-timers! Eastside room for local oldies waiting to be discovered by Mr. Peabody and Sherman.

Wildrose
1021 E Pike St, 324-9210
(map: GG7)

Hetero-friendly lesbian tavern with (usually) women-oriented musical entertainment as well as a blend of rock, folk, and jazz.

DESSERT, COFFEE AND TEA

B & O Espresso
204 Belmont Ave E,
322-5028 (map: GG6)
Every day

See Restaurants chapter.

The Boiserie
17th Ave NE and NE
45th St (Burke Museum),
543-9854 (map: FF6)
Every day

Some places are filled with such a palpable sense of history and romance that they seem to have been there forever. That's the "Bwoz," a civilized coffeehouse in the basement of the venerable Burke Museum. The walls are lined with ornate carved-pine panels from an 18th-century French chateau. At communal tables students and professors nobly study, drinking good espresso and enjoying cookies, thick wedges of carrot cake, Mazurka bars, and other sweets. Classical music lilts in the background; there's a cream dispenser by the door. Tables turn every 40 minutes once classes begin; the place closes at 8pm most nights (5pm on weekends). Outdoor tables are lovely in the spring.

Cafe Allegro
4214½ University Way
NE, 633-3030
(map: FF6)
Every day

Some say Dave Olsen, owner of the Allegro, is responsible for Seattle's coffee epidemic. In 1975 he opened one of the city's first coffeehouses in an alleyway next to the UW. He started buying his coffee from a small, four-year-old company called Starbucks. Twelve years later, he was asked to oversee the buying and roasting of their precious beans. Regulars—and most customers here are just that—swear by this rather sparse spot with average sweet offerings. The Allegro invites perpetual students to come for hours to study or philosophize, but it's rather intolerant of newcomers unfamiliar with its scene.

Cafe Counter Intelligence
Pike Place Market,
622-6979 (map: J8)
Every day

The food at Counter Intelligence is quite good, but that's not the point. Two flights above Pike Place Market, this narrow cafe is really about personality, panache, and viewpoint, the last in the most literal sense of the word. From this urban aerie you can watch the Market bustle by, and feel its energy and its pulse, in a protected, voyeuristic sort of way. Best not to be in a hurry here, or too fashionably strapped. The food is luxuriously fresh and carefully prepared and arranged. Crumpets with nut butter and fruit, for example, sounds deceptively simple, but what you get is a plate with a little vat of flavorful, freshly ground nut butter, two yeasty-chewy toasted crumpets, and a slice of perfectly ripe, seasonal fruit. At lunch there's often a special soup (gazpacho with an avocado and cucumber base painted with shreds of white Cheddar and red bell peppers, for instance), a miso soup, and a couple of open-faced sandwiches. Beyond the usual espresso permutations, you can choose blends like Bean Spasm, which marries cocoa, espresso cubes, milk, ice cream, pecans, and shaved chocolate.

Cafe Dilettante
416 Broadway E,
329-6463 (map: GG7)
Every day

1600 Post Alley,
728-9144 (map: I8)
Every day

The name of this Seattle institution, begun by the grandson of the czar's chief chocolatier, is derived from the Italian word *dilettare,* to delight. And that's exactly what its sinfully rich (and expensive) truffles and buttercream–filled chocolates do—day or night (though the cakes and tortes sometimes look better than they taste and always cost more than they should). The Broadway location is packed with late-night romantics (until 1am on weekends) who nibble and dream across candlelit tables. The Post Alley cafe, just the thing for a mid-afternoon sugar low, closes at 11pm on weekends. No cigarettes, please. A small retail outlet at the candy factory (2300 E Cherry Street) sells seconds at reduced prices on weekends.

Cafe Sophie
1921 1st Ave, 441-6139
(map: I8)
Tues-Sun

See Restaurants chapter.

Cyclops
2416 Western Ave,
441-1677 (map: F9)
Tues-Sun

See Restaurants chapter.

Danken's Gourmet Ice Cream
4507 University Way NE,
545-8596 (map: FF6)
Every day

In a neighborhood crowded with ice-creameries, Danken's has risen above the rest to purvey rich, flavorful scoops that are creamy-textured (some say too creamy), never too sweet, and particularly good at capturing liqueur flavors (such as Bailey's Irish Cream). Espresso and frozen yogurt, too. Open late.

Elliott Bay Cafe
101 S Main St, 682-6664
(map: O8)

It's a cozy and somewhat contemplative place located in the basement of the fine Elliott Bay Book Company, with brick walls and padded nooks where you can huddle over coffee and a book for hours. The food (small sandwiches, vegetarian lasagne, or a tear of French bread with Brie) is third in line to the atmo-

Elliott Bay's Art 109 Cafe
109 S Main St, 682-6664
(map: O9)

sphere downstairs and the books upstairs. In addition, they've raised their prices out of the good deal category—the desserts are outrageous in price and confection (and tiny in portion). Best to hit this place at a crawl; the cafeteria line moves slowly. The newspaper rack has a superior stock.

Upstairs in Elliott Bay Graphics is an extension of this subterranean cafe, but instead of books and bricks this one's surrounded by prints and sunlight.

Espresso to Go (ETG)
3512 Fremont Pl N,
633-3685 (map: FF7)
Every day

This is Fremont, summarized in a stand-up-size espresso nook with two stools and a couple of newspapers. Locals visit this place for coffee and sweet bites throughout the day. In true Fremont form, the hours are flexible: it's usually open from whenever the baker gets there (usually around 4am) to whenever the last person leaves (usually around 6pm).

Fortnum's on Olde Main
10213 Olde Main St,
Bellevue, 455-2033
(map: HH3)

Where ladies lunch. A pretty little rose-and-chintz nook off Bellevue's fading Main Street, Fortnum's has been quietly developing a reputation among Eastsiders for inexpensive lunches and elegant desserts. For roughly $5 to $6 you can get a slice of creamy quiche Lorraine with a salad, or a serving of zucchini frittata, or a spinach walnut salad with a cup of homemade lentil soup. Desserts, however, are the coup de grace, to be savored with a cup of Fortnum's good coffee: mocha walnut meringue cake, a parfait glass of frothy lemon mousse, a sumptuous helping of bread pudding, and an assortment of fudgy, dreamy things that are baked inhouse and might be different each day. Light dinners Thursday and Friday only.

The Famous Pacific Dessert Company
420 E Denny Way (and
branches), 328-1950
(map: I1)
Every day

We have mixed feelings about this now-chain dessert and pastry dispensary. Famous Pacific Desserts (as self-impressed, incidentally, as the name) *did* introduce us to the ultimate indulgence, Chocolate Decadence, and for that we'll be forever indebted. After that, the showcase chocolate desserts tend to be perfunctory and the service can be startlingly poor (especially late nights at the Capitol Hill outpost; 420 E Denny Way, 328-1950). But we've also had some wonderful concoctions here: rich, incredibly silky cheesecakes, a custardy ice cream laden with chunks of chocolate, an Italian domed sponge cake with whipped cream inside. The catering service (only from the Denny location) gets high marks, as does the branch in Bellevue (10116 NE Eighth Street, 451-9001), which helps to fill the yawning lunch gap in that city with its menu of soups, salads, sandwiches, and hot dishes *and* now stays open until midnight on weekends. Queen Anne (127 Mercer St, 284-8100) and Capitol Hill are just for dessert.

Globe Cafe
1531 14th Ave, 324-8815
(map: HH6)
Wed-Sun

See Restaurants chapter.

Grand Illusion Espresso and Pastry
1407 NE 50th St,
525-9573 (map: FF6)
Every day

Attached to the last independent theater in town is the Illusion, where UW students (and their professors) rendezvous at the small tables, the fireside couch, or, on a warm afternoons, in the tiny courtyard outside. Light lunch selections such as quiche and soup change every day (artichoke and split pea, respectively, were good), and the scones, cookies, and fruit pies are favorites; however, most customers come for post-film conversation or late-afternoon quiet.

Harvard Espresso Gallery
810 E Roy St, 323-7598
(map: FF6)
Every day

Who would have thought that Broadway needed another espresso house? Michael Lyons and Everett Patterson have created a comfortable space across the street from the Harvard Exit that has in a relatively short time become a haven for regular filmgoers and arty Cornish students. They come not for the desserts (limited to a few pastries, cookies, and muffins) but for the good espresso drinks (including a few unusual ones, such as the Lebanese with cardamom, the Madras with cloves). And for the we're-all-friends-here atmosphere, which is fostered by the proximity of the tables and the eager conversation of the lingering clientele.

Honey Bear Bakery
2106 N 55th St, 545-7296
(map: EE7)
Every day

KIDS Virtually everyone who walks into the warm, sweet arms of the Honey Bear adopts the place as if it were his very own—from morning lattes and sugar-powdered whole-wheat sourdough cinnamon rolls to late-night steamed milk and German chocolate cake. Earthy yuppies, ageless hippies, and just plain good folk linger, converse, read, write, and listen to laid-back live acoustic music (weekends only), regardless of the lines out the door. Praise goes to the marionberry Danish with sweetened cream cheese and almonds on top, and to the moist, warm, and not too sweet cardamom coffee cake. White chocolate brownies are almost too sweet, but the banana bread's superb. The nonsmoking Honey Bear also serves hearty homemade soups and salads and stays open until 11pm.

Last Exit on Brooklyn
3930 Brooklyn Ave NE,
545-9873 (map: FF6)
Every day

The Last Exit provides a living history lesson on the Beat Generation. Little has changed here since it opened in 1967, not even its clientele: bohemian philosophers, poets, and chain-smoking chess champions who come because the espresso is good (hand-pulled and served in tall mugs), the conversation is radical, and the food is ample and cheap. Culinary ambitions are modest—healthful soups and an oozing pb&j—but The Exit has been famous for its large, soupy plates of apple pie and soft ice cream for as long as we can remember. Monday night's open mike night (the only night when conversation's discouraged). The espresso pullers can be lighting quick, but the slow table service is part of the package. Don't worry, though, you have until midnight (2am weekends) to stay, and no one is going to kick you out of your chair.

Pastry Case
4429 Wallingford Ave N,
547-7788 (map: FF7)
Tues-Sun

Just a small, bright, friendly neighborhood spot with a baker's dozen tables for enjoying quiet conversation and outrageous desserts: tangy lemony tarts, meltingly pleasing shortbread, and fair-sized slices of Watergate Cheesecake. No bugs in the Washington, DC, hotel namesake, just a recipe lifted from the chef's former place of employment.

Procopio Gelateria
1901 Western Ave (Pike
Market Hillclimb),
622-4280 (map: J9)
Every day

Seattle's original gelateria still serves the most civilized Italian ice cream in town, in a stylish little nook right off the Hillclimb. At least 16 flavors (seasonally rotated) of freshly made ice cream are always displayed, and if you can get past these positively first-class ices, you can choose from an assortment of luscious desserts. Beverages include a great wintertime hot spiced cider, a few Italian wines, champagne, and most espresso drinks. Open until 11pm Sunday through Thursday, midnight Friday through Saturday.

Queen Mary Teahouse
2912 NE 55th St,
527-2770 (map: EE6)
Every day

Neophyte restaurateurs Tom and Mary Harmon transformed an austere brown-and-white chocolate shop into a den of cranberry chintz, dark woods, and silk-flower arrangements. Tom is a financial adviser; Mary is a graduate of two respected Seattle community college culinary programs. She opened Queen Mary in an attempt to recapture the comfort of a childhood with an

English mother and grandmother, and the everpresent cup of tea. Harmon proves there is so much more to proper tea than just a cup of tea. An order ($1.75) brings forth a special blend in one of Harmon's bone-china tea pots, accompanied by a small tray laden with lemon wedges (in cheesecloth bags), milk, and castor sugar. Full tea ($13.95) includes a refreshing sorbet and a tray of assorted scones, toasted crumpets, tarts, and biscuits. Or just try one, perhaps a fresh fruit trifle, an enormous concoction of fresh fruit, sponge cake, pastry cream, and whipped cream. But as much as we would like it to be, all is not dessert at the Queen Mary. The small dinner menu (about half-a-dozen entrées) includes a rather tough beef tenderloin in an amateur version of chukar cherry sauce, good crab cakes with aioli mayonnaise, and Cornish game hen with lemon-thyme-hazelnut butter. The tea (and desserts) is why you return on those all-too-English, all-too-Seattle damp, chilly nights.

SBC Coffee
Westlake Center (and branches), 400 Pine St, 682-7182 (map: I6)
Every day

Starbucks' local rival resides on Vashon Island. SBC (which recently changed its name from Stewart Brothers Coffee at the behest of the trademarked Stewart's Private Blend in Chicago) devotes 80 percent of its business to selling wholesale to restaurants; however, their four coffee bars are some of the most stylish places in the city in which to sip this good brew: Pike Place Market, 500 Union, Bellevue Square, and the newest, most popular at the southwest corner of Westlake Center.

Septieme
2331 2nd Ave, 448-1506 (map: G8)
Every day

See Restaurants chapter.

Simply Desserts
3421 Fremont Ave N, 633-2671 (map: FF7)
Tues-Sun

A longtime supplier to local theaters, Simply Desserts' outlet cooks up a selection of classic pastries: chocolate espresso cake, berry and fruit pies, fudge torte, a white-chocolate strawberry cake that wins raves from everyone, and the best chocolate cake in the city. A tiny spot with an enormous reputation.

Starbucks
1325 4th Ave (and branches), 623-5427 (map: K6)
Mon-Fri

See Coffee and Tea in the Shopping chapter.

Still Life in Fremont Coffeehouse
709 N 35th St, 547-9850
(map: FF7)
Every day

See Restaurants chapter.

Teahouse Kuan Yin
1911 N 45th St, 632-2055
(map: FF7)
Wed-Mon

You can peruse the latest guide to India while sipping a dark ti kuan yin, or study a map of Japan while letting steep a pot of green shou-mei. It wasn't by chance that Frank Miller and Miranda Pirzada located "Seattle's first teahouse" beside the new home of Wide World Books. Former travel agents with a longtime interest in Asia, Pirzada and Miller taste-tested many teas in Asia before selecting the Kuan Yin offerings: a broad array of black teas, a slightly shorter roster of greens, a few oolongs, and some herbals. Complementing these is a multiethnic and very reasonably priced assortment of quiches, focaccia, humbao, and sometimes sushi. The mood is meditative but worldly; customers are invited to sit in leisurely and lengthy contemplation. Instruction in the ways of tea drinking is dispensed generously, if sometimes with a philosophical air.

Torrefazione Italia
320 Occidental Ave S,
624-5773 (map: O8)
Mon-Sat

622 Olive Way, 624-1429
(map: I6)
Mon-Sat

Torrefazione has become the dernier cri in Seattle in much the same way Starbucks did 15 years ago. The retail trade at Umberto Bizzarri's two-outlet operation is small and exclusive, and its lighter, smoother, less bitter coffee is relatively new to the Northwest palate. Bizzarri, who learned the craft from his father in Perugia and is now passing it on to his son Emmanuele, roasts only 1,200 pounds of beans a week.

Uptown Espresso Bar
525 Queen Anne Ave N,
281-8669 (map: GG7)
Every day

A toned-down funk of the sort you'd expect in Lower Queen Anne. The table lamps are gems; we like the hula one. Desserts aren't outstanding, but the quiet post-movie or theater crowd lingers over good coffee. Especially on a hot summer eve, when an iced latte can be made with espresso cubes. No smoking.

Veneto's
10116 NE 8th St,
Bellevue, 451-8323
(map: HH3)
Every day

Regulars are almost rabid about the coffee and biscotti at this chrome espresso bar near QFC. In part, we think, it's because there's nowhere else like it on the Eastside. Nowhere, that is, that pulls such a *great* cuppa java.

Would you like to order a copy of this book for a friend? There's an order form at the back of this book.

THE ARTS

ART IN PUBLIC PLACES

FREE Public artworks are everywhere in Seattle, in styles as varied as the emotions they inspire. Among the more than 1,000 works of art on public display in the city are decorative manhole covers, totem poles, classical statuary, and abstract forms cast in metal. The sheer quantity of public art is due in part to a 1973 city ordinance that calls for 1 percent of certain capital improvement funds to be spent on public art; corporate and private donors have also added to the collection. Consequently, every City of Seattle office building, almost every hotel or office tower lobby, and practically every park boasts a mural, sculpture, painting, relief, or collage—many by local artists. The Seattle Arts Commission (Seattle Center House, 305 Harrison Street, 684-7171, map: B6) puts out a free pamphlet called **FREE** *Steps to Enjoying Seattle's Public Art.*

Few works of public sculpture have enjoyed as much unbridled affection as Richard Beyer's *Waiting for the Interurban* (1978) in Fremont—the gray, huddled band of cast-aluminum trolley riders (Fremont Avenue N and N 34th Street, map: FF7) whose distinctly homely figures have become the symbol of the neighborhood (and unofficial symbol of Seattle, showing up as they do on everything from T-shirts to greeting cards). Some artworks get a cooler reception. Michael Heizer's *Adjacent, Against, Upon,* three massive hunks of granite sitting next to, leaning on, and lying atop three mammoth chunks of concrete, was the subject of a loud public outcry over spending tax dollars on rocks when it was installed on the waterfront at Myrtle Edwards Park (map: B9) in 1976. Now it's considered an integral part of the waterfront. And some artworks inspire the vehement loyalty of Seattleites, as occurred in 1987 when Seafirst Bank announced the sale of Henry Moore's *Three Piece Vertebrae* (1968) (1001 Fourth Avenue Plaza, map: M6) to a Japanese investor. Art activists protested, and the sale was blocked.

One good starting point for art lovers is the University of Washington campus (map: FF6), whose best-known sculptures include Phillip Levine's bronze *Dancer with a Flat Hat* (1971) near the Henry Art Gallery and Barnett Newman's *Broken Obelisk* (1967) in Red Square. Downtown has the largest concentration of public artworks, however. Standouts are Rodin's *La Terre,* in the main lobby of the Rainier Bank Tower (One Rainier Square, map: K6) and Alexander Calder's *Grand Crinkly* metal mobile on the plaza at Fourth and Blanchard. Walk north-south along Third, Fourth, or Fifth avenues for the grand tour of corporate plaza sculptures and fountains, including several by local artist George Tsutakawa. At Waterfront Park on Alaskan Way and Union Street (map: K8) stands Douglas Bennett's bronze *Christopher Columbus* (1978), a striking constructivist figure that the city reluctantly accepted from the Italian-American community after stalling for years due to aesthetic objections.

At Seattle Center (map: HH7), look for Ronald Bladen's *Black Lightning* (1980), Alexander Liberman's huge orange steel *Olympic Iliad* (1984), and the untitled red neon sculpture (1983) wrapped around the Bagley Wright Theater by Stephen Antonakos (map: A6).

The relationship between the individual and the environment—natural and created—is gracefully explored along the shoreline walk at the National Oceanic and Atmospheric Association (NOAA) facility at Magnuson Park. George

Trakas's *Berth Haven* treats the meeting of land and water, while the wind chimes in Douglas Hollis's *Sound Garden* add wind and sound to the experience.

DANCE

Allegro! Dance Festival
Broadway Performance Hall, 1625 Broadway, 32-DANCE (map: HH6)

This popular September-through-July series features the best of this region's dancers and independent choreographers, such as Long Nguyen, Wade Madsen, and Llory Wilson. The festival, established in 1985, consists of eight or more performances of new works, often with free preperformance lectures.

On the Boards
Washington Hall Performance Gallery, 153 14th Ave, 325-7901 (map: HH6)

Always fresh and daring, On the Boards produces distinctive works that merge dance, music, theater, and various visual media. Its rather makeshift space in the Central District also hosts touring avant-gardists (though some performances are held at Meany Hall). The sellout New Performance Series, October to May, brings in internationally known contemporary artists, while the Northwest New Works Festival in late spring and the 12 Minutes Max series (two quarterly performances) premiere compelling experimental pieces by regional composers, choreographers, and playwrights.

Pacific Northwest Ballet
Opera House, Seattle Center, 628-0888 (map: A6)

The big show in town has evolved into a company of national stature under the guidance of artistic directors Kent Stowell and Francia Russell, former dancers with the New York City Ballet. PNB has a distinct Balanchine bias, with many of that master's works in its repertoire. Russell, one of Balanchine's protégés, evokes the master's spirit through the precision, coolness, and attack of his dancers. **KIDS** PNB's widely acclaimed *Nutcracker* is performed at the Opera House every December—choreography by Stowell, sets and costumes by children's author/illustrator Maurice Sendak. Six repertory performances fill out the PNB season between October and May.

World Dance
Meany Hall, University of Washington, 543-4880 (map: FF6)

Three to five major dance groups are brought in every year as part of Meany's World Dance Series. The October-through-May series enjoys broad appeal and includes such tried and true top draws as the Alvin Ailey American Dance Theater, Pilobolus, and the dance troupes of Paul Taylor and Twyla Tharp.

GALLERIES

GALLERIES: ART

Seattle's burgeoning gallery scene is primarily concentrated in Pioneer Square. One good way to get to know them all is to attend a **FREE** Gallery Walk, held the first Thursday of each month, when new shows are previewed and refreshments are served.

Art Center Gallery
3 W Cremona St, Seattle
Pacific University,
281-2079 (map: FF8)
Mon-Fri or by
appointment

This not-for-profit gallery in SPU's art building features a smattering of well-known local artists and a good number of unknowns. Some student work too.

Arthead Art Gallery
5411 Meridian Ave N,
633-5544 (map: EE7)
Tues-Sat

Arthead is an intermediate stop for young artists (mainly local, including some UW graduate students) on their way up and looking to break into the downtown gallery scene. Exhibits range from painting and sculpture to photography.

Carolyn Staley Fine Prints
313 1st Ave S,
621-1888 (map: O9)
Tues-Sat

The specialty here is fine old prints, including maps, Japanese woodblocks, Depression-era prints, and botanical prints, all historically or decoratively interesting. Staley also features occasional book-art shows.

Center on Contemporary Art (COCA)
1309 1st Ave, 682-4568
(map: K8)
Tues-Sat

If you're seeking outrageous, in-your-face art, look no further. This vanguard arts group has staged radio-operated robot performances and turned the Seattle Art Museum into a huge filing cabinet. A recent "Modern Primitives" exhibit put COCA at odds with Senator Jesse Helms—and the public loved it. Many of COCA's offerings are staged off site. On some nights, the First Avenue space transforms into a dark and cryptic performance spot. Black attire is a must.

Cliff Michel Gallery
520 2nd Ave,
623-4484 (map: N7)
Tues-Sun

Cliff Michel's been debuting some of the best younger artists in Seattle, as well as more established ones (Mary Henry, James Lavadour, and Robert Maki) who've been unjustly neglected. Recently, this gallery has been representing a few of the area's finer photographers, too.

Cunningham Gallery
Cunningham Hall,

Named after famous Northwest photographer Imogen Cunningham, this campus gallery presents six one-

University of Washington,
545-1090 (map: FF6)
Mon-Fri

woman shows per year. All work—fiber, photography, and painting—is by Northwest women.

Davidson Galleries
313 Occidental Ave S,
624-7684 (map: O8)
Tues-Sun

1915 1st Ave, 441-6699
(map: I8)
Mon-Sat

The Occidental Avenue (Pioneer Square) location exhibits a special collection of 19th and early-20th-century American paintings, as well as a mixed bag of works by local and international artists, including some mainland Chinese painters. The gallery on First Avenue near Pike Place Market boasts every imaginable kind of antique print, from medieval illuminations to Japanese and Czechoslovakian designs and antique maps.

Foster/White Gallery
311½ Occidental Ave S,
622-2833 (map: O8)
Every day

Frederick & Nelson, 7th
Floor, 502 Pine St,
382-8538 (map: I5)
Every day

The major keeper of Northwest traditions, Foster/White mainly represents established regional artists (Callahan, Graves, Tobey). Glass works of a few Pilchuck artists are on permanent display.

Francine Seders Gallery
6701 Greenwood Ave N,
782-0355 (map: EE7)
Tues-Sun

Recently, Seders has been exhibiting new works by female and black artists such as Barbara Thomas and Pat DeCaro. She still represents many venerable members of the University of Washington art faculty, including Norman Lundin, Michael Spafford, and Karen Ganz.

Fuller/Elwood Gallery
316 Occidental Ave S,
625-0890 (map: O8)
Wed-Sat

Hard to look at, hard to follow, even hard to find (behind MIA Gallery in the Burke Building), but it's easy to appreciate Carol Fuller and Sean Elwood exhibits of works that might not otherwise be seen in Seattle. They feature intriguing Northwest artists and international names such as Chilean Alfredo Jaar, Andy Warhol, and Christian Bolanski.

Galleria Potatohead
2316 2nd Ave,
448-SPUD (map: G7)
Thurs-Sat

Young, interesting, and somewhat foolish. Billski (Bill Moore), Spike Mafford, and Jan Cook have moved their hodgepodge Ballard gallery to Belltown. You'll sometimes catch young ambitious artists such as painter Elizabeth Aurich.

Greg Kucera Gallery
626 2nd Ave, 624-0770
(map: N7)
Tues-Sun

Canny young gallery owner Greg Kucera does a brisk business in top-quality prints by blue-chip artists—Motherwell, Hockney, Stella, Rothenberg, Johns—but is just as apt to give space to promising local painters or

GALLERIES

sculptors. His thematic shows tend to be hot topics, exploring controversial images and social criticism. This is where you'll find the latest from New York.

Linda Farris Gallery
320 2nd Ave S, 623-1110
(map: P8)
Tues-Sun

Much of the cream of Seattle's vanguard talent is here—Andrew Keating, Randy Hayes—interspersed with shows by famous contemporary artists like Robert Rauschenberg and Andy Warhol. Farris also represents several Soviet artists.

Linda Hodges Gallery
410 Occidental Ave S,
624-3034 (map: O8)
Tues-Sun and by
appointment

Owner Linda Hodges's stable includes mostly mid-career artists from all around the Northwest, as well as a few Californians and New Yorkers. Some of these are very good, others vary. Theme shows and group shows are the main fare at this small gallery.

MIA Gallery
314 Occidental Ave S,
467-8283 (map: O8)
Tues-Sun

MIA's focus has shifted from ethnographic art to the work of self-taught "outsider" artists. The shows—sculpture, painting, art jewelry, and some way-out art furniture—all share a narrative, visionary quality.

911 Media Arts Center
117 Yale Ave N,
682-6552 (map: H1)
Tues-Fri

A vital link with contemporary multimedia art that evolved out of Anne Focke's legendary experimental art center of the early '70s called and/or, 911 emphasizes film, video, and audio. There's an editing and screening room with a huge video screen for the production and exhibition of electronic installations. Call ahead for a schedule of evening screenings. The Northwest's only art video library is available to members.

Photographic Center Northwest
2617 5th Ave, 441-7030
(map: E6)
Every day

This photography school and gallery arranges six to eight exhibits per year. National and regional photographers are featured, in addition to the center's own faculty and students.

Silver Image Gallery
318 Occidental Ave S,
623-8116 (map: O8)
Tues-Sun

The Silver Image Gallery is devoted to fine—albeit rather mainstream—photography by master and contemporary artists, including Edward Weston, Ansel Adams, and onetime Seattleite Imogen Cunningham. It also carries a good selection of posters and books.

Wilkey Fine Arts
108 Occidental Ave S,
343-9070 (map: O8)

Jeffry Wilkey has a blue-chip gallery on Madison Avenue in Manhattan showing older, well-known New York artists such as Tom Wesselman, Michael Goldberg,

*Tues-Sun (Mon by
appointment)*

Willem de Kooning. His suave West Coast outlet is
slick, maybe *too* slick.

William Traver Gallery
*2219 4th Ave,
448-4234 (map: G7)
Tues-Sun*

Look for exhibits by regional and national avant-garde
painters, sculptors, and glass artists in spring and fall,
multimedia group shows in summer, and the annual Pilchuck glass show in December.

Woodside/Braseth Galleries
*1101 Howell St,
622-7243 (map: I3)
Every day*

Strictly Northwest. Works by regional masters—Tobey, Horiuchi, Graves, Morris—and a selection of
other artists (Helmi, Ivey) abide in this 28-year-old
gallery, Seattle's oldest.

GALLERIES: CRAFT

Artworks Gallery
*155 S Main St, 625-0932
(map: O8)
Mon-Sat*

Artworks Gallery's Pioneer Square home hosts individual and thematic group shows of contemporary sculpture, ceramics, handmade paper, jewelry, and textiles.

**Christopher Pawlik/Native
Design**
*108 S Jackson St,
624-9985 (map: O8)
Tues-Sat and by
appointment*

The very knowledgeable owners have selected a wide
range of ethnic imports and primitive art for this gal-
lery/shop. The ever-changing collection runs the gamut
from African masks and musical instruments to textiles
from Indonesia and Mexico and Northwest Indian baskets. And much more.

Lakeshore Gallery
*15 Lake St, Kirkland,
827-0606 (map: EE3)
Every day*

Mostly local artists and craftspeople show in this Eastside lakefront gallery. Original watercolors, sculpture,
ceramics, jewelry, and blown glass are showcased.

Lynn McAllister Gallery
*416 University St,
624-6864 (map: K6)
Every day*

In her new space, McAllister has shifted her focus from
Northwest art in general to glass, glass, and more
glass. It's blown, cast, and modeled by Northwest
masters as well as national and international artists.

Northwest Craft Center
*Seattle Center, 728-1555
(map: A7)
Tues-Sun (every day
in summer)*

Ceramics are the focus here; juried shows change
monthly. You'll also find wood items and jewelry.
Rewarding gift shopping.

**Northwest Gallery of Fine
Woodworking**

This gallery is a showcase for exceptional Northwest
woodworkers (a new one is featured every two

202 1st Ave S, 625-0542
(map: O8)
Every day

317 NW Gilman Blvd,
Issaquah, 391-4221
(map: JJ1)
Every day

months), who create fluid-lined, superbly original tables, desks, chairs, cabinets, sideboards, screens, boxes, and other woodcraft. Cooperatively owned. There's now an Eastside outpost in Gilman Village.

GALLERIES: NATIVE AMERICAN

The Legacy (Alexis Hotel)
1003 1st Ave, 624-6350
(map: L8)
Mon-Sat

The historic collection of Northwest Indian and Eskimo items in The Legacy includes basketry, ivory carvings, masks, beadwork, and hunting and fishing implements. Also shown are contemporary ceramics, prints, blankets, and jewelry.

RJL, Northwest Coast Ethnic Art (Four Seasons Olympic Hotel)
411 University St,
682-5005 (map: L6)
Mon-Sat

RJL has a sizable selection of carved ivory and soapstone from Alaska, totem poles by local tribal artists, scrimshaw, jewelry, and masks.

Sacred Circle Gallery of American Indian Art
Daybreak Star Cultural
Arts Center, Discovery
Park, 285-4425
(map: FF9)
Every day

A profit-making arm of the United Indians of All Tribes Foundation, this gallery features contemporary Indian art with a fresh view, flavored with tribal heritages (and they just got major NEA funding, so future shows should be even more so). The annual Northwest Coast Exhibit brings in larger, even finer pieces.

Snow Goose Associates
4220 NE 125th St,
362-3401 (map: CC6)
Thurs-Sat (Sept-May);
summer by
appointment only

Snow Goose Gallery is a cozy display room crowded with art and artifacts of Alaskan and Canadian Eskimos and Northwest Coast Indians. Annual shows include a quick-selling fall exhibit of prints by Inuit artists from Cape Dorset on Baffin Island.

MOVIES

According to *Variety*, Seattle has more filmgoers per capita than any other city in America. The first-run fare is always up-to-date, and fine offbeat movies are almost commonplace. Seattle has helped many an "unreleasable" film prove its commercial viability, and a growing number of filmmakers regularly preview early cuts here.

The Seven Gables circuit accounts for a major chunk of Seattle's cinemas. Seven Gables, which started as one tiny storefront theater in the early 1970s, began to give the national chains bidding competition when it grew to own dozens of local screens by the late 1980s. In 1989 they were purchased by California-based Heritage Entertainment. The comfortable, flagship **Seven Gables** theater (911 NE 50th Street, 632-8820, map: FF7) still books many choice foreign films, while the multiplex theaters concentrate on interesting first-run material. In 1988, **The Egyptian** (805 E Pine Street, 323-4978, map: HH6) was one of the last Seven Gables acquisitions before Heritage moved in. This roomy theater in a grand old Masonic temple on Capitol Hill is the headquarters for Cinema Seattle, which runs the annual **Seattle International Film Festival** (324-9996). This May festival has become an indispensable fix for local film enthusiasts, and it brings in about 150 movies from all points of the cinematic compass, as well as an increasing number of film celebrities. The organizers pay especially close attention to what national cinema is hot. Other venues for the fest are primarily located on Capitol Hill, including the **Broadway Market Cinemas** (Broadway E, between E Harrison and E Republican, 323-0231) and the **Harvard Exit** (807 E Roy Street, 323-8986, map: GG6), Seattle's first luxury art theater (located in a former ladies club headquarters). The Exit is good for specialized programming. In 1980 a second auditorium, the **Top of the Exit**, was added to this charming old movie house.

Seattle hosts a handful of more thematically focused festivals, too. The **New Film Festival** at **New City Theatre** (1634 11th Avenue, 323-6800, map: GG6) runs experimental, cult, or locally produced shorts once a month. It's the only place in town to see Karl Krogstad's works. Greg Olson at the Seattle Art Museum (Volunteer Park, 625-8900) curates a regular film program (usually chosen around a theme or a director), including the sellout **Film Noir** series. Also held predominantly at SAM is the **International Festival of Films by Women Directors** in October (623-8733); the directors are more approachable during this smaller, more informal affair.

Among the city's many first-run houses, the **UA Cinema 150** (Sixth and Blanchard, 728-1622, map: G6) and Cineplex Odeon's **Cinerama** (Fourth and Lenora, 443-0808, map: G7) are prime locations for sink-into-your-seat, wraparound-big-screen viewing. With 10 theaters in one, the new **Metro Cinemas** (4500 Ninth Avenue NE, 633-0055, map: FF6) is able to snatch up a couple of the film fests favorites (and other lesser-known reels) probably never seen elsewhere. The only repertory film theater in town is the **Neptune** (1303 NE 45th Street, 633-5545, map: FF6), which is sure to show your favorite old flick at least once during the course of a year. One movie that never left the Neptune and probably never will is the *Rocky Horror Picture Show*, which plays at midnight on weekends to a raucous teen crowd in drag. The spiffy **Market Theater** (1429 Post Alley, 382-1171, map: J8) at Pike Place Market was once independent but has been acquired by Cineplex Odeon. The **Grand Illusion** in the University District (1403 NE 50th Street, 523-3935, map: FF6), the last truly independent theater in town, brings old classics, select foreign films, and even some late-night animation spots to its postage-stamp screen (which is best viewed from the love seat in the back row).

All places in this book are recommended; even "no stars" are worth knowing about.

MUSEUMS

Bellevue Art Museum
Bellevue Square,
Bellevue, 454-3322
(map: HH3)
Every day

Here's an art museum where you'd least expect it—on the third floor of a shopping mall. Some say the museum doesn't quite transcend the atmosphere, but for the most part, BAM has created its own niche with an interesting array of exhibits that favor Northwest artists and handicraft traditions from around the world. Recently, fountain designer and artist George Tsutakawa was honored with a retrospective here. The museum sponsors the Pacific Northwest Arts and Crafts Fair at Bellevue Square every July. It also offers occasional classes and lectures. Admission is $3 for adults, $2 for seniors, and free for students and kids. **FREE** Tuesdays are free for everyone.

Burke Memorial Washington State Museum
17th Avenue NE and NE
45th Street, University of
Washington, 543-5590
(map: FF6)
Every day

FREE The most popular attractions in this modest-sized natural history and anthropology museum are the dinosaur skeletons and Northwest Coast Indian artifacts, but the Burke's collection features cultural and archaeological materials from many other Pacific Rim cultures. Recently reopened with more gallery space and a new director, the museum has some ambitious exhibits planned, including a permanent natural history installation. Downstairs you'll find a gift shop and the Boiserie cafe, a superb resting spot. Admission is free except for special shows.

Center for Wooden Boats
1010 Valley St, 382-2628
(map: GG7)
Every day (closed
Mondays in winter)

FREE You can sail away with the exhibits at the Center for Wooden Boats, which has its own little harbor at the southern tip of Lake Union. This maritime museum, kept afloat financially by private donations and a contingent of volunteers, celebrates the heritage of small craft before the advent of fiberglass. Of the 75 vintage and replica wooden rowing and sailing boats in the collection, more than half are available for public use. Admission is always free. Rentals range from $8 to $25 an hour. Lessons in sailing, traditional woodworking, and boat building are offered for all ages.

Frye Art Museum
704 Terry Ave, 622-9250
(map: N3)
Every day

FREE Although the Frye primarily showcases weighty 19th-century European salon paintings from the collection of the late Charles and Emma Frye, this spacious gallery is gradually including more contemporary work. Its tastes, however, remain conservative. The collection includes paintings by three generations of Wyeths and contemporary nonnative Alaskan art. Admission is always free. The Frye sponsors the annual juried Puget Sound Area Exhibition.

Henry Art Gallery
University of Washington,
543-2280 (map: FF6)
Tues-Sun

This small, architecturally distinguished gallery on the southwestern edge of the UW campus has rotating exhibits that range from modern Chinese painting to African ritual objects. Northwest artists are often featured. The Henry's permanent collection is strong in 19th- and 20th-century paintings and prints, textiles, and ceramics. Admission is $4 for adults (UW students and faculty get in free). Carefully organized shows.

Museum of Flight
9404 E Marginal Way S,
764-5720 (map: KK6)
Every day

See Major Attractions in the Exploring chapter.

Museum of History and Industry
2700 24th Ave E,
324-1125 (map: FF6)
Every day

KIDS The amiable MOHAI is a huge repository of Americana (especially with the recent expansion of its Northwest Americana library). The collection of memorabilia and artifacts pertaining to the history of the Pacific Northwest includes a 1920s Boeing mail plane and an all-new exhibit on the great Seattle fire of 1889. Kids will enjoy the antique cars and marine equipment. Additional rotating exhibits are shown throughout the year. Admission is $3 for adults, $1.50 for kids. **FREE** Free on Tuesdays.

Nordic Heritage Museum
3014 NW 67th St,
789-5707 (map: EE9)
Tues-Sun

This museum, located in Scandinavian Ballard, focuses on the history of Nordic settlers in the United States, with rooms devoted to each of the Scandinavian countries. Exhibits include photographs, maritime equipment, costumes, and other memorabilia—anything from the sublime to the silly. Holidays often bring special events to the museum. Admission is $2.50 for adults, $1.50 for children.

Seattle Art Museum
E Prospect St and 14th
Ave E, 625-8901
(map: GG6)
Tues-Sun

See Major Attractions in the Exploring chapter.

Seattle Children's Museum
Center House, Seattle
Center, 441-1768

KIDS This imaginative learning center, located on the fountain level of the busy Center House, stresses participation in hands-on activities and exploration of other

(map: B6)
Tues-Sun

cultural traditions. The museum has several permanent features, including a Playcenter, a Neighborhood, and a soap bubble area. The variety of special programs— Mexican folk dancing, Native American games, Chinese storytelling, Japanese kite making—is impressive. The Imagination Station features a different artist every month guiding activities with various materials. Admission is $3.

Wing Luke Asian Museum
417 7th Ave S, 623-5124
(map: R6)
Tues-Sun

The Wing Luke museum is named after Seattle's first Chinese-American city councilman, who died in a plane crash in 1965. This sparkling little museum in the International District is devoted to the Asian-American experience in the United States, and the Northwest in particular. Rotating exhibits include art, antiques, and artifacts from Asian cultures and work by Asian-American artists. Excellent gift shop. Admission is $2.50 for adults, $1 for students and seniors. **FREE** Free on Thursdays.

MUSIC SERIES

Seattle has a thriving classical music scene and is quickly developing the kind of musical offerings worthy of a major city. The symphony and opera have entered the big leagues in recent years, and chamber music has become a local passion. Seattle is also a regular stop for major performers on tour.

Lately, the lack of performance space for the growing number of musical groups is becoming an uncomfortable problem. The Seattle Symphony is busily trying to raise money to construct an acoustically perfect concert hall, as the Seattle Opera House is booked almost every day of the year. The smaller orchestras, such as the Northwest Chamber Orchestra, are searching for an adaptable small space so that their musicians can have some continuity between rehearsal and performance. The following series continue to flourish despite this dearth of venues.

Early Music Guild
325-7066

The Early Music Guild is credited with making Seattle a center of early music performance, and has enjoyed great success as pre-baroque music becomes more and more popular. Its International Series consists of five concerts of medieval, Renaissance, baroque, and early classical music, and features top international players and ensembles, some playing instruments as old as the music. The organization also sponsors performances by local musicians.

International Chamber Music Series
Meany Hall, University of Washington, 543-4880 (map: FF6)

This six-concert series has featured such chamber-music legends as the Guarneri String Quartet and the Beaux Arts Trio, as well as rising stars such as the Emerson String Quartet and the Golub-Kaplan-Carr Trio. These popular concerts are scheduled fall through spring.

Ladies Musical Club International Artist Series
Meany Hall, University of Washington, 728-6411 (map: FF6)

Kreisler, Rachmaninoff, Horowitz, and an astounding roster of other musical giants have performed in this series since its inception in 1900. The annual series of five recitals has shifted its focus from big names and prize-winning musicians to up-and-coming young artists. You'll say you heard them here first. Performances are held at either Meany or Kane halls.

Marzena Performance Ensemble
Nippon Kan Theater, 628 S Washington St, 364-1856 (map: P6)

Its full name is the Marzena Performance Ensemble for Contemporary and Ethno-Music, Dance, Drama, and the Visual Arts, and as it suggests, it doesn't leave anything out. This ambitious group picks up where the bulk of Seattle's music scene leaves off, featuring contemporary classical and ethnic music combined with every discipline possible. For the time being, the group's own series has been telescoped into the Seattle Spring Festival of Contemporary Music, adding a variety of local, national, and international artists to the program. Since its inception four years ago, Marzena has attracted a small but devoted following.

Northwest Chamber Orchestra
343-0445

The NWCO, the only professional chamber orchestra in the region, was experiencing financial and artistic troubles, but recently it has tightened up its act. Under the new leadership of conductor Sidney Harth, the reestablished orchestra may find the musical focus it previously lacked. The orchestra presents a subscription series and special concerts, including the October baroque festival "Bach by Popular Demand." Performance locations vary.

Philadelphia String Quartet
527-8839

The mainstay of the Philadelphia String Quartet's popularity is undoubtedly the Olympic Music Festival, a series of summer concerts (with guest artists) held on a pastoral 40-acre farm on the Olympic Peninsula. Otherwise, the quartet—based in Seattle since 1966—doesn't have much of a following in the city. Some say that, due to frequent personnel turnover, the group hasn't been able to develop the synergy that comes

MUSIC SERIES

from playing together for a long time. But listening to classical music while reclining on a bale of hay *is* fun.

Santa Fe Chamber Music Festival in Seattle
Meany Hall, University of Washington,
622-1392 (map: FF6)

Santa Fe, the cream of the chamber music festivals, visits Seattle every August for one week of glorious music. The performers are fresh from Santa Fe's own festival, so this is relaxed, well-rehearsed music making. Regulars have included such distinguished musicians as violinist Ani Kavafian and the Mendelssohn String Quartet. The festival includes master classes and open rehearsals, and it features a different American composer-in-residence each year. The festival now extends itself into other seasons as well, with a touring "festival favorite" in the spring and a Music of the Americas concert in the fall at the Moore Theater.

Seattle Camerata
443-1026

Seattle Camerata presents three concert series that "put the chamber back into chamber music." Camerata Concerts feature nationally acclaimed chamber ensembles in such romantic venues as historic mansions, museums, and libraries. The Cafe Concerts series in fall and spring consists of local ensembles performing in intimate after-work concerts at Italia (1010 Western Avenue); the new Camerata Presents series features more formal, full-length evening concerts at the Nippon Kan Theater.

Seattle Chamber Music Festival
Lakeside School, 14050
1st Ave NE, 328-5606
(map: CC7)

Founded by University of Washington cello professor Toby Saks, this popular summer series is a showcase of local and international talent. The performances are spirited and often exceptional. Grace notes include preperformance dining on the lawn (bring your own picnic or buy a catered meal) and a minirecital before each concert. The acoustics in St. Nicholas Hall are only so-so, but for a gracious summer evening, you can't do better. This festival is almost always sold out.

Seattle Symphony
443-4747 (map: A6)

This granddaddy of the Seattle classical music scene has been a barometer of the city's growing stature in the music world. Under Maestro Gerard Schwarz, the 90-member symphony has reached a new level of consistency and artistic mastery and has gained recognition through tours and recordings. Schwarz has initiated several successful series—including Basically Baroque, Mainly Mozart, and the American Music Series—since he took the helm in 1984, so there's a package for every kind of music lover. Also worth noting is the symphony's Discover Music Series, one-hour concerts designed to introduce children to various themes in classical music, combined with attention-holding performances. Concerts are usually held in the 3,000-seat Opera House in Seattle Center or at the Moore Theater.

Seattle Youth Symphony
Opera House, Seattle Center, 362-2300 (map: A6)

One of the premier youth orchestras in the country, the Seattle Youth Symphony flourished for 28 years under the baton of Vilem Sokol, who retired in 1988. His successor is Ruben Gurevich, an Uruguayan-born conductor and violinist formerly based in California. Seattle's loyalties still seem to be divided between the old and the new conductors, but the main attraction is still the orchestra. These talented young musicians are usually dazzling with even the most demanding works.

OPERA

Seattle Opera
Opera House, Seattle Center, 443-4711 (map: A6)

The Seattle Opera has become a top-flight company under the leadership of Speight Jenkins, general director since 1983. Mounting a well-balanced program of five full-scale operas every season, the company also stages internationally acclaimed summer festival presentations, among them Wagner's *Ring* cycle and other large-scale works. The Seattle Opera's mostly sellout audiences have come to expect fresh and innovative productions.

THEATER

Theater is Seattle's liveliest art. In any given week, you might choose between a Broadway musical, a new performance art piece, a zany comedy, or a classic—done straight or with a time-warp twist. In Seattle biggest doesn't necessarily mean best, and the line between professional and gifted amateur is never distinct, so don't be afraid to experiment. For far-out—or just beyond the mainstream—theater, there are a number of smaller organizations producing a great deal of quality work. The LOFT (League of Fringe Theaters) Hotline, 637-7373, provides up-to-date information on performances, auditions, and workshops.

A Contemporary Theatre
100 W Roy St, 285-5110 (map: GG8)

ACT, which opens in May when the Rep is just about to shut down, sticks mainly to contemporary plays, particularly by young American and English playwrights.

More adventurous musicals are also an ACT specialty. The season always closes with *A Christmas Carol*, a Seattle tradition. The small auditorium (450 seats) and thrust stage are just right for intimate dramas, but the company plans to move to a new, two-theater downtown space at Second Avenue and Pike Street in early 1992.

Bathhouse Theatre Company
7312 W Green Lake Dr N, 524-9108 (map: EE7)

Arne Zaslove's talented Equity players pay offbeat homage to Shakespeare (*Macbeth* set as an early-19th-century western, for example), along with contemporaries, original musicals, and other classics, in a remodeled 1928 bathhouse on the shores of Green Lake. The five-play season runs February through December.

The Empty Space Theatre
107 Occidental Ave S, 467-6000 (map: EE7)

Small and widely noted, this group specializes in the new and out-of-the-ordinary but also presents stripped-down classics and works in translation. Many of the prominent names in Seattle theater cut their teeth here in the 1970s, during the Empty Space's hippest and most provocative years, and the theater remains a major forum for local playwrights. The six-play season runs October through summer in this 158-seat space.

The Group Theatre Company
The Ethnic Theater, 3940 Brooklyn Ave NE, 543-4327 (map: FF6)

Seattle's only theater group with a social agenda takes on such heavyweight subjects as apartheid, Central American politics, and developmentally disabled adults. Fortunately, that doesn't stop some of its shows from being great fun, too. There are five main-stage productions, September through June, in the 200-seat Ethnic Theater. Annual events include *Voices of Christmas*, a collection of sketches and personal stories illustrating how different people celebrate the holidays, and the annual Multi-Cultural Playwrights Festival in summer.

Intiman Theatre Company
Intiman Playhouse, Seattle Center, 626-0782 (map: A6)

Intiman focuses on both classics and thematically serious contemporary works in the recently renovated 424-seat Playhouse at the Seattle Center. Season runs May through November. Late night Fridays and Saturdays are reserved for the improv comedy theater group Theatersports (781-9273).

New City Theatre
1634 11th Ave, 323-6800 (map: HH6)

The New City Theatre on Capitol Hill offers a smorgasbord; it is a venue for performance art and unusual cabaret acts as well as straight plays. The season is practically year-round. Special performances include an annual juried directors festival and playwrights festival. The weekly New City Late Night Club, an eclectic variety show of new works—comedy, video, music, you name it—is the big rage in town (admission is *really* low). Theater Zero features work by young artists.

On the Boards
Washington Hall
Performance Gallery, 153
14th Ave, 467-8121

See Dance in this chapter.

Seattle Children's Theatre
PONCHO Theater, N
50th St and Fremont Ave
N, 633-4567 (map: EE7)

KIDS The nationally admired Seattle Children's Theatre, in the 280-seat PONCHO Theater at Woodland Park, draws almost equal numbers of adults and children with its innovative and often very sophisticated productions. The six-play season (September through June) features everything from fairy tales and classics to newly commissioned contemporary plays. Every run includes two shows with interpreters for the hearing impaired.

Seattle Gilbert and
Sullivan Society
Bagley Wright Theater,
Seattle Center, 322-8682
(map: A6)

The Gilbert and Sullivan Society produces one show per year (*Princess Ida* in 1990) in a 12-performance run in July. The cast and orchestra are volunteer performers who put on very professional productions (usually sellouts). If G & S is your cup of tea, these are said to be among the best productions in the country.

Seattle Repertory Theatre
Bagley Wright Theater,
Seattle Center, 443-2222
(map: A6)

The Rep is the oldest and biggest show in town, with a six-play, October-through-May season in the striking 856-seat Bagley Wright Theater. Under artistic director Dan Sullivan, the Rep's repertory is a blend of classic and modern, including world premieres and Broadway plays. Production values are invariably first-rate, sets spectacular. A concurrent Stage 2 season in the intimate PONCHO Forum consists of three plays.

University of Washington
School of Drama
University of Washington,
543-4880 (map: FF6)

The university's student productions are a good bet for both classics and contemporary plays—and a bargain, too ($4 to $7 a ticket). Productions by graduate students in the Professional Actor Training Program generally range from Shakespeare to Shaw: thesis productions by students of directing and stage production tend to be more avant-garde. The UW uses three campus theaters for drama—the Meany Studio Theater, Glenn Hughes Playhouse, and Penthouse Theater. The 11-play season runs late fall until June.

EXPLORING

EXPLORING CONTENTS

MAJOR ATTRACTIONS

DOWNTOWN

Between 1st Ave and 9th Ave, Yesler Way and Lenora St (map: H9–N9)

Seattle's recent growth has wrought visible changes throughout the city, but nowhere are they more apparent than in the downtown district. Downtown lies between the industrial sector south of the Kingdome and the Denny Regrade north of Lenora Street. Although many of the new office towers in the **Commercial Core** are corporate behemoths of the any-city style, hints of postmodernism are bringing the district an exciting new look. Two notable examples are the **Washington Mutual Tower** (Third Avenue and Seneca Street), with its hypnotic blue facade that reflects the day's changing light, and **Pacific First Centre** (Fifth Avenue and Pike Street), which elegantly dominates the Fifth Avenue skyline. Its light-filled lobby contains freestanding architectural ornaments, engaging chandeliers, and delightful glass sculptures. Three floors of exclusive shops, including Gucci's, provide excellent browsing, and the Palomino bistro tastefully drapes over both sides of the third floor escalator.

Towering above everything else is the 76-story **Columbia Center** (Fourth Avenue and Columbia Street). For a grand view, visit the observation platform on the 73rd floor. Check in with the security desk in the lobby ($3.50 adults, $1.75 children and seniors, weekdays only).

Five bus stations of the new **Transit Tunnel** opened in late 1990 to ease Seattle's menacing downtown traffic problem. Each station is a showcase of underground urban glamour. The controversial tunnel is outfitted with rails for future adaptation to a light-rail system.

The **Washington State Convention and Trade Center** (Eighth Avenue and Pike Street), a mammoth, glass-enclosed building, sprawls atop 12 lanes of expressway. Adjoining the complex is **Freeway Park** (Sixth Avenue and Seneca Street), one of Seattle's most original outdoor spaces. This extraordinary park forms a lid over thundering I-5—a feat of urban park innovation when it was constructed in 1976. Here, amid grassy "plateaus" and rushing waterfall "canyons," the roar of traffic disappears, and lunchtime brown-baggers find rejuvenating solace. Nearby, the new **Two Union Square** building (Sixth Avenue and Union Street) echoes the rhythm of Freeway Park with a courtyard and waterfall of its own. Also joining the army of serious architectural towers in the commercial district is the new 62-story **AT&T Gateway Tower** (Fifth Avenue and Cherry Street).

The **Retail Core** lies basically between Third and Sixth avenues from Stewart Street to University Street. Few cities of Seattle's size do a better job of retaining a large, spiffy, varied retail center—anchored by the big department stores (**Frederick & Nelson** at Fifth Avenue and Pine Street; **The Bon Marché** at Fourth Avenue and Pine Street; **I. Magnin** at Sixth Avenue and Pine Street; and the flagship **Nordstrom** at Fifth Avenue and Pine Street) and augmented by high-quality boutique enclaves (**Westlake Center** at Fifth Avenue and Pine Street and **Century Square** at Fourth Avenue and Pine Streets). Strings of smaller shops proceed up Fourth and Fifth avenues to **Rainier Square** (Fourth Avenue and Union

Street), an elegant three-story atrium at the base of the bank tower. Across University Street to the south is the **Four Seasons Olympic Hotel** (Fourth Avenue and University Street), the noble grand dame of Seattle hostelry, girded all about with boutiques of international pedigree. High tea in the Olympic's **Garden Court** (621-1700) or a Parisian lunch at Rainier Square's **Crêpe de Paris** (623-4111) make very civilized breaks while shopping.

Another retail district runs along First Avenue. At its north end is famous **Pike Place Market** (see listing in this section), which is spreading its retail tentacles southward along First and Western avenues toward Pioneer Square. **Waterfront Place** (First Avenue and Post Alley between Madison and Seneca streets) forms a centerpiece of shops, offices, and restaurants that surround the exquisite **Alexis Hotel**. This once blighted part of town is becoming a bastion of sophisticated urban retail—a reputation that will likely be enhanced by the opening in December 1991 of the downtown **Seattle Art Museum** in its stylish Robert Venturi–designed building (First Avenue and University Street; see review in this section).

PIKE PLACE MARKET

Pike St to Virginia St on Pike Pl (map: J7–I8)
Information: 1st Ave and Pike Pl, 682-7453

KIDS FREE If cities have souls, then Pike Place Market is Seattle's. It opened as an experiment in August of 1907, as a response to the demands of angry housewives who were tired of high food prices padded by middlemen. Bringing farmers and consumers together proved to be immensely successful, and soon fishmongers and shopkeepers joined the farmers' wagons along Pike Place. Later, the Market fell victim to supermarkets, hard times, and urban decay. Downtown developers planned to tear it down in the 1960s, but Seattle voters blocked the scheme, and in 1971 the Market was designated a 7-acre historical district. Since then, with generous federal urban renewal funds, the old buildings have gradually been restored. In the early '80s, the Pike Place Preservation and Development Authority, which owned the Market, ran out of money to complete the renovation and sought private investors to finish it. But in 1989 the deal turned sour. The investors demanded a higher return, and threatened to replace the PDA as manager. The PDA insisted it had sold only tax breaks, not authority over the Market. At press time, they were fighting it out in court, and the tomatoes are still in the stands.

So, despite relentless gentrification of the area, the oldest continuously operating farmers market in the United States still prides itself on being an incubator for small businesses—"the biggest mom 'n' pop store in town"—and no national or regional chain stores or franchise businesses are allowed. The Market's future, however, is now on unstable ground. Nearly 90 local farmers have permits to sell their produce at day stalls, over 250 permanent businesses operate there year-round, and about 200 craftspeople and artists sell handmade wares. The Market is open every day from early May to the end of December, and Monday through Saturday the rest of the year.

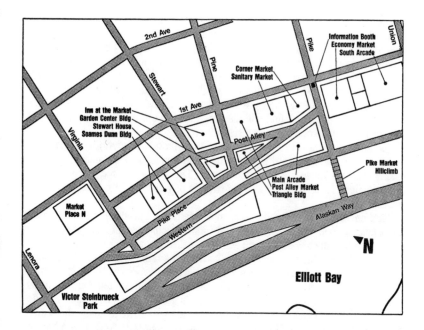

The people of the Market, the occupants of this "museum of humanity," are the main attraction—old seadogs who reminisce about the Market's lusty past; the boisterous Italian produce vendors who bark at the passersby; "Mae West," the beercan-hat lady; the street musicians, puppeteers, and mimes who turn the street corners into stages. The way to "do" the Market is to spend an unstructured day meandering its crannies, nibbling from its astonishing variety of ethnic and regional foods, browsing the shops, watching the people. If you visit before 9am you can watch the place come alive as the farmers set up; in spring and summer, shopping is best done (once most of the farmers have come) early on Saturday mornings. There's not much nightlife here, although many restaurants stay open in the evenings.

The starting point of your excursion will probably be determined by where you can find parking. It's almost impossible to get a space on Pike Place—don't even try, it's too congested—so splurge for a space in the new 550-slot parking garage on Western, with its elevator that opens directly into the Market. Or try one of the lots a little farther down Western Avenue, or First Avenue to the north.

The official entrance is at the corner of First Avenue and Pike Street, at the **Information Booth** (First Avenue and Pike Place, 682-7453), where you can pick up a map, advice on sights, or a self-guided tour pamphlet. **Read All About It** (624-0140), the Market's newsstand and official gossip station, anchors this busy corner, as does **DeLaurenti** (622-0141), the quintessential Italian deli, still run by an old-time Market family. To the south is the **South Arcade**, home to the upscale shops and condos that have spread forth from the historical district. Walking the other way, down the covered corridor, past artists' stalls and vegetable stands, you'll come to the elbow of the L-shaped Market. This is the start of the **Main Arcade**—the famous Pike Place Market sign is just above you—the most authentic area of the market, the most crowded, and home of the big bronze pig, which makes as good a meeting spot as any for folks with connections to make. Look down: the floor tiles under your shoes were part of a fund-raising project in 1986, when a $35 donation bought a person a little bit of immortality in the form of an engraved tile. Ronald and Nancy Reagan have one (they didn't have to pay), and outside DeLaurenti you'll find one tile for each of the prime numbers under 100, paid for by the wife of a mathematician.

The stairs lead down to the bowels of the Market, a labyrinth of shops and more offbeat enterprises. Funky clothes, old comic books, "junque" jewelry, talking parrots—these are the enticements. The shops become more upscale if you make it as far as the **Pike Market Hillclimb**, which leads to Western Avenue and the waterfront.

Back in the Main Arcade are more farmers: produce vendors called "highstallers," with beautifully arranged (don't touch) international produce; and local farmers at the low stalls, who sell seasonal, regional produce—local berries, sweet onions, Washington apples—direct from the farm. You'll likely pass some Market veterans along here: highstaller Dan Manzo, who was "born in a lettuce crate"; unofficial Market matriarch Pasqualina Verdi (who will tell you with Italian flair and authority how to cook the mustard greens you just bought); Indo-Chinese refugee farmers selling bok choy and other Asian vegetables; the "honey man" and the "herb lady." In the midst of this, on your left, don't miss a Market institution: **The Athenian** (624-7166), a smoky, working-class cafe that's been the favorite haunt of Market old-timers since 1909. The down-home food is OK, but the real draws are the marvelous view of Elliott Bay and the longest beer list in these parts.

In summer, the artists' and craftspeople's tables stretch down Pike Place to Virginia Street and **Victor Steinbrueck Park**, the splash of green that marks the northern border of the Market (see Parks and Beaches in this chapter). You're on a very fashionable corner here: **Cutters Bayhouse** (2001 Western Avenue, 448-4884) is the trendy, viewy restaurant just north (standing room only during the after-work stampede); exquisite, stylish **Cafe Sport** (2020 Western Avenue, 443-6000) is across the street; the **Market Place North Condominiums** are where the upwardly mobile live, the **Seattle Club** (2020 Western Avenue, 443-1111) downstairs is where they get fit. Cross Pike Place near **Pike and Western Wine Merchants** (441-1307) (where you can choose a good vintage for your crab picnic) and head back south past **Peerless** (it is) **Pie** (443-1801). If you wander inside this building, called the **Soames-Dunn**, you'll discover shops and ethnic eateries leading to a shady courtyard in the back. Here you'll find covered tables for **Emmett Watson's Oyster Bar** (448-7721), a folksy seafood joint named after the infamous Seattle journalist and raconteur. On a nice day, a cold beer and a half-dozen tiny Olympia oysters on the half-shell taste wonderful.

If you were to take a short detour here, up the wooden stairs to **Post Alley**, you'd find two of the gems of the ethnic restaurant scene in Seattle: the funky, likable trattoria/cabaret called **The Pink Door** (443-3241) (no sign, just a pink door); and **Kells** (728-1916), a rough-hewn Irish pub. Follow Post Alley on to where it meets Pike Place at the Sanitary Market; you'll pass **DeGraff Books** (441-0688), a good general bookstore, and **Cafe Dilettante** (728-0144), a branch of Seattle's famous chocolatier in the block of Post Alley just below the stylish, 65-room **Inn at the Market** (443-3600), Pike Place Market's only hotel. In the next block you'll pass the see-and-be-seen sipping bar at **SBC Coffee** (467-7700) and the entrance to an array of shops and eating places—including a very good regional gift shop, **Made in Washington** (467-0788)—in the somewhat more sterile arcade of the **Post Alley Market Building**. The upper reaches of this building contain a cluster of shops along First Avenue; down below, a passageway forms a back door to the colorful Sanitary Market. Here Post Alley disappears for a while as it crosses Pike Place, but you could meet up with it again in the hidden lower level of the Market elbow, by the classy, dimly lit Italian restaurant/bar **Il Bistro** (682-3049) and the arty **Market Theater**(382-1171), and follow it all the way to its terminus near Pioneer Square.

Back in the Soames-Dunn courtyard, take the door leading to the **Stewart House**, a renovated 1902 workingmen's hotel that's now used for low-income housing and commerce. Your path curves back around, past **Totem Smokehouse** (443-1710) (where you pick up smoked salmon or arrange to ship it home) and back onto Pike Place. Try to make it past the alluring aromas wafting onto the sidewalk from **Le Panier** (441-3669), the French bakery on the corner, and head for the **Seattle Garden Center** (448-0431), which stocks many hard-to-find bulbs and seeds. As you pass, note the premodernist, peach-colored, Art Deco structure that also houses **Sur La Table** (448-2244), a cook's emporium (and singularly bad place to find yourself in an earthquake). Continue on, past the **Triangle Building**—(stopping, perhaps, for a shoeshine at **Johnson's Shoe Repair**, 623-6542)—to the **Sanitary Market**, so named because horses were not allowed inside. This is an atmospheric, chaotic jumble of produce stands and eating places, including the delicious wares at the **Pike Place Market Creamery** (622-5029); **Jack's Fish Spot** (467-0514), which sells steaming cups of cioppino from an outdoor bar; and the **Three Girls Bakery** (622-1045), where the line for take-out sandwiches and chocolate macaroons might curl onto the sidewalk. Up the skylit staircase in the back is a shortcut to First Avenue and its string of vintage clothing, jewelry, and fashion stores.

Next door, to the south, is the last building in the historic stretch: the **Corner Market**, a picturesque structure of careful brickwork and arched windows that houses produce and flower stalls. There are a couple of restaurant finds hidden in its upper reaches: **Cafe Counter Intelligence** (622-6979), fine for breakfast and a lingering latte, and **Chez Shea** (467-9990), a pricey little restaurant and the most romantic nook in town.

PIONEER SQUARE

Jackson St to Columbia St along 1st Ave (map: 09–M8)

Pioneer Square, just south of the present downtown, has undergone several transformations since its days as an Indian village ("little crossing place"). Whites settled there in 1852 (after abandoning windswept Alki in present West Seattle), and the city flourished on the crest of the timber boom and the Alaska Yukon gold rush. The Pioneer Square seen today is not the original architecture, however: the entire core of the town was razed in the great fire of 1889 and rebuilt according to more architecturally coherent—and less flammable—standards.

Pioneer Square went into a long decline after the 1920s when "downtown" moved northward. It became an art gallery center in the 1960s, survived a proposal to turn it into parking lots and glass towers, and was declared a historic district in the early 1970s. Today it is one of the few extensive and stylistically consistent "old towns" in the nation, abounding in bookstores, gift shops, art galleries, antique shops, exotic rug stores, and nightclubs. Lawyers, architects, and media folk dominate the work force, while homeless transients fill the streets, drawn by a preponderance of missions (and park benches).

The real Pioneer Square, actually a triangle on the corner of First Avenue and Yesler Way, is adorned by a Victorian iron and glass pergola (a turn-of-the-century holdover from the days when trolley cars serviced this district) and a Tlingit Indian totem pole. Facing the square is the **Pioneer Building**, one of the most elaborate works of the post-fire reconstruction. It houses offices, a maze of antique shops on the lower level, and the headquarters of the **Underground Tour**, a touristy, subterranean prowl through the original streets of downtown (see Organized Tours in this chapter). On the sidewalk in front of **Merchants Cafe** (109 Yesler Way, 624-1515), Seattle's oldest restaurant, is a dandy shutterbug view of the **Smith Tower**, built in 1914 and distinguished for years as the tallest building west of the Mississippi. You can take the elevator up to the tower's 35th-floor observation deck to get the lay of the land. If you meander waterward you'll find a tasty breakfast or a late-night dinner at **Trattoria Mitchelli** (84 Yesler Way, 623-3883), an unofficial Pioneer Square landmark, open until 4am.

First Avenue is the main, tree-lined artery through the historic district, intersected by streets that terminate at the **waterfront** a block west. Heading south you'll see the **Northwest Gallery of Fine Woodworking** (202 First Avenue S, 625-0542), with its continually changing exhibits of exquisite handcrafted furniture and wood sculptures. **FireWorks Gallery** (210 First Avenue S, 682-8707) is another decor gallery, with beautifully crafted pottery. On the same block is the **Grand Central Arcade**, with two levels of tony, upscale retail—a far cry from its original function as a skid road, later row (you're in the district, incidentally, for which that term was invented) hotel. This block comes alive on weekend nights, as the restaurants on its west side metamorphose into jumping nightclubs.

Across Main Street is the **Elliott Bay Book Company** (First Avenue S and S Main Street, 624-6600), perhaps the finest bookstore in the Northwest and an authentic reflection of the artistic/literary sensibilities of this raw and stylish district. There's a cafe in its basement where browsers can eat quiche, sip coffee, and read their purchases. **Grand Central Mercantile** (316 First Avenue S, 623-8894), a quality kitchen emporium, and the whimsical **Wood Shop** (320 First Avenue S, 624-1763) are a couple of other worthy stops along this stretch.

West on Jackson Street is **Merrill Place**, Pioneer Square's high-rent district. Once Schwabacher's Hardware, the revitalized building conceals an enclave of apartments and **Il Terrazzo Carmine** (411 First Avenue S, 467-7797), an esteemed Italian restaurant with a romantic bar and terrace view of a fountain below. The **Empty Space Theater** has a home right across the street. If you retrace your steps eastward on Jackson you'll come to **Occidental Avenue South**, a sun-dappled, brick-lined pedestrian walkway studded with galleries. The first Thursday of every month this mall—indeed, all of Pioneer Square—fills up with art- (and scene-) appreciators who turn out for **FREE First Thursday Gallery Walks**, when galleries stay open late to preview new shows and serve refreshments. You can pause for a nosh at the chic, high-character Italian coffee bar **Torrefazione Italia** (320 Occidental Avenue S, 624-5773), or some tapas and perhaps an impromptu flamenco performance at **Cafe Felipe** (303 Occidental Avenue S, 622-1619).

Look southward from here, and you can't miss the 74,000-seat **Kingdome** (Fourth Avenue and S King Street, 296-3128), hailed by some as fine brutalist design, lambasted by others as Seattle's oversized cement orange-juice squeezer. Either way you look at it, you might enjoy a tour of the inside of this skyline-hogger ($2.50 for adults, $1.25 for kids)—its stratospheric reaches, its press box, and its colorful sports museum—which is offered three times daily in summer. **F.X. McRory's Steak, Chop and Oyster** (and bourbon) **House** (419 Occidental Avenue S, 623-4800) is the restaurant and watering hole of choice for gamegoers, a madhouse after Seahawks and Mariners victories.

Look up through the trees at the corner of Occidental and Main for a unique and nostalgic perspective on the heights of Seattle development, old and new: the **Smith Tower standing (from this angle) taller than the sleek black rise of one of the West Coast's tallest buildings, the Columbia Center.** Up a block, Occidental Avenue South segues into **Occidental Park**, a Northwest attempt at a Parisian park setting with cobblestones, plane trees, and park benches enough to accommodate all the street dwellers. The international feeling is enhanced by the occasional horse-drawn buggy or rickshawlike pedicab that breezes by. A more interesting park is tucked into a corner of Second Avenue: **Waterfall Gardens** (219 Second Avenue), where a (man-made) waterfall spills over large rocks in a cool urban grotto—a fine place for a picnic lunch.

WATERFRONT/SEATTLE AQUARIUM
Main St to Broad St along Alaskan Way (map: O9–D9)

Seattle's heart has always been in Elliott Bay, the lovely, deep harbor around which the city grew. After Puget Sound was discovered and named in 1792 by Captain George Vancouver, it gained a reputation as one of the world's most navigable ocean inlets, and Seattle became its dominant port of call. The city's dreams of commercial success have been intimately connected with its maritime access: first as a shipping point for logs, wheat, and coal, then as the outfitting base for the Alaska and Yukon gold rushes, and now as the Port contends with California for trade with the Pacific Rim countries.

Today the downtown waterfront is mostly a tourist boardwalk, the shipping piers having been relocated to the north and south ends of the harbor. The strip is lined with kitschy souvenir shops, harbor-tour operations, and endless fish 'n' chips counters—a layout that will soon be replaced by the new Waterfront Plan. A pedestrian promenade, maritime museum, world conference/trade center, and short-stay moorage marina are all part of the grand scheme. Until then, the waterfront is still a worthy attraction and a fine place for an invigorating, sea-gazing stroll.

At the south end of the strip is **Pier 48** (foot of Main Street), home of the for-mer Stena Line ferry which ran between Seattle and Victoria, BC, which at press time was up for sale. The waterfront side of the pier has an excellent interpretive display of the harbor's history and periscopes offering grand seaward views. Up the street is the city's main ferry terminal, **Colman Dock** (foot of Marion Street at Pier 52), where boats depart for Bremerton, Bainbridge Island, and Vashon (see Transportation in the Essentials chapter).

Just north, at Pier 54, are a couple of Seattle's most endearing landmarks. **Ye Olde Curiosity Shop** (682-5844) displays an unabashedly zany collection of odd-ities, knickknacks, and miscellaneous Northwestiana of the giant-clams-and-shrunken-heads ilk. **Ivar's Acres of Clams** (624-6852), with its breezy outdoor fish bar, was the first in a diverse local chain of seafood eateries for notorious raconteur, Seattle booster, friend to artists, and ace fish hustler Ivar Haglund. Though the fried fish may be the least appealing of his many legacies, this place is worth a stop for a cup of clam nectar, a whiff of salt air, and a scenic outlook.

Wade through the thick of the tourist boardwalk to the waterfront's main draw, the compact, well-designed **Seattle Aquarium** (Pier 59, 386-4320, open daily, adults $4.50, teens $2.50, 6- to 12-year-olds $1.75). There are illuminated dis-plays and convincing re-creations of coastal and intertidal ecosystems. In a domed room, you're surrounded by a tank in which sharks, snapper, octopi, salmon, and other Puget Sound inhabitants whisk by. Finally, you follow a salmon ladder to a marvelous topside vista of Elliott Bay and the superstars of the Aquarium: the cavorting seals (real hams) and the playful sea otters. The **Omnidome Theater** (622-1868), with its dramatic cinema-in-the-round looks at nature's spectacles, is also in the building.

In the fall of 1990 the privately run **Puget Sound Express** on **Pier 56** began reg-ular runs from Port Townsend to Seattle (and back) with weekday stops in King-ston (see listing in the Essentials chapter). Just north on **Pier 66**, home of the Port of Seattle's offices and several fish-packing enterprisesion to make room for the goodies of the future Waterfront Plan, at which time the Port offices will join the popular *Victoria Clipper* (see Ferries under Transportation in the Essentials chapter) in **Pier 69**. Next door is **Pier 70**, a picturesque barn of a pier—the most organized commercial/retail enterprise in the strip—with award-winning views.

Last comes **Myrtle Edwards Park** (see the Parks and Beaches section of this chapter). Here you can hop aboard the waterfront trolley for a ride on a quaint, old streetcar that runs along Alaskan Way to Main Street with several stops in be-tween, a 15-minute, 55 cent ride. Consider getting off at the Aquarium and cross-ing Alaskan Way for an ascent of the **Pike Market Hillclimb**, a jolly succession of shops and eateries that links the Pike Place Market with the waterfront—via end-less stairs.

Looking for a particular place? Check the index at the back of this book for individ-ual restaurants, hotels, B&Bs, shops, bars, parks, museums, galleries, neighbor-hoods, messenger services, nightclubs, and more.

FERRY TO BAINBRIDGE ISLAND

Riding a ferry is the best way to catch the sea breeze and Seattle's skyline and to get a feel for the accessibility and grandeur of Puget Sound. There's one (or more) leaving every hour from **Pier 52** (foot of Marion Street) to **Winslow on Bainbridge Island** (see Ferries under Transportation in the Essentials chapter). If you walk aboard and stay on for the round trip, you can get a hearty dose of wind in your hair and salt on your face inside an hour and a half. Or make a stop-off in Winslow and spend part of the day exploring the island's commercial center and ferry stop.

If you time your visit right, you can walk off the ferry and up Winslow Way to the **Streamliner Diner** (397 Winslow Way E, 842-8595), whose steamed-up windows beckon you in for brunches of home-fried potatoes and salsa omelets. A little farther on, imbibers can head for the estimable home branch of **Pegasus Espresso** (131 Parfitt Way SW, 842-3113) for coffee, or the deck of **The Saltwater Cafe** (403 Madison Avenue S, 842-8339) for a beer (skip the food, it's overpriced and merely passable). Shops line Winslow Way back to the ferry dock.

With a little more time you can take a deeper approach to the island. At once rural and suburban, Bainbridge is both a developer's bonanza and a recluse's dream, an odd mix of moneyed landowners who are in it for the view and the waterfront property and dreamy utopians wanting nothing more than their piece of the forest. One way to get a feel for the charming duality of the island (and still leave your car on the mainland) is to catch one of the **Kitsap ParaTransit** buses (1-800-422-2877), which meet all commuter ferries (call to arrange pickups during the day). For 25 cents you can take in the scenic ride as the school bus–like vehicle deposits residents at various stops around the island. It's probably a little more fun to take your car so you're guaranteed to hit the island's highlights: **Fay Bainbridge State Park** on the island's northeast corner (see Parks and Beaches in this chapter); **Fort Ward**, a prime spot for hikes and picnics; **Lynwood Center**, the island's lesser commercial enclave with Bainbridge's only movie theater and the **Four Swallows**, an excellent pub and eatery; the 150-acre **Bloedel Reserve** (be sure to make reservations: 842-7631); and **FREE Bainbridge Island Winery** (682 State Highway 305, 842-WINE), the only Puget Sound winery that grows its grapes on the premises (informal tours and tastings Wednesday through Sunday).

INTERNATIONAL DISTRICT

S Weller St to S Washington St between 2nd Ave S and 12th Ave S (map: HH7)

Once known as Chinatown, this neighborhood on the southeast edge of downtown is anything but a frenetic, neon-lit miniature Hong Kong or Taipei. It's small and unselfconscious, and serves neighborhood denizens with scores of tiny ethnic groceries and family-style restaurants, but offers little more in the way of standard tourist attractions. Thus it makes a refreshingly *real* place to visit.

The history of white treatment of Asians in Seattle is not a pleasant one. In the 1880s many Chinese were deported (returning only when their labor was needed to rebuild downtown after the great fire of 1889). Similarly, the Japanese were packed off to internment camps during World War II; when they returned, they

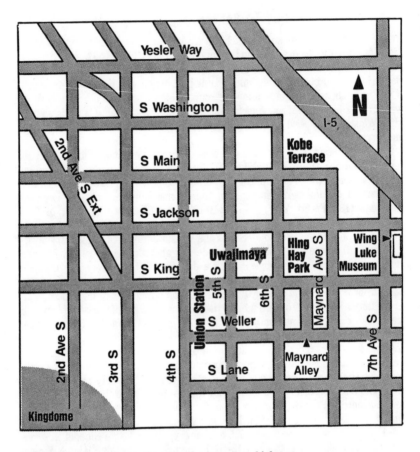

found their community replaced by the interstate highway.

Alongside reminders of this difficult past is more inspiring evidence of the distinguished artists and writers who have emerged from this pan-Asian cultural center. Seattle's International District is both a collection of distinct ethnic communities (the Chinese have their own newspapers and opera society, the Japanese have a theater) and a cohesive melting pot (a community garden, museum, and neighborhood playground are shared by all). A recent influx of Southeast Asian immigrants and refugees has further enriched the mix of Chinese, Japanese, Filipinos, and Koreans. This cultural renaissance has helped infuse the district with a new vibrance, which will likely increase now that the new bus tunnel's terminus at Fifth Avenue South and South Jackson Street connects the neighborhood to the rest of Seattle.

The centerpiece of the neighborhood is the vast emporium called **Uwajimaya** (519 Sixth Avenue S, 624-6248), the closest thing this country has to a real Japanese supermarket/department store. Inside the tile-roofed building is a playground for the Asian gourmet, with huge tanks of live fish and rare imported produce. A cooking school here is well regarded throughout the region. To get an idea of the engaging contrasts of the International District, cross the street to the tiny **Hoven Foods** (510 S King Street, 340-0774), which, in much humbler fashion, sells excellent fresh tofu and soybean milk. A few doors up is **A Piece of Cake** (514 S King Street, 623-8284), a bakery that has achieved local fame for its marvelous fresh mango cake (and draws many from the suburbs into the heart of the district). You're on the central thoroughfare of the International District now, which crowds on weekend mornings with families shopping at grocery and import stores that look as if they haven't changed in 50 years. This is a particularly good time for families to visit, to poke around in the mom 'n' pop markets and their yields of tantalizing Asian ingredients, and to stand in line for a jolly weekend brunch of dim sum. A traditional Chinese breakfast can be had at **House of Dumplings** (510 S King Street, 340-0774). Or try **Ocean City** (609 S Weller Street, 623-2333), typical of the huge, corporate-owned Cantonese restaurants known for decent dim sum and bright, eye-catching exteriors. The classy **House of Hong** (409 Eighth Avenue S, 622-7997), a bit farther east, is another good bet for dim sum. **Hien Vuong** (502 S King Street, 624-2611), across the street from Uwajimaya, is an excellent choice for Vietnamese fare. At **Kau Kau** (656 S King Street, 682-4006), glistening barbecued pork and roast ducks hang enticingly in the window. **Sea Garden** (509 Seventh Avenue S, 623-2100) serves some of the city's finest seafood. Finish the feast with a visit to the tiny **Mon Hei Chinese Bakery** (669 S King Street, 624-4156), whose ovens yield up fresh sweet bean cakes and lotus seed fritters.

King Street is also home to one of the district's many traditional herbalists, the **Korea Ginseng Center** (670 S King Street, 682-5003). Look around—all over are buildings reminiscent of the type built in China's urban centers in the 1920s, businesses on the first floor and apartments with balconies above. Some larger balconies are the locations of former Buddhist temples.

Up Seventh Avenue from here is the **Wing Luke Asian Museum** (407 Seventh Avenue S, 623-5124), named after the first person of Asian ancestry elected to public office in Washington. With rotating exhibits and a permanent display of photographs, the museum sensitively chronicles the experience of early Asian immigrants to the West Coast. Across Jackson Street to the west is the main Japanese district, where you will find a whimsical Japanese pre-World War II five 'n' dime, **The Higo Variety Store** (604 S Jackson Street, 622-7572), presided over for the last half-century by the Murakami family. This is also where many of the finest Japanese restaurants are clustered, the best of which is **The Mikado** (514 S Jackson Street, 622-5206), whose sushi and robata bars and omakase dinners attract crowds every night. North on Sixth Avenue is the **Nippon Kan Theater** (628 S Washington Street, 624-8800), known for its annual Japanese Performing Arts Series, and **Kobe Terrace Park**, with a noble stone lantern from Seattle's Japanese sister city of Kobe. Here, too, you'll get a splendid view of the district and Pioneer Square, including the **terraced gardens**, reminiscent of Asia in the compactness of their design and use of the terrain. The gardens were built in the late 1970s and parceled out to low-income elderly inhabitants of the district, who tend their tiny plots with great pride.

East of here on Jackson, the International District takes on a Vietnamese flavor. **Viet Wah Supermarket** (1032 S Jackson Street, 329-1399) may look like a poor cousin of Uwajimaya, but it has an excellent selection of fresh and packaged foods at very low prices, and it can boast the most comprehensive selection of Chinese and Southeast Asian ingredients in town. Seattle has a well-deserved reputation for its fine Vietnamese restaurants, and this is where you'll find many of them: **Hai Yen** (1233 S Jackson Street, 328-0757), **A Little Bit of Saigon** (1036 S Jackson Street, 325-3663), and the tiny **Pho Bac** (1314 S Jackson Street, 323-4387), with its excellent beef soup.

BROADWAY

Along Broadway, Pine St to E Roy St (map: HH6)

Along the spine of Capitol Hill lies **Broadway**, the closest Seattle comes to the spirit of San Francisco's Castro Street. Nearly written off to urban decay just a dozen years ago, Broadway has experienced a dramatic (some would say excessive) revival, establishing it as the heady center for the city's trendy alternative boutique and street culture. Its free-stepping spirit is perhaps best expressed in Jack Mackie's inlaid bronze **Dancing Feet**, offbeat public art appearing at intervals along the sidewalk, which allow the stroller to get in step with the cha-cha or the foxtrot down the boulevard. The haunt of punk-fashionable and mohawk-coiffed youth, the city's unofficial gay district, and the one place in town where the sidewalks are still filled after 10pm.

The commercial district extends roughly from **Seattle Central Community College** at Broadway and Pine to where Broadway becomes 10th Avenue East at East Roy Street, a lively eight-block walk or a slow-going drive. Best not to bring your car at all, since parking is rough (although the situation has been somewhat eased by two parking garages, one near SCCC at the corner of Harvard Avenue and Pine Street, the other farther north, beneath the Broadway Market. Parking, though, is not always a bargain; we suggest taking one of the many buses that stop in the area. Call Metro for schedules (see Telephone Numbers under Keys to the City in the Essentials chapter).

Northward, the district doesn't really begin to thicken until you see **Dick's Drive-In** (115 Broadway E, 323-1300), one of the last remaining preserves of Broadway's less assuming character (along with Ernie Steele's Checkerboard Room up the street) and home of the best greasy French fries in town. Food of all ethnic persuasions is available along Broadway, but one must take the minefield approach in pursuit of it, as some of the most promising-looking places tend to rest on their good looks. Sushi eaters should continue several blocks northward to stylish **Aoki** (621 Broadway E, 324-3633); Thai fanciers can find sufficiently tongue-searing dishes at **Siam on Broadway** (616 Broadway E, 324-0892); burger cravers will do well at **The Deluxe I Bar and Grill** (625 Broadway E, 324-9697), full of the spirit of old-time Broadway; Italian-food eaters will be satisfied with trips into **Testa Rossa** (208 Broadway E, 328-0878), home of the world's cheesiest stuffed pizzas. Two new bright spots among these seeming old-timers are **Pollo Rico** (420 Broadway E, 325-8712), featuring chicken and only chicken, starring in various South American dishes; and **The Oven** (213 Broadway E, 328-

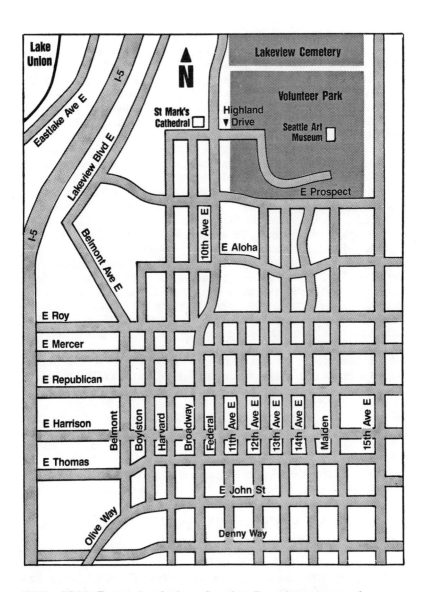

2951), a Middle Eastern fast-foodery of good quality and generous portions.

Food is one of the raisons d'être at the spanking new **Broadway Market** (401 Broadway E, 322-1610), which, Fred Meyer installation notwithstanding, stands as an imposing symbol of the continuing million-dollar enfranchisement of once-funky Broadway. There's even a multiplex cinema here, providing a pointed contrast with the old and ornate theaters that mark the north and south boundaries of the Broadway strip: **The Egyptian** (801 E Pine Street, 323-4978) and the **Har-**

vard Exit (807 E Roy Street, 323-8986), both of which screen excellent foreign films. The skylit Market features a few terrific shops—including **Comfort by Akiko**, a futon and pillow oasis, and **Seattle Floral**, a creative florist—but is best for getting a feel for the more Martian aspects of Broadway (not to mention the healing powers of wheatgrass juice) at the futuristic **Gravity Bar.**

Vintage and imported fashion, books, and home accessories are the focus of the best of the Broadway shops. **Opus 204** (225 Broadway E, 325-1781) purveys fashions and exotica from all over the world, while **Retro Viva** (215 Broadway E, 328-7451), **Chop Suey** (1828½ Broadway, 329-7839), and **Dreamland** (619 Broadway E, 329-8044) encourage our kitschy, retro sides. On the other side of the street are an excellent newsstand, **Steve's Broadway News** (204 Broadway E, 324-7323)—well stocked for hangers-out—and an eclectic bookstore, **Bailey/Coy Books** (414 Broadway E, 323-8842). Here you'll also see the browsable, high-end home accessories shop **Keeg's** (310 Broadway E, 325-1771).

Finally, you'll meander to Roy Street, bounded by the quaint stone **Loveless Building** and its sophisticated tenants: **Fast Forward** (701 Broadway E, 325-1313), a showcase for modern clothing, jewelry, and cards; and **Byzantion** (806 E Roy Street, 325-7580), a cozy Greek restaurant richly adorned with muted floor-to-ceiling friezes that depict Pushkin's fairy tale of Czar Saltan (this space used to house the Russian Samovar restaurant). Filmgoers and arty Cornish students gather at the **Harvard Espresso Gallery** (810 E Roy Street, 323-7598) next door for unusual coffee combinations in a comfortable space. A fittingly schmoozy capper to a day like this might be a cup of coffee and a bite of dessert at any one of the coffeehouses along the strip, which are as abundant in the pedestrian-heavy corners of Seattle as mushrooms in the rain forest. **Dilettante** (416 Broadway E, 329-6463) is a pricey Seattle tradition and the cafe of choice for those who prefer to mainline their chocolate. **Starbucks** (516 Broadway E, 323-7888) is another local success story, known and loved for its mellow coffee roasts. The best coffeehouse, however, isn't on Broadway at all, but resides on the corner of Belmont and Olive: **B & O Espresso** (204 Belmont Avenue E, 322-5028). Dim and bohemian, full of earnest conversations and a well-mixed bag of the variant characters who populate this hill, all sinking into such temporal delights as fat, fudgy cakes and creamy espresso—the B & O is a microcosm of eclectic Broadway.

SEATTLE ART MUSEUM/VOLUNTEER PARK AND DOWNTOWN

First Ave and University St (downtown, map: K8)/E Prospect St and 14th Ave E (Volunteer Park, map: GG6), 625-8901

Mature trees, circling drives, grassy lawns, and lily ponds make **Volunteer Park** the most elegant of Seattle's parks and as stately as the mansions that surround it. Designed by the Olmsted brothers of New York Central Park fame, Volunteer Park graces the top of Capitol Hill and offers sweeping views of the Space Needle, the Sound, and the Olympic Mountains. At the north end of the main concourse lies the elaborate **Volunteer Park Conservatory** (15th Avenue and Galer Street, 684-4743), with three large greenhouse wings filled with flowering plants, cacti, and tropical flora. **KIDS FREE** It's open (free of charge) to the public, and a treat for kids. At the other end is an old 75-foot water tower, which the hardy can climb for a splendid view of the city and beyond.

The centerpiece of the park is the **Seattle Art Museum**, an Art Deco gem in this woodsy setting and the flagship art museum of the region since 1933. By December 1991, the museum's permanent collections will be moved to the **new downtown museum** and the Volunteer Park establishment will close for remodeling for at least a year. The new 145,000-square-foot downtown building (University Street between First and Second avenues) is a "classical/whimsical" Robert Venturi–designed structure that is sure to propel the excellent museum into the same league as its other big-city peers. For the moment, SAM in Volunteer Park continues to mount 15 to 20 exhibits a year, from Japanese woodblock prints to Native American art and contemporary painting. The Katherine White Collection, a bequest of African art so vast it has to be exhibited serially, opened in 1984. By the end of 1991, these will be in place on four floors of the downtown museum (the fifth floor will be offices). The impressive Asian art collection will remain a permanent fixture in Volunteer Park once it reopens. The Volunteer Park museum is open Tuesday through Sunday, with tours at 2pm. Admission is $2 for adults, **FREE** free on Thursdays. Hours and admission of the downtown museum had not been confirmed at press time. The museum also sponsors lectures, concerts, and showings of documentary films and Hollywood classics.

WASHINGTON PARK ARBORETUM

2300 Arboretum Dr E, 543-8800 (map: GG6)

The **Washington Park Arboretum**, a lush retreat south of the University of Washington, doubles as a public park and a botanical research facility for the university. Bordered on one side by Lake Washington, the 200-acre preserve is a serene and lovely place for long walks in any season, but it is particularly spectacular in spring, when the flowers and fruit trees burst into vivid color. The Arboretum is crisscrossed by walking paths, from which you can see over 5,000 varieties of woody plants, trees, shrubs, and vines, many of them marked with their Latin and common names.

Any visit to the Arboretum should include the **Japanese Garden** (684-4725), just off **Lake Washington Boulevard E**, the road that winds north-south through the park. This secluded garden, built 30 years ago by Japanese architect Juki Iida, is a graceful composition of Japanese trees and shrubs, rockeries, tranquil pools, and granite lanterns. A waterfall below a 12-tiered pagoda flows down to a carp-filled lake with tiny islands and two small bridges. A cypress and cedar **teahouse** is opened for special occasions and demonstrations of the Japanese tea ceremony. The Japanese Garden is open every day in warm weather months from 10am; closing times vary. Cost of entry is $1.50.

Just across the road to the north is the start of **Azalea Way**, a pastoral promenade (where no jogging is allowed) amid azaleas, dogwood, and flowering cherry trees, branching off into groves of rhododendrons (the Arboretum's collection is world famous) and camellias—some in colors you may not have imagined existed in nature. Azalea Way ends at the new **Arboretum Visitor Center**, which has horticultural displays and information on the park, and is the jumping-off point for **FREE** free, naturalist-led tours of the garden (1pm Sundays). Only a few years old, the 10-foot by 60-foot Signature Bed charms visitors with a collection of plant life that changes each spring. Maintained by a different horticultural group each year, plantings vary, depending on the sponsor. Previous years' displays have included common annuals, exotic perennials, and a rock garden. The knockout Wallingford beds will go to the Good Shepherd Center next year, permanently.

From the visitors' center you can head back by the upper, less-trafficked road or continue your tour northward into the marsh and island area. This estuarine sanctuary is a haven for wildlife, canoeists, swimmers, fishermen, bird watchers, and picnickers—and you can explore it by boat **KIDS**, renting your canoe from the **University of Washington Waterfront Activities Center** (see Kayaking/Canoeing under Great Outdoors in this chapter).

UNIVERSITY OF WASHINGTON

NE 45th St and 17th Ave NE, 543-2100 (map: FF6)
Visitor Information Center: 4014 University Way NE, 543-9198

The University of Washington's parklike campus is one of the most beautiful and accessible in the nation. Just 15 minutes from downtown on the freeway, the 694-acre campus is the center of a vibrant and diverse community and is the Northwest's top general educational establishment. The university was founded in 1861 on a plot of land downtown and moved to its present site in 1895. It is known for its medical school and law school, as well as its programs in international relations, computer science, and forestry, among others. Total enrollment is about 34,000. The university has suffered serious financial setbacks in recent years, but the tight budgets don't show to a casual observer—the campus has matured into a horticultural and architectural showpiece.

The **main entrance** to the university is on 45th Street and 17th Avenue NE opposite **Greek Row**, a neighborhood of stately older mansions occupied mostly by fraternities and sororities. This is also one of the entrances to the campus parking network (another is located on 15th Avenue NE and NE 41st Street), which allows you to park near your intended destination, explore a little on foot, and pay just $4 for the day. To the right of the main entrance is the **FREE Burke Museum** (543-5590), which houses a good collection of Native American artifacts and natural history exhibits (see Museums in the Arts chapter), as well as a dandy basement coffeehouse and student haunt, **The Boiserie** (543-9854). Take a left on Stevens Way to begin the circuit around campus. In April this stretch of road is flanked by brilliant orange azalea blossoms. As you pass the art and music departments, you'll see the main undergraduate dormitories up ahead, a series of uninspired cement structures on some of the best view property in the city. Next to them you can see it yourself—the panorama of Lake Washington, the floating bridge, and the Cascades.

Continue along to the **Student Union Building (The HUB)** (543-1447), where you'll find a newsstand, a cafeteria, and a branch of the University Book Store. From there King Lane leads into the heart of the campus, the **Fine Arts Quad-**

UNIVERSITY OF WASHINGTON

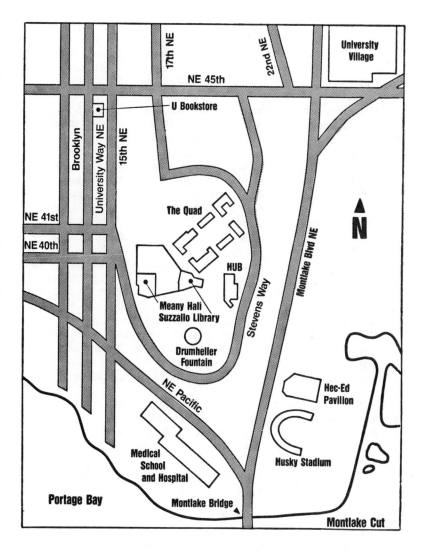

rangle. Home of UW liberal arts, the mellow Gothic buildings and grassy lawns surrounding the Quad look like a stage set for the classic collegiate scene, and the rows of gnarled flowering cherries open spring quarter with a dazzling pink display. Straight ahead and up the hill from here is **Denny Hall,** the oldest building on campus and home of the clock whose chimes can be heard every hour throughout the university area.

Turn left and walk down toward **Red Square,** a striking (if slippery when wet) marriage of brutalism with Siena's town square. The main parking garage is right beneath you. On your left is **Suzzallo Library,** the main research library, with its ornate exterior and stained-glass windows. Continuing around the square clockwise are the main administration building; **Meany Hall,** an exceptional venue for chamber music concerts and recitals; **Odegaard Undergraduate Library** (543-2060); and **Kane Hall,** site of many of the enormous lecture classes that are a mainstay of undergraduate education at the UW, as well as lecture series that are open to the public.

If you head back between Suzzallo and the administration building, you'll reach **Drumheller Fountain** (Frosh Pond), a pleasant stopping point surrounded by the UW's acclaimed **rose gardens.** Look south for another winning view, the aptly named **Rainier Vista.** To the left, in what appears to be a clump of large evergreens, is the **Sylvan Theater,** a lovely hidden glade and pausing spot watched over by four towering white columns. Rejoin Stevens Way at the vista and curve around to the right, past the Forestry Department, Botany Greenhouse, and the old architecture department, and out the west gate of the university. You've just seen the brains of the U District—now on to its nerve center.

One block up is **University Way NE,** known to all as **the Ave,** a series of long north-south blocks jammed with shops and restaurants. The Ave has taken on a rather soulless quality in recent years, as family-owned businesses, funky secondhand stores, and hippie head shops have given way to trendy franchise boutiques and fast-food outlets. Pockets of cultural diversity and bohemian academia can still be found at intervals, however, as in the several art-house theaters found throughout the area (see Movies in the Arts chapter), and the vast number of unusual ethnic restaurants, excellent bookstores, and coffeehouses. For a decade-dissolving trip, duck into **The Last Exit on Brooklyn** (3930 Brooklyn Avenue NE, 545-9873) or **Cafe Allegro** (4214½ University Way NE, 633-3030) for excellent espresso in the company of true denizens of the counterculture.

Retail on the Ave is hit-and-miss, but there are bright spots. **Folk Art Gallery/La Tienda** (4138 University Way NE, 632-1796) is full of select art objects and exotic crafts from several continents. On the next block is **Bulldog News** (4208 University Way NE, 632-6397), a browser's paradise where you can sip espresso while flipping leisurely through any of hundreds of periodicals on the stands. But the real bibliophile's dream is up the street at the **University Book Store** (4326 University Way NE, 634-3400), which occupies most of the block between 43rd and 45th streets. This and the Harvard Coop are engaged in perpetual rivalry for the title of biggest, best, and most varied bookshop in the country. In the blocks north of the major intersector, 45th Street, the best shops are **Windfall** (4712 University Way NE, 522-1220), a basement emporium with excellent discount merchandise, and **Danken's Gourmet Ice Creams** (4507 University Way NE, 545-8596), commonly considered the purveyor of the best rich scoops in Seattle. Until recently the area north of 50th was predominantly residential. Over the past few years, however, more of the ethnic restaurants have moved north to the slightly lower-rent district on the northern end of University Way: **The Chile Pepper** (5000 University Way NE, 526-5004), serving the regional cuisine of Mexico's upland state Guanajuato; **Tandoor** (5024 University Way NE, 523-7477), an authentic Indian restaurant; and **Silence-Heart-Nest** (5247 University Way NE, 524-4008), another Indian restaurant with a playful, inventive twist. At the farthest reaches of the Ave is the endearing **Il Paesano** (5628 University Way NE, 526-0949).

WOODLAND PARK ZOO

Park: N 50th St and Green Lake Way N, 684-4075
Zoo: 5500 Phinney Ave N, 625-2244 (map: EE7)

KIDS Guy Phinney was an Englishman who wanted to turn his property into something resembling a proper English country estate. Woodland Park retains much of its previous owner's vision; no matter that six-lane Aurora Avenue plows right through the middle of it, dividing the property into two distinct areas. The east side of Aurora is the site of most of the sporting activities (lawn bowling, tennis,

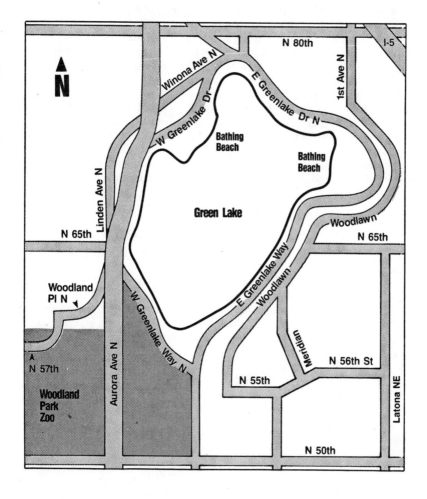

playing fields, mini-golf, picnic areas, and Green Lake). The west side has the formal rose garden, the **Poncho Theater** (see Theaters in the Arts chapter), and the impressive **Woodland Park Zoo.**

One of the 10 best zoos in the country, the Woodland Park Zoo has evolved in the last decade from a traditional animals-behind-bars facility into one that provides lifelike representations of natural habitats. Among them are a grassy **African savannah** populated with giraffes, zebras, and hippos (who wallow merrily in their own simulated mud-bottomed river drainage); a tropical jungle for primates; a state-of-the-art **marsh** for waterfowl and waders; and a heavily planted **lowland gorilla enclosure** (the largest display of its kind in the world), concealing a brooding troop of adults and their precocious offspring. Newest is the **Asian Elephant Forest,** an impressive home for the impressive pachyderms, whose 4.6 acres includes an elephant-sized pool for some large-scale splashing, a complete Asian forest, and a replica of a Thai logging camp. About two years down the jungle path, the zoo is planning to open a tropical rain forest exhibit, an ambitious project under construction at the moment. Visitors will be able to walk right into the forest floor, up through several layers of growth, and up to the tree canopy, seeing the various kinds of wildlife that reside in the different environments. Interspersed with these new exhibits are some less inspired leftovers from the 1950s (the feline house, for instance), which await updates of their own.

On a tamer scale, the **family farm** is a wonderful place for human youngsters to meet the offspring of other species during supervised sessions. The zoo also offers a rich schedule of family programming, including orientation walks, classes, special events, and lectures. The zoo food is of the concessioned variety (pleasing to kids but probably not to you). The entry fee for the Woodland Park Zoo is $4.50 for grown-ups and $2.25 for kids **FREE** (free for those under 6).

THE HIRAM M. CHITTENDEN LOCKS

3015 NW 54th St, 783-7059 (map: FF9)

FREE KIDS A little marvel out of an earlier industrial age, the **Hiram M. Chittenden Locks** in Ballard will make a big impression on folks from landlocked places. Pioneers had dreamed of joining **Lakes Union and Washington** to each other, and then to **Puget Sound** below. The channel between the lakes was completed in 1880—Lake Washington was lowered 9 feet in the process—and the locks were opened to great fanfare in 1917. Now more than 100,000 boats per year (both pleasure and commercial) ply the narrow passage of the **Lake Washington Ship Canal** on their way to or from the "water elevator," forming a sort of an informal regatta to entertain onlookers.

It is a captivating sight, watching the boats gently rise and fall. Puget Sound fluctuates between 6 and 26 feet lower than the channel, and the descent (or ascent) takes 10 to 25 minutes, depending on which lock is being used. Across the waterway in **Commodore Park,** the torrents generated by a **fish ladder** entice close to a million fighting salmon each year that are en route to their spawning grounds in Cascade Mountain streams. You can watch the fishes' progress from a viewing area with windows onto the ladder: salmon in summer (peak viewing for sockeyes is in early July) and steelhead in winter.

The locks are open from 7am to 9pm every day (call the **visitors' center** at the number above to find out times for the daily tours). The green lawns and tree-lined waterside promenade of the park, along with the impressive rose display at the **Carl S. English, Jr., Botanical Gardens,** make grand backdrops for summer picnics. See also Gardens in the Exploring chapter.

SEATTLE CENTER

Between Denny Way and Mercer St, 1st Ave N and 5th Ave N, 684-8582 (map: B6)

KIDS This 74-acre park on the edge of the Denny Regrade, just north of downtown, is the legacy of the 1962 World's Fair, one of the few to turn a profit and leave a permanent facility behind. The site was once a grounds for Indian gatherings; now it's the arts and entertainment hub of the city, and—even more significant to visitors—home of the Space Needle. Seattleites don't seem to mind its dated 1960s high-tech look, and various plans for its renovation have met with opposition from all angles (the absurdly expensive Disney plan for the center's face-lift was all but laughed out of the planning room).

It's open all hours with **FREE** no admission charge to get onto the grounds, but **parking** can be a problem. The cheapest lots are located on the east side. For events at the Opera House, Arena, and the Intiman Playhouse, the covered parking garage directly across Mercer Street from the Opera House affords easy ac-

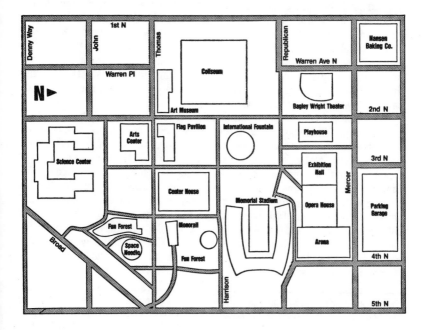

cess, but the egress is maddeningly long on busy nights. One way to circumvent the problem is to take the **Monorail** from downtown—a 90-second ride (see Transportation in the Essentials chapter) which leaves you next to the **Center House**. This cavernous building, with its vast selection of mediocre fast food (if you're starving, the Asian fare is the most reliable), is the province of conventioneers, preadolescent hangers-out, and, on many afternoons, senior citizens dancing to the strains of a big band. On the lower level of the Center House is the **Seattle Children's Museum** (see Museums in the Arts chapter) and the Center House Theater, which hosts children's performances.

Next to the Center House is the **Fun Forest** (closed in winter), a small-scale amusement park with rides and an arcade. Even if it's closed, the 520-foot elevator ride up to the **Space Needle Observation Deck** provides sufficient thrills and a heck of a view for your $4.75. (The ride is free if you're dining at the revolving **Space Needle Restaurant** or **Emerald Suite Dining Room**. But don't—the food is uninspired and overpriced.)

Just southwest of the Space Needle is the **Pacific Science Center** (443-2001), five white buildings grouped around shallow pools and graceful white arches. The Science Center was designed by Minoru Yamasaki—the architect responsible for the inverted-pencil Rainier Square tower downtown—and features engrossing hands-on science and math exhibits for school-age children and traveling shows aimed at all age groups. There are enough excellent displays, films, and demonstrations to keep a family occupied for most of a day. (Admission is $5 for adults, $4 for kids, and $3 for kids under 6.) Other attractions include the mammoth-screen **IMAX Theater** and laser shows set to music.

Head north from the Science Center to another learning-is-fun facility, **Pacific Arts Center** (443-5437). Here, kids and professional artists are united in hands-on learning situations—classes, workshops, and special programs in music, drama, visual art, and writing. There's a gallery, too, showcasing the works of young artists. Farther on is the **Flag Pavilion** (you'll know it when you see it), which has housed such blockbuster exhibits as King Tut and Son of Heaven; and the **International Fountain**, shooting up enormous jets of water, sometimes synchronized with classical music and lights.

From here you can't miss the building that looks like a collapsed tepee. This is the **Coliseum**, 15,000-seat home of trade shows, conventions, circuses, and rock concerts—but best loved as the raucous home court of the Seattle SuperSonics basketball team, that is, at least until their new arena is built near the Kingdome. Cultural institutions reside around the fountain on the northern edge of the campus. The newest and flashiest is the striking, neon-adorned **Bagley Wright Theater** (443-2210), home of the Seattle Repertory Theater Company (which you can arrange to tour, **FREE** free of charge, from September to May). The Rep's old digs, the **Playhouse**, is now a rental venue for Intiman and other companies, while the **Opera House** accommodates the Seattle Opera, Seattle Symphony, and Pacific Northwest Ballet. Beyond the square is the **Arena** and **High School Memorial Stadium**, site of high school football and soccer matches.

Seattle Best Places lists the finest establishments throughout Seattle and the Eastside, north to Edmonds, south to Federal Way, and west to Bainbridge Island.

MUSEUM OF FLIGHT

9404 E Marginal Way S, 764-5720 (map: NN6)

KIDS You don't have to be an aviation buff to enjoy the sheer physical spectacle of 20 full-size airplanes—including a 40,000-pound B-17—suspended from the ceiling of a stunning six-story glass and steel gallery. **The Museum of Flight**, 10 miles south of Seattle, is notable for its size, its sophisticated design, its impressive collection, and its unique location in a working airfield. Tour guides are quick to point out that the museum has no formal affiliation with **The Boeing Company**—the aircraft manufacturing monolith and mainstay of the Northwest economy—apart from its location at **Boeing Field** and its origination in **The Red Barn**, Boeing's humble first home in 1909. One cannot explore the fascinating history of Northwest aviation without paying ultimate homage to this local industry giant, however, and the airfield setting—with real aircraft taking off and landing all around you—is one of the most thrilling aspects of the museum.

The real theme here is how humans have fantasized about flight, and then gone about trying to achieve it. MOF takes you from the early legends of flight through the history of aviation, from pioneering stages to the present, with special emphasis on Pacific Northwest flight—military, commercial, and amateur. The collection includes a replica of the Wright brothers' original glider, and a 1917 Curtiss Jenny biplane. Don't miss the bright red 1950 Aerocar III, which converts from a car to a plane in 10 minutes.

The museum sponsors workshops, films, tours, and special programs. Open every day; adults pay $4, kids $3. Children will especially enjoy the hands-on learning areas with paper airplanes, boomerangs, and other toys that fly.

MOUNT RAINIER

98 miles SE of Seattle on Hwy 706, 1-569-2211

See Excursions in the Outings chapter.

THE GREAT OUTDOORS

BICYCLING

Despite its hilly topography, Seattle is teeming with avid bicyclists; in 1990, *Bicycling* magazine named Seattle the best North American city for cyclists. Many people cycle to work, and many more include cycling in their recreational pursuits. **Cascade Bicycle Club** (522-BIKE), one of the largest recreational cycling clubs in the nation, organizes group rides and special biking events, including the popular Seattle-to-Portland and Seattle-to-Vancouver, BC, rides. Call the club for a recorded listing of upcoming events.

FREE KIDS The Seattle Department of Parks and Recreation sponsors monthly **Bicycle Sundays** (the third Sunday *and* first Saturday of each month, May through September) along Lake Washington Boulevard, which is closed to auto traffic. Anyone with a bike is welcome to participate. It's a great family activity.

Racers should note that the Eastside boasts the only true bike-racing track this side of Portland, the 400-meter **Velodrome** (Marymoor Park, Redmond, 882-0706, map: FF1). Twice-weekly track races are held at the Velodrome from early May to the end of August, with race times of 7pm on Thursdays and 7:30pm on Fridays (when national-caliber riders often race). Spectators should bring $3 for admission (Fridays only) and a pad to protect themselves from the aluminum bleachers (or sit on the grass). Serious racers can also join any of the dozens of racing clubs in the area, two of the biggest being the **Puget Sound Cycling Club** (523-1822—Gregg's Greenlake Cycle, the team's sponsor) and **Avanti Racing Team** (324-8878).

The booming popularity of **mountain biking** in the past few years presents something of a dilemma to environmentalists as well as bikers. The very trails that provide an optimum off-road experience—quiet, remote, untouched—are those that often end up closed by the National Forest Service because of the damage caused by increasing numbers of bikers. Your best bet for staying abreast of trail closures is **TRIS** (Trail Users Information System), a computer program (updated weekly in prime outdoor sports months, less often in the winter) providing the latest trail information for mountain bikers, hikers, backpackers, and horseback riders. There are TRIS computers at all REI outposts, as well as at the National Parks Service Information Center (915 Second Avenue). It's free. REI will also refer you to specific ranger stations if you'd rather talk to a live person. The **Backcountry Bicycle Trails Club** (4210 191st Avenue SE, Issaquah 98027, 767-9815) organizes local rides for all levels of experience and is especially adamant about teaching "soft-riding" techniques, which protect trails from the roughing-up that can eventually cause their closure.

Following are some of the favored rides in the area; the city Engineering Department also publishes a biker's map of Seattle, which most bike stores carry. See also the trails listed under Running in this section.

Alki Strip
Alki Beach Park to
Lincoln Park
(map: II9–KK9)

This 6-mile West Seattle route from the beach at Alki to Lincoln Park is along a road wide enough for both bikes and cars, and now that cruising has been outlawed here, cycling is safer. Avoid the Alki beach area on sunny Sunday afternoons, when it is crowded and often littered with broken glass. Bicycles can be rented from **Alki Bicycle Company** (2722 Alki Avenue SW, 938-3322, map: II9), across the street from Alki Beach Park.

Bainbridge Island Loop
Start on Ferncliff at
Winslow Ferry Terminal
(avoid Hwy 305)

A pleasant 30-or-so-mile getaway for Seattle cyclists, this signed bike route follows fairly low-traffic roads around the island. This is the approximate route of Chilly Hilly, a February bike ride that officially marks the opening day of Seattle biking. Bikes can be rented at **Winslow Wheels** (Village Plaza, 842-3732), about a mile from the ferry terminal (take Ferncliff to High School Road).

Blue Ridge
Carkeek Park to Golden Gardens Park (map: DD8–DD9)

The view of Puget Sound and the Olympic Mountains beyond is spectacular on this ride of less than two miles. Try making a big loop, from Green Lake through the Greenwood district to Carkeek and Golden Gardens, then back by way of the Ballard Locks.

Burke-Gilman Trail
Gas Works Park to Kenmore Logboom Park (map: FF7–BB5)

KIDS It looks like a trail, but in spirit it's a park that provides a lush corridor of green from Gas Works Park on Lake Union to Kenmore's Logboom Park at the northern tip of Lake Washington. The 12.5-mile path is built on an old railway bed and offers a scenic route through the leafy University of Washington, along Lake Washington, and past neighborhood parks such as the family-oriented **Matthews Beach** (map: DD5). It's crowded—cyclists of all shapes and persuasions, joggers, walkers, and roller skaters (speed limit, 15mph). Cyclists often continue on to the Sammamish River Trail, which connects with the Burke-Gilman after a short jog on busy Bothell Way; the new connection between the two should be completely finished sometime in 1991. You can rent wheels at **The Bicycle Center** (4529 Sand Point Way NE, 523-8300, map: EE6), about one mile northwest of the University of Washington, just off the trail.

Elliott Bay Bikeway
Pier 86 to Pier 70 (map: HH8–GG8)

KIDS You get a grand view on this brief ride along Puget Sound. The trail is less than two miles long and passes between the Grain Terminal and loading dock. Start at the north end (off West Galer); buy the kids ice cream at Pier 70, then head back. Full of runners at noontime.

Lake Washington Boulevard
Madrona Park to Seward Park (map: HH6–KK5)

KIDS There are great views all along this serene 5-mile stretch between Madrona and Seward parks. The road is narrow part of the way, but the southern half (from Mount Baker Beach southward) has a separate asphalt path, which is safer for children. On Bicycle Saturdays and Sundays this latter portion is closed to traffic.

Mercer Island Loop
Along E Mercer Way and W Mercer Way (map: II4–KK4)

A new biker's tunnel leads to the I-90 bridge on the way to Mercer Island (the entrance is off Martin Luther King Jr. Way, through a sort of park of concrete monoliths). You'll ride over moderate rolling hills the whole length of this 14-mile loop. The roads are curving and narrow, and although motorists are accustomed to bikes, you should avoid rush hour. This is a great route for perusing the varied residential architecture of the island.

Sammamish River Trail
Near Bothell Landing,
Bothell to Marymoor
Park, Redmond
(map: BB3–FF1)

KIDS This very flat, peacefully rural route follows the quietly flowing Sammamish River for 9.5 miles. Stop for a picnic at the parklike Chateau Ste. Michelle Winery, just off the trail at NE 145th (bring your own lunch or buy one there). Bike rentals are available at **Sammamish Valley Cycle** (8451 164th Avenue NE, Redmond, 881-8442, map: EE2).

Seward Park
S Juneau St and Lake
Washington Blvd S
(map: JJ5)

Take this paved and traffic-free 2.5-mile road around wooded Seward Park, which juts out prominently into Lake Washington. The ride is extremely peaceful and can even be lonely.

FISHING/CLAMMING

Washington is famous for its salmon fishing. The salmon's battling cousin, the steelhead—a seagoing trout that spawns in fresh waters and is often mistakenly referred to as a salmon—is avidly pursued as well. To fish in this state, you need a Washington State fishing license and a punch card for salmon, steelhead, and sturgeon. You can get a license at most tackle shops and charter-boat companies, as well as chain sporting-goods stores such as Fred Meyer and Chubby & Tubby. It's a good idea to pick up a fishing regulation pamphlet along with your license to clarify the often confusing rules on catch limits and tackle. Another good resource is a local, up-to-date fishing journal called *Fishing and Hunting News* (624-3845). Fishing is allowed off all public docks in the area (see the Parks and Beaches in this chapter).

Steelhead are classified as game fish in Washington and fall within the jurisdiction of the State Department of Wildlife (600 Capitol Way N, Olympia 98504, 1-753-5713). Besides keeping watch on run sizes on the rivers and regulating catch limits, the department will answer your questions on steelhead fishing. The season is roughly June through mid-March. Some of the best rivers for steelhead fishing are: the Skykomish, Monroe to Index; the Skagit, a beautiful stretch of water between Sedro Woolley and Rockport; the Kalama, Green, and Cowlitz rivers to the south of Seattle; and the Hoh, Soleduck, Bogachiel, and Quillayute rivers in the rain forest of the Olympic Peninsula. For a pleasant introduction to steelhead fishing, you can hire a local guide to take you out (*Fishing and Hunting News* lists licensed guides).

Salmon are considered food fish and are therefore regulated by the Washington State Department of Fisheries (Room 115 General Administration Building, Olympia 98504, 1-753-6552). Under normal conditions, salmon fishing charters off the Pacific Coast surpass the smaller Puget Sound operations out of Seattle in both volume and excitement. Coastal towns from the northern tip of Neah Bay to Ilwaco at the mouth of the Columbia River—and especially Westport, the biggest fishing draw—are full of charter-boat operators, who will take you out on the high seas for about $45 to $65 per person. (Reservations—and Dramamine—may be necessary.) Puget Sound and the Strait of Juan de Fuca (with charter hubs of Sekiu and Port Angeles) have a longer salmon season, with a few special closures in summer.

Charter fishing operations closer to home include: **Major Marine Tours** (1415 Western Avenue, Suite 503, 292-0595), **Sea Charters Tackle & Marine** (115 W Dayton Street, Edmonds, 776-5611; 1728 W Marine View Drive, Everett, 1-252-4188), and the **Everett North Sound Charters** (2815 W Marine View Drive, Everett, 1-339-1275). You'll also find good salmon fishing on the Skykomish, Snoqualmie, Hoh, Soleduck, and Green rivers. The rules for freshwater salmon fishing vary widely depending on the lake or river, so consult the Department of Fisheries for specifics.

Shellfish are the edible treasures you can get without ever leaving the shore. **KIDS** Digging for clams and harvesting oysters and mussels are great family activities, and all you need is a small shovel or long-tined rake, a bucket, and a low tide. Seattle's public beaches are open for clamming year-round (butter clams are the big draw), unless pollution alerts are posted. **Alki Beach Park** (Alki Avenue SW, map: I19) is the most popular in-city spot, but the digging is good at public beaches in Edmonds, Mukilteo, Everett, and on Whidbey Island as well. **FREE** Clamming is free—unless you're going to the Pacific beaches for the endangered razor clams, in which case a license is required (available at Chubby & Tubby and Fred Meyer). There are daily limits on all other shellfish. Be warned: Clamming seasons are sometimes shortened or canceled altogether because of drastic decreases in the clam population, so you should consult the Department of Fisheries before setting off. There is also an ongoing danger of paralytic shellfish poisoning (PSP) caused by a microscopic organism that can turn the ocean water red, thus "red tide." The organism is great for bivalves but highly toxic for humans. Cooking does not reduce the toxin. Always call the **Red Tide Hotline** (1-800-562-5632) before going shellfishing, to learn which beaches are safe.

GOLFING

In addition to a number of fine public-access golf courses in Seattle and on the Eastside, many in wonderfully scenic surroundings, the region boasts two really challenging destination courses a little farther away: **Port Ludlow Golf Course** (9483 Oak Bay Road, Port Ludlow 98365, 1-437-2222) on the Olympic Peninsula, which is rated among the top courses in the United States; and **Semiahmoo Golf and Country Club** (8720 Semiahmoo Parkway, Blaine 98230, 1-371-7005), the spiffy, Arnold Palmer–designed course up north near the Canadian border. Day golfers should call for reservations.

Bear Creek Country Club
13737 202nd Ave NE,
Woodinville, 881-1350

An 18-hole, 6,900-yard semiprivate (and more expensive) course—the most challenging on the Eastside. All but the best golfers find it frustrating. PNGA 70.5, 72.0, 74.5, depending on which tees you use.

Bellevue Municipal Golf Course
5500 140th Ave NE,
Bellevue, 451-7250
(map: FF2)

This course (5,535 yards), the busiest in the state, is fairly level and easy. Eighteen holes, PNGA 66.6.

Jackson Park Municipal Golf Course
1000 NE 135th St,
363-4747 (map: CC7)

A speedy and easy course over lovely rolling hills. Eighteen holes, 6,592 yards, PNGA 68.2. Also has a short nine course.

Jefferson Park Golf Course
4101 Beacon Ave S,
762-4513 (map: JJ6)

You get great views of the city from the hilltop fairways of this enormously popular course, which looks easier than it is. Eighteen holes, 6,146 yards, PNGA 67.9.

Tyee Valley Golf Course
2401 S 192nd St,
878-3540 (map: PP6)

Right at the foot of the Sea-Tac runway, this easy course is perfect for a fast game between planes, but very noisy. Eighteen holes, 5,926 yards, PNGA men: 66.0, women: 70.6.

West Seattle Municipal Golf Course
4470 35th Ave SW,
935-5187 (map: JJ8)

A good, undulating 18-hole course just over the Duwamish River and tucked into a hilly valley, which makes for some surprising lies. 6,285 yards, PNGA 68.6. The toughest of the in-city courses.

HIKING

It's true: the hiking in Washington is superlative. Alpine lakes, rain forests, ocean cliffs, mountain meadows—all of these are within easy access of Seattle, and day hikers can count on reaching any of a score of trailheads within an hour or two. For this reason, the national parks, state parks, national forests, and wilderness areas nearby are heavily used, but conservation efforts have managed to stay a small step ahead of the abuse. Places like Mount Rainier National Park offer paved trails for the uninitiated, and car campers generally stick to short, low-elevation hikes. Forest Service wilderness staff often take the triage approach—

letting a few popular spots take a pounding while quietly applying their energy and money to preserving remoter areas. A lot of the credit goes to the community of hikers who maintain a strict creed of wilderness ethics.

One place to start if you're unfamiliar with the region is **Recreational Equipment Inc. (REI)** (1525 11th Avenue, 323-8333, map: HH6; 15400 NE 20th Street, Bellevue, 643-3700, map: GG1), which has a generous stock of hiking guides and US Geological Survey maps, as well as equipment (see Outdoor Equipment in the Shopping chapter). The **US Forest Service/National Parks Service Outdoor Recreation Information Office** (915 Second Avenue, Room 442, 442-0170, map: L8) offers trail reports, maps, guidebooks, and weather information, and its staff can direct you to a ranger station near your destination. The best hiking guides are published by **The Mountaineers** (300 Third Avenue W, 284-6310, map: A9), a venerable and prominent outdoors club. A Mountaineers membership costs $27 for the initiation fee and $34 annual dues and gives you access to skills courses, group hikes, and a variety of other membership privileges. Another good outdoor association is the Seattle branch of the **Sierra Club** (1516 Melrose Avenue, 621-1696, map: HH7). The **Washington Trails Association** (1305 Fourth Avenue, Suite 512, 625-1367, map: K6), a nonprofit outreach group, welcomes telephone inquiries about hiking.

The following are some nearby areas for hiking, described broadly by region:

Issaquah Alps
20 miles E of Seattle
off I-90

The most easily accessible from Seattle, these pretty Cascade foothills have dozens of day trails, frequented by both hikers and horses. Every week the **KIDS** Issaquah Alps Trails Club (PO Box 351, Issaquah 98027, 328-0480) organizes day hikes through the hills, ranging from short and easy to strenuous—a good way to introduce children to hiking.

Central Cascades
Between Snoqualmie
Pass and Stevens Pass

The best nearby backpacking is in this section of the Cascade Range, one or two hours east of Seattle off Highway 2 or I-90. The Central Cascades are mainly national forest and include a stretch of the **Alpine Lakes Wilderness**, a scenic marvel. A gorgeous section of the **Pacific Crest Trail** (which links Mexico with Canada) cuts through the wilderness along the mountain ridges.

North Cascades
Between Stevens Pass
and the Canadian border

The high trails in this area are most spectacular, reaching glaciers, old lookout shelters, and exhilarating panoramas that overlook the rest of the range. Seekers of solitude will find it here. The alpine flowers are at their best in early August, and the fall colors peak in early October, with snow following soon after.

Olympic Mountains

The Olympics are a bit of a longer journey from Seattle

Olympic National Park,
Olympic Peninsula

(plan on over two hours to get there via ferries), but are well worth the extra effort. Take your pick of glaciers, waterfalls, riverside hikes through the mossy rain forest, and alpine lakes similar to the Cascade tarns. Wildlife is abundant—you'll probably spot goats, deer, marmots, grouse, and, if you're lucky, a cougar or a bear. At **Hurricane Ridge** (Visitors' Center: 3002 Mount Angeles Road, Port Angeles 98362, 1-452-0330), a high point and hiking hub of the range, you'll also spot plenty of tourists. Rain is plentiful over the Olympic Range, so come prepared. For more information, see Olympic Peninsula under Longer Excursions in the Outings chapter.

South Cascades
Between Snoqualmie
Pass and the
Oregon border

In the South Cascades, **Mount Rainier** is the most popular hiking area. Rainier offers numerous trails, including a wonderful circuit around the base of the mountain (see Mount Rainier under Excursions in the Outings chapter). The rest of the South Cascades is a stunning contrast to the sections farther north. The rugged, more arid landscape is in many places reminiscent of Montana and the Southwest. Sadly, logging roads and clearcuts dominate the views, including those on the South Cascades segment of the Pacific Crest Trail.

HORSEBACK RIDING

KIDS Stables and outfitters abound on the Eastside and in the Cascade foothills. The following afford good doses of the outdoors, views, and picnicking opportunities.

Aqua Barn Ranch
15227 SE
Renton–Maple Valley
Rd, Renton, 255-4618
(map: OO1)

One of the oldest ranches in the area, Aqua Barn offers easy guided rides in the evenings and on weekends through 100 acres of pasture and foothills. The cost is $15 an hour; reservations are required. Anyone over age 8 can ride.

Kelly's Riding and Boarding
Ranch
7212 Renton–Issaquah
Rd SE, Issaquah, 392-
6979

A guide leads you along trails at the base of Squak Mountain for $15 an hour. Call for reservations.

Look for **KIDS**—*it means your child will especially enjoy this place or attraction.*

Tiger Mountain Outfitters
24508 SE 133rd St,
Issaquah, 392-5090

Specializes in three-hour rides to a lookout on Tiger Mountain. Most of the 10-mile round trip ($35 per person) is along logging roads, and the rest is in dense forest. No tykes under 10.

KAYAKING/CANOEING

There are dozens of navigable rivers in the region to kayak and canoe on, with names Walt Whitman would love, like the Skagit, the Nisqually, the Stillaguamish, the Hoh, and the Humptulips. There are also 10,000 or so lakes in the state. These sports require a good deal of instruction and preparation, so it's best to go with experienced boaters. One of the oldest kayaking clubs in the nation is the **Washington Kayak Club** (PO Box 24264, Seattle 98124, 433-1983), a safety- and conservation-oriented club that organizes pool practices, weekend trips, and sea- and whitewater-kayaking lessons in the spring. Dues are $20 per year, with an initiation fee of $15; you must have your own equipment.

Rental outfits are leery of renting whitewater kayaks to the public because of the obvious dangers (and resulting insurance) problems; some flat-out won't do it. You may occasionally find a place that will rent you a demo kayak if you've taken a whitewater course or have some proof of your experience.

Though they're not on Portage Bay anymore, the **Swallow's Nest** (2308 Sixth Avenue, 441-4100, map: G5) has canoes and kayaks for rent—along with the most knowledgeable guidance and advice on the subject—though it's more of a haul to the water from their new location. If you've never held a paddle before, they'll ask you to take one of their instructional clinics before you hit the water.

Around Seattle, several bodies of water provide more relaxed recreational opportunities for paddleboating that require little or no experience.

Montlake/
Arboretum

A cruise through the marshlands of the Arboretum (map: GG6) is the most peaceful (yet most popular) in-city canoe excursion. You can rent a canoe or rowboat ($3.50 an hour) across the Montlake Cut at the **University of Washington Waterfront Activities Center** (543-9433, map: FF6) behind Husky Stadium. Here the mirrored waters are surrounded by a mosaic of lily pads and waxy white flowers. Closer to shore, it's a lovely sight: vibrant yellow irises push through tall marsh grasses, ducks play under weeping willows. Pack along a picnic lunch and wander ashore to the **marsh walk,** a favorite bird-watching stroll from just below the Museum of History and Industry to the lawn of Foster Island. Be sure to have the canoe back by 8:30pm.

Green Lake

Green Lake's tame waters are a good place to learn the

basics. The **Green Lake Small Craft Center** (5900 W Green Lake Way N, 684-4074, map: EE7) at the southwest corner of Green Lake offers year-round canoeing and kayaking instruction and special boating programs. The **Seattle Canoe Club** (684-4074) operates out of here, with canoes and kayaks for members ($45 a year, previous paddling experience and float test required). **Green Lake Boat Rentals** (7351 E Green Lake Drive N, 527-0171), a Parks Department concession on the northeast side of the lake, also rents canoes and offers lessons (open every day, except in bad weather).

Lake Union

Lake Union offers fine paddling, great city views, and a lot of boat traffic. If you don't mind that, you can rent canoes at **Kelly's Landing** (1401 NE Boat Street, 547-9909, map: FF7) or **Northwest Outdoor Center** (2100 Westlake Avenue N, 281-9694, map: GG7) for use on Lake Union and in Portage Bay.

Lake Washington

This big lake has all sorts of shores for putting in, in addition to the **University of Washington Waterfront Activities Center** by the Montlake Cut (see Montlake/Arboretum above). On the southeast side, you can rent canoes, rowboats, paddleboats, and sailboards at **Coulon Beach Boat Rentals** in Renton's **Coulon Beach Park** (1201 Lake Washington Boulevard N, Renton, map: MM3).

Duwamish River

KIDS From Tukwila (where the Green River becomes the Duwamish) to Boeing Field (map: JJ7 to QQ5), this scenic waterway makes for a lovely paddle. Beyond Boeing, you pass industrial salvage ships, commercial shipping lanes, and industrial Harbor Island, until the river empties into Elliott Bay. Rent a canoe or kayak at **Pacific Water Sports** (16205 Pacific Highway S, 246-9385, map: OO6) near Sea-Tac Airport—the staff can direct you to one of several spots along the river to put your craft in. The current is sometimes strong, but not a serious hazard for moderately experienced paddlers.

Sammamish River

KIDS The trip up the gently flowing Sammamish Slough (map: BB5 to FF1) is quiet and scenic. Ambitious canoers can follow it all the way to Lake Sammamish, about 15 miles to the southeast, passing golf courses, the town of Woodinville, Chateau St. Michelle Winery, and Marymoor Park along the way.

Puget Sound

Seattle's proximity to the open waters and scenic island coves of Puget Sound is the main reason sea-kayaking is so popular here. Bainbridge Island's **Eagle Harbor** is a leisurely paddle in protected (albeit polluted) waters. Tiny **Blake Island**, a state park, is a short trip from Vashon Island, Alki Point, or Fort Ward Park on Bainbridge Island (see Parks and Beaches in this chapter). Birdwatchers can head to the calm waters of the **Nisqually Flats** south of Tacoma. And the **San Juan Islands** provide endless paddling opportunities, but the currents can be very strong—not for novices.

MOUNTAINEERING/CLIMBING

Washington offers climbers an unusually rugged and remote experience, with opportunities for both experienced climbers and first-timers in alpine and technical rock areas. The real climber's paradise is the **North Cascades**, including Mount Baker (see below) and other spires such as **Liberty Bell Mountain, Mount Shuksan, Forbidden Peak,** and **Glacier Peak.** A local alpine and rock-climbing guide service, **Alpine Ascents Unlimited of Seattle** (4013 Stone Way N, 633-0640, map: FF6), offers courses in avalanche safety and leads both summer and winter expeditions in the Northwest; they also provide the instruction for REI's Mountain School. REI rents some climbing equipment (see Hiking section). **The Mountaineers** (300 Third Avenue W, 284-6310, map: A9), the largest outdoor club in the region, is a superb resource, offering group climbs, climbing courses, and general information on these and other climbs—both in and out of the Northwest.

The Northwest is also of major importance to rock climbers. The **Vertical Club** (1111 Elliott Avenue W, 283-8056, map: A9) has simulated indoor climbing surfaces and is the first gym of its kind in the country; they'll also rent you rock shoes and give you instruction in climbing techniques. The man-made **University of Washington Climbing Rock** behind Husky Stadium and **Sherman Rock** at **Camp Long** (5200 35th Avenue SW, 684-7434, map: JJ8) are other in-city practice spots. **Orion Expeditions** (1516 11th Avenue, 322-9130, 1-800-553-7466) offers week-long camping and climbing trips in Washington and Joshua Tree, California's climber's paradise.

The following are the major peaks of the Washington Cascades, all volcanoes and all within three hours of Seattle:

Mount Adams

Information: Mount Adams Ranger Station, 2455 Hwy 141, Trout Lake 98650, 1-509-395-2501, 200 miles SE of Seattle

"Mount Rainier's little brother" is similar to Rainier in terrain, but smaller (12,326 feet) and much safer—a good day-long first climb. Many people scale Mount Adams as a practice run for Rainier; others do it just to ski down. Most climbers scale Adams on their own, but **Alpine Ascents Unlimited of Seattle** can take you up.

Mount Baker

*Information: North
Cascades Forest Service
and Park Service
Headquarters, 2105 Hwy
20, Sedro Woolley 98284,
1-856-5700, 100 miles
NE of Seattle*

Like Rainier, Mount Baker (10,778 feet) offers both well-traveled, standard alpine routes and rugged, highly challenging ascents, including long rock walls and ice faces. Baker's Coleman Headwall, at 2,500 vertical feet, is the longest ice face in the North Cascades. You can go with your own group, but registration is required at either the Forest Service and Park Service headquarters or at the **Glacier Public Service Center** (Box C, Glacier 98244, 1-599-2714). The climb can be done in one day. Many prefer to climb with **American Alpine Institute** (1212 24th Street, Bellingham 98225, 1-671-1505), which leads moderate to extremely difficult ascents of Mount Baker. Weekends are extremely crowded on the mountain—as many as 500 climbers could be climbing on any given day.

Mount Rainier

See Mount Rainier under Excursions in the Outings chapter.

Mount St. Helens

*Mount St. Helens
National Volcanic
Monument, Route 1, Box
369, Amboy 98601,
1-247-5473, 200 miles
south of Seattle*

At the 10-year anniversary of its eruption, the sight of what the blast left behind is still the most compelling reason to visit Mount St. Helens, which stands at 8,363 feet—over 1,300 feet shorter than it was on May 17, 1980 (see Mount St. Helens under Excursions in Outings chapter). It wasn't reopened to climbers until May 1987. Permits are required, and only a limited number are given out each day (for free). Most climbers take the Monitor Ridge Route up the south face to the rim of the volcano—a steep upward climb that can take seven hours round trip. After June, when the snow has disappeared, it's a long, dusty hike

RIVER RAFTING

In a region crisscrossed with rivers, it's no wonder that rafting has become one of the premier outdoor adventure sports. Rafting companies are sprouting up all over the state, particularly west of the Cascades, and they're willing to give you a taste of the waters for $50 to $80 a day. Each company has its own style of trip, though there are two basic types: peaceful float trips, often in protected and scenic wildlife areas, and trips through rapids, which vary in their degree of difficulty. Spring and early summer is the time for whitewater trips. Regular trips are scheduled on more than a dozen Washington rivers, including the Skagit, Sauk, Methow, Wenatchee, Skykomish, and Green, and rivers on the Olympic Peninsula.

The following are among the biggest rafting companies in the area:

Downstream River Runners
12112 NE 195th St,
Bothell, 483-0335,
1-800-732-RAFT (map:
AA3)

Downstream River Runners leads daytrips on 12 Washington and Oregon rivers, including the Green, Grande Ronde, Methow, and Klickitat. The scenic Skagit bald eagle float trips in winter (hot homemade soup included) make a great family expedition.

Northern Wilderness River Riders
23312 77th Ave SE,
Woodinville, 448-RAFT
(map: BB3)

A trip with the River Rafters promises a day full of rapids and world-famous (so they claim) guacamole at lunch. They'll provide everything you need—from wet suits to barbecue—and feature trips for every member of the family at every level of experience. In the winter, an 8-mile float trip from Marblemount to Rockport offers a chance to see over 200 bald eagles feeding on spawned-out salmon.

Orion Expeditions
1516 11th Ave, 322-9130,
1-800-553-7466
(map: GG6)

The veteran guides at Orion Expeditions give lessons and lead rafting trips in Washington, Oregon, Costa Rica, and on the Rio Grande in Texas.

ROWING

In a city graced with two large lakes, many people opt to exercise on the water instead of jogging through exhaust fumes or roller-blading around Green Lake. The water might not always be clean enough to swim in, but these days many athletes are finding a kinship with sleek, lightweight rowing shells that slice across the silver-black flat water of early morning. The **Seattle Parks and Recreation Department** (684-4075) runs, among other things, two rowing clubs: one on Green Lake out of the **Green Lake Small Crafts Center** (5900 W Green Lake Way N, 684-4074) and another on Lake Washington through the **Mount Baker Rowing and Sailing Facility** (3800 Lake Washington Boulevard S, 386-1913). Both operate year-round and offer all levels of instruction, host yearly regattas, and send their top boats to the nationals. On the outskirts of the city are two other rowing clubs, **Renton Rowing** (874-2992) and **Carillon Point Rowing Club** (822-0835), which also oversees a club out of **Chandler's Cove** on Lake Union (682-2031).

The **Lake Washington Rowing Club** (PO Box 45117, Seattle 98145-0117, 547-1583) is an excellent organization for self-directed self-starters. A coach is available three days a week, but the rest of the time you're on your own. Open to all levels (there's everything from a beginner orientation to an elite group training for international competition), with a very reasonable yearly fee. Another strong racing club—for postcollegiate, experienced rowers only—is the **Seattle Rowing Club** (PO Box 30003, Seattle 98103; men, 386-0244, women, 547-2021), which is launched out of Seattle Pacific University's boathouse.

On the less competitive side, **Rowing Northwest** (3304 Fuhrman Avenue E,

324-5800), located underneath the University Bridge, has introduced over 4,000 people to the sport since 1984. Instruction and monthly and daily rentals (and sales) are available for their open-water training shells. Numerous other women-only, men-only, or age-specific clubs thrive in the Northwest. For a full list, call Sarah Lopez, regional coordinator, Northwest Region of US Rowing, 722-1833.

RUNNING

If you enjoy scenic jogging, you're in the right city. Step out just about any door in the area, and you're on a good running course. The mild climate and numerous parks contribute to the appeal, but there is also a large and well-organized running community to link up with for recreation or competition.

Club Northwest's *Northwest Runner* is a good source for information on organized runs and a complete road race schedule, for those of you who hate to exercise alone or who just want to get the special T-shirt.

Racers, both casual and serious, can choose from a number of annual races (at least one every weekend in spring and summer). Some of the biggest are the St. Patrick's Day 4-Mile, the Emerald City Marathon in April, the 6.7-mile Seward-to-Madison Shore Run in July, the 8-kilometer Seafair Torchlight Run through the city streets in August, and the Seattle Marathon in November. Outside of Seattle, runners can test their mettle in the 12K Sound to Narrows Run in Tacoma or the Bloomsday Run in Spokane, the best-attended run of the year. One of the finest running outfitters in town, **Super Jock 'N Jill** (7210 E Green Lake Drive N, 522-7711, map: EE7), maintains a racing hotline (524-RUNS).

Listed below are some of the best routes for runners (see also the Bicycling section of this chapter).

Arboretum
Arboretum Dr E and Lake Washington Blvd E (map: GG6)

A favorite. You can stay by the windy main drive, Lake Washington Boulevard E, or run along any number of paths through the trees and flowers. The boulevard connects up with the scenic but steep E Interlaken Boulevard at the Japanese garden.

Green Lake
Latona Ave NE and E Green Lake Way N (map: EE7)

The 2.8-mile path around the lake is half for cyclists and half for pedestrians, runners, roller-skaters, baby strollers, and dogs. On sunny weekends, Green Lake becomes a recreational Grand Central—great for people-watching, but slow going. Early mornings or early evenings, the quiet trip around the lake may offer ducks and geese to be fed, mountain views, and a look at crew practices. The path connects with a bikeway along Ravenna Boulevard. A painted line establishes the cycling lane; runners can follow the boulevard's grassy median. For bike advice and rentals, stop by

▼

RUNNING

Gregg's Greenlake Cycle (7007 Woodlawn Ave NE, 523-1822) on the south side of Green Lake.

Kelsey Creek Park
13204 SE 8th Pl,
Bellevue (map: II2)

This pretty Eastside park has a main jogging trail plus offshoot paths that lead into the wooded hills.

Kirkland Waterfront
Along Lake Washington
Blvd, Kirkland
(map: FF3–EE3)

This is the Eastside's see-and-be-seen running stretch, along the water from Houghton Beach Park to Marina Park. A little over a mile each way.

Lincoln Park
Fauntleroy Way SW and
SW Trenton St
(map: KK9)

Various paths and roads go through this tree-filled park overlooking Vashon Island and Puget Sound.

Magnolia Bluff–Discovery Park
Along Magnolia Blvd
(map: GG9–EE9)

A striking run when in clear weather, this route offers vistas of the Olympic Mountains across Puget Sound. From the Magnolia Bluff parking lot run 2.1 miles, with some hills, to the other end of Discovery Park.

Medina–Evergreen Point
Along Overlake Dr and
Evergreen Point Rd,
Bellevue (map:
FF4–HH4)

A scenic run along nicely maintained roads offers views of Lake Washington and some of the area's most stunning homes. Two and a half miles each way.

Queen Anne Hill
Start at W Highland Dr
(map: GG8)

This loop around Queen Anne Hill is one of the city's most architecturally pleasing runs. It incorporates Highland Drive, Queen Anne Avenue, and other interesting parts of Queen Anne Hill in a 3-mile circuit on tree-lined streets and wide promenades. You'll pass the elegant Parsons Gardens and other small parks along the way.

Ravenna Boulevard
Green Lake Way N and
NE 71st St
(map: EE7–EE6)

Follow this course along the wide, grassy median strip beginning at Green Lake and dip into Ravenna Park's woodsy ravine at 25th Avenue NE, near the boulevard's end.

Warren Magnuson Park
Sand Point Way NE and
NE 65th St (map: EE5)

Magnuson Park, formerly part of the Naval Air Station at Sand Point, has many opportunities for running, including wide, paved roads and flat, grassy terrain—all nicely situated on Lake Washington. On clear days, the view of Mount Rainier is superb.

SAILING

Green Lake

Green Lake is a great place for a leisurely sail; the winds are usually gentle here, and the lake is no more than a mile across in any direction. The **Seattle Sailing Association** is headquartered at the **Green Lake Small Craft Center** (5900 W Green Lake Way N, 684-4074, map: EE7), at the southwest corner of the lake; they'll let you use their boats on Green Lake for a $20 annual membership fee and proof that you know a thing or two about sailing. The association also organizes its own classes and races.

Lake Union

FREE KIDS Lake Union is scenic but quite congested, and just about every other craft in the water will be bigger than yours. There are three prime sailboat rental outfits on the lake. The **Center for Wooden Boats** (1010 Valley Street, 382-BOAT, map: GG7) is a maritime museum (free admission) that rents out more than half its collection of vintage and replica wooden rowboats and sailboats. Rentals range from $10 to $25 an hour. Lessons in sailing, traditional woodworking, and boat building are also offered. **Kelly's Landing** (1401 NE Boat Street, 547-9909, map: FF7), open from Memorial Day to Labor Day (weather permitting), rents a good selection of sailboats (14 to 25 feet) for $10 to $20 an hour on weekends (prices are halved on weekdays—a great deal for an after-work sail). **Sailboat Rentals and Yacht Charters** (1115 N Northlake Way, 632-3302, map: FF7) is open year-round and has 14- to 42-foot sailboats for $20 to $60 an hour. Both Kelly's Landing and Sailboats Unlimited offer a few sailboats with outboard motors that can be taken through the Montlake Cut and into Lake Washington.

Lake Washington

Look toward Lake Washington on any sunny day, and you'll see a generous sprinkling of colorful sails all across the water. Many boaters like this body of water best, for its spectacular mountain views, romantic sunsets, dozens of coves, trendy dockside restaurants, and outrageously opulent waterfront homes. There's also room enough for every water-sport enthusiast. You can set sail from just about any waterfront park. Sailing lessons are available at **Mount Baker Park** through the Seattle Parks Department's **Mount Baker Rowing and Sailing Center** (3800 Lake Washington Boulevard S, 386-1913, map: II6). For a more extensive course, **Island Sailing Club** at Carillon Point offers 16 hours of instruction on 20-foot sailboats; at the course's end, you'll receive ASA certification and your own logbook. (2100 Carillon Point, Kirkland, 822-2470.) ISC is the only rental outfit on this lake.

SKIING: CROSS-COUNTRY

Cross-country enthusiasts can find wonderful skiing in the nearby Cascades, the Hurricane Ridge area of the Olympics, or on the drier snow and gentler slopes in Eastern Washington. Care must always be taken, however—this seemingly carefree form of recreation can be perilous. There is a constant danger of avalanches in the mountainous backcountry. Conditions change daily (sometimes hourly), so always call the Forest Service's **Northwest Avalanche Information Hotline** (526-6677) before setting out. Also check the driving conditions before you depart by calling 464-6010.

Most plowed parking areas near trailheads and along state highways require a **Sno-Park Permit**, which costs $10 per vehicle per season. These can be purchased at several local retail outlets or from the **US Forest Service/National Parks Service Outdoor Recreation Information Center** (915 Second Avenue, Room 442, 442-1070, map: M7). This office, open Monday through Friday, has information on trail and road conditions and sells parking permits and Forest Service maps.

Crystal Mountain Resort
PO Box 1, Crystal Mountain 98022, 1-663-2265, 76 miles SE of Seattle off Hwy 410

Although this area is better known for its downhill runs, cross-country skiers come for the big, broad, open areas of Silver Basin (just off chair 4). The ski patrol here will monitor your whereabouts if you check in and out, and for 50 cents they supply topographical maps of the area. No groomed trails.

Hurricane Ridge
Olympic National Park, 3002 Mount Angeles Road, Port Angeles 98362, 1-452-4501, ext 230, 17 miles S of Port Angeles on the Olympic Peninsula

This pinnacle in the heart of the Olympic Range is enormously popular. The views are spectacular, and there are good treks for all levels of skill among the several roads and trails. Ski and snowshoe rental equipment is available from the National Park concessionaires (no sleds for rent). The visitors' center at the above address has trail maps. In winter, the Hurricane Ridge Road is open only from 9am to 4pm on weekends and holidays. Call 1-452-9235 for a 24-hour report on conditions, as the road closes frequently due to weather. The weather at Hurricane Ridge changes erratically, so bring extra clothing. Snow tires are frequently required.

Methow Valley
Methow Valley Ski Touring Association PO Box 147, Winthrop 98862, 1-800-422-3048, 250 miles NE of Seattle off Hwy 20

One of the top cross-country spots in the state, the Methow Valley offers the charm of Vermont, the snow of Utah, and the big sky of Montana. Too far for a daytrip, the area is great for an entire weekend of touring along the 150 kilometers of groomed trails. The valley towns of Mazama, Winthrop, and Twisp offer plenty of rentals, lessons, guides, and lodges. Call Central Reservations for hut-to-hut skiing or housing rental reservations.

Mount Baker–Snoqualmie National Forest
Information: 915 2nd Ave, Room 442, 442-0170 (map: M7)

The US Forest Service offers a wide variety of marked cross-country trails here, with trailheads clustered along I-90 (Snoqualmie Pass) and Highway 2 (Stevens Pass). The Gold Creek and Bandera areas near I-90, with their open spaces and gentle slopes, are especially good for beginners.

Mount Rainier National Park
Tahoma Woods Star Route, Ashford 98304, 1-569-2211, 100 miles SE of Seattle

Several marked cross-country trails in the Paradise area—to Narada Falls, Nisqually Vista, and Reflection Lakes—have breathtaking views of the mountain but hilly and tough for novices. Park rangers lead snowshoe walks along the Nisqually Vista Trail from Paradise on winter weekends. Avalanche dangers increase off the marked trails. Rentals and instruction are available from Rainier Ski Touring (1-569-2283). For a taped report on road and weather conditions, call 1-569-2343.

Mountainholm Touring Center
PO Box 37, Easton 98925, 1-509-656-2346, 60 miles E of Seattle off I-90

For a fee you can use their two double-tracked groomed trails. One of them hugs the shore of scenic Lake Kachess, the other is a beginner's track. Instruction and rentals are available.

Ski Acres Cross-Country Center
PO Box 134, Snoqualmie Pass 98068, 1-434-6646, 47 miles E of Seattle off I-90

KIDS At this full-fledged cross-country center, you can rent equipment, take lessons, go on guided treks and, with the addition of the trails above newly acquired Hyak, enjoy 75 kilometers of trails (5 kilometers are lit for night track skiing). Particularly good for kids and other beginners.

All places in this book are recommended; even "no stars" are worth knowing about.

Wenatchee National Forest
Information: 915 2nd Ave, Room 442, 442-0170 (map: M7)

This area, which encompasses a huge portion of the Cascades east of Seattle, offers good trails, especially in the areas of Lake Kachess (off I-90) and Lake Wenatchee (off Highway 2, with 290 kilometers of trails), and near the alpine town of Leavenworth (also off Highway 2).

SKIING: DOWNHILL

They call it "Seattle Cement"—the rain-thickened, heavy snow of Cascade skiing areas. Some say that if you can ski it, you can ski anything. Even so, the weekend parking lots are plenty crowded. And despite the unpredictable weather, you can luck into a perfect day of fresh, light snow. Several of the ski areas on this side of the Cascades have weekend shuttle buses leaving from Seattle. All of the areas offer rentals; prices for a day of skiing vary from $18 to $25 (weekdays and nights are cheaper). If you plan to drive, carry tire chains and a shovel, and call 1-976-ROAD before you leave to find out about highway conditions.

On the eastern side of the Cascades, temperatures are considerably chillier, but the payoff is drier snow. Mission Ridge and White Pass ski resorts are the closest to Seattle. There are other areas at the eastern extremities of the state (including 49 Degrees North, Bluewood, and Mount Spokane). For longer ski vacations, travel north to British Columbia's Whistler and Blackcomb mountains, south to Oregon's Mount Bachelor, or east to Idaho's Schweitzer Basin.

The following is a list of the best ski areas in Western Washington. For daily updates on conditions in downhill areas, call the **Cascade Ski Report** (634-0200).

Alpental/Ski Acres/Snoqualmie Summit/Hyak
Information: 3010 77th Ave SE, Suite 201, Mercer Island 98040, 232-8182, 47 miles E of Seattle off I-90

KIDS At press time, this complex made up of three neighboring areas added a fourth with the purchase of the former PacWest ski area (Hyak) just east of Ski Acres. The new combination offers extensive choices for skiers of all abilities (total: 23 chairs and 12 rope tows). Linked by a free shuttle bus service on Friday evenings, weekends, and holidays, they all honor the same lift ticket. Alpental boasts some high-grade challenges, including the famous Internationale. Ski Acres offers intermediate to expert runs (try the Triple 60 chair for the steepest night skiing around), while Snoqualmie Summit's gentler slopes are ideal for children and beginning and intermediate-level skiers. With its two lifts and 75 kilometers of tracked and untracked cross-country ski trails, Hyak adds a fourth dimension to this mega-operation. A single-ride lift ticket gets you up to the excellent trails on Mount Catherine. For up-to-date snow conditions, call 236-1600.

Crystal Mountain Resort
PO Box 1, Crystal Mountain 98022, 1-663-2265, 76 miles SE of Seattle on Hwy 410

Crystal Mountain is the best ski resort in the state and the site of the 1972 World Cup Championship. This 7,002-foot vantage point at the top of Green Valley affords a tremendous view of Mount Rainier, and Mount St. Helens on a clear day. Ten chairlifts lead to extensive runs, beginner to expert. There's weekend night skiing all winter. Call 634-3771 for conditions.

Mount Baker Ski Area
1017 Iowa St, Bellingham 98226, 1-734-6771, 56 miles E of Bellingham off I-5

Mount Baker, the earliest area to open, is a terrific weekend destination, even though most of the lodging is in or close to Bellingham. Hours are limited to Fridays, weekends, and holidays. The view is remarkable. The runs are varied, but predominantly intermediate with bowls, meadows, and trails. No night skiing. Snow conditions: 1-671-0211.

Stevens Pass
PO Box 98, Leavenworth 98826, 1-973-2441, 70 miles NE of Seattle on Hwy 2

Challenging and interesting terrain makes Stevens Pass a favorite for many skiers. The conditions tend to be drier than at Crystal Mountain. Ten chairs lead to a variety of runs. The Double Diamond and Southern Cross chairs take you to some daunting expert slopes on the back side. For snow conditions, call 634-1645.

SWIMMING

See Parks and Beaches section of this chapter.

TENNIS: PUBLIC COURTS

Tennis is popular here, but not so much so that it is impossible to get a public court. There is only one indoor public tennis facility in Seattle: **Seattle Tennis Center** (2000 Martin Luther King Jr. Way S, 684-4764, map: II6), with 10 indoor courts and rates of $9 for singles ($11 for doubles) for 1-1/4 hours of play. The like facility in Bellevue is **Robinswood Tennis Center** (2400 151st Place SE, Bellevue, 455-7690, map: II2), with four outdoor and four indoor courts. The cost here is $9 per hour of singles ($12 for doubles).

Most public outdoor courts in the city are run by the Seattle Parks Department and can be used either on a first-come, first-served basis or reserved. Purchase of a one-year $15 reservation card enables players to make phone reservations up to two weeks in advance (684-4077). Otherwise, reservations must be made in person at the scheduling office of **Seattle Parks and Recreation** (5201 Green Lake Way N, map: EE7). Reservation fees are $3 per 1½ hours of court time. If it rains, your money will be refunded. Eastside outdoor public courts cannot be reserved in advance. The best time to play is early in the day; in spring and summer, the lineups start at around 3pm.

Here are the best outdoor courts in the area:

Ballard .... 14th Ave NW and NW 67th St (map: EE8)
Bryant .... *40th Ave NE and NE 65th St (map: EE5)*
Grass Lawn Park .... *7031 148th Ave NE, Redmond (map: EE2)*
Hillaire Park .... *15731 NE 6th St, Bellevue (map: HH1)*
Homestead Field .... *82nd Ave SE and SE 40th St, Mercer Island (map: II4)*
Killarney Glen Park .... *1933 104th Ave SE, Bellevue (map: HH3)*
Lincoln Park...................... *Fauntleroy Ave SW and SW Webster St (map: KK9)*
Lower Woodland Park .... *W Green Lake Way N (map: FF7)*
Luther Burbank Park .... *2040 84th Ave SE, Mercer Island (map: II4)*
Magnolia Playfield .... *34th Ave W and W Smith St (map: GG9)*
Marymoor Park...... *6046 W Lake Sammamish Pkwy NE, Redmond (map: FF1)*
Meadowbrook .... *30th Ave NE and NE 107th St (map: DD6)*
Norwood Village .... *12309 SE 23rd Pl, Bellevue (map: II2)*
Rainier Playfield .... *Rainier Ave S and S Alaska St (map: JJ5)*
Riverview...................................... *12th Ave SW and SW Othello St (map: KK7)*
Volunteer Park............................... *15th Ave E and E Prospect St (map: GG6)*

WINDSURFING

Definitely not for dilettantes, windsurfing takes athleticism, daring, and a lot of practice. The sport is big in this town, partly because the Northwest helped put windsurfing on the map. The **Columbia River Gorge** (about 200 miles south of Seattle) is the top windsurfing area in the continental United States (second only to Maui in the country), due to the strong winds that always blow in the direction opposite to the river's current—ideal conditions for confident windsurfers. Closer to home, good windsurfing can be enjoyed on virtually any body of water. Remember: always wear a wet suit or dry suit of adequate thickness for protection from cold, avoid offshore winds, and never sail alone.

You can sail your way into a great deal and some real quality instruction by taking a nine-hour course through the **New Waves Windsurfing School** (PO Box 3911, Bellevue 98009, 746-1989). After an hour lecture and two four-hour sailing sessions, you'll have earned a basic boardsailing certification and will be able to rent boards from the school at half the going rate. Other sailors must prove to New Waves that they have some competence in the sport. This safety-oriented school operates out of Bellevue and teaches on various lakes around Seattle and the Eastside.

A list of popular locations for windsurfing follows:

Green Lake   This is the best place for beginners—the water is warm
E Green Lake Dr N and   and the winds are usually gentle. Experts may find it

W Green Lake Dr N
(map: EE7)

too crowded, but novices will probably appreciate the company. You can take lessons and rent equipment at **Green Lake Boat Rentals** (7351 E Green Lake Drive N, 527-0171) on the northeast side of the lake.

Lake Union

Lake Union has fine winds in the summer, but you'll have to dodge sailboats, commercial boats, and seaplanes. You can rent equipment from **Bavarian Surf** (711 N Northlake Way, 545-9463, map: FF7) and take your board to **Gas Works Park** (N Northlake Way and Meridian Avenue N, map: FF7), the only public spot to surf from—but the walk from parking lot to shore is farther than at many Lake Washington beaches.

Lake Washington

Most windsurfers prefer expansive Lake Washington. Head to any waterfront park—most have plenty of parking and rigging space. **Magnuson Park** (Sand Point Way NE and 65th Avenue NE, map: EE5) on the Seattle side is favored for its great winds. At **Mount Baker Park** (Lake Park Drive S and Lake Washington Boulevard S, map: II6), you can take lessons at **Mount Baker Rowing and Sailing Center** (3800 Lake Washington Boulevard S, 386-1013), a public concession.

Choice Eastside beaches include Renton's **Coulon Beach Park** (1201 Lake Washington Boulevard N, Renton, map: MM3), where you can also rent boards and get instruction; **Houghton Beach Park** (NE 59th Street and Lake Washington Boulevard NE, Kirkland, map: FF4), with rentals nearby at **Ski Rack Sports** (1006 Lake Street S, Kirkland, 822-RACK, map: EE3); and **O.O. Denny Park** (NE 124th Street and Holmes Point Drive NE, Juanita, map: DD5).

Puget Sound

On Puget Sound, which is warmer than Lake Washington in the winter, windsurfers head for **Golden Gardens Park** (north end of Seaview Avenue NW, map: DD9) or **Duwamish Head** at **Alki Beach Park** (Alki Avenue SW, map: II9) in West Seattle.

GARDENS

Seattle's gardens sprout in the most unlikely places: a circle of bloom in an intersection, along busy streets and down alleyways, P-patches full of vegetables in otherwise vacant lots, gardens on campuses and corporate lawns, preserved family estates. The temperate climate of the area makes for adaptable and diverse plant life. The rhododendron (which grows in environments ranging from tropic to alpine) is Washington's state flower, and the largest collection of rhododendrons in the world is found south of the city in Federal Way. As a Pacific Rim city, Seattle also displays the influence of the Far East; this area has an impressive and extensive bonsai collection.

Following are descriptions of gardens found in this area, most of which are free to visitors.

The Bloedel Reserve
7571 NE Dolphin Dr,
Bainbridge Island,
842-7631
Wed-Sun

The Bloedels of Canada's MacMillan-Bloedel retired on this 150-acre Bainbridge Island estate. In the early 1980s it was turned over to the Arbor Fund, and is now open to the public. It's all very green and parklike, with the estate's manse, now a serene visitor's center, as its centerpiece. The Japanese Garden greets you with a guest house that subtly blends Japanese and Pacific Northwest traditions; nearby, the sand and stone Zen Garden invites contemplation. The native plants in the Moss Garden provide a wide range of textures. Bring binoculars to view inhabitants of the Bird Refuge. Only 150 visitors a day are permitted, and reservations are required. The reserve is open to the public Wednesday through Sunday (except federal holidays) from 10am to 4pm. Admission is $4 for adults, $2 for seniors and children. **FREE** Children under five are free.

Carl S. English Jr. Botanical Gardens
Hiram M. Chittenden
Locks, 3015 NW 54th St,
783-7059 (map: FF9)

Hundreds of seeds from all over the world were planted here by Carl S. English Jr., who began his collection during the Depression, compensating for the dearth of funds by trading seedlings and specimens with his colleagues.

The garden is never without color: even in winter the winter sweet bears fragrant, pale yellow flowers; in May, red horse chestnut trees line the main promenade of the garden's quarter-mile path. Picnics, weddings, and even band concerts take place on the generous lawns. The garden is open from 7am to 9pm every day; guided tours of the locks, fish ladder, and garden are given on weekends only, but special in-depth tours can be arranged. Admission is free.

The Gardens at Children's Hospital
Children's Hospital and
Medical Center, 4800
Sand Point Way NE,
527-3889 (map: EE5)

FREE It is unusual (and honorable) that such a handsome floral collection is maintained by a hospital administration, indeed an unlikely place for a notable garden. To find the perennial borders, drive the main roadway to Lot 3. Opposite this parking lot are descending steps bordered by native and imported plants that display unusual and hard-to-find perennials. About 100 feet in length and 30 feet wide, the borders are based on traditional English designs, with the plants grouped together for color, texture, and form. A rose arbor and sundial add lovely touches. Follow the roadway to Lot 6 at the southeast corner of the hospital to find the Heather Garden, with at least 50 varieties.

The Herbfarm
32804 Issaquah–Fall City Rd, Fall City, 1-800-866-4372

See Daytrips in the Outings chapter.

Pacific Rim Bonsai Collection
Weyerhaeuser Way S (Weyerhaeuser Company), Federal Way, 1-661-9377

FREE The country's largest timber concern also happens to be the owner of the West Coast's largest (so to speak) bonsai collection. More than 50 tiny trees are on display. A 999-year-old Sierra juniper, a 3-foot-high sequoia, and an entire miniature forest are among the treasures to be found here. Many of the trees are potted, so exhibits change regularly. Every other Sunday (April through November) professional bonsai artists demonstrate pruning, propagation, and caretaking techniques. Tours are Sunday at noon or by appointment. Open year-round from 11am until 4pm, Saturday through Wednesday (closed Saturdays in winter).

Rhododendron Species Foundation
Weyerhaeuser Way S (Weyerhaeuser Company), Federal Way, 1-661-9377

A center for the preservation, distribution, and display of rhododendrons (and other plants), the foundation sports the largest collection of rhodies in existence (500 species, 60 of them endangered). In 1974, the Weyerhaeuser Company donated this 24-acre site on the company headquarters property, 24 miles south of Seattle. Its woodland setting frames the immaculate beds arranged by species, subsection, and variety. Wide gravel paths wind around the two study gardens, which showcase a representative of each species on the grounds. Sharing the foundation's hours and courtyard is the Pacific Rim Bonsai Collection (see listing). Open year-round, 11am to 4pm Saturday through Wednesday (closed Saturdays in winter). Admisssion for adults is $2.50, students $2. Children under 12 are admitted free.

Seattle Tilth Demonstration Gardens
4649 Sunnyside Ave N

FREE This educational garden is a showcase for organic agriculture. Located at the south boundary of the Good Shepherd Center, a half-acre of nearly 1,200 varieties

(Good Shepherd Center),
633-0451 (map: FF7)

of plants thrives without chemicals. Informative signs tell how it's done as you walk the narrow paths. The garden speaks to the urban farmer, offering practical information on seeds and planting techniques. It's primarily reserved for vegetables, but there are also some flowers, fruits, and even a section devoted to common weeds. Tilth also reaches out to the community. For example, you can elect to become a "master composter," learning techniques to take back to your neighbors. Classes such as seed saving and food preservation are offered regularly to both adults and children. **KIDS** The Children's Garden lets young green thumbs practice organic and sustainable gardening, too. The gardens are open 24 hours, all year long.

Woodland Park
Rose Garden
5500 Phinney Ave N,
684-4040 (map: EE7)

The rose garden at the entrance to the Woodland Park Zoo (a somewhat smaller, more haphazard version of Portland's Rose Garden in Washington Park) is a test garden for the All-America Rose Selections. Each species is tested for two years, and at the end of the trial period, the plants that garner the most points for looks, disease resistance, fragrance, and other fine points are given names and become "official" roses. The entire garden boasts 266 rosaceous varieties on 2½ acres. Sniff out your favorite. The improved landscaping inside the zoo also makes for some very interesting botanical browsing.

Washington Park Arboretum
2300 Arboretum Dr E,
543-8800 (map: GG6)

See Major Attractions in this chapter.

PARKS AND BEACHES

FREE In 1884, Seattle pioneers David and Louise Denny donated to the city a 5-acre plot of land at what is now the corner of Denny Way and Dexter Avenue North, and Seattle had its first park. Since then the park system has grown to more than 5,000 acres, many of those acres designed by visionary park planners John Charles and Frederick Olmsted Jr. (sons of New York's Central Park mastermind, Frederick Law Olmsted). Seattle's parks range from the classical (Capitol Hill's Volunteer Park, the Washington Park Arboretum) to the recreational (Green Lake, Alki Beach) to the wild (Discovery Park, Seward Park) to the ingenious (Gas Works Park, Freeway Park). At last count there were over 300 parks in the city of Seattle alone. The following are the best. To find out more about any of them, call the Washington State Parks and Recreation Commission at 1-800-562-0990 or the appropriate Parks and Recreation Department. They are: King County, 296-4232; Seattle, 684-4075; Bellevue, 455-6881; Issaquah, 392-7131; Kirkland, 828-1217; Mercer Island, 236-3545; Redmond, 882-6401.

Alki Beach
Alki Ave SW (map: II9)

This 2½-mile strip of beach point marks the spot where the original white Seattle settlers first established homesteads. Now the beach has many faces, depending on the season: cool and peaceful in the fall, stormy in winter, and jammed with cyclists and skaters in the summer. It is also regularly thronged with teenagers, who hang out along the Alki Avenue strip (no more "cruising" allowed), lined with beachy eateries on one side, sandy beach on the other. Duwamish Head, at the north end of the strand, offers spectacular views, as does the Coast Guard–maintained **Alki Point and Light Station** (3201 Alki Avenue SW, 932-5800) at the tip of the point. **FREE** This is also one of the few Seattle beaches that allows beach fires (in designated fire rings). The scenic extension of Alki Beach continues southward along Beach Drive past windswept **Me-Kwa-Mooks Park** and on to Lincoln Park (see listing).

Bellevue Downtown Central Park
1201 NE 4th St, Bellevue (map: GG3)

This 6-acre park in downtown Bellevue reflects the community's desire for an oasis in a busy urban area. Tired shoppers from Bellevue Square across the street come to sit by the fountain, enjoy the large formal garden, or stroll by the 1,200-foot reflecting canal.

Blake Island State Park
*PO Box 277, Manchester 98353,
1-731-0770*

Once an ancestral camping ground of the Suquamish Indian tribe, this tiny island in Puget Sound is now a densely wooded wilderness state park. There are 30 campsites, plus boat moorage (there is no ferry service to the island, except for commercial runs to the privately operated Tillicum Village, described in the Organized Tours section of this chapter). Trails encircling the islet access about five miles of beaches.

Park at Bothell Landing
*9929 NE 180th St,
Bothell, 486-8152
(map: BB3)*

This quaint little community park across the Sammamish River from the Sammamish River Trail offers rolling green lawns for family picnics and Frisbee throwing, an amphitheater (with Friday evening concerts in the summer), a historical museum housed in a turn-of-the-century frame building, and a senior center. Canoes and small boats can tie up at the public pier, where the ducks await bread crumbs. There is limited parking at the site itself; a parking lot at 17995 102nd

Avenue NE, Bothell, on the south side of the river, has additional spaces.

Bridle Trails State Park
116th Ave NE and NE
53rd St, Kirkland,
827-2900 (map: FF2)

This 480-acre park is a densely wooded equestrian paradise laced with horse trails (one links up with Marymoor Park) and sporting an exercise ring. Though you may feel like an alien if you come to do anything but ride (even the private homes in the area all seem to have stables), the park also features picnic sites.

Camp Long
5200 35th Ave SW,
684-7434 (map: JJ8)

KIDS West Seattle's Camp Long, run by the Seattle Parks and Recreation Department, has a variety of broader functions: as a meeting/conference facility (a lodge holds 75 people in its upper room and 35 in the basement), a family vacation destination (10 bunk-bed-equipped cabins hold 12 people each at $75 a cabin), or simply a 68-acre rustic parkland. The park also offers weekend educational programs for kids. There's a climbing rock and a simulated glacier face for climbers who want to practice their technique.

Carkeek Park
NW Carkeek Rd and 9th
Ave NW (map: DD8)

Carkeek Park is 198 acres of wilderness in the northwest corner of the city. Forest paths wind from the parking lots and picnic areas to the footbridge spanning the railroad tracks, and then down a staircase to the broad beach. (Use caution around the tracks; trains run frequently through the park, and the acoustics can be misleading.)

Chism Beach Park
1175 96th Ave SE,
Bellevue (map: HH4)

KIDS One of Bellevue's largest and oldest waterfront parks, Chism sits along the handsome residential stretch south of Meydenbauer Bay. There are docks and diving boards for swimmers, picnic areas, a playground, and a large parking area above the beach.

Coulon Park
1201 Lake Washington
Blvd N, Renton,
235-2560 (map: MM3)

This arboreal park on the shore of Lake Washington is the prize of Renton's park system. It has won national awards for the arresting architecture of its pavilion and restaurant concession (an Ivar's Fish Bar), but is best loved for its beach. Log booms around the swimming area serve as protective barriers for windsurfers, and there is a boat rental facility.

Discovery Park
3801 W Government

FREE KIDS Formerly the site of Seattle's Fort Lawton Army Base, this densely foliated Magnolia wilderness has been allowed to revert to its premetropolitan natu-

Way, 386-4236
(map: FF9)

ral order. It is full of variety and even a little mystery—in 1982 a cougar was discovered in the park, and no one knew how it got there or how long it roamed free in the 534 acres. Self-guided interpretive nature loops and short trails wind through thick forests, along dramatic sea cliffs (where powerful updrafts make for excellent kite flying), and across meadows of waving grasses. The old barracks houses and training field are the few remaining vestiges of the Army's presence. Discover the park's flora and fauna yourself or take advantage of the scheduled walks and nature workshops conducted by park naturalists. Program topics range from beach life and forest plants to Indian lore; most are free or close to it. The **Daybreak Star Arts Center** (285-4425) sponsors Indian activities and gallery exhibits of contemporary Indian art in the Sacred Circle Gallery. There are two marvelously equipped kids' playgrounds, along with picnic areas, playfields, tennis and basketball courts, and a rigorous fitness trail. The network of trails is a favorite among jogging enthusiasts.

Fay Bainbridge State Park
15446 Sunrise Dr NE,
Bainbridge Island,
842-3931

About a 10-minute drive from the Winslow ferry dock on Bainbridge Island, Fay Bainbridge is a smallish (17-acre) park known for its camping areas and view of Mount Rainier and Seattle. The log-strewn beach has pits for fires; other features include a boat launch, horseshoe pits, and two kitchen shelters. It's a popular stop for cyclists on their way around the hilly isle.

Freeway Park
6th Ave and Seneca St
(map: L5)

See Downtown in Major Attractions in this chapter.

Gas Works Park
N Northlake Way and
Meridian Ave N
(map: FF7)

KIDS What do you do when the piece of property with the grandest skyline and lakeside view in the city is dominated by a greasy old gas-processing plant? You turn it into a park, of course. Conceived in the spirit of the amusement parks of old, Gas Works Park represents urban reclamation at its finest. Consequently, it's one of the city's most delightful parks, with a grassy mound for kite flying, a large picnic shelter (call 684-4075 to reserve space), a wonderful play barn, and a front-row seat on one of Seattle's patented views. Against a sky full of dancing kites, even the looming works look oddly handsome. The threat of lurking soil pollutants, which closed the park in 1984, has been ruled out, provided you don't eat the dirt.

Golden Gardens
North end of Seaview Ave
NW (map: DD9)

Alki Beach's spiritual counterpart to the north, Golden Gardens teems with tanning humanity on summer weekends. A breezy, sandy beach, boat ramp, beach fire pits, and the pretty waters of Shilshole Bay are the biggest lures, although fully half of the park's 95 acres lie to the east of the railroad tracks along the wooded, trail-laced hillside.

Green Lake
E Green Lake Dr N and
W Green Lake Dr N
(map: EE7)

KIDS When the sun shines and the jogging, tanning, and roller-skating crowd musters en masse, the greenbelt around Green Lake looks like a slice of Southern California that's been beamed to the button-down Northwest. Even on dreary days the 2.8-mile circuit around the lake can be jammed with the Nike-and-Walkman set. What is now the center of Seattle's exercise culture is the remnant of a large glacial lake that was well on its way to becoming a meadowland when the pioneers arrived (hence the name). The city scrapped plans to turn it into a golf course or storm drain for I-5, and decided to bolster its declining waters with surplus from city reservoirs. This makes for balmy dunking (though on warm days the water can be rather ripe), superlative sailing and windsurfing, and a great place to people-watch. Although the tennis courts, soccer field, indoor pool and recreation center, outdoor basketball court, baseball diamond, putt-putt golf course, boat rental, thriving commercial district, and considerable car traffic around the lake make it feel like an urban beach resort, you can usually find one or two lonely grassy patches for a picnic. There's a well-equipped kids' playground on the northeast side. Limited parking can be found in three lots: the northeast lot (Latona Avenue N and E Green Lake Way N, the most crowded), northwest lot (7312 W Green Lake Way N), and the south lot (5900 W Green Lake Way N).

Kelsey Creek Park
13204 SE 8th Pl,
Bellevue (map: II2)

KIDS Kids are in their element at this excellent nature park, comprised of 80 acres northeast of the I-90/405 interchange. In addition to a variety of parkland habitats (marshy forests, open grassy glades, wooded hillsides), two barns and a farmyard provide a petting zoo where children can see newborn calves, goats, lambs, and piglets in the spring. Kelsey Creek and numerous footpaths (good for jogging) wind throughout. A delicate Asian garden and an original 1888 pioneer log cabin add cultural and historical dimensions.

Kirkland Waterfront
Along Lake Washington Blvd, Kirkland (map: DD4)

A string of parks, from Houghton Beach to Marina Park at Moss Bay, lines the shore of Kirkland's beautiful Lake Washington Boulevard. The kids feed the ducks and wade (only Houghton Beach has lifeguards); their parents sunbathe and watch the runners lope by. This is as close to Santa Cruz as the Northwest gets.

Lake Sammamish State Park
20606 SE 56th St, Issaquah, 455-7010

The sprawling beach is the main attraction of this state park located at the south end of Lake Sammamish. Shady picnic areas, grassy playfields, barbecue stands, and volleyball courts are the excellent secondary draws. Large groups must reserve day-use areas—the place can be overrun in summer. Issaquah Creek, fine for fishing, runs through the park's wooded area.

Lake Washington Parks
From Madison Park at E Madison St and 43rd Ave E to Stan Sayres Memorial Park at 3800 Lake Washington Blvd S (map: GG5–JJ5)

This string of grassy beachfronts acts as collective backyard for several of the neighborhoods that slope toward Lake Washington's western shore. **Bicycle Saturdays and Sundays** take place in the summer, when the route from Colman to Seward Park is open to bicycles (closed to cars 10am to 6pm). **Madison Park**, the site of an amusement park and bathing beach early in the century, has shed its vaudeville image and is now a genteel neighborhood park, with a roped-in swimming area and tennis courts. If you head west on Madison and turn left onto Lake Washington Boulevard, you'll wind down to meet the beach again, this time at **Madrona Park** (Lake Washington Boulevard and Madrona Drive), a grassy strip with a swimming beach, picnic tables, a (summer only) food concession, and a dance studio. Farther on is **Leschi Park** (Lakeside Avenue S and Leschi Place), a nicely manicured city park that occupies the hillside on the other side of the boulevard and offers great views of the Leschi Marina and the dazzling spinnakers of the sailboats. Another greenbelt, **Colman Park** (36th Avenue S and Lakeside Avenue S), marks the start of the seamless strip that includes **Mount Baker Park** (Lake Park Dr S and Lake Washington Blvd S), a gently sloping, tree-lined ravine; the hydroplane racing mecca—once a marshy slough, now a manicured park and spectator beach—called **Stan Sayres Memorial Park**; and the lonely wilderness peninsula of Seward Park (see listing).

Lincoln Park
Fauntleroy Ave SW and

KIDS Lincoln Park, a 130-acre jewel perched on a pointed bluff in West Seattle, offers a network of walk-

SW Webster St
(map: LL9)

ing and biking paths amid grassy forests, recreational activities from horseshoes to football to tennis, and expansive views of the Olympic Mountains from seawalls or rocky beaches. There are tide pools to be inspected and beaches to roam, and the kids will delight in the playground equipment. Don't miss the (heated) outdoor saltwater Colman Pool (summer only), which began as a tide-fed swimming hole.

Luther Burbank Park
2040 84th Ave SE,
Mercer Island (map: II4)

KIDS Luther Burbank's undulating fields and endless land-and-lake recreational areas occupy a goodly chunk of the northern tip of Mercer Island and make it the Eastside's favorite family park. There are picnic shelters, nicely maintained, tennis courts, an outdoor amphitheater for summer concerts, a first-rate playground, several playing fields, docks for boat tie-ups (the haunt of the sun-worshiping teens in summer), and green meadows that tumble down to the shore.

Magnuson Park
Sand Point Way NE and
65th Ave NE,
(map: EE5)

This 193-acre park fronts Lake Washington just south of Sand Point Naval Air Base, with a mile of shoreline, a boat launch, a playing field, and six tennis courts. Adjacent to the north is **NOAA (the National Oceanic and Atmospheric Administration, 526-6046)**. There you'll find a series of unique artworks along the beach (see Public Art in the Arts chapter). One, **Sound Garden**, is composed of state-of-the-art sculptures fitted with flutelike aluminum tubes that create eerie "music" when the wind blows. The site is open every day from 6:30am and is a hauntingly wonderful spot to sit on a blue whale bench, listening to wailing wind chimes and watching the sun come up over Lake Washington.

Marymoor County Park
6046 W Lake
Sammamish Pkwy NE,
Redmond, 296-2966
(map: FF1)

KIDS This vast expanse of flat grasslands and playfields is located in rural Redmond, a city considered by many to be the bicycle capital of the Northwest. Marymoor has the Northwest's only velodrome (see Bicycling under Great Outdoors in the Exploring chapter) and serves as the starting point of the Sammamish River bike (or jogging or horseback-riding) trail. There are a lot of other resources here too: the Marymoor Historical Museum (885-3684), picnic facilities, a popular area for flying remote-control model airplanes, and about a zillion playing fields.

Map locators refer to the fold-out map included in this book. Single letters refer to the Downtown Seattle map; double letters refer to the Greater Seattle map.

Myrtle Edwards Park
Alaskan Way between W
Bay St and W Thomas St
(map: B9)

Myrtle Edwards and the adjacent **Elliott Bay Park** provide a front lawn to the northern part of downtown. This breezy and refreshing strip is a great noontime getaway for jogging (the two combined form a 1.25-mile trail), picnicking on sea-facing benches, or just strolling. Parking at the Pier 70 lot just south of Myrtle Edwards is at a premium, but the Waterfront Streetcar stops there.

Ravenna Park
20th Ave NE and NE
58th St (map: EE6)

This steep woodland ravine strung between residential districts north of the U District is a lush rural antidote to the city above. At the west end is **Cowen Park** (University Way NE and NE Ravenna Boulevard), with its tennis courts and play and picnic areas. Trails along burbling Ravenna Creek lead to the eastern end of the park and more picnic areas, a wading pool, and playing fields.

Saltwater State Park
25205 8th Pl S, Kent,
764-4128 (map: RR7)

Folks use this 88-acre Puget Sound–front park for clamming (call ahead for red-tide report), picnicking, camping, hiking in the forested uplands, or scuba diving in the underwater reef. The views of Vashon Island and the summer sunsets are spectacular.

Seward Park
Lake Washington Blvd S
and S Juneau St
(map: JJ5)

KIDS This spectacular wilderness occupying a 277-acre knob of land in southeast Seattle gives the modern-day Seattleite an idea of what the city must have looked like centuries ago. There are times when the park is imbued with a primal sense of permanence, especially on misty winter days when the quiet of a solitary walk through the old-growth Douglas fir forest is broken only by the cries of a few birds. But other times—hot summer Sundays, for instance—Seward turns into a frenzy of music and barbecues. You can drive the short loop road to get acquainted with the park, past the bathhouse and beach facilities; the **Seward Park Art Studio** (722-6342), which offers classes in the arts; some of the picnic shelters (call 684-4075 for reservations); and some of the trailheads, which lead to the fish hatchery, the outdoor amphitheater, and into the forest preserve. Cyclists and runners can make an even better loop on the scenic 2½-mile lakeside trail encircling the park.

Schmitz Park
SW Stevens St and

Just east of West Seattle's Alki Beach is this 50-acre virgin nature preserve, full of raw trails through thickly

Admiral Way SW
(map: II9)

wooded terrain. The largest western redcedars and hemlocks here are likely to be about 800 years old—seedlings when Richard the Lionhearted was leading his troops on the Third Crusade. It's a marvelous place for contemplation and nature study. No playgrounds, picnic areas, or other park amenities.

Victor Steinbrueck Park
Western Ave and Virginia St, 684-4080 (map: H8)

Pike Place Market's greatest supporter and friend is the namesake behind this splash of green at the north end of Pike Place Market. With the Alaskan Way Viaduct right below, the park can be quite noisy during peak traffic hours. It is also a favorite hangout for street people. Despite those caveats, the park's grassy slopes and tables make a fine place for a Market picnic, and the view of the blue bay and ferry traffic is refreshing.

Volunteer Park
15th Ave E and E Prospect St (map: GG6)

KIDS See Major Attractions in this chapter.

Washington Park Arboretum
E Madison and Lake Washington Blvd E, 543-8800 (map: GG7)

See Major Attractions in this chapter.

Waterfall Gardens
219 2nd Ave S, 624-6096 (map: P8)

How many city downtowns can boast a park with a 22-foot crashing waterfall, even an artificial one? The waterfall in this tiny Pioneer Square park was built to honor the United Parcel Service, which started in this location in 1907. It does crash (this is no place for quiet conversation), and the benches do fill up by noon on weekdays (there's a small concession stand here), but it makes for a marvelous little nature fix in the middle of a busy urban day.

Waterfront Park
Pier 57 to Pier 61 on Alaskan Way (map: J9)

A multilevel park that spans three piers between the Aquarium and Pier 57 provides a break from the bustling activity of the rest of the waterfront. The park contains a tree-encircled courtyard, raised platforms with telescopes for a voyeur's view of the bay and islands, plenty of benches and picnic tables, and—strange for a park in this town—not a blade of grass.

Weyerhaeuser/King County Aquatics Center

This aquatics center was originally built for the 1990 Goodwill Games. Its three different pools are now open

650 SW Campus Dr,
Federal Way, 1-927-5173

for public use (except when there are state or national competitions being held). The diving pool stages a 1-, 3-, 5-, 7.5-, and 10-meter platform, and a 1- and 2-meter spring board; the Olympic-size competition pool is one of the nation's fastest due to the surge gutters that prevent much wave action; the recreation pool is handicapped-accessible—it's 0 to 4 feet deep and runs a bit warmer than most for therapeutic purposes (anywhere from 82 to 86 degrees).

Woodland Park
5500 Phinney Ave N,
684-4800 (map: FF7)

KIDS See Woodland Park Zoo under Major Attractions in this chapter.

ORGANIZED TOURS

AIR TOURS

Chrysler Air
1325 Fairview Ave E,
329-9638 (map: E1)

Jim Chrysler does his main business in charters to Canadian fishing camps—and has for 24 years—but he also does a $27.50, 20-minute exhaustive airborne tour of Seattle (UW, Lake Washington, Kingdome, the waterfront, Magnolia, the Locks, Shilshole, Green Lake, and back to Lake Union). There's also a two-hour tour down to Mount St. Helens (price varies according to number of people).

Kenmore Air
6321 NE 175th St,
486-1257 (map: BB5)

1838 Westlake Ave N,
486-8400 (map: GG7)

The largest seaplane operator in the area, Kenmore Air has a fleet of 15 planes that makes scheduled and charter flights around Puget Sound, including sightseeing excursions over the city, from seaports in north Lake Washington and Lake Union. The popular city tour lasts 20 minutes and costs $78 for three passengers or fewer, $90 for four or more. A one-way passage to the San Juan Islands is $51 per person on a scheduled flight, or $180 for a charter for one to three people. Go standby to the San Juans for $30 per person, or sign up for a daytrip package (including lunch and dinner on San Juan Island) for $99.

Lake Union Air Service
950 Westlake Ave N,
284-0300 (map: GG7)

A half hour of Seattle from the air. Seaplanes depart from Lake Union, circle over all of the area's main attractions, from the Ship Canal to Shilshole to the University of Washington campus and Lake Washington. The pilot narrates the excursion. Reservations can be made on the day of the trip, for a minimum of two people. Cost is $150 per half hour for up to six passengers.

Sound Flight
Renton Municipal Airport, Renton
827-7179

Up to 10 passengers can arrange their own pilot-narrated floatplane tours of Seattle, Mount Rainier, the San Juan Islands, Mount St. Helens, or the North Cascades. Prices (from $24 to $139 per person) depend on the number of people and extent of the tour.

BOAT TOURS

Gray Line Water Sightseeing
Pier 57, 441-1887 (map: J9)

This two-and-a-half-hour harbor cruise aboard the 65-foot tour vessel M/V *Sightseer* includes a trip from Lake Union through the Locks to the Seattle waterfront. The season lasts from April to October, with charters the rest of the year ($15.50 per person). Reservations are needed for parties of over 15.

CLOSED

Major Marine Tours
Pier 54, 292-0595 (map: L9)

Harbor tours (June through September) on board the 100-foot *Emerald Sea* include an informative narrative composed by the Museum of History and Industry, and a barbecue. Cost is $6.50. Major Marine also offers sport- and bottom-fishing charters year-round (reservations required for the charters).

Seattle Harbor Tours
Pier 55, 623-1445 (map: L9)

These excellent tours run six times daily (June through September) and give hard facts about Seattle's waterfront instead of the usual unbroken stream of groaning puns. The narrated trip on the *Goodtime* vessels lasts one hour and costs $7.50 (slightly less for seniors and juniors). Charters are available for groups of 50 to 500.

Spirit of Puget Sound
2819 Elliott Ave (Pier 70), 443-1439 (map: D9)

Cruise International brings its newest luxury ship to Seattle. With 10 other ships harbored from Boston to Los Angeles, these professionals have entertainment figured out. This 600-passenger luxury ship sails nightly (depending on availability and weather) for two- to three-hour tours of the Sound in a style akin to that of a deep-sea cruise liner: a full-service restaurant, entertainment, and dancing. Lunch cruises run $16.25 to $20.35, dinner cruises from $35.65 to $39.75.

*Look for **KIDS**—it means your child will especially enjoy this place or attraction*

Tillicum Tours
Pier 56, 329-5700
(map: K9)

KIDS Get a (slightly stagey) glimpse into North Coast Indian heritage with this cruise to Tillicum Village in Blake Island Marine State Park, birthplace of Chief Sealth. Artifacts and crafts, forest trails, Indian dances, and a traditional salmon bake dinner served in a cedar longhouse highlight the four-hour trip. Tours are seasonal; call for information. Cost is $32 for adults, less for kids.

Virginia V Foundation
624-9119

Numerous cruises a year are scheduled aboard the stately *Virginia V* passenger steamer: Octoberfest, July Fourth, New Year's Eve, Christmas, Seafair, and Maritime Week tugboat races in Seattle and Olympia. There are summertime dinner/dance cruises and twice-monthly jazz cruises. Cost starts at $25. Boarding places vary according to season. Call for reservations.

MOTOR TOURS

Gray Line of Seattle
720 S Forest St, 624-5813

This touring agency offers several choice trips: Mount Rainier ($31 per person), the Boeing plant ($17 per person), the popular Seattle City tours ($27 for six hours, or $16 for two and a half hours), overnighters to Victoria, BC, and more. Free pickup at several downtown hotels.

WALKING TOURS

Chinatown Discovery
236-0657

Vi Mar Travel conducts three-hour walking tours of the International District, with dim sum lunch at a Chinese restaurant included. Reservations required. Tours begin at 10:30am, but evening tours (with a Chinese dinner) are also available. Tours run Tuesday through Saturday. Cost is $18 for adults, $12 for kids.

The Underground Tours
610 1st Ave, 682-4646
(map: N8)

KIDS These tours are mostly one story down, the level of the city before it was rebuilt after the great fire of June 6, 1889. (Poor drainage at the old, lower level made the higher streets imperative.) It's all pretty cornball, but you'll get a salty taste of the pioneers' eccentricities and some historical insights in spite of the bad puns. The tours begin at Doc Maynard's Public House and run one and a half hours. Reservations are recommended. Tour times vary seasonally. Cost is $4 for adults, less for students, children, and seniors.

SHOPPING

SHOPPING CONTENTS

ACCESSORIES AND LUGGAGE

Bergman Luggage
*1930 3rd Ave (and
branches), 448-3000
(map: H7)*
Every day

If it's made of leather or intended for travel, this long-time family-run business has it at discount prices: belts, bags, attaché cases, carry-ons, wallets, travel accessories, and suitcases galore. There's something for every pocketbook, and there's luggage repair service at three of the eight branches.

Bree
*Westlake Center,
340-0719 (map: I5)*
Every day

A European bagmaker brings to Seattle its own line of purses, totes, briefcases, portfolios, and satchels that last a lifetime—with a one-year guarantee. Natural pale blond cowhide (which darkens and softens with age) and trimmed leather goods in classic styles. Prices are steep but fair.

Byrnie Utz Men's Hat Store
*310 Union Ave, 623-0233
(map: K6)*
Mon-Sat

Byrnie Utz provides that civilized flourish that has all but disappeared from modern dressing. With anywhere from 500 to 1,000 styles, men can find everything from Harrison Ford's hat in *Raiders of the Lost Ark* to John Wayne's Stetson. The shop is one of the last full-line hat shops on the West Coast, and one of the largest in the United States.

**The Coach Store (Four
Seasons Olympic Hotel)**
*417 University St,
382-1772 (map: L6)*
Mon-Sat

Classic, beautifully tooled bags, belts, and accessories are displayed on floor-to-ceiling bookshelves. This branch is owned by the Coach factory, so new styles arrive early for test marketing. The salespeople are helpful and down to earth, but prices are not.

Fast Forward
*1918 1st Ave, 325-1313
(map: I7)*
Every day

Local artists provide most of the jewelry, clothing, and trinkets in this eclectic store, now in a more spacious downtown location. A good selection of scarves and perky hats for women.

Fini
*525 Pine St, 623-4216
(map: J5)*
Mon-Sat

Unusual high-fashion jewelry, gloves, scarves, hosiery, belts, and handbags. Everything from exotic tribal pieces to refined hand-painted silk scarves. Salespeople are eager to assist and can produce some choice surprises from a cache in the back.

InSync
1418 1st Ave, 292-0770

Sophisticated, cutting-edge accessories (primarily from New York and Europe, but some from local artists) are

---

Send us your feedback and tips on the report form at the back of this book.

(map: J8)
Mon-Sat, every day
from Memorial Day
to Labor Day

found in this shop. Look here for a belt buckle, hair clip, or bolo tie to finish an outfit.

Metro Man
401 Broadway E
(Broadway Market),
328-1417 (map: GG7)
Every day

What began as a humble tie-cart has grown up to meet the demands of the metropolis. Geometrically designed ties are still present, but the store also stocks an armload of leather belts and a thoughtful collection of contemporary watches, playful tie tacks, and uncommon pins. Do you dare to give cotton Bullwinkle boxers?

Personal Adornments
Gilman Village,
Issaquah, 392-9907
Every day

An outstanding store for wearable art, handcrafted by selected artists from all over the US; the wide range of unusual and lovely things includes men's caps, hand-painted silks, and avant-garde jewelry. You'll also find art for the home: wall art, pottery, and glassware.

Simms & Marchesi
999 3rd Ave, 623-1676
(map: M7)
Every day

2 Union Square,
224-4330 (map: K5)
Mon-Sat

Thirteen years of partnership have resulted in a winning formula: Simms lives in Seattle, Marchesi in Italy. Their imports—mostly handbags and some other accessories—come directly from Italian fashion houses. Prices are steep, but you can't find classic, elegant merchandise like this anywhere else in town.

WE Hats
105 1st Ave S,
623-3409 (map: N8)
Every day

A delightful mix of kitsch and quality. The walls are covered with wacky hats, many made in the minifactory upstairs, including the popular ones with duckbills, well-made fedoras and top hats, and berets. Earrings, umbrellas, nylons—even a spider web design—and great glasses round it all out. What a browse.

ANTIQUES

Almost Antiques
6019 15th Ave NW,
783-5400 (map: EE8)
Every day

This modest Ballard storefront with scrolled signage on the side of the building has room after room of gilt mirrors, tapestried love seats, lamps, dining sets, and everything mahogany.

Antique Importers
640 Alaskan Way,
628-8905 (map: M8)
Every day

Direct importing from England and Denmark (each item hand-selected by the store's own buyers) ensures that the stock of mainly pine furniture and stained glass is of excellent value and respectable quality. Good prices; mostly standard items, with a few rare finds. New shipments every three weeks.

Antique Liquidators
503 Westlake Ave N,
623-2740 (map: D2)
Mon-Sat

Without a doubt this is the largest store in town, with 30,000 square feet of sales and storage space. New merchandise arrives constantly to meet the high demand for practical furnishings (mostly Danish and English) and small household accessories. Endless variety and good prices, but don't expect perfect quality.

Apogee
4224 E Madison St,
325-2848 (map: GG6)
Tues-Sat

Madison Park's neighborhood attic has a room full of beautifully chosen and displayed gifts and antiques, behind which is a stash of chic clothes (Eileen Fisher, Max Sport). Every store should have such style.

Bob Alsin Antiques and Interiors
1015 Western Ave,
624-9799 (map: L8)
Mon-Sat

Reproductions and special orders are the larger part of the business, but a discriminating selection of English and French country furniture, paintings, and Oriental rugs makes this store a full-service antique dealer. They also have an interior-design arm. Don't look for bargains here.

Cobblestone Used Furniture
7320 Greenwood Ave N,
789-0853 (map: EE8)
Wed-Mon

From the outside, it resembles a huge garage. Inside, you'll see chairs and desks stacked literally to the very high ceiling. A refinisher's delight and an excellent source for those who are in the market for reasonable home and office furniture. One whole block big.

Craftsman Antiques
1520 E Olive Way,
324-4961 (map: HH6)
Mon-Sat

A thorough collection of pieces from the American Arts and Crafts Movement of 1900 to 1915, with a concentration on decorative arts and furniture made of Kentucky white oak. Because this style is so well represented in Seattle, this dealer buys many of his antiques locally. Expect exceptional quality.

The Crane Gallery
1203-B 2nd Ave,
622-7185 (map: L7)
Mon-Sat

Crane is highly respected in the business for its fine Asian antiques and artifacts. Paintings, ceramics, bronzes, ivory, jade, and furniture from around the Orient are museum quality and appropriately priced.

Daily Planet
3416 Fremont Ave N,
633-0895 (map: FF8)
Every day

A medley of vintage collectibles and Art Deco memorabilia covers every square inch of this eccentric Fremont enclave. For 20 years, owners Richard Friend and Jan Colehas have filled this unique shop with jukeboxes, Victrola music machines, lamps, chandeliers, light fixtures, and scads of other objects.

David Weatherford Antiques and Interiors

A Capitol Hill mansion provides a resplendent showplace for exquisite 18th-century English and French

133 14th Ave E,
329-6533 (map: HH6)
Mon-Sat

furniture, as well as Oriental rugs, porcelain, and screens, and art glass. A resident design team advises clients on how to gracefully integrate antiques with present furnishings.

English Style Antiques and Interiors
1219 E Pine St, 623-3179
(map: J1)
Mon-Fri

An eclectic mix of carefully selected tapestry pillows, candlestick lamps, painted furniture, silver teapots, and botanical prints from various periods gives this shop a wonderful sense of old English style. Restoration of English antiques is the specialty of the house.

CLOSED

David Gaines
1121 1st Ave, 464-0807
(map: L8)
Mon-Sat

Formerly Gaines Halliday, this classy shop carries the finest and some of the most expensive 18th- and 19th-century European antique furniture and art in the Northwest. Prices range from $100 to $30,000.

Honeychurch Antiques
1008 James St, 622-1225
(map: N4)
Mon-Sat

John Fairman runs this excellent shop, whose second location—run by Fairman's parents—is in Hong Kong. He has the largest selection of 19th-century Japanese and Chinese furniture in the Northwest, but the store's attraction lies in its blend of Asian fine art, folk art, and furniture. Occasionally the shop puts on shows of early Chinese ceramics and Japanese woodblock prints. The reputation for integrity and quality is well deserved.

Jean Williams Antiques
115 S Jackson St,
622-1110 (map: O9)
Mon-Sat

The distinctive collection of French, English, and American 18th- and 19th-century furnishings that was once Sixth Avenue Antiques is now showcased in this commodious Pioneer Square storefront. Handsome fireplace mantels, mirrors, and other classic accent pieces fill in the crannies, distinguishing this shop as extremely well stocked. You can get French and English handmade reproductions here at half the cost of genuine antiques.

Marvel on Madison
69 Madison St, 624-4225
(map: M8)
Tues-Sat

The shop is small, but the Japanese antiquities are so well displayed you have the feeling you're in a Japanese home. Screens, tea sets, tansu chests, and a unique collection of jewelry set with Chinese semiprecious stones are all personally selected by owner Marvel Stewart. Affordably priced.

N. B. Nichols and Son
1924 Post Alley,
448-8906 (map: I8)
Mon-Sat

The sign in Post Alley sums it up: "Antiques, Fine Imported Objects, & Extraordinary Junk." From 11th-century, BC, Egyptian antiquities to English garden figurines, this barny store stocks the junk of the world.

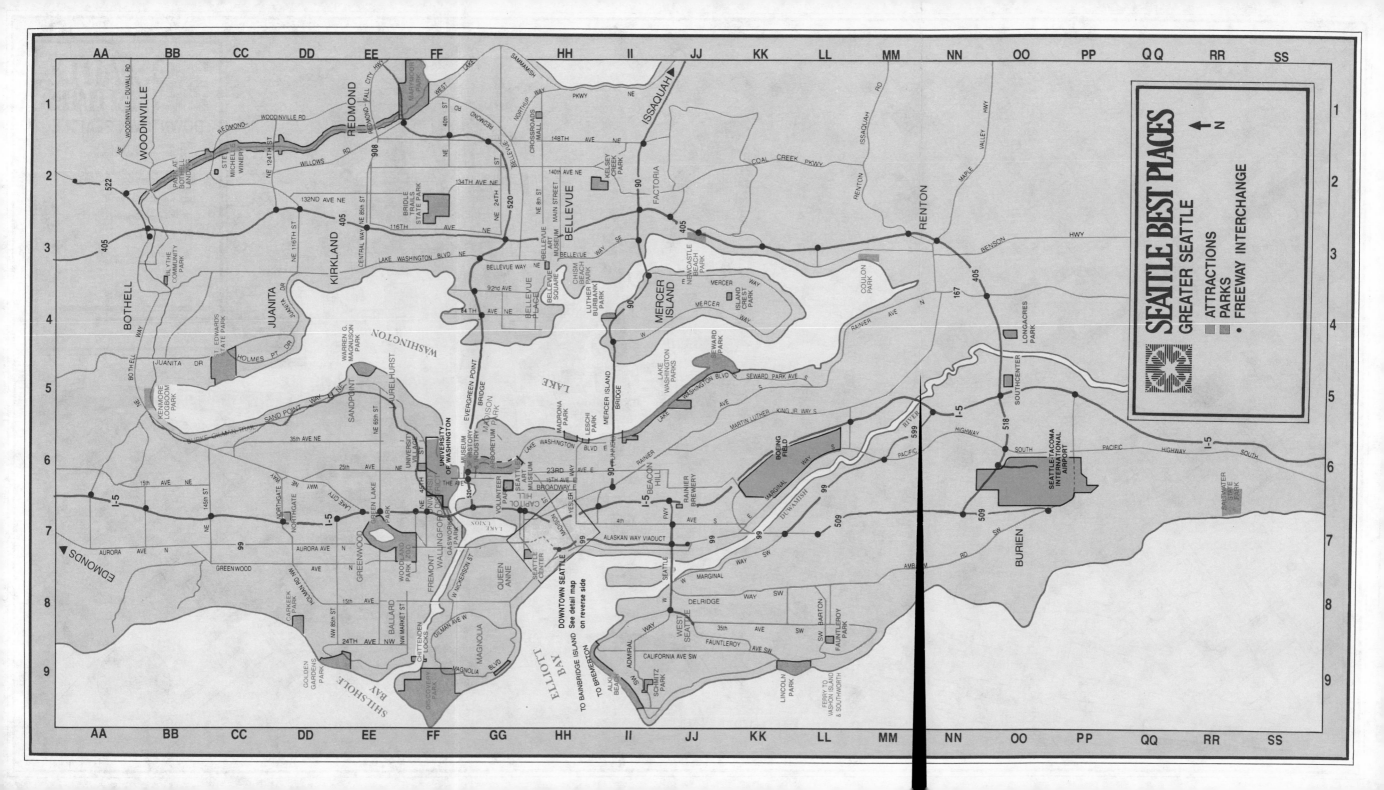

Don't expect to find flawless treasures, but do expect an interesting conglomeration of European, Asian, and African Old World belongings—some truly lovely.

Partners in Time
1201 2nd Ave,
343-3300 (map: M8)
Every day

Come here for country pine furniture imported from England, Austria, Germany, and Holland. Also Oriental carpets, Japanese porcelain, and other collectibles.

Pelayo's
7601 Greenwood Ave N,
789-1999 (map: EE8)

8421 Greenwood Ave N,
789-1333 (map: EE8)
Every day

Pedro Pelayo specializes in Danish country pine furniture from the 19th and 20th centuries. Scandinavian and Spanish crockery, bric-a-brac, wine jugs, and benches can be found along with brass and copper accessories. Home of the never-ending red-tag sale.

Stuteville Antiques
1518 E Olive Way,
329-5666 (map: HH6)
Tues-Sat, or by
appointment

Some may remember Marshall Stuteville from Globe Antiques. These days he brings to his own shop an impressive collection of Georgian period furniture as well as Continental and American pieces. The authenticity of every item, including the smaller silver and porcelain items, is evident. He also offers a restoration service.

Wicker Design Antiques
515 15th Ave, 322-2552
(map: HH6)
Wed-Sat, and by
appointment

The store has limited hours, but not limited service; its dealers are some of the handful of experts on the West Coast who buy, sell, and restore old wicker furniture—chairs, sofas, rockers, and the occasional Victorian baby buggy. Finder service, too.

APPAREL

A Grand Affair
10218 NE 8th St,
Bellevue, 453-7300
(map: HH2)
Every day

It's fun to dress up in sequined outfits, especially if you don't have to *buy* them. There are no Bob Mackie creations on hand here, but this shop is one of the few that rent glitzy formal (and bridal) wear. The standard five-day rental conveniently takes partygoers from the night before the event to the Monday after, and includes coordinated jewelry and a handbag. The in-between is up to you.

Abercrombie & Fitch (Four Seasons Olympic Hotel)
421 University St,
623-2175 (map: K6)
Every day

When aristocrats dress sporty, it's usually in something with the Abercrombie & Fitch label. It's pricey stuff but nicely crafted, and it's displayed alongside the kind of gifts you'd bring your hostess for a weekend in the Hamptons (including three imported croquet sets).

Ann Taylor
Pacific First Centre,
623-4818 (map: J5)
Mon-Sat

Classic, reliable, predictable. Here's the place to go for timeless clothing in luxurious fabrics. A fine selection of Joan & David shoes.

Baby & Co.
1936 1st Ave, 448-4077
(map: I7)
Every day

Baby & Co. visually dominates this trendy corner of town with some of the best window displays in the city. Inside, walls are festooned with chichi playclothes evocative of New York and Paris street life. Besides new-wave trappings, the store carries handsome pieces in silk, rayon, and cotton in an increasing number of classic styles, some to comfortably cover both sexes. Sales help at Baby can be obsequious, and prices are flagrantly inflated.

Banana Republic
508 Union St, 622-2303
(map: J6)

Bellevue Square,
Bellevue, 453-0991
(map: H3)
Every day

It's a jungle in here. You'll find fabrics besides khaki in colors brighter than olive drab in these outposts of San Francisco's upstart outfitter—the company's response to waning enthusiasm for the relentless safari theme. Still, Banana Republic remains a gold mine of weekend thump-around clothes, all extremely well constructed and of all-natural fabrics. Too crowded for comfy shopping; you're always bumping into palm trees.

Barney's of New York
1420 5th Ave (Pacific
First Centre), 622-6300
(map: J5)
Mon-Sat

The leader of New York City retailers and the pride of distinctive shoppers has created a handful of satellite shops across the country—and still maintains its integrity as an innovator. Barney's mixes, as *Money* magazine says, haute and hip, bold architectural design and phenomenal customer service. This is the first outlet on the West Coast (another's opening in Beverly Hills in 1993). The inventory still has high style to spare, with preciously displayed shoes, suits, and accessories. Always one step ahead of the time and three leaps ahead of your wallet.

Betsey Johnson
1429 5th Ave, 624-2887
(map: J5)
Every day

Twist and shout. Seattle's once pallid fashion scene gets an extra-high-voltage jolt of fun with stretch, funk, spandex, push-up bras, short flippy skirts, and leggings, displayed in an ultrabright retail space.

Bonneville's
114 Lake St, Kirkland,
822-7002 (map: EE3)
Every day

Beauty and a sure sense of style pervade Bonneville's, both in ambience and in merchandise. Colorful and unusual scarves; sequined, beaded, or appliquéd tops; and tons of accessories are displayed side by side with Oriental carpets, antique wood furniture, silk flowers, and Japanese parasols. Truly lovely stuff.

Brooks Brothers
1401 4th Ave,
624-4400 (map: K6)
Mon-Sat

The only Brooks Brothers north of San Francisco is ensconced in the heart of downtown. Its famous conservative lines of men's fashions are well geared to Seattle's climate. Tremendous depth of inventory, a fine special-order system, two terrific sales a year (two weeks in June and the week after Christmas), and gracious service amid sedate surroundings are the store's trademarks. Some good women's lines, too.

Brotman's
Columbia Tower, 623-
3866 (map: M7)
Mon-Fri

Wardrobe consultation is available free (after hours, by appointment) at this women's shop, which has a strong inventory of contemporary, fashionable/executive lines such as Jones of New York, Tahari, and Paul Stanley. They offer the working woman professional polish without severity.

Burberrys
409 Pike St, 621-2000
(map: J6)
Mon-Sat

The famous trench-coat maker has only 16 retail stores in the US, and none as needed as this one. There's a full line of men's furnishings and assorted women's separates (primarily skirts and sweaters), as well as the trench coats, umbrellas, handbags, and scarves, all endowed with the trademark Burberry plaids.

Butch Blum
1408 5th Ave, 622-5760
(map: K6)
Mon-Sat

The shop that first taught Seattleites how to be fashionable, Butch Blum features the fashion-forward, predominantly European clothes of established designers as well as avant-garde newcomers. Almost all the lines they carry are exclusives to Seattle; you can depart without fear of seeing yourself cloned all over the city—and a good thing, too, at these prices. The shop can be rather intimidating, but owners William and Kay Smith-Blum employ a friendly, helpful staff.

Carol Gilmour
7803 SE 27th St, Mercer
Island, 232-9255
(map: II4)
Mon-Sat

A tasteful selection of sportswear, suits, dresses, and sweaters hangs in the burnished closets of this snug island shop. Sales staff are helpful without hovering. Great accessories add polish.

Country Gentleman
911 Bellevue Way NE,
Bellevue, 455-2969
(map: HH3)
Every day

A capacious, classic Bellevue shop with mostly men's traditional clothing (suits, sport coats of quality). Where Bif and Skip will shop after they graduate.

Dakota
601 Union St, 224-1677

Racks and racks of tasteful designs in lush natural fabrics distinguish this small boutique. Dakota favors classic clothes and accessories—all from American designers—with a contemporary touch.

(map: K4)
Mon-Sat

196 Bellevue Square,
Bellevue, 462-1677
(map: HH3)
Every day

Design Products Clothing
208 1st Ave S, 624-7795
(map: O8)
Mon-Sat

Sumptuous sweaters, paper-thin suedes and leathers, and an outstanding array of blouses offset slick tailored apparel at Design Products Clothing. This snazzy boutique in Pioneer Square also carries limited menswear and some local designer clothing.

Dita Boutique
603 Broadway E,
329-2777 (map: HH6)
Every day

Dita's has a wide array of innovative silhouettes, many imported from Italy, Germany, France, Belgium, and Japan. Twenty- and 60-year-olds shop side-by-side here; the selection is rooted in a style, not an age.

The Forum Menswear
95 Pine St, 624-4566
(map: I8)
Every day

Casual, fashionable guys come here first for a good selection of not-too-expensive European clothes and accessories for men, including San Remo and Louis Raphael suits. European socks, belts, and ties help finish the look. Salespeople are quite anxious to please.

Georgiou
Westlake Center,
622-8441
(map: I5)
Every day

Georgiou's own line of designs are made from wools, silks, and other natural fabrics, specializing in suits, dresses, and separates. Excellent selection of petites.

Gucci Inc.
Pacific First Centre,
682-7365
(map: J5)
Mon-Sat

From the gold signature handles on the elegant glass entryway of this shop to the trademark handbags, Gucci is the insignia for fine Italian leather goods and accessories. Luxe housewares, clothing, leather goods—it's all here.

Helen's (Of Course)
1302 5th Ave, 624-4000
(map: K6)
Mon-Sat

Bellevue Place, Bellevue,
462-1400 (map: HH3)
Every day

Fashions from the pages of *W* fill this elegant marble showcase, with labels from the world's most famous couture houses (Oscar de la Renta, Escada Boutique, Valentino Boutique). Helen's is the choice for Seattle's worldliest—and wealthiest—fashion mavens. Dress accordingly, or you may get snubbed by the shop girl.

Jeffrey Michael
Rainier Square (and
branches), 625-9891

This *Gentleman's Quarterly* kind of place hasn't sold its soul to abject trendiness. Jeffrey Michael carries suits to sportswear by top designers, wonderful sweaters,

(map: K6)
Every day

diverse outerwear, and accessories. It's all beautifully presented and pitched by friendly salesfolks. Other locations are in the big malls.

Jessica McClintock Boutique
400 Pine St (Westlake Center), 467-1048
(map: I5)
Every day

Scarlett O'Hara would swoon here. Dresses with lots of lace, puffy sleeves, sweeping skirts, taffeta, and satin. Need we say more?

Jordan
1427 5th Ave, 628-6411
(map: J6)
Mon-Sat

Jordan serves an absolutely crucial function in this town: it is the one place that shows us the view from the edge. Owner Jacqui Cohen is committed to the highest fashion, from Japan and Italy, and includes Jordan's own lines of men's and women's clothing. The avant-garde designs are architectural, the fabrications diverse. It's all displayed in a spare, narrow, bitingly elegant space on Fifth Avenue. We don't know who *buys* it (the stuff is expensive, and far, far out)—we're just glad it's here.

Klopfensteins
1332 6th Ave (and branches), 682-3397
(map: I6)
Mon-Sat

This bastion of fashion for men offers quality, mainstream style for pinstripe tastes, with standard lines of fine American brands and some European garments. Correct, unimaginative, necessary. Other branches grace the big suburban malls.

Laura Ashley (Four Seasons Olympic Hotel)
405 University St, 343-9637 (map: L6)
Mon-Sat

Laura Ashley invented the look that defines a type: demure and country elegant. At the Seattle outpost in the Four Seasons Olympic Hotel, you shop for the ever-popular floral print smocks, dresses, pajama pants, and sweet white blouses, as well as home decorations made from the same signature prints. Kids' clothes (including togs for budding mama's boys), crisp nighties, and bridal gowns share space with linens, wallpaper, lamps, and floral perfume.

Littler
Rainier Square, 223-1331 (map: K6)
Mon-Sat

Littler has long catered to a mature, upper-income clientele, with a mixture of conventional styling in top-quality fabrics and dressy evening wear. The Jaeger line is exclusively available in Washington in its own shop within Littler's women's section. Men shop here for Oxford cloth suits, among other things. Where Republicans shop.

All places in this book are recommended; even "no stars" are worth knowing about.

The Limited and Express
400 Pine St (Westlake Center), 624-6064 (map: J5) Every day

The biggest Limited in the country has three floors of fashion-forward apparel at reasonable (sometimes fabulous) prices. Somehow, the pants are always flattering.

Local Brilliance
1535 1st Ave, 343-5864 (map: I8) Every day

Full of the individual tastes of owner/designer Renata Tatman, Local Brilliance showcases the best Northwest designers, so you can get originals at affordable prices. Jewelry, belts, and scarves add panache.

Lord's
10520 NE 8th St (Bellevue Place, 454-1234 (map: HH3) Every day

This fine men's shop, servicing Bellevue for over 25 years, has beautifully cut suits and sport coats by Louis Roth, Corneliani, and others, as well as a larger-than-ever sportswear selection. Look in their new shop in Bellevue Place for the new line of Bally of Switzerland or the Northwest exclusive of the St. Croix line.

Lu/Barbary Stenderu
1401 1st Ave, 682-4099 (map: J8) Mon-Sat

Stenderu stresses the *wearable* in wearable art, cutting her hand-painted, block-printed, or screened silks in simple designs. Where else could you find one-of-a-kind chiffon shorts? Diana Graves's jewelry (formerly sold at Orbit) has quite a following. A singular operation, from the pretty paper bags to the bill dressed in a hand-decorated envelope.

Mario's of Seattle
1513 6th Ave, 223-1461 (map: J5) Every day

Practically a stop on the party circuit, Mario's is a high-energy boutique that specializes in a studied, spunky casualness, even in the workday clothes they offer. Sumptuous Italian suits tend to be overpriced, but the suit sales are great. Look here for Basco and Giorgio Armani for men, and Donna Karan, Zanella, and Moschino for women. Then upstairs for soup and a sandwich at Stella Rossa (see Restaurants chapter).

Marlee
University Village, 522-6526 (map: FF6) Every day

915 Bellevue Way NE, Bellevue, 453-1195 (map: GG3) Every day

Marlee carries many local, very affordable designers, including Deliane Klein, Marylou Ozbolt, Storer, Seattle Gear, and dozens of others, as well as lines of playwear and dressier clothes, and a few career-dressing styles. There is a large display of belts, and lots of fun, affordable jewelry to finish off any outfit.

Nelly Stallion
4538 University Way NE,

A faithful customer of Nelly Stallion, Hiroko Ima, resurrected this store after the first owners went bankrupt in 1990. The rest remains unchanged. Nelly's buyer

633-3950 (map: FF6)
Every day

prowls the garment district of New York and flies the finds to this stunning shop before anyone else in town has them. Consequently, Nelly Stallion has won the hearts of Seattle's most stylish, who look upon the annual sales as seasonal events. High points are the superb shoe and vintage watch selections, beautiful separates, some dresses, and pretty lingerie. Original, elegant, savvy—a glimmer of style on the hopeless Ave.

Newport House
Factoria Square,
Bellevue, 747-6333
(map: II3)
Every day

It's one of the stores on the Bellevue Ladies Circuit, but Newport House, with its sporty bent, appeals to a slightly younger clientele. Elegant, upper-end lines like Calvin Klein and Karen Alexander fill up the racks. It's the reason to go to Factoria.

Nubia's
1507 6th Ave,
622-0297 (map: J5)
Mon-Sat
4116 E Madison St,
325-4354 (map: GG6)
Mon-Sat

Nubia's eclectic inventory has a common thread of relaxed sophistication with an ethnic flavor; the clientele knows its own style and feels comfortable wearing it. The best natural textiles distinguish this garb, be it drapey resort wear by Zonda Nellis or tailored outerwear by Nikos. Many of Nubia's accessories are designed to complement the clothing.

Opus 204
225 Broadway E,
325-1782 (map: GG7)
Every day

A striking array of art, wearable and otherwise, distinguishes this outstanding Capitol Hill boutique. Owners Vija Rekevics and Nancy Souther assemble unique fashion and artifacts from all over the world. The clothes are of beautiful wools, cottons, and linens—often spare and simple in design, always interesting.

Pendleton
Bellevue Square,
Bellevue, 453-9040
(map: HH3)
Every day

1313 4th Ave, 682-4430
(map: K6)
Mon-Sat

For Pendleton wool lovers, this shop has it all: a wide selection of very classic clothing for men and women, along with scarves and accessories.

Polo—Ralph Lauren
Rainier Square,
587-0200 (map: K6)
Mon-Sat

Lauren's storefront in Seattle carries the polo-playing seal of approval and has the latest creations for men and women—not the department store, mass-produced lines, but preferred pieces from the Lauren Collection. Very pricey, very lovely.

Send us your feedback and tips on the report form at the back of this book.

SRH Caravan
Bellevue Square,
Bellevue, 455-2939
(map: HH3)
Every day

This cluttered nook is the brightest spot in Bellevue Square. Here you'll find a rhinestone pendant looking quite natural on a butter-silk baseball shirt, an orange chintz purse draped enticingly over a South American basket. It's very high-fashion stuff, tweaked with the ethnic flavor of all sorts of exotic ports of call. It's also expensive. So crowded with merchandise you'll think a bomb dropped here.

Stefanel
1525 6th Ave,
623-2655 (map: J5)
Every day

Stefanel specializes in wool jerseys, beautifully patterned leggings, sweaters, and a collection of summer-weight cotton knits in imaginative hues and cabbage-rose prints. Also, a selection of casual, refined—and very Italian—clothes for men.

The Talbots
Rainier Square,
464-1456 (map: K6)
Mon-Sat

Bellevue Square,
Bellevue, 455-5058
(map: HH3)
Every day

Bright, well-appointed stores offer fine women's fashions from the famous mail-order house. These clothes are classic but not unexciting, with pretty new twists on preppie themes. The petite and large-size sections are thoroughly stocked, and it's a good place to pick up faux-pearl jewelry.

Totally Michael's
Rainier Square, 622-4920 (map: K6)
Mon-Sat

Clothing for sophisticates, at work (beautifully tailored suits and separates), at play (relaxed, oh-so-chic casuals), and after dark (evening and party dresses). The small, whimsical home accessories section has whitewashed baskets, dhurrie rugs, and country pine and willow accessories.

Uno
1927 1st Ave, 728-9420
(map: I7)
Every day

Duo
2209 1st Ave, 448-7011
(map: H7)
Mon-Sat

Donald Fletcher's small shop on First Avenue displays a very precious selection of Italian-tailored menswear from classic gray flannel slacks to bright orange tweed coats. Three blocks north is its mate, Duo. Roni Vincent-Fletcher's shop is a spacious (almost spare) interior with oriental rugs draped over wood floors, and displays glisten with costume jewelry, watches, and clothes that you might wear to First Thursdays.

What's That
8117 161st Ave NE,
Redmond, 881-3034
(map: EE1)
Mon-Sat

Owner Lenoir Perara specializes in dressing women in moderately priced alternative clothing with accessories to complement the looks. Suits have softer lines here, and the casual clothes are chosen with a creative flair. She has a keen eye for fashion and obtains her stock from all over the world.

The Yankee Peddler
1516 5th Ave (and branches), 622-8712 (map: J6)
Every day

The Yankee Peddler was thriving long before the advent of *The Preppie Handbook*, and assuredly it will endure long after. Quintessential classics—the tweed jacket, Oxford shirt, corduroy pants, and Shetland sweater—are just some of the accoutrements it stocks for a provincial East Coast look. A good depth of inventory in both the men's and women's sections. Branches in University Village and Madison Park.

ZebraClub
1901 1st Ave (and branches), 448-7452 (map: I8)
Every day

An inspired cacophany of audio and visual trends of the 1980s, this is the sort of place you'd expect to find in Hollywood or Soho. Fashionable street clothes from local manufacturers (International News, Code Bleu) are displayed on stage-lit platforms, and video equipment is everywhere. There's even a hair salon back there somewhere, and (what else?) an espresso cart outside. Two other stores, Z Club in Westlake Center (623-4371) and Club 101 at 101 Stewart Street (448-CLUB), provide similar sensory overload experiences.

AUCTIONS

Bushell's Auctions
2006 2nd Ave, 448-5833 (map: H7)
Mon-Fri

Mary Bushell's auction house is open to all, with auctions most Tuesdays at 10am and occasionally at 7:30pm, depending on what's being sold (there are more antiques in the evenings). The merchandise (which comes from estate liquidations and private sales) consists of a great variety of household items, some antique, some contemporary: dishes, glassware, rugs, bedroom sets, and more. Real treasures can be found here, but you have to know your stuff because there's little help from salespeople. Previews are noon to 5pm Fridays, 8am to 7pm Mondays.

Pacific Galleries
2121 3rd Ave, 441-9990 (map: H7)
Call for schedule/by appointment

Twice a year the owner flies to Europe to bring back housewares, art, and furniture, which are featured in the monthly auctions. Many of these are antiques—Pacific Galleries is the largest antique auction gallery in the Northwest. They auction items in every price range, from 50 cents to thousands of dollars. Preview from the catalog, or at the house the weekend before each auction.

Renton Auction
Call for location, Renton,

Robert Losey had to move out of his space on Longacres Way. At press time, he was operating his business from the basement of his home, with plans to

271-5182 (map: MM3)
Fri-Sat

be in a new location soon. Once settled, everything should run as before. Auction time's every Saturday night at 6:30pm. Containerloads of antiques and secondhand furniture from Great Britain—drop-leaf and draw-leaf tables, armoires, occasional tables, dining room chairs, bowls, you name it—go under the hammer at a brisk pace. Appliances and new furniture are auctioned after the antiques. It's a marathon affair, often going into the wee hours, but you'll have a lot of fun watching the colorful auctioneer and the crowds of auction hounds. If the new space is anything like the old you'll need to dress warmly and bring a pillow. Preview from 10am on, Friday and Saturday.

Satori Fine Art Auction
2305 5th Ave, 443-3666
(map: F6)
Mon-Fri, Sun

An auction at Satori used to be a low-key, refined affair; now it's a good-humored show, as much fun to watch as to take part in. The items are on consignment from private estates and may include antique furniture, coins, jewelry, fine art, porcelain, Oriental rugs, even some real estate. Coffee is served throughout. Preview items from 10am to 7pm on Monday and Tuesday and 12pm to 5pm on Sunday; auctions are Tuesday at 7pm.

BAKERIES

A La Francaise
University Village,
524-9300 (map: FF6)
Every day

87 S Jackson St,
447-1818 (map: O8)
Every day

Buttery croissants and the best French bread in the city are the hallmarks of this established French bakery. The Pioneer Square location is primarily wholesale; the University Village retail shop also carries a selection of all-butter pastries, fresh fruit tarts, and a wonderful sour cream chocolate cake with ganache icing. As we went to press, rumors of a third location near Pioneer Square were wafting our way.

A Piece of Cake
514 S King St, 623-8254
(map: R6)
Wed-Mon

Adored for its light, fresh, fruit-filled sponge cakes (mango is the best), A Piece of Cake in the International District also bakes Napoleon and Black Forest cakes, as well as authentic Chinese pastries.

Arthur's Bakery
138 107th Ave NE,
Bellevue, 454-9661
(map: HH3)
Mon-Sat

Arthur's, an Eastside institution, has grown up with Bellevue. Reasonably priced, first-rate breads, pastries, and dessert tarts are the draw, and the bakery does a thriving business in specialty cakes.

The facts in this edition were correct at presstime, but places close, chefs depart, hours change. It's best to call ahead.

▼
BAKERIES

B & O Espresso
204 Belmont Ave E,
322-5028 (map: GG6)
Every day

2352 California Ave SW,
935-1540 (map: II9)
Every day

See Restaurants chapter.

Boulangerie
2200 N 45th St, 634-2211
(map: FF7)
Every day

At this authentic French bakery you can count on excellent crusty loaves, buttery croissants, and muffins. Their seigle noix—a dense, light rye bread with walnuts—is superb with cheese. Boulangerie has been acquired by a grocery store chain, but that hasn't affected the quality. The place is always busy.

Brenner Brothers Bakery
12000 NE Bellevue
–Redmond Rd,
Bellevue, 454-0600
(map: GG3)
Every day

Excellent challah, rich cream puffs, cheese pastries, and filled strudels are just some of the offerings in this kosher bakery. There's a deli with a small selection of specialty foods, too: rye bread, lox, pastrami, matzoh, and other kosher supplies.

Exquisite Desserts
2800 E Madison St (and
branches), 328-0518
(map: GG6)
Mon-Sat

This healthful bakery isn't of the carob-and-granola school; this is the next generation of healthful goods. They specialize in baked goods (lush cakes with satiny frostings, chocolate jelly rolls, and excellent pies) made with either fruit-juice concentrates (which can be tolerated by diabetics and hypoglycemics) or artificial sweeteners for calorie counters (less successful). A new outlet will be opening in Bellevue's KHOL Center (NE Eighth Street and NE 100th).

The Famous Pacific Dessert Company
420 E Denny Way (and
branches), 328-1950
(map: I1)
Every day

See Dessert, Coffee, and Tea in Nightlife chapter.

Grand Central Bakery
214 1st Ave S,
622-3644 (map: O8)

See Restaurants chapter.

Great Harvest Bread Company
5408 Sand Point Way
NE, 524-4873
(map: EE6)
Every day

A real, no-frills bakery with 14 varieties of excellent bread—most whole wheat (Great Harvest stone-grinds its wheat on the premises), one salt-free, all good for you. There is a small sit-down counter with newspapers, scones, muffins, and coffee available.

Greenwood Bakery
7227 Greenwood Ave N,
Seattle, 783-7181
(map: EE7)
Tues-Sun

Tough to say *how* far we'd drive for eye-popping, mouth-watering fruit tart with Grand Marnier custard, but suffice it to say we've encountered patrons from as far away as Capitol Hill. The whole-wheat sourdough bread is an excellent excuse for a sandwich. Cookies are small and traditional; pastries border on decadent.

Honey Bear Bakery
2106 N 55th St, 545-7296
(map: FF6)
Every day

See Dessert, Coffee, and Tea in Nightlife chapter.

John Nielsen Pastry
1329 3rd Ave, 622-1570
(map: K7)
Mon-Sat

A marvelous downtown bakery and old-fashioned coffee shop with authentic Danish pastries, petit fours, and specialty cakes at great prices. Come early for a breakfast pastry, hot from the oven.

Lake Street Bakery
6 Lake St, Kirkland,
827-0890 (map: EE3)
Every day

Lake Street Bakery serves up giant blueberry muffins, cinnamon rolls, apple walnut coffee cakes, and a spread of specialty cakes. Espresso, too.

Larsen Brothers Danish Bakery
8000 24th St NW (and
branches), 782-8285
(map: EE9)
Every day

The best Scandinavian bakery in town is getting more visible every day, with products available in most QFCs. Still, quality is high, with moderately priced Danish pastries, coffee cakes, Kringler, light cookies, and great breads (particularly the eight-grain and Swedish rye).

Le Panier Bakery
Pike Place Market,
441-3669 (map: J8)
Mon-Sat

In addition to the most enticing aromas in town, Le Panier turns out fine (if expensive) baguettes, arguably Seattle's best; unusual breads (notably the onion and walnut rye); fruit tarts; and French amandine croissants from the hearth ovens.

Madison Park Bakery
4214 E Madison St,
322-3238 (map: GG6)
Tues-Sat

Truly a neighborhood bakery (with a slightly German slant), with good cinnamon rolls and rye breads, and room to sit down with a cup of coffee and a pastry.

Marzi Tarts
2323 N 45th St, 328-2253
(map: FF7)
Mon-Sat

A little bit naughty and a little bit fun. As such, this erotic bakery does a bang-up business making cakes for men's and women's stag parties. White or chocolate cakes are topped off with buttercream frosting and a marzipan sculpture of your most, er, edible body parts.

Would you like to order a copy of this book for a friend? There's an order form at the back of this book.

Peerless Pie
Pike Place Market,
443-1801 (map: J8)
Every day

See Restaurants chapter.

CLOSED

Seattle Bagel Bakery
1302 Western Ave,
624-2187 (map: K8)
Every day

Unofficially the most authentic bagel in town—and absolutely the best bagel *deal* in town—is at this take-out and lunch-in spot underneath the Market. Seventeen kinds, from pumpernickel to poppy seed. Slab 'em with cream cheese and lox, if you please, but those gooey garlic cheesy ones are just right all alone.

Simply Desserts
3421 Fremont Ave N,
633-2671 (map: FF7)
Tues-Sun

See Dessert, Coffee, and Tea in Nightlife chapter.

Spot Bagel Bakery
1815 N 45th St, 525-3775
(map: FF7)
Every day

Lots of folks like this little spot in Wallingford Center; it's even stood the test with finicky Easterners who think they know what a bagel's 'sposed to be. These big, doughy spheres are infused with orange poppy seeds, jalapeño, or seeded with whole garlic cloves.

The Store Next Door
4405 Wallingford Ave N,
547-3203 (map: FF7)
Every day

Next door to Julia's in Wallingford, that is. Far from being in Julia's shadow, however, the bakery actually concocts the wonderful cinnamon rolls, breads, and cookies devoured every day in all of the now three Julia's locations. Except here, you don't have to wait in line for a table.

Tio's Bakery and Cafe
2379 Eastlake Ave E,
325-0081 (map: GG7)
Every day

What started in early 1990 as a place to reap the Julia's overflow has, in very little time, become a pleasant morning Eastlake stop *instead* of Julia's. A harpist or guitarist often provides unobtrusive music on weekends, and the hazelnut bread (available by the slice for toast), oatmeal scones, and morning glory muffins filled with carrots, apples, or currants furnish equal satisfaction.

BODY CARE

The Body Shop
Bellevue Square,
Bellevue, 637-9535
(map: HH3)
Every day

Anita Roddick's franchise has had an almost cultish following for the past 14 years. Devotees have been known to make pilgrimages to Vancouver, BC, just to get their hands on—and in—the Body Shop's naturally based products. Now they need go no further than

Bellevue Square (an excessive place so very different from the sensible ideology of this store). The Body Shop's the purveyor of environmentally safe, biodegradable body and hair care products packaged in recyclable or reusable bottles.

Crabtree and Evelyn
Bellevue Square,
Bellevue, 451-8457
(map: HH3)
Every day

Westlake Center,
682-6776 (map: I5)
Every day

The shelves of this pretty shop are lined with imported luxuries that taste and smell delicious. Besides gourmet food items and lovely potions for the bath, Crabtree and Evelyn has an extensive line of home fragrances: room sprays, sachets, incense, and potpourri. The place to buy a bridal gift.

Garden Botanika
Westlake Center,
624-8292 (map: I5)
Every day

Bellevue Square,
635-0284 (map: HH3)
Every day

Three environmentally concerned Northwest natives began this skin and body care company in late 1990, riding on the coattails of other naturally concerned skin care shops. No animal products, no controversial animal testing, no petroleum products, and minimalist packaging—with big-time plans for national expansion.

Parfumerie Elizabeth George
1424 4th Ave,
622-7212 (map: J6)
Mon-Sat

First, Elizabeth George tests your skin's pH content, then she matches a fragrance to you and helps you learn to wear it. From her little room in the lobby of an office building, George sells one of the top lines of designer match scents (less expensive versions of the originals) and specializes in custom and hard-to-find perfumes. Beautiful atomizers and a line of lotions.

Parfumerie Nasreen
1005 1st Ave, 682-3459
(map: M8)
Mon-Sat

Fittingly situated off the lobby in the Alexis Hotel, Parfumerie Nasreen is the only all-perfume store in the city. They stock close to 400 different fragrances, many from exotic lands, in all price ranges.

The Soap Box
4340 University Way NE
(and branches), 634-2379
(map: FF6)
Every day

A fragrant emporium of perfumed soaps, bath oils, lotions, decorative pillows, calendars, and novelties for the bath. You can always find a gift here; they'll mix any scent you like into a lotion or oil. Also located in Bellevue Square, Pike Place Market, and downtown.

BOOKS/MAGAZINES/NEWSPAPERS

Art in Form
2237 2nd Ave,

Located in Belltown, the heart of Seattle's artist district, Art in Form has the largest, most in-depth selec-

441-0867 (map: G7)
Mon-Sat

tion of contemporary art publications in the city. The store stocks several museum catalogs, art magazines, and critical titles. They also run a well-connected international mail-order business. Check their window periodically for installations by local artists.

Bailey/Coy Books
414 Broadway E,
323-8842 (map: GG7)
Every day

1317 Madison St,
682-4334 (map: HH7)
Mon-Sat

Respected by book buyers and booksellers alike, Bailey/Coy offers a wide spectrum and an eclectic mix. Excellent fiction and literature (including mystery and sci-fi), poetry, lesbian and gay studies, and philosophy. Look here also for coffee table books, child care, gardening, and cooking.

Beatty Bookstore
1925 3rd Ave,
728-2665 (map: I6)
Mon-Sat

One of the largest general used-book stores in Seattle, Beatty has a huge inventory that includes one of the best bibliography sections on the West Coast. Excellent regional, art, philosophy, and cookbooks, too. They pay well for the used books they buy, ask fair prices for the books they sell, and are very knowledgeable about their inventory.

Beks Bookstore
Rainier Square,
624-1328, Mon-Sat
(map: K6)
Mon-Sat

Beks II
1201 3rd Ave
(Washington Mutual
Tower), 224-7028
(map: K7)
Mon-Fri

An uptown bookstore to match its location: the stock leans toward business, travel, Northwest books, and current fiction and nonfiction best-sellers. Service is friendly and knowledgeable. A miniversion of Beks, Beks II is in a great spot to grab a potboiler for the commute home after a hard day of stock trading.

Blackbird
3130 E Madison Ave,
325-3793 (map: HH6)
Every day

Joseph Antoine-Zimbabwe sells strictly African and African-American literature from his small, well-stocked store on Lake Washington.

**Bowie & Weatherford
Booksellers**
314 1st Ave S,
624-4100 (map: O8)
Every day

The newest bookstore in town sells the oldest and rarest books in town (dating back to 1475). M. Taylor Bowie, known for his outstanding collection of out-of-print and antiquarian books, joined Richard M. Weatherford last year to stock out-of-print books, maps, and west-of-the-Mississippi ephemera. It's not exclusive: there are items ranging from $5 to $70,000. A catalog is issued frequently for mail orders. Appraisals available (informal ones are free of charge).

Brentano's
400 Pine St (Westlake Center), 467-9626 (map: I6)
Every day

This is Waldenbooks' upscale version of itself. It started in New York City, then spread to San Francisco and eventually Seattle (the only one in the Northwest).

Bulldog News and Fast Espresso
4208 University Way NE, 632-6397 (map: FF6)
Every day

Broadway Market, 328-2881 (map: HH6)
Every day

Between 1,800 and 2,700 titles are stocked at this indispensable Ave newsstand: periodicals, foreign magazines, and newspapers. They also sell espresso to sip while you browse. The other branch is a kiosk literally at the heart of the Broadway Market.

Cinema Books
4753 Roosevelt Way NE, 547-7667 (map: FF6)
Mon-Sat

A specialty bookstore located under a movie theater could sell only one thing: film-related books and magazines, screenplays, posters, stills, and technical books for filmmakers. Truly a movie-lover's paradise.

City News
10116 NE 8th St, Bellevue, 455-9683 (map: HH3)
Every day

Harriett Bryant has the best selection of foreign and domestic magazines and newspapers on the Eastside, as well as some books. Service is well informed.

Collector's Bookstore
Pike Place Market, 622-5182
Mon-Sat (every day May-Dec)

Not your typical bookstore, Collector's specializes in cookbooks, sci-fi, fantasy, horror, and signed and limited editions (some—like a specially commissioned Stephen King/Barbara Kruger collaboration with a digital watch embedded in a steel cover—running as high as $2,400).

David Ishii, Bookseller
212 1st Ave S, 622-4719 (map: O8)
Every day

A select group of used, out-of-print, and scarce items reflects the tastes and interests of David Ishii—fly-fishing and baseball, primarily. He carries the city's largest collection of books on the subjects and is one of the few downtown sources for Everett Giants tickets.

DeGraff Books
999 3rd Ave, 682-6882 (map: M7)
Mon-Fri

Pike Place Market 441-0688 (map: J8)
Mon-Sat, every day in summer

A general bookstore, located in the business and tourist centers of the city, with good selections in travel, literature, and regional books. The larger location in the Market has more titles, as well as a note card and magazine selection.

BOOKS/MAGAZINES/NEWSPAPERS

East West Book Shop
6417 Roosevelt Way NE,
523-3726 (map: EE7)
Every day

Based on the East West store in Palo Alto, Seattle's version is a good place to thumb through alternative and off-the-wall books by authors who are either crazy or geniuses, and sometimes a bit of both. One of the most comprehensive Jungian psychology selections in town. Friday night speakers' forums focus on topics from spiritual healing to near-death experiences.

Elliott Bay Book Company
101 S Main St, 624-6600
(map: O8)
Every day

KIDS Seattle's premier bookstore opened in 1973 as a rough-hewn one-room shop near the corner of First Avenue and Main. From day one it has offered a broad selection in a relaxed, literary atmosphere. When Elliott Bay Graphics moved around the corner, the bookstore took over its space. This move effectively doubled the store's size, making a total of four rooms, with more science and technical books, computer books, and art and history books. The kids' book nook moved downstairs, and last year Elliott Bay opened two lofts for bargain and travel books.

Today Elliott Bay stocks over 100,000 titles, making it the second-largest independent bookstore in the state. Service is smart and efficient; they'll field any question, wrap and send your entire gift list, and even help you set up your own reading group. The quarterly newsletter, *Book Notes*, runs staff book reviews, profiles authors, and announces recent paperback releases. **FREE** Readings and signings occur several times a week at 7:30pm. These are free, and the schedule is printed out on your receipt. Recent authors have included Kurt Vonnegut, T.Coraghessan Boyle, and Barbara Kingsolver.

The newest addition to the bookstore is the 109 Elliott Bay Art Cafe (where Graphics moved), which is part graphics store, part frame shop, and part cafe. At press time the menu was the same as that of the comfortable, book-lined cafe downstairs, another big draw (see Dessert, Coffee, and Tea in Nightlife chapter). Open late.

Flora and Fauna
121 1st Ave S,
623-4727 (map: N8)
Mon-Sat

This Pioneer Square basement offers the largest selection of books on natural history and the life sciences you'll find anywhere on the West Coast, possibly in the country. New, used, and rare books—it's all here, aardvarks to zebras, in over 25,000 titles. Buy or sell.

The facts in this edition were correct at presstime, but places close, chefs depart, hours change. It's best to call ahead.

Fortuna Books
113 Lake St, Kirkland,
827-7294 (map: EE3)
Every day

New and used books and current periodicals share the shelves in this Kirkland bookstore. In addition to buying and selling, they will search for out-of-print books. A strong foreign language section.

Gilman Village Books
317 NW Gilman Blvd,
#42, Issaquah, 392-3766
(map: JJ1)
Every day

An excellent general bookstore that makes the difference with service. Owner Sally Oljar works double-time for customers who request special orders or rapid delivery, or who simply want it wrapped for a special occasion (and it doesn't have to be Christmas).

The Globe Books
5220 University Way NE,
329-3586 (map: FF6)
Mon-Sat

You'll find a broad selection in the humanities (especially literature and reference books) and a growing section of natural science books in this U District new and used bookstore. Don't be intimidated by the specialized inventory; this is a wonderfully unstuffy place and a real labor of love. Browse through the antique maps and reproductions, too. Trades are welcome.

Half-Price Books and Tapes
4709 Roosevelt Way NE,
547-7859 (map: FF7)

156th Avenue and NE 8th
St (Crossroads Mall),
Bellevue, 747-6616
(map: GG1)
Every day

No evasiveness here. Two locations sell books at half price (they buy overstocks, remainders, and used ones at far less). The University District branch has a large selection of classical literature. They also have a huge line of discounted new and used software (located next door in the U District, in the same store at Bellevue).

Horizon Books
425 15th Ave E,
329-3586 (map: GG6)
Every day

A roomy bookstore with an emphasis on literature, criticism, history, mysteries, and philosophy, and as much secondhand science fiction as any place on the West Coast.

International Books–Multilingual Resources
3237 Eastlake Ave E,
323-5667 (map: GG7)
Tues-Sat (Sept-Feb),
Wed-Sat (March-Aug)

This store, which features learning materials, cassettes, dictionaries, and grammar books in close to 50 languages, is fascinating and complete. Western languages (including Russian, Greek, French, Spanish, Italian, Swedish, Danish, and German) are represented in the huge inventory of literature and children's books.

Island Books
3014 78th St, Mercer
Island, 232-6920

KIDS A good general bookstore with a lot of personal service, such as gift-wrapping and mailing. Besides a fine assortment of children's books (the largest on the

(map: II4)
Mon-Sat.

Eastside), nice touches for kids include a playhouse and story hours on Saturdays throughout the year.

Left Bank Books
Pike Place Market,
622-0195 (map: J8)
Every day

From buttons to bumper stickers to books, variety is the rule in this alternative bookstore in the Corner Market building. The emphasis is on politics of a reddish hue; there's also pretty good new and used social science, poetry, and fiction sections.

M. Coy Books
117 Pine St, 623-5354
(map: J8)
Every day

Michael Coy, formerly of Bailey/Coy, takes bookselling seriously, and he's crafted his retail business into a fine art; he knows how to make you feel good about the books you read, and often suggests others of the same genre. An espresso bar in back is one of the few in Seattle to use Coloiera beans.

Magazine City
1901 3rd Ave,
441-4235 (map: I7)
Every day

The inventory consists of about 3,000 publications—the state's largest selection of US and foreign periodicals. Open until 10:30pm weekdays.

Main Street Kids Books
10217 Main St SE,
Bellevue, 455-8814
(map: HH3)
Mon-Sat

KIDS Former employees of Children's Hospital Andy Pickard and Kari Peterson opened this bookstore primarily for kids under 12 (with a strong parenthood section) a year ago. There's a play area that becomes a stage once a month for Saturday storytelling.

Parkplace Books
348 Parkplace Center,
Kirkland, 828-6546
(map: EE3)
Every day

KIDS Co-owner Ted Lucia is a book rep who decided to open a new account about four years ago—his own. A general bookstore that pays close attention to children's books and mysteries.

Peter Miller Architectural
and Design Books
and Supplies
1930 1st Ave, 441-4114
(map: H8)
Every day

In an elegantly spare space, Peter Miller's shop carries not only the best local selection of new, used, and out-of-print architectural books (one of the few such specialized outlets in the country), but also a collection of European and Japanese gadgets and drafting supplies. Ask about the catalog.

Read All About It
Pike Place Market,
624-0140 (map: J8)
Every day

An enormous selection of local, national, and international papers and magazines is displayed at this colorful newsstand in Pike Place Market (right across from DeLaurenti). A Market institution with a jolly staff.

Red and Black Books
432 15th Ave E,

As much of an awareness outlet as a bookstore, this volunteer collective shelves books you may not find in

322-7323 (map: GG6)
Every day

other stores. Books, newspapers, pamphlets, buttons cover leftist politics, gay/lesbian issues, and, for that matter, almost any issue with a radical bent. There's plenty of reading matter on abuse and addiction recovery, as well as kids' books and a play area.

Second Story Books
Wallingford Center,
547-4605 (map: FF7)
Every day

KIDS A terrific general bookstore with excellent children's, regional, and fiction sections. Ask about joining the rental library, or come for an autograph party. Good displays draw you in, and the big, comfy armchairs invite you to stay.

The Secret Garden
Children's Bookshop
7900 E Green Lake Dr N,
524-4556 (map: EE7)
Every day

KIDS The Secret Garden is the oldest exclusively children's bookstore in the city, and it continues to grow. The selection is fine here; special events (musical performances, classes, signings, and the occasional reading) are entertaining. Their heart is in the right place: half of the profits benefit schools in Mexico and Haiti.

Shorey Bookstore
1411 1st Ave, 624-0221
(map: J8)
Every day

Shorey's, one of the world's largest general antiquarian bookstores, has been in existence since 1890, and has an inventory that's now over a million volumes. In the past, all those titles have made for organizational chaos, and some volumes have been poorly handled. However, an imminent move from Union Street to a bigger, more visible location in the south arcade of Pike Place Market will hopefully mitigate the problem.

Spade and Archer
810 3rd Ave, #440,
682-7064 (map: M7)
By appointment only

Mystery and crime fans, grab your magnifying glasses and head to this detective and crime-related bookstore. They sell collectible books and also sponsor the Belltown Film Festival.

Steve's Broadway News
204 Broadway E,
324-7323 (map: GG6)
Every day

Steve Dunnington's news nook has become a newshound's source for current issues of periodicals, from regional magazines to Australian dailies. No back issues. Open every day from 8am until 11pm, 364 days of the year (closed Christmas).

Titlewave
7 Mercer St, 282-7687
(map: A7)
Tues-Sun

At first we commended Titlewave for its bold move to the same block as Tower—now we see it as brilliant. If you can't find it at Tower, Nickie Jostol will do a book search for you. Her store sells only out-of-print and used books.

Look for **KIDS**—*it means your child will especially enjoy this place or attraction.*

Tower Books
20 Mercer St, 283-6333
(map: A7)

10635 NE 8th St,
Bellevue, 451-1110
(map: HH3)
Every day

Russ Solomon's chain that's not really a chain, as there's no central buying here. Still, we don't understand why a store with far and away the best computer book selection in the city (the Bellevue branch is even better) doesn't have a computerized inventory. A good general book selection, too, with an obvious bias toward mysteries, sci-fi, and sports. Open until midnight every day of the year, even holidays.

University Book Store
4326 University Way NE,
634-3400 (map: FF6)
Mon-Sat

990 102nd Ave NE,
Bellevue, 646-3300
(map: HH3)
Every day

KIDS The largest bookstore in Washington happens to also be one of the largest college bookstores in the country. The U Dub's own has a vast selection (the textbook, arts, and technical books departments are particularly distinguished) that *is* a bit overwhelming at first. (The children's department is not as extensive as it used to be.) Don't hesitate to ask for help, but browse on your own, too. There's a stationery department with all manner of supplies, as well as surprisingly well stocked camera, computer, record, sporting goods, clothes, and gift sections. The newer branch across the lake is smaller in comparison and does not carry textbooks or have the buy-back service; they do carry an extensive general literature selection, as well as large gift and clothing departments. On the Ave, the bookstore is open until 9pm on Thursday; the Bellevue branch is open until 9pm every weeknight.

Wide World Books and Maps
1911 N 45th St, 634-3453
(map: FF7)
Every day

All of the employees are seasoned wanderers, so advice on trips and travel is part of the service. Aside from a vast array of travel books, you'll find a complete range of accessories, including globes, maps, posters, a passport photo service, and luggage. The serene Teahouse Kuan Yin next door is the perfect place in which to contemplate future journeys.

CAMERAS

The Camera Show
7509 Aurora Ave N,
782-9448 (map: EE7)
Tues-Sat

This used-camera shop presents a continually changing stock of cameras and gear, from collector's items to late-model equipment. Proprietor Ed Olson knows virtually everything about the trade. Hours are short: 12pm to 6pm, Tuesday through Saturday.

CameraTech
5257 University Way NE,

Once a camera repair shop and photography gallery, CameraTech now concentrates mostly on repairs (the

526-5533
(map: FF6)
Mon-Sat

new hired techs occupy part of the former gallery space). A good selection of refurbished cameras for sale alongside racks of accessories. Same-day or custom black-and-white developing.

Cameras West
1908 4th Ave,
622-0066 (map: I6)
Every day

The best discount prices in town and a good selection of major brands make this *the* best place for amateurs to shop for a new camera. They also carry a large inventory of video equipment.

14309 NE 20th St,
Bellevue, 641-6677
(map: BB7)
Every day

Glazer's Camera Supply
430 8th Ave N,
624-1100 (map: GG7)
Mon-Sat

A knowledgeable staff purveys the city's broadest professional selection of darkroom supplies and cameras. Rental equipment is also available. They have the lowest prices around on film and paper, too.

Photographic Center Northwest
2617 5th Ave, 441-7030
(map: D7)
Every day, closed Sun in August

Besides carrying photo supplies, this place offers the only rental darkrooms available in Seattle. Do-it-yourselfers can try black-and-white, color, and cibachrome printing from both slides and negatives. They offer technical assistance or will do the developing for you at slightly lower prices than other labs.

CANDIES AND CHOCOLATES

Cafe Dilettante
416 Broadway E (and
branches), 329-6463
(map: GG7)
Every day

See Dessert, Coffee and Tea in Nightlife chapter.

The Confectionary
University Village,
523-1443 (map: FF6)
Every day

KIDS An old-fashioned parlor shop with unique candies imported from all over the world, interspersed with old favorites. A variety of licorice and gummies, dried fruits, hard candies, jelly beans, taffy, low-calorie and sugarless candies, and pecan and macadamia nut brittles. Great service.

Fran's Chocolates
2805 E Madison St,
322-6511 (map: GG6)
Tues-Sat

Fran Bigelow's magnificent creations are hand-dipped, using Belgian chocolate; true chocoholics, recognizing the best in the city, head here first. The East Madison chocolatier is known especially for her truffles and European creams, at great prices. Chocolate tortes and Gold Bars, too.

Godiva Chocolatier
Bellevue Square,
Bellevue, 646-8837 (map:
HH3)
Every day

This is the only shop in the Northwest devoted exclusively to Godiva, the chocolate as rich in cachet as in calories. Chocolate sauces and espresso, as well.

The Sweet Addition
Gilman Village,
Issaquah, 392-5661
Every day

This large candy shop carries a variety of imported Swiss chocolates and domestics from San Francisco. It's a licorice lover's heaven, but dozens of chewy, gummy, hard, and sugarless candies, as well as pastries, pies, and cakes, draw just as many fans. The addition also serves a soup/salad/sandwich-style lunch every day, which regulars report is creative and consistently good.

Temptations
410 Broadway E,
323-4880 (map: GG7)
Mon-Sat

10116 NE 8th St,
Bellevue, 455-4844
(map: HH3)
Every day

KIDS The place to fill up a stocking or Easter basket, because it's all here: Boehm's hand-dipped chocolates, Fran's Gold Bars, Joseph Schmidt chocolates, jelly beans, cordials, dried fruits, nut confections, hard candies, gumballs, and, at the Broadway location, freshly baked cookies.

CHILDREN'S CLOTHING

012 Benetton
Bellevue Square,
Bellevue, 454-5632
(map: HH3)
Every day

This children's version of the très chic adult chain is housed in the same store as an adult branch, under separate ownership. Clothes are fun if criminally pricey: 100 percent wool or cotton, mix-and-match, unisex clothing made by Italian designers.

Alley Kids
1904 Post Alley,
728-0609 (map: J8)
Mon-Sat

Shop here to ensure your tot will not see his same vogue outfits on children all over the city: Alley Kids prides itself on continual updates and revisions of its unique-to-the-city clothing lines. Some are French designers, others local (such as the popular Cotton Caboodle), but all are stylish and made from natural fibers. This is where you will find Nini Bam Bini and Guess clothing for children.

Babakies
12528 Lake City Way
NE, 362-4525
(map: DD6)
Mon-Sat

Named for an Afrikaans term meaning "little babies," Babakies specializes in infant and toddler wear. Lots of cute prints on natural fabrics and all the rest. Expectant mothers will also find everything in nursing accessories and some maternity wear.

CLOSED

Basic
1828 Broadway E,
323-7261 (map: HH6)
Every day

Basic cotton in not-so-basic styles. Offbeat and upbeat, this alternative children's wear includes such finds as alphabet and cupid-patterned T-shirts, Department of Peace bloomers, and Frankenstein-patterned leggings.

Boston Street Baby Store
535 W McGraw St (and
branches), 284-9291
(map: GG7)
Every day

This is a true baby supply store, with new and consignment specialty brands that can't be found in department stores. Locally made, one-of-a-kind clothing (sizes 0 to 14). Toys, books, tapes, and strollers, too, from over 1,600 consigners. A great place to find furniture at factory close-out prices. Branches are in Bellevue, Kirkland, and the Wallingford Center.

The European Child
125 Central Way,
827-2012, Kirkland
(map: EE4)
Mon-Sat

These European lines are modish, one-of-a-kind, and conservative. Selection is sweet and of good quality. They also sell a few accessories.

Fine Threads
2660 NE University
Village Mall, 525-5888
(map: FF6)
Every day

Here's the largest selection of classic, high quality boys' and young men's clothing in the Northwest. Fine Threads carries junior sizes for males aged 6 to 96. This is where to shop for his first suit, if you are willing to pay a man's price.

Kids in the Park
4105 E Madison St,
324-0449 (map: GG6)
Mon-Sat

This pricey but imaginative little shop in Madison Park concentrates on high-end European children's clothing and accessories. Plenty of cute little-girl wear: slips, nighties, bathing suits, and tiny leotards.

Le Petit Bateau
1324 5th Ave, 625-9643
(map: K5)
Mon-Sat

Bellevue Square,
Bellevue, 453-0708
(map: HH3)
Every day

This is where wealthy matrons buy presents for their grandchildren. Le Petit Bateau carries well-designed, expensive, and irresistible clothing from Europe and top-quality domestic lines for the little preppy. There are handknits, too, and occasionally you'll find some really lovely heirloom pieces. Both stores carry sizes from infant to 6X.

Li'l People
400 Pine St (Westlake
Center), 623-4463
(map: I5)
Every day

Whimsy and cotton knits prevail here. Baggy bloomers and leggings in charming prints and bright solid hues, patchwork cardigans, fleece jumpsuits, and inventive headgear for Jughead or Romeo.

Me 'N Mom's
1021 NE 65th St,

This store carries sizes newborn through 14, with a concentration on sizes 6X and under. They specialize in

524-9344 (map: EE6)
Every day

100 percent cotton playwear, such as the exclusive line Flapdoodles. Both new and (good condition) consignment. Individually oriented.

Merry Go Round Baby News
11111 NE 8th St,
Bellevue, 454-1610
(map: HH3)
Every day

A Seattle-area institution that may not be terribly imaginative, but makes up for it with a wide selection of quality clothes (through size 14 in Bellevue, size 7 in Lynnwood) and furnishings.

18905 33rd Ave W,
Lynnwood, 774-2797
Every day

Sprouts for Kids
Gilman Village,
Issaquah, 392-2049
Every day

There's an exuberant selection of clothing, accessories, and gift items in every price range at this shop—from necessities to one-of-a-kind articles handmade in Austria, baby towels to an antique cradle.

COFFEE AND TEA

MarketSpice
Pike Place Market (and
branches), 622-6340
(map: J8)
Every day

MarketSpice, famous for its aromatic teas in more than 100 flavors, also carries an extensive line of coffee beans, spices from all over the world, and "Healthy Heart" salt-free seasonings, formulated by the shop's own Yvonne Kennedy. In the Main Arcade.

Pegasus Coffee
131 Parfitt Way SW,
Bainbridge Island,
842-3113
Every day

Beans are roasted at the original Pegasus on Bainbridge Island and delivered fresh daily to the downtown outlet, where 18 varieties of coffee are always on hand Monday through Friday. They have recently expanded their tea selection and are beginning to offer home-baked goods.

711 3rd Ave, 682-3113
(map: N7)
Mon-Fri

SBC Coffee
Pike Place Market (and
branches), 467-7700
(map: J8)
Every day

See Dessert, Coffee, and Tea in Nightlife chapter.

Starbucks
Pike Place Market (and
branches), 448-8762
(map: J8)
Every day

The local roaster with a national reputation, Starbucks can be credited with establishing Seattle as the notorious coffee-drinking town that it is. Good blends (36 of them) are the reason. You'll also find the best in brewing accessories, several imported teas, and coffee by the cup. A few branches serve sandwiches made by the venerable Schwartz Brothers; others have various sweets and breakfast breads.

The Tea Cup
2207 Queen Anne Ave N,
283-5931 (map: GG7)
Mon-Sat

It seems that Seattle is kicking the coffee habit and moving over to teas. This is the third teahouse we know of that's opened up in the past year. Bulk teas for here or to go (there are seven on tap, but only two tables and a stand-up bar). They'll even steam you up a tea latte.

Teahouse Kuan Yin
1911 N 45th St, 632-2055
(map: FF7)
Wed-Mon

See Dessert, Coffee, and Tea in Nightlife chapter.

Torrefazione Italia
320 Occidental Ave S,
624-5773 (map: P8)
Mon-Sat

See Dessert, Coffee, and Tea in Nightlife chapter.

622 Olive Way, 624-1429
(map: I5)

CONSIGNMENT AND DISCOUNT

Between Friends
818 3rd Ave, 624-2220
(map: M7)
Mon-Sat

Between Friends, in the financial district, carries primarily career clothing (designer and department store labels), all in good condition. Periodically the owners add some new designer merchandise, culled from women's stores that have closed—resulting in some really good deals.

The Clothes Connection
11026 NE 11th St,
Bellevue, 453-2055
(map: HH3)
Mon-Sat

Contemporary men's and women's consignment fashions at very good prices are the emphasis here, with a keen eye toward the working woman. The big hitters (Ellis, Vitadini, Nipon) all have berths.

Costco Wholesale
4401 4th Ave S (and
branches), 622-1144
(map: I17)
Every day

Not everyone can be a member here (in order to join you must be the manager or owner of a business, a public service employee, or a member of a credit union or like association), but if you qualify you'll be in consumer heaven. Nothing isn't here—you've got appliances of all sorts, clothes, sporting goods, car tires and auto accessories, books, garden equipment and

CONSIGNMENT AND DISCOUNT

plants, jewelry, and bulk (and we mean *bulk*) groceries—all at prices 10 to 50 percent below retail, displayed quite functionally in an enormous warehouse.

Dark Horse
11810 NE 8th St,
Bellevue, 454-0990
(map: HH3)
Every day

With close to 30 years of business behind it, Dark Horse keeps to its extremely high standards, offering high-fashion designer clothing and better labels. Styles are so current it's hard to believe they've had time to be owned already, and you don't have to dig to find quality labels such as Missoni, Calvin Klein, Nipon Boutique, and Molly Parnis. There's a small men's section along one wall.

Don Shingler Inc. (The Down Factory)
1101 E Pike St, 322-0800
(map: HH6)
Mon-Sat

The Down Factory is a manufacturer and marketer of down products, selling first-quality apparel—parkas, vests, pants, tops, and warm-ups—quilts, and comforters. Apparel prices average 25 percent below retail.

Furie Limited
2810 E Madison St,
329-6829 (map: GG6)
Tues-Sat

There is an excellent selection of new and lightly used designer clothing at this Madison Valley natural-fibers shop. Everything (women's clothes, accessories, shoes, lingerie, bathing suits) is in pretty good shape

Gentlemen's Consignment
2809 E Madison St,
328-8137 (map: GG6)
Tues-Sun

This, the only men's consignment shop in the state, sells moderate to upper-end clothing, emphasizing business clothes and accessories. You can find Polo, Armani, a lot of Nordstrom labels, as well as tailor-made suits in sizes 36 to 56. Suspenders, belts, cufflinks, and ties finish the look.

J. Thompson
1501 4th Ave (and
branches), 623-5780
(map: I6)
Mon-Sat

A softer version of John T. Malloy's Dress for Success is espoused at J. Thompson, where sporty and professional wear for women doesn't seem like it should be this inexpensive. Especially good deals on women's coordinates, all very stylish.

4081 Factoria Square
Mall (128th Ave SE)
(map: II2)
Every day

Kathy's Kloset
4751 12th Ave NE,
523-3019 (map: FF7)
Every day

4738 42nd Ave SW,

Kathy Robertson's shop has a great reputation among consignment shoppers, who look to her for classic, professional, and fun clothing that's off-priced, used, new, and sometimes trendy. Women can find everything they need here, including makeup, shoes, coats, and

937-2637 (map: JJ8)
Every day

lingerie. The West Seattle branch does not keep the same high standards.

Loehmann's
3620 128th Ave SE,
Bellevue, 641-7596
(map: II2)
Every day

This women's off-price clothing store offers some of the most incredible bargains around, from Perry Ellis sweaters to Calvin Klein dresses to Jag sportswear and much, much more. It's inconsistent—sometimes you can't find anything, while at other times you can't stop buying. Be forewarned that the dressing rooms are communal and the staff watch you like hawks; but they're usually happy to offer advice and a critical eye. Don't miss the Back Room of elegant evening wear.

Marshall's
15801 Westminster Way
N, 367-8520 (map: BB7)
Every day

Shop carefully, and you'll pick up excellent bargains on staples: accessories, men's pants, and women's sweaters. Much of this is just so much stuff to fill up a rack, but when you find a $15 black turtleneck or a pair of $10 jeans, your heart will be warmed. Branches are in Redmond, Tukwila, and Lynnwood.

Pacific Trail Outlet Store
1310 Mercer St,
682-8196 (map: F1)
Mon-Sat

A factory outlet shop for Seattle's fine Pacific Trail Sportswear. Come here for good bargains on coats and jackets in all different fabrics; kids' polo shirts and shorts, and a good selection of ski overalls.

Pavilion Mall
17900 Southcenter Pkwy,
Tukwila, 575-8090
(map: OO5)
Every day

There's nothing but bargains in Washington's only off-price shopping mall, down by Southcenter. Under one roof you find shops that specialize in kids' clothing, linens, cosmetics, imports, toys, jewelry, hair care, accessories, anything you can think of. Particularly notable are the Bergman's and Marshall's outlets, and an enormous Nordstrom Rack.

The Rack
1601 2nd Ave (and
branches), 448-8522
(map: I7)
Every day

The Rack carries clearance merchandise from the Nordstrom stores at up to 70 percent off full price, but that's not why it's so good. Certain lines are bought in bulk just for the Rack stores, which allows for jaw-dropping prices on designer clothing. The downtown Rack occupies several floors, with a marvelous shoe selection and shoe repair service.

Ragamoffyn
127 Park Lane,
Kirkland, 828-0396
(map: EE3)
Mon-Sat

Ragamoffyn offers an unbeatable combination: high-quality, well-selected clothes at low prices. It's all so well presented that it takes a moment to realize you're in a resale shop. Owner Gisela Tipton uses close to 800 consignees, who keep her shop stocked with career and casual separates, shoes, and accessories.

Redress Shop
513 156th Ave SE,
Bellevue, 746-7984
(map: HH1)
Every day

In addition to the play- and business clothes, Redress has the only consigned selection of bridal, bridesmaid, and mother-of-the-bride dresses on the Eastside. Upper-end to moderate.

Savvy Boutique

8072 163rd Ave NE,
Redmond, 883-6441
(map: EE1)
Mon-Sat

Half of what Savvy sells is new boutique clothes; the other half is the consignment clothing for women. They carry business clothing made by Jones of New York and Calvin Klein, as well as casual sportswear.

Take Two Consignment
430 15th Ave E,
324-2569 (map: HH6)
Every day

Here's a Capitol Hill outlet that features good-quality, selectively chosen merchandise and factory seconds. In the new larger quarters, the spectrum stretches from business to casual clothing, all in excellent shape. Salespeople are eager to help.

DEPARTMENT STORES

The Bon Marche
3rd Ave and Pine St (and
branches),
344-2121 (map: I6)
Every day

Recent cosmetic upgrades throughout several Bon stores have made the Bon into a much more stylish and upscale place. The Bon is big (nine floors on a city block) and offers a full complement of services: tire center, free delivery in the downtown area, pharmacy, shoe repair, optometrist, engraving service, travel service, post office, picture framing, three remodeled restaurants, a beauty salon, liquor store, and a bakery. It's the everyman's department store in town, specializing in good-looking, moderately priced merchandise, and a lot of it. The Cube and the Tiger Shop stock excellent selections for juniors, including a good representation of local sportswear manufacturers. Toyopolis is a miniature FAO Schwartz with a play area for kids. Particularly noteworthy are all women's departments (they've extended their women's shoe department and have one of the largest Liz Claiborne selections on the West Coast); the linen, lingerie, and fine furniture departments are large, varied, and attractive. You can find Baccarat crystal in glassware. Prices are generally lower here than at the other department stores in town. And the bathrooms are more like suites in a grand hotel.

The facts in this edition were correct at presstime, but places close, chefs depart, hours change. It's best to call ahead.

Frederick & Nelson
5th Ave and Pine St (and branches) 682-5500
(map: I5)
Every day

Now back in local hands, Frederick & Nelson has finally emerged from a dark period of corporate ownership to reintroduce some of the grand traditions that made it a Seattle institution: a doorman to assist with packages, Frango chocolates made in the store, spring and fall international fashion shows, the Steuben Glass Shop (a Northwest exclusive), and the Wide World Shop featuring unusual and traditional antiques.

Ten floors in the downtown store feature top apparel designers, stunningly showcased; an extensive lingerie department; outstanding men's and children's departments; and five restaurants (including the Arcade Cafe with its Frango milkshakes and the Tea Room, the grande dame of the full-service store restaurants). Not to be missed is the basement Arcade, with a wine shop, bakery, delicatessen, cooking school, espresso bar, tobacconist, shoe repair, candy counter, housewares section, and an outstanding book department. The Ticketmaster outlet is now on the ninth floor. And at Christmas, Frederick & Nelson emerges as a local tradition, loved and remembered for its gorgeous decorations, amusing animated window displays, strolling minstrels in Dickensian costumes, and wide-eyed children waiting to see Santa.

I. Magnin
601 Pine St, 682-6111
(map: J5)
Every day

Small, tasteful Magnin is the company's northernmost branch, and from the clean-lined marble facade to the dignified and spare designer floor it exudes calm and class. The first floor is the most lively, with a large leather department, handbags featuring the Northwest exclusive Louis Vuitton, a fur salon, cosmetics, jewelry, gifts, less expensive accessories, and a marginal men's department. Upstairs it gets pricier but offers a very complete selection of clothing for women. Other exclusives include Adolfo and Hanai Mori, both on the designer floor. Service is proper and professional.

Nordstrom
5th Ave and Pine St (and branches), 628-2111
(map: J6)
Every day

This locally owned success story owes much of its popularity to the famous Nordstrom emphasis on service. The "Ask Me I Know" booth, located on the main floor, provides visitors with maps and brochures in eight languages. The extremely helpful sales staff is very well informed about current fashions and the store's merchandise, and they dress to emphasize the point. Nordstrom's success has led to two spinoff operations: The Rack (see Discount Shopping in this chapter) and Place Two, with more moderate and junior lines.

Nordstrom started business as a shoe store, and shoes are still its specialty. These shoe departments are the best in the city, with a tremendous range of style and price and no shortage of hard-to-find sizes. Women's fashions are displayed in a series of departments, each with a well-defined feeling all its own—Savvy, Collectors, Gallery, Brass Plum, Point of View, and Individualist Sportswear. The Bellevue and Tacoma stores have a new Encore department, clothing specifically for larger women. Men can outfit themselves to Northwest Ivy League specifications (and in the popular Nordstrom-label suit, a Seattle wardrobe mainstay) in three departments. Even Chanel has a berth, a Northwest exclusive in the second floor of the downtown store. A smattering of beautifully chosen gifts and gourmet foods is found in the Boardwalk department. And the Nordstrom Cafe is often packed at lunch under the rigidly enforced "seven-minute food rule."

Watch for the excellent sales throughout the store, which have come to be known as Northwest events: Nordstrom's anniversary (July), half-yearly for women (June and November), and half-yearly for men (June and January).

ETHNIC MARKETS AND DELIS

Beacon Market
2500 Beacon Ave S,
323-2050 (map: I16)
Every day

An impressive array of products from Taiwan, Japan, Korea, Singapore, Thailand, and the Philippines. The seafood section is small, and they carry very few housewares, but there is produce and extensive canned and dried foods. Prices are very reasonable, drawing customers from all over the Seattle area.

Borracchini's Bakery
2307 Rainier Ave S,
325-1550 (map: I16)
Every day

Remo Borracchini's spot makes fresh pasta and a variety of country breads, and stocks Italian canned goods and wines. The bakery is an institution, primarily for its sheet cakes, cheaper and faster than any place else in town, but ordinary in quality.

The British Pantry
8125 161st Ave NE,
Redmond, 883-7511
(map: EE1)
Mon-Sat
119 W Dayton St,
Edmonds, 771-3967
Tues-Sat

In addition to the tearoom and charming restaurant, The British Pantry carries groceries from the mother country: pickled onions, Fox's biscuits, Marmite, cane sugar syrups and treacle, Robertson's ginger preserves, Nabob tea.

C'est Cheese
7525 SE 24th St, Mercer
Island, 232-9810
(map: II4)
Every day

Larger quarters allow an even better selection of cheeses, wine, imported biscuits, and other gourmet take-out items.

Continental Store
5014 Roosevelt Way NE,
523-0606 (map: FF7)
Mon-Sat

A German deli with excellent cheeses, sausages, mustards, sauerkrauts, breads, pastries, chocolates, and pickled everything. Some gift items, too, including bath oil, German deodorants, and beer steins.

Cucina Fresca
Pike Place Market,
448-4758 (map: I8)
Every day

The smell of garlic draws you in. Scoop up lunch or a dinner pint to go of the cool salads, such as marinated eggplant or mushrooms, a wide selection of entrées (from chicken piccata to vegetable tortes), and inventive pastas, such as red pepper, gold beet, or kosher garlic linguine. Just don't say "ahhh."

DeLaurenti
Pike Place Market,
622-0141 (map: J8)
Mon-Sat

317 Bellevue Way NE,
Bellevue, 454-7155
(map: HH3)
Mon-Sat

DeLaurenti has been an institution in the Market since 1944. People prowl through the narrow aisles in pursuit of unusual canned items, outstanding cheeses, olives, imported pasta, wines, and deli meats. Service is cheerful and expert. It's more international than Italian, but Mediterranean lines are the specialty. The wine department has one of the city's strongest selections of Italian labels, along with California, Washington, and French wines; the Bellevue location has fewer bottles.

El Mercado Latino
Pike Place Market,
623-3240 (map: J8)
Mon-Sat

This cramped little space in the Sanitary Market stocks items unique to Caribbean, South American, Spanish, and Creole cuisines—bags of black beans, bottles of salsas and fruit syrups, canned chiles, and South American coffee.

Johnsen's Scandinavian Foods
2248 Market St,
783-8288 (map: FF8)
Mon-Sat

A magnet for Ballard Scandinavians, it's noted for baked goods, imported herring (as well as their own pickled herring), Scandinavian cold cuts, and lefse (a flat potato bread).

Kosher Delight
1509 1st Ave, 624-4555
(map: J8)
Mon-Fri

Everything's kosher: matzoh ball soup, knishes, lox, bagels, and other eat-in fare, as well as packaged items and catered affairs. Closed on the Sabbath.

Larry's Market
10008 Aurora Ave N (and
branches), 527-5333

Breaking ground as a supermarket that's really an ethnic market, Larry's is truly a treasure, stocking wild greens, unusual produce, healthy foods (a line of Orien-

(map: DD7)
24 hours

tal macrobiotic products), and rare ethnic flavorings (Indian curries, Thai spices), in addition to mainstream supermarket offerings. Branches are in North Seattle, White Center, Totem Lake, and by Sea-Tac Airport. The newest one, in Bellevue, designed by Carlson/Ferrin Architects, has a temperature-controlled wine room, offers cooking classes, and arranges the cereals by sugar content.

Matzoh Momma Deli and Restaurant
509 15th Ave E,
324-6262 (map: GG6)
Every day

See Restaurants chapter.

The Mexican Grocery
Pike Place Market,
441-1147 (map: J8)
Mon-Sat

This quirky place in the Market's Soames-Dunn Building carries a small amount of chiles and other products traditionally Mexican, yet it is a good source for other ingredients not found elsewhere. Clientele is largely non-Hispanic. Here's where you'll find the Tortilla Factory's wonderful homemade tortillas.

Oriental Mart
Pike Place Market,
622-8488 (map: J8)
Mon-Sat

Turn into the Corner Market (where you see the jumping paper snakes), and there's Oriental Mart, a good place to become familiar with Asian cuisines. Owner Mila Apostol, from the Philippines, is familiar with every item and ready with advice. The Japanese line is incomplete, but everything else is well stocked and accessible for Westerners. An adjoining lunch counter sells adobo and other Filipino plates.

Pacific Food Importers
1001 6th Ave S,
682-2022 (map: II7)
Tues-Sat

Frugal gourmet's delight: wholesome prices on pasta, tomatoes, bulk spices, and other prime ingredients.

Pasta & Company
University Village (and branches), 523-8594 (map: FF6)
Every day

See Restaurants chapter.

Pike Place Market Creamery
Pike Place Market,
622-5029 (map: J8)
Mon-Sat

Seattle's only dairy specialty shop is a good one. Here you'll find wonderfully rich heavy cream, unsalted butter, raw goat's milk cheese, and yogurts, kefirs, and ice creams in a variety of natural flavors. Located in the Sanitary Market.

Salute deli
7500 35th Ave NE,
522-8580 (map: FF6)
Every day

One mile up the street from Rafaele Calise's charming Italian restaurant is his take-out deli with pizzas, Italian sandwiches, and antipasti to go. There's a good selection of Italian cheese, meats, and sausages too.

Scandinavian Specialties Products Inc.
8539 15th Ave NW,
784-7020 (map: DD8)
Mon-Sat

Salted lamb, fish balls, lingonberries, cloudberries, cheeses, homemade potato sausage, lutefisk, and other authentic fare are available at this specialty store, in addition to a catering service.

The Souk
Pike Place Market,
441-1666 (map: J8)
Mon-Sat

11730 Pinehurst Way,
367-8387 (map: DD6)
Every day

Four Pakistanis operate this esoteric store with a tremendous inventory of Middle Eastern and Indian delicacies: bulgur in varying degrees of coarseness, spices, teas, orange and rose waters, olives. A new Pinehurst location, too.

Truffles
3701 NE 45th St,
522-3016 (map: EE6)
Mon-Sat

See Restaurants chapter.

Tsue Chong (Rose Brand) Company Inc.
801 S King St, 623-0801
(map: R5)
Mon-Fri

In Rose Brand's high-quality Chinese noodle shop, they sell dried Northern-style wheat noodles, fresh and dried Southern ones (made of wheat, rice, or bean flour), fresh wonton wrappers, and dumpling skins. Fortune cookies and canned goods fill out shelves.

Uwajimaya
519 6th Ave S,
624-6248 (map: R7)
Every day

15555 NE 24th St,
Bellevue, 747-9012
(map: GG1)
Every day

Here's the mainstay of the International District, the "Super Safeway" of its neighborhood. They sell tapes and CDs, makeup, small electrical appliances (rice cookers, woks), and run a crack cooking school, but the real distinction is in the fresh-fish tanks and produce bins—you'll find geoduck, live prawns and crabs, bitter melon, water chestnuts, durian, and all the makings for sushi. Service is quite knowledgeable.

Viet Wah Supermarket
1035 S Jackson St,
329-1399 (map: HH6)
Every day

It isn't classy or fancy, but it's the best Chinese and Southeast Asian grocery store in town. You can find all the ingredients you need, including fresh seafood, at very reasonable prices.

The Wedge
University Village,

The Wedge specializes in local products such as Cougar Gold cheese, made at Washington State University, and the Wedge's own smoked Monterey Jack and

523-2560 (map: FF6)
Every day

herbed cream cheese. The meats, cheeses—200 varieties in all—fresh breads, pâtés, wines, and imported beers make great picnic combinations. A very professional catering operation.

Welcome Supermarket
1200 S Jackson St,
329-7044 (map: HH6)
Every day

A completely authentic International District Vietnamese grocery owned by Chinese. This is where you find great buys on bulk frozen shrimp and a terrific selection of exotic greens. Best to know what you need and how to recognize it before you go.

FABRIC AND KNITTING SUPPLIES

Calico Corners
104 Bellevue Way SE,
Bellevue, 455-2510
(map: HH3)
Every day

3225 Alderwood Mall
Blvd, Lynnwood,
778-8019
Every day

First and second quality—second quality has only very minor flaws—decorator fabric for the home. If you don't see material you like, order from their samples selection. Their workrooms will do the sewing for you if you don't want to do it yourself.

Designers' Fabrics
1800 4th Ave,
467-6100 (map: II6)
Every day

15600 NE 8th St,
Bellevue, 747-5200
(map: HH1)
Every day

Downtown's only fabric store is an excellent one. It caters to the kind of folks who sew their own dress-for-success suits or one-of-a-kind wedding dresses. They offer a large selection of bridal fabrics and imported laces and can give the customer the know-how to create a masterpiece.

In the Beginning Fabrics
8201 Lake City Way NE,
523-8862 (map: EE7)
Every day

Here you'll find the best selection of calicoes and cottons in Seattle. Their specialty is quilts, and they sell the fabrics, teach the classes, and own the library to assist the public. In the new location they've added an extensive collection of natural dress fabrics, and a broad selection of domestic and imported wool challises.

Jehlor Fantasy Fabrics
730 Andover Park W,
Tukwila, 575-8250
Mon-Sat

This is the stuff dreamwear's made of: liquid sequin, hand-beaded laces, lamé, metallic glitz. A fantastical fabric store for evening wear and costumes. A large spandex department that will be, well, expanding soon.

The Loft
99 Front St N, Issaquah,

A complete quilting department is featured here, along with good general troubleshooting and advice. The Loft

392-5877
*Mon-Sat, and last Sun of
every month*

now offers decorator fabrics from Waverly, suitable for draperies and light upholstery. For those too lazy to take a class, ready-made Amish quilts are sold here.

ML Mallard
*1012 Western Ave,
621-0632 (map: L8)
Mon-Sat*

*17 102nd Ave NE,
Bellevue, 455-2138
(map: HH2)*

The strengths in Kerry Ferguson's stylish shop are beautiful knitting yarns, original patterns for knitting and needlepoint projects, and a wide range of esteemed classes for beginner to design knitters.

The Needle Works
*2818 NE 55th St,
523-9535 (map: FF6)
Mon-Sat*

This store has snob appeal, with a good selection of natural-fiber, imported yarns and high-fashion knitting patterns. The needlepoint section—including hand-painted canvases—is improving.

The Old Yarn Shop
*106 102nd Ave SE,
Bellevue, 454-3636
(map: HH4)
Mon-Sat*

Anything you might want for knitting can be found here: yarns, needles, books, small classes, and customer service from knowledgeable and patient employees who can answer any question.

Shamek's Button Shop
*1201 Pine St, 622-5350
(map: J2)
Mon-Sat*

The only button shop on the West Coast carries bone, wood, plastic, glass, pewter, and coin buttons, along with shell, tusk, and horn. Custom-made belts are the most expertly crafted in town, and the buckle selection is like nobody else's. Good buttonhole service.

Tricoter
*3121 E Madison St,
328-6505 (map: GG6)
Mon-Sat*

Tricoter seems much happier in its new Madison Street location near the Arboretum, since it's not an I-want-to-save-money-so-I'll-knit store. It's very much fashion knitting, with a small but dazzling selection of fine yarns from Germany, Japan, France, and Italy. Good design and finishing classes.

The Weaving Works
*4717 Brooklyn Ave NE,
524-1221 (map: FF6)
Every day*

It's crowded with yarn, and everything you need for dyeing, spinning, weaving, and knitting—including advice and classes, which makes this store popular with knitters. They also carry basketry supplies.

FLORISTS AND NURSERIES

Ballard Blossom
*1766 NW Market St,
782-4213 (map: EE8)
Mon-Sat*

In the flower business for years and years, this Ballard florist purveys a fine variety of plants and cut flowers, but no garden supplies. Service is top-notch, and they are open until 8pm Monday through Friday.

FLORISTS AND NURSERIES

Bay Hay and Feed
10355 Valley Rd,
Bainbridge, 842-2813
Every day April-June,
Mon-Sat July-March

Half of this country store sells feed for animals; the other half is a small, growing nursery with very attentive service and unusual plants. The large plant selection changes frequently for such a small nursery.

City People's Garden Store
2939 E Madison St,
324-0737 (map: GG7)
Every day

See Hardware in this chapter.

Crissey Flowers and Gifts
2100 5th Ave, 448-1100
(map: G5)
Mon-Sat
416 University St,
728-6661 (map: K6)
Mon-Sat

For everything from office bud vases to exotic custom arrangements, Crissey is *the* established florist in town. Prices are higher, but reflect the outstanding quality of the products, the knowledge and skill of the employees, and the fact that the flowers are so well handled that they will last a long time. Both locations carry a good supply of gifts (baskets, vases, and the like), silk and dried flowers, and clean-lined arrangements.

Furney's Nursery
21215 Pacific Hwy S (and
branches), 878-8761
(map: PP6)
Every day

Furney's, an excellent, top-flight nursery, is the place to buy trees and shrubs: 17 planted acres on Pacific Highway South (and another 75 in Oregon), plus some stock from wholesalers, makes the nearly 50-year-old family business a mainstay of Seattle gardens and gardeners. Bare-root fruit trees, balled-and-burlapped deciduous trees, field-grown evergreens, shrubs, and shade and flowering trees are stocked in abundance.

Kimura Nursery
3860 NE Bellevuet
Redmond Rd, Redmond,
881-6508 (map: FF1)
Every day

This pastoral (read "out-of-the-way") Redmond nursery features three greenhouses devoted to bargain greenery. You can't find better prices on indoor palms, ficus trees, dracina, bamboo palms, and smaller indoor or outdoor plants, including a nice selection of bonsai.

Megan Mary Olander Florist
222 1st Ave S,
623-6660 (map: O8)
Mon-Sat

Arrangements from this Pioneer Square florist look as if they were just gathered from a luscious English garden. Using unusual plant materials, the staff makes an extra effort to make the most of your budget, which doesn't have to be very much.

Molbak's Greenhouse and Nursery
13625 NE 175th St,
Woodinville, 483-5000
(map: BB2)
Every day

The superstore of nurseries, Molbak's is distinguished by the sheer quantity of plants alongside unusual and interesting garden products. Staff lacks the deep knowledge found at more specialty stores, but quite helpful in such a voluminous place. Browsers will find that they

Seattle Garden Center
Pike Place Market,
448-0431 (map: J8)
Every day

have been well treated here. Flowering plants are Molbak's forte, and it has gained destination status for its glorious profusion of Christmas pointsettias and great sales. Pike Place Market's Garden Center does big business in seeds of all kinds.

MsK Rare Plant Nursery
20066 15th Ave NW,
546-1281 (map: AA8)
By appointment only

The owner, the wife of a botanist at the University of Washington, recently discontinued mail-order service here to concentrate on the 3,000-plus unusual plants that thrive in her 4-acre nursery. Don't look for geraniums or peonies—this is where you go for maidenhairs and polystichums, catsuras and saxifrages, all of which she grows from seeds or cuttings.

Ness Flowers
4544 University Way NE,
632-7733 (map: FF7)
Every day

Since 1936, the Ness family has arranged flowers for weddings, proms, and funerals from this bustling corner of the Ave. There is the standard array of merchandise: flower settings, green houseplants, novelty gifts, and hospital vases. The specials on the shelves outside the store are usually a very good deal. Open until 9pm Monday through Friday.

Pike Place Flowers
Pike Place Market,
682-9797 (map: J8)
Mon-Sat

Pike Place Flowers in the Corner Market Building carries the widest range and best overall quality of blossoms at the Market. They'll wire all over the US, Canada, and Europe.

Swanson's
9701 15th Ave NW,
782-2543 (map: DD8)
Every day

Swanson's is getting better all the time. They stock a good range of annuals, perennials, and house and garden plants, but not many of each. They are pouring ever-increasing energy into a landscaping center, for which they certainly have the plants and the know-how.

Wells-Medina Nursery
8300 NE 24th St,
Bellevue, 454-1853
(map: GG3)
Every day

The best local nursery there is: excellent range and prices, complemented by a knowledgeable, helpful staff. Gardeners can find a variety of plants, especially perennials, the nursery's specialty. A notably wide variery of our state flower, the rhody, and wonderful sales, too.

West Seattle Nursery
5275 California Ave SW,
935-9276 (map: KK8)
Every day

West Seattle Nursery carries plenty of indoor and outdoor plants, especially varieties with colorful leaves or flowers. They also carry hand tools, fertilizers, herbicides, and other garden care products, with some gift items as well.

FURNITURE

Abodio
*1223 Western Ave (and
branches), 587-0516
(map: K8)
Every day*

Furnishings that are loosely modeled on Conran's pattern of contemporary simplicity and functional design fill this waterfront warehouse. The main floor is a maze of wall systems, country and modern beds, computer cubicles, rugs, and couches. They specialize in contemporary and upbeat traditional pieces, with a good supply of kids' furniture. Prices are in the middle range.

**Aventura International
Home Furnishings**
*10328 Main St, Bellevue,
455-3472 (map: HH3)
Tues-Sun*

This is a contemporary furniture store with an emphasis on design, and room for pieces not found anywhere else in the Northwest. Here you'll stumble across silver from Germany, Italian suede sofas, Noguchi lamps, and African baskets—a colorful, eclectic mix. They do custom work as well.

Current
*1201 Western Ave,
622-2433 (map: K8)
Every day*

If your taste runs to high-tech black matte, Memphis design geometry, or neoclassical granite, you'll be in contemporary heaven at Current. The store specializes in state-of-the-art lighting, also avant-garde wall units, chairs, desks, tables, rugs, and beds. The unfinished concrete and brick interior is an appropriately spare showroom for all of the Italian imports.

Del-Teet Furniture
*10308 NE 10th Ave,
Bellevue, 462-5400
(map: HH3)
Every day*

Once the pride of Capitol Hill's Broadway, Del-Teet now has its showroom in Bellevue, with an emphasis on classic-contemporary Northwest items. Leather love seats, Japanese antique tansu, and rosewood dining sets represent the cross section of furnishings. Furniture can be custom-made here to specifications, and an interior design service is provided for clients.

Kasala
*1505 Western Ave,
623-7795 (map: J8)
Every day*

*1014 116th Ave NE,
Bellevue, 453-2823
(map: GG3)
Every day*

Kasala emphasizes moderate prices and modern, space-conscious lifestyles. Its collection includes contemporary, trendy European home accessories—concentrating on lighting systems—glassware, gift items, and furniture.

Books in the Best Places series read as personal guidebooks, but our evaluations are based on numerous reports from local experts. Final judgements are made by the editors. Our inspectors never identify themselves (except over the phone) and never accept free meals or other favors. Be an inspector. Send us a report.

Masin Furniture
220 2nd Ave S,
622-5606 (map: O8)
Every day

10245 Main St, Bellevue,
450-9999 (map: GG2)
Every day

This traditional furniture store's extensive showrooms display the full range of classic furniture styles—Henredon, Drexel Heritage, and Karastan carpets. The proficient staff offers free in-home consultations.

Nido
1426 Alaskan Way,
623-6144 (map: J8)
Every day

Primarily a showroom for Chicken and Egg Productions, which manufactures sturdy and elegant log pine furniture, both children and adult size. The logs are hewn and peeled by kids at YMCA Camp Orkila on Orcas Island, and the proceeds (all of them) go to the prevention of harm to children by way of the Children's Trust Fund. To help feather your nido (and theirs) there are lots of other worldly treasures in this gentle space, which has an unlikely—and workable—air of Santa Fe, Japanese, and Italian villa combined.

Pennsylvania Woodworks
17705 140th Ave NE,
Woodinville, 486-9541
(map: BB1)
Every day

901 Fairview Ave N
(Chandler's Cove),
340-1613 (map: D1)
Every day

Each piece here is individually made by the Amish (yes, the people who don't believe in cars, telephones, or electricity); hence they're simple, traditional designs in solid woods (no veneers), and some handmade quilts and rugs.

Roche Bobois
1002 Western Ave,
622-7166 (map: M8)
Every day

Here's where professional athletes and others of like megabuck status come to fill their homes with Italian leathers, high-gloss lacquers, and neoclassical marble. Roche's European dining rooms, bedrooms, and living rooms are first-cabin luxury, bringing elegance and selection to those who can invest. Service is professional, as befits the inventory.

GIFTS AND STATIONERY

All Wrapped Up
211 Pine St, 447-CARD
(map: I7)
Every day

A comprehensive greeting card selection (check the beauties upstairs) and every gift-wrapping accessory imaginable keep customers rolling into this downtown card shop. But it's the little extras—Gumby, Slinky, Teaberry gum, and old musicals on the sound system—that give this place personality and bring back your childhood memories.

GIFTS AND STATIONARY

Bazaar Des Bears
1909 1st Ave, 443-0596
(map: I7)
Mon-Sat

This is a world of bears and sachets, hatboxes and pot-pourris, lace collars and baskets, all handpicked and romantically displayed by owner Michelle Durkson Clise, the author of several popular children's books.

Belle Provence
Country Village, Bothell,
483-4696 (map: AA4)
Every day

Tucked inside quaint Country Village is this spirited and artful shop. Old world hatboxes, belts, hair bows fashioned from antique fabrics, Limoges boxes, Beatrix Potter books, and fragrant potpourris line the shelves and provide both collectors and browsers an abundant shopping experience.

Burke Museum Store
University of Washington,
685-0909 (map: FF6)
Every day

Housed inside the Burke Museum at the northwest corner of the campus, the gift store follows the museum's lead. Look for their permanent collection of Northwest Coast Indian art, silk-screen prints, basketry, and wooden boxes, and don't miss the geological specimens and dinosaur replicas.

de Medici/Ming Fine Paper Company
1222 1st Ave, 624-1983
(map: L7)
Mon-Sat

Walking into this shop is like going into your Victorian great-aunt's attic (albeit a well-kept one) and finding some of the stationery she used for bread-and-butter notes. Handmade Japanese rice paper pressed with butterfly wings vies for your attention with rare Italian and vintage Chinese ceremonial papers. For the really passionate, there are papermaking classes, as well as calligraphic services. No ordinary stationer, this.

The Disney Store
Westlake Center,
622-3323 (map: I5)
Every day

Save the airfare to Anaheim or Orlando. Mickey and friends show up on watches, slippers, suspenders, cotton briefs, and tennis outfits for children. Stuffed Goofy, Pluto, and Donald, too.

Elliott Bay Stationery Store
Westlake Center,
587-4001 (map: I5)
Every day

2724 1st Ave S,
624-4423 (map: II7)
Mon-Sat

Leather anything and everything for the office: photo frames, desk sets, appointment books, and planners. Boxed writing paper for conservative occasions, and all sorts of custom printing.

Exclusively Northwest
415 Stewart St, 622-9144
(map: I6)
Mon-Sat, Sundays in
the summer

As much a gallery as a store, this corner of the Times Square Building showcases nicely chosen Northwest art and crafts, including clothing, Native American art, sculpture, pottery, jewelry, foodstuffs, and more.

Explore More Store (Pacific Science Center)
Seattle Center, 443-2870
(map: C7)
Every day

Don't let the educational benefits of browsing here deter you from a visit—it's fun, too. The shop ties in with the Pacific Science Center exhibits, so you'll find minerals, astronomy paraphernalia, dinosaur items, and other science-related toys and books for children. The collection of crystals is extensive and affordable, compared with those of the New Age specialty stores.

FireWorks Gallery
210 1st Ave S, 682-8707
Every day

Westlake Center,
682-6462
Every day

FireWorks shows a compelling array of ceramics, from the wild and whimsical to the more elegantly functional. A browse through here is the best introduction you'll find to the choicest local work, as well as that of outside talent. Jewelry here is some of the most fun in town; FireWorks also makes forays into fiber art, woodworking, and furniture.

Flying Shuttle
607 1st Ave, 343-9762
(map: N8)
Every day

Wondrous finds here, primarily of handwoven clothing, rugs, and jewelry. The last is crafted from a wide range of media, including paper, glass, ceramics, and beads. A wonderful place to find a gift.

Fox Paw
160 Winslow Way W,
Bainbridge Island,
842-7788
Every day

Owner Linda Allen has created an eclectic place to shop, with her assortment of artwork, jewelry, books, photo frames, note cards, linens, and lace.

The G Swan Inc.
2025 1st Ave, 448-7950
(map: H8)
Mon-Sat

Think of this fragrant froufrou shop when you need an English country–inspired gift. In addition to photo frames, soaps, and baskets, there's a small collection of vintage vanity accessories, such as sterling hairbrushes and hand mirrors.

Hat & the Heart
2806 E Madison St,
325-9909 (map: GG6)
Tues-Sat

Ingrid Savage and Diane Glenn search the world to bring unique flavor to their wondrous shop. Primitive folk art mixes with antique and art furniture, and, at Christmas, artful stockings from antique fabric, striped satin, and old buttons and charms.

Made in Washington
Pike Place Market,
467-0788 (map: J8)
Every day

Gilman Village,
Issaquah, 392-4819
Every day

And everything is—from crafts and local books to food-stuffs and wine. The selection is vast, and gift packages can be assembled for those who have the misfortune of being anywhere else.

GIFTS AND STATIONARY

Metropolis
7220 Greenwood Ave N
(and branches), 782-7002
(map: EE8)
Every day

Contemporary greeting cards (many by Northwest artists and photographers), gift wrap, and party supplies for every possible occasion are the specialties at Metropolis. The store is popular, with additional branches in Wallingford Center and West Seattle's Jefferson Square.

Mr. Peepers
6200 Sand Point Way
NE, 522-8202
(map: EE5)
Mon-Sat

They begin with an extensive selection of dollhouses (ranging from $1 to $30,000) and carry out the theme with an assortment of miniature furniture and dolls. Christmas decorations are the other big deal.

Museum of Flight Store
9404 E Marginal Way S,
764-5720 (map: LL6)
Every day

A barnstorm of aviation books: general, military, and literary. Models and posters are geared to all ages, from little plastic planes for kids to fairly complex airplane models for adult hobbiests. There's also a little outlet in Westlake Center.

The Nature Company
2001 Western Ave,
443-1608 (map: H9)
Every day

Right in the heart of the city is a paradise for the nature lover. Shoppers lose themselves as they handle the telescopes and globes, study the minerals and fossils, play with the nature-related toys, sort through the posters and books, and check out the distinctive timepieces. Five-year-olds will be delirious with joy when they see the dinosaur toys.

Northwest Discovery
142 Bellevue Square,
Bellevue, 454-1676
(map: HH3)
Every day

Elements Gallery
10500 NE 8th St,
Bellevue, 454-8242
(map: HH3)
Every day

An Eastside showcase for local artists' work, which features a fine woodwork collection of boxes, cribbage boards, and mirrors. Porcelain, silver, and beaded jewelry are of distinctive design and reasonably priced. Elements, in a more refined gallery atmosphere, displays hand-blown glass, pottery, and wall art.

PANACA Gallery
Bellevue Square,
Bellevue, 454-0234
(map: HH3)
Every day

The focus of PANACA (Pacific Northwest Arts and Crafts Association) has shifted from fine art paintings to crafts and artifacts; handcrafted pottery, blown glass, baskets, and handmade jewelry, beautifully produced by Northwest and Southwest craftspeople.

Paper Cat
214 1st Ave S, 623-3636
(map: N8)
Every day

This is a one-stop stationery shop, where you'll find loads of greeting cards, note paper, stickers, wrapping paper, and thousands of rubber stamps. A selection of fine imported stationery and handmade note cards, too.

The Paper Tree
Bellevue Square,
Bellevue, 451-8035
(map: HH3)
Every day

A tasteful selection of note cards, stationery, invitations, and frames is coolly displayed in this mall nook. Handsome desk accessories and fine writing instruments augment the inventory—although the shop would probably survive just fine solely on its custom-order business.

Riley's
7811 SE 27th St, Mercer
Island, 232-0833
(map: II4)
Mon-Sat

The quintessential suburban gift shop, but classier than most, Gloria Riley's store is strong on gifts for babies (that happened when she became a grandmother), china and crystal, accent pillows, good note cards, and other gifts for sophisticates. A men's section carries a variety of accessories.

Seattle Pen
1424 4th Ave, Suite 527,
682-2640 (map: J6)
Mon-Sat

There are only three stores on the West Coast that sell only pens. Here's a terrific collection of vintage fountain pens, ink, and leather pen cases. Owner Todd Craver provides repairs when needed and engraves at the store.

Sharper Image
1501 4th Ave, 343-9125
(map: J6)
Every day

What you used to drool over in their catalog can now be picked up and squeezed at this inventive adult gadget store. Among their most popular items are a table that will give you the best $1,995 full-body massage you've ever had and a pocket-size electronic telephone book—just the necessities, you understand, for life in the fast lane. Tuesdays they auction the floor samples.

Silberman/Brown
Rainier Square,
292-9404 (map: K6)
Mon-Sat

10220 NE 8th St,
Bellevue, 455-3665
(map: HH3)
Mon-Sat

This stationer's stationer offers an elegant array of stationery and desk accessories, with several choices for special-order monograms and engravings. Invitations for all occasions and a handsome selection of picture frames are hallmarks. Very accommodating, and they even carry the hard-to-find and hard-to-live-without Filofax line.

Tilden
401 15th Ave E,
323-7526 (map: HH6)
Every day

Tilden has earned its reputation as a classic gift store by continuing to focus on the kinds of items that make the best gifts: textiles, crystal, candles, glass, note cards, art jewelry, and housewares. It's all displayed well and priced with integrity.

The Weed Lady
122 4th Ave S, Edmonds,
775-3800
Mon-Sat

Set in an old-fashioned, arbor-guarded house off the main street, this shop is fragrant with potpourris, dried everlastings, soaps. It also carries small pottery pieces displayed on wooden shelves and around the floor. The owner is especially creative with dried floral arrangements and does an outstanding job for weddings (ask to see her photo album). The Weed Lady offers seasonal (fall and spring) classes in floral design, and her garden in the back of the store is a quiet oasis in Edmonds's suburban flow.

Wing Luke Asian Museum Store
407 7th Ave S, 623-5124 (map: R6)
Tues-Sun

Ethnographic artifacts such as baskets and jewelry from Japan, Korea, Indonesia, and China are available at the Wing Luke's small, excellent shop, which is intelligently stocked by the museum curator and an experienced import buyer. You *might* find some elegant robes and kimonos among the T-shirts and posters.

Ye Olde Curiosity Shop
Pier 54, Alaskan Way, 682-5844 (map: N9)
Every day

This "world-famous" Seattle attraction (since 1899) is a novelty stop for more than tourists. It's a veritable kitsch museum, housing a remarkable collection of Northwest Indian and Eskimo art, ivory, and soapstone, plus imports, totem poles, and other curios. Weird and wonderful things are found among the souvenir junk.

HARDWARE

Ballard Hardware and Supply
5229 Ballard Ave NW, 783-6626 (map: EE8)
Mon-Sat

A hardware store for the hard-core: if you need pipe fittings, this is the place to go, but there's nothing to touch up the kitchen with. You'll get professional service, if you know what you want.

Chubby & Tubby
3333 Rainier Ave S (and branches), 723-8800 (map: I16)
Every day

To call Chubby & Tubby a hardware store doesn't do it justice, since this local chain, with branches in North Seattle and White Center, virtually carries one of everything—from clothes to croquet sets—at working-man's prices. Cheapest Christmas trees in town.

City People's Mercantile
500 15th Ave E, 324-9510 (map: GG6)
Every day

City People's Garden Store
2939 E Madison St, 324-0737 (map: GG6)
Every day

This aptly named emporium stocks a bit of everything: from cards and office supplies to clothing, not to mention your basic hardware, lawn, and garden supplies. As close to a general store as we have in this city. Avid gardeners and gift shoppers alike will find everything they need at the Madison location, including Crabtree & Evelyn products and organic, nontoxic fertilizers.

Fremont Hardware
3517 Fremont Ave N,
632-1200 (map: FF7)
Mon-Sat

This neighborhood store has been equipping the Fremont crowd with home and garden supplies and hardware for over 80 years. Now a True Value; the owners are still friendly—and so are the prices.

Gowan's Greenwood Hardware and Glass
7201 Greenwood Ave N,
783-2900 (map: EE7)
Every day

An excellent, full-line hardware store with an extensive line of hot-water tanks, garden tools, sleds, paint, insulation, fittings, fixtures, and antique tools. The salesman who says, "If you don't see it, it's somewhere," is right on the mark.

Hall's Ace Hardware
9000 Roosevelt Way,
522-3324 (map: DD7)
Every day

A no-frills hardware store that favors plumbing and electrical supplies for the do-it-yourselfer. This and the friendly staff have made it popular with North End homeowners for 40 years.

Hardwick's Swap Shop
4214 Roosevelt Way NE,
632-1203 (map: DD7)
Tues-Sat

This hardware store, your best bet to beat the high cost of tools, has just about anything to stock and run a home, from furniture and fire irons to sinks and toilet seats. New and used.

Kirkland True Value Hardware
424 Kirkland Ave,
Kirkland, 822-6011
(map: EE3)
Every day

Kirkland Hardware draws clientele from all over the Eastside with its low-price offerings on a variety of quality paints, electrical and plumbing items, lumber, and housewares. They're enthusiastic and friendly folks, respected by local patrons and fellow hardware store owners alike.

Madison Park Hardware
1837 42nd Ave E,
322-5331 (map: GG6)
Mon-Sat

No ordinary hardware store, Madison Park Hardware is the friendly center of commercial life in this close-knit, single-family neighborhood. Proprietor Lola knows Madison Park like nobody else does, and her shop caters well to its needs, with a good selection of kitchen and gift items, decorator baskets, toys, and pet supplies to supplement the standard hardware stuff. Usually closed most of January.

McLendon's
710 S 2nd St, Renton,
235-3555 (map: MM3)
Every day

This hardware megaemporium has been in business for nearly 60 years, which makes it something of an area institution and well worth the trek to Renton. They have everything and a lot of it, including electrical and plumbing supplies and lumber.

Pacific Iron and Metal
2230 4th Ave S,

It's eclectic: cork, chicken wire, doors, rope, Plexiglas, Styrofoam, and seconds, plus a bin of discounted odd-

628-6256 *(map: II7)*
Every day

ities. But if you've taken on some serious remodeling, you'll get excellent help with your specifications.

RR Hardware
6512 15th Ave NE,
522-7810 (map: EE6)
Every day

A neighborhood store with a wood stove, Coke machine, and kids out front makes a fine place to browse or pick up a few yard tools. There's not much in the way of cookware, but other than that it's well stocked. Besides, it's one of the last of a dying breed: an old-fashioned hardware store with a fix-it shop and a handyman service.

Tashiro's Japanese Tools
1024 S Bailey St, 762-
8242 (map: Q6)
Mon-Sat

As its name suggests, this store specializes in high-quality Japanese woodworking tools and cutlery—shears, carving chisels, fine sashimi knives, and more. Open Monday through Saturday from 11am until 5pm.

Tweedy and Popp Ace Hardware
1916 N 45th St, 632-2290
(map: FF7)
Every day

The only touch of whimsy in this compulsively well organized store is the Yankee Clipper sleds hanging high on the wall. For the suburbanite with an impeccable house and garden, this store has everything, including kitchen sinks and bright green lawn mowers.

HEALTH FOOD

Central Co-op
1835 12th Ave, 329-1545
(map: GG2)
Every day

This Capitol Hill independent co-op is in its 12th year. In addition to a large organic produce department, it offers a wide range of macrobiotic products and is an excellent source for special dietary needs (salt-free, sugar-free, wheat-free, and other alternatives). Non-members are welcome, but pay a slightly higher price.

The Grainery
13629 1st Ave S, Burien,
244-5015 (map: OO8)
Mon-Sat

The Spendloves have been in business in Burien for 15 or so years. They grind some of their own flours and carry a large selection of grains, beans, raw honeys, and many hard-to-find items. In their central kitchen they offer classes and frequently demonstrate milling and grinding, dehydrating, and bread making.

Magnano Foods
Pike Place Market,
223-9582 (map: J8)
Mon-Sat

A great place in the mezzanine of the Main Arcade for buying bulk pasta, rice, beans, flours, grains, nuts, coffees, teas, and spices. Their bulk olive oil is a real bargain.

Marlene's Market and Deli
31839 Gateway Center

Marlene's new, bigger place is a nutritional gold mine, with a large book section, natural cosmetics, vitamins,

Blvd S, Federal Way,
839-0933 (map: SS6)
Every day

herbs, bulk grains, spices, raw dairy products, and organically grown produce. A natural-foods lunchroom is attached to the store.

Nature's Pantry
10200 NE 10th St,
Bellevue, 454-0170
(map: GG3)
Every day

The Eastside's finest and most comprehensive natural-food outlet features low-priced fresh produce, whole-grain baked goods, vitamins, cheeses, natural cosmetics, all-natural pet foods, a large book selection, and a deli/bakery.

Pilgrim's Garden Grocer
4217 University Way NE,
634-3430 (map: FF7)
Every day

5607 20th Ave NW,
782-6377 (map: EE8)
Mon-Sat

A virtual health supermarket that's been on the Ave for 17 years, it offers a wide selection of natural groceries, vitamins, imported cheese, and bulk food (and food for bulking up), as well as fresh-squeezed juices. There's one in Ballard, too.

Puget Consumers' Co-op
6504 20th Ave NE (and
branches), 525-1450
(map: EE7)
Every day

Member-owned and -operated (nonmembers can shop here too, but not at the same savings), this 30-year-old cooperative has grown to five stores (Ravenna, Kirkland, Green Lake, Seward Park, and View Ridge) and offers a wide variety of health-food items at competitive prices. Best known for bulk food supplies, PCC also has additive- and chemical-free meats, organically grown produce, and the lowest milk prices in town. View Ridge, Kirkland, and West Seattle have extensive delis.

Rainbow Grocery
409 15th Ave E,
329-8440 (map: HH6)
Every day

This folksy grocery features healthy natural-food products at competitive prices. Especially fine is the dairy department, with raw cream and several varieties of cheese. Service is exceptionally attentive.

HOME ACCESSORIES

Addisons
Northgate Mall,
362-0707 (map: DD7)
Every day

This superb kitchen and giftware shop stocks linens, dinnerware, and tabletop items, all well chosen and functional. Bridal registry available.

Crystallia
Bellevue Square,
Bellevue, 454-5687
(map: HH3)
Every day

It's one of the most complete selections of world-renowned crystal, glass, and Lucite accessories you'll find in the Northwest—Waterford, Orrefors, Sasaki. Service is great, and if they don't have what you're looking for, they'll find someone who does.

HOME ACCESSORIES

Design Concern
1420 5th Ave #201
(Pacific First Centre),
623-4444 (map: J8)
Mon-Sat

An eclectic collection of items fills this high-tech, two-level store, but all share at least one feature: unique, top-notch design. Bathroom scales, pens, housewares, jewelry, and wares such as Braun and Royal Copenhagen. The gallery downstairs has design shows.

Domus
Bellevue Square,
Bellevue, 454-2728
(map: HH3)
Every day

Alderwood Mall,
Lynnwood, 775-6144

An extremely well chosen lot—wine glasses, linen towels, jewelry, note cards, furniture, china, aprons, cutlery—in Bellevue Square's best housewares store. Affordable, with a sleek, modern inclination. You could lose yourself in here for hours.

Egbert's
2231 1st Ave, 728-5682
(map: G8)
Mon-Sat

You'll rarely see the same thing twice at this unlikely Belltown address, but you can be assured of finding fine, creative, good-quality items all the time. An Italian leather chair sets off a Scandinavian light wood dining room table; jewelry from around the world approaches museum quality; textiles from Africa mix with folklore-inspired bronzes. There is even some clothing thrown in for good measure. The potpourri style is executed quite successfully by owner Jim Egbert, whose eclectic tastes run the gamut from whimsical to functional.

Frank and Dunya
3418 Fremont Ave N,
547-6760 (map: FF7)
Tues-Sun

Quirky Frank and Dunya are the owners' departed dogs, and their likenesses perpetually, cheerfully greet all comers to F and D. The store is filled with hand-made furniture and mostly locally crafted accessories. Everything in here is a character piece—overwhelmingly so. Expensive and worth it.

Hold Everything
1420 5th Ave, #202
(Pacific First Center),
682-8915 (map: J6)
Every day

The Williams-Sonoma people have come out of the kitchen. Just walk into the store and you'll feel more organized. They carry places to put stuff—cedar shoe racks, bright floral closet bags, folding bookshelves, expando spice risers. Catalog, too.

J.F. Henry Shop
4540 California Ave SW,
935-5150 (map: I19)
Mon-Sat

J.F. Henry's bright interior attracts West Seattle shoppers looking for popular and traditional place settings: Noritake, Mikasa, Lenox, and other mainstream collections, plus a bountiful assortment of glassware, crystal, and accessories. Brides can register here.

Keeg's
310 Broadway E,

This Capitol Hill mainstay equips Seattleites with all the pricey necessities for modern small-scale living:

325-1771 (map: GG6)
Every day

kitchenware, gourmet treats, children's toys, leather accessories, contemporary lighting, rugs, flatware, tables and chairs, and more, including wrapping paper and note cards. Just the place to find ginger graters and Mexican tortilla warmers.

Market Graphics
1935 1st Ave, 441-7732
(map: I8)
Every day

From da Vinci to pop art, Market Graphics carries contemporary and classic art reproductions. Helpful owners provide special service to businesses decorating with posters.

Miller-Pollard Interiors
University Village (and branches), 527-8478
(map: FF6)
Every day

Now in three locations, this Seattle treasure continues to delight browsers with its restrained good taste. Clean-lined antiques (with a special affection for Danish pine) intermix with comfortable chintz pillows; country kitchen tables are bedecked with wooden bowls; table linens complement the flatware, dinnerware, and stemware. The U Village and Bellevue locations have the heaviest concentration of furniture. Design consultation available.

Pottery Barn
1420 5th Ave (Pacific First Centre), 682-9312
(map: J6)

Another Williams-Sonoma offspring specializing in tabletop and living space accoutrements for the Modern Home: stenciled cotton rugs, bold vases, and a wide array of glass- and stemware.

The Well Made Bed
1427 Western Ave,
343-5066 (map: J8)
Every day

990 102nd NE, Bellevue,
455-3508 (map: HH3)
Every day

No beds. No comforters. No nightstand gewgaws. Only beddings—sheets, duvets, pillow slips, and dust ruffles. They carry or can special-order bed linens from any American manufacturer, one gorgeous and pricey French line, and sometimes even discontinued patterns. If you are concerned about where you spend one-third of your life, albeit unconscious, let this place tuck you in.

Zanadia
Wallingford Center,
547-0884 (map: EE6)
Every day

Zanadia carries a wide range of contemporary, reasonably priced kitchen and lifestyle accessories, as well as rugs, clocks, mirrors, magazine racks, picture frames, garbage cans, and other can't-do-withouts.

IMPORTS

Anglomania
Gilman Village,
Issaquah, 392-2842
Every day

Owner Susan Jarrett loads up with authentic British goods on her twice-yearly jaunts to the mother country. A proper collection of English bone china (Royal Doulton, Royal Albert, and other lines), Irish porcelain,

Cottontail Corner
Gilman Village,
Issaquah, 392-3818

British woolen sweaters, bumper stickers, tea biscuits, and much more fill the shelves. A second store, Cottontail Corner, carries nothing but Beatrix Potter figurines. Remember Appley-Dappley?

Asia Gallery
1220 1st Ave, 622-0516
(map: K7)
Mon-Sat

Owner Tony Ventura, in his annual forays to the Orient, picks up fine Asian antiques, plus folk arts, ethnic textiles, and some contemporary (mostly Asian) jewelry. Evening hours are arranged by appointment.

Cibol
Pike Place Market,
682-5640 (map: J7)
Mon-Sat

The good-looking, low-priced, imported clothing in this small Market shop (on the mezzanine level of the Main Arcade) comes from Latin America, India, Greece, Bali, Mexico, Guatemala, and South and Central America—just about everywhere except the Orient. Alpaca sweaters are great deals, a lot of color and warmth at very reasonable prices. The accessories are imports, too: jewelry, bags, and scarves.

Folk Art Gallery/La Tienda
4138 University Way NE,
632-1796
(map: FF6)
Mon-Sat

One of the nation's premier import shops, La Tienda is loaded with clothing, crafts, jewelry, and musical instruments from everywhere, including a fair amount of work from US folk artists. The displays are fascinating—shelves of hand-thrown pottery, a few imported children's toys, African drums, silk scarves—and the owner is delighted to speak Spanish with customers.

Galway Traders
7518 15th Ave NW,
784-9343 (map: EE8)
Every day

Goods from Ireland and art from the American Southwest share space in this Ballard house-turned-shop. Successfully, too: the six rooms are filled to the brim with crafts, imports, and foodstuffs. From Ireland come woolens, capes, Aran sweaters (the best collection in the area), Belleek china, dolls, books, and the largest collection of Celtic records north of San Francisco. From the Southwest come Navajo pottery and haunting Indian tapes, gorgeous tiles, and other art. Then pick up the makings of a meal: oatmeal and Irish tea, blue corn tortillas and salsa.

Hands of the World
Pike Place Market,
622-1696 (map: J8)
Every day

A bright shop in the lower level of the Main Arcade, Hands of the World carries beautiful crafts and home accessories imported primarily from third-world countries. The emphasis is on jewelry and art, including masks and carvings, along with other imported accessories. Closed Sundays January through April.

Look for **KIDS**—*it means your child will especially enjoy this place or attraction.*

Higo
604 S Jackson St,
622-7572 (map: Q6)
Mon-Sat

Think of a Japanese Woolworth's in the International District, and that's Higo, a 50-plus-year-old Seattle institution. There are soup bowls, chopsticks, rice steamers, and other utensils along with kimonos, shoes, and postcards of Mount Fuji.

Monsoon
4536 University Way NE,
633-2446 (map: FF6)
Every day

Nancy and Eric Gorbman travel abroad three times a year to bring back treasures from Indonesia, Thailand, Japan, India, Pakistan, and Nepal, but they don't exclude local designers. Monsoon is the only place in Seattle where you'll find handmade Nepalese sweaters and Japanese baseball shirts. Lovely accessories—including a marvelous selection of sterling silver jewelry set with stones—from India, Nepal, Pakistan, and Thailand. Tons of beads from everywhere.

Prima de Mexico
68 Madison St, 682-6294
(map: M8)
Mon-Sat

Mexican furniture, pottery, jewelry, and folk art are the order of the day at Prima de Mexico. It's all handcrafted in Mexico and imported directly to the US. Especially popular are the pottery selections—which come in all sizes, shapes, and colors—and the masks from all over Mexico, made of stone, wood, or metal.

Pyramid Imports
106 Pine St, 448-8447
(map: I7)

The softest of cottons can be found here in the pure Egyptian cotton pajamas. Other items from Egypt include clothing, loungewear, earrings, and cloth bags at low prices.

JEWELRY

Alvin Goldfarb Jeweler
305 Bellevue Way,
Bellevue, 454-9393
(map: HH3)
Mon-Sat

The owner learned his trade as a gemologist at Friedlander, his wife's family's business. Now on his own for 10 years, Alvin Goldfarb provides unerring personal attention and quality. Many of Bellevue's affluent won't go anywhere else.

Beau Bangles
1420 5th Ave, #206
(Pacific First Centre),
682-4434 (map: J5)
Every day

Barrie Galantie's high-fashion accessories shop on the second floor of Pacific First Centre features one-of-a-kind jewelry, scarves, and jackets from local to New York designers.

Ben Bridge
4th and Pike (and
branches), 628-6800
(map: J6)
Mon-Sat

The best place for diamonds is Ben Bridge, in the same downtown location since 1912. Their diamonds range from inexpensive to expensive, and service is very informative. Mountings are fairly traditional, but custom design work is offered.

Carroll's
1427 4th Ave,
622-9191 (map: K6)
Mon-Sat

Carroll's sparkles with unusual finds from all over the world; it's one of the most fascinating and lovely gem stores in Seattle. You might discover an antique silver picture frame or a set of antique Oriental gaming pieces. There's also a classy selection of watches, rings, bracelets, necklaces, and gemstones, which make the store a favorite with wealthy matrons. Service is appropriately stuffy.

Facere Jewelry Salon
(Seattle Sheraton Hotel)
6th Ave and Pike St,
624-9779 (map: K5)
Mon-Sat

Facere Jewelry Art
1501 4th Ave,
624-6768 (map: J6)
Mon-Sat

Proprietor Karen Lorene has long been Seattle's leading authority on antique jewelry, and her original shop, Vanity Fair on Pier 70, was the place to buy it. Now, at her Seattle Sheraton store, she carries primarily antique (Victorian) jewelry; her Century Square shop carries contemporary jewelry art. She offers appraisals, classes, and antique jewelry repair.

Fox's Gem Shop
1341 5th Ave, 623-2528
(map: K6)
Mon-Sat

If there really were a diamond as big as the Ritz, here's where you'd find it. Fox's is an elegant shop with stiff prices. Their specialties: glittering gemstones and dazzling diamonds. You dress up to shop here. A gift section has silver for all occasions and a large selection of clocks. The only Tiffany's boutique in the Northwest.

Friedlander Jewelers
1400 5th Ave (and
branches), 223-7474
(map: J5)
Mon-Sat

A landmark in Seattle since 1886, Friedlander Jewelers is one of the best. Besides an overwhelming selection of watches, rings, and fine crystal, the shop offers custom design and repair. One hundred years of practice makes perfect—or close to it—and five branches.

Gem Design Jewelers
14310 NE 20th St, Ste B,
Bellevue, 643-6245
(map: GG3)
Mon-Sat

Owners Shauna and Richard Miller deal in original and custom designs and stone remounting. Also a nice line of earrings, gold necklaces, and individual stones.

Gold & Silver Shop
526 1st Ave N,
284-2082 (map: A7)
Mon-Sat

Traditional to ultramodern jewelry is fabricated in-house here. Diamonds are an especially good value because the shop buys directly from contacts in Israel. Gemstones, too.

Goldman's Jewelers
1521 1st Ave, 682-0237
(map: J7)
Mon-Sat

Jack Goldman carries exciting, state-of-the-art jewelry, much of it made by local artists (his own designs included). Expect to find unusual gems and colored stones, custom and artist inlay work, and an extensive clock selection. Goldman's ships all around the world.

Lillian's Pearl Shop
504 Pike St, 682-1043
(map: J5)
Mon-Fri

Lillian's has a broad assortment of cultured pearls in many colors and sizes. The shop strings pearl necklaces to any length (and can repair broken strings); also jade and lapis pieces. Hours are short: weekdays from 11am to 4pm.

Michael Wm Farrell, Jeweler
324 15th Ave E,
324-1582 (map: HH6)
Mon-Sat

5420 Sand Point Way
NE, 524-8848
(map: EE5)
Mon-Sat

A friendly shop, always full of clients buying and admiring the excellent selection of vintage watches. They're assembling an impressive collection of sterling silver hollowware, as well as vintage American signature jewelry. They also do custom repairs.

Philip Monroe Jeweler
519 Pine St, 624-1531
(map: J5)
Mon-Sat

The top of the line when it comes to custom jewelry (which makes up 95 percent of its business), this small shop has an air of restrained elegance. Occasionally their lovely selection of unusual and antique jewelry hangs from the arms of exquisite Oriental figurines.

Turgeon Raine Jewelers
Fourth and Pike
Building, 447-9488
(map: J5)
Mon-Sat

Designer jewelry and custom design work are the reasons to go up nine floors in the Fourth and Pike Building to Turgeon Raine. There's something here for all ages. The jewelry has a creative, artistic feel.

KITCHENWARES

City Kitchens
1525 4th Ave,
328-1138 (map: J6)
Every day

A general purpose kitchen store where selected commercial and specialty cookware lines are sold at some of the lowest prices in the city.

A Cook's Tour
Pier 56, 622-2838
(map: K9)
Every day

This spacious, gadget-filled waterfront store has everything you need for a well-equipped kitchen, from stemware to storage containers to stock pots. The helpful staff, the long hours (until 10pm every night), and the salty air make this a particularly relaxing place to shop.

Grand Central Mercantile
316 1st Ave S,
623-8894 (map: O8)
Every day

A gold mine of imported kitchenware, cooking accessories, and dinnerware, plus a broad selection of knives and unusual knickknacks. Well thought of by cooks.

Send us your feedback and tips on the report form at the back of this book.

Kitchen Kitchen
Bellevue Square,
Bellevue, 451-9507
(map: HH3)
Every day

A spinoff of the superlative housewares store Domus, Kitchen Kitchen carries at everything that belongs in a kitchen, from the practical to the frivolous. Mixing bowls, pots, and cookbooks vie for space with cookie cutters and refrigerator magnets. Lots of classes.

Magnolia Kitchen Shoppe & Cooking School
3214 W McGraw St,
282-2665 (map: GG8)
Mon-Sat

Magnolia Kitchen Shoppe has a wide selection of unusual and modern kitchen supplies and giftware, as well as a catering and carry-out service. The cooking school, which employs up to a dozen teachers, has an excellent reputation among the town's elite cooks.

Mr. J's Kitchen Gourmet
10116 NE 8th St,
Bellevue, 455-2270
(map: HH3)
Every day

A veritable warehouse of tasteful domestic and imported pots, pans, glassware, plates, flatware, cooking aids, processors, and trendy gadgets. Classes are offered in fall, winter, and spring.

The Mrs. Cooks
University Village,
525-5008 (map: FF6)
Every day

This neighborhood kitchen store concentrates on top-quality cookware and utensils, besides carrying a respectable collection of cookbooks, giftware, and excellent kitchen linens. Salespeople are knowledgeable.

Sunshine Kitchen Company
14625 NE 20th St,
Bellevue, 641-4520
(map: GG2)
Every day

Owner Hal Sadis opened his kitchen supply shop in the same building as the Sunshine Bakery; the aroma of baking brioches and baguettes will inspire you to purchase his crockery, copper molds, heavy kitchen equipment, and other necessities.

Sur La Table
Pike Place Market,
448-2244 (map: I8)
Every day; closed Sun,
Jan, Feb, and March,
more or less

A delightfully crammed, Continental-feeling storefront in the Garden Center Building has all the essential (and nonessential) equipment for cooks: candy molds, Cuisinarts, cake pans, muffin tins, copper pots, dish towels, potholders, imported aprons, and lots of cookbooks. Author appearances yield occasional cooking demos. Service is skilled in the art of kitchen advice.

Williams-Sonoma
Westlake Center,
624-1422 (map: I5)
Every day

A line formed just to get *inside* when this catalog retailer opened its Seattle doors—a long-standing favorite of cooks looking for French porcelain or the latest in kitchen wizardry. The shop also stocks a small collection of gourmet foodstuffs, glassware, and linens.

LINGERIE

Bella Notte
1011 1st Ave (Alexis

A glamorous lingerie boutique with a wonderful variety of styles and sizes, ranging from decadent to demure.

Hotel), 343-9536
(map: L8)
Mon-Sat

They feature the Natori line (many floral appliqué patterns) in both silk and polyester; elegant, sexy Adagio silks; and nice soft cottons.

Boxer Bay
1420 5th Ave, Ste #202
(Pacific First Centre),
625-9418 (map: K5)
Mon-Sat

Lingerie, of sorts, for men. Boxer Bay has its own label of silk boxers, loungewear, and ties, as well as luxuriously thick cotton terry robes that are favorites for men and women. Mother-daughter team Rein and Cynthia Hillis have plans for expanding their one-of-a-kind concept to Colorado and California.

Nancy Meyer
1318 5th Ave, 625-9200
(map: K6)
Mon-Sat

This eclectic boutique has about as much square footage as the walk-in closets of some of its patrons, but it manages to stock a surprising selection of the finest designer and imported lingerie. The tasteful luxury displayed here has made it a favorite among the physically and fiscally fortunate.

Victoria's Secret
Westlake Center (and
branches), 623-6035
(map: I5)
Every day

Women have grown to expect two things from VS: cotton that isn't frumpy and tasteful lingerie that doesn't cost a fortune. Intimate apparel here runs the from sport bras to skimpy silk nighties to hug-size bathrobes.

Westminster Lace
1501 4th Ave,
622-4476 (map: J5)
Every day

Most of the products here are "touched with lace": linens, tablecloths, lingerie, doilies, tray covers, dust ruffles, and on and on. Antique or not, everything has a Victorian feeling. Products are expensive but not excessively, and come in a range of prices—the handkerchief supply contains one for $5 and one for $50.

MEAT

A & J Meats and Seafoods
2401 Queen Anne Ave N,
284-3885 (map: GG8)
Tues-Sat

Regarded as the best in town, A & J Meats has a wonderful selection of specialty items as well as top-quality basic cuts (the beef and lamb are superb). They make all their own wieners and lunch meats (both pure beef), chicken Cordon Bleu, stuffed pork chops, meat loaves, and sausages of all types (including fruit), as well as doing all their own applewood smoking.

Bavarian Meats
Pike Place Market,
441-0942 (map: J8)
Mon-Sat

A large selection of sausages from bratwurst to knackwurst in the north end of the Market.

Brodeen's Quality Produce & Delicatessen
128 5th Ave S, Edmonds, 778-0202
Every day

You just have to look at something in this friendly produce and cheese store in Edmonds and a staff member will probably come up and slice it open and give you a taste. Everything's very high quality here. A return to the good old days.

Bud's Fine Foods
4000 E Madison St, 322-8361 (map: GG6)
Tues-Sat

Recently relocated from downtown Bellevue, Bud's is collecting a Seattle following for its fine butcher shop and quality delicatessen under one roof.

Cascioppo Brothers Italian Meat Market
2364 NW 80th St, 784-6121 (map: EE8)
Every day

Seattle's only Italian meat vendor and a longtime Ballard tradition carries several lines of imported Italian specialty foods. The Italian sausage is spicy and excellent, the choice of many Italian restaurants in town.

Don & Joe's
Pike Place Market, 682-7670 (map: J8)
Mon-Sat

Located under the clock in the Main Arcade, Don and Joe's is the best butcher in the Market. Their smoked ham, fresh turkeys, and lamb chops are superb. Friendly service ensures hordes of satisfied regulars.

Fischer Meats and Seafoods
85 Front St N, Issaquah, 392-3131
Mon-Sat

This 1910 Issaquah institution is the place to go for chicken—it's delivered fresh daily, as is the seafood. Fischer also makes their own German, Italian, and potato sausages.

Honey Bee Hams
700 108th Ave NE, Bellevue, 462-1212 (map: HH3)
Mon-Sat
2650 University Village Mall, 523-3070 (map: FF6)
Every day

Ham like you've never tasted comes out of these shops, honey glazed and succulent. They also do smoked poultry and a buzzing lunchtime sandwich trade. Low on atmosphere, but high marks for efficiency and—most importantly—taste.

Market House Corned Beef
1124 Howell St, 624-9248 (map: I2)
Mon-Sat

A very unpretentious place that sells simply terrific corned beef. The emphasis here is on wholesale, but they do retail corned beef in any amount.

The Meat Shop
6522 Fremont Ave N (and branches), 789-5834 (map: EE7)
Every day

This workers cooperative is the most complete supplier of organic meats in the Pacific Northwest. The beef, pork, lamb, and poultry are raised without hormones, antibiotics, and other additives; most of the ham, bacon, wieners, and sausages are produced without sodium nitrate or other preservatives.

Seattle Super Smoke
2454 Occidental Ave S,
625-1339 (map: II7)
Mon-Sat

Seattle Super Smoke caught on so feverishly with Seattle palates that it had to move to much larger quarters. Its main business is wholesale, but you can also buy this deeply smoky, alderwood-redolent poultry and meat out of a retail deli. The barbecue sauce is a fine accompaniment.

Torino Sausage
700 S Dearborn St,
623-1530 (map: HH7)
Mon-Sat

A family-run company that specializes in freshly made sausages (no preservatives). Watch while you wait or order up on a hoagie roll.

OUTDOOR GEAR

Alpine Hut
2215 15th Ave W,
284-3575 (map: GG8)
Mon-Sat

Alpine Hut's business is pretty evenly divided between selling new items and renting used gear—ski gear in winter, wet suits and bike wear in summer. They don't have a lot of everything, but the owner is friendly and the store aims to please.

Crossings
716 N 34th St, 547-3819
(map: FF7)
Mon-Sat

While the emphasis is on sailing, these crew outfits work nicely for *almost* any kind of boating endeavor. The outerwear keeps you dry on deck and the natural fiber fabrics keep you dapper.

The Crow's Nest
1900 N Northlake Way,
632-3555 (map: FF7)
Every day

6010 Seaview Ave NW,
783-6262 (map: EE9)
Every day

This large marine hardware store specializes in yachting accessories, clothing, foul-weather gear, and hardware. There's another branch in Everett.

David Morgan
11812 Northcreek Pkwy
N, Bothell, 485-2132
(map: BB4)
Mon-Sat

Here is where you buy the plush, functional waxed cotton Warwick and Sandringham shooting jackets and Buxton riding coats. Also look for British ordinance survey maps, Filson clothing (the prime outdoor wear made in Seattle), Akubra hats, and Welsh wools. Everything for the well-heeled horseman, huntsman, or all-purpose outdoorsman.

de la Rosa's Northwest Cycle
1100 E Pike St, 329-2453
(map: J3)
Mon-Sat

A Capitol Hill bike shop featuring several European lines as well as equipment and bikes for everyone. They cater to commuters, recreationalists, and racers.

Easy Rider
15666 W Valley Hwy,
Tukwila, 228-3633
Mon-Sat

The largest West Coast manufacturer of canoes and kayaks, Easy Rider offers its complete line of 35 different styles, factory direct to the public. Factory pickup offers savings of at least 15 percent on first-quality vessels, 25 to 30 percent on seconds. There are whitewater, lake, saltwater, all-purpose, family, and hunting styles in 13- to 18½-foot lengths.

Eddie Bauer
Rainier Square (and
branches), 622-2766
(map: K6)
Every day

Once Seattle's very own, Eddie Bauer is now a national chain (owned by Spiegel Inc.) with a like-sized reputation. You used to shop here for fine goose-down sleeping bags, comforters, and pillows, but now you come for outdoor fashion: goose-down jackets, vests, and parkas, along with shorts, rugby shirts, and other sportive ensembles. All are very high quality, dependable, and pricey. In addition, their 200 stores sell some fishing rods, backpacking equipment, sports accessories, knives, sunglasses, and shoes. The downtown Eddie Bauer's outlet store sells merchandise at 40 to 70 percent reductions.

Elliott Bay Bicycles
2116 Western Ave,
441-8144 (map: G8)
Mon-Sat

7904 E Green Lake Dr N,
524-4270 (map: EE7)
Every day

Intimidating to novices, Elliott Bay is the Cadillac of bike stores. It's regarded as something of a pro shop; they sell bikes to cyclists who know what they're doing, and do enough of it to justify the high prices. Among its other attributes, the shop is home base for Bill Davidson, a nationally known frame builder.

Fast Lady Sports
15600 NE 8th St,
Bellevue, 641-9696
(map: GG2)
Every day

Fast Lady has the most complete selection of women's clothing and footwear for running, cycling, swimming, tennis, and aerobic workouts. The supportive, friendly staff dispenses accurate information and advice.

Feathered Friends
1516 11th Ave, 324-4166
(map: HH6)
Every day

1417 1st Ave, 622-0974
(map: J7)
Mon-Sat

These are the top-of-the-line down products in the city; every expedition that climbed Mount Everest from January to August of 1988 was wearing Gore-Tex down suits made by Feathered Friends. The First Avenue branch sells bedding and comforters; the one on Capitol Hill specializes in sporting goods, sleeping bags, and climbing equipment.

Gregg's Greenlake Cycle
7007 Woodlawn Ave NE
(and branches), 523-1822
(map: EE7)
Every day

Gregg's is a high-volume, high-pressure Seattle institution, perhaps (at least initially) by virtue of its Green Lake location. They have such a large inventory that they can handle the entire family: bikes for kids, all-terrain and Japanese-, Italian-, and American-made racing cycles, along with Seattle's largest collection of touring bikes. Because of its sheer volume, it's the best first stop when you're hunting for a bicycle. If you do buy from them, you'll get great follow-up service (better than they've supplied before). The Green Lake location has a large clothing and accessories department and rents bikes, roller skates, and skateboards. There are branches in Bellevue and on Aurora.

Il Vecchio
140 Lakeside Ave,
324-8148 (map: HH6)
Tues-Sat

Visually, George Gibbs's bicycle shop in Leschi looks more like an art gallery than a bike shop. The Weinstein-designed store is minimalist in appeal—there are very few bikes here—and maximal in quality (and price): Italian racers, Belgian-made Eddy Merckx, and sometimes Seattle original Glenn Erickson.

The Magic Spoke
7009 Roosevelt Way NE,
527-2100 (map: EE6)
Tues-Sat

Sally Hildt has gained a reputation for her quick, honest bicycle repairs and wheel building. All types of bikes and bicyclists benefit from this thorough-service ethic.

Marine Center
1150 Fairview Ave N,
682-1150 (map: HH7)
Every day

Discount prices and a helpful staff at this large Lake Union store keep nautical types in equipment, clothing, and foul-weather gear for a variety of boating needs.

Marmot Mountain Works
827 Bellevue Way NE,
Bellevue, 453-1515
(map: HH3)
Every day

Marmot outfits the skier, backpacker, and mountaineer with cross-country skies, packs, tents, boots, crampons, ice axes, and more—all for sale or rent. Prices for outerwear are some of the highest around; however, deals can be found on some ski accessories, such as climbing skins for the backcountry. An excellent selection of climbing hardware. Large enough to have everything you need, though the staff (while knowledgeable) is clumsy: they either hover or ignore.

Mercer Island Cyclery
2827 80th Ave SE,
Mercer Island, 232-3443
(map: JJ4)
Every day

The island's neighborhood bike shop has gained a reputation for being *the* place to go for mountain (all-terrain) bikes—it's credited with starting the craze in this area—but it also offers several other models. The shop is small; you're always bound to be talking to one of the owners, both of whom are enthusiastic cyclists and eager to help.

The North Face
1023 1st Ave, 622-4111

A well-known name in backpacking equipment design, The North Face also has down clothing and bags, out-

(map: L8)
Every day

door apparel, and skiwear. The store has rentals to meet virtually any mountaineering equipment need, including maps and books. The feeling here is one of a yuppified REI, but that doesn't mean they aren't serious about products and service.

Pacific Water Sports
16205 Pacific Hwy S,
246-9385 (map: OO6)
Mon-Sat

A landbound spot on the Pacific Highway South strip is an unlikely location for this burgeoning waterplay shop. Here advanced and novice paddlers outfit themselves with the boat (kayaks or canoes), the suit (wet or dry), and even the class (sea or whitewater). Excellent instruction ranges from canoe basics to intensive whitewater excursions. Exceptionally friendly service and advice. Rentals, too.

Patrick's Fly Shop
2237 Eastlake Ave E,
323-3302 (map: GG7)
Mon-Sat

Fishing enthusiasts think of this shop as the premier source of information on area fly-fishing and how to tie those flies. Patrick's offers workshops (including a new one on rod building) and just plain old-fashioned friendly fishing stories and advice.

R & E Cycles
5627 University Way NE,
527-4822 (map: FF7)
Every day

Mountain Bike Specialists
5625 University Way NE,
527-4310 (map: FF7)
Every day

Nationally known for their bicycle frames, owner Angel Rodriguez and frame builder Glenn Erickson specialize in singles, tandems, and racing bikes at R & E. It's also a good shop for wheel building. Mountain Bike Specialists next door carries only mountain bikes; repairs are done down the street at Seattle Bike Repair (527-0360), and seconds are sold at 2nd Gear (527-1536) around the corner. A crack, thorough operation.

Recreational Equipment Inc. (REI)
1525 11th Ave (and
branches), 323-8333
(map: HH7)
Every day

The nation's largest co-op (15 West Coast stores, just over two million members) has expanded its stock to include more clothing and sportswear, but you'll still find everything you need for mountaineering, backpacking, camping, cross-country skiing, and other outdoor pursuits. The Capitol Hill emporium is an excellent source for maps, trail food, and outdoor books. Anyone can shop here, but members pay only $10 to join and receive at least a 10 percent yearly dividend on their purchases. Founded in 1938 by a group of Seattle mountaineers who wanted to import European equipment, the co-op was presided over for years by Everest-conqueror Jim Whittaker, and is still staffed by knowledgeable outdoorspeople. Rentals at good prices, too. There are smaller branches in Bellevue, Federal Way, and, the most recent addition, Lynnwood.

Ricky Young Surfboards
14 102nd Ave NE #2,
Bellevue, 453-2346
(map: GG3)
Mon-Sat

Yes, there's surfing in Washington (and Oregon). Ricky Young, a nationally ranked surfer in the '60s, is the sport's top local promoter and adviser. Young manufactures his own boards (accessories and rentals, too) and sells a California line for both short- and longboard surfers. This is a *real* surf shop.

Scuba Sports Expeditions
241 Sunset Ave N,
Renton, 228-7332
(map: MM3)
Every day

The local hub of diving activity concentrates on skin diving, wet suits, and underwater photography. They offer various classes and also sponsor group dives, tropical trips, and a buddy system for divers without partners. Scuba equipment sales, rentals, and repairs.

Seattle Athletic and Exercise
842 Northgate Way (and
branches), 364-5890
(map: DD2)
Every day

Everything from one-pound weights to $7,000 exercise machines, including exercise mats, rowing machines, treadmills, and other high-quality exercise equipment. Customers are trained in how to use their new purchases. Branches are in Bellevue and just south of Southcenter Mall.

Super Jock 'N Jill
7210 E Green Lake Dr N,
522-7711 (map: EE7)
Every day

Sports medicine clinics and doctors send their patients here for proper shoe fitting: these salespeople know their merchandise and understand the mechanics of running and power-walking. A podiatrist is in the store once a week to answer questions and help with problems. The selection of other merchandise (running gear, bathing suits) is smaller, but often this is the one place in town to carry a specific item. They are also a good source on races, routes, and training.

Swallows' Nest
2308 6th Ave, 441-4100
(map: G6)
Every day

A specialty climbing shop, Swallows' Nest outfits backpackers, cross-country skiers, and mountaineers with rental or sales merchandise. Second only to Marmot Mountain Works, they will special order. Kayaking and canoeing are the other big focus. There's more room at their new downtown nest.

Trek
300 Queen Anne Ave N,
281-7870 (map: A8)
Mon-Sat

Adventure travel is *in*, so a store is born. Inexpensive clothing and accessories from Nepal to take back to Nepal. It's the helpful advice and low-key atmosphere that keep customers returning for their backpacking needs—whether for the Himalayas or the Cascades.

Warshal's Sporting Goods
1000 1st Ave, 624-7300
(map: M7)
Mon-Sat

A downtown dinosaur, Warshal's has been holding down the corner of First and Madison forever. You come here for virtually any sporting-goods need, along with unadvertised discounts, hunting and fishing licenses, and a fine selection of darkroom supplies and photography equipment. In-house repair service for fishing reels and firearms is another draw. The regular-joe atmosphere appeals in this high-gloss part of town.

West Marine
6317 Seaview Ave NW,
789-4640 (map: EE9)
Every day

1000 Mercer St, 292-8663
(map: D2)
Every day

Cal Marine has a well-established reputation as a sailing-equipment supplier, with a full line of marine supplies for powerboats and sailboats, and accessories for both: binoculars, winches, line (for sails or for tying up), outboards, dinghies, sports boats up to 12 feet, and more.

Wilderness Sports
14340 NE 20th St,
Bellevue, 746-0500
(map: GG2)
Mon-Sat

Top-quality cross-country skiing and mountaineering equipment, clothing, and books are offered year-round, at lower prices than anywhere else. You can also rent almost everything, with rental fees applied to the purchase price. Free classes and seminars are held at the store. The staff is more interested in promoting outdoor sports and educating you than in making a profit. Seriously.

Wiley's Waterski Shop
1417 Trenton St,
762-1300 (map: LL6)
Mon-Sat

Wiley's sells waterskis out of a garagelike South End store. Wet suits, dry suits, slalom skies, ropes, and life preservers complete the selection. They will custom-make bindings for customers.

Wright Brothers Cycle Works
219 N 36th St, 633-5132
(map: FF7)
Tues-Sun

You can have reliable bike repairs done here or, for a small fee, join this cooperative and do your own bike maintenance with their tools and space. Owner Charles Hadrann and his staff are known for wheel building, informative repair classes, and good advice. Low prices on parts. Closed Sundays and Mondays in winter.

RECORDS

Bop Street Records & Tapes
5512 20th Ave NW,
783-3009 (map: EE7)
Mon-Sat

Here, in the site of the old Ballard Record Store, you'll find a stock of albums, 78s, CDs, cassettes, and tens of thousands of 45s.

Bud's Jazz Records
102 S Jackson St,
628-0445 (map: O8)
Every day

Established in 1982 by Chicago refugee and jazz buff Bud Young, Seattle's first and only jazz, all-jazz, and nothing-but-jazz store is the biggest of its kind west of

Chicago. It has one of the best inventories in the country; with around 15,000 titles, Bud's is *the* place. Musicians argue here over the unlisted sidemen on old Charlie Parker records, and Bud's keeps an exhaustive jazz library to settle the argument. The free search service has a great track record. Spend the afternoon.

Cellophane Square
1315 NE 42nd St,
634-2280 (map: FF7)
Every day

Bellevue Square,
Bellevue, 454-5059
(map: HH3)
Every day

Here's the closest thing to Berkeley's Telegraph Avenue selection in used jazz and rock. A lot of stock, both vintage and new, and fast turnover, quality merchandise, and friendly, knowledgeable staff.

Golden Oldies
201 NE 45th St (and
branches), 547-2260
(map: FF7)
Every day

An enormous selection of rock, country and western, big band, and jazz albums and singles. They've got music from 1910 to the present, but the main attractions are hits from the 1940s, '50s, '60s, and '70s. These historians will search nationwide for your favorite record from seventh grade.

Peaches
811 NE 45th St,
633-2990 (map: FF7)
Every day

2232 NW Market St,
784-9517 (map: EE8)
Every day

KIDS This record supermarket used to be owned by a chain, but it's now the best independent store (with outposts in Ballard and the U District) for folk, children's, and women's music. Bargain cutouts in soul and rock. A lot of local rock.

Platters
8064 Lake City Way NE,
523-9900 (map: EE6)
Mon-Sat

Here's where to find the city's largest stock of 12-inch singles and unused oldie 45s. In the waning days of vinyl, if anyone's got it, they do.

Rubato Records
10672 NE 8th St,
Bellevue, 455-9417
(map: HH3)
Every day

This shop is named for a musical term meaning "without a steady beat"—the owners swear they didn't know the *other* Italian translation of the word ("stolen records") until years after they opened. You *will* find some steals here in quality used music of all types.

Silver Platters
14603 NE 20th St,
Bellevue (and branches),
643-3472 (map: GG1)
Every day

Silver Platters has the country's largest selection—virtually everything on the market—of compact discs. There's also a large selection of laser video discs. Silver Platters is in the Northgate Mall and Southcenter Mall neighborhoods, too.

Tower Records
500 Mercer St (and branches), 283-4456 (map: B4)
Every day

KIDS One side of this Records R Us emporium is classical—a well priced, good selection. The popular side has pop and a wall of jazz. It's a good first-look place for folk, country, children's, and women's music. There's also a strong rock (local, old, and new wave) orientation. Cutouts, too. It may be the supermarket of record stores, but there's always at least one good, informed clerk on duty, and it's open until midnight every night. Also in the U District, Bellevue, and Tacoma.

SEAFOOD

City Fish
Pike Place Market, 682-9329 (map: J8)
Every day, May-Dec; Mon-Sat, Jan-April

With a reputation for the highest-quality fish, Gary Levy's place in the Main Arcade does a brisk business, with many steady customers. Overnight shipping to anywhere in the country.

Edmonds Fish Market
130th 5th Ave S, #124, Edmonds, 771-5830
Mon-Sat

Not a huge selection, but a reliable source staffed by folk who know their fish. One of the only places to buy Alaskan spot prawns or abalone in Edmonds.

Jack's Fish Spot
Pike Place Market, 467-0514 (map: J8)
Mon-Sat

With the help of sister Gretchen (of Gretchen's Of Course), Jack's Fish Spot in the Sanitary Market has opened a walk-up seafood bar. He still offers an excellent seafood selection, has the Market's only live shellfish tanks, and is the only place thereabouts that will smoke salmon for you.

Mutual Fish Company
2335 Rainier Ave S, 322-4368 (map: II6)
Mon-Sat

Mutual Fish, lovingly run by the Yoshimura family, provides some of the widest selection and freshest seafood in the city. Prices are good, they know all about packing for air freight or carry-home, and they take great care to keep live products fresh and pure.

Pacific Fish House
617 S Dearborn St, 382-4632 (map: HH7)
Mon-Sat

Pacific is a mammoth supplier to restaurants, so it always has an enormous supply of seafood on hand, of all levels of quality. This retail outlet is a bit overwhelming, but you can find excellent fish here if you are skilled at spotting quality.

Pike Place Fish
Pike Place Market, 682-7181 (map: J8)
Mon-Sat, every day in the summer

Wide selection of scrupulously fresh fish, plus smoked and kippered seafood. They are likely to have some local rarities, and they pack and ship for the traveler. Located in the Main Arcade and identifiable by the fish flying through the air.

Port Chatham Packing Company
632 NW 46th St,
783-8200 (map: FF8)
Mon-Sat

Julia Child discovered the satiny cool-smoked salmon this place has been turning out for years, and they've done land-office business ever since. It's hard to find in Ballard, but is a fascinating old-fashioned place to visit. They'll take care of your gift needs for the next decade.

University Seafood & Poultry
1317 NE 47th St,
632-3900 (map: FF7)
Mon-Sat

The best of local catches always seems to find its way to this U District fish market—and you pay for it. Always fresh, and you'll find delicacies here no other shop has managed to get. Game birds, eggs, and wine, too.

Wild Salmon Fish Market
1735 W Thurman St,
283-3366 (map: FF8)
Every day

This shop buys all its fresh salmon from local fishermen right here at the terminal, so you stand a pretty good chance of getting the real, wild thing. If you're particular, you may want to check, as the occasional hatchery-raised item slips through the nets.

SHOES

Bally of Switzerland (Four Seasons Olympic Hotel)
1218 4th Ave, 624-9255
(map: L6)
Mon-Sat

Bally's white marble entryway and beige interior are forbidding: a cathedral for shoes. But the staff is friendly and the merchandise is superb. Shoes range from dancing slippers to jogging shoes; accessories from dress-for-success briefcases for women to leather jackets for men. Need we say it's expensive?

Church's English Shoes
520 Pike St, 682-3555
(map: J5)
Mon-Sat

The perfectly proper English shoes here range from fine leather loafers to opera pumps, at prices not scaled for the budget-conscious.

Duncan and Sons Boots and Saddles
541 1st Ave S, 622-1310
(map: P9)
Mon-Sat

There are 30 varieties of boots in this 90-year-old boot shop—one of the largest selections in downtown Seattle—for men, women, and children. All price ranges are represented, from $80 to $500. Most are handmade in Texas.

Florsheim Shoe Shop
Northgate Mall (and branches), 363-1355
(map: DD7)
Every day

Reasonable prices for well-made men's shoes; business and dress shoes, but nothing trendy.

John Fluevog Shoes
1611 1st Ave, 441-1065

Fluevog's footwear, designed by the owner and made in England, constitutes the wildest selection in town: leopard skin, bright green, square toes, pointed toes.

(map: I8)
Every day

So outrageous, folks may stop you on the street and ask, "Where did you get *those?*"

MJ Feet's Birkenstock Store
4334 University Way NE,
632-5353 (map: FF7)
Every day

Pike Place Market,
624-2929 (map: J8)
Every day

This is where you get those sturdy Birkenstock sandals, all styles and (earth) tones. To make up for the spartan-looking shoes, this cheerful shop carries a lot of jazzy socks by Hue and the like, plus a small selection of clothing and lingerie. It's also a good place to get durable, hard-to-find Danish schoolbags.

Maggie's Shoes
610 Pike St, 628-9614
(map: J5)
Mon-Sat

68 Pine St, 728-5837
(map: I8)
Mon-Sat

Maggie journeys to Italy twice a year to send back the latest from the country that knows fine footwear. The result: a spectrum of flats and pumps with subtle flair at reasonable prices.

San Marco
1509 6th Ave, 343-9138
(map: J6)
Every day

One of the most high-style shoe stores in town ("Nordstrom's Salon meets John Fluevog"), San Marco carries a superb selection of French and Italian women's and men's shoes, suave and classic to punk-trendy. All are stunningly showcased, and the service is quite thoughtful.

Ultima
2025 First Ave, 441-0485
(map: H8)
Mon-Sat

Georgio Brutini
1408 1st Ave, 682-9259
(map: J8)
Every day

Ultima is the ultimate in inventive Italian leather design, heavy on the Studio Paolo, Via Spiga, Paloma, and Kenneth Cole. There are also several fine lines for the well-shod male at prices that are astonishingly reasonable ($30 to $120).

SPECIALTY SIZE CLOTHING:
LARGE/TALL/MATERNITY/PETITE

Barisof
606 Pike St, 467-7377
(map: J5)
Mon-Sat

Owner Nancy Barisof knows the plight of shopping for the petite woman—all 4-foot-9 of her. Consequently she buys from an insider's point of view, stocking her San Francisco–style boutique with sophisticated fashion-forward items for women 5-foot-4 and under.

Donna Grande
Westlake Center,

The most stylish outfitter of large (size 14 to 24) women carries Paul Stanley and Jackie Bernard suits

682-2147 (map: L8)
Every day

and other designers' lines. There is an emphasis on career dressing. Everything is upscale and flattering, and the service is thoughtful and thorough—all of which you pay dearly for.

Fifth Avenue Maternity
415 Pike St, 343-9470
(map: J6)
Every day

When women don't want to give up style for nine months, they drain the savings account and head for this excellent shop. Some styles are easily belted and attractive to wear after the baby is born.

High & Mighty Store
Alderwood Mall,
Lynnwood, 771-5115
Every day

Expert, personalized service and good brands such as Ratner and Crown distinguish this menswear shop for tall and large men.

Village Maternity
University Village,
523-5167 (map: FF6)
Every day

Village Maternity stresses versatility, affordability, and long-term wear; most clothes can be worn even after the baby comes. A good mix of sporty, dressy, and business clothes includes the popular Japanese Weekend line. There are some all-cotton children's clothes, too.

Vogue La Grande
15600 NE 8th St,
Bellevue, 746-6632
(map: HH2)
Every day

With a moderate to high-end inventory of fashions by Jones of New York, French Vanilla, and others, this boutique outfits large women with up-to-date, fashionable clothing. A good selection of career clothing.

Your Hidden Closet
1075 Bellevue Way NE,
453-5999 (map: HH3)
Mon-Sat

It's a great idea: a women's large-size consignment shop, so weight droppers can drop their larger clothes, too. It was a quick success; volume has doubled since opening four years ago. They sell a wide range of merchandise (including lingerie, shoes, and purses) in a correspondingly wide range of quality.

STEREOS/AUDIO EQUIPMENT

Car Toys
307 Broad St, 443-2726
(map: D7)
Every day

The ultimate in car stereos sounds good enough to go in your living room. Car Toys does a great deal of business in custom work; however, for the less audio-obsessed, they do carry more common brands like Alpine, Sony, and Rockford Fosgate. Branches in Bellevue and Lynnwood, too.

Definitive Audio
6017 Roosevelt Way NE,
524-6633 (map: EE6)
Tues-Sat

The smart-not-slick sales at Definitive reflect a certain Zen, and indeed, one of the owners majored in philosophy at college. This is Seattle's oldest dealer in high-end systems; prices are on the same end.

Hawthorne Stereo
13107 Northup Way,
Bellevue, 881-3916
(map: HH3)
Every day

Perhaps the most particular of all the stereo component stores. Brand names are less important than quality, as they carry many of the upper-end (lesser-known) systems, too. Salespeople are friendly and eager to impart their (extensive) knowledge.

Magnolia Hi-Fi
6322 Roosevelt Way NE
(and branches), 525-0080
(map: EE6)
Every day

An almost undisputed favorite that has created a virtual electronic ghetto on Roosevelt (and with branches in Bellevue and Southcenter), Magnolia stocks several durable brands and can put together systems for the uninitiated. Reports of excessive hard sell and condescending salespeople have surfaced from time to time, but beneath it all they usually know what they're talking about. Excellent follow-up service.

Speakerlab
6307 Roosevelt Way NE,
523-2269 (map: EE6)
Every day

Speakerlab's specialty is, naturally, speakers. They'll custom-design a set for you, or sell you a kit to make your own. The small store also sells some audio and video equipment in all price ranges.

TOYS

American Eagles
2220 NW Market St,
782-8448 (map: EE9)
Mon-Sat

The largest hobby shop in the country specializes in historical hobbies and model railroads. Owner Michael Edwards stocks over 87,000 different items, including a regiment of 22,000 miniature soldiers, and lots and lots of models.

Animal Tracks
Westlake Center,
623-6825 (map: I5)
Every day

A menagerie of darling stuffed animals in traditional and not-so-traditional forms (aardvarks or parrots, anyone?). Books, games, and other amusements are scattered about the shop.

Archie McPhee
3510 Stone Way N,
547-2467 (map: FF7)
Mon-Sat

A life-size Bozo sets the tone. This is contemporary kitsch at its wacky best, where you get glow-in-the-dark dinosaurs and rubber slugs. It's a great place to stock up on cheap toys and party favors; ask for a catalog. Plenty of grown-ups confess shameful inclinations to losing themselves among the whoopie cushions.

The Disney Store
Westlake Center,
622-3323 (map: I5)
Every day

A place that drives parents Disney. Nonstop patter from multiple video screens playing the latest Walt Disney clips. The G-rated clerks also sell Disney-inspired gadgets and garb. Kids love it.

Don's Hobbies
University Village,
525-7700 (map: FF6)
Every day

A gold mine for the hobbyist, Don's has radio-controlled boats, model airplanes, motorized race cars, and American and European electric trains in all the usual gauges. Models of all kinds and system toys by Fischer, Brio, and more draw a faithful clientele from all over.

Eastside Trains
10600 NE 68th St,
Kirkland, 828-4098
(map: EE3)
Mon-Sat

Trains, trains, trains. For train lovers young and old, this shop is one of the best places in the region to shop. The business chugged along for eight years out of the owner's home; it's now full speed ahead in the new Kirkland location.

Fantastic Games and Toys
3333 184th St SW,
Lynnwood, 775-4871
Every day

Fantastic specializes in board games—Risk, Monopoly, Scrabble—with an emphasis on strategy games. They have a selection of novelty toys (windup walking teeth), seasonal items (squirt guns), and small toys (dice).

Great Winds Kite Shop
402 Occidental Ave S,
624-6886 (map: P9)
Every day

Kites of all kinds live in this friendly Pioneer Square shop. It's a whimsical, wonderful place where you can also get kite-making kits, windsocks, boomerangs, and plenty of good advice.

The Great Wind-up
Pike Place Market,
621-9370 (map: J8)
Mon-Sat, every day
in summer

For the kid in every adult. The Great Windup is full of every kind of wind-up and battery-operated animated toy imaginable (you can hear the whirring and chirping from a few doors away), as well as the usual nostalgia toys: Slinky, Sea Monkeys, Pez, and Gumby. In the Economy Market Atrium.

Imagination Toys
1815 N 45th St, 547-2356
(map: FF7)
Every day

A real find for wonderful, well-made toys by Brio, Gund, and the always popular Lego. Activity toys by Playmobil, dolls by Pauline, games, and puzzles.

Juggle Bug
7506-J Olympic View
Drive, Edmonds,
774-2127
Mon-Fri

No flaming torches or knives here, but this *is* the place for those with the bug. Every tossable thing from balls and pins for experts to bean bags for novices.

KidsKraft
1711 N 45th St, 632-5160
(map: FF6)
Mon-Sat

KidsKraft carries toys that nurture creativity and peace—you won't find war toys or media clones here. The focus is educational, but the emphasis is on serious fun: reams of colored and special-effect papers, jugs of

---

All places in this book are recommended; even "no stars" are worth knowing about.

nontoxic paints, all kinds of building sets, puzzles, games, and (for the precocious youngster) beginning foreign language tapes.

Learning World
500 Westlake Ave N (and branches), 464-1515
(map: D2)
Every day

The best purveyor of basic, educational toys (craft supplies, chemistry sets, abaci, and flash cards), Learning World also sells Fisher-Price and Playskool brands. Other branches are in Sea-Tac Mall, Lynnwood, and Bellevue Square.

Magic Mouse
603 1st Ave, 682-8097
(map: N8)
Every day

Top-of-the-line toys, chosen by a professional child, fill the shelves of this marvelous Pioneer Square store: Steiff animals, Corolle dolls, Brio wooden train sets, and Marklin electric trains. The stuffed-animal collection includes over 100 styles of teddy bears alone. There is a selection of developmental baby and preschool toys, art supplies, games and puzzles, kids' books, windup toys and stocking stuffers, and even a tub stocked with water toys, to try before you buy.

Thinker Toys
10680 NE 8th St, Bellevue, 453-0051
(map: HH2)
Every day

The intelligently chosen, upper-end inventory has a little bit of everything: kites, games, trains, dolls, books, and so on. Open until 9pm on weekdays.

A Train House
2020 2nd Ave, 441-1151
(map: H7)
Mon-Sat

A Train House carries varied merchandise, some of it antique or rare, for the toy train enthusiast—tracks, cars, and all accoutrements. Be sure to look at the bargain table for especially good buys. It's a savvy operation; they have good connections with big-time collectors and run a good repair service.

The Wood Shop
320 1st Ave S, 624-1763
(map: O8)
Every day

Well-crafted, sturdy wooden toys by Pacific Northwest artisans are stocked side by side with imported European items. This fun family-run shop is particularly known for its puppets, including Furry Folk Fred the Bear and Chuck the Dog. Beautiful Nativity scenes are imported from all over the world.

Zippity Zoo
Bellevue Square, Bellevue, 455-5150
(map: HH3)
Every day

The name is perfect: there are enough stuffed animals to stock any zoo, and the store is a constant hum of activity, with animals, kids, and parents everywhere. Stickers, puppets, books, T-shirts, and videos round out the selection.

VINTAGE/RETRO

Deluxe Junk
3518 Fremont Ave N,
634-2733 (map: FF8)
Every day

Not to be taken seriously, Deluxe Junk is trashy, exuberant, and kitschy. The clothes, from the 1930s through the 1960s, have, if not grace, a lot of style, and the stock rotates seasonally (heavy tweed coats and handmade sweaters in winter, cool cotton shirts and straw hats in summer). This huge former funeral parlor also has lots of room for furniture and collectibles.

Dreamland
619 Broadway E,
329-8044 (map: HH7)
Every day

The best used-leather selection in the Northwest is at Dreamland, including real bomber jackets and Eisenhower jackets. It's the only vintage shop for truly cool men; a few choice army/navy items are thrown in for good measure. Look here for one of the largest vintage watch collections in the area.

Foreign Intrigue
108 James St, 625-9960
(map: N8)
Mon-Sat

Foreign Intrigue is like a department store for Art Deco: jewelry, furniture, lamps, cocktail and smoking accessories, statues, clocks, chrome accessories, they're all here (but no clothing, alas). No reproductions, and furniture is in original condition if possible.

Fremont Antique Mall
3419 Fremont Pl,
548-9140 (map: FF7)
Every day

Mark Salo let the community of Fremont shape the look of his antique store in the basement of the Fremont Building. The results? It's more, well, collectibles than antiques. There are over 25 dealers, with vintage clothing and toys, dinnerware and appliances from the 1950s, Oriental rugs, and even a little bit of the *real* stuff here and there.

Guess Where
615 N 35th St, 547-3793
(map: FF7)
Every day

Mostly men's clothing and accessories—one of the best selections in the city. Everything is high quality: a vintage alligator trunk, perfectly broken-in cowboy boots, Ward Cleaver cardigans, groovy Hawaiian shirts. A few contemporary items and some furniture are mixed in, too.

Isadora's
1920½ 1st Ave, 441-7711
(map: I8)
Every day

Laura D'Alesandro's shop is distinguished by her understanding of and passionate attention to a period (the 1900s to the 1950s), and no "filler." The museum-quality clothing at Isadora's is elegant and truly stunning, including gowns and tuxedos. She has a space in the Fremont Antique Mall as well (see listing).

Look for **KIDS**—*it means your child will especially enjoy this place or attraction.*

VINTAGE/RETRO

Madame & Company
117 Yesler Way,
621-1728 (map: N8)
Tues-Sat

Vintage clothing is treated with respect, knowledge, and love by the people at Madame & Company, a fact recognized by collectors, shoppers, and Hollywood costumers, all of whom frequent the store. Mother-daughter owners Carol and Deborah Winship carry inventory up to the 1940s (though you'll be carefully screened if you want to see the 19th-century museum-quality pieces in the back). Lingerie, furs, evening wear, and antique wedding dresses are carefully restored before being marked for sale. Check out the lace yardage, collars, buttons, hats, and other accessories, or just indulge yourself in a highly satisfying browse.

Retro Viva
1511 1st Ave (and
branches), 624-2529
(map: J8)
Every day

A funky shop with men's and women's clothing and accessories from every era, Retro Viva is your first stop when you need a leopard-skin bra from the 1960s. Jewelry—some costume, some collector's—fills seven display cases. Clothing is well priced, and customers are told if a piece is damaged. Other stores are on Broadway and the Ave.

Rhinestone Rosie
606 W Crockett St,
283-4605 (map: GG8)
Tues-Sat

Rhinestone Rosie rents, buys, and sells an exceptionally large and complete inventory of rhinestone treasures in all colors, shapes, and sizes. Her specialty is buying broken pieces of jewelry and repairing them herself before selling them for low prices; she is the only store on the West Coast with this rhinestone repair service. If you have lost a stone out of a favorite piece, she can probably find a replacement for you.

Ruby Montana's Pinto Pony
603 2nd Ave, 621-7669
(map: O7)
Every day

The five-and-dime of vintage objects. Ruby Montana sells wonderfully awful things from the 1900s through the 1960s with a dash of the present here and there: kidney-shaped sofas, lava lamps, marlin and mooseheads to hang on walls, and the largest salt and pepper shaker selection on the West Coast. There's also a treasure trove of vintage 1970s and 1980s smaller merchandise: note cards, lamps, clocks, and other novelties. Postcards galore.

Tootsie's
609 2nd Ave, 682-0807
(map: O8)
Every day

In her new location, owner Sandra Gengler maintains a good network of quality sources for her clothing and accessories from the Victorian era to the present. Some new clothes mix with excellent vintage cashmere sweaters, costume jewelry, formalwear, and a full line of alligator accessories.

Vintage Clothing
*6501 Roosevelt Way NE,
522-5234 (map: EE7)
Every day*

A lavish collection of Victorian through 1950s apparel is available for sale *or* rent from a savvy staff who can add just the right touch from their large accessories supply: a feather boa, sunglasses, the perfect hat. Everything is top-of-the-line.

WINE AND BEER

The Cellar
*14411 Greenwood Ave N,
365-7660 (map: CC7)
Every day*

Joe Marleau is one of the city's most established wine merchants, and his store is one of the few that carry such a deep collection of wine-making, beer-making, and liqueur-making equipment and books. He has an extensive mail-order service and will ship anywhere in the world.

DeLaurenti
*Pike Place Market,
622-0141 (map: J8)
Mon-Sat*

*317 Bellevue Way NE,
Bellevue, 454-7155
(map: HH3)
Mon-Sat*

See Ethnic Markets and Delis in this chapter.

Esquin Wine Merchants
*1516 1st Ave S, 682-7374
(map: II7)
Mon-Sat*

Owner Rand Sealey frequently flies off to France to purchase wine directly from the chateaus, thus acquiring wines no one else has. (His German and Italian selection is equally good.) You'll find close to 800 different labels, case discounts, free tastings twice a week, and outstanding sales. Prices are very good, and it's a great place to find a bottle in the $5 to $15 range.

European Vine Selections of Washington
*522 15th Ave E,
323-3557 (map: GG6)
Tues-Sun*

Begun in a Fremont basement specifically to provide low-cost, low-overhead wines, this shop has moved to Capitol Hill but still holds on to the same concept. The supply is a little limited but very carefully selected, and the owners sample virtually every wine they sell so that they know what they're recommending.

La Cantina
*University Village,
525-4340 (map: FF6)
Every day*

*10218 NE 8th St,
Bellevue, 455-4363
(map: HH3)
Mon-Sat*

Although under separate ownership, both stores are exactly what a small specialty shop is all about. Owners are knowledgeable, and in getting to know regular customers are able to make suggestions based upon the customers' tastes. They have good wine at great prices, with an emphasis on French bottlings.

WINE AND BEER

Le Sommelier
3131 E Madison St,
324-WINE (map: GG6)
Mon-Sat

Drop into this wine store for some bottle-buying advice or a sampling of the dozen or so vintages Tim Summers has open for the day—best enjoyed with crudités or a slab of salmon mousse and crackers at the counter.

McCarthy and Schiering
6500 Ravenna Ave NE,
524-0999 (map: EE6)

2209 Queen Anne Ave N,
282-8500 (map: GG8)
Mon-Sat

Dan McCarthy, a veteran of Seattle's wholesale wine business, just opened his second outlet on top of Queen Anne. As with his Ravenna store, he opened it with the intention of finding the very best wines on the market, then selling them at prices as low as those of most grocery stores. It's a tribute to his expertise, as well as his pricing, that the shop is such a success. Regular in-store tastings, a knowledgeable staff, and a special rate for "Vintage Select" club members add appeal. A good place to find a rare bottle; California is as well represented as France.

Mondo's World
4223 Rainier Ave S,
725-5433 (map: JJ5)
Tues-Sat

Scores of faithful customers come here to order wine by the caseload at some of the best prices in town. Proprietor Jerry Banchero presides over the cramped quarters with enthusiasm and hosts occasional beer and wine seminars. There are some extraordinarily good deals here, especially on cases of Bordeaux.

Pike & Western Wine Merchants
Pike Place Market,
441-1307 (map: J8)
Mon-Sat

Managing partner Ron Irvine is *the* authority on Northwest wines; he is frequently called on to judge wine competitions, and he writes a wine column for a Northwest publication. The store carries an excellent selection of classic French and some German wines, especially the French "country" wines.

Queen Anne Thriftway
1908 Queen Anne Ave N,
284-2530 (map: GG7)
24 hours

Grocery stores around Seattle are developing amazingly deep cellars, and this superlative independent does one of the best jobs. Wine manager Mark Takagi oversees an ever-changing selection (better than in many wine shops), including many of the current hits. In addition, Thriftway carries over 100 varieties of beer, including fresh microbrews. Open 24 hours (but no alcohol is sold between 2am and 6am).

Books in the Best Places series read as personal guidebooks, but our evaluations are based on numerous reports from local experts. Final judgements are made by the editors. Our inspectors never identify themselves (except over the phone) and never accept free meals or other favors. Be an inspector. Send us a report.

LODGINGS

▼

LODGINGS CONTENTS

HOTELS

DOWNTOWN

Alexis Hotel
1007 1st Ave,
624-4844 (map: L8)
Expensive; AE, DC,
MC, V; checks OK

Few cities can boast of a hotel as elegant as the Alexis, a gem carved out of a lovely turn-of-the-century building in a stylish section of downtown near the waterfront. It's small (54 rooms), full of tasteful touches (televisions concealed in armoires, complimentary sherry upon arrival), and decorated with the suave modernity of Michael Graves's postmodernist colors. You'll be pampered here, with Jacuzzis and real-wood fireplaces in some of the suites, a steam room that can be reserved just for you, nicely insulated walls between rooms to ensure privacy, and a concierge at the ready. Other amenities include complimentary continental breakfasts, a morning newspaper of your choice, shoeshines, a guest membership in the nearby Seattle Club ($15), and a range of dining options, from elegant Northwest cuisine to a steak house. No convention facilities: the Alexis favors well-heeled travelers on the Stanford Court–Pierre circuit who prefer quiet poshness. It is a hotel where the front desk people always know your name and will solve any problem (they're especially helpful with advice about the city).

However, the Alexis is still not a hotel of world-class performance. The staff is very young and lacks the air (and polished skill) of seasoned help. Lately, we've gotten reports of understocked rooms and loud air-conditioner noise. And there are no views. We suggest booking a room that faces the inner courtyard—rooms facing First Avenue can be noisy. Or book one of the 32 condos five doors down in the jointly managed Arlington Suites, spaces geared for longer stays with views, kitchens, and (for a little bit extra) full Alexis maid and room service.

Four Seasons Olympic Hotel
411 University St,
621-1700 (map: L6)
Expensive; AE, DC, MC,
V; checks OK

The Olympic has been a Seattle landmark since the 1920s. It has been refurbished in a style befitting its earlier grandeur; the rooms (450 on 11 floors) are now quite spacious, softly lit, and tastefully furnished in period reproductions. Welcome touches include valet parking, 24-hour full room service, a stocked bar, chocolates on your pillow, complimentary shoeshine, and a terry-cloth robe for each guest. A team of well-informed concierges offers uncommonly good service; indeed, the staff exudes just the right blend of unobtrusiveness and thorough care.

The public rooms are grand verging on gaudy: armchairs, potted plants, marble galore, tapestries, wood paneling. You can lounge amid the swaying palms in the skylit Garden Court, taking high tea if you wish. The showcase dining room, the Georgian Room, is a handsome space; downstairs is the livelier Shuckers, an oyster bar with excellent mixed drinks. There are several elegant meeting rooms (the ornate Spanish Ballroom for large affairs), and retail spaces off the lobby make for the best boutique shopping in town. A classy health club rounds out the amenities with a pool, Jacuzzi, and licensed masseuse. Prices are steep, especially considering there are few views, but this is Seattle's one venerable, world-class contender, and the service (and location) cannot be bested.

Holiday Inn Crowne Plaza
6th Ave and Seneca St,
464-1980 (map: L5)
Expensive; AE, DC,
MC, V; checks OK

★★

This hotel bends over backward for the repeat and corporate visitor. The upper-floor rooms, which are corporate, comfortable, and very clean, have been refurbished in striking maroons, mauves, and dark wood and receive a lot of individual attention: free papers, a lounge, and their own concierge desk (at a slightly higher price). Lower-floor guests stay in spacious but rather bland rooms, and though concierge services are available to all, there's no lower-floor desk. The lobby is elegant and comfortable, the staff attentive and accommodating. In addition to the pleasant Parkside Cafe, the pricier Parkside Restaurant was scheduled to open at press time. Conference rooms and parking (for a fee) are available. The location is ideal—right downtown, near the freeway, and two blocks from the Convention Center.

Inn at the Market
86 Pine St, 443-3600
(map: I7)
Expensive; AE, DC,
MC, V; checks OK

★★★

It's become one of the finest places to stay in the city, largely because of the location. You are right in the famous Pike Place Market, looking out over its rooftops to the lovely bay beyond. The hotel is small—65 rooms—so service can approximate that of a country inn; and you won't feel oppressed by conventioneers (there are limited conference facilities, in the form of one meeting room and one outdoor deck). The architecture is quite good (by the local firm of Ibsen Nelsen), with oversized rooms, bay windows that let even some of the side rooms enjoy big views, a Laura Ashley lobby, and a configuration that is a modern version of a medieval inn built around a central courtyard. Opening off the courtyard are smart shops, a sumptuous spa, and the elegant Campagne restaurant (see Restaurants chapter).

The Inn struggled in its first years, but now its management is under the Alexis folks. There is no complimentary breakfast and, with no in-house kitchen, room service is a problem (order breakfast from the Gravity Bar, the rest from nearby du jour or Cutters). But there are great places to discover right out the door, especially in the morning, when it all resembles a bustling Parisian market. A hotel in America's finest public market is a marvel.

Inn at Virginia Mason
1006 Spring St, 583-6453
(map: HH7)
Moderate; AE, DC,
MC, V; checks OK

Up until about two years ago, most people who stayed at the Inn at Virginia Mason were sick—or at least friends or relatives of those who resided at Virginia Mason Hospital. Since its $1.5 million renovation, however, it's been open to the general public. The standard rooms are quite small and modest (and smell a bit antiseptic), but the suites are a good deal at $149. Try for the one on the rooftop floor with a fireplace in the living room, bar, TVs, and a behind-the-city view of the Sound. There's not much of a lounge (it's mostly the pleasant Rhododendron Restaurant), but you're an easy walk from downtown shops and restaurants. There's access to Virginia Mason from the hotel, and some of the hospital staff services are on the main floor, but it does offer respite from the downtown bustle, even if you're not affiliated with Virginia Mason.

Mayflower Park Hotel
405 Olive Way,
623-8700 (map: I6)
Expensive; AE, DC,
MC, V; checks OK

Renovations have paid off at this handsome 1927 hotel right in the heart of the downtown shopping district. A coolly elegant lobby opens onto Oliver's (bar and lounge) on one side, and Clipper's, one of the prettiest breakfast places in town, on the other. Rooms are small, bearing charming reminders of the hotel's past: lovely Oriental brass and antique appointments; large, deep tubs; thick walls that trap noise. Modern intrusions are both for better and worse: double-glazed windows in all rooms to keep out traffic noise, and the addition of undistinguished furnishings in many of the rooms. The deluxe rooms are slightly bigger and have corner views; aim for one on a higher floor or you may find yourself facing a brick wall. Prices, $100 to $275 for doubles, are average for this part of town, and $18 more gets you a guest membership in an athletic club four blocks away.

The Seattle Hilton
1301 6th Ave, 624-0500
(map: K5)
Expensive; AE, DC,
MC, V; checks OK

This hotel has been criticized because its entrance lobby sits above the parking garage while its guest lobby (no windows) is on the 12th floor. Still, the bay windows in each room give these digs a homey feel, and the location is central. All the rooms recently have been redone in the mauves of the 1980s, and rooms with northern exposure offer views of Lake Union, Puget Sound, and ferries (if you stretch a bit). The higher you stay, the higher you pay. Top of the Hilton Lounge is a popular nightclub.

Seattle Sheraton Hotel and Towers
1400 6th Ave, 621-9000
(map: K5)
Expensive; AE, DC,
MC, V; checks OK

Seattle's Sheraton is an 841-room tower rising as a sleek triangle, the Convention Center in its shadow. It, too, aims at the convention business, so the rooms are smallish and standard, and the emphasis is on the meeting rooms, VIP floors upstairs, and the restaurants. Banner's restaurant offers mainstream continental fare, plus a 27-foot-long dessert spread; Gooey's is the disco; and Fullers, adorned with outstanding Northwest paintings, is perhaps the city's finest restaurant (see Restaurants chapter). The overall architecture is bland and confusing, but Northwest artists have been commissioned to decorate the walls.

Service is quite efficient. Convention facilities are complete, and the kitchen staff can handle the most complex assignments. Snootier business travelers will want to head for the upper four "VIP"floors (31–34), where a hotel-within-hotel offers its own lobby and considerably more amenities in the (same size as economy) rooms. The top floors feature a health club and a private lounge with a knockout city panorama. You pay for parking.

Sorrento Hotel
900 Madison St,
622-6400 (map: M4)
Expensive; AE, DC,
MC, V; checks OK

When the Sorrento opened in 1909—in time for the Alaska Yukon Pacific Exposition—it commanded a bluff overlooking the young city and Puget Sound. For years thereafter, it was the most elegant hotel in the city, with Renaissance architecture modeled after a castle in Sorrento, Honduras mahogany in the lobby, and a famous dining room on the top floor. The place faded badly, though, and the view was lost as the city grew up around the hotel. Then in 1981 it was fixed up and reopened. They couldn't bring back the view, but they brought back its beauty. Downstairs there's a clubby restaurant. The mahogany lobby is now a lounge that is a fine place for talking or afternoon tea. The rooms, 76 of them, are decorated in muted, tasteful coziness with a slight Oriental accent. We recommend the 08 series of suites, in the corners. Suites on the top floor make elegant quarters for special meetings or parties—the showstopper being the $700 penthouse, with its grand piano, patio, Jacuzzi, view of the bay, and luxurious multiple rooms. The location, uphill five blocks from the heart of downtown, may be inconvenient, but it's quieter. The main restaurant, The Hunt Club, now boasts an improved menu and food more worthy of the lustrous setting (see Restaurants chapter).

Stouffer Madison Hotel
515 Madison St,
583-0300 (map: M5)
Expensive; AE, DC, MC,
V; checks OK

★★½

This large hotel at the southeast edge of downtown successfully conveys a sense of warmth and intimacy inside. The lobby, dressed in signature greens and peach, is tasteful and uncluttered, upstairs hallways are softly lit, and the rooms sport elegant marble countertops, coffered ceilings, and wood cabinetry. Extras include feather pillows, oversized towels, coffee, and morning papers. The pricey "Club Floors" (25 and 26) offer exclusive check-in privileges, concierge services, hors d'oeuvres and continental breakfast at "Club Lounge," a library, and the best views (although views from most rooms are quite good). Comfortable conference facilities, parking (for a fee), free in-town transportation, and a concierge on duty round out the offerings. Prego, on the 28th floor, offers a surprisingly fine selection of seafood (see Restaurants chapter).

WestCoast
Camlin Hotel
1619 9th Ave, 682-0100
(map: I4)
Moderate; AE, DC,
MC, V; checks OK

★½

Like many older hotels in Seattle, this 1926 grande dame has been remodeled and made soundproof with double-glazed windows. (The elevator and the ventilation system, however, both hark back to an earlier era.) Though there are no conference facilities, the Camlin appeals to the business traveler (the large rooms have small sitting/work areas), and it's a good buy for the money. Rooms have been redecorated with sophistication, featuring spacious closets and spotless bathrooms; those whose numbers end in 10 have windows on three sides. Avoid the cabanas (they're small and dreary and for smokers) and room service, which is quite slow. Rooftop dining in the Cloud Room. The downtown location is closer to the retail district and Convention Center than to offices.

WestCoast Roosevelt Hotel

1531 7th Ave,
621-1200 (map: H5)
Moderate; AE, DC, MC,
V; checks OK

Gone is the grand skylit lobby that so distinguished the Roosevelt when it first opened its doors in 1930; new owners who reopened it in 1987 deemed that space better suited to Von's Restaurant (a McRory's-type outpost). The new lobby is low-ceilinged and cramped, but elsewhere the WestCoast installation has somewhat preserved the Roosevelt's Art Deco sensibilities. The hotel's 20 stories have been redivided for the contemporary traveler, but standards are still almost comically small. The deluxes (only $20 more than a standard) are a better choice, with adjoining sitting areas; the 11 superior-class rooms each boast a Jacuzzi, a separate sitting area, and a perspective northwest toward Puget Sound. There are only two floors that are nonsmoking (4 and 14); you can request nonsmoking, but it's never guaranteed. Considering its proximity to the Convention Center and the shopping district, the Roosevelt's prices—$79 to $109—are decent, but the service could use some polish.

WestCoast Vance Hotel

620 Stewart St, 441-4200
(map: I6)
Moderate; AE, DC,
MC, V; checks OK

½

Another WestCoast mission to save a forgotten downtown hotel. In 1990, they spent $7 million restoring the hotel to its original elegance. Most of the work, it seems, was done on the lobby—a pretty entrance. The rooms are small and spartan; the deluxe has a double bed, TV, and full bath—no table, no chairs, no dresser. Sweet, but cramped. The north-facing rooms above the fifth floor are the best, with a view of Queen Anne and the Space Needle. Valet parking. At press time, there was no room service, though they were working on a contract with the Italian restaurant next door, Salute in Città.

Westin Hotel

1900 5th Ave,
728-1000 (map: H5)
Expensive; AE, DC,
MC, V; checks OK

★★★

Westin, a major international chain, is headquartered in Seattle, so this flagship hotel has quite a few extras. The twin cylindrical towers may be called corncobs by the natives, but they afford spacious rooms with superb views, particularly above the 20th floor. Convention facilities, spread over several floors of meeting rooms, are quite complete. There is a large pool, along with an exercise room supervised by conditioning experts. On the top floors are some ritzy, glitzy suites. The location, near shopping and the Monorail station, is excellent. Trader Vic's is still here (one of the better ones in the chain), as well as a posh restaurant, The Palm Court (see Restaurants chapter). For more casual dining try the good (though overpriced) Market Cafe, and perhaps later a drink at Fitzgerald's, the long, dark cocktail bar.

DENNY REGRADE/SEATTLE CENTER

Best Western Executive Inn
200 Taylor Ave N,
448-9444 (map: F5)
Moderate; AE, DC,
MC, V; Checks OK

Remodeling and new paint have turned the large and spacious rooms mauve, rose, and teal in this cheerful inn. Now that the rooms are done they're working on the lobby and restaurant. Doubles cost $83. The executive suites ($94 to $130) have couches, wet bars, refrigerators, and whirlpool baths. Food, liquor, and free parking. Being in the shadow of the Space Needle is good if you're here for an event at Seattle Center.

Best Western Loyal Inn
2301 8th Ave, 682-0200
(map: F5)
Inexpensive; AE, MC, V;
checks OK

Rooms trimmed in blue and mauve, large indoor whirlpool surrounded by new gray tile, 24-hour sauna, and an adjoining sun deck give this standard motel a boost. No restaurant, coffee shop, or bar, but Seattle Center is nearby. Some rooms have wet bars and refrigerators. A family place with doubles ($62 to $88).

Edgewater Inn
Pier 67, 2411 Alaskan
Way, 728-7000 (map: F9)
Moderate; AE, DC,
MC, V; checks OK

Alas, you can't fish from the famous west windows of this waterfront institution anymore. The place has been spiffed up quite a bit (so no more fish-cleaning in the rooms), giving the lobby and rooms a rustic tone, with bleached oak and overstuffed chairs. It's like an urban motel (parking is free), but with a serviceable restaurant and a decent bar with a piano. Waterside rooms are quietest, with the best views and $125-to-$175 price tags. The Edgewater is just two blocks from the *Victoria Clipper* terminal.

Sixth Avenue Inn
2000 6th Ave, 441-8300
(map: H5)
Moderate; AE, DC,
MC, V; checks OK

This sprightly motor inn, catering to tourists and conventioneers, is done up in blues and tans. Some rooms have brass beds, and service is professional and friendly. There's less street noise on the east side. Room service, restaurant, free parking, and a good location near retail on one side, movie theaters on the other.

Warwick Hotel
401 Lenora St, 443-4300
(map: H6)
Expensive; AE, DC, MC,
V; checks OK

The Warwick is part of an international chain of hotels that aims its pitch at the corporate traveler; unfortunately, the result is somewhat characterless. Comfortable rooms are large and relatively soundproof, with marble bathrooms (the original owners had a quarry) and executive amenities. Rooms above the sixth floor have terrific views. The pool in the health club is too shallow for play and too short for laps, and the lobby is a jumble. On the whole it's not worth the big money, except for the 19th-floor Queen Victoria Suite, with its elegant appointments and panoramic view (good for private parties, too). The restaurant, Liaison, has decent service and serviceable food but no surprises. You pay for parking, but they run a 24-hour courtesy van service for downtown appointments. One of the few downtown establishments that allow small pets (ask first).

UNIVERSITY DISTRICT/NORTH END

Edmonds Harbor Inn
130 W Dayton St,
Edmonds, 771-5021
Moderate; AE, DC,
MC, V; checks OK

Strategically located near the Edmonds ferry and train terminals (20 minutes north of Seattle) is an attractive choice for a night in Edmonds: 61 large rooms, oak furnishings, continental breakfast, and access to a nearby athletic club. Get directions—the place is near the harborfront, but a little difficult to find in the gray sea of new office and shopping developments. No views.

Meany Tower Hotel
4507 Brooklyn Ave NE,
634-2000 (map: FF7)
Moderate; AE, DC, MC,
V; checks OK

Old-timers might not recognize their favorite U District hotel, formerly the University Tower. The distinguished 1930s design remains, but inside there are double-glazed windows and air conditioning, and the whole place—lobby and rooms—is quite cloyingly turned out in shades of peach. Each room has a bay window with a good view, and those on the south side are sunny. The bathrooms sparkle. You're one block from shopping on the Ave, two blocks from the University of Washington campus. The hotel's restaurant, The Meany Grill, is newly prettified with brass and deep green, but the food isn't much. The bar boasts a big-screen TV in the lounge for sports fans.

AIRPORT AREA

Doubletree Inn and Plaza
16500 Southcenter Pkwy,
Tukwila, 246-8220
(map: PP4)
Moderate; AE, DC, MC,
V; checks OK

The Doubletree, fixed between I-5 and the Southcenter shopping mall, is two hotels. The Plaza has handsome luxury suites ($99 to $156) with refrigerators, TVs (you pay per cable movie), and small wet bars. Southeast-facing rooms have views of Mount Rainier. There's a Jacuzzi and a sauna at the Plaza; the pool is across the street in a secluded courtyard at the Doubletree Inn, the more plebeian sibling. The woody Northwest lobby is nice, but rooms here ($69 to $104)

are average; avoid the north-facing ones, which hum with the sounds of I-5 and offer views of the Frederick & Nelson department store. Service is quite friendly.

Holiday Inn of Renton
800 Rainier Ave S,
Renton, 226-7700
(map: NN4)
Moderate; AE, DC,
MC, V; checks OK

★

A spirited, friendly staff gives this up-to-date but average mid-rise hotel some personality. The public rooms are done in mauve and burgundy; all the rooms have been refurbished. Spend the night before you leave from Sea-Tac, and you can park here free while you're away. Corporate-oriented.

Hyatt Seattle
17001 Pacific Hwy S,
244-6000 (map: OO6)
Expensive; AE, DC,
MC, V; checks OK

★

The upgraded coffee shop, dining room, and lobby give this low-lying hotel a certain splash, but the rooms lean toward the dark side. Courtyard pool, sauna, and massage are available. Avoid rooms across from the United Airlines hangar.

Sea-Tac Holiday Inn
17338 Pacific Hwy S,
248-1000 (map: PP6)
Moderate; AE, DC,
MC, V; checks OK

½

The lobby's been opened up and toned down; the remodeled rooms are tastefully done, for a hotel chain. Don't miss the time-warp revolving restaurant with its singing waiters. Avoid rooms with a southwest exposure—too much street noise.

Sea-Tac Red Lion Inn
18740 Pacific Hwy S,
246-8600 (map: PP6)
Expensive; AE, DC,
MC, V; checks OK

★

In true Red Lion tradition, it's gargantuan (850 rooms) and caters to conventioneers. You may pass Willy Loman in the dark, cavernous halls, but the tower rooms have been rather nicely redone in pastels. The east-facing rooms have views of the Cascades. Suites are available for parties. There is room service from 5am to past midnight, three full restaurants, two lounges, and an airport limo service.

Seattle Airport Hilton Hotel
17620 Pacific Hwy S,
244-4800 (map: PP6)
Expensive; AE, DC,
MC, V; checks OK

★★

This streamlined building miraculously manages to create a resort atmosphere along an airport strip. Plush rooms (at posh prices) circle a large, landscaped courtyard with pool and indoor/outdoor Jacuzzi. The architecture is by the distinguished national firm of SOM. Exercise room and meeting and party rooms available. A versatile menu offers Continental cuisine.

Seattle Marriott at Sea-Tac
3201 S 176th St,

Another megamotel, but on a human scale. The Alaska motif is warm, though somewhat cluttered in the lobby.

241-2000 (map: PP6)
*Expensive; AE, DC,
MC, V; checks OK*

Rooms are standard but suites are spacious. A pool and a courtyard area are part of an enormous covered atrium; there are also two Jacuzzis, a sauna, and a well-equipped exercise room. Lobby bar open until 2am.

EASTSIDE

The Bellevue Hilton
*100 112th Ave NE,
Bellevue, 455-3330
(map: HH3)
Expensive; AE, DC,
MC, V; checks OK*

With every amenity in the book, the Bellevue Hilton is the best bet on the Eastside's Hotel Row. Rooms are tastefully done in soft, warm colors; extras include use of a nearby health and racquet club, free transportation around Bellevue, 24-hour security and room service, cable TV (or movies) in every room, and three restaurants. Meeting rooms recently have been renovated. Doubles run from $97 to $105; parlor suites, at $225, have sitting rooms, partial kitchens, and dining tables.

Bellevue Holiday Inn
*11211 Main St, Bellevue,
455-5240 (map: HH3)
Moderate; AE, DC,
MC, V; checks OK*

This understated two-story motel neither stimulates nor overloads the senses; many regular visitors to Bellevue won't stay anywhere else. The units are arranged campus-style around a well-manicured lawn and heated pool. The suites are nothing special; the fancy dining room, Jonah's, is better than most.

Bellevue Red Lion Inn
*300 112th Ave SE,
Bellevue, 455-1300
(map: HH3)
Expensive; AE, DC, MC,
V; checks OK*

If you can get past the gaudy entrance and Vegas-style lobby of this 353-room monster hotel, you might enjoy your stay here. Rooms are unusually large and tastefully decorated in mauve and gray. Good convention facilities, a swinging disco, and spectacular suites make this one of Bellevue's most popular meeting spots.

**Best Western Greenwood
Hotel**
*625 116th Ave NE,
Bellevue, 455-9444
(map: HH3)
Moderate; AE, DC,
MC, V; checks OK*

A revamp has nicely updated the interiors in this midscale Bellevue hotel, just a jump off of I-405, but service here can be curt. Still, the Greenwood stands out for its nightlife (Deeter's is one of Bellevue's favorite dance emporiums; Thursday is comedy night) and 15 two-level townhouse suites ($99 to $174), with fireplaces and wet bars. Rooms facing the courtyard are much pleasanter than those with parking lot vistas.

**The Club
on Yarrow Bay**
*4311 Lake Washington
Blvd NE, Kirkland,
827-4603 (map: FF3)*

This is really an apartment complex, but 30 of the 300 units are set aside as "executive suites." The location is lovely—right on the shores of Lake Washington in Kirkland's poshest neighborhood—and a few rooms offer glimpses of Yarrow Bay. There are one- and two-

Moderate; AE, MC, V; checks OK

 ★½

bedroom suites, some with fireplaces. All have queen-size beds, kitchens, cable TV, and access to tennis courts, pool, Jacuzzi, and saunas. Exercise room available. Boat slips are extra.

Hyatt Regency at Bellevue Place
NE 8th St and Bellevue Way, Bellevue, 462-1234 (map: HH3)
Expensive; AE, DC, MC, V; checks OK

 ★★½

Hyatt Regency is just one part of Kemper Freeman's splashy, sprawling retail-office-restaurant-hotel-health-club complex called Bellevue Place. It's a 382-room hotel with 24 stories (the highest in Bellevue), which offers all the extras: two pricier "Regency Club" floors, two big ballrooms, and several satellite conference rooms, an adjoining health club (for a $10 fee), and an excellent restaurant, Eques. The best rooms (doubles start at $155) are those on the south side above the seventh floor. Plenty of people come to Bellevue just to shop—and now they have a place to stay.

La Residence Suite Hotel
475 100th Ave NE, Bellevue, 455-1475 (map: HH3)
Moderate; AE, MC, V; checks OK

 ★

Conveniently located across from the region's best shopping (Bellevue Square), this 24-room facility is a homey alternative to commercial super-hotels on the Eastside. The owner has added contemporary European furniture in pursuit of a more international ambience. Rooms have kitchens, separate bedrooms, and large closets, making the hotel popular for longer stays (but there is no minimum stay). Laundry facilities and free parking.

Woodmark Hotel
1200 Carillon Point, 822-3700 (map: EE3)
Expensive; AE, DC, MC, V; checks OK

 ★★★

On the eastern shore of Lake Washington, this new hotel resembles any new office building. Nearby there's still a lot of construction at Carillon Point, and parking access is a bit of a maze, but inside one encounters the soft touches of a fine hotel: 100 plush rooms (the best have lake views) with fully stocked minibars, VCRs (with complimentary movies available at the front desk), baths equipped with a *second* TV, terry-cloth robes, and oversized towels, with service (from laundry to valet) to match. They serve a full breakfast—with a newspaper—and if you get late-night cravings, the refrigerator is yours to raid.

Downstairs on the lake level there's a comfortable living room with a grand piano and a well-tended fire. The hotel has it's own restaurant, too, the Carillon Room, but you'll be happier going next door to Yarrow Bay Restaurant and Beach Cafe (a sibling of Ray's Boathouse at Shilshole Bay) or Ristorante Stresa (the Eastside version of Luciano Bardinelli's Settebello; see Restaurants chapter).

INNS AND BED & BREAKFASTS

Bed and breakfast is a marvelous way to discover a new city—through its natives, in its neighborhoods. Many of the B&Bs are independents, but far more can be reserved through two bed and breakfast registries: **Pacific Bed & Breakfast Registry** (701 NW 60th Street, Seattle 98107, 784-0539), which includes among its listings a sailboat in the San Juans and viewy Capitol Hill and Queen Anne Victorian homes; and **Travellers' Bed & Breakfast** (PO Box 492, Mercer Island 98040, 232-2345), which offers a waterfront cottage 10 minutes from downtown, a Tudor mansion in West Seattle, and many more. Most rates start at $50 for two people. Most are also listed in the **Washington State Bed & Breakfast Directory** (2442 NW Market Street, Seattle, 98107). Here are a few of our favorites.

LAKE UNION

MV Challenger
Henry Pier at Chandler's Cove on Lake Union (behind Benjamin's),
340-1201 (map: C1)
Moderate; AE; checks OK

★½

This friendly little retired tugboat docked at the south end of Lake Union is the city's only bunk and breakfast. When you come aboard, owner Jerry Brown may offer you a refreshment from the hardwood bar and a seat in the conversation pit—a sunken living space with two couches and a fireplace. His engine room is a gleaming nautical beauty; up top there's a deck, ideal for lolling in the sun.

As for sleeping, you have two boat choices (three in winter). We prefer the classic tug, where you might stay in the unbelievably small main-floor berths (two bunk rooms, one double, which share a head). Better is the suite state-room, with its own bath, VCR, and stereo, and the newly renovated wood-paneled "upstairs" rooms. However, the nearby yacht is more spacious—and more contemporary—with two berths (each with big double beds). Wintertime guests overflow (Jerry's tug is often full) into the *Alaska Adventurer*, which summers as a charter fishing boat. Jerry makes breakfast in the *Challenger*'s galley, using a diesel-powered stove and a microwave oven. In the evening, it's a pleasant stroll to Lake Union's growing number of restaurants. A very Seattle experience.

QUEEN ANNE HILL

The Williams House
1505 4th Ave N,
285-0810 (map: GG8)
Moderate; AE, DC,

In its 89-year history, this south-slope Queen Anne residence has also done stints as a gentlemen's boardinghouse and an emergency medical clinic for the 1962 Seattle World's Fair. Doug and Sue Williams still own

MC, V; checks OK

the establishment; however, they've moved out and have turned the management over to the reliable Ruth McGill. There are five guest rooms, four with views and two with private baths. The enclosed south sun porch is a nice meeting spot. Brass beds, original fixtures, fireplaces, ornate Italian tiles, and oak floors hark back to the home's Edwardian past. You will get a full breakfast.

CAPITOL HILL

Gaslight Inn
1727 15th Ave
325-3654 (map: HH6)
Inexpensive; AE, MC, V;
checks OK

Praised by repeat guests and bed-and-breakfast owners alike, the Gaslight is one of the loveliest, most reasonably priced, and friendliest bed and breakfasts in town. Trevor Logan and Steve Bennett have polished this turn-of-the-century mansion into a nine-guestroom jewel, six with private baths, all decorated in distinct styles—some contemporary, some antique. Outside are three decks and a large heated swimming pool. No pets or kids. Smoking is OK.

Landes House
712 11th Ave E,
329-8781 (map: HH6)
Moderate; MC, V; checks
OK

The Landes House, named after Bertha Landes, Seattle's only woman mayor (1926–1928), remained in the Landes family until 1965. Dick Hurlocker and Tom Hanes opened it and the house next door a year and a half ago, turning the two grand residences into a bed and breakfast facility (run more like a small inn). Seven out of the nine rooms have their own baths. The stately houses are connected on the side by a deck with a year-round, 24-hour hot tub. Our favorite rooms are two city-facing ones with an adjoining deck. The contemporary-design common areas—a spacious hard-wooded living room with fireplace, a drawing room with a grand piano, and an impressive dining area—are in the Landes house, where a light breakfast is served. Off-street parking.

Roberta's
1147 16th Ave E,
329-3326 (map: HH6)
Moderate; AE, DC,
MC, V; checks OK

Roberta is the gracious, somewhat loquacious lady of this Capitol Hill house a few blocks from Volunteer Park, the Seattle Art Museum, and the funky Broadway district. Inside it's lovely: gleaming refinished floors throughout, a comfortable blue couch and an old upright piano, books everywhere, and a large oval dining table and country-style chairs. Of the five rooms, the blue-toned Hideaway Suite (the entire third floor) with window seats, a sitting area with a futon couch and a small desk, and a full bath with a tub, is our favorite. Others prefer the one in peach tones with an antique desk, bay window, love seat, and queen-size brass bed. Early risers will enjoy the Madrona Room, with its morning sun and private bath. All five rooms have their own private baths (note the ceramic sinks), but one room's privy is across the hall. In the morning, Roberta brings you a wake-up cup of coffee, then later puts out a smashing full breakfast (no meat, though), maybe homemade cinnamon rolls or grainy raisin bread with blackberry jam. No children. No smoking except on the porch.

Salisbury House
750 16th Ave E,
328-8682 (map: HH6)
Moderate; AE, MC, V;
checks OK

A welcoming porch wraps around this big, bright Capitol Hill home, an exquisite hostelry neighboring Volunteer Park. Glossy maple floors and lofty beamed ceilings lend a sophisticated air to the guest library (with a chess table and a fireplace) and living room. Up the wide staircase and past the second-level sun porch are four guest rooms (one with a canopy bed) that share two large baths. Our favorite is the Rose Room, with its bay window and walk-in closet; if you can stand this much purple, the Lavender Room comes in second. Breakfast is taken in the dining room or on the sunny terrace. Classy, dignified, and devoid of children (under 12) and pets.

Shafer Mansion
907 14th Ave E,
329-4628 (map: HH6)
Moderate; AE; checks OK

This 1912 mansion, located one block from Volunteer Park, is elegantly yet comfortably furnished, with Oriental rugs in the vast oak dayrooms and a billiards room that warms up with a copper-hooded tile fireplace. A grand staircase is flanked by wood and ivory elephant carvings picked up by owner H. Lee Vennes on his travels abroad. All five rooms are on the second floor; three have their own baths. The Elliott Bay Suite features a splendid view of its namesake. Lee serves a blueberry muffin breakfast every day except Monday.

NORTH END/UNIVERSITY DISTRICT

Chambered Nautilus
5005 22nd Ave NE,
522-2536 (map: FF6)
Moderate; AE, DC,
MC, V; checks OK

This blue 1915 Georgian colonial (with a new coat of paint), on a hillside street in the U District, offers six airy guest rooms furnished beautifully with antiques. Four open onto porches with tree-webbed views of the Cascades. It's a fine place to stay in the U District, though you are just across the street from shared housing units, and a few blocks from Fraternity Row, so it can get noisy here during rush (other times, it's surprisingly quiet). Bunny and Bill Hagemeyer serve a full breakfast and complimentary afternoon tea. A spacious public room, meeting facilities, and an enclosed porch/reading room with soothing chamber music round out this tasteful hostelry.

Chelsea Station
4915 Linden Ave N,
547-6077 (map: FF8)
Moderate; AE, DC,
MC, V; checks OK

Innkeepers Dick and Marylou Jones have converted an elegant fourplex near the Woodland Park Zoo into a five-bedroom bed and breakfast. Upstairs accommodations include two spacious suites, one with a small kitchen. Noise from busy 50th street can be intrusive. In a downstairs sitting parlor is a desk with a phone for guests who need to transact business. The Joneses provide full breakfasts, king-size beds, an enclosed hot tub, and friendly advice on local excursions and dining. Children over 12 are welcome. No pets. No smoking.

The College Inn
Guest House
4000 University Way NE,
633-4441 (map: FF7)
Inexpensive; AE, DC,
MC, V; checks OK

Burgundy carpets, window seats, antiques, and pastel comforters create a cozy if somewhat spartan atmosphere in this hospitable inn designed along the lines of a European pension. Housed in a renovated 1909 Tudor building that is on the National Register of Historic Places, it's in the heart of the lively U District, with a cafe and rathskeller pub below. (Late-night noise travels quite handily into west-side rooms.) Each room has a sink but no toilet, TV, radio, or phone (for the musically inclined there's an upright piano in room 305). Bathrooms are at the end of each hall, and a guest living room is tucked away on the fourth floor. A generous continental breakfast is included—a good deal at these budget prices.

Lake Union B&B
2217 N 36th St, 547-9965
(map: FF7)
Moderate; MC, V;
checks OK

Shoes off. If you don't have any socks, they're provided. Then sink into the white cloud of carpet and couches of this modern three-story house not far from Gas Works Park—a refreshing break from the Victoriana that plagues most B&Bs. There are two rooms upstairs, both stunning, though one—with its solarium, fireplace, and a view of Lake Union and Seattle skyline from the Jacuzzi or peeked at through the residing telescope—is probably Seattle's finest *affordable* bedroom. There's a sauna in the downstairs bath.

Pinkham's Pillow
202 3rd Ave S, Edmonds,

This clean, ageless home is right in the heart of downtown Edmonds, two blocks from the waterfront, with

774-3406
Moderate; MC. V;
checks OK

views of Puget Sound. Don't worry about the name: Pinkham's Pillow does lean toward lace and ruffles, heart-shaped rugs and antique-style furnishings, but still remains comfortable and uncluttered, with an over-riding sense of organization and welcome. Each of the five guest rooms—Melissa, Shannon, Lacey, Joy, and Adria, named after the owners' daughters—has a private bath; Lacey has handicapped access. Prices are $56 to $86 and include breakfast.

BAINBRIDGE ISLAND

Beach Cottage B&B
5831 Ward NE,
Bainbridge Island,
842-6081
Moderate; no credit cards;
checks OK

Right across Eagle Harbor from the ferry-stop town of Winslow is this charming, flower-bedecked four-cottage setup, each with a queen-size bed, kitchen (stocked with breakfast fixings), logs for the fireplace, and stereo. Two are right on the beach, and all four boast a view of Eagle Harbor and its marina (the brand-new two-bedroom on the hill even views Seattle and Mount Rainier on clear days). Each goes for $75 for two people ($95 for four). Smoking is allowed (pets and children aren't), and there's a rowboat for use.

The Bombay House
8490 Beck Rd NE,
Bainbridge Island,
842-3926
Moderate; AE, MC, V;
checks OK

Located near Fort Ward State Park on the south end of the island, the Bombay House has a hearty dose of the country-hideaway mood that's so much of the bed and breakfast mystique. It's a sprawling turn-of-the-century house with a widow's walk, set in a lavish flower garden with a rough-cedar gazebo overlooking scenic Rich Passage. The large living room has a huge fireplace, and all five bedrooms are done up in country antiques (three have private baths). The vast second-floor Captain's Suite has a wood parlor stove and claw-footed tub. Innkeepers Roger Kanchuk and Bunny Cameron are friendly hosts; their breakfast includes homemade muffins and breads, and fresh fruits. Smoking is restricted.

WEST SEATTLE

Hainsworth House
2657 37th Ave SW,
938-1020 (map: II9)

This 1906 Tudor mansion has excellent views of downtown Seattle (and the West Seattle industrial area) and lovely landscaped grounds. It's a massive 18-room house; however, there are only two guest rooms

Moderate; AE, MC, V; checks OK

($75 and $85), each with a porch and private bath (though only one has a view—an incredible view). Owners Carl and Charlotte Muia pamper you with coffee or tea brought to your room when you wake up, and serve champagne with breakfast. No smoking, no unmarried couples. Make friends with the little mutts, stay out of the two kids' rooms, and you're set.

Villa Heidelberg
4845 45th Ave SW, 938-3658 (map: II9) Moderate; no credit cards; checks OK

Leaded glass windows, beamed ceilings, Puget Sound views, and a wraparound covered porch distinguish this 1909 minimansion in West Seattle, built and named by a German immigrant. The three guest rooms ($45 to $65) share one bathroom. One has an Olympics-facing sundeck, the other has a fireplace and a phone. Owners John and Barb Thompson serve a breakfast of popovers and fruit, waffles, or French toast. Look for extras like a bouquet of roses on the table, grown in their own beautifully landscaped garden.

EASTSIDE

Cedarym
1011 240th Ave NE, Redmond, 868-4159 (map: EE1) Inexpensive; MC, V; checks OK

★★

We wish this magnificent bed and breakfast had more than two rooms. It's a brand-new Colonial, situated amid gorgeously cultivated grounds with a wide lawn and arbor (often used for weddings), and a dandy spa-in-gazebo highlighted by bursting rhodies and roses and a ring of tall cedars. Inside, Mary Ellen and Walt Brown have re-created a Colonial homestead, right down to the gleaming pine plank floors, hand-forged lift latches, and the enormous brick cooking hearth in the family room (which Mary Ellen really uses). The Tulip and Anchor rooms feature big, comfortable beds, TVs, sitting areas overlooking the grounds, and a shared bath. The Browns make uncommonly cordial hosts.

Mercer Island Hideaway
8820 SE 63rd St, Mercer Island, 232-1092 (map: KK4) Inexpensive; no credit cards; checks OK

It definitely feels like a homestay, but a notch more luxurious than most. Mary and Bill Williams offer one suite and one smallish room in their sprawling Mercer Island home. The suite has its own entrance and an adjoining fireplace room and would make a comfortable base for a long stay. A lot of windows and pastels lighten up the public rooms; a full breakfast is served around the lazy Susan every morning. Pristine Pioneer Park is just down the road. Call first; winter hours are sporadic due to the Williams's wanderlust.

Shumway Mansion
11410 99th Pl NE,
Kirkland, 823-2303
(map: DD3)
Moderate; AE, MC, V;
checks OK

When Richard and Salli Harris heard that developers wanted to demolish this historic 1909 building to make room for condos, they hauled the four-story house to a safe location near Kirkland's Juanita Bay. Now it's a gracious bed and breakfast with an equal emphasis on seminars and receptions. Seven guest rooms are furnished with antiques (each has a private bath) and antique-filled public rooms that overlook the bay (just a short walk away) and the lower parking lots. The ballroom downstairs is often used for weddings or special meetings. In summer, it opens onto a flowering patio. A full breakfast is served in the dining room on table linens. The Columbia Athletic Club (available for guest use) is a block away; downtown Seattle is 20 minutes away. Children over 12 are welcome. No pets or smoking.

The Wildflower
25237 SE
Issaquah–Fall City Rd,
Issaquah, 392-1196
Inexpensive; no credit
cards; checks OK

Laureita Caldwell has decorated the four guest rooms of her log-house bed and breakfast in floral themes, based on plants native to Issaquah: the Strawberry Room, the Fern Room, the Daisy Room, the Rose Room. The latter boasts the classiest decor (although it shares a bath with Daisy); all rooms have raw pine walls, charming window seats (great for reading), and handmade quilts. Downstairs there's a cozy common room where guests can relax by the wood stove. All this and breakfast too for $50.

The massive cabin sits quite impressively in the lonesome woods just north of Issaquah—a terrific base camp for travelers torn between the mountains and the metropolis.

CONDOMINIUMS

Alexis Hotel
1007 1st Ave,
624-4844 (map: L8)
Expensive; AE, DC,
MC, V; checks OK

See Downtown Lodgings in this chapter.

The Hotel Alternative
2453 152nd Ave NE,
Redmond, 867-9200
Moderate; AE, DC,
MC, V; checks OK

This condominium rental service lists fully equipped apartments in Renton, Redmond, Bellevue, and Seattle. Weekly maid service, linens, and recreational-facility use are included. A three-day minimum stay is required.

CONDOMINIUMS

Pacific Guest Suites

915 118th Ave SE, Mill Creek, 454-7888
Moderate; AE, DC, MC, V; checks OK

Pacific rents condos in Seattle, Bellevue, and Redmond. Most locations have pools, exercise facilities, Jacuzzis, and weekly maid service. Valet and grocery shopping service are available at every location. Fee depends on length of stay.

WestCoast Plaza Park Suites

1011 Pike St, 682-8282 or 1-800-426-0670
Expensive; AE, DC, MC, V; checks OK

unrated

At press time, the newest hotel to open its doors in downtown Seattle was the Plaza Park Suites, a step away from the Washington State Convention Center. It's geared toward extended stays (they'll quote prices by the month, if you like), so each room is, in one way or another, a suite (even the studios). Each has a sitting area, kitchen, and a downy bedroom (with a *second* TV). Some have fireplaces, others boardrooms. Whatever you want, from groceries to an extra phone line for your modem, can be arranged. This suite hotel has all the amenities of a full-service hotel: conference rooms, exercise rooms (sauna and Jacuzzi too), laundry and valet service, and a restaurant. Shorter stays are welcome.

OUTINGS

OUTINGS CONTENTS

DAYTRIPS

BOEING/PAINE FIELD

FREE To some, Boeing is synonymous with Seattle. Of the 160,000 people employed worldwide by the nation's largest electronic, computer, and aerospace corporation, 103,000 live and work in the Puget Sound area. Twenty-two thousand of these are part of the three-shift crew in the world's largest building, at Everett's Paine Field, which manufactures 747s and 767s (with future plans for 777s). It's the only plant in commercial aviation that conducts tours.

Here on this 1,026-acre site are eight office buildings, four warehouses, two storage buildings for the plane's interiors, two paint hangars, and the main assembly building. As you'll learn on the 1½-hour tour, the main building stands 11 stories tall (the doors themselves are the size of a soccer field), covers 62 acres (or 90 football fields), and spans 291 million cubic feet—the largest building, by volume, in the world (you could fit 4½ Kingdomes inside). You'll view planes (a new one rolls out the door approximately every four days) in all stages of assembly, from a mere fuselage to a fully painted, ready-to-test-fly airplane.

Tours, which begin with a 25-minute video on Boeing's history, are free. Space is limited (especially during July and August), so tickets must be picked up at the tour center the same day (I-5 exit 189, head west on Highway 526 for 3½ miles; 342-4804). No children under 10.

BREWERIES

FREE The West Coast is the heartland of "craft brewing" in this country, and some say the Northwest is even more sophisticated about the art of microbrewing than tony Los Angeles. Brewpubs in Seattle currently number five: Trolleyman in Fremont, Noggin's in Westlake, Big Time Brewery and Ale House in the University District, the Pacific Northwest Brewing Company in Pioneer Square, and at press time, the Seattle Brewing Company opened its Duwamps Cafe on Lower Queen Anne, an addition that should firmly establish Seattle as a hub on the boutique brewery map.

Still, the local brew that enjoys the biggest commercial status is Seattle's own (sort of—it's now owned by an Australian conglomerate) Rainier Beer. You can smell hops as you drive by the **Rainier Brewery** (3100 Airport Way S, 622-2600, map: JJ6) on I-5, marked by the red neon "R." The brew's local reputation is based more on hometown pride and its original, brilliantly wacky advertisements (now replaced with disappointing Hollywood versions) than its flavor, but it's still many Seattleites' beer of choice. **FREE** The 30-minute weekday tours of the facility are free and include a tour of the beer house, taste testing in the tap room (kids get root beer), and an orientation film.

The real fun (and flavor) is found in the microbreweries, however. The first to come to this city was **Red Hook Brewery** (3400 Phinney Avenue N, 548-8000, map: FF7), which opened in Ballard in 1982 but recently moved to larger quarters in Fremont. This is where they make Red Hook Ale, Black Hook Porter, Ballard Bitter, and a host of special seasonal brews. You can watch the process on one of the frequent public tours. **The Trolleyman**, Red Hook's own pub, is a wonderfully comfortable, smoke-free atmosphere where the beer is complemented by good food (see Restaurants chapter).

Hale's Ales (109 Central Way, Kirkland, 827-4359, map: EE3) on the Eastside welcomes visitors to its small facility in Kirkland, where production was recently relocated from the original quarters in Colville in northeastern Washington. No tours are offered, but you may be able to talk someone into showing you around. Hale's turns out a dozen beers, the most popular being the Pale Ale, Special Bitter, Celebration Porter, and Moss Bay Amber Ale—which you can watch being made through windows from the adjoining **Kirkland Roaster & Ale House** (111 Central Way, Kirkland, 827-4400, map: EE3). (See Restaurants chapter).

A ferry ride away is the esteemed **Thomas Kemper Brewery** (22381 Foss Road NE, Poulsbo, 1-697-1446; get to the Kitsap Peninsula via ferry to Bainbridge Island). **FREE** Kemper produces lager beers and offers free tours and tastings on weekends.

CARNATION

KIDS An autumnal, country escape into the Dairy Bowl starts at the **Carnation Research Farm** (28901 NE Carnation Farm Road, 788-1511), 25 miles northeast of Seattle (take the Preston–Fall City exit off I-90; look for the giant cow statue). Self-guided tours of Washington's best-known dairy are permitted between 10am and 3pm every day except Sunday (when the cows sleep in), March through October. You'll wind past tractors, haystacks, livestock, the calf nursery, and the maternity barn, see cows being milked, and learn all about the pasteurization process. Kids love it, and the grounds include a lovely formal garden.

The place to picnic nearby is **Tolt River/John A. MacDonald Memorial Park** (31020 NE 40th Street, 333-4198), a woodsy retreat with meandering trails and an old-fashioned suspension bridge across the Tolt River. **The Original Brown Bag Restaurant and Bakery** (4366 Tolt Avenue, 1-333-6100), located in a historic 1913 clapboard building, is a fine place to pick up the picnic—especially since the return of its original owners and Thelma, the baker of the cinnamon rolls.

End your trip with a drive through the fertile Cascade farmlands. In October be sure to visit the Two Brothers pumpkin patch, part of the **Game Haven Greenery** (7110 310th Avenue NE; one mile north of town on Carnation Farm Road, 333-4313), a great place to select your jack-o'-lantern.

EVERETT BASEBALL

KIDS In the vintage mill town of Everett (30 miles north of Seattle on I-5), the Great American Game is still played the way you remember it: on grass, outdoors, under the sky. The **Everett Giants Baseball Club** (PO Box 1346, Everett 98206), a minor league, class-A satellite team of the San Francisco Giants, plays mid-June through August in **Everett Memorial Stadium** (39th Street and Broadway; take exit 192 off I-5). Games start at 7pm weekdays, 2pm Sundays (call 1-258-3673 for tickets and season schedule). While the on-field antics may fall short of the (slightly) more polished professionalism of the M's, the price is right ($2.50

for kids, $4 for adults, reserved seats slightly higher) and the fans are charged up. There's always a promotional event halfway through—you know, fireworks, a big-bucks raffle giveaway, or a Beat the Walker race—making Everett baseball (next to Muckleshoot bingo) the hottest ticket in the Northwest. Even the hot dogs are good. Tickets are available in Seattle only at Peaches (811 NE 45th Street) or David Ishii, Bookseller (212 First Avenue S).

FISHERMEN'S TERMINAL

A most authentic attraction, Seattle's bustling Fishermen's Terminal (1735 W Thurman Street, 728-3395, map: FF8) is the busiest of its kind in the North Pacific. It sits in protected Salmon Bay, the last stretch of the Lake Washington Ship Canal before it reaches the Ballard Locks and empties into Puget Sound.

Pick a weekday morning to drive to **Miles American Cafe** (4019 21st Street W, 282-0655), which overlooks the terminal, for a full fishermen's breakfast. Outside, the commercial fishing boats come and go. After breakfast, head out to the crowded piers to inspect the hundreds of trollers, gill-netters, and crab boats that make up the Northwest's most active fleet. Hardened fishermen will be repairing their nets and scrubbing their vessels, preparing to return to sea. The revamped terminal includes new docks, a large public plaza (with interpretive panels detailing the development of the local fishing industry), an energetic seafood restaurant (and a fish 'n' chips annex), and a barnlike retail/office complex—but the working soul of the place remains. At the **Wild Salmon Fish Market** (1800 W Emerson Place, 283-3366), only feet from the boats, you can purchase the freshest catch of the day for your dinner.

THE HERBFARM IN FALL CITY

Shady, rural roads beyond the interstate lead to **The Herbfarm** (32804 Issaquah–Fall City Road, Fall City; 25 miles east of Seattle, 784-2222 or 1-800-866-4372), where simple, centuries-old horticulture meets sparkling culinary innovation. Some years ago, Bill and Lola Zimmerman outgrew their shady lakeside lot and moved to an old farm in Fall City. Here Lola's backyard herb business took root and sprouted, spreading to 17 display gardens all over the grounds and into several greenhouses—until finally it flowered (under the direction of the Zimmermans' son Ron and his wife, Carrie Van Dyck) into an elegant lunchtime restaurant, where herbal harvests grace each carefully crafted dish and reservations are as hard to come by as fresh French tarragon in winter (see Restaurants chapter).

FREE KIDS Even if you can't sample the food, you can still come appreciate this rustic herbal Eden. Over 630 varieties of herbs and 120 varieties of succulents and sedums are grown in theme gardens. The oldest, the Herb Garden, displays culinary and medicinal herbs, and flowers for drying. Others include the Silver Garden (herbs with gray foliage or white flowers), the Fragrance Garden, the Thyme Garden, the Good Cook's Garden (culinary herbs), the Edible Flowers Garden, the Pioneer Garden (those herbs that the early pioneers grew from seed), and the Shakespeare Garden (herbs mentioned in his works). All are demonstration gardens on a home scale, so you can see how to grow the herbs yourself; samples are sold in the herb shop (which Bill originally built out of the old garage on the property). Tours of the gardens and greenhouses (offered weekends during spring and summer, or by appointment for groups) include fascinating herbal lore and legend; a surprising assortment of classes and workshops teach everything from crafting dried herb wreaths to cultivating herbal medicines. Kids probably won't appreciate the elaborate luncheons, but they'll love the grounds, watched over by a couple of gentle llamas (available for rides on special occasions; call first) and full of gracious picnic spots. Hayrides and harvest festivals are seasonal diversions.

ISSAQUAH

This small, thriving suburb, tucked up against the Cascade foothills, retains a bit of the character of its coal-mining days. Tiger, Squak, and Cougar mountains—Issaquah's scenic "Alps"—are just a short walk from Issaquah's growing downtown and recreational opportunities (these range from seasonal mushroom hunting to hang gliding). But it's hiking that draws most folks. (See Hiking and Climbing under The Great Outdoors in the Exploring chapter.)

A trip to Issaquah should include a visit to the **FREE KIDS Edelweiss Chalet** of Julius Boehm, the Austrian-born candymaker who set up **Boehm's Chocolates** (Boehm's Candy Kitchen, 255 NE Gilman Boulevard, 392-6652; take exit 17 off I-90) here in 1956. You can tour Boehm's chalet home with its sizable collection of paintings, statues, and artifacts, and the chocolate factory, complete with samples of the famous candies. Buy some to eat in the adjoining garden.

FREE KIDS In the fall, don't miss the **Issaquah State Salmon Hatchery** (125 W Sunset Way, 1-392-3180), where you can view the chinook and coho thrashing up the fish ladder. A festival in October celebrates the return of the salmon (see Calendar chapter). In spring the hatchery's pools swarm with guppy-sized youngsters. Open every day; admission is free.

The **Cougar Mountain Zoo** (19525 SE 54th Street, 391-5508; closed Mondays and Wednesdays), once an educational facility with a petting zoo, is now open to the public. It houses numerous birds and animals, including many endangered species. The Formosan deer—extinct in its native Taiwan—just gave birth to a fawn in 1990.

Issaquah's other big draw is **Gilman Village** (317 Gilman Boulevard, Issaquah, 1-462-0594), a boutique assemblage of 30-some converted farmhouses and bungalows dating from 1910 to 1935. It's all very tony and upscale—a favorite of "destination shoppers"—with excellent gift shops, clothiers, and small, decent eateries where you can stop for lunch. Nearby, stop at the **Gilman Antique Gallery** (625 NW Gilman Boulevard, 391-6640), a converted grocery store filled with antiques and kitsch from all periods. **Lake Sammamish State Park** (20606 SE 56th Street, Issaquah, 455-7010) is a good place for a swim on a summer's afternoon.

Looking for a particular place? Check the index at the back of this book for individual restaurants, nightclubs, lodgings, shops, attractions, and more.

LAKE UNION

KIDS FREE Lake Union (map: FF7–GG7) is the most central of Seattle's bodies of water, and the one most imbued with historical romance. It's also a flotsam-littered, grimy working lake; the boatyards that linger there are evidence of its industrial past. Its working character is passing, however, with much nostalgic gnashing of teeth, and spiffy view restaurants are staking claim along its shores. Consequently, from different angles—a window table at a glittering eatery, the prow of a wooden rowboat, the grassy flanks of a lakeside park, or the pier of a working dry dock—schizophrenic Lake Union takes on many different guises. There's great variety in an exploration of its shores.

Unfortunately, those shores are not easy for a pedestrian to reach, but the explorer can enjoy them on a drive. The southeast corner is the most accessible from downtown (via Westlake Avenue) and therefore has become the lake's commercial hub. A shiny new complex of restaurants crowds the shore, with excellent views of the lake and its docks. This is also where the **seaplane charters** take off (see Transportation in the Essentials chapter) and where you can rent a classic wooden rowboat or sailboat from the **Center for Wooden Boats** (1010 Valley Street, 382-BOAT, map: GG7), a maritime museum that rents its exhibits for sailing on the lake. Speedier vessels are available for rent from any number of other lakeside outlets, but the Center merits a stop to view its pretty boat shop, the old dry-docked lumber schooner *Wawona*, and maybe cadets a-drilling at the nearby Naval Reserve station.

The west shore of the lake is another eaters' destination (with **Triples**, 1200 Westlake Avenue N, 284-2535, map: GG7, drawing singles in droves), but is less accessible to pedestrians. Instead, head up the east shore, along Fairview Avenue. The efficient-looking vessels docked at Blaine Street are among nine **floating survey ships** belonging to the National Oceanographic and Atmospheric Administration (NOAA). You may be able to arrange a guided tour of one on a weekday during the winter (call 442-7657).

The pretty pocket park (big enough for one blanket's worth of picnic, that's all) at the end of the next street, East Newton, marks the start of Lake Union's famous **houseboat strip**, a remnant of a floating community that once stretched along the Duwamish River and Lake Washington as well. Floating shacks were once a cheap, sequestered haven for water rats, bootleggers, prostitutes, and impoverished university students. Some houseboats are still hand-hewn in the old fashion, but over the years, enclaves of designer boxes (looking like condos washed off the Kirkland hillsides) have grown, vinelike, from the shore. (Remember: these picturesque homes and their walkways are private, so respect property rights.) There are more public pocket parks along this strip, at the feet of East Lynn and Roanoke streets.

But the grand park is on Lake Union's north shore: sprawling **Gas Works Park**, an industrial eyesore ingeniously transformed into a picnicker's and kite-flyer's heaven. Climb the grassy mound to enjoy the mosaic sundial and a view of the downtown towers just two miles away. The **Burke-Gilman biking and jogging trail** cuts east from Gas Works, a wonderful path winding clear up to Lake Washington's north edge.

Westward, past more dock trade, lies a wholly different attraction: funky Fremont. Once a seedy mini-Haight Ashbury, this district (connected to Westlake Avenue by the most garish bridge in town) is now undergoing a Pioneer Square–style renaissance of restaurants and shops, making Fremont a terrific, if slightly offbeat, outing. It boasts the city's most popular and populist sculpture, **Waiting for the Interurban** (1978), along with highly browsable antique, secondhand, and retro-kitsch stores with names like **The Daily Planet** (3416 Fremont Avenue N, 633-0895, map: FF7) and **Deluxe Junk** (3518 Fremont Avenue N, 634-2733). From here a pleasant park strip along the **Ship Canal** wends toward the old Scandinavian fishing enclave of Ballard, its famous locks, and the Sound beyond.

LANGLEY (WHIDBEY ISLAND)

KIDS Seekers of an island idyll needn't travel all the way to the San Juans when **Whidbey Island** is as close as a drive to Mukilteo, 20 miles north of Seattle (see Transportation in the Essentials chapter). From there you take a short ferry ride to Clinton on Whidbey Island. From **Clinton** it's a 10-minute drive to **Langley**, the Lake Wobegon of rural Whidbey Island, and a dandy day trip for the family.

The main street is a browser's paradise of classy antique and gift shops, along with the **Clyde Theater** (221 First Street, 1-321-5525), which hosts periodic local theater productions in addition to its regularly scheduled films. Swap stories with John Hauser of **Moonraker Books** (209 First Street, 1-321-6962). **Whidbey Island Antiques** (115 Anthes Avenue, 1-221-2393) has beautiful old wood furniture, and the burgeoning **Star Store** (201 First Street, 1-321-5222), a genuine mercantile outpost under whose banner thrive two other businesses: **Star Store Grocery and Deli** (1-321-5222) and the **Star Store Bistro** (1-221-2627), a Deco oasis in quaintsville with an outdoor deck and a snappy menu. **Annie Steffen's** (101 First Street, 1-321-6535) displays sumptuous handcrafted and woven goods. And there are two interior design stores owned by the same designer, Linda Lundgren: **Islandesign** (111 First Street, 1-321-5121) and **In the Country** (315 First Street, 1-221-8202).

Cafe Langley (113 First Street, 1-221-3090), a Middle Eastern restaurant, is a busy, garlicky spot that has quickly become a popular dinner stop. Join natives for a brew at the charmingly dumpy **Dog House Backdoor Restaurant** (230 First Street, 1-321-9996), along with a burger and fries. Or take a picnic to **Double Bluff Beach**, north of Langley—just the place to fly a kite, spot a bald eagle, watch a Puget Sound sunset, or stroll the length of an unspoiled sandy beachfront. If one day isn't enough, there are numerous excellent bed-and-breakfast inns here. Or you can try for a room at the newer **Inn at Langley** (400 First Street, 1-221-3033), which marries a little bit of Northwest ruggedness with Pacific Rim tranquillity.

NORTHWEST TREK

KIDS This remarkable natural habitat, a 600-acre preserve near Eatonville (11610 Trek Drive E, Eatonville, 1-832-6116; 55 miles south of Seattle off Route

161) is made up of pastures, peat bogs, swamps, ponds, and forests. Here bison, bighorn sheep, caribou, moose, elk, and deer roam "free," while human visitors view (and photograph) them from trams. Naturalists narrate the hour-long, 5.5-mile trip, which is exciting for both kids ($4) and adults ($6.25). Also in the park are nature trails, a number of walk-through exhibits, a gift shop, and the **Fir Bough Cafe**, the in-park food concession that does a serviceable job with breakfasts and burgers. You might combine this visit with a trip to Mount Rainier (see Excursions in this chapter), just another 60 miles up the road.

POINT DEFIANCE PARK (TACOMA)

FREE KIDS Situated on a slender finger of land that juts dramatically into Puget Sound is Point Defiance Park (5400 N Pearl Street, Tacoma, 1-591-3690), one of the most inspired city parks in the country. The 700-acre wilderness park was admirably planned and is being maintained to absorb heavy use without heavy damage. As a result, Point Defiance is Tacoma's greatest civic treasure, a vast natural playground that tops the best parks in Seattle. It also makes a perfect daytrip from King County, best planned around a fair-weather picnic. Stop at the **Antique Sandwich Shop** (5102 N Pearl Street, 1-752-4069) on the way for your lunch: meat-loaf sandwiches, lemonades, and wedges of cheesecake (they also serve the best clam chowder in Tacoma). The only problem will be in deciding in which spot in this verdant park you should put down your blanket.

A one-way 5-mile drive (fine for biking, closed to motorized vehicles on Saturday mornings) and hiking trails wind through the wilderness, sweeping out now and again for views of the Sound, the Olympic Peninsula, and Vashon Island. **Fort Nisqually**, a restored Hudson's Bay Company fur trading post from 1833, sits on a cliff with a commanding view of the **Tacoma Narrows** waterway. Inside is a museum with artifacts from the old Northwest fur trade. A lumber museum, **Camp Six** (1-752-0047), features original loggers' bunkhouses and an operating 1929 steam train that chugs around the camp. In addition there's a rocky swimming beach with a picnic area, a boathouse with all sorts of boats for rent, tennis courts, splendid formal gardens, and a children's **Never Never Land** (1-591-5845), where 31 Mother Goose scenes are nestled in 10 acres of woods (open in summer).

Most impressive is the **Point Defiance Zoo and Aquarium** (1-591-5337; $5.50 admission), which is known for excellent displays of both native Northwest species and more exotic animals such as arctic muskox and a beluga whale. The family-oriented Boathouse Grill Restaurant (5910 N Waterfront Drive, 1-756-7336), owned and run by the Parks Service, is next door to the ferry landing.

OLYMPIA

Olympia, the state capital, sits along the protected waters of Budd Inlet, the southernmost finger of Puget Sound. It is a scenic, friendly, and livable city, whose destiny was settled in 1853 when it won out over competitors such as Yakima, Ellensburg, and Vancouver to become capital of the Washington Territory, and later, Washington State. Now there are plenty of reasons to visit

Olympia—the attractive campus of **The Evergreen State College** (Evergreen Parkway, 1-866-6000) and the spectacular 5.7-mile bird-watching hike in the **Nisqually National Wildlife Refuge** (100 Brown Farm Road, 1-753-9467), to name two—but an entire outing can be planned around a visit to the seat of state government.

FREE The classic dome of the **Legislative Building** is at the center of the grounds. Replete with bronze and imported marble, the bold Romanesque structure houses the state Senate and House of Representatives in annual winter sessions. Their debates can be critiqued from visitors' galleries. To the east of the Legislative Building rises the pillared **Temple of Justice**, seat of the state Supreme Court. To the west is the red brick **Governor's Mansion**, which the architects scorn but the people love, as was discovered a few years ago when someone suggested tearing it down. It is open to visitors on Wednesday afternoons from 1pm to 2:45pm. **FREE** Free tours of the mansion and the other buildings of the Capitol group can be arranged by calling 1-586-8687. Finish up with a visit to **Wagner's Bakery and Deli** (1013 S Capitol Way, 1-357-7268) for a big ham sandwich on German rye or one of Rudy's exquisite cream horns, to go or eat in.

Handsomest of the newer state buildings is Paul Thiry's squarish **State Library**, behind the Legislative Building. Open to the public during business hours, it contains a striking abstract mural by Washington's best-known painter, the late Mark Tobey. In its Washington Room are artifacts from the state's early history, a collection of books by Washington authors, and a mural by the late Kenneth Callahan—one of his best—detailing events in state history. The **FREE State Capital Museum** (211 W 21st Avenue, 1-753-2580), formerly a lumber baron's residence, displays an excellent collection of Native American baskets and periodically shows the work of Northwest artists.

In Olympia proper, the opening of the **Washington Center for the Performing Arts** (on Washington Street between Fifth Avenue and Legion Way) has brought new life to the downtown area. In the same block is the **Marianne Partlow Gallery**, a leading outlet for contemporary painting and sculpture. Across Fifth Avenue, the **Capitol Theatre** (1-754-6670), a onetime movie house, provides a showcase for the offerings of the Olympia Film Society, as well as locally produced plays and musicals. Toward the harbor, at the corner of North Capitol Way and West Thurston Street, is the lively **Olympia Farmers Market**. Open Tuesday through Sunday from 10am to 3pm, except in winter, it's filled with South Sound produce, flowers, and crafts.

Wholly different in character is **West Fourth Avenue**, between Columbia and Water streets, a hangout for students and ex-students, artists and would-be artists, gays, lesbians, and counterculture members. At the corner of Water Street is **Childhood's End**, a gallery for arts and crafts, and across from it is **Percival's Landing**, where the city has created a new waterfront park. A boardwalk extends from the moored craft of the Olympia Yacht Club to the mainland and continues out to the working port. Here you can climb a tall viewing tower to survey the whole of Olympia's harbor, from the snowy Olympic Mountains to the north all the way back to the Capitol Dome.

The Tumwater Division of the **Pabst Brewing Company** is just outside Olympia

(Schmidt Place and Custer Way, Tumwater, 1-754-5000), a perfect diversion for an afternoon; take one of the free tours offered every day, and enjoy the free beer afterwards.

KIDS In Tenino, 8 miles south of Tumwater, is **Wolf Haven** (3111 Offut Lake Road, 1-264-4695; admission is $3 for adults, $2 for kids), an educational and research facility that teaches wolf appreciation and studies the question of whether to reintroduce them into the wild. The public is invited to see the wolves or join them in a "howl-in." No petting allowed—remember, these are wild animals. For $20 a year, you can participate in the Adopt-a-Wolf program.

SNOQUALMIE AND THE FALLS

In this lovely country where the dairyland folds into the mountains, you begin to understand how the Cascades got their name. Against this alpine backdrop 30 miles east of Seattle is the quiet little former mill town of Snoqualmie (take the Snoqualmie Falls exit north from I-90), once best known for its falls, just northwest of the town, and now familiar to most as the setting for *Twin Peaks*.

The diner serves Twin Peaks Pie, and even the banks sell its T-shirts. The 268-foot **FREE Snoqualmie Falls** is a thundering spectacle just up the road. You can admire it from a covered observation deck above, or at the base of a steep, wooded trail that winds to the bottom of the gorge. The window tables at **Salish Lodge at Snoqualmie Falls** (37807 SE Fall City–Snoqualmie Road, 1-888-2556) also offer magnificent overlooks. Unfortunately, they have always been much better than the food; however, with the recent appointment of a new chef from The Herbfarm, the food might (finally) begin to at least equal the view. The Salish's adjoining 91-room inn is a good choice for luxury-loving overnighters, but homier 10-guest-room accommodations are nearby at **The Old Honey Farm** (8910 384th Avenue SE, 1-888-1637), with pastoral outlooks across the meadows of a 34-acre farm.

The area is rife with possibilities for engaging side trips. May through September, the **KIDS Puget Sound and Snoqualmie Valley Railroad** (PO Box 459, Snoqualmie 98065, 1-888-3030, 1-746-4025) operates its vintage steam trains, which leave from the distinctive 1890 depot and chug through thick woods, over bridges, past farms, and to the top of the spectacular falls. The 10-mile round trip includes a stop at **Railroad Park**, a depot in charming **North Bend**. Both stations have railroad artifacts and old engines on display. Fares are $6 for adults, $4 for kids.

The **FREE Snoqualmie Winery** (1000 Winery Road, Snoqualmie, 1-888-4000), about five miles southwest of the town, offers free tastings every day. This is only the winery headquarters (the actual production takes place in Matawa in Eastern Washington, hence, no tours), but the grounds are an ideal picnic destination, with a stunning panorama of the Snoqualmie Valley and the surrounding Cascades. Sausage, cheese, and other edibles are available at the gift shop.

Finally, **Snoqualmie Pass**, the historic, low-lying transmountain route of the Indians, is a fine starting point for hikes. In winter, four ski areas offer the closest downhill and cross-country skiing for Seattle skiers (see Great Outdoors in the Exploring chapter).

SUQUAMISH MUSEUM

KIDS In a forested setting near Agate Pass on the Kitsap Peninsula is the Suquamish Museum (Highway 305 off Sandy Hook Road, Suquamish, 1-598-3311), focusing on the history of the region's original inhabitants, the Puget Sound Salish Indians. A visit to the museum makes a marvelous daytrip: you take the ferry to Winslow on Bainbridge Island, then drive north on Highway 305 to the Port Madison Indian Reservation. The ongoing exhibit "The Eyes of Chief Seattle" treats the alternative, pre-European history of the region through graphics, transcribed oral histories, and artifacts. A slide show narrated by tribal elders richly complements the exhibit. Outside, a quarter-mile-long nature trail is flanked by edible and medicinal plants. The museum is open every day during warm-weather months, Wednesday through Sunday in winter; admission is $2.50.

The grave of **Chief Seattle (Sealth)** can also be found nearby, on the grounds of St. Peter's Catholic Mission Church adjacent to the town of Suquamish. Twin dugout canoes rest on a log frame over a stone that reads: "The firm friend of the whites, and for him the city of Seattle was named." In late summer, the Suquamish people hold their **Chief Seattle Days** celebration, continuing a tradition passed down to them by their forebears. Singing, dancing, canoeing, and a salmon bake (over alderwood pits) make up the feast, which is open to all visitors.

VASHON ISLAND

KIDS This bucolic, faintly countercultural isle is a short ferry ride from either Seattle or Tacoma (see Transportation in the Essentials chapter), and Vashon is wonderful for exploring by bicycle, though the first long hill up from the ferry dock is a killer. Few beaches are open to the public, but Dockton County Park (Stuckey Road and SW 260th Street) on Maury Island makes one nice pausing spot, and there's a lonely beach at Point Robinson (SW 243rd Place and Skalberg Road) presided over by a Coast Guard–maintained lighthouse.

FREE You could spend an entire day just touring all the island-based companies that market their goods both locally and nationally. **K2 Corporation** (19215 99th Avenue SW, 1-463-3631) gives tours of their ski manufacturing plant twice a day on Tuesdays and Thursdays, May through October. **SBC Coffee** (Vashon Center, Island Highway, 1-463-3932), which recently changed its name from Stewart Brothers Coffee to SBC (an acronym that Jim Stewart claims now stands for Seattle's Best Coffee), will show you around if they're in. **Wax Orchards** (131st Street SW, north of 232nd Street, 1-463-9735) makes preserves, natural sugarless sweeteners, apple cider, and fruit syrups. **Maury Island Farms** (Island Highway, 1-463-9659) cans fruit toppings and preserves. Many of these island products are available at **The Country Store and Farm** (20211 Vashon Highway SW, south of Vashon Center, 1-463-3655), a wonderful old-fashioned general store that also stocks potted herbs, gardening supplies, and natural-fiber apparel. Across the street is **Sound Food Restaurant** (204th Street SW at Island Highway, 1-463-3565), a mellow, wood-floored lunch stop with healthy soups, salads, sandwiches, and aromatic home-baked goods. Good espresso, too.

Round out your day with a return ferry trip from Vashon's other terminal, at

Tahlequah (99th Avenue SW, on the south end of the island), to Tacoma's magnificent **Point Defiance Park** (Pearl Street off Highway 16). (See Point Defiance Park in this section.) From there, retrace your rural route back to Seattle or shoot up the concrete I-5 corridor in a quarter of the time.

WHALEWATCHING

KIDS Gray whales cruise the Washington coast like clockwork twice a year during their migrations from their feeding grounds in the Bering Sea to their breeding domain off the shores of Baja, and back. Their predictability has resulted in both their near demise (during the whaling days at the turn of the century) and their amazing revival (at last count there were more than 21,000 grays).

Fortunately, whales have become less of a sport and more of an art. Whale watching requires only a good pair of binoculars (or a sharp pair of eyes), a good dose of patience, and a preferably windless day. Spring (March to May), as the playful whales meander north, is often the preferred season for whalewatching only because of the milder weather. The southward migration (late October to mid-December) offers an equally good opportunity to view these impressive mammals.

From shore, look for their spouts and occasionally a tail. Good whalewatching promontories include Ilwaco's North Head Lighthouse, Kalaloch, and Cape Flattery; however, the whales' movements are more expressive close-up. Over a half-dozen charter operations with knowledgeable skippers run out of Westport, a two-hour drive southwest from Seattle. For boat tours, plan on spending at least two hours out at sea (warm clothes are needed, even in summer). The Westport Chamber of Commerce (1-268-9422) has a complete list of the area's charters (roughly $25 a person).

More evasive, but in some ways a more exciting find, is the **orca**, or killer whale. These year-round residents of Puget Sound travel in family groups, known as pods, for their entire lives. Although they're occasionally sighted from the decks of a Washington State ferry, your chances of spotting a pod of these playful black and white creatures are far better in the San Juan Islands. Off San Juan Island, there are three resident pods (88 whales in all, including six calves born in 1990), which are often visible between June and September; their appearances then become more sporadic. **Lime Kiln Park**, on the southwestern end of the island, is America's only official whalewatching park.

The **Whale Museum** (PO Box 945, Friday Harbor 98250, 1-378-4710) offers exhibits on the natural history of whales and information about whalewatching.

WINERIES

FREE Washington's growing reputation as an excellent wine-producing region is a recent development. Although the first European grapes were planted here in the late 1800s, fledgling wine-making efforts were doomed by limited demand, and Washington vintners resigned themselves to producing ordinary dessert wines instead. It wasn't until the late 1960s that the potential of Washington's soil and climate was fully appreciated and the first real premium wines were made here. The number of wineries has since ballooned from a handful to more than 70, and Washington has become the second-largest wine-producing state in the country (after California). Most of this is happening in the sun-soaked Yakima River and Columbia River valleys east of the Cascades, but increasingly the Seattle area oenophile can find good tastings close to home.

At Pike Place Market, the retail outpost of **Staton Hills Winery** (1910 Post Alley, 443-8084, map: I8) hides behind one of Post Alley's trendy storefronts. There's a gift shop and a tasting room, but no tours (production takes place in Eastern Washington), although visitors can drop in anytime for a tasting.

A great number of wineries are concentrated on the Eastside. **Chateau Ste. Michelle** (14111 NE 145th Street, off Highway 202, 2 miles outside Woodinville, 488-1133, map: CC2) is the state's largest, occupying showplace headquarters on the 87-acre estate of local industrialist Henry Stimson. The chateau's wines have settled into a dependable (if somewhat unimaginative) style, but the facility itself offers the most comprehensive tour north of Napa Valley. The manicured grounds are beautiful and provide lovely picnicking opportunities. You can buy picnic food to go with your wine in the gourmet shop on the grounds. You'll get a different perspective on Ste. Michelle from across the street—at the **Columbia Winery**, that is. Recently moved from Bellevue, this is one of the pioneer wineries in the region. Their varied picnic facilities, where you can sprawl out after a wine-tasting (14030 NE 145th Street, Woodinville, 488-2776), offer a pretty view of Ste. Michelle's grounds.

Two smaller Woodinville wineries provide interesting counterpoint. **French Creek Cellars** (17721 132nd Avenue NE, Woodinville, 486-1900, map: BB2), in downtown Woodinville, offers informal drop-in tours every day. **Salmon Bay Winery** (13416 NE 177th Place, Woodinville, 483-9463) is too small an operation for tours, but you can sample their dry whites and cabernet sauvignon between noon and 5pm daily.

Kirkland's **Covey Run at Moss Bay** (107 Central Way, Kirkland, 828-3848, map: EE3) is the tasting room (open every day) for Eastern Washington-produced Covey Run wines. You can combine your visit with a stop at Hale's Ales, the microbrewery next door (see Breweries in this section).

One of the most innovative local vintners is **Paul Thomas Winery** (1717 136th Place NE, Bellevue, 747-1008, map: GG2), widely recognized for both its classic vinifera wines (cabernet sauvignon and merlot are noteworthy) and its unusual dry fruit wines. Informal tours and tastings are held Tuesday through Saturday.

Two other very worthwhile winery stops in the region are **Snoqualmie Winery** (see Snoqualmie and the Falls in this section) and **Bainbridge Island Winery** (see Ferry to Bainbridge Island under Major Attractions in Exploring Chapter).

Books in the Best Places series read as personal guidebooks, but our evaluations are based on numerous reports from local experts. Final judgements are made by the editors. Our inspectors never identify themselves (except over the phone) and never accept free meals or other favors. Be an inspector. Send us a report.

EXCURSIONS

MOUNT RAINIER

Mount Rainier, the abiding symbol of natural grandeur in the Northwest, is regarded with an almost religious reverence in these parts. Native Americans, who once inhabited the mountain's subalpine meadows, tell of the great goddess Tahoma, who fled her husband (Mount Baker) in a jealous rage but stretched her neck and looked back so many times along the way that she grew enormously tall. She finally stopped where she is today, 100 miles southeast of Seattle, and planted a garden around her. Today that "garden" is the 378-square-mile **Mount Rainier National Park** (98 miles SE of Seattle on Highway 706, 1-569-2211), a lushly forested reserve with the 14,411-foot-high active volcano as its centerpiece. From Seattle the view of the peak is often obscured by clouds or haze (the mountain creates its own weather), so when it appears it overwhelms the landscape and imparts to Seattleites a renewed sense of the dominance of nature in this region.

There are now four ways to experience the mountain: tour it by car, see it by train, hike its flanks, or climb to the summit. By far the favorite choice is to drive the two and a half hours to the National Park (entrance fee, $5). The most popular—and populated—visitor center is the one at **Paradise** (1-569-2211), which at 5,400 feet features the most complete tourist services, including a circular visitor center with a 360-degree view of the park and countrified accommodations (May to October) at the **Paradise Inn** (Highway 706, call 1-569-2272 for reservations). Paradise also features a network of easy hiking trails that wind past waterfalls, massive glaciers, and, in summer, through wildflower-laden meadows. (The road to Paradise is also open all winter, when the rest of the park is closed, so you can cross-country ski, snowshoe, or go inner-tubing; but be sure to carry tire chains in case road conditions require them.) The **Sunrise** visitor area at 6,400 feet offers another take on the peak, from the northeast side. It's the highest point in the park open to automobiles (though the road's closed when the snow falls, approximately mid-October through mid-June). Pack a picnic if you come—the food at both visitor centers is mediocre at best. The **Mount Rainier Scenic Railroad** is a good way to view Mount Rainier (there's a dinner train, too), but it never gets as close to the mountain as you'd like it to; call for reservations, 1-569-2588.

Those in search of more tranquil communion with the mountain can choose from 305 miles of more remote trails within the park. The best known of these is the spectacular **Wonderland Trail**, which makes a 95-mile circle around the mountain, passing through meadows of wildflowers, across streams, and past glaciers and alpine lakes. Backcountry permits, available at the ranger stations and visitor centers, are required for overnight camping. The park also has several **campgrounds**: at Ohanapecosh, White River, Cougar Rock, and Sunshine Point (the only one open year-round).

Finally, you can climb the mountain. There are two ways to do this: with **Rainier Mountaineering** (summer: Paradise 98397, 1-569-2227; or winter: 201 St. Helens Avenue, Tacoma 98402, 1-627-6242), the concessioned guide service; or in your own party after registering at one of the Mount Rainier National Park ranger stations (1-569-2211). Unless you can prove you're qualified to do it on your own—and this is a big, difficult, and dangerous mountain on which lives are lost every year—you must climb with the guide service. In a one-day training session they will teach you everything you need to know to make the climb; all you need is a sound heart. The climb itself takes two days and can be done any time from late May to mid-September.

MOUNT ST. HELENS

Washington State's now more famous mountain, the temperamental Mount St. Helens, simmers about two hours south of Seattle off I-5. On a clear day it is well worth the trip to see what remains of this mountain a decade after the incredible eruption of May 18, 1980 (it's 1,300 feet shorter than before the blast). The US Forest Service's wood-and-glass visitor's center (5 miles east of I-5 at exit 49, 1-274-6644; 1-274-4038 for weather conditions) sits in a stand of timber in the Gifford Pinchot National Forest near Silver Lake. The center commemorates the blast with excellent exhibits: a walk-through volcano, hundreds of historical and modern photos, geological and anthropological surveys, and a film documenting the mountain's destruction and rebirth. A network of trails, some of which accommodate wheelchairs, are good for short, scenic strolls.

For an even better view from the north, the side on which the blast carved out a crater 2 miles across and half a mile deep, take the I-5 turn east on Route 12 into Randall, then take Route 25 to connect with 26, which will lead you to **Windy Ridge**; park at the end of the road (closed winters). Many of the trails have been created or reconstructed to allow further exploration.

The big thrill is to see the volcano from the air—which can be arranged at any of the numerous charter flight companies in the nearby towns of Kelso and Longview—or to climb it (see Mountaineering/Climbing under Great Outdoors in Exploring chapter).

NORTH CASCADES

The Cascade Range is a source of great pride for both Eastern and Western Washingtonians, even though this lumpy barrier has created a vast division—economic, meteorological, and psychological—between the halves. One loop trip, a swing east across the mountains to the **Columbia River** then north and west back through the glorious **North Cascades**, is possible only in summer, when the **North Cascades Highway** is open. However, when the apple blossoms are blooming around Wenatchee in the spring, and the deciduous trees redden the forests near Leavenworth in the fall, you should set out to explore segments of the grand loop.

From Bothell at the north end of Lake Washington, jog eastward on Highway 522 until it meets up with Route 2, which follows the **Skykomish River** up to the ski resort of **Stevens Pass**. The old railroad towns along the highway offer little more than some big ice cream cones and camping provisions, but there are plenty of hiking trails that lead off from the pass or near Lake Wenatchee (see Hiking under Great Outdoors in Exploring chapter). From Stevens Pass to the Bavarianized village of **Leavenworth**, Route 2 becomes one of the most beautiful roads in the state, as it winds along the rapids of the Wenatchee River with the mountains looming beyond. It is especially dramatic in the fall, when the trees are ablaze with color. The numerous shops and restaurants in Leavenworth make for fine lingering (we favor the burgers and brews at **Gustav's Onion Dome Tavern**), but the town is best known as a base for all manner of Northwest outdoor pursuits: river rafting, climbing, spectacular hiking, riding, or late-season cross-country skiing. If you want to spend the night, try for a woodstove-heated room in the log **Mountain Home Lodge**.

Continuing east, pass lovely, mountain-ringed **Cashmere**—last of the great small towns—en route to **Wenatchee**, the apple capital of Washington. Here, the mighty basalt coulees of the **Columbia River** are set off by lacy orchards of fruit blossoms in the spring. You can get the best view of the river valley from **Ohme Gardens** (just north of town), a rocky promontory festooned with small, beautifully cultivated gardens from all climes. A good place for dinner is the **New Orleans Kitchen**, or when in Wenatchee, eat as the Wenatcheeans eat—at **The Windmill**, the last of a dying breed of classic American steak houses. You may want to finish the evening with a twilight drive up Route 97 as it follows the thundering Columbia to the town of **Chelan**, at the foot of Lake Chelan. The lake is a silvery wonder, thrusting like a fjord into the towering Cascades. Cruise it on an old-fashioned tour boat, *The Lady of the Lake*, or overnight at **Campbell's Lodge**, the venerable resort sprawled along its shore. The lake is jammed in the summer, so be warned.

Here the route turns again westward, entering the dry and remote valley of the **Methow River**. The Methow Valley is cross-country skiers' heaven (see Skiing under Great Outdoors in the Exploring chapter) blanketed with rolling rangeland and woven with trout streams. **Winthrop**, the "metropolis" of the valley, is gussied up to quasi–Wild West effect. It features the fully remodeled **Sun Mountain Lodge**, a four-seasons resort cantilevered 1,500 feet above the valley, with a knockout view and spacious rooms (most with their own fireplaces). As you progress farther west, Route 20 becomes the **North Cascades Highway** (closed in winter, short on food and gas anytime), justly famous for its awe-inspiring alpine vistas (especially the view from the **Washington Pass Overlook**) and trailhead access—indeed, one of the great highways in the country. As it descends toward the **Skagit River Valley**, you get fine views of **Ross Lake**, site of some engineering marvels by Seattle City Light.

The road comes down through the lush farmland of the Skagit, as beautiful a river valley as the state can offer, and the place to go for bald eagle watching (see River Rafting under Great Outdoors in Exploring chapter). Route 20 meets up with I-5 at **Burlington** for a quick 80-minute run south to urban civilization.

NORTH PUGET SOUND

For a day or weekend excursion, the corridor from Seattle to **Bellingham** offers myriad branching-off spots—east into the foothills of the Cascades, west toward the shimmering islands of Puget Sound—and unbeatable glimpses into Washing-con's beguiling small-town soul. First stop on a zigzag tour might be **Whidbey Island**, reached by ferry from **Mukilteo** (an hour north of Seattle). This long landfall is distinguished by its rolling farmland, sandy beaches, viewpoint parks, and more bed and breakfasts per capita than you might've thought possible.

Langley is the nicest village here (see Whidbey Island under Daytrips in this chapter). Its main street is studded with resort-town shops, and it offers a couple of charming accommodations, the newest of which is the Inn at Langley, and the **Whidbey Inn**, which clings magnificently to a bluff. At the northernmost tip of the island is **Deception Pass**, a treacherous and spectacular bridged gorge surrounded by an excellent state park for hiking and picnicking.

At this juncture you can head still westward to **Anacortes**, the beachside town best known as the ferry stop for the **San Juan Islands** (see description in this section), or east to **La Conner**. A trading post and fishing town since 1867, La Conner has reinterpreted its destiny to be that of a tourist mecca—benches and outdoor courtyards dot the main street (which runs alongside the Swinomish Slough), upscale country shops and eateries cater to seasonal inhabitants. Still, La Conner hasn't sold its soul; it's taken on some of the flavor of an art colony and retains a somewhat relaxed atmosphere (though you might not agree if you visit on a sunny weekend afternoon). The bakery at the cutesy **Calico Cupboard** is the place to pick up a shortcake bar or a bearclaw to go. Or drop in at Martin Hahn's esteemed **Black Swan**. Country accommodations (there's rarely a last-minute room to be found) are best at **The Heron** and **La Conner Country Inn** and a half dozen or so bed and breakfast inns. To help accommodate the increasing number of visitors, the **Channel House** is being constructed alongside the Swinomish Slough (scheduled to open summer of 1991).

La Conner, along with **Mount Vernon** to the east, is also regarded as the centerpiece of flower production in the **Skagit Valley**, whose fertile flatlands and meadows explode each April with the colors of blooming tulips, irises, and daffodils, against a backdrop of the snowy North Cascades.

One way to enjoy the region is to tour it on a bike; it's a flat, easy, and scenic pedal. Ambitious cyclists might continue farther north to **Chuckanut Drive**, a curving, coast-hugging stretch of road that features sweeping views of Puget Sound and the San Juan Islands (and a few restaurants, such as the legendary **oyster bar**). Chuckanut winds right into **Bellingham**, a livable city blending the provincial (stately old houses and neighborhood parks) and the enlightened (home of **Western Washington University**) to charming effect. We recommend an Italian meal at **Il Fiasco** and an overnight at the **Schnauzer Crossing** estate.

From here you're just half an hour from **Blaine** and its flagship resort, **Inn at Semiahmoo**, whose most appealing features are an outstanding, Arnold Palmer –designed golf course and breathtaking cruises to the San Juan Islands. You're just a few minutes from the border of British Columbia.

OLYMPIC PENINSULA

Even if you never get any closer to them than the view from Queen Anne Hill, you'll appreciate the Olympic Mountains on Seattle's western horizon; their jagged, snowy peaks loom like the set in some fantasy epic. The Olympic Peninsula can be an inhospitable place to live (thanks to isolation, winter gales, and rainfall that exceeds 200 inches a year), but it makes a breathtaking place to visit, when you can look at all that fog and drizzle as mood-enhancing.

The most direct route is via ferry to **Bainbridge Island**, where signs lead to the Hood Canal Bridge. On the way you'll come to **Poulsbo**, a corny but cheerful "historic" Scandinavian village with perhaps more murals per square foot of wall than any place outside the Vatican. The flashiest sits over **Sluy's Bakery**, along with the inscription "Giv Os Idag Vort Daglige Brod." Shops offer craftsy gifts in a similarly Nordic vein, and the nearby wharf provides a pretty stroll. If you want to spend the night (and enjoy a lavish, multicourse meal) in rural elegance, try the nearby **Manor Farm Inn**, on a working farm just north of Poulsbo.

Continue toward the **Hood Canal Bridge**, which sank spectacularly several years ago and was reopened in 1982. **Port Townsend** should be your next stop. Imbued with a salty, irreverent air, this historic port is full of graceful Victorian mansions and is home to an inordinate number of artists, writers, and other non-conformists (along with, we'll wager, the ghosts of sea dogs long departed), and bed and breakfast establishments. Port Townsend hosts a string of festivals and offers galleries, antique shops, bookstores, and a wooden boat–building school.

Of the legion bed and breakfasts, **The James House** continues to be one of the most pleasant (ask for a room with a view). When hungry head for the comfortable **Fountain Cafe**, though the best breakfasts are served at the **Salal Cafe**. **Fort Worden**, on the northern outskirts of town, hosts the bang-up summer arts series put on by **Centrum**. The Fort also provides terrific picnic grounds on beach or bluff.

Following the perimeter of the peninsula you're soon in **Sequim** (rhymes with "whim"), the driest town on the west side of the state (thanks to its spot in a "rain shadow") and, consequently, retirement heaven. **Dungeness Spit**, 6 miles northwest, is the longest sandspit in the country and a national bird refuge.

Port Angeles, an unpretentious, rough-edged working port, is a jumping-off point to the **Olympic National Park**. The park fills the interior of the peninsula and, along with inclement weather, ensures it a low human population and a huge amount of wildlife. Follow signs to the park headquarters, then up 17 miles of winding precipices to a subjective height that few mountains with twice the altitude can offer (the Olympics only make the 6,000- to 8,000-foot range). **Hurricane Ridge**, with restroom and snack facilities, is the hiking hub in these mountains (see Mountaineering under Great Outdoors in Exploring chapter), and the site of truly awesome vistas. A privately run ferry (Blackball) regularly runs between Port Angeles and Victoria (see Transportation in Essentials chapter).

A long side trip on Route 112 will bring you to **Neah Bay** on the Makah Indian Reservation; there are good salmon fishing opportunities here. This area, however, is best known for its museum and research center, which houses artifacts from an abortive (closed for budget cuts) archaeological dig at **Lake Ozette**. In 1970 the dig unearthed fascinating remnants of an ancient Makah Indian fishing village. **Cape Flattery**, at the peninsula's tip, is the end of the road. It's heralded as the most perfect land's end in the United States, with the longest unbroken expanse of water before it.

Highway 101 takes you along the southern length of glimmering Lake Crescent. And not far west and inland you'll find the **Sol Duc Hot Springs Resort,** where spartan accommodations are secondary in appeal to the tiled mineral hot-spring pools. If you push on around the peninsula on Highway 101, you'll see some of the eeriest scenery this planet allows: the perpetual, lushly desolate **rain forest,** most spectacular along the Bogachiel, Hoh, Queets, and Quinault river valleys. Moss-dripping, 300-foot firs and cedars, ribboned with ever-present fog and mist, create a melancholy mood in the forest.

Highway 101 heads inland about midway down the peninsula to lovely **Lake Quinault,** dammed by a glacial moraine. On its shore is the massive, cedar-shingled **Lake Quinault Lodge,** a historic resort with a venerable past. From here you can head back to Seattle via Aberdeen, Olympia, and Tacoma, or explore the coastal beaches north on State Highway 109 or south on State Highway 105.

THE PALOUSE

Thousands of years of winds deposited rich dust on rounded volcanic mounds, creating the rolling hills of southeast Washington—still known to many as **the Palouse** (which in French means "waves of blowing grass"). It's not grass but grain that the wind brushes in golden strokes up and down the hills. Stunning sunsets of deep orange and red cast a surreal light over these farmlands. The best times to travel through the Palouse are spring, when the green winter wheat carpets the hills, or fall, when the soft sun of Indian summer dances on the golden fields.

Though most of the area's diversions are of the small-town genre, there are several natural sites worth knowing about. The **Juniper Dunes Wilderness,** about 15 miles northeast of Pasco, is a 7,140-acre wilderness area that includes some of the biggest sand dunes (up to 130 feet high) and the state's largest natural grove of western junipers, some of them 150 years old. This geographic phenomenon, protected under the 1984 Washington Wilderness Act, is what remains of an ecosystem that once stretched 400 square miles south to the Columbia and Snake rivers. The Bureau of Land Management prohibits camping and fires in the park, as there is almost no water. The most scenic portion of the wilderness area is a short hike (2 miles) northeast of the parking area. Be sure to contact BLM before you set out, 509-353-2570.

In winter, people come to cross-country ski in the Blue Mountains and downhill at the nearby **Ski Bluewood** (509-382-4725). The area, not prime ski territory by some standards, is impressive for Eastern Washington; it gets more than 300 inches of snow a year, and has three chair lifts and a vertical rise of 1,125 feet.

About 30 miles southwest of Dayton is **Walla Walla** (a native phrase meaning "many waters"). The valley of the Walla Walla is an important historical area: Lewis and Clark came by in 1805, fur trappers set up a fort in 1818, and in 1836 Marcus Whitman built a medical mission west of the present town, where he and his wife, Narcissa, were murdered by Nez Percé Indians in the famous massacre of 1847. The town itself was founded in 1858 and has grown into a pleasant vale with fecund wheatlands all around (lentils, too) and a college anchoring the city. **Whitman College,** a private liberal arts college, lends a quiet dignity to the community, and the lovely woodsy campus is an excellent place for a stroll.

On the west edge of town is **Fort Walla Walla Museum** (Myra Road, 509-525-7703), a pioneer village that houses a museum with thousands of farming artifacts. **Whitman Mission National Historic Site,** 7 miles west of town, sketches out the story of the mission and massacre. The visitors' center is the only building, though the simple outline of the mission on the ground is strangely affecting (off US Route 12, follow the signs, 509-522-6360). Birders should visit the exotic birds at the **Pioneer Park Aviary** (at Alder and Division streets, 509-527-4527).

The townfolk are equally proud of the **Walla Walla Symphony**—touted as the oldest continuously operating symphony west of the Mississippi River—and the well-known **Walla Walla sweet onions.** So proud of these truly sweet alliums, in fact, that they throw a festival in the onions' honor in late July.

Grapes grow here too, and consequently some excellent **wineries** have sprouted throughout the region, most known for their cabernets, merlots, and chardonnays: Leonetti Cellar (1321 School Avenue, Walla Walla, 509-525-1428), Biscuit Ridge Winery (11 miles east of Walla Walla on Highway 12, Dixie, 509-529-4986), Woodward Canyon Winery (Highway 12, Lowden, 509-525-4129), Waterbrook (south of Lowden, off McDonald Road, 509-522-1918), and L'Ecole Number 41 (Lowden, 509-525-0940).

Pullman sprawls across the hills in the heart of the Palouse. The Palouse's largest town retains some of its cowpoke image but also has an international reputation as a university town, swelling with some 16,000 **Washington State University** students each September. Activities in Pullman, understandably, center on the university. On campus, you'll find the contemporary **Museum of Art** in the Fine Arts Center, which has mostly regional and faculty shows, the **Museum of Anthropology** in College Hall, the fascinating **Maurice T. James Entomological Collection** in Johnson Hall, and the extensive **Marion Ownbey Herbarium** in Herald Hall. Most opt for a tour of the **Beef, Dairy, and Swine Center** (509-335-5714), a controlled farm with dairy and beef cows. The center is tied in closely with the veterinary school, which has developed an excellent equestrian program (geared particularly to racehorses). On a hill above the university is the **Jewett Observatory** (509-335-8518), run by a couple of experts in black holes, and in Troy Hall there's **Ferdinand's,** famous for its milk shakes, Cougar Gold cheese, and ice cream—all made from WSU's own dairy herd (open weekends only).

Martin Stadium, home of the WSU Cougars football team, can now hold Pac 10 Conference–sized crowds; the baseball team plays on the new **Bailey Field** near the 12,000-seat **Beasley Performing Arts Coliseum,** venue for both the basketball team and frequent rock concerts (800-325-SEAT for tickets and an events calendar).

For a commanding view of the gentle Palouse, take the winding drive on Highway 195 (9 miles north of Colfax) to the top of the windy **Steptoe Butte.** Not far from Steptoe is the 105-acre **Palouse Falls State Park,** where the Palouse River pours over a 198-foot basalt cliff (higher than Niagara Falls) into a steep-walled basin. The falls are most spectacular from late winter to early autumn. Just downstream, near the confluence of the Palouse and Snake rivers, is the **Marmes Rock Shelter,** where remains of the earliest-known inhabitants of the Western

Hemisphere were discovered by archaeologists. This site is only accessible by canoe (canoe up the Palouse River from Lyons Ferry State Park).

SAN JUAN ISLANDS

Where Puget Sound meets the riptides of the Strait of Juan de Fuca and the Strait of Georgia, the San Juan Islands glisten like emerald stepping-stones across the waters. The archipelago lies just a couple of hours north of Seattle, but the passage across the Sound ensures a mood of exotic isolation that spells weekend heaven for city-frazzled Seattleites. That mood is bolstered by a slight change in climate: the islands are at the north end of the famous Juan de Fuca "banana belt," under a rain shadow that allows more sunshine and less rain than in Seattle. The islands also exude a contagious countercultural air that can't help but relax you after such mundane annoyances as, say, interminable lines for the chronically late (and expensive) ferries. Seaplanes and charter boats can also take you islandward (see Transportation in the Essentials chapter).

From the embarkation point of **Anacortes**, the first ferry stop is **Lopez Island**. Flatter and quieter than its fellows, Lopez beckons cyclists who come to purr past meadows of sheep, cattle, geese, and Shetland ponies on a 30-mile circuit that can be done in a day. Lopez also attracts kayakers, many of whom push off from the sandy shore of **The MacKaye Harbor Inn** to explore the nearby waterways, then come back for a dinner of surprising finesse and a countrified room for the night.

The only major island (there are 168 minor ones) with a tourist trade smaller than Lopez's is **Shaw Island**; it has neither resorts nor eateries, but there's a county park for camping and probably the only ferry landing in the country run by Franciscan nuns. Next up is **Orcas Island**, largest and hilliest of the isles. Though less urban than San Juan Island, it's far more tourist-attuned. **Rosario Resort** is Orcas's best-known resort, but it's almost always deluged with tour buses and presents a far less beguiling experience than, say, the beachy **Beach Haven Resort**, the elegant (but inland) **Turtleback Farm Inn**, or the funky, minimalist **Doe Bay Village Resort**, renowned for its hot springs. Shops and eateries are centered in **Eastsound**; we suggest a meal at the elegant **Christina's** or the New Mexican–style **Bilbo's Festivo**.

Orcas's greatest prominence, however, is geographic: the 2,409-foot **Mount Constitution**, whose granite lookout tower offers a grandstand view of the splendor of the islands. Surrounding the mountain is **Moran State Park**, with campsites and lakes for fishing.

Last stop (short of Canada) is **San Juan Island**, whose **Friday Harbor** ferry stop is the nearest thing on the islands to a town. In addition to an amiable stack of restaurants, craftsy galleries, and little hotels, "Friday" also boasts a **Whale Museum** and **whale-watching park**, from which you can view migrating orcas and minkes. The wonderfully imaginative **Cafe Bissett** is the one really distinguished restaurant in these islands; **The Duck Soup Inn** and **Springtree Eating Establishment and Farm** are close seconds. At the island's opposite end is the vintage, Gatsbylike **Roche Harbor Boatel and Resort**, but the bed and breakfasts that have sprung up all over the island present all sorts of lodging alternatives.

VICTORIA, BC

Though often besieged by tourists, the Anglophile's dream town of Victoria, on British Columbia's Vancouver Island, still makes a grand international daytrip or weekend getaway and combines many of the elements that make the Northwest so appealing. Getting there, for instance, is one of the best parts: you can zoom up quite scenically via seaplane or hydrofoil (see Transportation in the Essentials chapter) or board the Stena steamship from downtown Seattle.

The stately **Empress Hotel** dominates the scene as you enter Victoria's harbor; a regal property that recently underwent a sorely needed $45 million remodel, which made it a far more pleasant place to stay. But remember, you're in Victoria's authentic tourist mecca (linked by a conservatory to the new 1,500-person **Victoria Conference Centre**), so don't expect tranquil surroundings. High tea at the Empress is also overrated, and inundated with tourists. More intimate accommodations can be had at **The Oak Bay Beach Hotel**, where guests immerse themselves in Old World English charm, or **Abigail's** or **The Beaconsfield**—twin inns where luxury and pampering are the order of the day.

Plan to spend a Victoria visit browsing the English-tinged specialty shops along **Government Street**, ambling among the antiques on **Fort Street**, taking high tea in veddy proper English fashion, or chatting up the friendly (mostly elderly) locals at a brewpub. **La Petite Colombe** is centrally located for a fine French lunch; our dinner recommendations include the excellent, high-energy **Herald Street Caffe** or, a bit farther afield and much spendier, the elegant **Chez Daniel**.

An excellent information kiosk, **Tourism Victoria**, located right where the ships dock on Wharf Street, dispenses dependable information on sights. They will tell you, rightly, that **The Provincial Museum** is one of the finest in the country, with elaborately reconstructed street scenes from 1900, exhibits on early logging operations, and a stunning Northwest Coast Indian exhibit. Even antsy kids love it. **Butchart Gardens**, 17 miles north of the city in Brentwood Bay, is truly lovely and actually lives up to the hoopla and tourist attention. Plan to visit late in the afternoon (Burchart closes at 11pm in the summer), after the tourists have left. If your tolerance for tour buses is very low, you might rent a bike and wind north along the coast for winning views of the Strait of Georgia. It will give you an idea of the rugged beauty of this island, of which Victoria gives only a hint.

ESSENTIALS

▼

ESSENTIALS CONTENTS

TRANSPORTATION

AIRPLANES: SEATTLE-TACOMA INTERNATIONAL AIRPORT

Sea-Tac Airport (map: OO6) is located 13 miles south of Seattle, barely a half-hour freeway ride from downtown. Successful expansion over the past decade has turned it into one of the most convenient major airports in the country. It now serves more than 15 million passengers a year. A computer-controlled subway system links the main terminal to two adjoining satellite terminals; allow an extra 10 minutes to reach gates in those terminals.

The Seattle–King County Convention and Visitors Bureau operates an **airport information booth** by the baggage claim to provide tourist information. **FREE Travelers Aid**, on the ticketing level, offers assistance weekdays from 9:30am to 9:30pm and weekends from 10am to 6pm. Besides providing free information for getting around town, the organization will escort children, elderly people, and handicapped travelers within the airport for a $20 fee. **Sea-Tac's Operation Welcome** sends bilingual staff to meet incoming international flights and help foreign passengers with customs and immigration procedures. The **KIDS airport nursery**, on the ticketing level of the main terminal near the Northwest Gift Shop, has space for changing and feeding children. Chairs, couches, and cribs are provided free of charge.

For exhaustive information on airport services and operating conditions, call the **Skyline information line** (431-4444) from a push-button phone. You can choose from a long list of recordings on everything from parking availability to paging. The airport **Lost and Found** (433-5312) is located on the mezzanine level of the main terminal and is open from 8am to 12pm and 1pm to 4pm every day.

The **Sea-Tac parking complex** is a short walk from the main terminal through enclosed walkways. The first half hour of parking is free; after that it costs $2 for two hours, up to a maximum of $10 a day. Long-term parking is generally limited to 30 days. Credit cards are not accepted. Metered parking on the south end of the passenger pickup drive is available 24 hours a day at $1 an hour.

For less expensive **long-term parking**, try the numerous commercial parking lots in the vicinity of the airport. The following operate 24 hours a day and offer free shuttle service for their parking and car-rental patrons: **Budget Rent A Car** (17808 Pacific Highway S, 244-4010), **Thrifty Car Rental and Airport Parking** (18836 Pacific Highway S, 246-7565), **Mini-Rate Airport Parking** (20620 Pacific Highway S, 248-2442), **Dollar Airport Parking** (17600 Pacific Highway S, 433-6767).

The easiest way to get to Sea-Tac from downtown and vice versa is on the **Gray Line Airport Express** (626-6088). Going to the airport, the shuttle stops every half hour at the Stouffer Madison, Holiday Inn Crowne Plaza, Edgewater, Best Western Executive Inn, Four Seasons Olympic, Hilton, Sheraton, Westin, Warwick, and Roosevelt, in that order, from about 5am until midnight. It runs from about 6am to midnight from the airport baggage area, also at half-hour intervals. More runs are added in the warmer months. The ride is about 50 minutes from the Stouffer Madison to Sea-Tac. Cost is $11 round trip, $6 one way. Children pay $8.50 round trip, $4.50 one way.

Shuttle Express (622-1424 or 1-800-942-0711) provides door-to-door service to and from the airport, serving the entire greater Seattle area. The cost ranges from $14 from within the city to $18 one way from the Eastside and other outlying suburbs. Make reservations 24 hours ahead for trips to the airport. The shuttle from Sea-Tac operates 24 hours and requires no advance notice.

The Eastside is served by the **Suburban Airporter** (455-2353), which runs from the Bellevue Red Lion Inn to Sea-Tac every half hour to 40 minutes, 5:15am to 11:15pm. Call a day in advance for pickup at other Bellevue hotels. Cost is $9.50 one way and $15.50 round trip for adults, $5 one way and $9 round trip for children. Kids who can travel on your lap ride free. The shuttle will also pick up from Eastside homes and offices and at designated points in Bellevue, Kirkland, Totem Lake, and Redmond. Cost is $12 to $17, depending on distance. The shuttle from Sea-Tac (5:50am to 12:30am) departs from the baggage claim area.

Metro Transit (447-4800) offers the cheapest rides to the airport (Fare is $1.00 one way, $1.50 during rush hour), via two routes: the #174 (every half hour, seven days a week; can take up to an hour from downtown) and the #194 Express (a 30-minute ride that runs until midafternoon on weekdays, and infrequently on weekends; call for schedules). Both originate on Ninth Avenue at Stewart Street near the Greyhound depot, and make several stops along Stewart and along Second Avenue up to Pioneer Square. They stop on the baggage level of the airport.

AIRPLANES: CHARTER

Most airplane and helicopter charter companies are based at **Boeing Field/King County International Airport** (296-7380, map: KK6). Others can be found at the Renton City Airport, Thun Field in Auburn, and Snohomish County Airport (Paine Field). Services include flying lessons and aircraft rentals. Call the **Seattle Automated Flight Service Station** (767-2726) from a push-button phone for up-to-date weather reports and flight-related information.

AIRPLANES: SEAPLANES

See Organized Tours in the Exploring section

BUSES: METRO TRANSIT

It is exceptionally easy to get around downtown Seattle without a car. **Metro** (821 Second Avenue, 447-4800) operates close to 200 bus routes in Seattle and King County, most of them running at half-hour intervals. Many of the coaches are wheelchair accessible. Bus stops have small brown signs designating route numbers, and many have schedules posted. The fare is 75 cents in the city ($1.00

during peak commuter hours), $1.00 if you cross the Seattle city line ($1.50 peak). Exact fare is required. Seniors, youths, and handicapped riders are eligible for discount cards. Printed schedules and information on discounts and monthly passes are available at Metro headquarters and at more than 500 other locations in the greater Seattle area.

FREE One of Metro's most valued services is the **Ride Free Area** in downtown's commercial core. In the area bordered by the Waterfront, the freeway, Jackson Street to the south, and Battery Street (near Seattle Center) to the north, you can ride free on any Metro bus. In 1990, Metro completed a **bus tunnel** under downtown. The L-shaped tunnel, lying within the Ride Free Area, has five stations, from the Washington State Convention and Trade Center at Ninth Avenue and Pine Street to the International District. By bringing a large number of buses "downstairs," the tunnel is expected to relieve much of downtown's traffic congestion. The tunnel is also designed to accommodate a future light-rail system.

Metro also operates the **KIDS Waterfront Streetcar**. The vintage 1927 Australian mahogany and white ash trolleys run along Alaskan Way on the waterfront from **Myrtle Edwards Park** to **Pioneer Square** to Fifth and Jackson. They depart at 15-minute to half-hour intervals from 7am (weekdays) or 9am (weekends) until 6pm or 7pm, with extended hours in the summer. The ride takes 20 minutes from one end to the other and costs 75 cents (exact change only). Metro monthly passes and discount permits are good on the streetcar.

KIDS The downtown **Monorail**, which connects Seattle Center to the retail district, was a space-age innovation of the 1962 World's Fair. The 90-second, 1.2-mile ride is a great thrill for kids and remains the only stretch of rapid transit in town. A smart way to avoid the parking hassle at Seattle Center is to leave your car downtown and hop on the monorail at **Westlake Center** (400 Pine Street, map: J6). Adults pay 60 cents one way, kids under 5 are free. Trains leave every 15 minutes from 10am to midnight in summer, until 9pm weekdays and midnight weekends the rest of the year.

For trips from as far out as Darrington and Skykomish, **Community Transit** runs inexpensive buses on a regular schedule. Fare is $1.35 to Seattle from any point outside the city; within Snohomish County, 60 cents. Call for schedule and information (778-2185, 1-800-562-1375).

BUSES: OUT OF TOWN AND CHARTER

Greyhound Bus Lines (811 Stewart Street, 624-3456) has the greatest number of scheduled bus routes connecting Seattle to other cities. The station is within walking distance of the downtown retail core. For package service, call 628-5555. **Trailways** (728-5955) runs one scheduled southbound bus per day out of the Greyhound terminal.

Seattle has a number of **charter bus companies** that offer local and long-distance transportation. The following are among the most competitive: **Gray Line of Seattle** (624-5077), **Greyhound Charters** (628-5534), and **Cascade Trailways** (838-3465).

FERRIES

KIDS No activity better captures the spirit of Seattle than a ferry ride—both for commuters who rely on them as transportation to their jobs and for sightseers who ride them to enjoy the sunset and the city skyline. **The Washington State Ferry System** is the largest in the country (eight routes serve 20 terminal locations) and transports 18 million passengers a year. There are often more cars than space; as a walk-on passenger, your fare will be much cheaper, and you'll catch the ferry you want. (Cyclists pay slightly more.) Food service is available on almost all routes (beer and wine on some), but it's mediocre and overpriced.

Listed below are some of the destinations from Seattle and environs, with one-way summer prices for a car and driver. For **schedule and route information,** call 464-6400 or toll-free 1-800-542-7052. Schedules vary from summer to winter (with much longer lines in summer); credit cards are not accepted. Passengers to Canada must bring a passport or other proof of US citizenship.

Seattle–Winslow (Bainbridge Island)

The handiest daytrip from Seattle, this crossing takes 35 minutes and is often loaded with commuters. Jumbo ferries leave frequently from Pier 52 (map: M9) on the Seattle waterfront; cost is $6.65 one way for car and driver and $3.30 round trip for walk-on passengers. (See Ferry to Bainbridge Island under Major Attractions in the Exploring chapter.)

Seattle–Bremerton (Kitsap Peninsula)

This run, with its good views of the Navy Shipyard, also departs from Pier 52 (map: M9). The auto ferry takes 60 minutes and costs the same as the Bainbridge Island trip; the passenger-only ferry takes 35 minutes and costs $3.30 round trip.

Edmonds–Kingston (Kitsap Peninsula)

Kingston, close to the northern tip of the Kitsap Peninsula, is reached from Edmonds (about 15 miles north of Seattle; take the Edmonds–Kingston Ferry exit from I-5 and head northwest on Highway 104). The crossing takes 30 minutes and costs $6.65 one way for car and driver and $3.30 round trip for walk-on passengers.

Fauntleroy– Vashon Island–Southworth (Kitsap Peninsula)

Vashon, an idyllic retreat west of Seattle, can be reached from Pier 52 in downtown Seattle or from Fauntleroy in West Seattle. Pier 52 offers a passenger-only ferry that sails several times daily (cars must travel via Fauntleroy). The crossing takes about 30 minutes and costs $3.30 round trip. Vashon is the first stop on a trip from the Fauntleroy terminal in West

Seattle (exit 163 off I-5, map: LL9) to Southworth on the Kitsap Peninsula. The trip to Vashon takes 30 minutes, Southworth is reached in another 10 minutes (cost for either stop is $6.65 one way for car and driver, $3.30 for walk-on passengers). If you bring your vehicle along, you can drive south on Vashon to the **Tahlequah terminal.** A 15-minute ferry ride from here lies **Point Defiance Park,** on the outskirts of Tacoma ($4.50 one way). (See Daytrips section in the Outings chapter.)

Mukilteo–Clinton (Whidbey Island)

Mukilteo is 26 miles north of Seattle (take exit 189 from I-5). The 20-minute passage to pretty Whidbey Island costs $4.50 one way.

Keystone (Whidbey Island)–Port Townsend (Olympic Peninsula)

From Keystone, 25 miles up island from Clinton, another ferry reaches Port Townsend, one of the most enchanting towns in the state. The crossing takes 30 minutes and costs $6.65 one way for car and driver and $3.30 round trip for walk-on passengers.

Seattle–Kingston–Port Townsend (Kitsap Peninusula–Olympic Peninsula)

The Puget Sound Express (PO Box 930, Port Townsend, 98368, 1-385-5288, 1-800-628-1826) runs its twice-daily commuter boats during the week—with an extra trip on weekends—from Port Townsend to Pier 56 in Seattle and back; once during each round trip, they stop in Kingston (weekdays only). No cars on this trip, but they'll take bikes and freight (round trip, $33; one way, $20; bikes, $5).

Anacortes–San Juan Islands–Sidney, BC (Vancouver Island)

The San Juan Islands are reached by ferry from Anacortes (82 miles northwest of Seattle, exit 230 off I-5). The boat stops at Lopez, Shaw, Orcas, and San Juan islands for fares from $6.95 to $9.50 one way. Once a day (twice in summer), the ferry continues on to Sidney on British Columbia's Vancouver Island, just 15 minutes by car from Victoria. It returns in the early afternoon. During the summer, you can reserve space for your car on this crowded run. The tariff is $31.25 for the trip from Anacortes to Sidney (walk-on passenger fare is $6.05).

Seattle–Victoria, BC (Vancouver Island)

The *Victoria Clipper* and *Victoria Clipper II* (448-5000, 1-800-888-2535) is currently the only ferry service to Victoria from Seattle. They run two smooth-sailing, passenger-only catamarans and there are plans to add a fourth in the summer of 1991. Their 2½-hour voyages go up and back twice daily, all year round ($39 one way in winter, $44 in summer). Reservations are necessary, and if you make them two weeks in advance, you'll save $20 on a round-trip ticket.

Port Angeles (Olympic Peninsula)– Victoria, BC (Vancouver Island)

Black Ball Transport's MV *Coho* (1-457-4491) makes two runs daily in winter and spring and four runs daily in summer from Port Angeles to Victoria ($23 for car and driver one way, $5.75 for walk-on passengers).

TRAINS

Catch the train at King Street Station (Third and Jackson, map: P8) at the edge of the International District. For passenger information and reservations, call Amtrak at 1-800-872-7245. For baggage offices, package express, and lost and found, call 382-4128.

KEYS TO THE CITY

CATERERS

Of all the caterers in town, perhaps the most respected is **Market Place Caterers** (3001 E Yesler Way, 324-5900, map: 07), run by Joe McDonnal, who is as dependable (and creative) as he is artistic. **Catering by Mangetout** (1104 19th Avenue E, 329-1227, map: HH7) is known for elegant, beautiful presentation; try **Gretchen's Of Course** (1333 Fifth Avenue, 623-8194, map: K6) for the expertise of Gretchen Mathers, the best-known caterer in town. On the Eastside, **The Upper Crust** (10900 NE Fourth Avenue, Bellevue, 454-1686, map: HH3) colorfully caters many of the high-ticket parties in Bellevue. For other recommendations, see the Index preceding the Restaurants chapter.

CHILD CARE

KIDS Day Care Referral Service (461-3207) recommends licensed day-care operators Monday through Friday, 9am to 1pm. Two excellent day-care services are **Panda Dial-a-Sitter** (325-BEAR) and **Rent-a-Mom** (547-4080). **Nanny Brokers** (25620 SE 157th Street, Issaquah, 624-1213) is a placement service that can find the best live-in care for your child, wherever you live.

CHURCHES

The **Church Council of Greater Seattle** (4759 15th Avenue NE, 525-1213, map: FF6) provides referrals, by denomination, for the greater Seattle area.

CITY OF SEATTLE COMPLAINTS AND QUESTIONS

The **Citizen Service Bureau** (600 Fourth Avenue, Room 105, 684-8811, map: 07) hears complaints about the city, from potholes in the road to your humble opinion on the Metro Sewage Plant. It will refer you to the agency that can best handle the problem.

CONSULATES

The major ones are the **Canadian Consulate** (412 Plaza 600, Sixth Avenue and Stewart Street, 443-1777, map: I5), the **French Consulate** (400 E Pine Street, 323-6870, map: J1), the **British Consulate** (First Interstate Center, eighth floor, 999 Third Avenue, 622-9255, map: M7), the **Japanese Consulate** (1301 Fifth Avenue, Suite 3110, 682-9107, map: K7), and the **Mexican Consulate** (2132 Third Avenue, 448-3526, map: G7).

DATING SERVICE

Matchmaker in the Market (94 Pine Street, 621-9101, map: J8) lends a touch of credibility—and exclusivity (fees are $900 a year)—to the dating game, employing a combination of questionnaires, interviews, and videos to make matches.

DELIVERY

Most nonchain pizzerias deliver within a small radius of their operations. Your best bet is **Romio's Pizza** (2001 W Dravus Street, 284-5420; 917 Howell Street, 622-6878; 616 First Avenue, 621-8500); if you're anywhere in Queen Anne, Magnolia, Interbay, Capitol Hill, Eastlake, or downtown, one of their three branches will rush a fresh, hot dinner out to you. Of course, there's always **Pizza Hut**; call any branch to find out the branch nearest you.

Your options, however, are not limited to the pie. **The General's Bar-B-Que** (2023 E Madison Street, 328-2414) trucks chicken, barbecued beef, hot links, and pork ribs all over Seattle (there is a minimum order). And for something *really* different, the Seattle- and Redmond-based **Entrées** (881-0929 for orders) provides attractively packaged meals delivered to your door by a fully outfitted chef. The main dishes are in the $6–$15 range and come with a seasonal vegetable and bread; pastas come with bread only. Each dish also comes with precise microwave and oven instructions (for a little extra, they'll cook it for you); a $10 minimum order earns free delivery in downtown Seattle, the University District, Bellevue, and Redmond. Call for a menu.

DISCRIMINATION

The **Seattle Human Rights Department** (105 14th Avenue, 684-4500, map: HH7) helps people who feel they have been discriminated against on the basis of race, age, sex, religion, marital status, political or sexual orientation, handicaps, and so on.

DRY CLEANERS AND TAILORS

The Four Seasons Cleaners, named best in the *Weekly* Reader's Poll, has five locations throughout the area: 1800 E Olive Way, 322-3200 (map: GG7); 2203 Eastlake Avenue E, 324-4341 (map: GG7); 11016 Meridian Avenue N, 364-3636 (map: DD7); 14602 15th Avenue NE, 365-8588 (map: BB7); and 7800 Sunset Highway SE, Mercer Island, 232-7666 (map: II4). Max Custom Tailoring (310 Stewart Street, 624-4393, map: I6) provides the same service for men, Monday through Friday.

FOREIGN EXCHANGE

Money-changing facilities are available at almost every major bank. Deak International (906 Third Avenue, 623-6203, map: M7; 10630 NE Eighth Street, Bellevue, 462-8225, map: HH3; and 2505 S 320th Avenue, Federal Way, 941-8878) is a foreign exchange broker. Several foreign banks also have branches in Seattle: Bank of Tokyo (1201 Third Avenue, Suite 1100, 382-6000, map: L7), Hokkaido Takushoku Bank (1001 Fourth Avenue, Suite 3920, 624-0920, map: L6), Hongkong & Shanghai Banking Corp. (705 Third Avenue, 622-8490, map: N7), Sumitomo Bank (1201 Third Avenue, Suite 5320, 625-1010, map: L7), and Taiyo Kobe Bank (900 Fourth Avenue, 682-2312, map: M6).

FOREIGN VISITORS

There is a multitude of services for the foreign visitor or resident who does not speak English as a first language. The American Cultural Exchange (3123 Eastlake Avenue E, 726-0055, map: GG7) provides English-language classes (Intensive English Language Institutes) for foreigners who want to study here. They also run the downtown Language School (where English-speakers can learn any of up to 16 languages) and arrange for summertime exchanges and visits by foreigners to American homes. Another American Cultural Exchange service, the Seattle Translation Center, provides both interpreters and written translations. The Central Seattle Community Health Centers (105 14th Avenue, 324-7835) is an umbrella organization for two hospital translation services, the Community Health Interpretation Service (324-7835), which provides translators for all the major Indo-Chinese languages, and Hospital Interpretation Services (324-7705), a 24-hour service providing translators for hospital patients (call 324-7835 before 8:30am or after 5pm in an emergency). The Milmanco Corp. (651 Strander Boulevard, Suite 100, 575-3808) can help those involved in international business who are in need of technical written translations (from foreign languages). Rates vary. The FREE Red Cross Language Bank (323-2345) is a volunteer-operated institution that provides on-call interpretive assistance at no charge in emergency and crisis situations.

GROCERY DELIVERY

The Medina Grocery (800 Evergreen Point Road, Bellevue, 454-3101, map:

HH4) delivers free of charge within the city of Bellevue with a minimum order of $20. At this time there is no grocery delivery to the downtown area.

HANDICAPPED AID

The **Resource Center for the Handicapped** (20150 45th Avenue NE, 362-2273, map: AA6) provides vocational training and placement services for handicapped citizens. The **Easter Seal Society** (521 Second Avenue W, 281-5700, map: GG8) sells *Access Seattle,* a guidebook listing local buildings with handicapped access. One copy is free if you stop by, $1 otherwise.

INFORMATION

Seattleites are known to be helpful to visitors; if that doesn't suffice, try the **Westlake Information Center,** on the third level of Westlake Center, for a wealth of Seattle information, from where to eat cheaply to what in the world a geoduck is. **Seattle Public Library Quick Information Line** covers a larger territory; dial 386-INFO to find out the answer to anything you could possibly think to ask. **The Seattle Survival Guide** (published by Sasquatch Books and available in bookstores) is a thorough, reliable resource for anyone who wants to get anything at all done in this maze of a city.

LEGAL SERVICES

Lawyer Referral Services (623-2551) puts customers in touch with lawyers who are members of this association. The cost is $20 for the first half hour, with a *pro bono* program for low-income clients. **Evergreen Legal Services** (464-5911) is a federally funded program that provides free consultation for clients with very low incomes.

LIBRARIES

KIDS There are 24 branches of the Seattle Public Library system located throughout the city, offering—besides books—lectures, films, and many other activities. Call the individual branches for specific events or questions. The **FREE Main Branch** (1000 Fourth Avenue, 386-4636, map: M6) leads tours Wednesdays and Saturdays at 2pm and has a Quick Information number, 386-INFO. For mobile library service, call 684-4713. The **King County Public Library** (General Information, 684-9000) has 36 branches countywide, as well as a traveling library service.

LIMOUSINE SERVICE

Washington Limousine Service (8016 Ashworth Avenue N, 523-8000, map: EE7) has been in business for 35 years, providing safe and efficient service.

Look for **FREE**—*it means this attraction or event is free of charge.*

LOST CAR

Begin by calling 684-5444 to find out if your car is listed as towed and impounded in auto records. If they have no record, it's been stolen—call 911.

MEDICAL/DENTAL SERVICES

Medical Communications Service (622-6900) can put you in touch with a doctor 24 hours a day. Dentist Referral Service (443-7607) provides comparable dental assistance. Chec Medical Centers (drop-in health clinics) have eight locations around town. Call 643-9140 for the address and phone number of the Chec nearest you.

NEWSPAPERS

The two dailies in town have merged their business functions under a joint operating agreement, but maintain entirely separate editorial operations. *The Seattle Times* (1120 John Street, 464-2000, map: F2) is the evening paper, heavy on graphic style and strong on features. It offers FREE free tours during the school year (call 464-2285; reservations required). The early-morning *Seattle Post-Intelligencer* (101 Elliott Avenue W, 448-8000, map: B9) is dowdier, but often quicker with local news. Both papers have improved markedly in recent years, although the differences between them have shrunk. *Seattle Weekly* (1931 Second Avenue, 441-5555, map: H7) provides coverage of politics, the arts, and civic issues, and has recently spawned a counterpart on the Eastside, *Eastsideweek* (123 Lake Street S, Kirkland, 827-5550). Both hit the newsstands on Wednesdays. Also on the Eastside, the Bellevue *Journal-American* (1705 132nd Avenue NE, Bellevue, 455-2222, map: GG2) provides a local voice and a hedge against the hegemony of the *Times*.

PET BOARDING

Pets Are Inn (PO Box 98198, 839-PETS) is a licensed network of screened private caretakers who will board your cat or dog (any breed, but no biters) in their own homes. They also ship and receive animals at the airport.

PUBLIC OFFICIALS

Seattle's mayor is Norm Rice (600 Fourth Avenue, 12th floor, 684-4000, map: O6). The King County Executive is Tim Hill (516 Third Avenue, 296-4040, map: O7). The Seattle City Council consists of: George Benson (684-8801), Tom Weeks (684-8805), Paul Kraabel (684-8807), Jane Noland (684-8803), Sue Donaldson (684-8806), Dolores Sibonga (684-8802), Sam Smith (684-8800), Jim Street (684-8808), and Cheryl Chow (684-8804). All have offices at 600 Fourth Avenue (map: O6). The members of the King County Council are: Audrey Gruger, District No. 1 (296-1001); Cynthia Sullivan, District No. 2 (296-1002); Brian Derdowski, District No. 3 (296-1003); Lois North, District No. 4 (296-1004); Ron Sims, District No. 5 (296-1005); Bruce Laing, District No. 6 (296-3457); Paul Barden, District No. 7 (296-7777); Greg Nickels, District No. 8

(296-1008); and **Kent Pullen,** District No. 9 (296-1009). All have offices at the King County Courthouse at Third and James (map: O7).

PUBLIC RESTROOMS

These are difficult to find downtown, with a couple of exceptions: at the base of the ramp in the Main Arcade of **Pike Place Market** (Pike Street and Western Avenue, map: J8) and at **Freeway Park** (Sixth Avenue and Seneca Street, map: L5). Many larger parks also have public facilities (although most are only open until dusk).

SALON CARE

In-home **Personal Care Services** (285-3582) brings hair care, manicures, pedicures, and other salon services to the privacy of your home, hospital bed, or hotel room.

SENIOR SERVICES

The **Senior Information Center** (1601 Second Avenue, 448-3110, map: I7) provides a list of resources available to seniors. **The Mayor's Office for Senior Citizens** (618 Second Avenue, 684-0500, map: N7) provides programs for low-income seniors, employment programs, educational workshops, social events, notary services, and other resources.

SERVICE STATIONS-ALL NIGHT

Downtown, **Mike Beasley's Chevron Service** (Denny Way and Stewart Street, map: H2); in the North End, **Lynnwood Shell** (19930 44th Avenue W, Lynnwood, 778-2243); in the South End, **Tukwila Texaco** (13138 Interurban Avenue S, 244-3520, map: MM5); on Mercer Island, **Sunset Chevron** (7725 Sunset Highway SE, Mercer Island, 232-2810, map: II4); in Edmonds, **Westgate Chevron** (9930 Edmonds Way, Edmonds, 778-2700); in West Seattle, **West Seattle Shell** (9200 35th Avenue SW, 935-2729, map: II9).

SHOE REPAIR

Shoe Stop, with cheerful, while-you-wait service, has several locations throughout the area, including Capitol Hill (425 Broadway E, 328-9496, map: HH6); downtown (926 Third Avenue, 467-6114, map: M7); and Bellevue (Bellevue Square, 451-1985, map: HH4).

TELEPHONE NUMBERS

AAA of Washington 448-5353
AIDS Hotline 587-4999

Alcoholics Anonymous............................ 587-2838
Ambulance 911
Amtrak 1-800-872-7245
Animal Control 386-4254
Auto Impound 684-5444
Better Business Bureau 448-8888
Birth and Death Records 296-4769
Blood Bank.. 292-6500
Chamber of Commerce 389-7200
Child Protective Services Crisis Hotline 721-4306
City Light.. 625-3000
City of Seattle Information..................................... 386-1234
City Parks Information and Scheduling Office 684-4075
Coast Guard 286-5450
Coast Guard 24-Hour Emergency................... 1-800-592-9911
Community Information Line 447-3200
Crisis Clinic 461-3207
Customs.. 442-4676
Dial-A-Story (Seattle Public Library) 386-4656
Directory Information....................... 1-555-1212 (25 cents per call)
Domestic Violence Hotline................................. 1-800-562-6025
DWI (Drunk Drivers) Hotline............................ 1-800-223-7865
Emergency Feeding Program................................. 723-0647
Environmental Protection Agency.......................... 442-1200
FBI... 622-0460
Fire... 911
Housing Hotline... 296-7640
Immigration and Naturalization Service 442-5956
Internal Revenue Service...................................... 442-1040
Locksmith, 24-Hour AAA Locksmith 325-1515
Lost Pets... 386-7387
Marriage Licenses... 296-3933
Metro Information... 447-4800
Missing Persons.. 633-1009
Northwest Ski Report 634-0071
Passports 442-7941
Planned Parenthood 328-7700
Poison Center.. 526-2121
Post Office Information 285-1650
Rape Relief... 632-7273
Red Cross.. 323-2345
Red Tide Hotline 1-800-562-5632
Seattle–King County Convention and Visitors Bureau.................... 461-5840
Seattle–King CountyDepartment of Public Health 296-4600
Self-Defense (Alternatives to Fear) 328-5347

Look for FREE—it means this attraction or event is free of charge.

Sexual Assault Clinic 223-3047
Shelter for Battered Women (New Beginnings) 522-9472
Sports Organizations:
   Longacres Park (horse racing).. 226-3131
   Seattle International Raceway (cars) 631-1550
   Seattle Mariners (baseball)... 628-3555
   Seattle Seahawks (football) 827-9777
   Seattle SuperSonics (basketball) 281-5850
   Seattle Thunderbirds (hockey) 728-9121
   University of Washington Huskies 543-2200
University of Washington... 543-2100
State Patrol.. 455-7700
Suicide Prevention... 461-3222
Ticketmaster... 628-0888
Time.. 1-976-1616 (30 cents a call)
Travelers Aid Society.. 461-3888
Voter Registration... 344-5282
Washington State Ferries 464-6400
Weather.. 526-6087
Zip Code Information.. 285-1650

TELEVISION STUDIO AUDIENCES

FREE **KING-TV**, the local NBC affiliate (333 Dexter Avenue N, 448-5555, map: D4), has three open-audience shows: a lighthearted morning interview program "Seattle Today," a weekly community affairs show called "Celebrate the Differences," and the local comedy sensation "Almost Live" (call 448-5555 for tickets). The local CBS affiliate, **KIRO-TV** (2807 Third Avenue, 728-7777, map: D8), offers one open-audience program, "Sports TV," a weekly sports magazine show; call 728-8338 for tickets. **KOMO-TV**, the ABC affiliate (100 Fourth Avenue N, 443-4000, map: D7) has two: "Northwest Afternoon," an interview show (one of only two in the country offering complete soap opera updates; 443-8333), and the good, often controversial "Town Meeting" (443-4186). Call each station for information on free tours.

TOWING

Lincoln Towing (609 Fairview Avenue N, 622-0415, map: E1) provides Seattle with 24-hour towing. **Eastside Towing** (12816 NE 21st Place, Bellevue, 747-3191, map: GG3) provides the same service for Bellevue and the Eastside.

UNIVERSITIES

The **University of Washington**, the largest of the Washington State public universities, has an Information Center (4014 University Way NE, 543-9198, map: FF6) and the second-largest university bookstore in the country (4326 University Way NE, 634-3400). **Seattle Pacific University** (3307 Third Avenue W, map:

FF8) is a private college associated with the Free Methodist Church; their information line is 281-2000. **Seattle University**, a private Catholic school located at the corner of Broadway and Madison in Capitol Hill (map: N1), has a general information line at 296-6000.

VETERINARIANS, EMERGENCY AND WEEKEND SERVICE

Downtown, contact **Emergency Seattle Veterinary Hospital** (1101 Westlake Avenue N, 284-9500, map: FF7); in the North End, **Emergency Service Hospital/Northeast Veterinary Hospital** (9505 35th Avenue NE, 523-1900, map: DD6); in the South End, **Emergency Veterinary Service/South Seattle** (112 SW 157th Avenue, 246-1211, map: OO7); on the Eastside, **Arrowwood Animal Hospital** (2975 156th Avenue SE, Bellevue, 641-8414, map: II2).

BUSINESS SERVICES
CONFERENCES, MEETINGS, AND RECEPTIONS

Most hotels and inns and many restaurants have meeting rooms for rent. (See Private Rooms index heading preceding Restaurants chapter.) The following is a list of other rental facilities appropriate for business meetings, private parties, and receptions. Private functions can also be held at branches of the Seattle Public Library, most museums, the University of Washington (which has numerous halls, auditoriums, and meeting rooms), and other educational facilities.

The Atrium
5701 6th Ave S, 763-0111
(map: JJ7)

The Atrium holds up to 900 people (cocktail party–style) in a skylit, three-story covered courtyard with plenty of tall greenery. A great place for weddings, parties, and reunions. You must use the Butcher restaurant kitchens for catering. Good PA system.

Battelle Seattle Conference Center
4000 NE 41st St,
525-3130 (map: FF6)

Battelle Memorial Institute, a nonprofit research organization, operates this fully equipped conference facility on its attractive, 18-acre wooded grounds not far from the University of Washington. Battelle has 25 guest rooms, and the 11 carpeted conference rooms can accommodate up to 110 people. Catering is provided by Battelle. Rental policies are geared toward conferences of one day or longer. No weddings, but business-sponsored receptions are OK.

Camp Long
5200 35th Ave SW,
684-7434 (map: JJ8)

See Parks and Beaches section of Exploring chapter.

CONFERENCES, MEETINGS, AND RECEPTIONS

Chateau Ste. Michelle
1411 NE 145th St,
Woodinville, 488-4633
(map: CC1)

In the quaint Manor House on the grounds of this East-side winery—an original early-1900s farmhouse—you can hold a meeting or reception for up to 80 people. The house boasts hardwood floors, a cozy fireplace, and formal gardens on either side. The Barrel Room accommodates gatherings of up to 250. Both rooms include custom, in-house catering.

Chinese Room
Smith Tower, 506 2nd
Ave, 622-4004 (map: O7)

Resembling a Chinese museum with its deep-red carpets and hand-carved wooden furniture, this sky-level room in the classic 1914 Smith Tower is a stunningly elegant backdrop for a party. Other features include ceramic ceiling tiles, an outside wraparound balcony, and express elevator service (complete with tuxedo-clad elevator operator). The Chinese Room accommodates 150 for cocktail party–style receptions. Bring your own caterer.

Court in the Square
401 2nd Ave S, 467-5533
(map: P8)

A glassed-in alley between two brick buildings, the Court in the Square has a classy French Quarter ambience. A retractable glass roof allows for dancing under the stars. It's available evenings and weekends for parties of up to 300; all catering is done by the very high quality in-house restaurant. A favorite among wedding planners, who must book six months to a year in advance.

Daughters of the American Revolution House
800 E Roy St, 323-0600
(map: GG6)

Weddings and dance parties are the main events in this classic Capitol Hill mansion, patterned after George Washington's Mount Vernon. Downstairs is Colonial and genteel; rent it by itself or along with the barny upstairs ballroom for a total capacity of 250 people. Bring your own caterer and sound system; they have two pianos. Midnight curfew.

Gold Creek Lodge
16020 148th Ave NE,
Woodinville, 296-2976
(King County Recreation)
(map: BB2)

The wooded trails of Gold Creek Park surround this rustic, pine-paneled room. The place holds 60 people for a meeting or reception, and two huge lofts sleep 30 (bring your own sleeping bags).

Kiana Lodge
14976 Sandy Hook Rd
NE, Poulsbo, 598-4311

The waterfront lodge and longhouse at Kiana on the Kitsap Peninsula have a genuine Northwest flavor. You can even dock your boat right in front. The specialty is alder-grilled salmon dinners for large groups (up to 1,000). Kiana is usually booked several months in advance for weekend weddings. No overnight accommodations.

Langston Hughes Cultural Center
104 17th Ave S,
684-4757 (map: HH6)

A large multipurpose room, 287-seat theater, and restaurant-capacity kitchen are available for rent at this Seattle Parks Department facility. At press time the center was being remodeled; scheduled to reopen in spring 1991. Fees are reasonable and determined on a sliding scale.

Longacres Park
1621 SW 16th St,
Renton, 624-2455
(map: OO4)

Four large rooms facing the racetrack are available for private receptions and meetings year-round, as long as the Emerald Racing Association continues to lease the facility from Boeing. The largest room holds 400 people; combine rooms for a capacity of 1,000. Longacres does the catering. A popular spot for reunions and proms.

Lutheran Bible Institute
Providence Heights,
Issaquah, 392-0400

Religious groups and nonprofit organizations can rent this comfortable Issaquah conference facility with rooms seating 12 to 400 people. The institute has dorm rooms and motel-style lodgings, dining rooms, a gym, and an indoor swimming pool. No smoking or alcohol consumption anywhere on the grounds, but you can eat (they provide catering).

The Meeting Place in the Market
93 Pike St, Suite 307,
447-9994 (map: J8)

Located in the renovated Economy Market Building in Pike Place Market, The Meeting Place has two unprepossessing rooms (one with a bay view) for rent on an hourly basis. They can be used separately or together, with a maximum capacity of 200. No in-house catering service, but they'll assist you with planning. The facility has a small pantry with a microwave oven and a refrigerator.

Museum of Flight
9404 E Marginal Way S,
764-5706 (map: LL6)

This museum (see listing in the Exploring chapter) houses an impressive cross-section of aviation history; you can hold a meeting for up to 3,000 people in the Great Gallery, where these great machines are hung. A stroll around the balcony above the gallery takes you to the view lounge (a view, that is, of Boeing Field to the east and Mount Rainier to the south), with its handsome chrome wet bar. Best atmosphere: the Red Barn, original home of Boeing, where a stripped-down Curtiss Jenny occupies center stage. Bring your own caterers, but they'll help out with the planning.

Museum of History and Industry

Located on Lake Washington near the Arboretum, the museum rents out a 460-seat theater/auditorium and a

2700 24th Ave E,
324-1126 (map: FF6)

carpeted room that accommodates 200 people. The room has an adjoining kitchen. Meetings and parties only, no wedding receptions. Facilities are rented in eight-hour blocks. Plenty of parking in the museum lot.

Robinswood House
2432 148th Ave SE,
Bellevue, 455-7850
(map: II2)

A comfortable, furnished two-story house that holds up to 120 people for parties is part of a well-tended 60-acre park. Parts of the house can be rented for smaller gatherings on weekdays (closed Monday), but on weekends the entire facility is rented as a unit. Robinswood is a popular place for weddings but is not well suited to live band music. Bring your own caterer.

Seattle Aquarium
Pier 59, Waterfront Park,
386-4320 (map: J9)

Several hundred people can party right in the exhibit area, amid the fish and octopi. The underwater dome is an especially atmospheric spot for wedding ceremonies. The Aquarium also has a conference room that will hold 20 people, and a 242-seat auditorium. Available evenings only; bring your own caterer.

Seattle Art Museum
Volunteer Park, E
Prospect St and 14th Ave
E, 625-8911 (map: GG6)

The Garden Court is an open, airy room perfect for receptions; you can arrange to have the two adjoining galleries open for wandering. The activities room has a kitchen and a bay window overlooking the park, and the auditorium (which seats 220) is equipped with all the necessary audiovisual equipment. The Volunteer Park building is due for renovation when the new downtown museum opens; no word as yet on the future status of the meeting rooms.

Seattle Center
305 Harrison St,
684-7202 (map: GG7)

The largest and most varied meeting and conference center in the city, Seattle Center can handle just about any need, from round tables for 8,000 to small monthly workshops. The center also can provide audiovisual equipment, catering services, planning assistance, and support staff.

Seattle Trade Center
2601 Elliott Ave,
441-3000 (map: E9)

The Seattle Trade Center, with over 50,000 square feet of flexible space, rents out mostly for large trade fairs and exhibitions. It will also accommodate conferences, seminars, and banquets for 50 to 700 people. Use their catering or bring your own. No audiovisual equipment available.

Skansonia
2505 N Northlake Way,

This retired Washington State ferry, permanently docked on Lake Union next to the Lakeside Restau-

545-9109 (map: FF7)

rant, is available for groups of up to 500. Besides the romance of it all, there's a large dance area, dining room, parlor, two garden decks, grand piano, full stereo system, working fireplace, and a postcard view of the city. Weddings and corporate parties are its main business. In-house catering is available. Wheelchair accessible.

Snoqualmie Winery
1000 Winery Rd,
Snoqualmie, 1-392-4000

The keg-filled wine cellar dresses up well for special occasions, the retail shop has a nice fireplace, and the terraced lawn has a wonderful view and picnic tables.

Space Needle
Seattle Center, 443-9800
(map: C6)

The rooms themselves aren't much, but turn outward for a spectacular 360-degree view from 100 feet up. There are three rooms with a total capacity for about 250; the Space Needle provides all catering.

St. Thomas
Conference Center
14500 Juanita Dr NE,
Bothell, 823-1300
(map: CC5)

This former seminary sits on 50 wooded acres next to a large state park on the northeastern end of Lake Washington. It is available to nonprofit groups only. Five conference rooms hold 30 to 150, and there are overnight accommodations for up to 22 people. Buffet meals are served three times a day; reception catering available.

Stimson-Green Mansion
1204 Minor Ave,
624-0474 (map: L2)

This stately turn-of-the-century brick Tudor mansion was home to two of Seattle's prominent industrialist families—the Stimsons and the Greens—and is now a designated historical site. Since the early 1980s, the 35-room house has been open for public tours and used for meetings, parties, and weddings. We like it best on wintry evenings, when the place is infused with a rich, cozy glow. It's pricey, but it exudes opulence.

Union Station
401 S Jackson St,
623-2434 (map: Q7)

Entertain up to 1,500 of your closest friends in the enormous Great Hall of Union Station, once the Grand Central of the Northwest. Special Events Catering provides the food service. With its high ceilings, mosaic tile floor, and stately ambience, Union Station is a top-choice venue for political fund-raisers, wedding receptions, and corporate parties.

Washington State
Convention and
Trade Center

This gargantuan new facility draped across I-5 has reception rooms that accommodate 50 to 4,000 people, exhibit halls, press facilities, conference rooms, ballrooms, indoor parking for 900 cars, and wheelchair ac-

*800 Convention Place,
464-5305 (map: L5)*

cessibility. Catering is available. The center is within walking distance of all major downtown hotels.

COMPUTER RENTALS

Bit-by-Bit Computers
*15092 NE 40th St,
Bldg Q, Redmond,
881-5353 (map: FF1)
Mon-Fri*

Rentals by the week or month, delivery to anywhere in the state. IBM, Compaq, Apple Macintosh, and IBM-compatibles. A complete system with printer runs about $70 to $175 a week. Free on-site repair, no in-house rentals. Known for accommodating service.

BCSR
*15660 NE 36th St, Suite
105, Redmond, 885-3454
(map: FF1)
Mon-Fri*

Business Computer Systems Rentals rents IBM, Compaq, Apple Macintosh, Toshiba, and Zenith by the day, week, or month. One- to three-year leasing available, also rent-to-buy. No in-house rentals, but they'll deliver to you and make on-site repairs. Pricier than most other computer rental places.

COPY SERVICES

Kinko's
*4125 University Way NE
(and branches), 632-0374
(map: FF6)
Every day.*

Kinko's has three locations near the University of Washington, one on Capitol Hill, and one downtown. The main U District store is open 24 hours, the others are open late. Services include copying, in-house typewriter rentals, résumé service, and passport photos. Service is quick and friendly, but the quality of the work can vary.

Superior Reprographics
*1925 5th Ave (and
branches), 443-6900
(map: I5)
Mon-Sat*

A complete graphics and copy center, with black-and-white and color copying, offset and diazo printing. Delivery within city limits. No color copies on weekends.

MESSENGER AND DELIVERY SERVICES

**Bucky's Messenger and
Delivery Service**
*448-9280
Mon-Fri*

Speedy service from radio-dispatched bicycle couriers. Delivery of messages and packages up to 20 pounds throughout Seattle and to the Eastside. Cars will deliver up to 400 pounds to Tacoma, Everett, and Bremerton.

Elliott Bay Messenger

Considered the best and fastest bicycle courier service

728-8505
Mon-Fri

downtown. Weight limit 20 pounds. Rush deliveries within a half hour, regular delivery within an hour. Car deliveries to all of the Puget Sound area.

Federal Express
282-9766
1-800-238-5355.
Mon-Sat

Worldwide delivery and next-day service within the continental US and to parts of Alaska and Hawaii and Puerto Rico. Eight offices in greater Seattle, three of them downtown. Limit 150 pounds per package on express items; no limit on two-day service. The toll-free number is for 24-hour customer service.

Fleetfoot Messenger Service
728-7700
Mon-Fri

Riders on radio-dispatched mopeds will deliver up to 20 pounds downtown. Car delivery of packages up to 60 pounds as far as Everett, Tacoma, Woodinville, and Issaquah. Quick service.

SECRETARIAL SERVICES

Business Service Center
1001 4th Ave Plaza, 32nd Floor, 624-9188
(map: M6)
Mon-Fri

Provides a range of secretarial services, including word processing, answering service, mail service, telex, and fax. Also rental of office and conference space by the hour, day, or long term.

Executive Quarters
411 University St, Suite 1200, 467-9378
(map: K6)
Mon-Fri

Geared toward business executives, this reputable outfit occupies the 12th floor of the Four Seasons Olympic Hotel. A full range of secretarial services, plus office and conference room rentals.

SEL, A Secretarial Service
1409 140th Pl NE, Suite 103, Bellevue, 643-3792
(map: GG2).
Mon-Fri

SEL provides word processing, typing, copying, fax, dictation service, and answering service. Pick up and delivery available. All jobs are done withing 24 hours unless rush service is requested; off hours jobs are no problem. Executive suites can be leased by the month.

CALENDAR

CALENDAR CONTENTS

JANUARY

Average daily maximum and minimum temperatures: 44, 34
Average rainfall: 6.04 inches

Chinese New Year
International District,
623-8171 (map: R6)

FREE In January or February (depending on the lunar calendar), the International District greets the Chinese New Year with a fanfare of festivals, displays, and a lively parade complete with lion dancers.

Imagination Celebration/Arts Festival for Kids
Center House, Seattle Center, 684-7200 (map: C6)

FREE KIDS For two days in January, kids and their parents can participate in hands-on learning activities including arts, crafts, and music.

FEBRUARY

Average daily maximum and minimum temperatures: 49, 37
Average rainfall: 4.22 inches

Artstorm
Downtown, 623-0340 (map: HH7)

FREE The Downtown Seattle Association sponsors more than 200 arts events at over 100 locations the last two weeks of the month. Scheduled activities include architectural tours, gallery walks, concerts, films, workshops, performances, and seminars throughout the city. It's all free.

Chilly Hilly Bike Ride
Bainbridge Island,
522-BIKE

Held the third Sunday in February, this 30-mile family ride sponsored by the Cascade Bicycle Club has come to be recognized as the opening day of bike season. Up to 4,000 cyclists fill the morning ferries to Winslow. Don't expect it to be warm or flat.

Fat Tuesday
Pioneer Square,
622-2563 (map: N8)

Seattle's own week-long Mardi Gras celebration brings a colorful parade, local crafts, and the beat of Cajun, jazz, and R & B music to the streets and clubs of Pioneer Square. Several nightclubs levy a joint cover charge, and some of the proceeds benefit Northwest Harvest, a local food bank. Held the week before Lent.

Northwest Flower and Garden Show
Washington State Convention and Trade Center, 789-5333 (map: K4)

This enormous horticultural happening occupies almost five acres at the Convention Center throughout Presidents Day weekend. Landscapers, nurseries, and non-commercial gardeners outdo themselves with over 300 demonstration gardens and booths. Shuttle bus service is available from Northgate and South Seattle. General admission is $7, evenings $5.

Seattle International Raceway
31001 144th St SE, Kent, take exit 142A east off I-5; 631-1550
(map: RR2)

SIR's season begins in February and continues with a busy schedule of races through the good-weather months. Though the dirt track for motorcycles is not much, the nine-turn, 2¼-mile road racing track (originally built in 1959 for sports-car racing) is a very good facility. Open February through October.

Washington State Games
Call for location, 682-4263

What originated as the Washington Centennial Games are now the Washington State Games, a yearly event held in February (the summer games are in mid-August). Eventually, the events will find permanent homes, but for now, expect changes from year to year. The winter games feature downhill and cross-country skiing events; the summer games consist mostly of traditional Olympic sports.

MARCH

Average daily maximum and minimum temperatures: 51, 37
Average rainfall: 3.59 inches

NW Buddy Werner Ski Racing Championships
Call for location, 392-4220

KIDS An alpine ski event designed just for the younger members of your family. About 300 kids from ages 7 to 12 compete in the frosty event. Come out and watch Olympic hopefuls give it their all. Races are held in Washington, Oregon, or Idaho.

Saint Patrick's Day Dash
From Jake O'Shaughnessey's, 100 Mercer St, to the Kingdome, 763-3333
(map: A7–Q9)

In a festive atmosphere, the greatest number of participants of any local run follow the easy 4-mile course along the waterfront.

Saint Patrick's Day Parade
City Hall to Westlake Center, 623-0340
(map: N7–J6)

This downtown parade features bagpipes, singing, dancing, and the laying of a green stripe down the center of Fourth Avenue.

Whale Migration
For information, call Westport Chamber of Commerce, 1-268-9422

From March to May, the gray whales return to Alaska from Baja, where they winter and calve. Along the Washington coast are a number of excellent whale-watching spots; some towns, such as Westport, offer charters specially for whale-seekers. The return migration happens from October to December, less favorable for whale-watching due to the weather.

Whirligig
Center House, Seattle Center, 684-7200 (map: C6)

FREE KIDS From mid-February through early April, this indoor winter carnival fetes the coming of spring with rides, music, and games just for kids. The entertainment is free; rides cost a quarter apiece.

APRIL

Average daily maximum and minimum temperatures: 57, 41
Average rainfall: 2.40 inches

Daffodil Festival Grand Floral Parade
Tacoma, 1-627-6176

The Daffodil Festival, a springtime tradition for over 55 years, celebrates the fields of gold in the Puyallup Valley. One of the largest floral parades in the nation visits downtown Tacoma, Puyallup, Sumner, and Orting, all in one day.

Longacres Park/Horse Racing Season
Longacres Racetrack, Renton; take I-5 south from Seattle, exit at Southcenter and head east, off I-405; 226-3131 (map: O04)

KIDS In the fall of 1990, Boeing purchased this splendid racecourse to make space for the construction of an office park. At press time, Boeing had agreed to make the track available to thoroughbred racers for one more year (maybe two), while a new track is being sought. The 1991 season will run from April through September under the management of the Emerald Racing Association. The beauty of Longacres is in the variety of places to sit, walk, horse-watch, people-watch, eat, drink, and place bets. Even kids are allowed on the premises with adults. Post time is 5pm Wednesday through Friday, 1pm weekends, and the cost of grandstand admission is $3.25.

Seattle Mariners Baseball Season
Kingdome, 628-3555 (map: Q9)

The crowd is predictably loyal, even for a team whose performance is not so predictable. Although the playing can be truly inspired, the outlook for the next few seasons isn't particularly bright. The season lasts from early April through the first week of October (game time is 7:05pm or 7:35pm weeknights, 1:35pm on Sundays and occasional weekdays). Bring your own peanuts (Kingdome food is too expensive and not that good) and prepare to get lively if you're sitting in the left field stands. Tickets are cheap ($4.50 to $10.50).

Skagit Valley Tulip Festival
Mount Vernon, 60 miles
north of Seattle via I-5,
1-42-TULIP

FREE When the 1,500 acres of tulip fields burst into brilliant color in early April, Mount Vernon seizes the moment and entertains visitors with a street fair and parades. Makes a particularly nice—and flat—bicycle trip.

Yakima Spring Barrel Tasting
Various wineries, Yakima
(call for map),
509-829-6027

FREE In late April, 20 wineries from Union Gap to Kiona hold special open houses in order to educate the public on the finer points of wine-making. Both owners and wine-makers are on hand to explain the process, and wines from the barrel—some two or three years away from maturity—are available for tasting. Individual wineries add entertainment and food.

MAY

Average daily maximum and minimum temperatures: 64, 46
Average rainfall: 1.58 inches

Bicycle Sundays
Lake Washington Blvd,
684-7092
(map: II5–KK5)

FREE KIDS Every third Sunday and first Saturday of the month, May through September, winding tree-lined Lake Washington Boulevard is closed to autos from the Arboretum to Seward Park, and cyclists truly own the road. Wonderful for families.

Bike Racing at the Velodrome
Marymoor Park,
Redmond, 882-0706
(map: FF1)

Track racing is a much more watchable sport than road racing, and many nights at this lovely course include national-caliber racers. The season runs from the first Friday in May through the last Sunday in August. (See Bicycling under Great Outdoors in Exploring chapter.)

International Children's Festival
Seattle Center, 684-7346
(map: C6)

KIDS This popular event brings in children's performers from all over the world. Crafts, storytelling, puppet shows, and musical and theater performances (some free) entertain kids and their parents for six days in early May.

Nordstrom Beat-the-Bridge Run
University of Washington,
628-1490 (map: FF6)

Hordes of local athletes participate in this local late-May/early-June favorite, a 2-mile fun run or 4-mile walk along a winding U District course; if you don't "beat" the University Bridge (the drawbridge opens to signal the end of the race), you don't finish. Registration is in mid-May.

Northwest Folklife Festival

FREE The largest folk fest in the nation runs throughout Memorial day weekend, and brings diverse folk-art tra-

Seattle Center, 684-7300 (map: C6)

ditions (dance, music, crafts, and food) to stages all over Seattle Center. Excellent.

Opening Day of Yachting Season
Lake Washington/Lake Union; Seattle Yacht Club, 1807 E Hamlin St, 325-1000 (map: GG7)

FREE Boat owners from all over the Northwest come to participate in this festive ceremonial regatta, which officially kicks off the start of the nautical summer. Arrive early to check out the world-class University of Washington rowing team in racing form. Registration for the parade is free.

Pike Place Market Festival
Pike Place Market, 587-0351 (map: J8)

FREE KIDS The Pike Place Market Merchant Association sponsors a free celebration of the Market on Memorial Day weekend: food and drink aplenty, as well as clowns and jazz musicians and an entire Kid's Alley chock-full of activities.

Poulsbo Viking Fest
Poulsbo; 12 miles northwest of Winslow on Hwy 305, 1-779-4848

FREE In mid-May Puget Sound's "Little Norway" celebrates Scandinavian independence with a weekend of folk dancing, live music, a carnival and parade, and a lutefisk-eating contest.

Rhododendron Festival
Port Townsend, 385-2722

This is the oldest festival in town, and it improves every year. Highlights of this week-long event include a Rover Run (dog and owner), beard contest (scruffiest, longest), adult tricycle race, keg put, carnival, senior citizen coronation and dance, and more. The Grand Finale is a classic parade; the Anti-Climax Grand Finale is the 12K Rhody Run. See all of the Rhododendron Queens' cement handprints in downtown Port Townsend.

Seattle International Film Festival
Citywide, 324-9996

Founded in 1976 by Darryl MacDonald and Dan Ireland, the Seattle International Film Festival brings films for every taste—arthouse to slapstick—to Seattle theaters every May. Fans of the obscure will appreciate the SIFF's archival treasures and independent films. Series tickets go on sale in January (Cinema Seattle, 801 E Pine Street, Seattle 98122).

Ski-to-Sea Festival
Bellingham, Mount Baker to Bellingham's Marine Park, 90 miles north of Seattle on I-5; 1-734-1330

A Bellingham civic festival over Memorial Day weekend that revolves around an 80-plus-mile five-event relay race including skiing, running, cycling, canoeing, and sailing.

University Street Fair
University Way NE,
523-4272 (map: FF6)

FREE This juried festival, which takes place on the third—and usually the hottest—weekend in May, features over 400 artists' booths in a 10-block area. Street mimes and clowns hold court in the crowd, which is as rich and varied as the selection of crafts.

JUNE

Average daily maximum and minimum temperatures: 69, 51
Average rainfall: 1.38 inches

Centrum Summer Arts Festival
Port Townsend, northeast tip of Olympic Peninsula, Hwy 20 off US Hwy 101; 1-385-3102

From June through September, one of the most successful cultural programs in the state enlightens thousands, with a multitude of workshops held by the nation's leading artists and musicians. For fiddlers, there's the Festival of American Fiddle Tunes. Jazz musicians can hone their skills at the Bud Shank Workshop or listen to the music at Jazz Port Townsend, one of the West Coast's foremost mainstream jazz festivals. Workshops are held at Fort Worden State Park; performances are on the park grounds or in various locations around town. There are also a writers conference and theater performances.

Chamber Music Northwest
Portland, Oregon; information: 520 SW 6th Ave, Suite 1112, Portland, OR 97204; 503-223-3202

One of the finest summer festivals in the country, distinguished by the caliber of its performances, takes place in Portland at Reed College and the Catlin Gabel School late June through late July.

Everett Giants Baseball
Everett Memorial Stadium, Everett, 1-258-3673

This Class A minor-league affiliate of the San Francisco Giants plays real baseball on real grass in real sunshine from mid-June through August. In 1990, the 1,800-seat Everett Memorial Stadium was enlarged to 2,400 seats to accommodate the ever-growing number of fans. Tickets are only $4.00 for adults, $2.50 for kids 14 and under; reserved tickets are a little more.

Fremont Arts and Crafts Fair
N 34th St, 632-1285 (map: FF7)

FREE The most colorful of the Seattle neighborhood fairs, this one is full of the quirky flavor of Fremont— live music, clowns, jugglers, mimes, and local crafts.

Garlic Fest
Ocean Park, 3½ hours

This two-day affair attracts about 7,000 people each year. A street fair, live music, garlic-peeling contest,

southwest of Seattle,
1-665-5477

oyster shucking, and helicopter rides are just a few of the events that will keep you busy all day. A garlic-eating contest may keep your enemies at bay.

Mainly Mozart Festival
Meany Theater,
University of Washington,
443-4740 (map: FF6)

In mid-June, the Seattle Symphony presents a three-week tribute to Mozart and other late-18th-century composers, in a hall well suited to such a repertoire. Tickets are around $15.

Mercer Island Summer Arts Festival
8236 SE 24th Ave,
Mercer Island, 232-6354
(map: JJ4)

FREE This artists-at-work festival, sponsored by the Mercer Island Visual Arts League, is usually held the last weekend of June in downtown Mercer Island. Displays include handmade toys, jewelry, pottery, and stained glass in over 200 crafts booths.

Microbrewery Festival
The Herbfarm, Fall City,
784-2222

Fourteen breweries from the Northwest, Canada, and Utah offer samples of their wares, along with beer food (barbecued chicken, knockwurst) and oompah beer music. Six dollars buys you six taste tickets and the chance to wander around the herb gardens.

Out to Lunch
Parks around Seattle,
623-0340

FREE From late June to early September the Downtown Seattle Association brings local musicians to area parks to entertain brown-baggers. Over 60 concerts feature jazz, classical music and show tunes, modern dance and calypso. Just the thing to break up stir-crazy summer days in the office.

Seattle Chamber Music Festival
Lakeside School,
328-5606 (map: CC7)

See Music Series in the Arts chapter.

Seattle-to-Portland Bicycle Ride (STP)
522-BIKE

There is a 10,000-rider limit for this 200-mile bike ride from Seattle to Portland sponsored by the Cascade Bike Club. Complete the course in one or two days (overnight facilities are provided at the halfway point). Registration is first come, first served, and in the past couple of years the limit has been reached.

Special Olympics
Call for location,
362-4949

In 1968 an act of Congress created the organization known today as the Special Olympics. It has since grown to be the largest single sports training and competition program in the world for the mentally retarded. The June event is the biggest competition in the state.

JULY

Average daily maximum and minimum temperatures: 75, 54
Average rainfall: .74 inches

Bellevue Jazz Festival
Bellevue Downtown Park, 10201 NE 4th St, 451-4106 (map: HH3)

Top Northwest jazz artists entertain outdoors for three days, the third weekend in July. Tickets are cheap ($5) and one concert is free.

Bite of Seattle
Seattle Center, 232-2982 (map: C6)

A big chomp fest brings cheap nibbles from over 60 restaurants to Seattle Center in mid-July. All tastes are under $4.

Chinatown International District Summer Festival
Hing Hay Park, International District, 725-1456 (map: Q6)

FREE KIDS This extravaganza in mid-July celebrates the richness and diversity of Asian culture with dancing, instrumental and martial arts performances, taste-of-Asia food booths, and arts and crafts. A Children's Corner features puppetry, storytelling, and magic shows; various craft demonstrations (classical ikebana, a Japanese tea ceremony, basket weaving, calligraphy, and Hawaiian lei-making) take place in the Cultural Corner.

Darrington Bluegrass Festival
Darrington; information: Bluegrass Association, Box 519, Darrington, WA 98241; 80 miles north of Seattle off I-5; 1-436-1077

Every summer during the third weekend in July, bluegrass fans from all over the country turn their attention to the tiny town of Darrington, nestled in the Cascade foothills. Terrific, foot-stomping, thigh-slapping bluegrass music is played outdoors by the country's best musicians. Apply early for camping permits ($10); tickets are $25 per person.

Emerald City Flight Festival (Flightfest)
Boeing Field, near the Museum of Flight, (map: NN6), 764-5703

KIDS More than just an air show, Flightfest encourages families to look, listen, and eat. There's always an aircraft in the sky—with occasional aerobatics—and entertainment on the ground. Headliners in past years have included the Apollo-Soyuz mission cosmonauts and the Golden Knights Parachute Team.

Emerald City Marathon
Starts and finishes at Husky Stadium, 285-3212 (map: O7)

It's not the Boston, but this challenging and scenic course gives local—and some nationally known—athletes a run for their money. Over 1,000 runners test their mettle on a circular route that winds its way through some of Seattle's most beautiful parks (Gas Works, Mount Baker, Myrtle Edwards, Lake Washington Boulevard, the Arboretum).

Fourth of Jul-Ivar Festival and Fireworks
Myrtle Edwards Park,
587-6500 (map: HH8)

FREE KIDS Arguably the best fireworks display in Seattle is visible over Elliott Bay on the evening of the Fourth. Take a bus to avoid traffic hassles and get a spot early; the pyrotechnics start shortly after dark. During the day, various games (including, in the spirit of Ivar himself, a fishing derby), concerts, and food booths keep the waterfront lively.

Fratelli's Fireworks
Lake Union, 324-5939

FREE KIDS Ever since the Fratellis began firing up some competition to the annual Ivar-works, those blessed with views of Elliott Bay and Lake Union have been debating over which is better. Allegiance to Ivar's is strong, but Fratelli's fireworks, choreographed with a laser show to the tunes of the Seattle Symphony, have quickly garnered loyal fans.

King County Fair
King County
Fairgrounds, Enumclaw;
take I-5 south to Auburn
exit, Hwy 104,
1-825-7777

KIDS The oldest county fair in the state is also its best, featuring five days of live music with country headline acts, a rodeo, 4H and FAA exhibits, a loggers show (remember ax-throwing contests?), crafts, and food. Begins the third Wednesday of July.

Lake Union Wooden Boat Festival
1010 Valley St, south end
of Lake Union, 382-2628
(map: GG7)

For three days, around the Fourth, the Center for Wooden Boats lures the nautically minded with rowing, sailing, and team boat-building competitions, plus workshops, food, and crafts. Spectators can board various wooden boats (including the *Wawona*, a schooner built in 1897) or ride the *Makah*, a 14-person dugout whaling canoe. Water taxis shuttle people from events to demonstrations during the day. Donations of $2 per person or $5 per family are suggested.

Marymoor Heritage Festival
Marymoor Park,
Redmond, 296-2964
(map: FF1)

FREE KIDS The rich ethnic heritage of the Puget Sound area comes to life over the Fourth of July, with food, crafts, and music in the pastoral setting of Marymoor Park. There's plenty to fascinate kids; admission is free, though parking on the grounds sets you back $3.

McChord Air Show
McChord Air Force Base,
Tacoma,
1-984-2350

Come see the real-life *Top Gun* pilots in action as the F-16s do their thing. Watch military demonstrations from an all-services attack demo to antique aircraft, and get your picture taken in the cockpit of a jet.

Nordstrom Anniversary Sale

A bona fide Northwest event—folks actually line up for this annual sale at Seattle's favorite store. Prices on up

5th Ave and Pine St,
628-1490

coming fall apparel are excellent. Happens for two weeks in late July.

Olympic Music Festival
Quilcene; 11 miles west of the Hood Canal Bridge on Hwy 104, take Quilcene exit, 527-8839

The Philadelphia String Quartet opens its season with one of Puget Sound's premier music festivals, held in a turn-of-the-century barn nestled on 40 acres of pastoral farmland near Quilcene on the Olympic Peninsula. Sit in the barn on hay bales ($14.50) or spread a picnic on the lawn ($6). The festival spans 10 weekends. Bring a blanket.

Pacific Northwest Arts and Crafts Fair
Bellevue Square, Bellevue, 454-4900 (map: HH3)

FREE The Northwest's largest arts and crafts fair covers Bellevue Square with an excellent juried selection of West Coast arts and crafts and a juried exhibition in the Bellevue Art Museum, the last weekend in July.

Pilchuck Open House
The Pilchuck School, 1201 316th St NW, Stanwood, 1-445-3111 (summer), 621-8422 (winter)

In 1971 glass master Dale Chihuly came to Pilchuck to teach glassblowing to a handful of students. Since then, this internationally renowned summer school has expanded its curriculum to include all facets of glass art, taught by artists in residence. The school is open to the public just twice every summer, when visitors are invited to demonstrations and slide shows. These open houses usually take place the third Saturdays in July and August; bring a picnic lunch to Pilchuck's lovely 40 acres. In October, there's an auction at Seattle's Sheraton Hotel, with works by Pilchuck's artists.

San Juan Island Dixieland Jazz Festival
Friday Harbor, San Juan Island, 1-378-5509

A three-day festival, $35 for all three days, sponsored by the San Juan Island Goodtime Classic Jazz Association, brings fans out to enjoy the jazz of yesteryear, mid- to late July.

Seafair
Citywide, 728-0123

FREE KIDS Seattle's frenzied summer fete has been around since 1950 and—to the chagrin of many locals—isn't likely to go away. The hoopla begins on the third weekend of July with the milk carton races at Green Lake and ends the first Sunday in August when the hydroplanes tear up the waters of Lake Washington. Bright spots include a couple of triathlons, some excellent ethnic festivals: Bon Odori, late July; Chinatown International District Summer Festival, mid-July; Hispanic Seafair Festival, late July; Black Mardi Gras (mid-July); and the Torchlight Parade (Friday before the hydroplane races), which is a full-scale march in the downtown area and a kid's delight. Practically all Seafair events are free.

Shore Run
Seward Park to Madison Park along Lake Washington Blvd,
467-4399
(map: JJ5-GG5)

The first Sunday after July 4th, this popular 6.7-mile run benefiting the Fred Hutchinson Cancer Research Center attracts 1,000 walkers and 3,000 runners—as much for the run as for the T-shirt, always an artful status symbol among Seattleites.

AUGUST

Average daily maximum and minimum temperatures: 74, 54
Average rainfall: 1.27 inches

Evergreen State Fair
Monroe; take I-405 north from Bellevue to Hwy 522, then northeast to Monroe; 1-794-7832

KIDS For 11 days, late August through Labor Day, the Monroe fair features country music headliners, roping and riding, stock car races, a lumberjack show, a carnival, and a chili cook-off. Great fun.

Gig Harbor Jazz Festival
Celebrations Meadow, Gig Harbor; south on I-5 to Tacoma, west on Hwy 16 over Tacoma Narrows Bridge; 1-627-1504

The grassy natural amphitheater makes a great setting for a festival that draws national jazz artists. Boat owners can sail up to the site.

Men's USTA Challenger Series and Washington State Open Tennis Tournament
922 McGilvra Blvd E (Seattle Tennis Club), 324-3200 (map: GG6)

The top players in Washington and the men's western pro circuit compete side by side during the first week in August at the exclusive Seattle Tennis Club. The Open is free; tickets for the Challenger Series range from $1 to $5, and it's worth the admission just to stroll the idyllic grounds. Order tickets well in advance.

RSVP (Ride from Seattle to Vancouver, BC, and Party)
From UW to UBC, 522-BIKE

It's two days and 185 miles from Seattle to Vancouver, BC, and the Cascade Bicycle Club makes the trip worth the sweat with a reception and buffet at the end. On the third day, the Vancouver Bicycle Club offers optional rides around their beautiful city. Register early; there's a 700-rider limit.

Santa Fe Chamber Music Festival
Meany Hall, University of Washington, 622-1392 (map: FF6)

See Music Series in the Arts chapter.

**Washington State Games
(summer)**
*Call for location,
682-4263*

See February in this chapter.

**Washington State
International Kite Festival**
*Long Beach, 3½ hours
southwest of Seattle,
1-642-2400*

KIDS On the last day of this colorful, high-flying week, the Festival of Kites attempts to break its own record for number of kites in the air. Every day is a different event, from lighted kites to handcrafted kites to stunt fun and games. The glorious spectacle is free to watch, but flying your own will cost you $17. The entire Long Beach peninsula is booked from January in anticipation of this week, so plan (way) ahead.

SEPTEMBER

*Average daily maximum and minimum temperatures: 69, 51
Average rainfall: 2.02 inches*

Bumbershoot
*Seattle Center, 684-7200
(map: C6)*

The longest multi-arts festival north of San Francisco is a splendid, eclectic celebration. Select craftspeople, writers and poets, and performing artists entertain the hordes on stages throughout Seattle Center over the long Labor Day weekend.

**Caribbean Festival—A Taste
of Soul**
*Myrtle Edwards Park,
329-8818 (map: DD5)*

Be transported to the islands during one of Seattle's most temperate months. Let yourself be tempted by luscious Caribbean and African foods while calypso, soca, gospel, and reggae music soothe your soul. There's a limbo contest if you're feeling flexible; otherwise, you can just pretend the winds off the Sound are the gentle breezes of Montego Bay.

Ellensburg Rodeo
*Ellensburg, 115 miles
east of Seattle on I-90,
1-800-637-2444*

The biggest rodeo in these parts brings riders in from far and wide for four days of Wild West events over Labor Day weekend. Cost of admission for the big, flavorful event is $9 to $13, depending on your seat.

Husky Football Season
*Husky Stadium,
University of Washington,
543-2200 (map: FF6)*

Beginning in September, the UW's indomitable "Dawgs" play football in the 73,000-seat Husky Stadium. Thousands of loyal fans (students and alums) will have gotten there before you, so purchase tickets for the big games well in advance ($17 except for the USC and Oregon games, which are $20); when the Huskies are home, the games are on Saturdays. Always be prepared for rain, no matter how sunny the day starts out, and try to team up on transit (parking can be miserable). Lovely views of Lake Washington and the Cascades entice a lot of fans to pack a picnic and arrive at the game by boat, or tailgate in the parking lot.

Leavenworth Autumn Leaf Festival
Leavenworth; 120 miles east of Seattle via 405 north to Hwy 522, then east on Hwy 2; 509-548-5807

FREE The last weekend of September is a grand time for a drive through the Cascade Mountains to Leavenworth, a mountain town gussied up Tyrolean-style and home of the festival celebrating the glory of the deciduous trees in full color. A parade, arts and crafts, and Bavarian music are all a part of the festivities. Most events are free.

The Puyallup Fair (Western Washington State Fair)
35 miles south of Seattle via I-5, 1-841-5045

KIDS This 17-day extravaganza beginning in early September is the rural county fair you remember from your childhood, only bigger. Rodeo, music, barnyard animals, carnival rides, exhibits, and vast amounts of food (including the legendary scones) make for kid— and grown-up—heaven.

Seahawks Football Season
Kingdome, 827-9766 (map: R9)

Chuck Knox's Seahawks may play conservative ball (and may have seen better seasons than the next few promise to be), but the fans' loyalty is steadfast. Consequently it's nearly impossible to get tickets ($19 to $35), and Kingdome-area parking is a crunch. The season starts in September (preseason games in August) and runs through December; games are Sundays at 1pm. Best bet is to take a free bus from downtown— and avoid scalpers.

Thunderbirds Hockey Season
Seattle Center Arena, 728-9124 (map: B5)

After football gets under way, the Thunderbirds jump in to provide Seattle with a taste of the Western Hockey League. It's not the NHL, but the action on the ice is full of youthful dedication. Games are mostly on weekends; the season lasts from late September through March (or into May if the 'Birds make it to the playoffs). Tickets range from $6.50 to $9.50.

OCTOBER

Average daily maximum and minimum temperatures: 60, 45
Average rainfall: 3.43 inches

Arboretum Bulb Sale
Parking lot of the Visitor Center, Seattle Arboretum, 543-8800 (map: GG6)

It's a wonderful sale of specialized bulbs, and imports from Holland. Loyal customers go year after year, the first weekend in October, for expert advice from folks who know their stuff.

Greek Festival
St Demetrios Church, 2100 Boyer Ave E, 325-4347 (map: GG6)

For three days in early October, enjoy traditional Greek food and festivities galore at this noble Byzantine church. Church tours, folk dancing performances, music, arts and crafts, and wonderful baklava make this a favorite neighborhood event.

International Festival of Films by Women Directors
Seattle Art Museum (map: GG6) and other locations, 623-8733

Despite its surge in popularity, this festival has retained its feel of intimacy. Films are shown in small theaters, and the directors usually make appearances for discussion afterward. There's no political agenda to this internationally recognized series, but provocative and challenging films by rising stars and established artists are guaranteed to make you think.

Issaquah Salmon Days
Issaquah; 15 miles east of Seattle on I-90; 392-7024

KIDS Issaquah celebrates the return of the salmon the first weekend of October, with a parade, food, crafts, music, dancing, displays, and shows. A special Kid's Fair keeps the tykes entertained with pony rides and face painting, and the hydro races at Lake Sammamish are fun for kids of all ages. At the state fish hatchery you can get excellent views of the chinook and coho thrashing up the ladder.

Mushroom Show
Information: Center for Urban Horticulture, University of Washington 98195, 522-6031

Sponsored by the Puget Sound Mycological Society, this fest in mid-October celebrates the height of the mushroom foraging season in the Northwest, featuring 150 to 300 mushroom species. Locations vary.

NOVEMBER

Average daily maximum and minimum temperatures: 50, 39
Average rainfall: 5.60 inches

Husky Basketball Season
"Hec" Edmundson Pavilion, University of Washington, 543-2200 (map: FF6)

The women's team, according to some sports fans, is the best show in town—last year they finished fifth in the nation and drew substantial crowds. The men have some mediocre seasons behind them and a relatively new lineup; they should play much better as they mature. The season for both Dawg-teams lasts from early

November through early March (varying nights) and tickets are cheap ($5 to $10).

Model Railroad Show
Pacific Science Center,
443-2001 (map: C7)

KIDS A slew of model train setups and clinics on how to make whistles, scenery, and train people bring out the kid in all of us ($6) over Thanksgiving Day weekend.

Seattle SuperSonics
Basketball Season
Seattle Center Coliseum,
281-5850 (map: C6)

From early November to late April, Seattle's home team tears up the courts. In the past, the Sonics have played smart, competitive, uneven basketball; they have a bright future, so grab tickets early ($5 to $30). Games are at 7pm.

Start of Ski Season
Cascade Mountains

First snows blanket the ski resorts around mid-November, and the season usually lasts through April. For more information on specific ski areas, see the Great Outdoors section of the Exploring chapter.

DECEMBER

Average daily maximum and minimum temperatures: 46, 36
Average rainfall: 6.33 inches

A Christmas Carol
ACT, 100 W Roy St,
285-5110 (map: GG7)

KIDS This festive production, based on an original adaptation written for ACT, has become a holiday tradition for many families and sells out every year. Runs from Thanksgiving to Christmas Eve.

Christmas Lighting
Leavenworth,
509-548-5807

Crafts, music, and food are part of this ceremony kicking off the Christmas season. Around 4:45 (usually on the first and second Saturdays of the month), the Bavarian village square is officially lit up for the season. In addition, you'll find all the ingredients for a traditional holiday: roasted chestnuts, sleigh rides, Santa and Mrs. Claus and Scrooge. All's free except the sleigh rides and evening concerts after the ceremony.

Christmas Ship
Beaches citywide,
684-4075

FREE One of Seattle's cherished Christmas traditions comes to life every December, as area musical groups serenade folks gathered at various shores. Call ahead.

Community Hanukkah
Celebration
Stroum Jewish

KIDS The arts and crafts, Hanukkah wares, games for children, and latke brunch are just the side attractions. The most significant thing about this event is the

Community Center, 3801 Mercer Way, Mercer Island, 232-7115 (map: JJ4)

numbers—that is, the thousand or so people who come every year to the largest community Hanukkah celebration around. Everyone is welcome to take part in the *haimishe* (friendly) feeling the area's Jewish community creates when it gathers together for its festival of lights. You'll also find a vast selection of books on all aspects of Jewish life. The symbolic candle-lighting is quite moving.

The Nutcracker

Pacific Northwest Ballet, Seattle Opera House, 547-5900 (map: C6)

KIDS This annual PNB production has become another Northwest tradition and is particularly known for the spectacular set designs of Maurice Sendak. A good introduction for children to the ballet. Early December through Christmas; tickets go on sale in early October.

INDEX

Steve's Broadway News, 282
Stevens Pass, 240
Still Life in Fremont Coffeehouse, 123
Stimson-Green Mansion, 404
Stone Way Cafe, 123
The Store Next Door, 275
Stouffer Madison Hotel, 345
Streamliner Diner, 124
Stuteville Antiques, 263
Subito, 124
Suicide Prevention Hotline, 399
Sunlight Cafe, 125
Sunset Cafe, 125
Sunshine Kitchen Company, 317
Super Jock 'N Jill, 324
Superior Reprographics, 405
Suquamish Museum, 372
Sur La Table, 317
Surrogate Hostess, 125
Sushi-Ten, 126
Swallows' Nest, 229, 324
Swanson's, 300
The Sweet Addition, 285
Swingside Cafe, 126
Szechwan Garden, 127
Szmania's, 127

T

Tailors, 394
Taj Mahal India Restaurant, 127
Takara, 128
Take Two Consignments, 291
The Talbots, 270
Tandoor Restaurant, 128
Tanooki Cafe, 129
Targy's Tavern, 159
Tashiro's Japanese Tools, 309
Tatsumi, 129
Tatsumi Express, 129
Tea, 287
The Tea Cup, 288
Teahouse Kuan Yin, 177
Teger's, 130
Telephone numbers (important), 397

Television studio audiences, 399
Temptations, 285
Tennis, Men's USTA Challenger Series, 419
Tennis, Washington State Open Tennis Tournament, 419
Tennis: public courts, 240
TestaRossa, 130
Thai Chef, 131
Thai Heaven, 131
Thai Palace, 131
Thai Restaurant, 132
Thai Terrace, 132
Thai Thai Restaurant, 132
The Legacy (Alexis Hotel), 187
Theater, 194
Thinker Toys, 333
Thirteen Coins, 133
Thomas Kemper Brewery, 364
Thompson's Point of View, 133
318 Tavern, 160
Three Girls Bakery, 133
Thumpers, 160
Thunderbirds Hockey Season, 421
Ticketmaster, 399
Tiger Mountain Outfitters, 229
Tilden, 306
Tillicum Tours, 256
The Timberline, 170
Tio's Bakery and Cafe, 275
Titlewave, 282
Tlaquepaque, 133, 160
Togetsu, 134
Tokyo Japanese Restaurant, 134
Tommy Thai, 135
Tootsie's, 335
Top of the Exit, 188
Top of the Hilton, 170
Torino Sausage, 320
Torrefazione Italia, 177
Toscana, 135
Toscana Deli, 135
Tosoni's Cafe, 135
Totally Michael's, 270
Tower Books, 283
Tower Records, 327
Towing, 399
Toyoda Sushi, 136
Toys, 331

Trader Vic's, 136
A Train House, 333
Trains, 392
Transportation, 387
Trattoria Mitchelli, 136
Trek, 324
Tricoter, 298
Triples, 137, 160
The Trolleyman Pub, 137, 160
Truffles, 138
Tsue Chong Company, 296
Tugs Belmont, 171
Tump Nak Thai, 138
Turgeon Raine Jewelers, 316
Tweedy and Popp Ace Hardware, 309
The Two Bells Tavern, 139, 160
Tyee Valley Golf Course, 226

U

UA Cinema 150, 188
Ultima, 329
Umberto's, 139
The Underground Tours, 256
The Unicorn, 160
Union Bay Cafe, 139
Union Square Grill, 140
Union Station, 404
Universities, 399
University Bar and Grill, 161
University Bistro, 171
University Book Store, 283
University District, 354
hotels, 348
University of Washington, 214
climbing rock, 231
School of Drama, 196
Waterfront Activities Center, 229
University Seafood & Poultry, 328
University Sports Bar and Grill, 171
University Street Fair, 414
Uno, 270
Uptown Espresso Bar, 178

DID YOU ENJOY THIS BOOK?

Sasquatch Books publishes books and guides related to the Pacific Northwest. Our titles are available at bookstores and other retail outlets throughout the region, or from the publisher at the address below. Here is a partial list of our current titles:

Northwest Best Places
Restaurants, Lodgings and Touring in Oregon, Washington, and British Columbia
David Brewster and Stephanie Irving

Portland Best Places
A Discriminating Guide to Portland's Restaurants, Lodgings, Shopping, Nightlife, Arts, Sights, Outings, and Annual Events
Stephanie Irving

Seattle Survival Guide
The Essential Handbook for City Living
Theresa Morrow

Seattle Cheap Eats
300 Terrific Bargain Eateries
Kathryn Robinson and Stephanie Irving

Washington Homes
Buying, Selling, and Investing in Seattle and Statewide Real Estate
Jim Stacey

Field Guide to the Gray Whale
The Oceanic Society

Field Guide to the Orca
David Gordon and Chuck Flaherty

To receive a Sasquatch Books catalog, or to inquire about ordering books by phone or mail, please contact us at the address below:

Sasquatch Books
1931 Second Avenue
Seattle, WA 98101
(206) 441-5555

SEATTLE BEST PLACES REPORT FORM

Based on my personal experience, I wish to nominate/confirm/disapprove for listing the following restaurant, shop, nightspot, sight, or other:

_____

_____

_____

_____

(Please include address and telephone number, if convenient.)

REPORT:

(Please describe food, service, style, comfort, value, date of visit, and other aspects of your visit; continue on overleaf if necessary.)

I am not concerned, directly or indirectly, with the management or ownership of this establishment.

Signed _____

Address _____

_____

Phone Number _____ Date _____

Send to: Stephanie Irving, editor
Seattle Best Places
1931 Second Avenue
Seattle, WA 98101